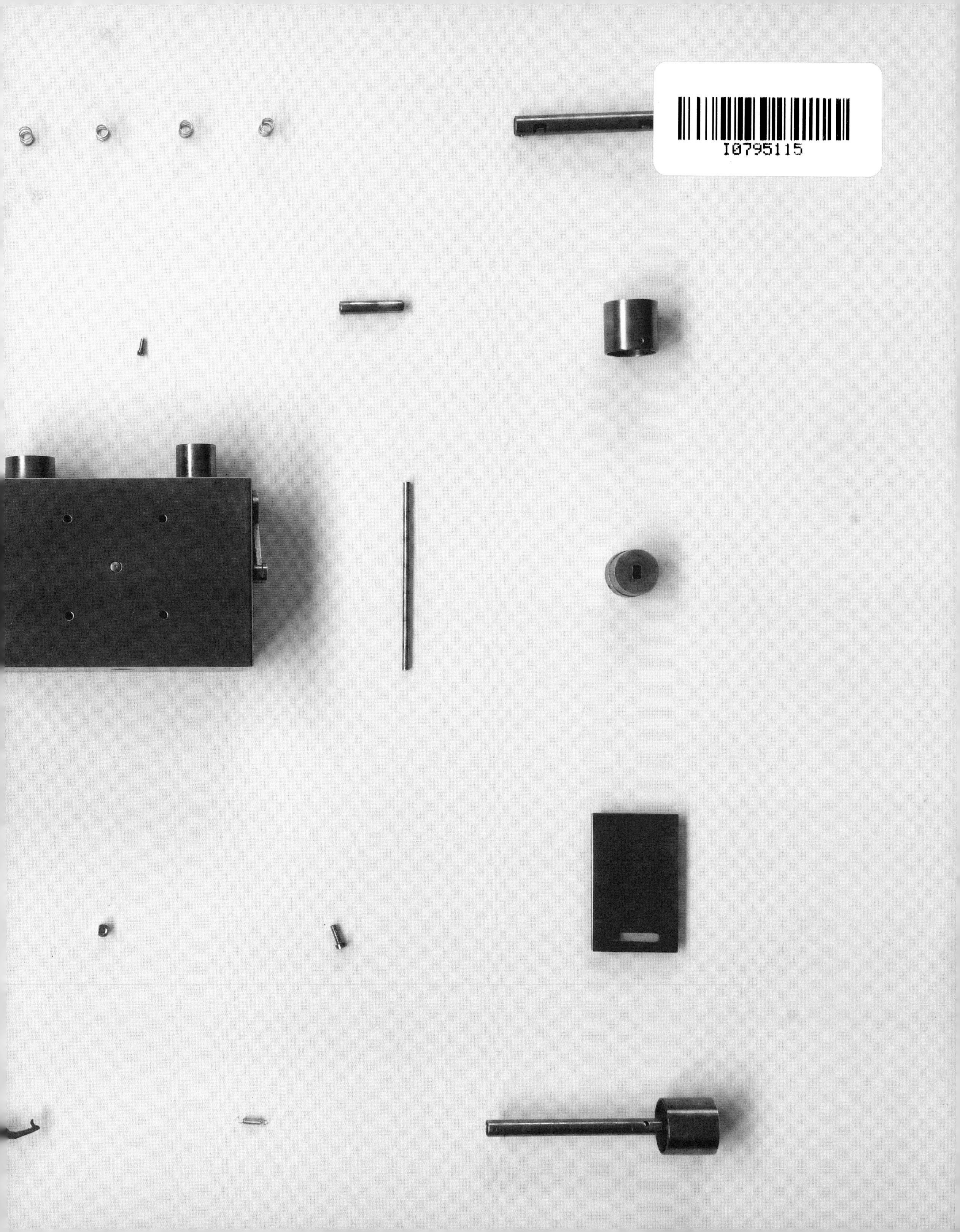

MULTIPLE
EXPOSURES

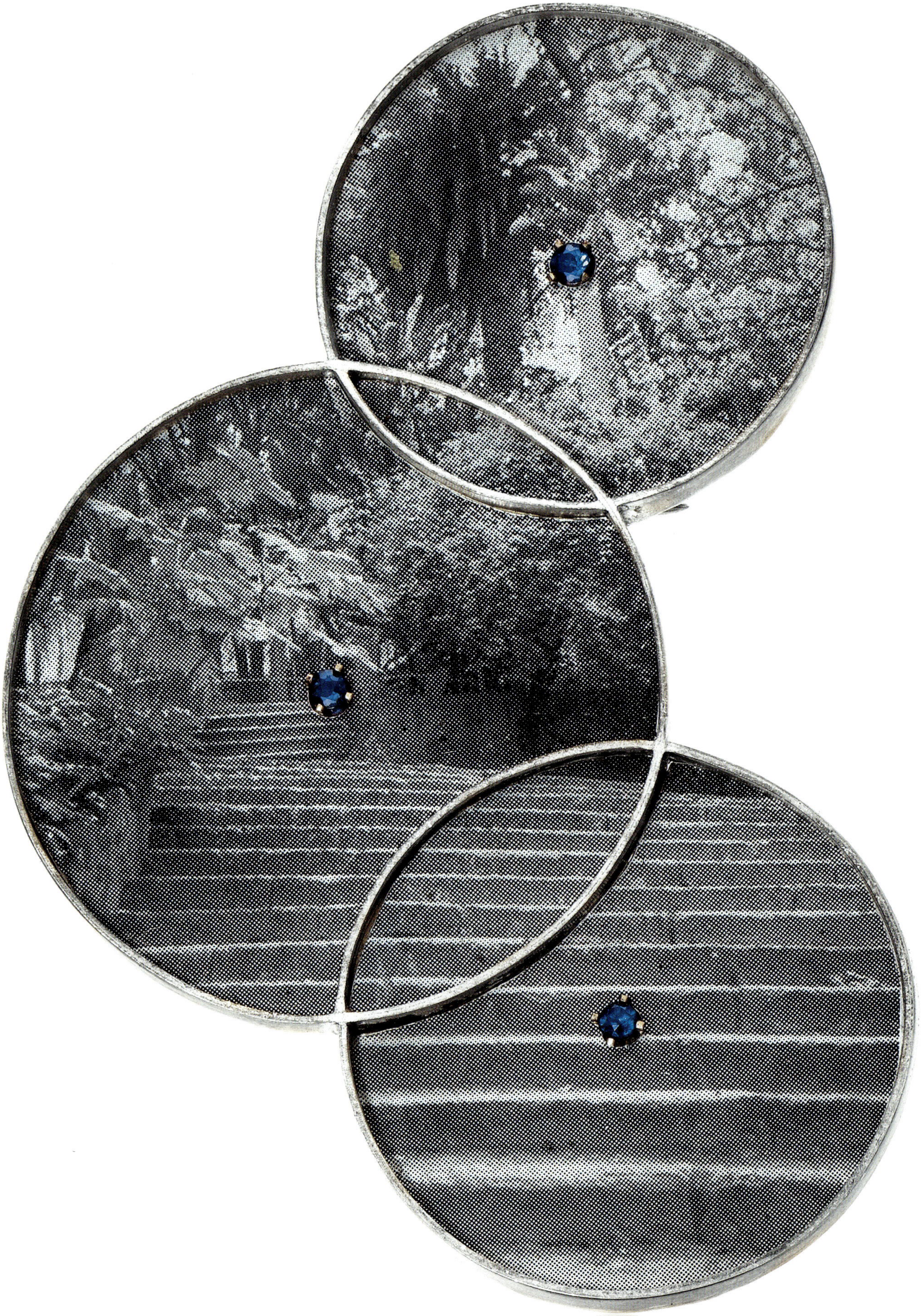

MULTIPLE EXPOSURES
JEWELRY AND PHOTO-GRAPHY

URSULA ILSE-NEUMAN

OFFICINA LIBRARIA IN COLLABORATION WITH
THE MUSEUM OF ARTS AND DESIGN, NEW YORK 2014

Museum of Arts and Design
2 Columbus Circle
New York, New York 10019
www.madmuseum.org

museum of arts and design

Officina Libraria
Via Carlo Romussi 4
20125 Milan, Italy

OFFICINA
LIBRARIA

Multiple Exposures: Jewelry and Photography is the catalogue for the exhibition organized by the Museum of Arts and Design. The exhibition is on view at the museum from May 13 through September 14, 2014.

Published in the United States of America by the Museum of Arts and Design.

Printed in Italy by Petruzzi Stampa, Città di Castello (PG) on acid-free paper, and typeset in *Documenta*, designed by Frank Blokland, and *National*, designed by Kris Sowersby. Color separations by Eurofotolit, Cernusco sul Naviglio (MI). Production coordination by Marco Jellinek.

ISBN MAD: 978-1-890385-28-6
ISBN OFFICINA LIBRARIA: 978-88-97737-292

Library of Congress Control Number: 2014940137

Sponsors
Support for *Multiple Exposures: Jewelry and Photography* has been provided by Hasselblad, Kara Ross NY, Betsy Z. and Edward E. Cohen, Washington Square Hotel, The Swiss Arts Council Pro Helvetia, The Dutch Culture USA Program by the Consulate General of The Netherlands in New York, Creative New Zealand, Janet Kardon, and Frame Finland. Additional support is made possible in part through the generosity of the Inner Circle, one of the Museum's leadership support groups.

EDITOR
Nancy Preu

BOOK DESIGN
HvADesign, NY
Henk van Assen with Anna Wexler
and Igor Korenfeld

FRONT COVER
Wafaa Bilal
3rdi (implanted camera), 2010
Silver, ABS, high-speed USB cable
2 x 1 1/4 in. (5.1 x 3.2 cm), camera
36 in. (91.4 cm), length
Collection of the artist

FRONTISPIECE
Bettina Speckner
Untitled (brooch) , 2004
Artist's photograph etched on zinc, silver, sapphires
2 3/4 x 2 x 1/4 in. (5.1 x 7 x 0.5 cm)
The Olnick Spanu Collection, New York

All measurements: height x width x depth, unless otherwise noted.

TABLE OF CONTENTS

FOREWORD

SINCE ITS FOUNDING IN 1956, the Museum of Arts and Design has had a long and proud history of exhibiting jewelry—a discipline that encompasses many techniques and forms, but operates always in relation to the body. Whether as ornament, status-marker, or critical device, jewelry is one of the most intimate and immediate means for artists and designers to articulate the relationship between people and the world around them. Today, we include jewelry regularly in our programming—particularly through our Tiffany and Co. Foundation Gallery, which offers both changing exhibitions and a large selection from our outstanding permanent collection.

As part of our ongoing commitment to the field, we now present *Multiple Exposures: Jewelry and Photography*. This groundbreaking exhibition is the first to examine the union of contemporary jewelry and the photographic image. The exhibition and its accompanying catalogue demonstrate the creative possibilities that result from hybrid practices. Photography and jewelry each have their own histories, technical repertoires, and theoretical implications. In *Multiple Exposures*, we show how each of these mediums is informed and enlarged by an engagement with the other.

The works included, both historical pieces and recent creations by over eighty international art jewelers, suggest the richness of this encounter. The examples selected for the exhibition and catalogue traverse a remarkably wide range, from traditional and even sentimental formats (such as the locket) to entirely new formats afforded by digital technology.

My particular thanks go to Ursula Ilse-Neuman, MAD's Curator of Jewelry. To say that I have learned a great deal from Ursula would be an understatement: I began my own association with this institution in 1995, as a volunteer intern, and she, as a newly appointed member of the staff, was one of the curators overseeing my work. In over two decades at the museum, Ursula has shown extraordinary passion, support, and expertise. Her accomplishments have not been limited to contemporary art jewelry by any means, but it is here perhaps that her impact has been strongest. Thanks to her work in curating exhibitions and building the collection, the museum has taken an important leadership role in the field.

As with any exhibition at MAD, the entire staff—from development officers to the facilities team—should be acknowledged for their roles in making this project possible. Here I would like particularly to recognize the contributions of Holly Hotchner, under whose directorship the project was conceived; David McFadden, our recently retired William and Mildred Lasdon Chief Curator and Vice President of Collections and Programs; and Lowery Stokes Sims, our new William and Mildred Lasdon Chief Curator.

From our Development Department, thanks are due to Alan Yamahata, Vice President of Major Gifts; Sophie Henderson, Vice President of External Affairs; and Anna Starling, Director of Institutional Giving. Thanks go as well to Ellen Holdorf, Registrar; Carla Hernandez, Associate Registrar for Exhibitions; and Cathleen Lewis, Vice President of Education. Special thanks to the artists, whose works are so beautifully shown in the exhibition and catalogue; to our authors—Liesbeth den Besten, Mark Alice Durant, Jutta-Annette Page,

Suzanne Ramljak, Lyle Rexer, Lowery Stokes Sims, and Ellen Maurer-Zilioli; and to the many private and institutional lenders who generously made their holdings available to the Museum. Thanks are also due to editor Nancy Preu, whose expertise informs the catalogue from beginning to end; graphic designer Henk van Assen and his staff at HvADesign for brilliantly interpreting the message of the exhibition in their catalogue design; and exhibition designer Rupert Deese, who conceived a remarkable sculptural installation that is entirely in tune with the themes of the show.

Our deep gratitude goes to Hasselblad and Kara Ross NY for generous support of the exhibition, and we additionally wish to thank Washington Square Hotel, Betsy Z. and Edward E. Cohen, the Swiss Arts Council Pro Helvetia, the Dutch Culture USA Program by the Consulate General of The Netherlands in New York, Creative New Zealand, Janet Kardon, Frame Finland, and members of the Museum's Inner Circle for making the exhibition possible.

Finally, we honor and thank MAD's Board of Trustees for their unfaltering leadership and generous support of exhibitions and programs. Their substantial investment in the Museum allows MAD to continue operating and presenting at the high caliber that they, MAD members, visitors, donors, partners, and local and international audiences have come to expect and enjoy.

GLENN ADAMSON
Nanette L. Laitman Director,
Museum of Arts and Design

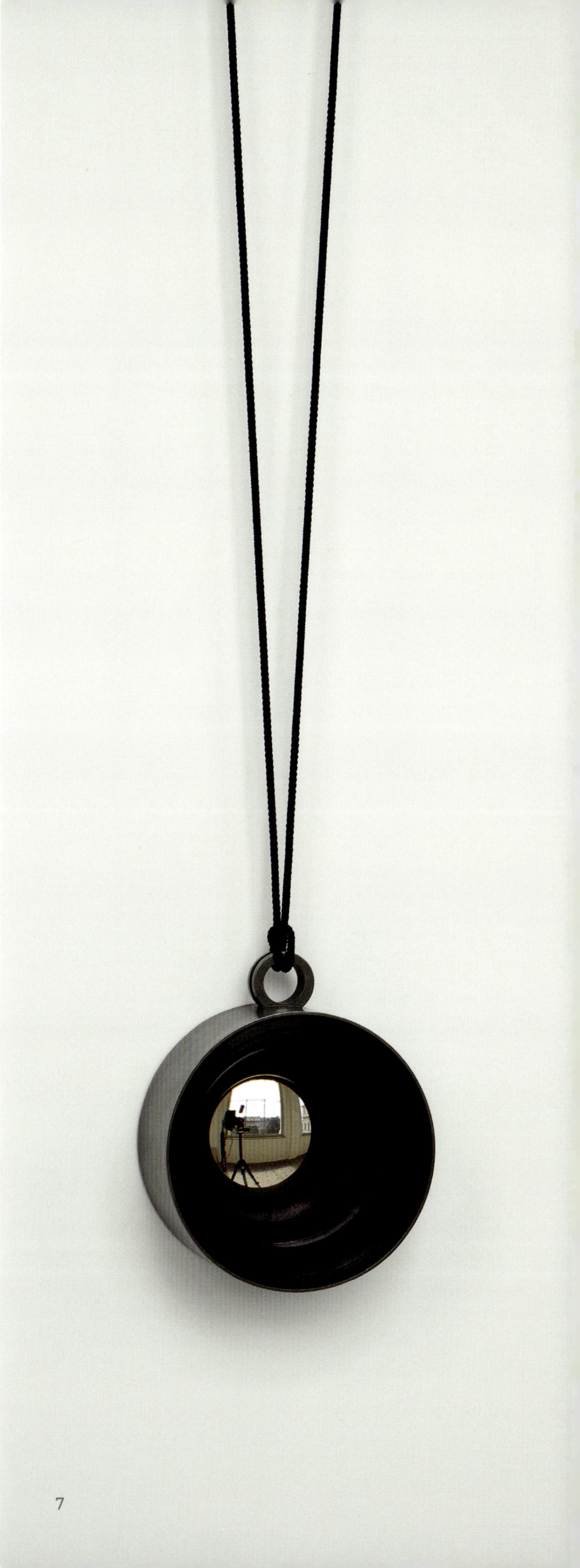

Jiro Kamata
Spiegel Pendant, 2010
Camera lens, mirror, blackened silver, stainless steel, nylon string
2 in. (5 cm), diameter
Collection of Susan Grant Lewin

ACKNOWLEDGMENTS

THE SPARK THAT GENERATED this exhibition was ignited four years ago when I opened a family locket to find a photograph of my great-grandmother that I had not known was there. This chance discovery spurred me to seek out examples of art jewelry in which photography figures prominently, and my search revealed the growing number of jewelry artists who incorporate photographic images into their work in order to enrich their artistic vocabulary. Drawing upon the abundance of imagery available today, from vintage daguerreotypes to analog and digital photographs, X-rays, and Internet jpegs, the artists whose work was selected for *Multiple Exposures: Jewelry and Photography* express a stimulating range of ideas realized with a great diversity of materials and innovative jewelry-making approaches.

My sincere thanks go to the many individuals and organizations who so generously supported me and my "jewelry team" as we tracked photo jewelry the world over. I am especially grateful to the artists whose creativity has inspired us and whose achievements we celebrate. Their belief in the importance of this project sustained us through many challenges.

At the Museum of Arts and Design, I am thankful for the support of the museum's new director, Glenn Adamson, who kindly assisted with last-minute preparations. My sincere thanks go also to former director Holly Hotchner and former chief curator David Revere McFadden.

I want to express my gratitude, in particular, to project manager Sophia Merkin, whose professionalism, infectious optimism, and tenacity were invaluable in bringing the exhibition and catalogue to fruition. My heartfelt appreciation extends as well to Barbara Paris Gifford. Her personal commitment and high standards during her one-year curatorial residency supported us all, and her contributions to this project would require a page of their own. In addition, a host of assistants, notably Allison Hollinger and Shelley Selim, and many hardworking interns were instrumental in reaching our goal.

I am grateful to the entire dedicated MAD staff for their energy and skill, uppermost among them Lowery Stokes Sims, William and Mildred Lasdon Chief Curator; Elizabeth Kirrane, Assistant Curator; Alan Yamahata, Vice President, Major Gifts; Sophie Henderson, Vice President, External Affairs; Megan Skidmore, Manager of Major Gifts; Anna Starling, Director of Institutional Giving; Georgia Wright, Director of Partnerships; Rafael Flores and Tiffany Jow, Development Associates; Claire Laporte, Director of Public Affairs; Cathleen Lewis, Vice President of Education; Ellen Holdorf, Registrar; Carla Hernandez, Associate Registrar; and the many staff members who worked tirelessly behind the scenes to ensure that this project would become a reality.

We are fortunate to have had the assistance of an extraordinary group of experts to realize this publication and exhibition. Seven outstanding authors—Liesbeth den Besten, Mark Alice Durant, Jutta-Annette Page, Suzanne Ramljak, Lyle Rexer, Lowery Stokes Sims, and Ellen Maurer-Zilioli—have contributed new insights and scholarship to the jewelry field. My utmost thanks to editor Nancy Preu, whose elegant wordsmithing and love of craft and design grace this book from cover to cover. Book designer Henk van Assen's creativity and eye for beauty are on full display in a transformation of manuscript and images that will never cease to astound me. Foremost in my mind and heart is Rupert Deese, who has my warmest appreciation as a longstanding friend and brilliant exhibition designer. A highly regarded painter, he agreed once again, in collaboration with artist-fabricator Eric Lindveit, to share his talents with the museum and our visitors.

Finally, I thank Kara Ross and all private and institutional funders, as well as the members of MAD's Inner Circle, for the crucial support and encouragement they have provided along the way.

URSULA ILSE-NEUMAN
Curator of Jewelry, Museum of Arts and Design

LENDERS

INSTITUTIONAL LENDERS

CODA Museum Apeldoorn
Apeldoorn, The Netherlands

Cultural Heritage Agency of The Netherlands
Amersfoort, The Netherlands

Deutsches Goldschmiedehaus Hanau
Hanau, Germany

George Eastman House, International Museum of Photography and Film
Rochester, New York

Hiko Mizuno College of Jewelry
Tokyo, Japan

The Metropolitan Museum of Art
New York, New York

Mint Museum
Charlotte, North Carolina

Museum Arnhem
Arnhem, The Netherlands

Museum of Fine Arts Boston
Boston, Massachusetts

Museum of Fine Arts, Houston
Houston, Texas

Renwick Gallery of the Smithsonian American Art Museum
Washington, D.C.

Stedelijk Museum 's-Hertogenbosch
's-Hertogenbosch, The Netherlands

SUPŠ A VOŠ TURNOV, The Secondary School of Applied Arts and The College of Craft Turnov
Turnov, Czech Republic

Tyler School of Art, Temple University
Philadelphia, Pennsylvania

PRIVATE LENDERS

Susan C. Beech
Drs. Karl and Heidi Bollman
Gail Brown
Sandra Donnell
Helen Williams Drutt
Vincent Fremont
Cathy Gordon
Mr. and Mrs. Lou Grotta
Daile Kaplan
Susan Kempin
Ulrike Knab
Natalie Knight Collection
Helen Kornblum
Susan Grant Lewin Collection
Gina Matchitt
Eija Mustonen
Ursula Ilse-Neuman
Olnick Spanu Collection
Robert L. Pfannebecker
Ron Porter and Joe Price
Claire L. Ramsey
Rotasa Trust Collection
Angela Schaefer
Kiff Slemmons
Giorgio Vigna Trench Art Collection
Sally von Bargen

GALLERY LENDERS

Friedman Benda
New York, New York

Galerie Rob Koudijs
Amsterdam, The Netherlands

Galerie TACTILe
Geneva, Switzerland

Gallery Loupe
Montclair, New Jersey

Gallery S O
London, United Kingdom

Hamish McKay Gallery
Wellington, New Zealand

Jeremy Rowe Vintage Photography
New York, New York

Maurer Zilioli—Contemporary Arts
Munich, Germany

Ornamentum Gallery
Hudson, New York

Sienna Patti
Lenox, Massachusetts

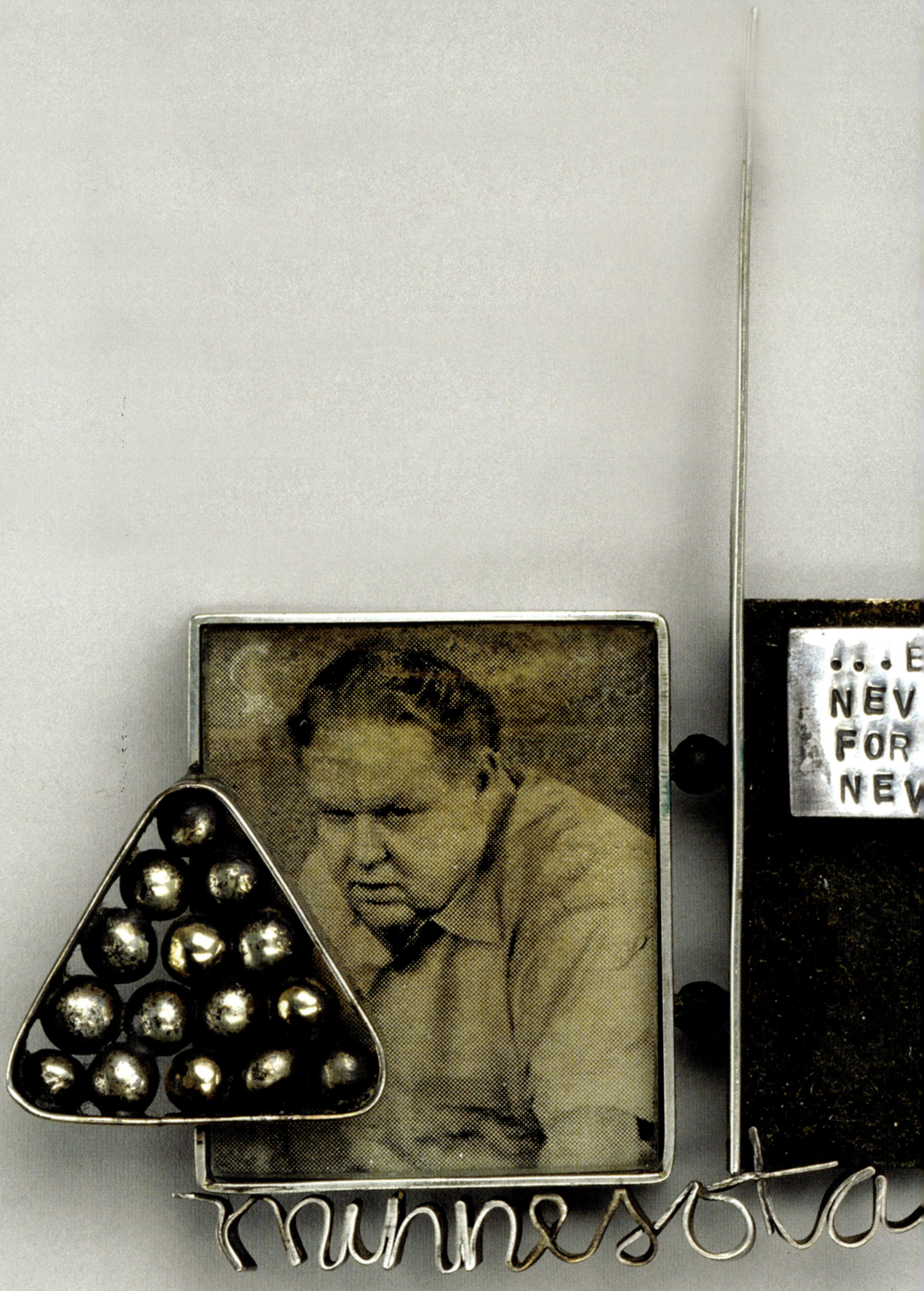

minnesota

"...A SCINTILLATING FUSION OF OBJECT AND IMAGE..."

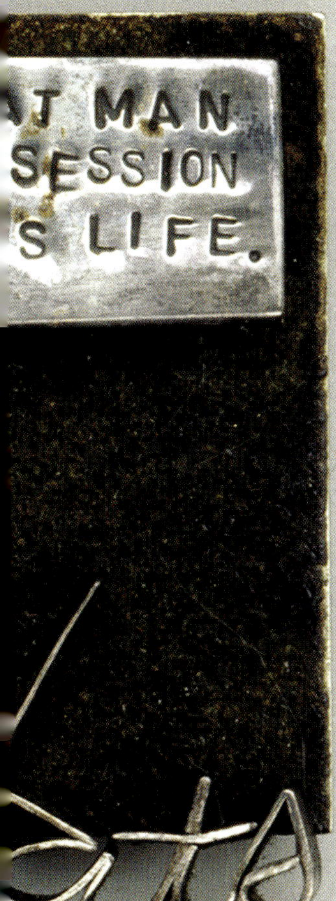

THE IMAGE TRANSFORMED CONTEMPORARY PHOTO JEWELRY

Every act of perception is
to some degree an act of creation, and
every act of memory
is to some degree
an act of imagination.

—GERALD M. EDELMAN AND GIULIO TONONI

URSULA ILSE-NEUMAN

JEWELRY HAS A HISTORY that extends more than eighty thousand years, and over the millennia it has brought a vast array of materials into its fold. Photography, on the other hand, has had less than two centuries to develop, and unlike jewelry, which is grounded in the tangible world of bodies and solid matter, it is based on light and the subjectivity of perception. In spite of their distinct histories and traits, or rather because of them, the union of these two mediums has resulted in a potent synergy that has reshaped jewelry. *Multiple Exposures: Jewelry and Photography* captures the artistic strength embodied in this scintillating fusion of object and image.

Soon after its invention in the 1830s, photography found a ready role within wearable ornament. By the 1840s, photo jewelry had become an enormously popular means of documenting and preserving memories of people and places and of authenticating historical events. As Lyle Rexer puts it in his catalogue essay on early photo jewelry, "In this age of an emerging middle class, photography joined hands with that other rapidly expanding medium of self-regard and self-presentation, jewelry."[1]

Since this bond was first created, both jewelry and photography have evolved and grown with the introduction of new technologies. No longer deemed a magical medium, photography is now so commonplace that we feel inundated by images rather than being thrilled by them. Because the human body is the site of our experiences, of our sense of identity, and the boundary between the self and the outside world, the act of wearing an image integrated into an intimate form makes a profound and immediate impact on both the wearer and the viewer. In tandem, jewelry and photography are providing unique insight into today's increasingly visual and rapidly shifting cultural terrain.

From the beginning, photography was prized for the verisimilitude it affords. The notion of a photograph as a dispassionate representation of reality was soon brought into question, however, by artists and writers who recognized that photographs do not represent a singular reality but are inherently shaped by the subjectivity, intentional or not, of the photographer. Today it is accepted that photographs are not mere facsimiles of the original subject captured through the lens of the camera, but are also shaped through the lenses of memory, experience, and consciousness.

Recognizing that perception is intricately bound with an individual's sensibility and background, and taking advantage of this fact rather than viewing it as a shortcoming, contemporary jewelry artists select and manipulate photographs from today's virtually infinite supply. Harnessing the visual clues and symbols contained within images, and carefully working them into one-of-a-kind settings, they develop alternate realities expressive of their own aesthetic sensibilities, beliefs, values, and emotions, as well as of current cultural and global concerns. The distinctive mark of the maker's hand introduces a fresh framework and context for each photograph—whether an early daguerreotype, a vintage snapshot, or a recent digital image—and establishes a narrative that, in many cases, does not depend on fidelity to the actual subject. By inviting viewers to react and interpret their creations from both universal and personal perspectives, contemporary jewelry artists establish a collaboration between maker and wearer that may well be the strongest such bond in the world of art and design.

• • •

The photographic images in the works in *Multiple Exposures* range from vintage daguerreotypes, ambrotypes, and ferrotypes to postage stamps and magazine cutouts, pictures taken by the artists themselves or downloaded from the Internet, and color photocopies, Polaroid images, and pinhole photographs. To meet the challenge of affixing such fragile materials onto lasting substrata, artists use complex processes such as photo-etching on silver, zinc, and nickel; kiln-fusing onto glass and enamel; photo-transferring onto various backings, including polymer clay, enamel, aluminum printing foil, sheet metal, and silk; photo-enameling; encasing half-tone reproductions in PVC; and printing digital images on aluminum.

The freedom that contemporary jewelry artists enjoy in using any material or technique to create works that may be precious or non-precious, narrative or abstract, decorative or grotesque, personal or socially charged, is traceable only to the mid-twentieth century. The American studio jewelry movement began in the 1940s and accelerated in the decades following World War II, when a group of artist-craftsmen turned their backs on traditional jewelry forms and precious metals in rejection of jewelry's deep-rooted associations with wealth and status. Driven to democratize jewelry and free it from conventional forms and materials, they changed the paradigm by aligning their craft with concepts adopted from the fine arts and design. This included the use of photographs, a practice central to early twentieth-century art movements, particularly Dada, which sought to blur the boundaries between life and art, and Surrealism, which used photography to explore the intersection of dreams and reality.

Working without the benefits or constraints of a long-standing goldsmithing tradition, American jewelers discovered new formal approaches and enlisted unorthodox materials such as industrial metals, plastics, and found objects. Beginning in the 1960s, American jewelry makers, including Don Tompkins (NOS. 33, 34), J. Fred Woell (NO. 32), Robert Ebendorf (NOS. 35, 36), and later Kiff Slemmons (NO. 54), adopted a collage or assemblage approach that often included nineteenth-century vernacular tintypes or clippings from magazines and newspapers. By incorporating photographs in this way, such jewelers were engaged not in literal storytelling but in stimulating the viewer's imagination through the associations of the often enigmatic images in combination with found objects.

The narrative aspects of jewelry were championed mainly in the United States. By contrast, European jewelers during this period concentrated more on abstract compositions and the conceptual aspects of jewelry. Photography was used as a means of documenting their unconventional and even radical approach to jewelry as body ornament, including its performative aspects, and also as a means of promulgating it. In the 1960s, Dutch jewelers Gijs Bakker and Emmy van Leersum began to use photographs to disseminate their revolutionary designs, which promoted the use of industrial materials such as aluminum, steel, rubber, and plastic and were inspired by the pared-down shapes of modernist art and mass production.

• • •

Since the works in *Multiple Exposures* are primarily content driven, this book is organized into subjects that are commonly associated with photography and that continue the main pictorial genres in art history—portraiture, landscape, and the figure—but with a contemporary sensibility. Other sections focus on pieces using approaches characteristic of such twentieth- and twenty-first-century artistic practices as recycling and repurposing; the appropriation of images from art and popular culture; and the exploration of the cultural role and performative aspects of jewelry through still and moving images.

Complex Identities

> *A portrait! What could be more simple and more complex, more obvious and more profound.*
>
> — CHARLES BAUDELAIRE

When photography emerged in the nineteenth century, it began a reorientation of portraiture that continues today. As discussed in "Saving Face," Suzanne Ramljak's essay in this volume on contemporary photo portrait jewelry, jewelry artists are keenly interested in how we perceive the people who look back at us from objects of personal adornment.[2] A remarkable range of subjects peers out from these wearable forms: the artists themselves, their friends and family, celebrated figures, the anonymous and long forgotten, and even society's outcasts.

The act of placing a portrait within a piece of jewelry worn on the body alters the context and the way the image is perceived. This transformation is evident in a number of works in *Multiple Exposures* in which vintage photographs play the central role. Some are placed in collages and assemblages, together with assorted found objects, creating an intriguing puzzle for the viewer; others become characters in a formal scenario with materials that establish a recognizable narrative.

The people in vintage photographs stare out from the past, but leading photo jewelry proponent Bettina Speckner often blocks their gaze with opaque materials such as jasper, thus cancelling the subject's identity (NO. 42). The decorative power of jewelry transports these history-laden portraits into the existential ambiguity of the twenty-first century.

It is worth noting that early photographic portraits were not always stiffly posed and serious. Victorian-era photographers created a sensation when they developed the ability to combine images from multiple negatives to create novelty

FIG. 1

Nineteenth-century headless portrait.

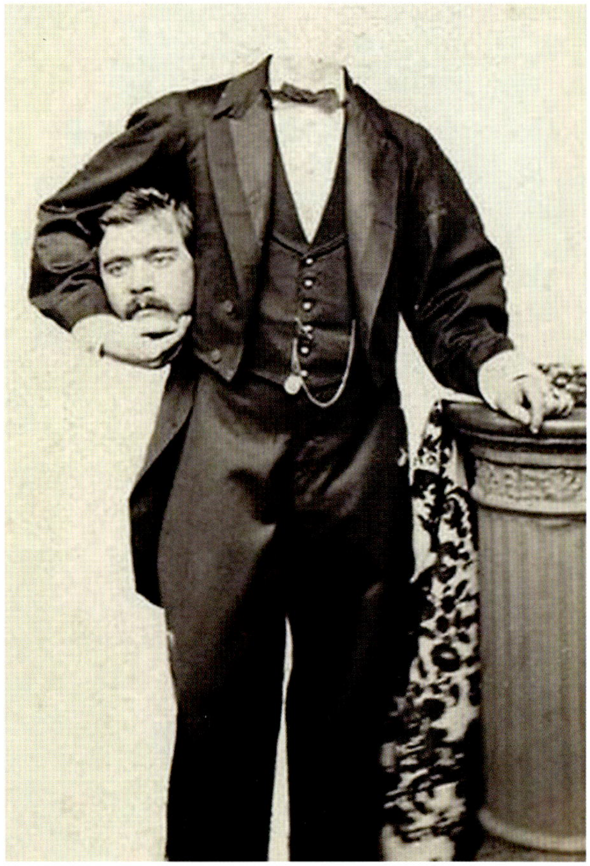

portraits and trick photos. Instead of formal poses, their eager clients readily sought out such amusements as "headless photographs" showing men and women whose chopped heads are skewered, served on platters, or simply carried by their owners (fig. 1). Another type of vintage photography that incorporated special effects was the "spirit photograph." These doctored double exposures purportedly captured ghostly apparitions that were otherwise invisible to the human eye. Such photographs were accepted as proof of the paranormal and duped many gullible believers, including Sir Arthur Conan Doyle (1859–1930). An actual spirit photograph is featured in the *Spectre Woman* brooch by contemporary jewelry artist Keith Lo Bue (NO. 47).

Depicting personal, social, and cultural relationships is a central concern for jewelry makers who enlist photo portraiture. Through such work they show their close connections to family and friends, provide commentary on celebrity, and encourage us to conjure up our own histories. Placing such personal works in jewelry, however, raises the question of whether it is appropriate for someone else to wear them. It is incumbent on the artist to transmit a shared humanity through his work that allows wearers and viewers to accept an unknown individual as a symbol of a larger idea.

The issue of ownership of personal images and histories has become even more critical with the ubiquity of smartphones and cameras. Whether social media are inherently anti-social is a matter of ongoing debate in the growing conflict between the desire for privacy and the voyeuristic fascination in seeing others in unguarded private moments—such as that seized by Thomas Gentille in the New York City subway (NO. 66). Privacy and voyeurism are also cogently addressed in Jordan Doner's surveillance jewelry with built-in spy camera and viewing monitor (NOS. 51, 52).

Corporal States

> *Your body is not a temple. It's an amusement park. Enjoy the ride.*
>
> — ANTHONY BOURDAIN

The human form is a source of inspiration, meaning, and metaphor for photo-jewelry artists who address a broad spectrum of contemporary concerns about the human body through representations ranging from the literal to the symbolic. Wearing jewelry increases our consciousness of the body's physical and temporal nature and gives tangible reality to our existence as biological organisms. In a rapidly evolving contemporary world characterized by flux and disintegration, artists are led to depict the self as changeable and fragmented, in contrast to earlier images of a fixed and stable identity. The sense that one's persona is constantly changing and that only a fraction of it can be captured by the camera is reflected when jewelry artists choose to portray themselves in casual, humorous, or even self-mocking poses, as Bernhard Schobinger has done through the addition of a red clown's nose to his commuter ID card (NO. 19), a gesture recalling the explorations of identity by artist/photographer Cindy Sherman.

Historically, the partial or fragmented form suggested a search for a whole that had vanished. It was manifest in the Romantic era's yearning for the lost age of antiquity as epitomized in the remains of classical statues and the ruins of ancient Rome. A parallel has been suggested between focusing on these fragments of classical sculptures and focusing on isolated parts of the human body, in that both imply a longing for some absent but idealized subject. A witty expression of this longing is provided by Gijs Bakker's 1982 *Embrace* necklace (NO. 62). A playful alternative to the conventional wedding ring, this necklace features a life-sized photograph of Bakker's torso that is designed to surround the neck of a beloved.

There is a clear connection between seeing the body in fragments, as it frequently appears in postmodernist works, and viewing it in medical diagnostic imagery. X-rays, microscopes, sonograms, and other medical scans reveal unseen aspects of our bodies that not only compel us to consider our frailties and mortality, but also force us to think about who we really are. In making medical images wearable, jewelry artists imbue them with a sense of wonder, bringing out qualities that unite us and allow the wearer to reclaim dominion over his body. Such aspects of photo jewelry are addressed in Lowery Stokes Sims's essay "Wearing the Body."[3]

Scoping the Land

> *The question is not what you look at,*
> *but what you see.*
>
> —HENRY DAVID THOREAU

Landscapes might seem impersonal and misplaced in jewelry, but jewelers are drawn to their evocative content as well as their references to specific times and places. From photography's inception, the objectivity of landscape photographers has been questioned with regard to their intended impact on the viewer. When Ansel Adams (1902–1984) was asked why there are no people in his landscapes, he responded, "There are always two people in every picture: the photographer and the viewer."[4] There is no escaping the photographer's presence. Although the photographs of Alfred Stieglitz (1864–1946), who championed photography as an art form, are unmanipulated, they are not documents but expressive reflections of his emotional state at the moment he snapped the shutter, and they are also not above allegorical allusion.

No photographers are involved, however, as the cameras that Google mounts on cars canvas the world's neighborhoods, automatically capturing fleeting moments that reflect a random instant in time (fig. 7). Artist Jon Rafman, who uses these Google Street Views for his photo projects (fig. 6), adds perspective and introspection to photographs that were taken by chance and lack a photographer's influence. Rafman believes that the very act of framing gives things meaning, and by reintroducing the human gaze on these scenes, he reasserts the importance and the uniqueness of the individual in interpreting their content.[5]

Iraqi-born Wafaa Bilal undertook a different and radical approach when he had a small silver camera surgically implanted on the back of his head (NO. 138). Doubling as an unlikely body ornament and timed to take minute-by-minute images, it recorded scenes from his daily life in New York for a full year following his departure from Baghdad. The personal images he uploaded in real time can be seen as a symbolic reference to the people and places we all leave behind.

As opposed to the uncritical, accidental framing of a Google Street View or Wafaa Bilal's automatic snapshots, the landscapes and cityscapes in contemporary photo jewelry reflect the artist's studied choice of where to focus, often revealing hidden and subtle aspects in the original photographs. Contemporary jewelry artists may intervene further by introducing incongruous spatial and temporal elements, as in Jantje Fleischhut's addition of wind turbines to a nostalgic setting in order to form a new, imaginary place (NO. 85). Several of the artists in *Multiple Exposures* focus on cityscapes, extracting patterns and colors from buildings to create decorative elements that bring out and augment their architectonic vocabulary. Others are drawn to dramatic, unspoiled vistas or to those in transition due to human intrusions that become metaphors for ruin and reconstruction. In her *Transformations* neckpiece, New Yorker Kara Ross celebrates the metamorphosis of an urban eyesore into a soaring new development. The neckpiece includes actual rubble from the building site along with photographs of the demolition that is the prelude to rebuilding (NO. 88).

Jewelry makers are sensitive to the ways in which photography can reconfigure memory, presenting images that cloud or even replace actual memories of our experiences of them. As Ellen Maurer-Zilioli notes in "Remembered Places—Imagined Spaces," many of these jewelers "tread the fine line between fantasy and objectivity, constantly fashioning new supposed circumstances."[6] Some use photographs to preserve memories of places visited, while others create imaginary places, choosing pictures that have the power to stimulate the mind and allow viewers to enter fantasy realms. Bettina Speckner generally uses her own photographs in evocative scenes that create a timeless atmospheric effect by employing outmoded or abandoned techniques such as photo-enameling or photo-etching on zinc (NOS. 76, 77). The most complete transformation from photograph to jewelry has been accomplished in Mari Ishikawa's gold and silver rings, which she forges from tracings of photographs of trees that inspire her (NO. 78).

Appropriation

> *Immature poets imitate; mature poets steal.*
>
> — T.S. ELIOT

Throughout history, artists, composers, and writers have been inspired to draw from and alter the work of others, an artistic process that has been made even easier today through the global proliferation of imagery via printed media, television, and the Internet. Photo jewelry, by definition, involves the co-option of photographs and images, with the jewelry-making process itself lending a new meaning to the original, a dynamic discussed in Jutta-Annette Page's essay "The Appropriated Image in Contemporary Jewelry."[7]

Beginning in the 1980s, Gijs Bakker, a pioneer and leading exponent of such reworking, began appropriating images and laminating them in PVC to create jewelry. His iconic works in this vein include a necklace in which Michelangelo's Sistine Chapel Adam rests on a gold circlet (NO. 109). A brooch with a photograph by Bruce Weber of a naked man throwing a bucket of water over his back is studded with diamonds that sparkle like droplets of water (NO. 58), a stunning contrast of a cheap throwaway with an object of enduring luxury. He further explored the capacity of the photographic image to embody and confer value and association by making wearable jewelry from photographs of luxurious jewelry and famous high-karat necklaces (NO. 97).

Ramon Puig Cuyàs, in his UTOPOS brooch *Nº 1279*, uses sections cropped from Internet images of Old Master paintings to explore the way we perceive the world and to question whether scientific thinking is more "accurate" than an artist's intuition. One brooch pairs a detail from Domenico Ghirlandaio's 1485 painting *Portrait of a Young Woman*, representing Renaissance humanism, with a visualization of Einstein's gravity field (NO. 100). Puig Cuyàs argues that since "rational science" has had to confront the mysteries of quantum physics and its relation to consciousness, perhaps it is time to accept the value of artists' insights in charting our place in the cosmos. It is remarkable to find these profound and challenging thoughts encapsulated in a small wearable object.

The Second Lives of Camera Paraphernalia

> *Use it up, wear it out, make it do,*
> *or do without.*
>
> —OLD NEW ENGLAND PROVERB

It is perhaps not surprising that the photographic instrument—the camera—would itself become the raw material for jewelry making. Realizing the camera's symbolic and material richness, jewelers demonstrate an ingenious sense for turning hard-edge mechanical components into striking body adornment. This particular interest is part of a growing movement that celebrates the repurposing of outdated, mass-produced consumer goods into handcrafted one-of-a-kind wearable objects. Inherent in such recycling is the discovery of the poetic wealth in the materials we cast aside and a challenge to their transient value and built-in obsolescence through new investment in compositional and technical creativity. Although less directly related to a narrative interpretation than jewelry containing photographs, jewelry made from camera parts, particularly from pre-digital cameras, retains its own fascination. As Mark Alice Durant conveys in "Lost Lenses and Orphaned Apertures," these discarded relics "are not simply archaic curiosities or nostalgic objects; they are talismans of memory, catalyzing agents of photography's power and magic."[8]

An appreciation of the experience and power accrued in camera lenses lies at the heart of Jiro Kamata's jewelry. The artist believes that the cast-off lenses he uses are repositories of memorable moments in people's lives (NOS. 122, 123). Similarly, Jaimie MacDonald drastically reconfigures plastic film canisters to reflect the landscapes she photographed near her childhood home in the Scottish Highlands (NO. 120). On a parallel front, Hyun-Seok Sim handcrafts fully functional cameras that reflect the almost fetishistic love that some people have for their cameras (NOS. 126A, 126B), albeit a passion that may be waning in today's world of low-cost but highly functional digital cameras.

Jewelry, like photography, has evolved and grown with the introduction of new technologies, and in this digital age, the pace of technological change is breathtaking. Whereas high-tech advances used to take place primarily in remote laboratories, today's technologies are rapidly realized as changes in our daily lives. In this regard, the race for personal, "wearable technology" is heating up, and video earrings and brooches now allow the wearer to project "selfies" or to use live webcams to throw images of viewers back at them. The small, mass-produced mechanisms that are begining to flood the market mimic standard rings or bracelets without endowing them with any personal significance. What distinguishes art jewelry from wearable tech is the eye and hand of the artist, for whom the idea or concept is paramount.

Jewelry beyond the Object

> *Invisible threads are the strongest ties.*
>
> —FRIEDRICH NIETZSCHE

When worn, a piece of jewelry sends messages about the attributes and character of the wearer that depend on and change with the social context. The cultural and performative facets that are inherent in how jewelry is perceived have been explored creatively through photo documentation.

In 1973, Gijs Bakker enlisted photography to present what is considered the first example of conceptual jewelry. His *Shadow Jewelry* was an ephemeral work that is known primarily through photographs and lacked the monetary value or permanence of traditional jewelry (fig. 4). Bakker stated that the idea originated from the "wish to make an invisible piece of jewelry, at last to find a form on the body which changes the body, making it more visible than the piece of jewelry."[9] A gold wire, which Bakker presented in a jewelry box, was the instrument for making the actual work, which was the impression left on the skin after wrapping the wire around different body parts. Photographs provided documentary evidence of Bakker's creations, as they did during that era for other artists with whose work Bakker was familiar, including Bruce Naumann, a participant in *Documenta 4* in 1968.

Another early example of jewelry as performance art that now survives only through photographs is Peter Skubic's *Jewelry under the Skin*, which entailed the surgical insertion

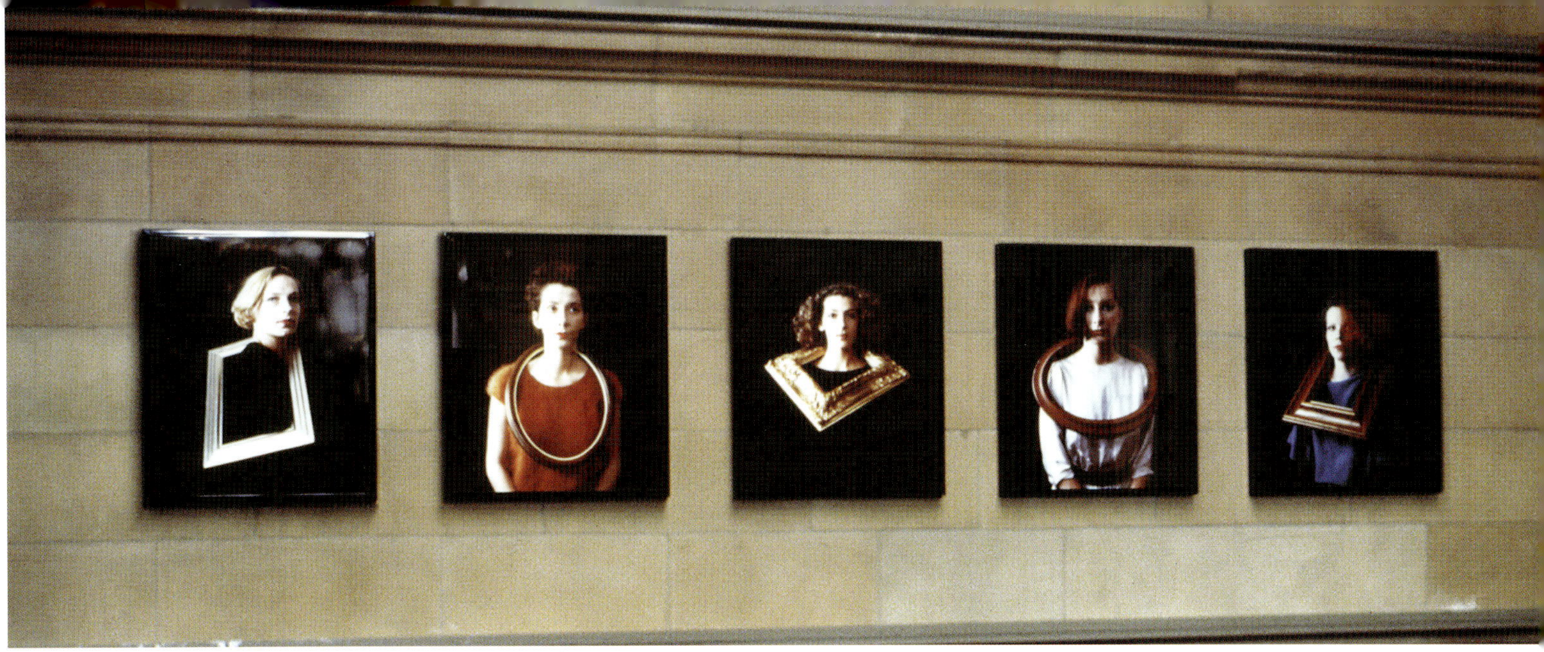

into his forearm of a stainless-steel "jewel" that he wore from 1975 to 1982 (fig. 5). Skubic's intention was to question the essential nature of the medium by comparing invisible forms of jewelry—including his implant—with prominent outward changes to the body, such as ornamental scars, piercing, and tattooing.

No other jewelry artist has utilized photographs with as much ingenuity as Otto Künzli, one of the most provocative and influential figures in the field over the past forty years. Early in his career, Künzli, like Bakker, sought ways of expressing the intrinsic meaning of jewelry and freeing it from historical conventions. In 1976, Künzli took a cardboard box full of tape, wires, and wooden rods to a photo booth in the main Munich train station in order to try out various configurations and combinations on his own body, an investigation he documented in his *Automatenfotos* (fig. 3). An accomplished goldsmith, Künzli effectively dematerialized the physical object and rejected the formalism traditionally associated with its making, as Bakker did in his invisible jewelry. Künzli's goal was not to produce a permanent piece of jewelry, but to create a series of photographs that recorded the effect of shapes on the body without regard for the material limits or techniques required to make an enduring wearable object. This disavowal of jewelry objects was in keeping with broader artistic tendencies of the period.[10]

Continuing his explorations through photography, in 1984, Künzli placed unframed photographs of young ladies within replicas of antique, gilded picture frames and presented them in his *Schönheitsgalerie* [Gallery of Beauties] installation (fig. 2). By allowing the picture frames to replace necklaces, this witty take on the Nymphenburg Palace's portraits of Munich's most beautiful women, painted from 1827 to 1850, takes an ironic look at the associations of rank and social status that are implicit in such historical portraits.

The important documentary role of photography for performative jewelry projects that were begun by Gijs Bakker, Otto Künzli, and Peter Skubic continues in contemporary practice, as discussed in Liesbeth den Besten's essay "Jewelry through the Lens."[11]

FIG. 2
Otto Künzli
Die Schönheitsgalerie installation, Kelvingrove Art Gallery and Museum, Glasgow Scotland, 1992.

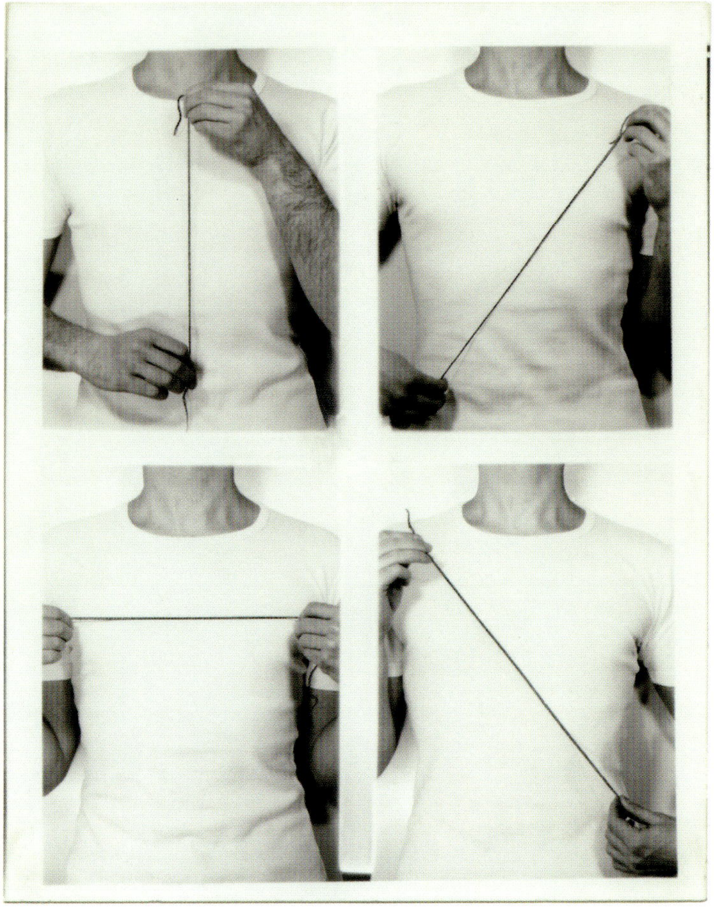

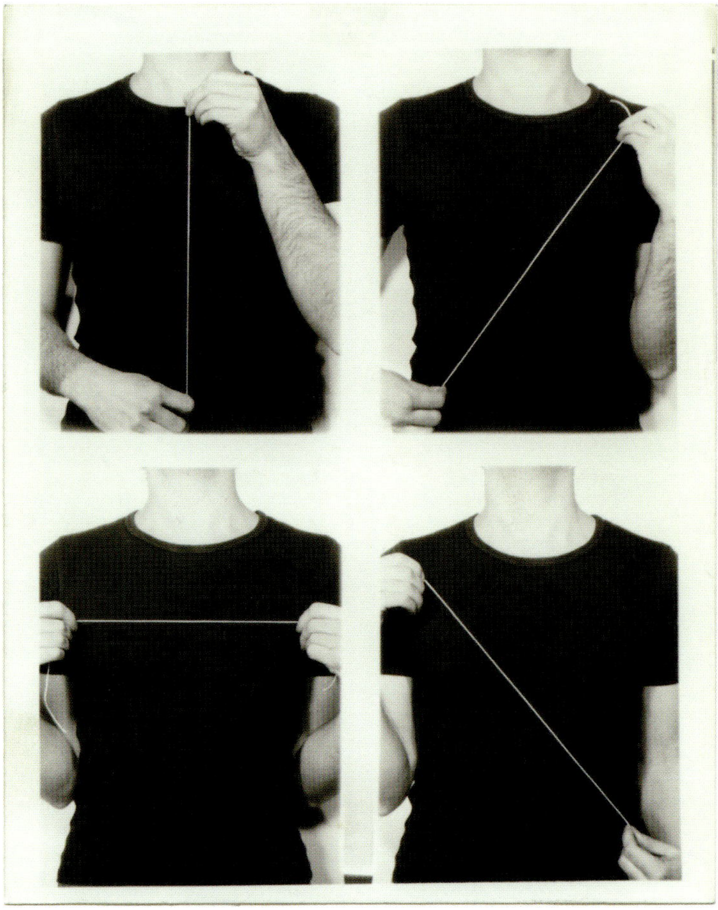

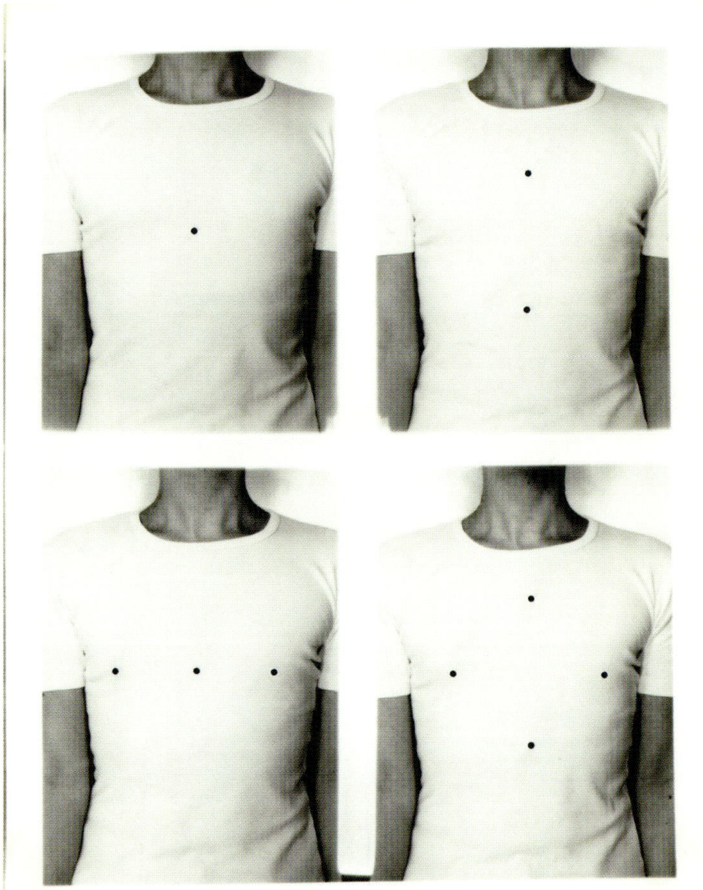

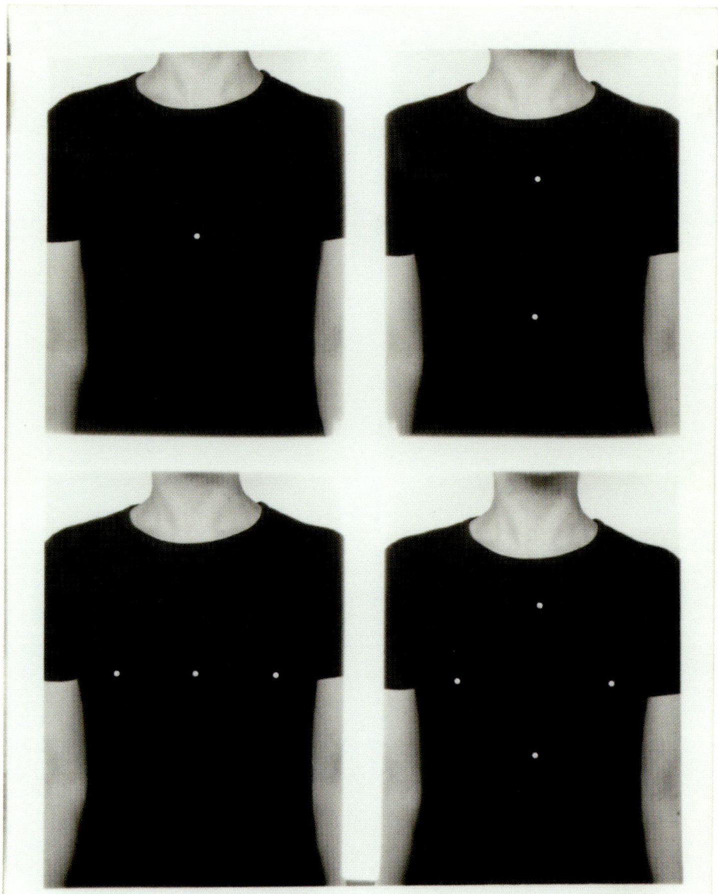

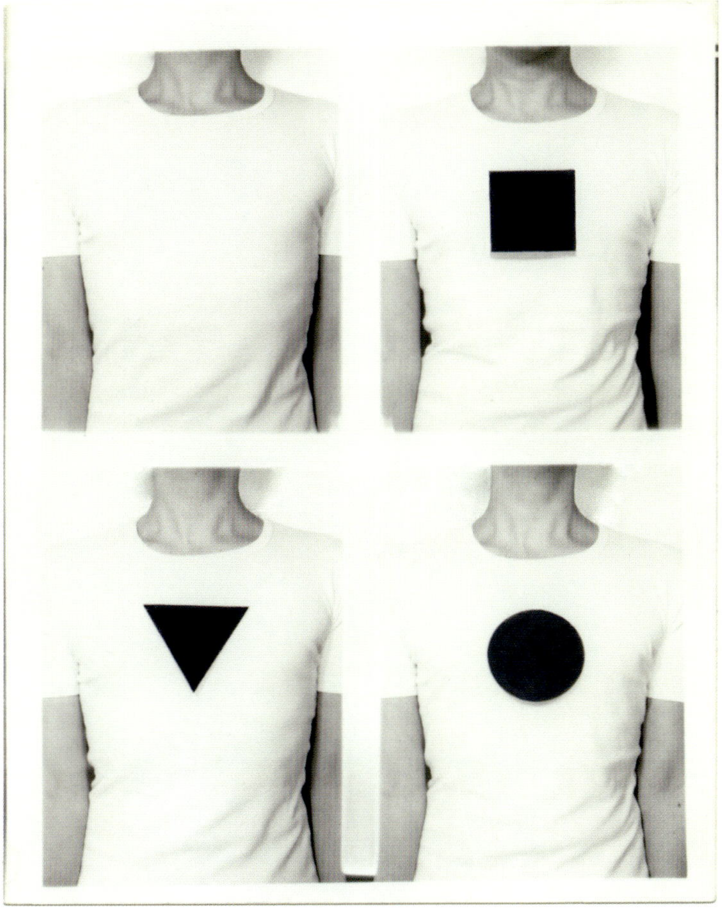
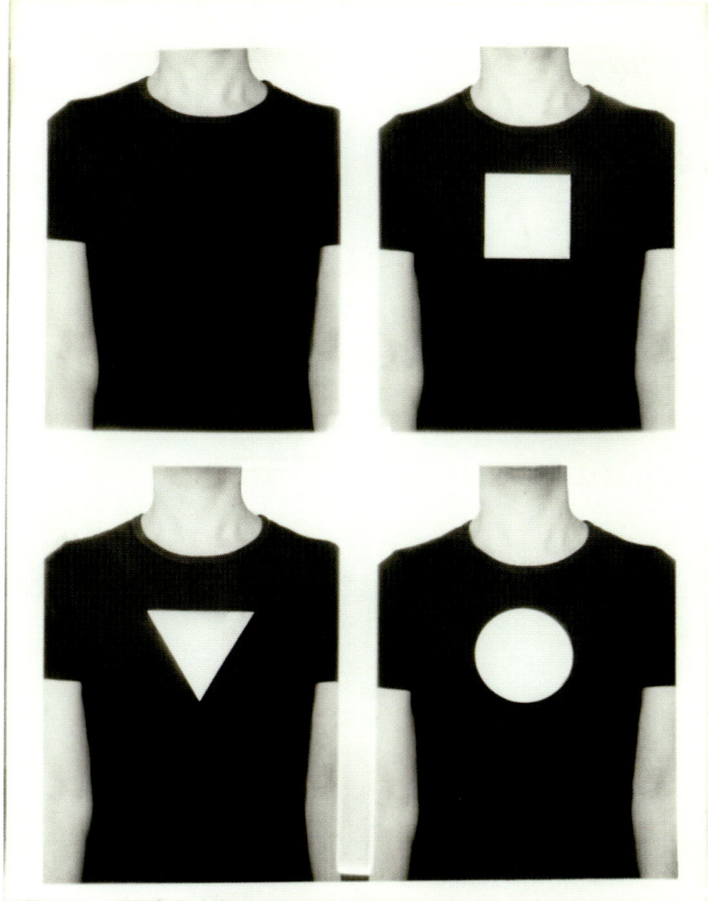
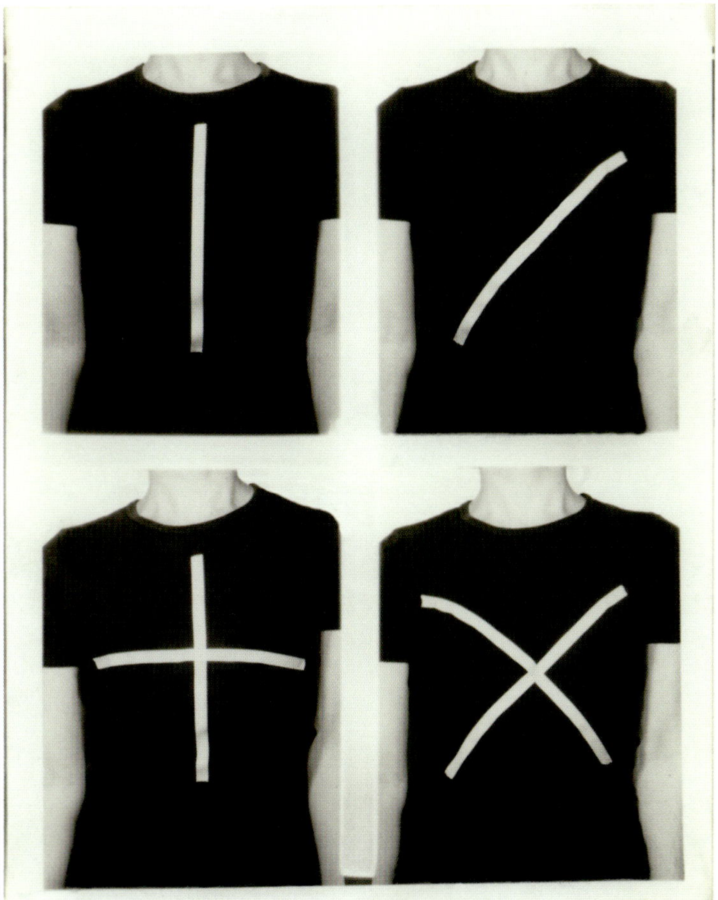
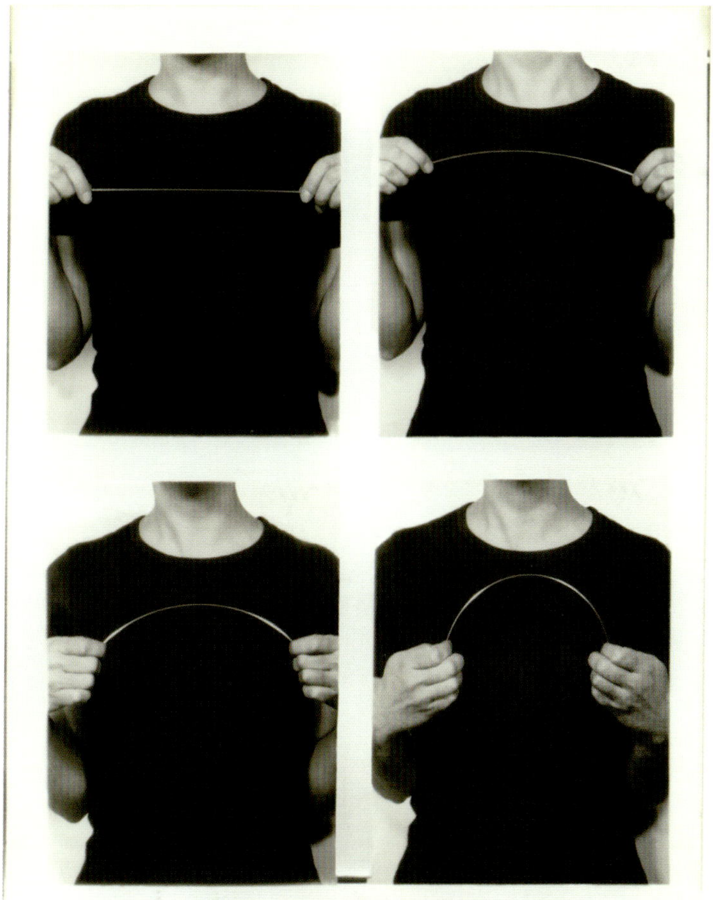

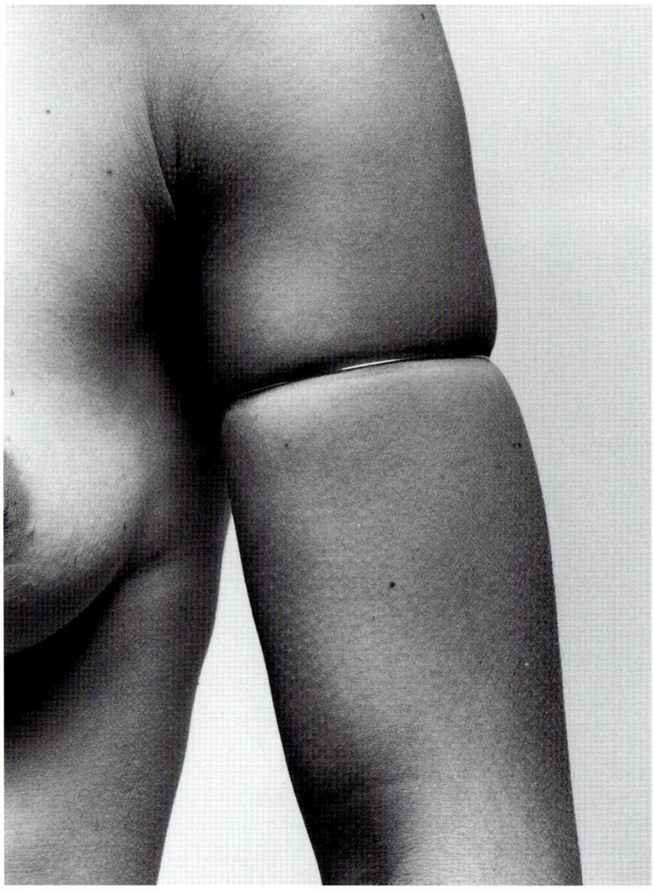

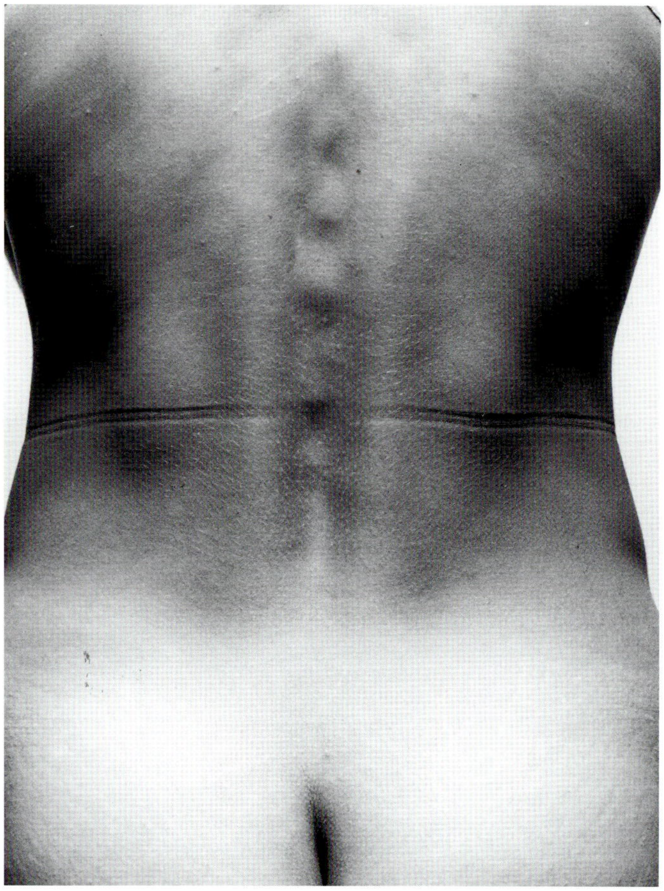

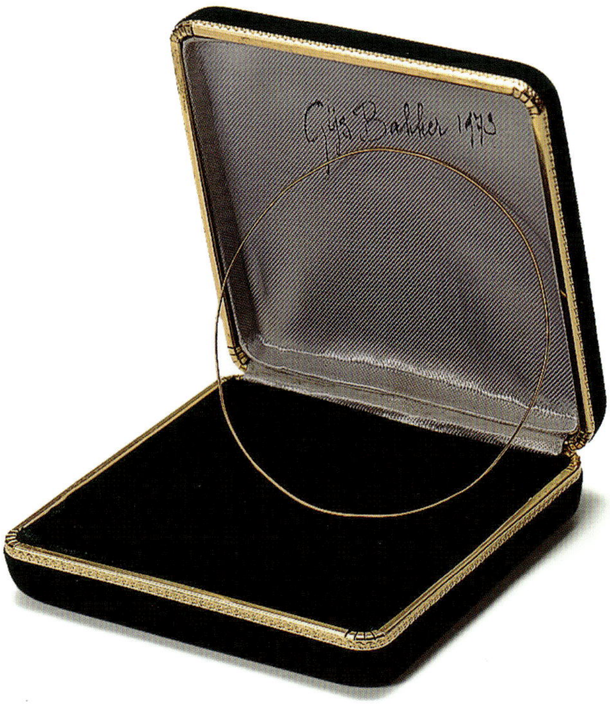

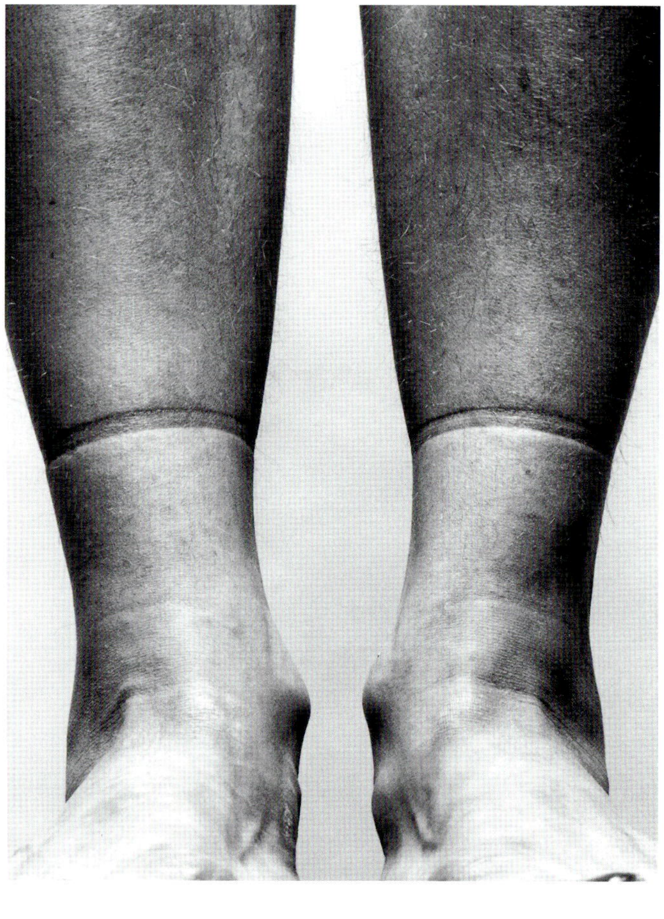

FIG. 4

Gijs Bakker

Shadow Jewelry (waist and ankles)

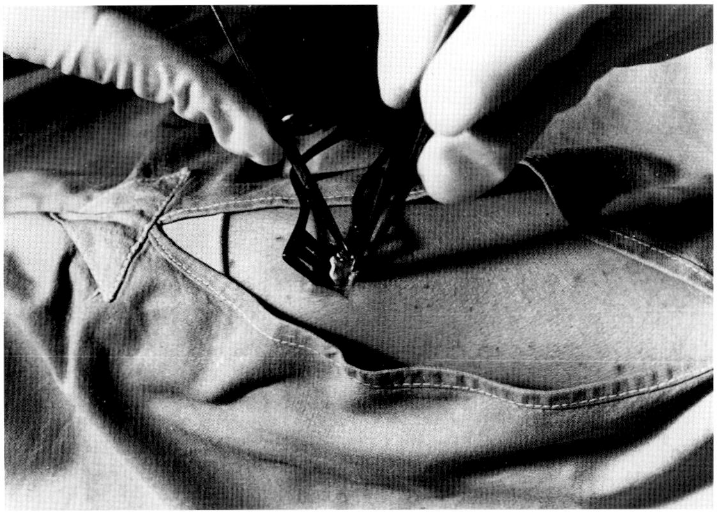

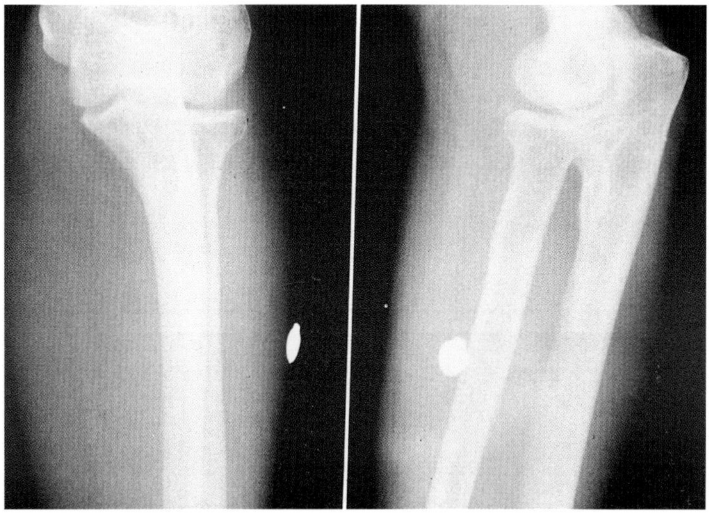

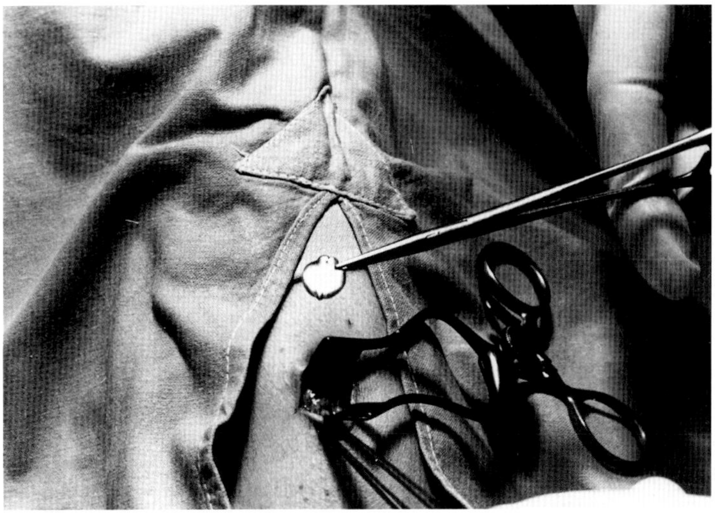

FIG. 3 PREVIOUS SPREAD

Otto Künzli

Automatenfotos, 1976

Photographs taken in a photo booth

in the Munich train station

5 x 3 3/4 in. (12.5 x 9.7 cm), each

four-image block

Collection of the artist

FIG. 4 OPPOSITE PAGE

Gijs Bakker

Shadow Jewelry, 1973

Bracelet, worn and displayed

Yellow gold 585

3 in. (7.7 cm), diameter

Courtesy of Gijs Bakker

Gijs Bakker

Shadow Jewelry, 1973

Waist and ankles

Courtesy of Gijs Bakker

FIG. 5 ABOVE AND LEFT

Peter Skubic

Jewelry under the Skin, 1975

Photographs and X-ray of steel "jewel"

implanted in the artist's lower arm

Courtesy of Peter Skubic

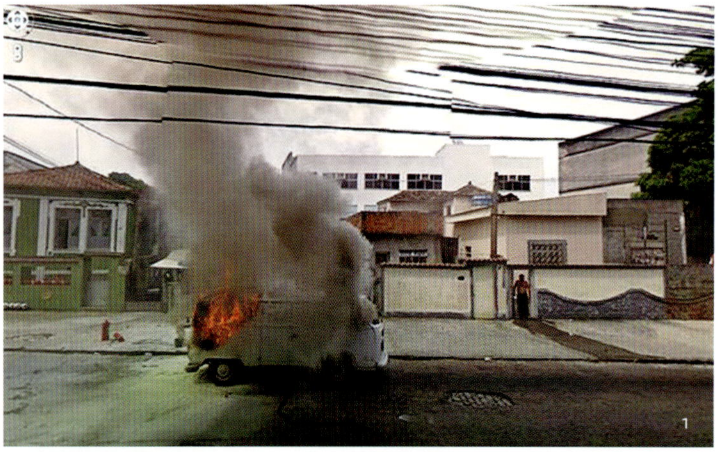

1

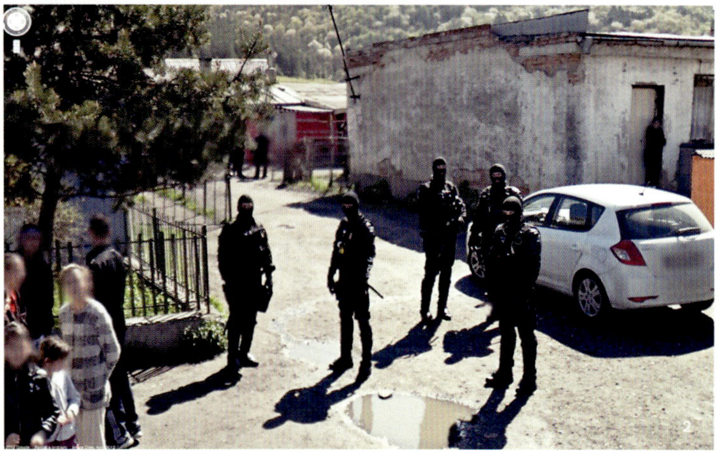

2

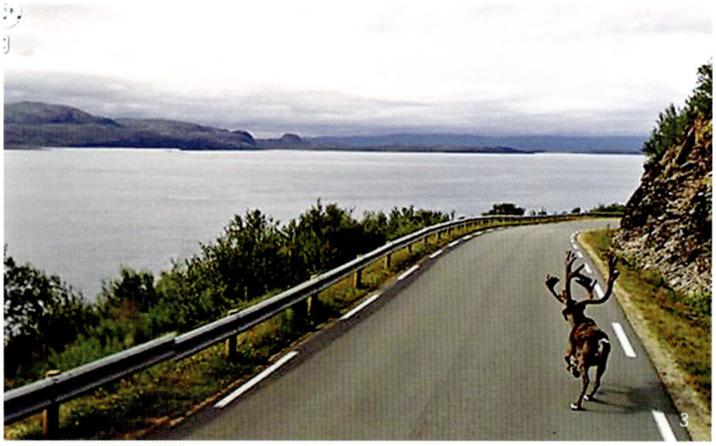

3

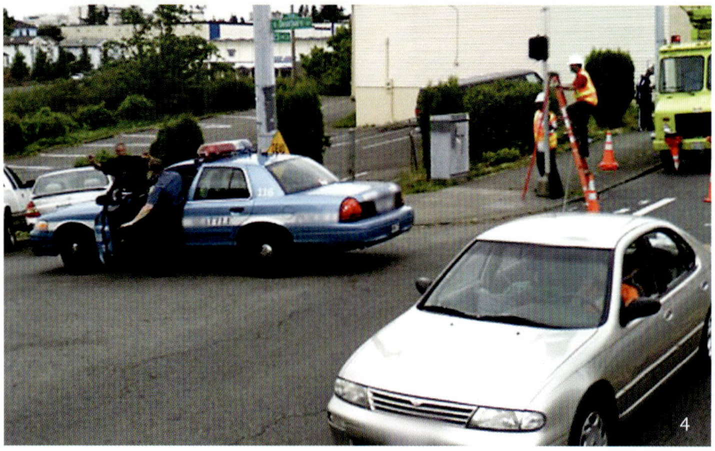

4

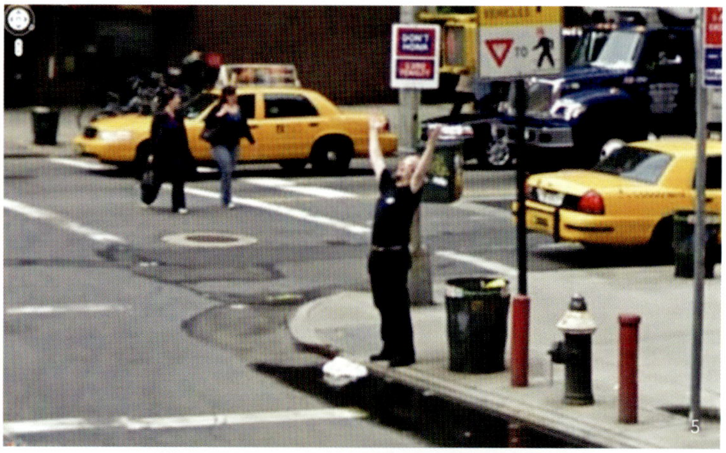

5

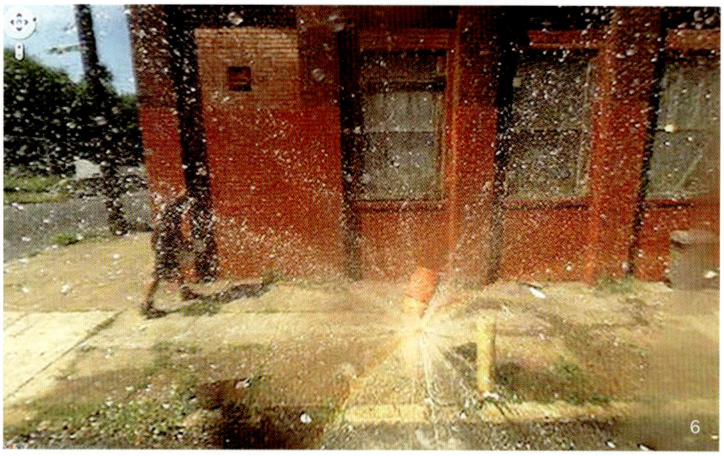

6

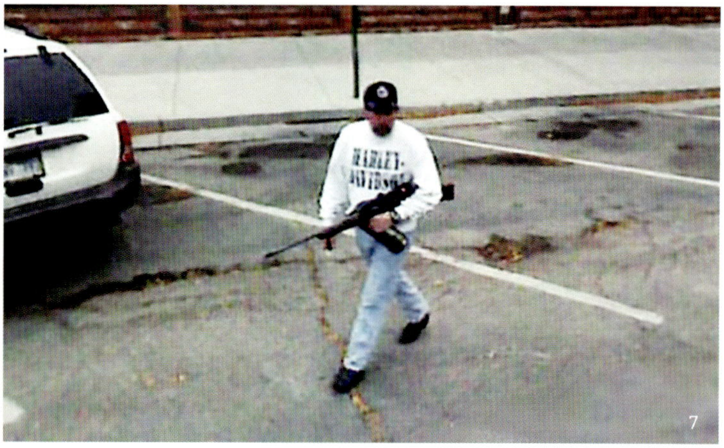

7

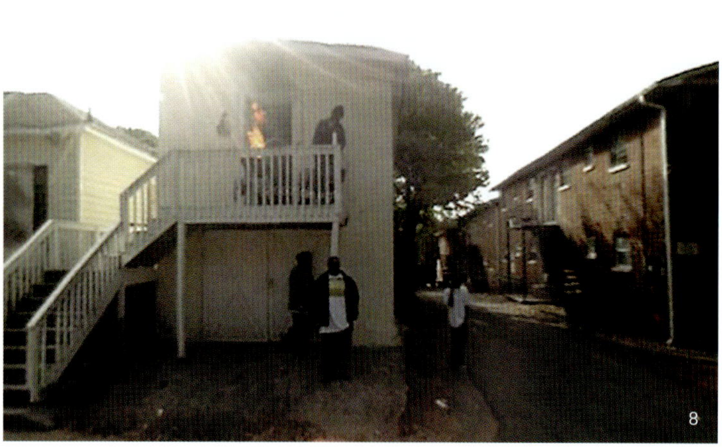

8

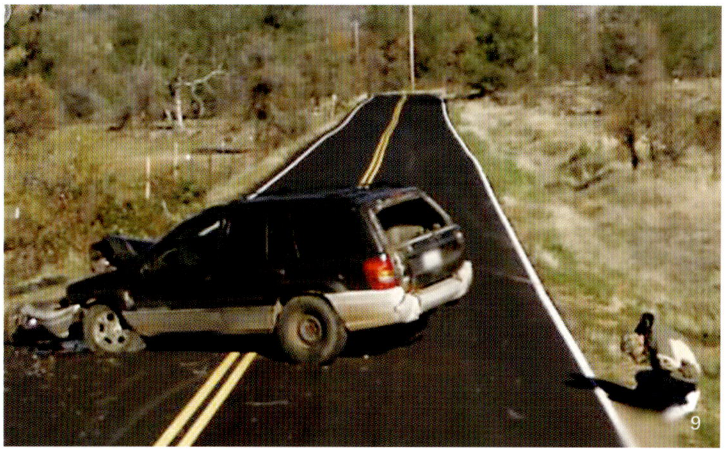

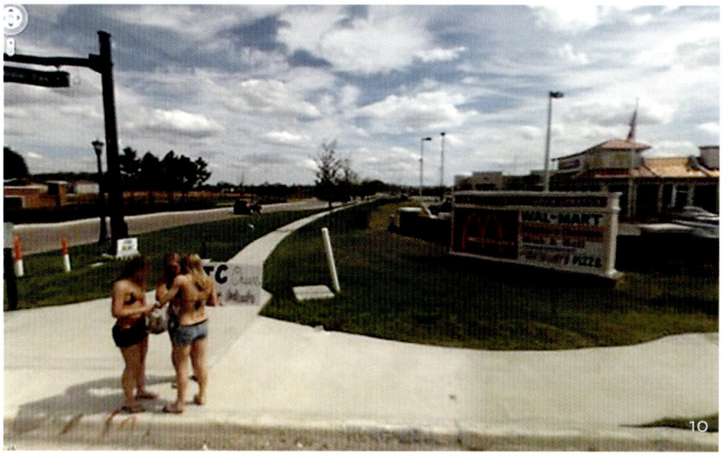

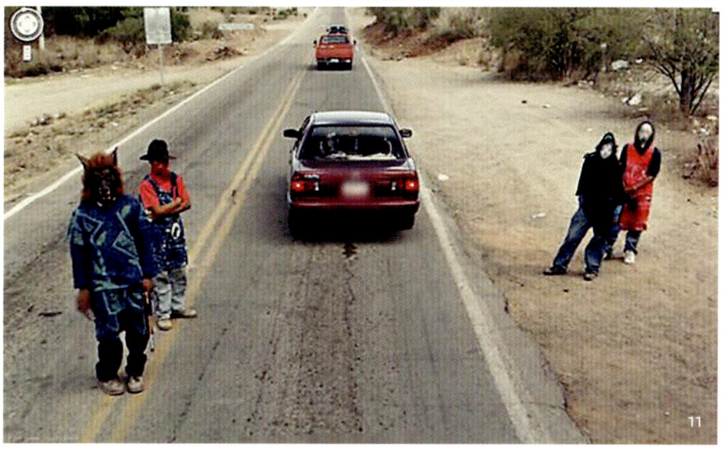

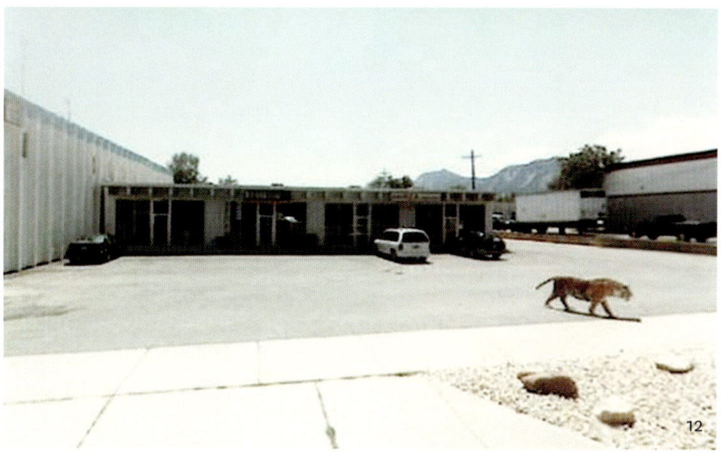

FIG. 6

Jon Rafman

Google Street View Project

Archival pigment prints mounted on Dibond®

40 x 64 in. (101.6 x 162.6 cm), each

Courtesy of Zach Feuer Gallery, New York

FROM TOP TO BOTTOM, LEFT TO RIGHT

1
9 Rua Pereira da Costa
Rio de Janeiro, Brazil, 2010

2
75 Na Podskaiku, Humenne
Presov Region, Slovakia, 2012

3
Rv 888
Finnmark, Norway, 2010

4
3012 23rd Avenue South
Seattle, Washington, n.d.

5
214 9th Avenue
New York, New York, 2010

6
3004 North Hope Street
Philadelphia, Pennsylvania, 2010

7
Main Street
Rapid City, South Dakota, 2009

8
26 Little Street, Southeast
Atlanta, Georgia, n.d.

9
28052 Oak Run Road
Central Shasta, California, 2010

10
South Avalon Park Boulevard
Union Park, Florida, n.d.

11
Nacozari de García-Moctezuma
Sonora, Mexico, n.d.

12
3081 Valmont Road
Boulder, Colorado, 2012

FIG. 7 BELOW

Google Street View Camera

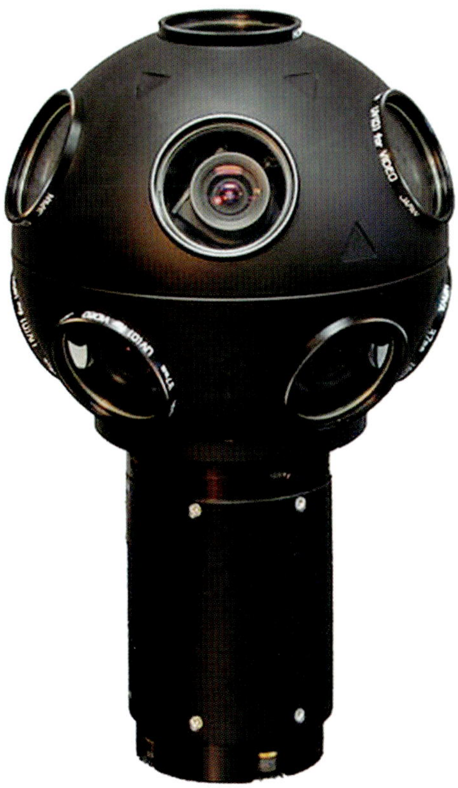

Recent examples of photographs being used as a vehicle for exploring jewelry's functions include Noa Zilberman's *Wrinkles* (NO. 137), a video and still photography project that examines the aging process of the human face. In it, Zilberman creates a facial map of future wrinkles by placing fine golden lines where her wrinkles will eventually occur, undermining the function of jewelry to beautify. Where Künzli used his photographic *Schönheitsgalerie* to critique jewelry as status symbol, Zilberman upsets the notion of jewelry as beautifier.

The hollow quest to gratify desire with rare gems and precious metals underlies Lauren Kalman's photographs and videos. Kalman, who calls her work "transgressions on the body," uses video to examine the grotesque aspects of beautification. As her *Tongue Gilding* video progresses, it is clear that what appears to be beautiful gilding is actually a form of torture, which, over the course of history, has often been the flip side of beauty (NO. 134).

Sarah Turner's *If One Could Wear a Marching Band* is a necklace projected on the body as a way to free herself from dependence on physical objects (NO. 139). Going beyond conventional constraints, she invites us to imagine a world where one could actually wear a full marching band. Such projections not only document a performance or once existing jewelry object, but also point to a new direction in jewelry in which the glitter and sparkle of gems are replaced by wearable light and color.

Although she trained as a goldsmith, Suska Mackert rarely makes jewelry, turning instead to photography and video to focus on its representative and symbolic aspects. In her video *To Be on Display*, Mackert suggests how the familiar, seductive jewelry brand names and logos of advertisements gain greater presence than the objects themselves (NO. 149). Her videos portray jewelry's complex associations on both intimate and societal levels.

The simple act of putting jewelry on and taking it off presents beautiful and poetic images in Esther Brinkmann's video *The Present Is the Only Thing Without an End* (NO. 131). At the opposite pole, video can be used to parody those who flaunt jewelry for its own sake, as is the case with Gisbert Stach's *Fitting*, in which a victim is crushed by the weight of accumulated but superficial luxury (NO. 133). An examination of the physical and metaphoric aspects of jewelry through photography and film helps to underscore the enduring importance of this wearable art form in our culture.

Since its invention, photography has been a transformative technology. The jewelry in *Multiple Exposures* harnesses that power, culling images from every source imaginable to introduce a world of new ideas, new materials, and new techniques. Today's photo jewelry embodies stimulating insights into subjects relevant to contemporary life. With its central focus on personal meaning, and its prime relationship to the body, photo jewelry has a unique position as a locus of intimate interactions in an increasingly impersonal and image-saturated world. Situated at the pulsating junction of photography and jewelry, the works in *Multiple Exposures* allow us to see the world of images all around us through a more human lens.

Ursula Ilse-Neuman *is Curator of Jewelry at the Museum of Arts and Design.*

1

Lyle Rexer, "Science, Sentiment, and Status: Early Photo Jewelry," in *Multiple Exposures: Jewelry and Photography*, 32–40.

2

Suzanne Ramljak, "Saving Face: Photo Portrait Jewelry," in *Multiple Exposures: Jewelry and Photography*, 54–57.

3

Lowery Stokes Sims, "Wearing the Body," in *Multiple Exposures: Jewelry and Photography*, 100–104.

4

Ansel Adams, interview by Victoria and David Sheff, *Playboy* 30, no. 5 (May 1983): 67–87, 222–26.

5

Scott Indrisek, "Out There: Taking It to the (Virtual) Streets," *Blouinartinfo* (September 28, 2010), http://www.blouinartinfo.com/news/story/122661/out-there-taking-it-to-the-virtual-streets.

6

Ellen Maurer-Zilioli, "Remembered Places, Imagined Spaces," in *Multiple Exposures: Jewelry and Photography*, 130–36.

7

Jutta-Annette Page, "The Appropriated Image in Contemporary Jewelry," in *Multiple Exposures: Jewelry and Photography*, 166–69.

8

Mark Alice Durant, "Lost Lenses and Orphaned Apertures: Apparatus Transformed," in *Multiple Exposures: Jewelry and Photography*, 194–98.

9

Ralph Turner, *Contemporary Jewellery: A Critical Assessment 1945–1975* (London: Studio Vista, 1976), 160.

10

Lucy Lippard, *Six Years: The Dematerialization of the Art Object from 1966 to 1972* (New York: Praeger, 1973).

11

Liesbeth den Besten, "Jewelry through the Lens," in *Multiple Exposures: Jewelry and Photography*, 218–22.

The epigraph that appears with this essay is from Gerald M. Edelman and Giulio Tononi's book *A Universe of Consciousness* (New York: Basic Books, 2001).

The sources for the display quotes on pages 16 through 20 are:

Charles Baudelaire as quoted in *Baudelaire: Selected Writings on Art and Artists*, translated by P. E. Charvet (Cambridge: Cambridge University Press, 1972), 290.

Anthony Bourdain in *Kitchen Confidential: Adventures in the Culinary Underbelly* (New York: Harper Collins, 2007).

Henry David Thoreau journal entry for August 5, 1851, in *The Journal of Henry David Thoreau* (Boston: Houghton Mifflin Co., 1906), 373.

T. S. Eliot, "Philip Massinger," in *The Sacred Wood: Essays on Poetry and Criticism* (New York: Alfred A. Knopf, 1921); Bartleby.com, 2000 (http://www.bartleby.com/200/sw11.html).

Old New England proverb in Wolfgang Mieder, *Proverbs Speak Louder Than Words: Folk Wisdom in Art, Culture, Folklore, History, Literature and Mass Media* (New York: Peter Lang, 2008), 161.

Friedrich Nietzsche as quoted in *Friedrich Nietzsche: Collected Works* (Berlin: Walter de Gruter GmbH & Co., 1999), 219.

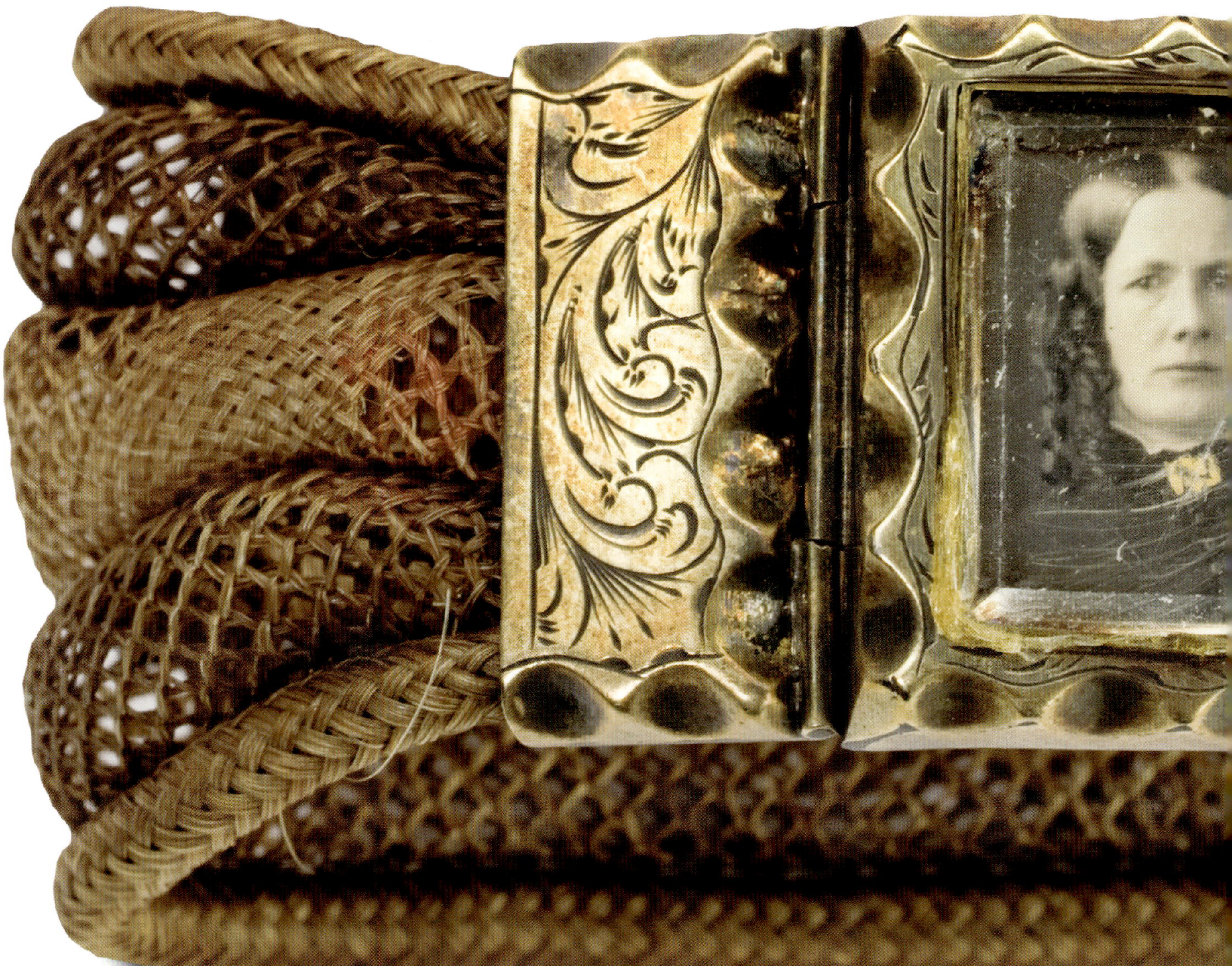

"...WHAT WAS THE MAGIC GOOD FOR?..."

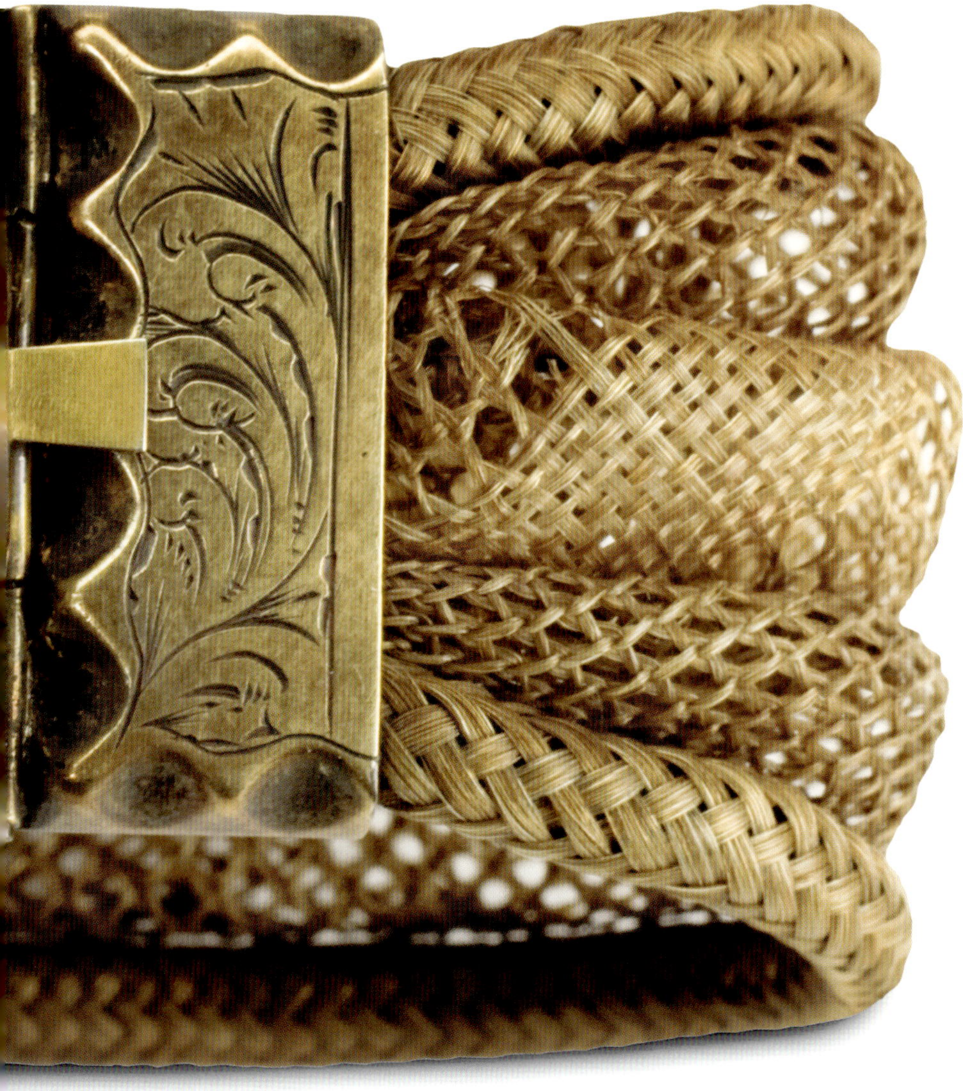

SCIENCE, SENTIMENT, AND STATUS EARLY PHOTO JEWELRY

LYLE REXER

WILLIAM HENRY FOX TALBOT (1800–1877), a pioneer in the development of early photographic processes, called the new medium of photography "a little bit of magic realized."[1] So it must have seemed in the *annus mirabilis* of 1839, when it was announced that both Talbot and the Frenchman Louis-Jacques-Mandé Daguerre (1787–1851), an entrepreneur and panorama painter, had succeeded in recording permanent images through capturing light on a surface. Daguerre's process came first, a method for making a one-of-a-kind image on a copper plate coated with silver and exposed in a camera, the eponymous daguerreotype. Talbot followed soon after with the description of a process he called photogenic drawing, the production of negative images on paper via sunlight and chemicals. Daguerre's remarkable, shimmering apparitions and Talbot's strangely hued monochromatic stains on paper carried what no artist, however talented, could ever achieve: the direct and exact description of visible reality.

The question was what was the magic good for? To what use could it be put? One of the most fascinating answers combined the parallel pursuit of beauty and economic gain with personal expression and broad social trends. Starting in the 1840s and continuing through the nineteenth century, jewelry incorporating the new medium of photography enjoyed tremendous popularity. It was worn by almost every stratum of society in Europe, England, and the United States, from Queen Victoria to the matriarch of a rural farm family, from a club-going gentleman to an up-and-coming salesman. The meteoric rise of this genre of adornment was the result of a revolutionary technology meeting societies undergoing profound political and economic changes. These changes affected the status and aspirations of individuals as well as deeper attitudes toward time, memory, loss, and death. One expression of these shifts was a pervasive desire for realistic images, a desire satisfied most poignantly and elegantly by photo jewelry.

A Useless, Desired Art

In its simplest embodiment, a photograph is an image formed by light that has been captured on a sensitized surface. A lens is not required in order to focus the light, although it makes the process more precise, and more controllable. The earliest cameras were no more than small boxes with a pinhole-size perforation to admit light. Applied to a thin piece of paper, the emulsion produced a negative image. This could serve as a template for the exposure of another coated surface to yield a positive. Almost any surface could receive an image to create a photograph, from leather to leaves to wood, but the most popular supports during the first four decades of photography were paper, glass, and metal. All were used in jewelry.

It is a testament to the fascination with photography that so many people were trying to invent it. Historian Pierre Harmant identified no fewer than twenty-four candidates for "first photographer,"[2] and there were experiments with the chemistry of the medium at least a hundred years before Daguerre's announcement. Other contemporaries, including Thomas Wedgwood (1771–1805), of the porcelain manufacturing family, experimented with the medium, and Samuel Morse (1791–1872), inventor of the telegraph code, introduced it to the United States. The main barrier seems not to have been capturing images but fixing them so that they would not continue to darken after their first exposure to light. Once the problem was solved by a friend of Talbot's, Englishman John Herschel (1792–1871), and the chemistry perfected, the gates opened, and a flood of images deluged Europe and the United States and spread literally around the world—this in spite of the fact, again, that no one was quite sure what the images were good for.

Talbot thought he knew. He patented a negative-positive paper process and in 1844 set up an ambitious business in Reading, England, to sell prints and publish editions of his multivolume *The Pencil of Nature*. The business managed to sell copies of his book but soon wound up running in the red. It wasn't until glass plate negatives were introduced in the 1850s that paper photography achieved widespread application, including in jewelry.

The daguerreotype was a different story. Daguerre turned over the patent for his process to the French government, which in turn released it to the world (although it was later patented in England). In exchange, he received a life pension, and the free availability of his secrets prompted a kind of craze among the public for making daguerreotypes. Newspapers in Paris parodied the hordes of amateurs and professionals crowding the street corners of the city with their large, unwieldy daguerreotype cameras. In a famous review of the Salon exhibition of 1859, the poet Charles Baudelaire (1821–1867) inveighed against the spread of photography among the public and especially against photographers' pretensions to art.[3] In the United States, the luminaries of early photography established commercial practices—Mathew Brady (1822–1896) in New York and the team of Albert Southworth (1811–1894) and Josiah Hawes (1808–1901) in Boston, among others. On lower Broadway in Manhattan, dozens of daguerreotype studios dedicated to making portraits lined the street, each promising pictures that, in the words of a Brady advertisement, "display all the artistic arrangements of the highest efforts of the painters."[4]

It is estimated that by the mid-1850s, several million daguerreotypes had been made, and in this expansion, photography began to discover its applications. Art was only one of them. The medium was used to catalogue

FIG. 1

Artist unknown, 1860s

Reproduced from West and Abbott, *Antique Photographic Jewelry* (New York: West Companies, Inc., Larry J. West, 2005).

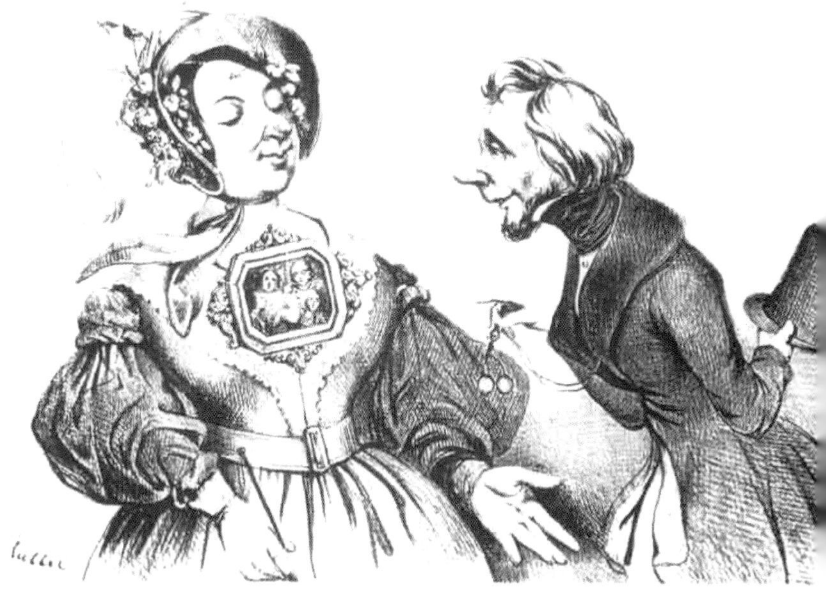

"Sir . . . have you seen my new photo jewelry?"

historical architecture; record foreign and exotic scenes and peoples; document police proceedings; survey the sun, moon,and stars; and provide a highly graphic and widely disseminated form of pornography. Above all, through an industry of portrait-taking, photography showed people what they looked like (NOS. 2, 3). For the first time in human history, the ordinary person could reasonably expect to have a permanent representation of himself and his family. In this age of an emerging middle class, photography joined hands with that other rapidly expanding medium of self-regard and self-presentation, jewelry.

Birth of a Genre

It is difficult to pinpoint exactly when photographs were first combined with jewelry, but by the mid- to late 1840s photographic studios and fine jewelers, including prestigious houses in France and England, were advertising settings for photographs. The elite silversmith Charles Christofle (1805–1863) was involved in both ends of the process, not only creating custom and manufactured settings but also producing the daguerreotype plates themselves. Photographs, usually portraits, appeared in lockets, earrings, brooches, bracelets, watchcases, cuff links, tiepins, hair combs, clutches, jewelry cases and boxes, telescoping gold pencils (NO. 7), and even vinaigrettes (NO. 8).

The daguerreotype was ideal for jewelry because it was itself a stunning creation. Oliver Wendell Holmes, Sr. (1809–1894), novelist, physician, and father of the famous American jurist, described it as "a mirror with a memory."[5] A piece of copper plated with silver and sensitized to light provided an exceptionally precise image on a surface that shimmered with reflected light. It was often elaborately framed, sometimes with gold, and fitted with a case incorporating a wide range of materials from velvet, leather, and mother-of-pearl to gutta-percha. Jewelry was in essence but an alternative display mount for the image, albeit an especially attractive

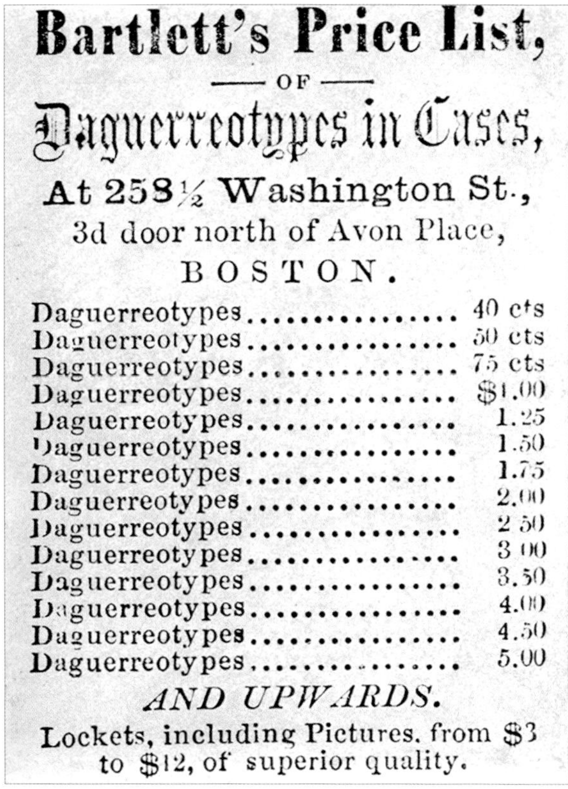

Bartlett's Price List,
OF
Daguerreotypes in Cases,
At 258½ Washington St.,
3d door north of Avon Place,
BOSTON.

Daguerreotypes.................	40 cts
Daguerreotypes.................	50 cts
Daguerreotypes.................	75 cts
Daguerreotypes.................	$1.00
Daguerreotypes.................	1.25
Daguerreotypes.................	1.50
Daguerreotypes.................	1.75
Daguerreotypes.................	2.00
Daguerreotypes.................	2.50
Daguerreotypes.................	3.00
Daguerreotypes.................	3.50
Daguerreotypes.................	4.00
Daguerreotypes.................	4.50
Daguerreotypes.................	5.00

AND UPWARDS.
Lockets, including Pictures, from $3 to $12, of superior quality.

FIG. 2
Bartlett's Price List, 1856–58.
Collection of Larry J. West

one, since the best settings were made with silver or gold and adorned with precious stones. The result was a compounded brilliance of image and staging.

The variety and accessibility of photo jewelry increased even more after 1851, when Englishman Frederick Scott Archer (1813–1857) invented a process for coating glass plates with an ether-based solution and then with silver salts to make them light sensitive. The wet collodion process, as it was known, yielded a negative of great tonal range and detail that could produce multiple positive prints. Backing the glass with a dark color produced an image that "read" as a positive. This was called an ambrotype. The same technique could also be applied to a thin piece of iron coated with black lacquer to produce the misleadingly named tintype. Both tintypes and ambrotypes were cheaper to produce than daguerreotypes, while the paper print had the virtue of being reproducible. This opened the door to the mass production of imagery for personal adornment—in political and military badges, campaign buttons, and cheap commemorative pins of all kinds. The paper print, ambrotype, and tintype rapidly replaced the daguerreotype, in jewelry and everywhere else, and by the late 1860s, the daguerreotype was commercially extinct.

Most of nineteenth-century photo jewelry was purchased out of photography studios or medium-priced jewelry stores, not from fine jewelers. Many pieces lack the maker's or manufacturer's name. The workmanship, although often handsome, is relatively simple and unrefined. The jewelry historian Joyce Jonas notes that throughout most of the nineteenth century, the majority of fine mountings in the United States were imported from Germany, England, or France. European mountings were often imported unfinished, and jewelers or wholesalers added final touches.[6] Over time, as methods of mass production improved, the United States developed its own mass-market mountings.

This increase of consumer choices dovetailed perfectly with a growing demand for jewelry among women. Not only were the wives of successful professionals buying and wearing jewelry as an important mode of publicly displaying their personal wealth, women were also entering the workplace as never before, including the burgeoning field of photography. This growth of the middle class and the increasing social prominence of women in that class spurred the market for all manner of adornments.[7]

Photographers were there to supply the demand for tokens of status and affection. Their studios constituted a new outlet for retail jewelry. Some thirty-one hundred professional photographers were listed in the United States alone as of 1860, and most of them offered photo jewelry.[8] Indeed, New York's most popular daguerreotypist, Jeremiah Gurney (1812–1895), began his career as a jeweler and switched to photography, perhaps to take advantage of both avenues of the trade. A glimpse inside Bartlett's of Boston, a typical upper-tier photo studio of the period, indicates how a customer would have acquired photo jewelry.[9] The gallery advertised lockets for three to twelve dollars and offered a wide range of detailing (fig. 2). Some of the mountings would have come from manufacturers like E. and H. T. Anthony of New York, which offered a comprehensive catalogue of jewelry settings for photographs, from brooches and swivel pins to scroll rings and spring lockets. Bartlett's would likely have worked with local jewelers on more intricate items. Customers would have come to Bartlett's because their jewelry prices were right or more likely because of the attractiveness of the settings they offered. For specialty items the jeweler himself might have been present to help make the sale.

To take the picture that would be displayed in the jewelry—often an image no more than an inch or an inch and a half in height, or even smaller—the photographer would use a camera with multiple lenses in order to make several images on a single plate. This insured at least one useable image from a sitting and most likely more if several pieces were to be made. It was a delicate matter to cut the tin, silver, or glass plate apart, especially since the images would have to be shaped to fit a particular mount. For a final touch, the portrait might be hand-tinted, possibly by a female assistant working in the studio. With a delicate touch of pink to the cheeks, the beloved simulacrum would be brought to life.

If the piece were crafted in England, however, the entire portrait, not just the cheeks, would likely have been colored. The difference between European and American photo jewelry—and especially between unique pieces and

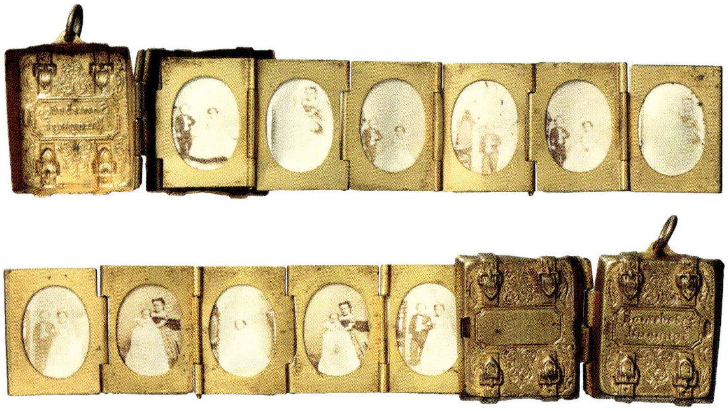

FIG. 3

From the photography studio of Mathew B. Brady (1822–1896)
Miniature Wedding Album of General Tom Thumb and Lavinia Warren (pendant), ca. 1863
Albumen silver prints, brass
1 1/8 x 7/8 x 3/8 in. (2.7 x 2.0 x 1.0 cm), album closed
The Metropolitan Museum of Art,
Joyce F. Menschel Photography Library Fund, 1999 (1999.89)

mass-produced items—is striking. As a rule, European pieces were more design-intensive, sporting elaborate scrollwork and engraving, with more edges and angles and more complex shapes.[10]

Lavish specialty settings could be purchased from well-known jewelers such as Phillips, Brogden, and Streeter, as well as from Garrard, the jewelers on whom Queen Victoria bestowed the title Crown Jeweller.[11] In the United States, Tiffany (often working with manufacturers in New Jersey) created one-of-a-kind settings, and in Paris, center of the fashion world under Napoleon III, Vever, Cartier, Boucheron, and others catered to an elite clientele. For middle-class customers from the mid-nineteenth century on, newly inaugurated department stores in London, Manchester, Dublin, Paris, New York, Chicago, and Philadelphia, among other cities, sold jewelry settings for photographs at fixed prices. It prompts the question, why did the nineteenth century especially find photo jewelry so compelling?

Designs for an Ocular Age

The philosopher Ralph Waldo Emerson (1803–1882) may have put the answer best when he called the period "an ocular age." The vast majority of photo jewelry is portraiture, and it represents a period when seeing and being seen took on broader social significance. This was the period of the *carte de visite*, introduced in 1854. The small photo calling card not only announced a person's name and presence but also confirmed his or her social status by representing the bearer's physical appearance. These became wildly popular and in mass reproduction helped confer a kind of celebrity status on a wide range of public figures, from stage actresses to military commanders. The rise of a new class of manufacturers and commercial managers seeking social prominence and prestige occurred against the backdrop of an expanding illustrated press, a press that made Queen Victoria herself the first true media superstar by obsessively documenting her marriage, childbearing, and extended bereavement. Jewelry often picked up where the press left off. A popular item was a miniature album of photos that could be worn as a locket commemorating the wedding of the tiny General Tom Thumb, a stage figure promoted by P. T. Barnum, and another small person, Lavinia Warren (fig. 3).

For a society increasingly preoccupied with looking at pictures of itself and its celebrities, the binocular locket could serve as a symbol. These pieces came with a built-in magnifying lens, so that friends and acquaintances could better see the socially displayed image. They solicited and facilitated the gaze. Cartoons of the day showed men peering overzealously at the photo necklaces that adorned ample female bosoms (fig. 1).

The desire for specific visual description went hand in hand with a burgeoning cult of sentiment that reflected the rising importance of *individuals*, their interior, emotional lives and their external attachments and relations. Long before photography, painted miniatures had supplied the objects of sentiment and recollection. Indeed, miniatures and photo jewelry coexisted well into the nineteenth century, fulfilling a similar keepsake role. Queen Victoria herself collected both.

A striking example was the bracelet with painted miniature produced by the Frenchman Honoré Bourdoncle (1823–1893) in 1855 as a gift to the queen, who later gave it to her daughter, Princess Beatrice (fig. 4). Adorned with diamonds and rubies, the intricate setting for the tiny hand-painted portrait shows a high level of workmanship, yet its base metal is neither gold nor silver but aluminum. Novel at the time, this metal was both decorative and easy to work.

One of the most fascinating pre-photographic chapters involves so-called eye jewelry, painted miniatures that represented the eye of a loved one (figs. 5, 6). They provide an apt metaphor for the position of representational jewelry at the beginning of Emerson's ocular age, for they blur the line between public display and private sentiment. The eye brooch revealed an object of affection—a lover or spouse—but preserved his or her privacy because only the couple themselves could identify the image. Often these miniatures were decorated with pearls, symbolizing lovers' tears.

The sheer availability of photographic pieces, however, soon rendered the painted miniature a precious curiosity from the past. Yet there was a deeper reason for the eclipse. Photographic likenesses added a new—and perhaps crucial—level of documentary immediacy, a more precise individuality, indeed, an unprecedented means of remembrance. As Elizabeth Barrett wrote of daguerreotypes in 1843, "It is not merely the likeness which is precious . . . but the association and the sense of nearness involved in the thing . . . *the very shadow of the person* lying there fixed forever!"[12] Until photography, most people remembered friends and loved ones by remembering *them*. Soon it became more convenient (and cheaper than a painted miniature) to refer to a photographic image. A watchcase with a child's picture on the inside or a locket with facing photographs of a couple "kissing in the dark until liberated into the light of the loved one's gaze," in the words of

FIG. 4
Honoré-Severin Bourdoncle (1823–1893)
Bracelet with Miniature Portrait of Queen Victoria, ca. 1855
Watercolor on ivory, aluminum, brass, diamonds, rubies, enamel, gold
$2^{5}/_{8}$ in. (6.5 cm), width
By kind permission of the Duke of Buccleuch & Queensberry KBE

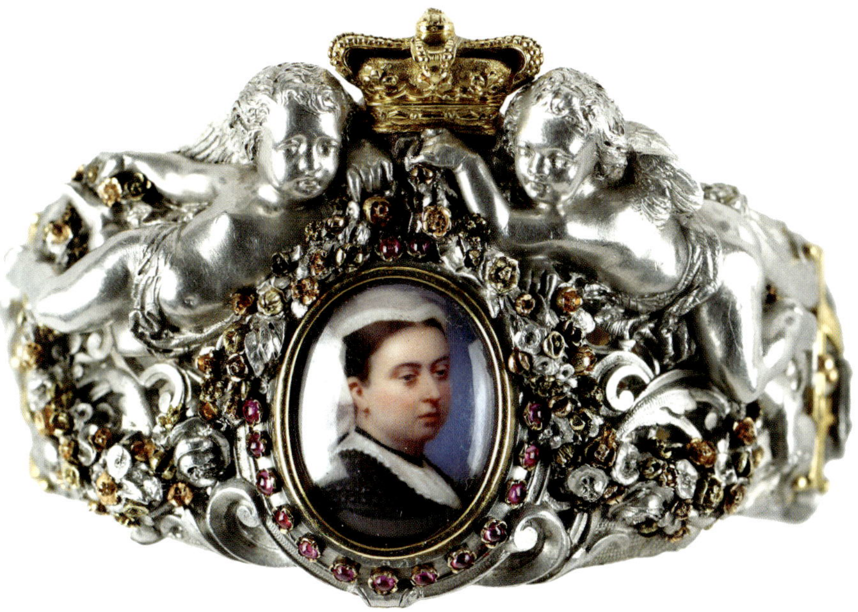

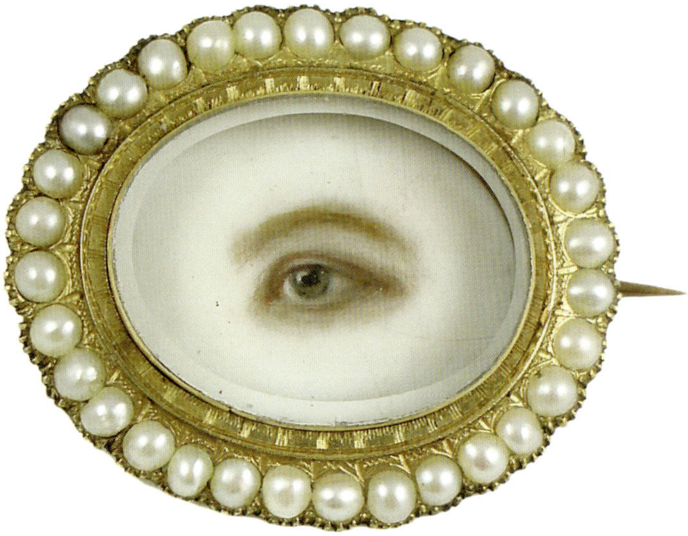

FIG. 5
Artist unknown
Brooch with Eye Miniature, ca. 1845
Watercolor on ivory, gold, pearls, rock crystal
7/8 x 1 in. (2.2 x 2.5 cm)
Collection of Cathy Gordon

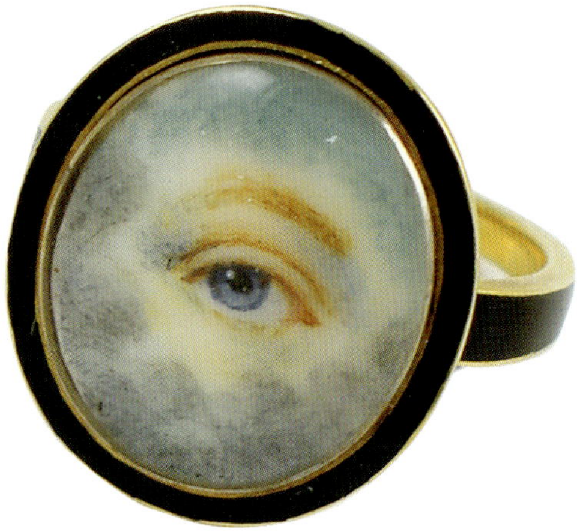

FIG. 6
Artist unknown
Mourning Ring with Eye Miniature, 1800
Watercolor on ivory, black enamel, gold, rock crystal
3/4 in. (1.7 cm), height; 2 1/4 in. (5.7 cm), diameter
Collection of Cathy Gordon

photo historian Geoffrey Batchen,[13] signaled the rise of private contemplation of intimate others—and a new, technologically enhanced capacity to hold them in mind.

At the same time, jewelry became a vehicle for communicating one's personal situation and values according to a "language" of materials, colors, and settings. The clever physical mechanisms of the pieces themselves further enabled the wearers to draw the lines between public and private realms. A beautiful example is a brooch from the 1860s bearing the gilt-highlighted enlistment portrait of a young Union soldier (NO. 5). Mounted on a swivel setting, it might have been worn face-forward during the day, almost as a badge, promoting ideas of patriotism, honor, sacrifice, and family. In the evening, it would likely have been reversed so that the image was close to the mother's heart, a turning inward of sentiment and memory.[14] A pair of onyx earrings whose dark color emphasized the somberness and formality of mourning complemented the brooch. This was an ensemble of image and symbol that transformed its wearer in the communication of loss.

The ability of photographs to stand in for the represented subject produced its profoundest emotional impact in mourning jewelry. Author Mary Brett puts it succinctly: "No era in history has had its living more immersed in dying than the Victorian era."[15] Death was a constant companion through conflicts such as the Civil War and the Crimean debacle, severe outbreaks of disease, and high infant mortality rates. Small wonder, then, that jewelry displaying recently deceased children or infants was so popular (NO. 4). Queen Victoria wore mourning for the remainder of her life after the death of Prince Albert in 1861 and was a singular force in popularizing the custom of commemorative photo jewelry in England. In the United States, a small industry grew up around commemorations of Abraham Lincoln. Lincoln was the first widely photographed president, guiding the country through the most tumultuous and bloody time in its young history. The national trauma resulting from his assassination after years of civil war prompted an outpouring of grief that was embodied in homemade mourning pins and badges (NO. 6). The sentence laid upon photography was quasi-theological. As an advertising slogan of the time put it, "Secure the Shadow ere the Substance fade. / Let Nature imitate what Nature made."[16]

People took the injunction literally. Hair of the deceased was often incorporated into memorial pieces, transforming them into reliquaries, and hair of the living as well as the deceased was woven into decorative bands for bracelets. The trade in human hair for jewelry was brisk. In creations like the woven hair bracelet with its delicate daguerreotype portrait (NO. 1), image and materials work together to produce an effect that is both primitive and decorative. Human hair augments the power of the picture to reconvene the absent other. The bracelet hovers between the evocation of a loved one and her literal restitution. From these natural strands the reverential fabric of memory was woven.

The very commonplaceness, the sheer ubiquity, of photographs probably contributed to their diminished prominence in fine jewelry in the twentieth century, although paradoxically this availability has had quite the opposite effect in contemporary art jewelry. In any case, we have ways of communicating status and identity now that were not available in the nineteenth century. It is hard to imagine, for example, that a piece of popular jewelry sporting a tourist photograph of a city like Osterode am Harz, Germany, would excite the admiration or the curiosity it probably did at the end of the nineteenth century, when global tourism was not yet a mass phenomenon (NO. 9), yet photo jewelry has remained popular throughout the twentieth century and into the twenty-first. Examples such as African-American celluloid portrait buttons from the 1930s (NO. 17) and First and Second World War "trench rings" sporting pictures of soldiers' wives, families, and sweethearts testify to the evocative power of photo jewelry (NOS. 10–16). Trench jewelry especially reminds us of the emotional history of war's relation to all keepsake photography, not only to the mourning pieces already discussed but also to the images carried into battle and those sent to family and loved ones from the front. Trench jewelry was fashioned by the soldiers themselves out of cheap and available metals such as the brass casings from cartridges and aluminum, which was soft enough to engrave. This they did in their own styles, often with the name of the battlefront and the date. Portraits could be cut out of paper photographs and pasted into the jewelry. In the age of the iPhone, when an entire personal archive can be carried in a pocket, it is unlikely that a version of trench jewelry would find much of a market among contemporary combat troops (though the pieces would have no batteries to run down). Yet precisely because of the simplicity and directness of their sentiment, these pieces speak to us with an added poignancy. Once meant to memorialize and celebrate specific individuals, they are now part of our cultural heritage. They illustrate the ongoing process by which memory—individual and collective—is becoming ever more thoroughly photographic.

Lyle Rexer *is a photo historian, critic, and lecturer, and a faculty member at the School of Visual Arts in New York City.*

1

In Gail Buckland, *Fox Talbot and the Invention of Photography* (Boston: David R. Godine, 1980), 32.

2

In Geoffrey Batchen, *Burning with Desire* (Cambridge, Mass.: MIT Press, 1997), 35.

3

Aaron Scharf, *Art and Photography* (London: Penguin Books, 1974), 145.

4

Larry J. West and Patricia A. Abbott, *Antique Photographic Jewelry: Tokens of Affection and Regard* (New York: West Companies, 2005), 153.

5

Oliver Wendell Holmes, "Doings of the Sunbeam," quoted in Beaumont Newhall (ed.), *Photography: Essays and Images* (New York: Museum of Modern Art, 1980), 54.

6

West and Abbott, *Antique Photographic Jewelry*, 124.

7

Charlotte Gere and Judy Rudoe, *Jewellery in the Age of Queen Victoria: Mirror to the World* (London: British Museum Press, 2010), 82.

8

West and Abbott, *Antique Photographic Jewelry*, 142.

9

Ibid.,137.

10

Ibid., 95.

11

Gere and Rudoe, *Jewellery in the Age of Queen Victoria*, 7–8.

12

In John Wood, *America and the Daguerreotype* (Iowa City, Iowa: University of Iowa, 1991), 96.

13

Batchen, *Burning with Desire*, 66.

14

Daile Kaplan, *Pop-Photographica: Photography's Objects in Everyday Life* (Toronto: Art Gallery of Ontario, 2003), 28.

15

Mary Brett, *Fashionable Mourning Jewelry, Clothing, and Customs* (Atglen, Penn.: Schiffer Publishing, 2006), 8.

16

Beaumont Newhall, *History of Photography from 1839 to the Present* (Boston: Little, Brown, 1982), 32; see also Jay Ruby, *Secure the Shadow* (Cambridge, Mass.: MIT Press, 1995), for an extended discussion of postmortem photography.

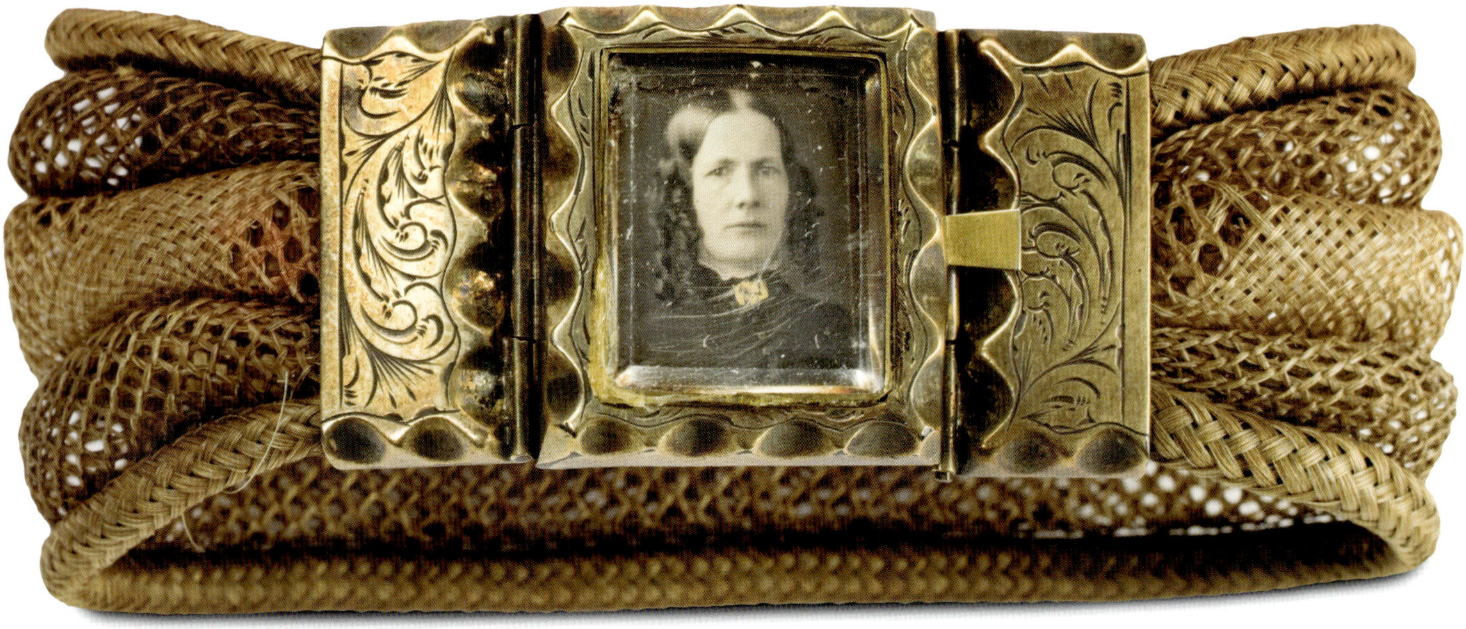

1 ABOVE

Unidentified artist

Bracelet inscribed "Lizzie," ca. 1850
Daguerreotype, gold-plated brass mount, woven hair, glass
5/8 x 1/2 in. (1.5 x 1.3 cm), image
1 1/4 x 6 1/4 in. (3.0 x 16.0 cm), open
Collection of George Eastman House, 1969:0214:0011

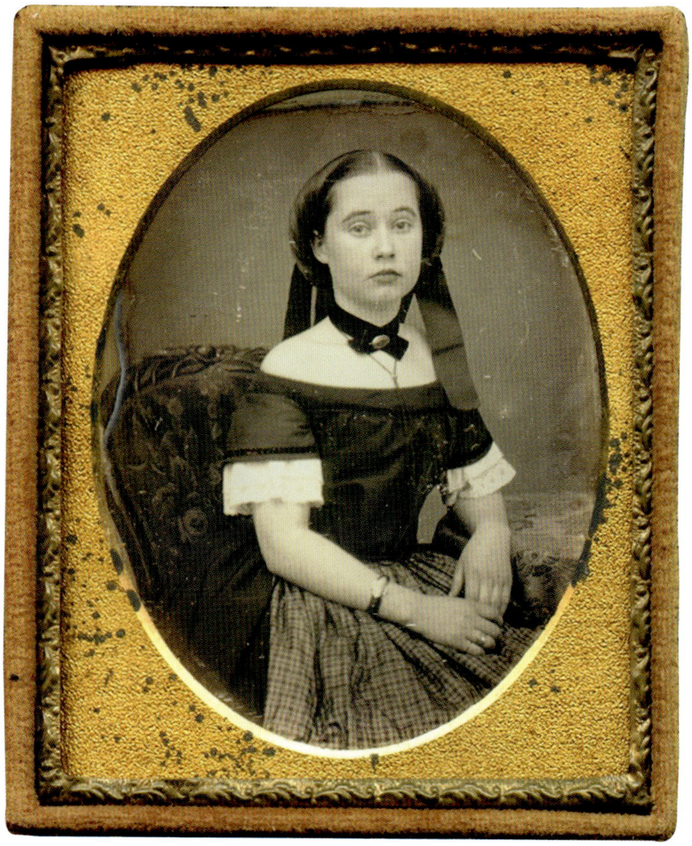

2 RIGHT

Photographer unknown

Studio Portrait of Unidentified Young Woman, ca. 1855
1/9 plate daguerreotype in half case
2 1/2 x 2 in. (6.4 x 5.1 cm)
Collection of Jeremy Rowe Vintage Photography

3 RIGHT

Unidentified artist
Pendant with Portrait of Mother and Two Children, ca. 1855
Daguerreotype, gold plate, hair, glass
$2\frac{1}{8} \times 1\frac{3}{4}$ in. (5.3 x 4.2 cm), image (oval)
$2\frac{1}{4} \times 1\frac{3}{4}$ in. (5.5 x 4.4 cm), mount (oval)
Collection of George Eastman House, 1977:0243:0005

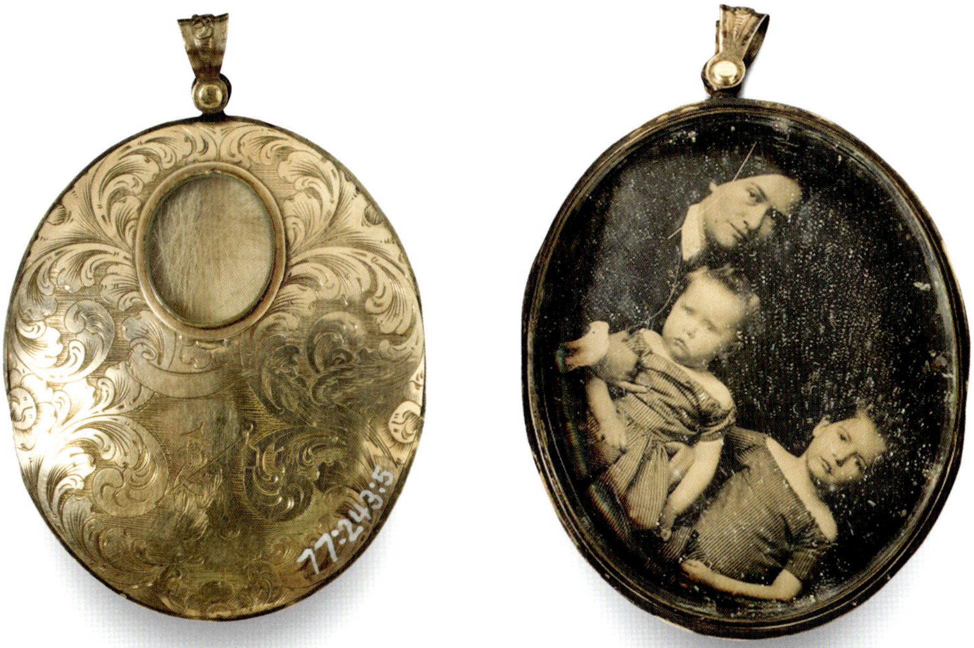

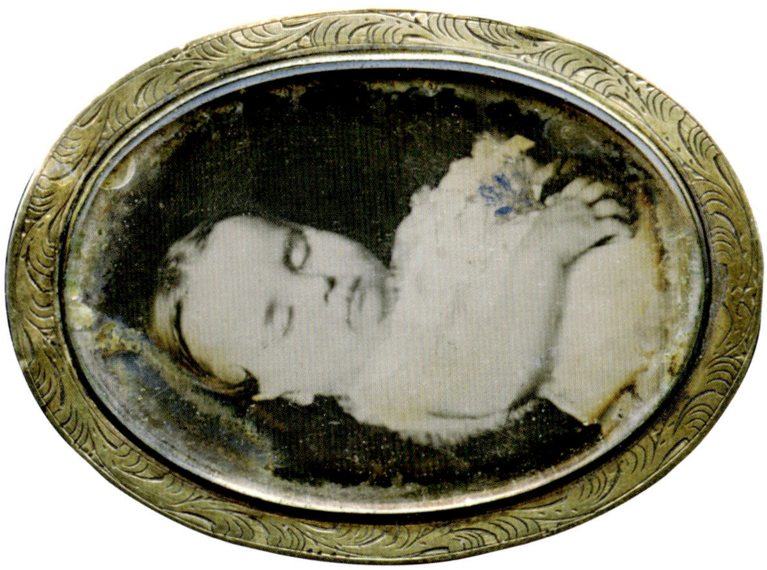

4 RIGHT

Photographer unknown
Maker unknown
Brooch with Postmortem Image of Young Child Holding Flowers, ca. 1855
Daguerreotype, gold-plated metal, enamel
$1\frac{3}{4} \times 1\frac{3}{8}$ in. (4.4 x 3.5 cm)
Collection of Jeremy Rowe Vintage Photography

5 BELOW

Photographer unknown
Maker unknown
Swivel Brooch with Portrait of Union Soldier, Irish Regiment, ca. 1863
Ambrotype, white onyx, black onyx (on back), electroplated gold
3 x 1 1/2 x 1/4 in. (7.6 x 3.8 x 0.6 cm)
Collection of Daile Kaplan

5 RIGHT

Maker unknown
Earrings, ca. 1863
Black onyx, white onyx, electroplated gold settings
1 1/4 x 3/4 x 1/4 in. (3.2 x 1.9 x 0.6 cm)
Collection of Daile Kaplan

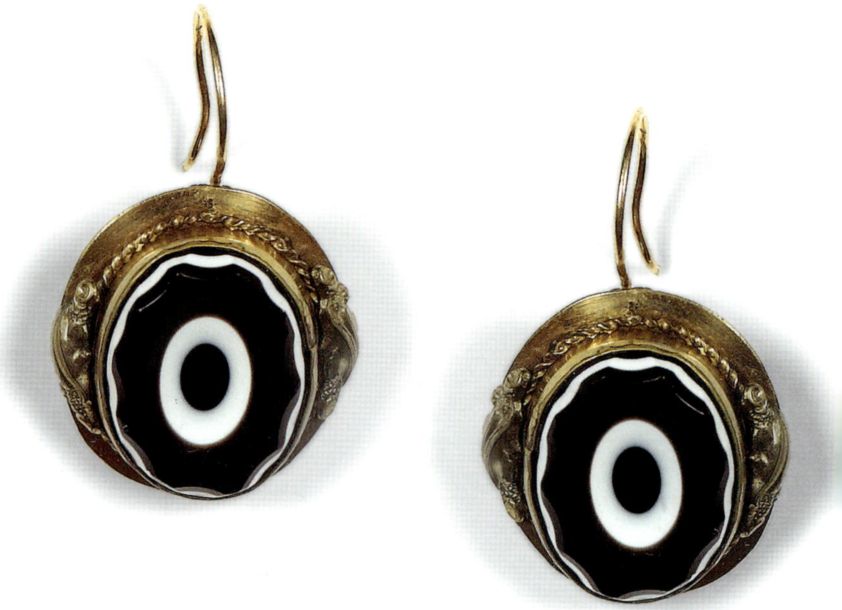

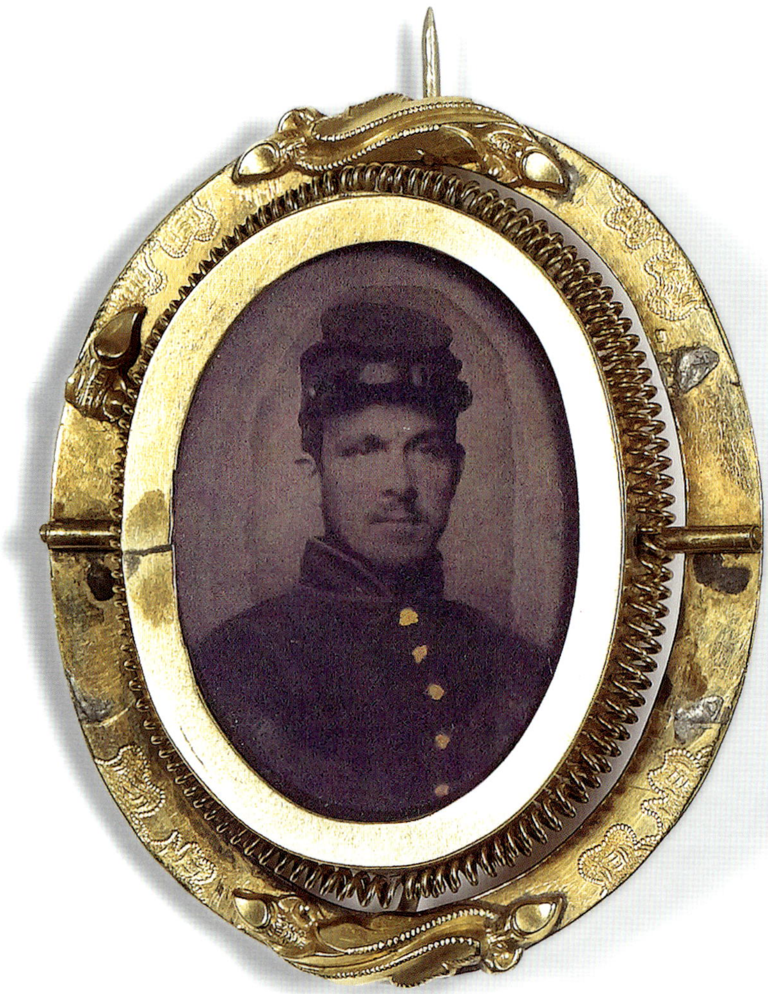

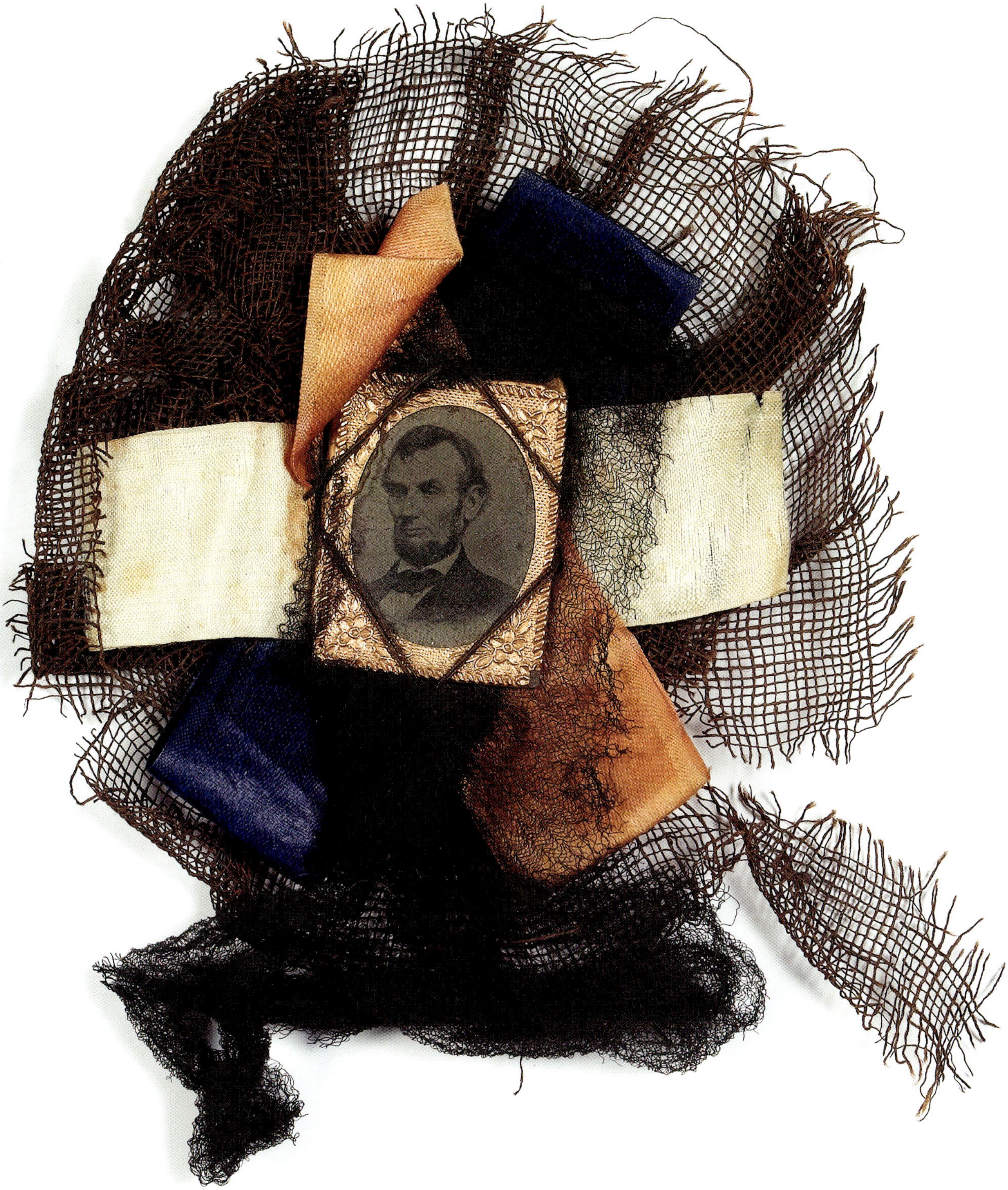

6

Photographer unknown

Maker unknown

Mourning Badge with Portrait of Abraham Lincoln, 1865

Tintype, gingham, black ribbons

4 1/2 x 3 1/2 in. (11.4 x 8.9 cm)

Collection of Daile Kaplan

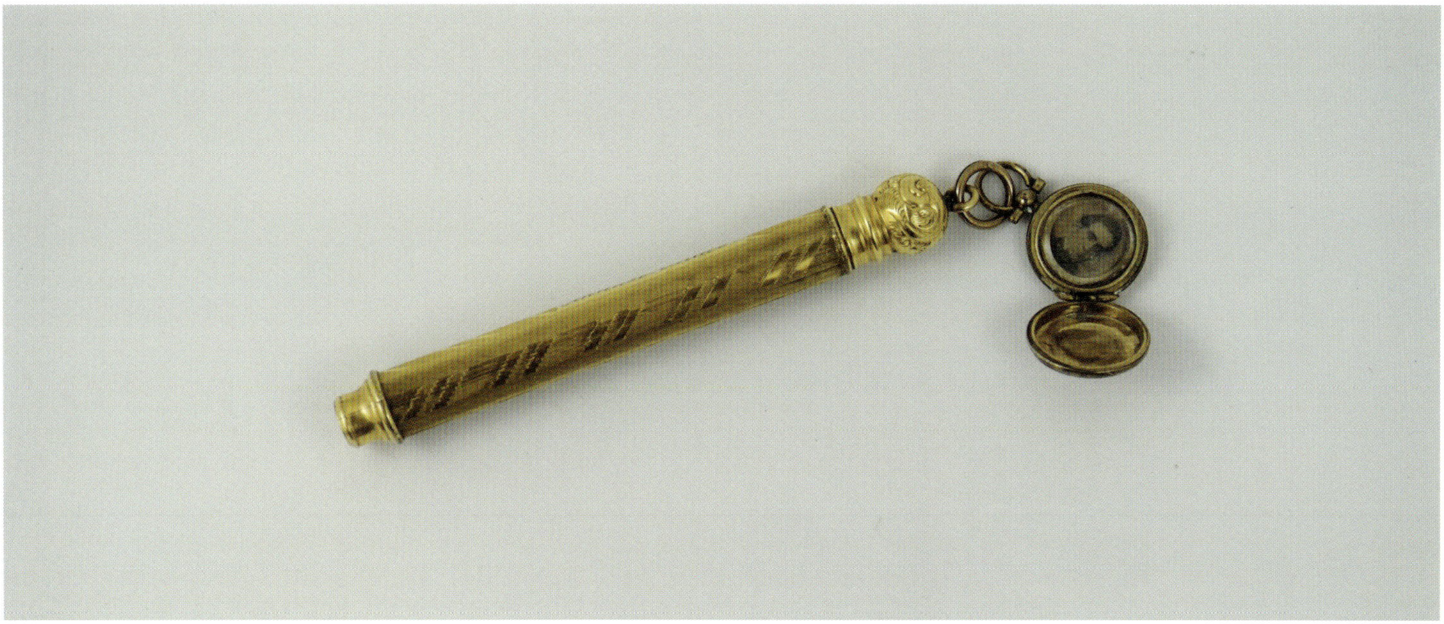

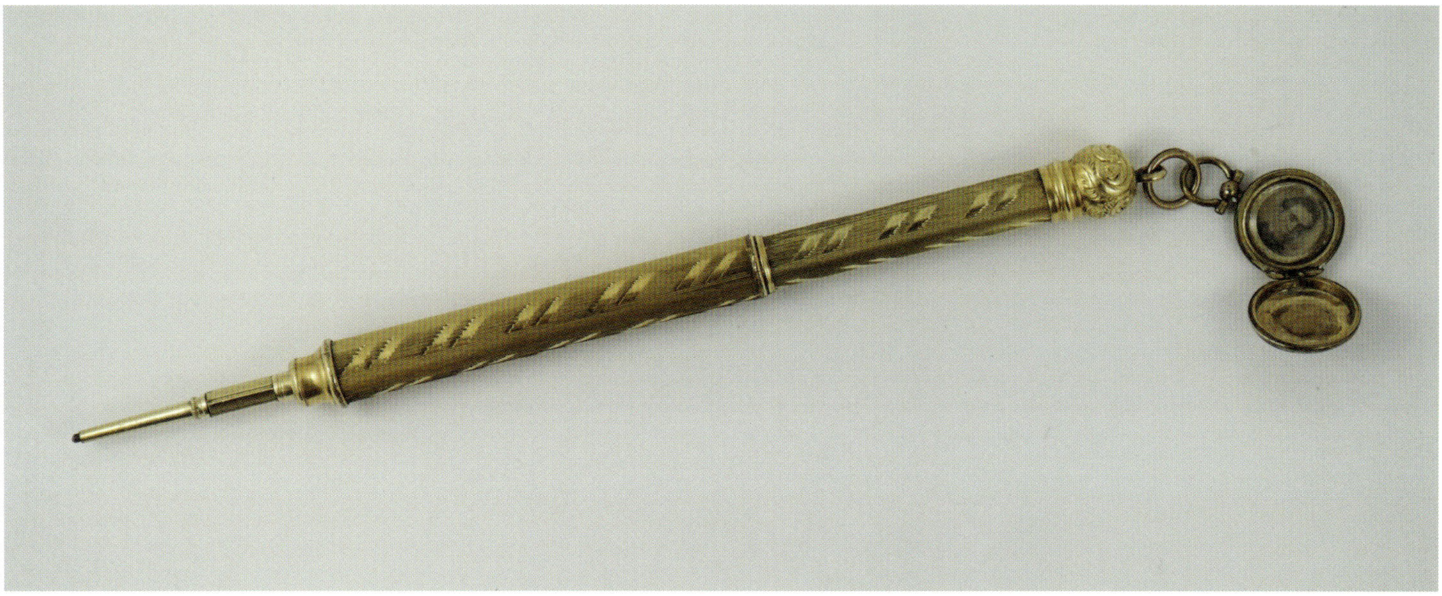

7

Photographer unknown

Maker unknown

Telescoping Gold Pencil with Locket, 1870–80 (image ca. 1850)

Daguerreotype, gold

2 1/2 in. (6.4 cm), length, pencil closed

4 3/4 in. (12.1 cm), length, pencil extended

1/2 in. (1.3 cm), diameter, locket

Collection of Thomas Harris

8 RIGHT

Photographer unknown

Maker unknown

Anchor-shaped Vinaigrette (pendant), ca. 1855

Ambrotype, sterling silver setting, glass

3 x 2 x 1/2 in. (7.6 x 5.1 x 1.3 cm)

Collection of Daile Kaplan

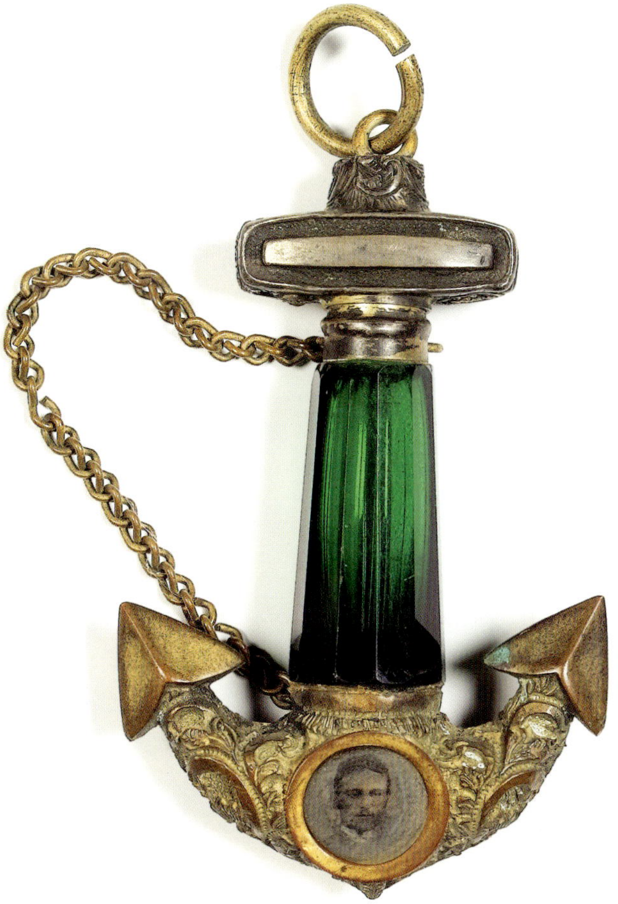

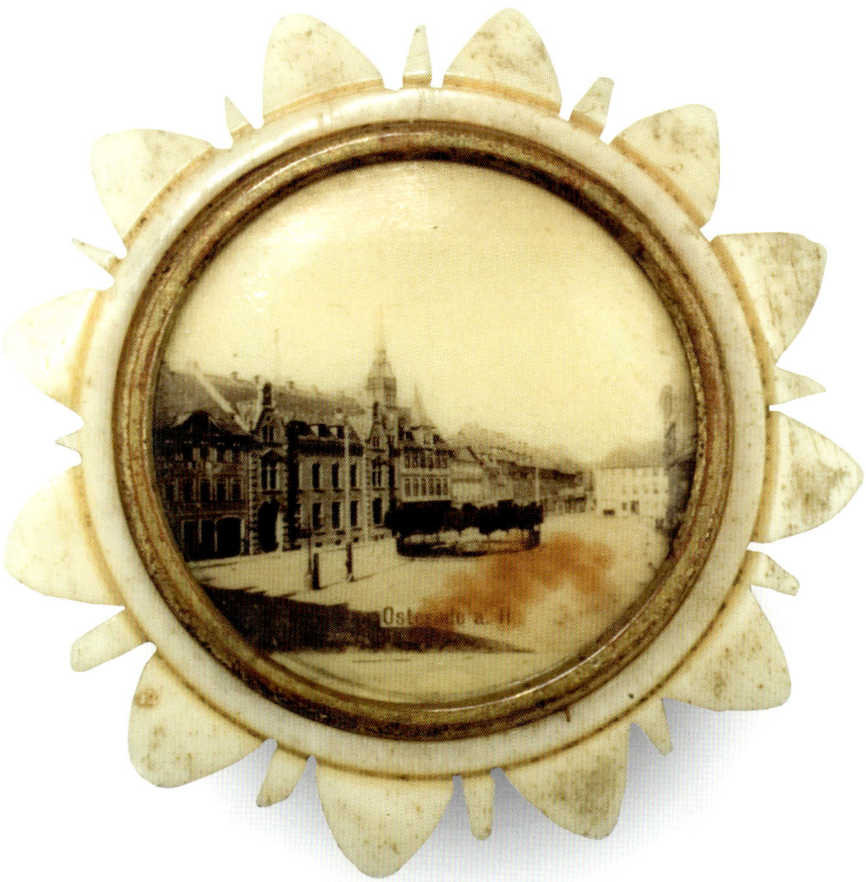

9 LEFT

Unidentified artist

Photographic Button of Osterode am Harz, Germany, ca. 1900

Albumen print, bone, brass, silver

3/4 in. (1.8 cm), diameter, image

1 1/8 in. (2.8 cm), diameter, mount

Collection of George Eastman House, 1969:0214:0017

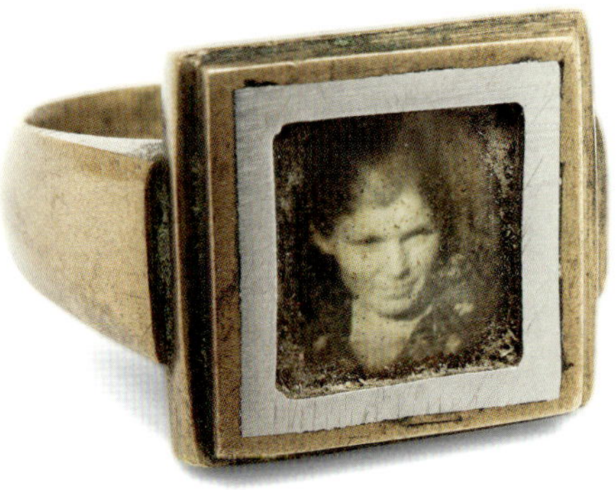

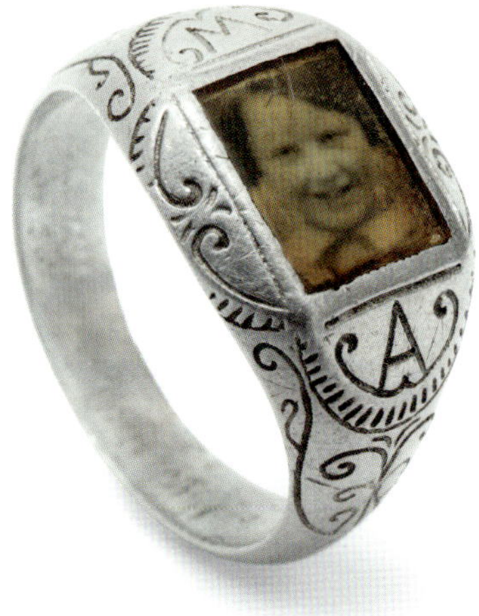

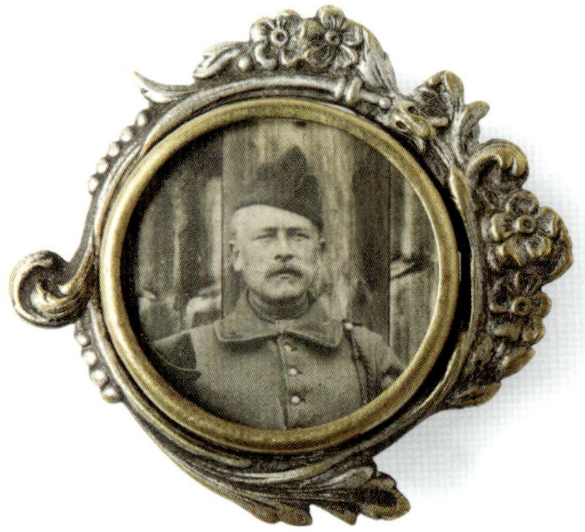

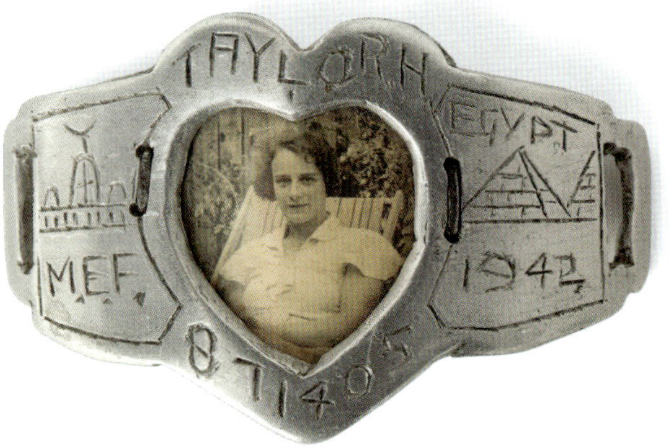

10 TOP

Photographer unknown

Maker unknown

Trench Art Ring, 1939–45

Gelatin silver print, brass, aluminum, steel, transparent plastic

1 in. (2.4 cm), height; 3/4 in. (1.7 cm), diameter

Giorgio Vigna Trench Art Collection, Milan

11 BOTTOM

Photographer unknown

Maker unknown

Trench Art Brooch, 1914–18

Gelatin silver print, silvered brass, glass

1 1/4 x 1 3/8 x 3/8 in. (3.2 x 3.4 x 0.8 cm)

Giorgio Vigna Trench Art Collection, Milan

12 TOP

Photographer unknown

Maker unknown

Trench Art Ring, 1914–18

Gelatin silver print, aluminum, transparent plastic

1 in. (2.5 cm), height; 1 in. (2.5 cm), diameter

Giorgio Vigna Trench Art Collection, Milan

13 BOTTOM

Photographer unknown

Maker unknown

Trench Art Bracelet, ca. 1942

Gelatin silver print, aluminum, transparent plastic

1 3/8 x 2 1/4 in. (3.5 x 5.6 cm)

Giorgio Vigna Trench Art Collection, Milan

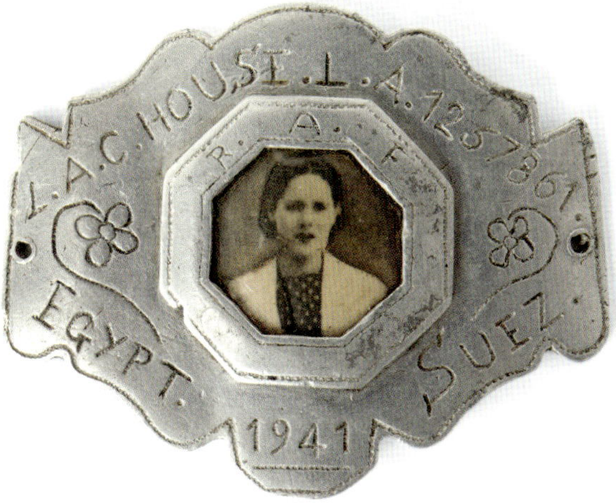

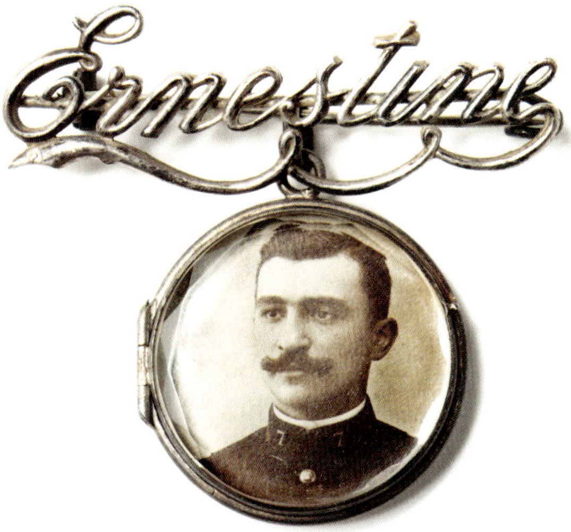

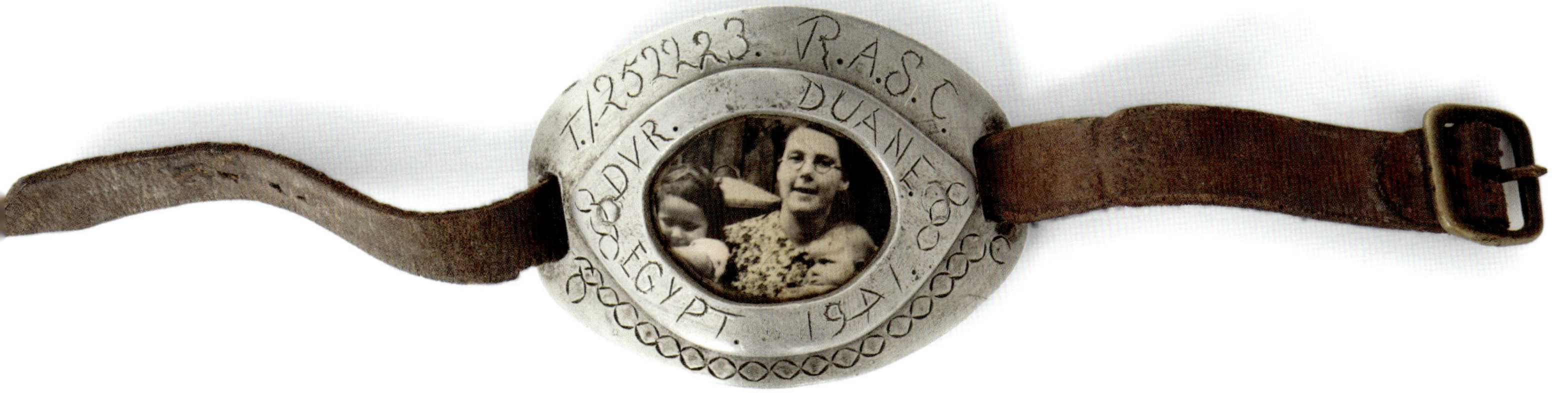

14 TOP

Photographer unknown

Maker unknown

RAF Trench Art Bracelet, 1941

Gelatin silver print, aluminum, transparent plastic

$1\frac{1}{2} \times 1\frac{7}{8}$ in. (3.8 x 4.6 cm)

Giorgio Vigna Trench Art Collection, Milan

15 BOTTOM

Photographer unknown

Maker unknown

Trench Art Bracelet, 1939–45

Gelatin silver print, aluminum, leather, steel, transparent plastic

$2 \times 7\frac{7}{8}$ in. (5 x 20 cm)

Giorgio Vigna Trench Art Collection, Milan

16 ABOVE

Photographer unknown

Maker unknown

Trench Art Brooch, 1914–18

Gelatin silver print, brass, glass, dried flowers

$1\frac{3}{4} \times 1\frac{3}{4}$ in. (4.5 x 4.5 cm)

Giorgio Vigna Trench Art Collection, Milan

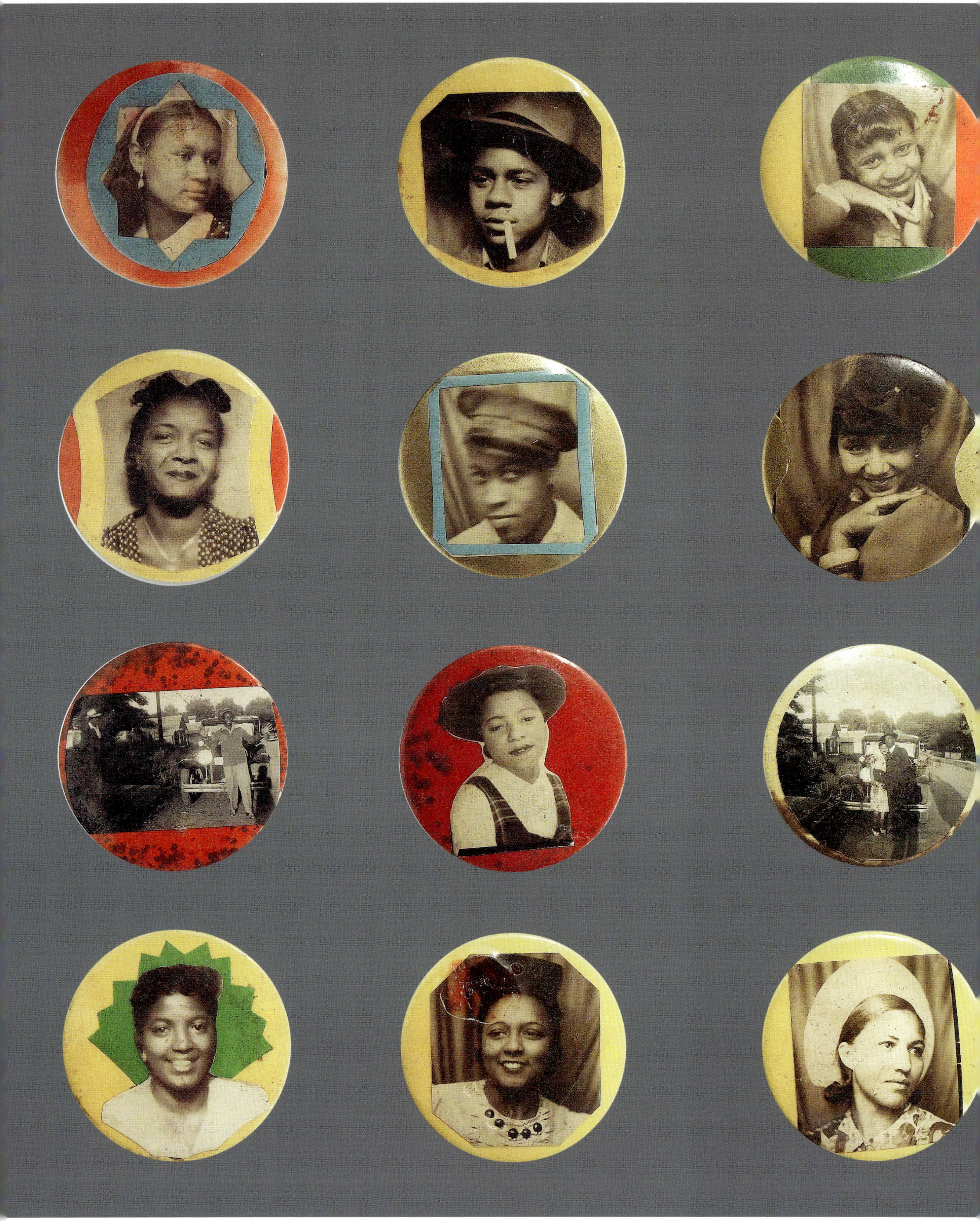

17 OPPOSITE PAGE

Photographers unknown

Makers unknown

Twelve Buttons, 1930–1940

Analog photographs, celluloid, metal

$1^1/_2$ in. (3.8 cm), diameter, each

Collection of Daile Kaplan

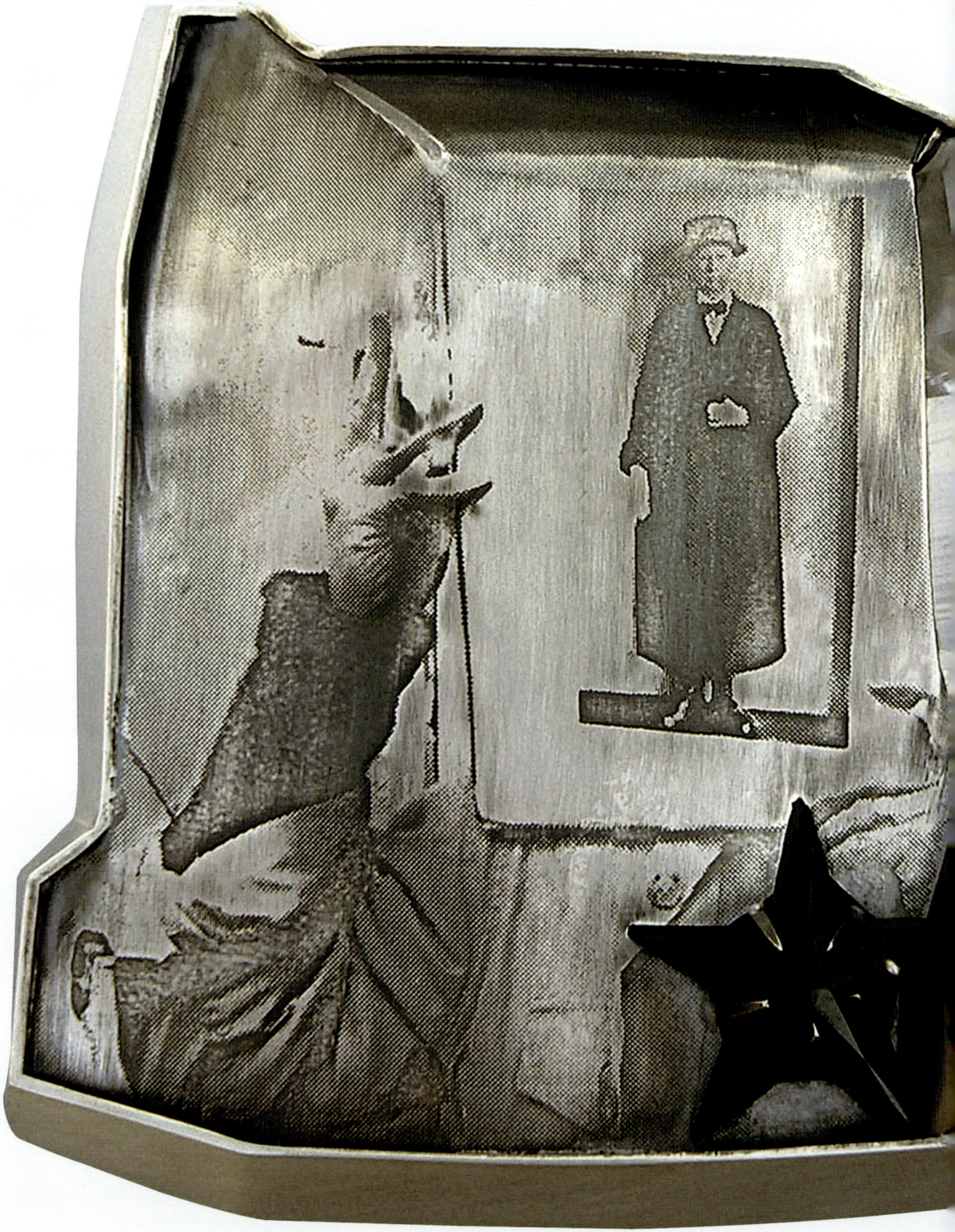

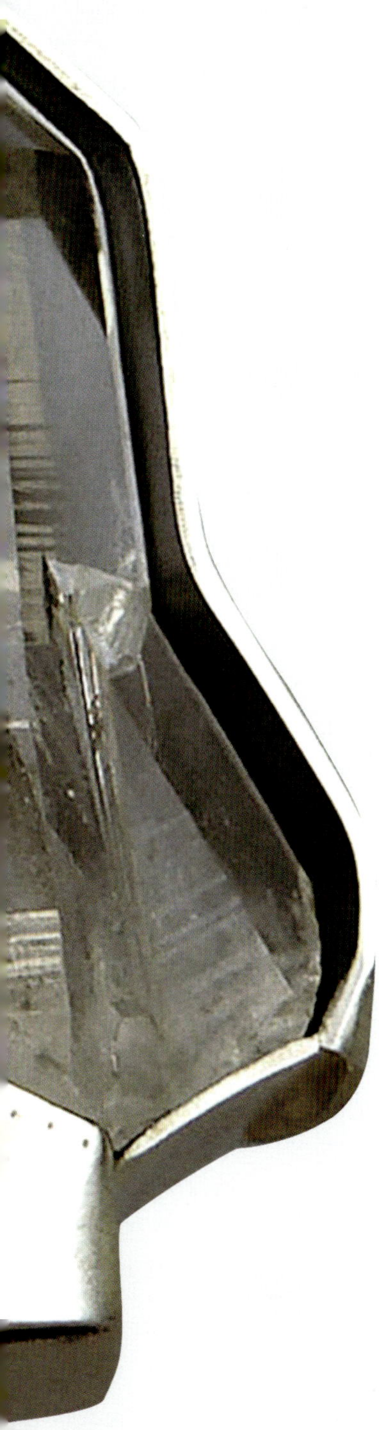

"... THEIR IDENTITIES HAVE EVAPORATED OVER TIME ..."

SAVING FACE
PHOTO PORTRAIT JEWELRY

SUZANNE RAMLJAK

THE CREATIVE CONJUNCTION of jewelry, photography, and portraiture yields a heady compound, ripe with association. When merged into a single object, these three artistic genres trigger a complex interplay between opposing elements, among them private/public, past/present, subject/object, and absence/presence. Along with generating dichotomies, such jewelry also raises essential questions: Why affix another person's image upon one's body? How do we identify with those with whom we adorn ourselves? What does it mean to wear a stranger's likeness, or that of a beloved? Are we sporting the jeweler or the portrait subject?

Deep biological roots underlie the practice of donning people's faces. In fact, researchers have posited an innate neural mechanism designed to read and decipher human features. Whether or not this decoding capacity is inherent at birth, we are naturally drawn to and responsive to facial expression for our social success and ultimately for survival. Our fixation on the visages of others persists even after they have died, as witnessed in death masks and other funerary renderings, from which portraiture originates in Western art.

The age-old quest to reproduce appearances got a boost in the nineteenth century, when photography provided a prime means of capturing a sitter's semblance. By the mid-1800s, photo portraiture had become widespread, and the images lent themselves to prevailing customs of wearing keepsake ornaments and painted portrait jewelry. Such photographic portraits enable the contemplation and display of loved ones as part of everyday dress. This newfound ability to preserve a human likeness gained urgency in an era marked by memorializing and mourning, especially when life expectancy was so short.

Photographic portrait jewelry still performs this essential task of negotiating loss and carrying our grief into public, as observed after the 9/11 attacks when mourners openly wore portraits of the deceased (fig. 1). Numerous contemporary artists enlist photographic jewelry for this traditional purpose, making keepsakes that pay homage to late family or friends. Among works in this vein are Sonya Clark's *Remembrance* (NO. 27) and pieces by Iris Nieuwenburg (NO. 28), Joyce Scott (NO. 37), and Pamela Morris Thomford (NO. 39). In Ashley Gilreath's draping necklace, *I Am Who They Were*, a transparent glass and decal portrait gallery allows the wearer's skin to show through and complete the ancestral photographs (NO. 40). To extend the tradition of commemoration, today's artists employ imaging modes and technologies such as photo etching, digital photography, and video.

This memorial role notwithstanding, our current rapport with photo portraits is distinctly altered from that of the past. Whereas photographs were once rare and precious, now the cultural landscape is densely strewn with photos, which appear on every possible surface from T-shirts to taxicabs. Indeed, the sources for the contemporary portrait works in this exhibition encompass photo ID cards, advertisements, filmstrips, newspapers, and postage stamps.

Within our Facebook era we are inundated with photos of other people, and this public intrusion into private space often leads to facial overload. Personal lives are becoming increasingly publicized via social networks and various forms of exhibitionism, foremost through reality TV. "Private life," according to Roland Barthes, is "nothing but that zone of space, of time, where I am not an image, an object."[1] Today it is becoming extremely difficult to avoid being objectified as an image. The inherent intrusiveness of imaging other people is staged in Jordan Doner's *Surveillance Pendant*, which harbors a tiny video camera that covertly records those who cross its lens (NO. 52), while the accompanying "Display" cuff allows the wearer to view illicitly captured images on a small LED screen (NO. 51).

Whereas we once wore portraits of only those we knew, mass media now provides access to a vastly expanded visual family. Accordingly, we can opt to identify with strangers or public figures with whom we feel strong kinship. Such identification is a key dynamic in the wearing of photo portraiture. Jewelry's inextricable link to the human body forges a strong union between owner and work, possessor and possessed. Because jewelry is an art form that comes with a face attached, the wearer becomes implicated with the subject, especially when it is another human being.

What, then, is conveyed when we bedeck ourselves with portraits of those whom we've never met? In some instances, this co-optation serves as a tribute to the photographed personage, as found in Don Tompkins's *Janis Joplin* and *Minnesota Fats* (NOS. 33, 34). Beverley Price's highly invested *Nelson Mandela* neckpiece also pays homage through its fusion of a traditional Xhosa collar type and photographs documenting highlights of the great statesman's life (NO. 25). Other pieces use photos of anonymous faces to represent a cultural group or era, such as J. Fred Woell's *Come Alive, You're in the Pepsi Generation* (NO. 32). The artist and wearer declare an allegiance to such depicted figures, as if sporting a campaign button to support a candidate. The act of adorning oneself with prominent personalities runs rampant in Hally McGehean's dress, *Everyone Who's Anyone* (fig. 2), which compiles well-known faces from magazines into a wearable *Who's Who* of present-day culture.

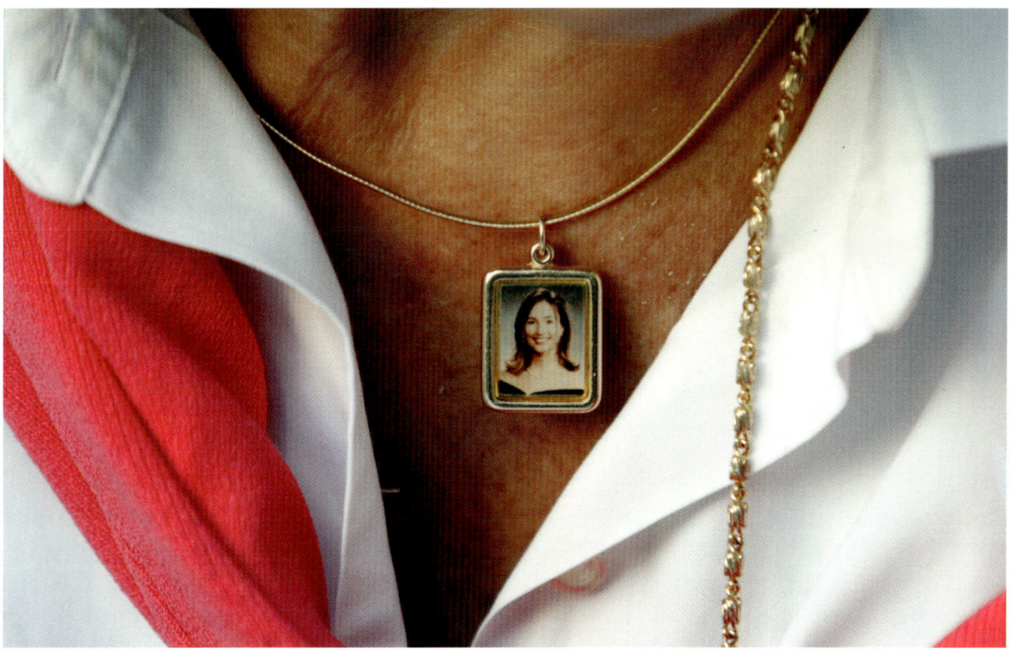

FIG. 1
REUTERS / Jessica Rinaldi, New York
"Liza Adams wears a necklace with a portrait of her daughter, Mary Lou Hague, 26, killed during the 9/11 attacks on the World Trade Center in New York. September 11, 2001."

When the portrait subject is infamous, not just famous, a new set of issues arises. While it is conceivable that one could identify with a cultural leader, affinity with child molesters or criminals is harder to fathom. This quandary is posed by Shari Pierce's neckpiece *34 Sex Offenders and 2 Sexual Predators from within a 5-Mile Radius* (NO. 50) and by Peter Deckers's *Ten Most Wanted* ring (NO. 49). In both, the portrait photograph is derived from mug shots posted to help apprehend outlaws. Wearing the ID photos of these social deviants helps broadcast their menace, while raising questions about the company we keep.

At the opposite pole of these notorious figures are the anonymous souls who populate the tintypes and silver prints of bygone years. There is a poignant irony in the fate of these faces; originally photographed to preserve their memory, their identities have evaporated over time. Portraits of the now unknown are the centerpieces of Bettina Speckner's, Robert Ebendorf's, and Bernhard Schobinger's jewelry, where they become subjects for free association and sentimental musings (NOS. 42–44, 35, 36, and 26). Like human Rorschachs, these nameless characters elicit our own hopes and memories.

The process of identification grows further entangled when the person portrayed is the artist him- or herself. While art serves like a hazy mirror reflecting the beholder's views, it also embodies a reflection of its original maker. "All photographs are self-portraits," claimed photographer Minor White,[2] but some more explicitly so than others. A number of today's jewelers have produced engaging photo self-portraits, including Bernhard Schobinger, Fritz Maierhofer, Ruudt Peters, and Martin Papcún. In each of these cases, the artist has aestheticized him- or herself into a portable object, packaging identity in a form to be worn. Whereas some self-portraits prove defacing in the very act of depiction—like Schobinger's commuter card photo half-eclipsed by a clownish red nose (NO. 19)—others reveal a more earnest intent, as do Maierhofer's portrait bracelet made as a gift for his mother (NO. 20) and Papcún's rings made for his friends (NOS. 22, 23). All of these works seek to propagate the artist's own self-image, an aim blatantly fulfilled in the edition of face pins created by Peters, suggestively titled *Ritual* (NO. 18). To wear a jeweler's self-portrait is to get the artist squared—both as an object-maker and a subject of interest.

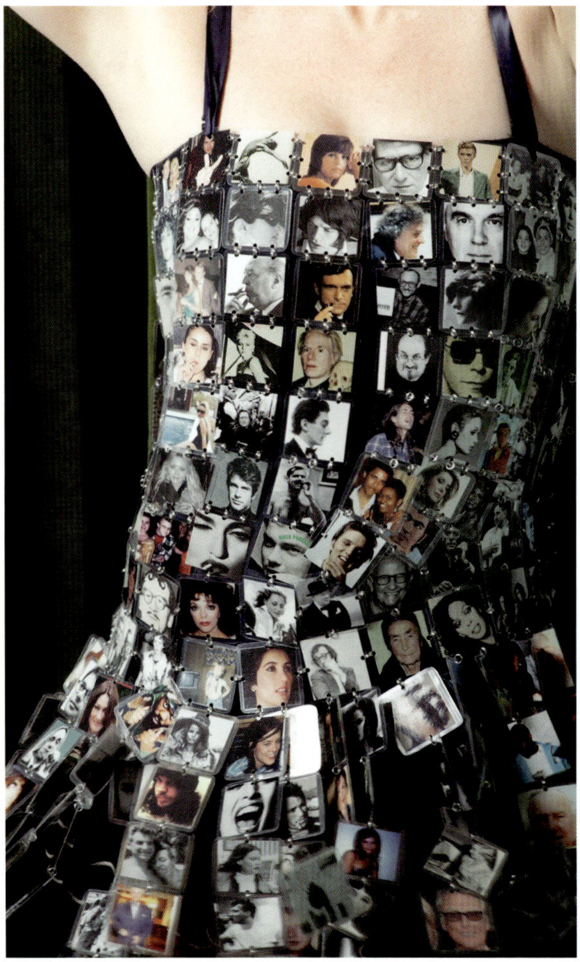

FIG. 2
Hally McGehean
Everyone Who's Anyone (dress), 2010
522 laminated magazine cut-outs, stainless steel split rings, silk ribbon straps
$1^{3}/_{4}$ in. (4.4 cm), each cut-out; size 2
Collection of the artist

Although the bond between a wearer and portrait subject is largely psychological, it also involves a physical dimension. Jewelry's direct contact with human skin heightens the communion one feels when wearing another's semblance; two bodies brush against each other across distance and time. The photographic portrait is literally a "print," with a causal connection to the originating body. Every photograph results from a "physical imprint transferred by light reflections onto a sensitive surface," affirms Rosalind Krauss. "The photograph is thus a type of icon, or visual likeness, that bears an indexical relationship to its object."[3]

Photographs have been rightly compared to relics and function similarly to preserve remnants of an individual. This capturing of human life is most pronounced in photo portrait jewelry that also contains physical matter from the subject. Geoffrey Giles's *Self-Portrait, Cultivated Perception*—a photo bracelet that documents the artist's transformative haircut—includes actual clippings from Giles's head (NO. 21). Other works preserve photographs in elaborate casings that sanctify the treasured image, as found in Eleanor Moty's opulent brooches (NOS. 45, 46) and the intricately layered setting by Truike Verdegaal (NO. 53). With or without real bodily fragments, subjects within portrait jewelry are like specimens under glass, akin to embalmed corpses primped for open-casket display.

As much as photographs are thought to harbor life, they also signal loss and the passing of time that cannot be regained. Our effort to save the lives of others through photographic portraiture ultimately betrays us, and we are left with the dry taste of death. As Susan Sontag famously stated, "All photographs are memento mori."[4] This deathly essence pervades Babette Boucher's *Souvenir* brooches from her Dead Class series, portraits of her mother's classmates from the 1940s (NOS. 29, 30, 31). Equally tinged with morbidity is Loes van Riel's and Robert Pfuelb's *Saturday, 20 June, 1942*, titled after a dated entry in Anne Frank's diary (NO. 24). Sally von Bargen's devastating *Elegy*—with over forty-two hundred portraits of American men and women who died in Iraq under the Bush administration—is a wearable memorial to the human casualties of war (NO. 41). Even when the depicted person is not deceased, the photo can remind us of a vanished past or fleeting moment that is gone for good.

Neither dead nor alive, the faces in photographs appear as haunting specters, echoing from another realm. When we put on these portraits, we adorn ourselves with ghosts whose spirits waft about us. The spectral nature of these photo apparitions is underscored by titles such as Keith Lo Bue's *The Spectre Woman*, Klaus Bürgel's *Ghost Ring*, and Nancy Worden's *The Revenants* (NOS. 47, 48, 38).

Photo portrait jewelry casts a potent spell, resulting from a blend of bodily touch and intangible trace, presence and absence. It invites viewers and wearers to ponder the limits of both life and death, as we encounter frozen faces affixed to breathing beings.

Suzanne Ramljak, *an art historian and writer, is currently editor of* Metalsmith *magazine and curator of exhibitions at the American Federation of Arts, New York.*

1
Roland Barthes, *Camera Lucida: Reflections on Photography*, Richard Howard, trans. (New York: Farrar, Straus and Giroux, 1981), 15.

2
Minor White, *Documentary Photography: Time Life Library of Photography* (New York: Time Life Books, 1972), 231.

3
Rosalind Krauss, "Notes on the Index: Part I," in *The Originality of the Avant-Garde and Other Modernist Myths* (Cambridge, Mass: MIT Press, 1986), 203.

4
Susan Sontag, *On Photography* (New York: Dell Publishing, 1977), 15.

RUUDT PETERS

Ritual

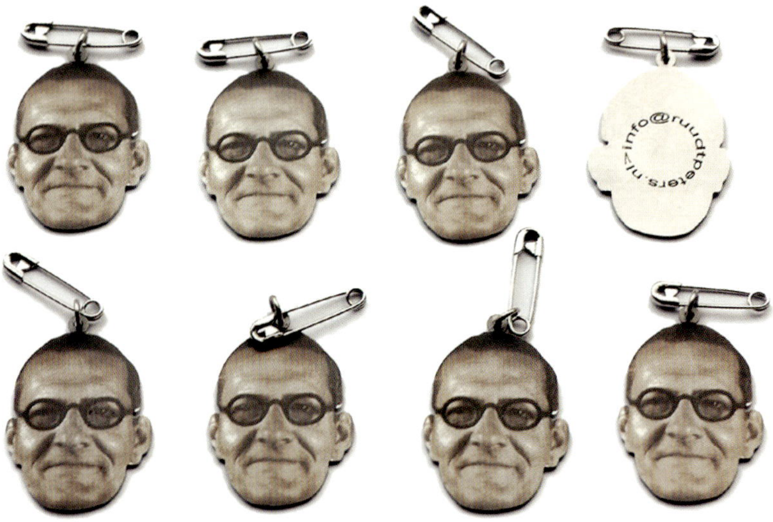

When I was a baby, my mother would pin a medal of the Virgin Mary on my undershirt every morning as a devotional ritual. I reinterpreted this practice by laser-screening my own face on a stainless steel medallion to create a type of business card that I can pin on people after a good meeting.

18

Ruudt Peters
Ritual, 2007
Digital self-portrait, laser engraved onto stainless steel, safety pins
1 3/8 x 7/8 in. (3.5 x 2.3 cm), each
Stedelijk Museum 's-Hertogenbosch

BERNHARD SCHOBINGER

Self-Portrait with Nose

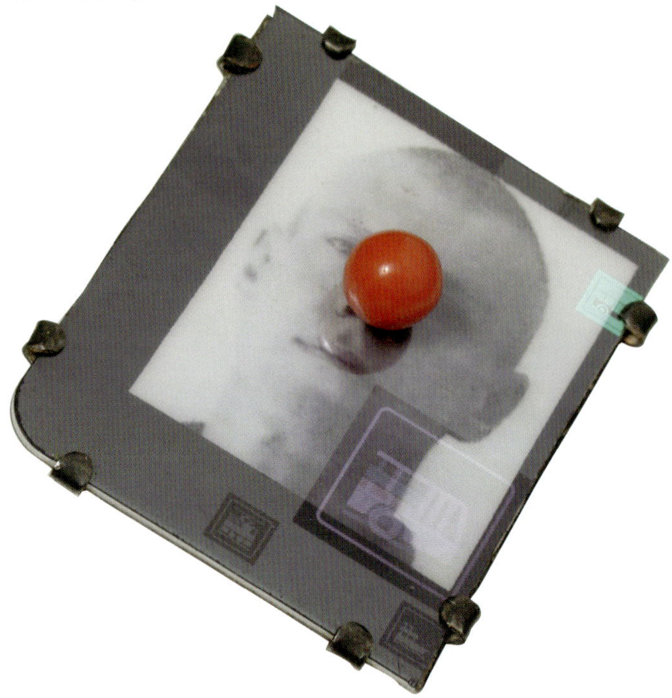

19

Bernhard Schobinger
Self-Portrait with Nose (brooch), 2010
Digital photograph on commuter card, hologram, silver, coral
1 1/8 x 1 1/8 in. (2.7 x 2.7 cm)
Courtesy of Gallery S O

FRITZ MAIERHOFER

Portrait of the Artist

I made this bracelet as a present for my mother when I came back to Vienna after living in England for three years. The picture was taken in Germany, near Rosenheim, where I had an exhibition and met up with fellow jewelers Otto Künzli, Gerd Rothmann, Helfried Kodré, and Lisa Defner Kodré. The softness and malleability of the green material that is fused onto the acrylic fascinated me, and I took advantage of this feature in fashioning the way the bracelet opens and closes.

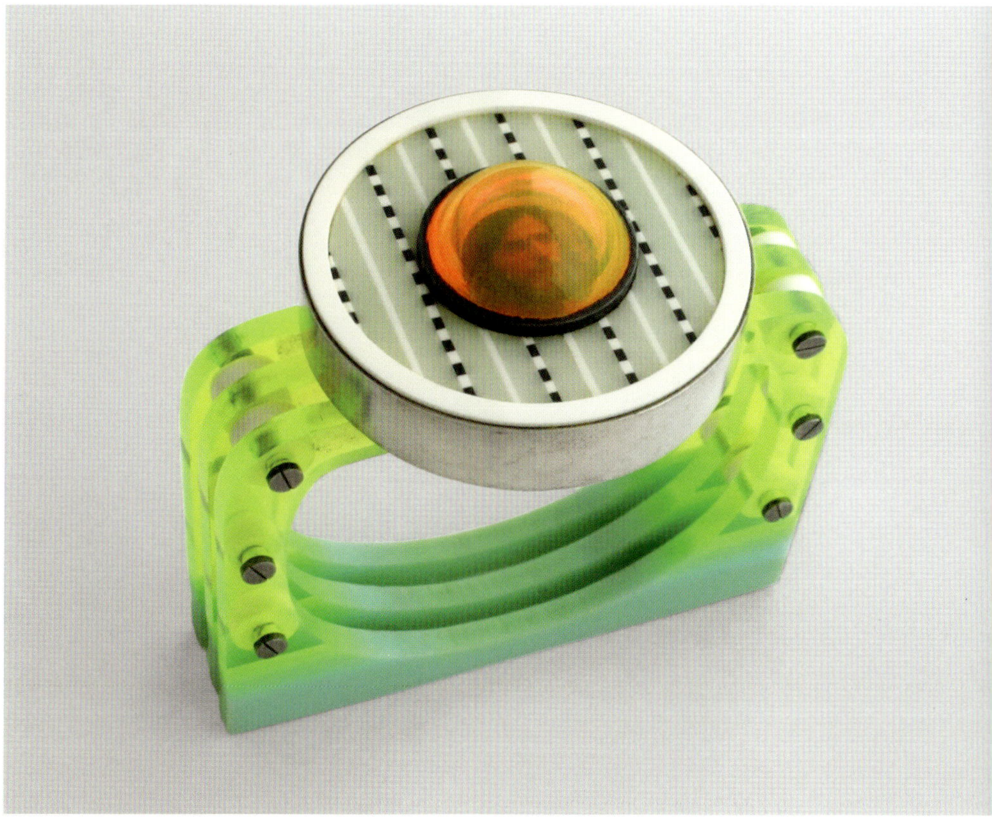

20
Fritz Maierhofer
Portrait of the Artist (bracelet), 1971
Analog photograph, acrylic, silver
$2^{3}/_{4}$ x $2^{5}/_{8}$ in. (7 x 6.7 cm)
Collection of the artist

GEOFFREY GILES

Self-Portrait, Cultivated Perception

The concept for this piece came about as a result of my being invited to participate in a charm bracelet-themed exhibition. At the time, I had been growing my hair for nearly ten years without ever brushing or cutting it. It was a period in my life when I realized firsthand how prejudice is often shaped by perception, how inner morality and belief systems are not always reflected by one's persona.

This bracelet represents the finality of that lesson for me. Eight separate cubes enclose a lock of my hair, and attached to each is a photograph chronicling its cutting. This very personal piece encapsulates a moment in my life, an instance of clarity within the transition between precedent and prospect.

The photographs for this piece were cut from a contact sheet. They are enclosed in frames made from 18k yellow gold and sterling silver, set under acrylic, and strung together on a single dreadlock.

21

Geoffrey Giles
Self-Portrait, Cultivated Perception (bracelet), 2003
Contact sheet photographs, hair, 18k yellow gold, oxidized sterling silver, acrylic
7 in. (17.8 cm), diameter
Collection of Mint Museum, Charlotte, North Carolina. Museum Purchase: Funds provided by Susan C. Beech and Exchange Funds from the Gift of Dr. and Mrs. Raul C. Aizcorbe

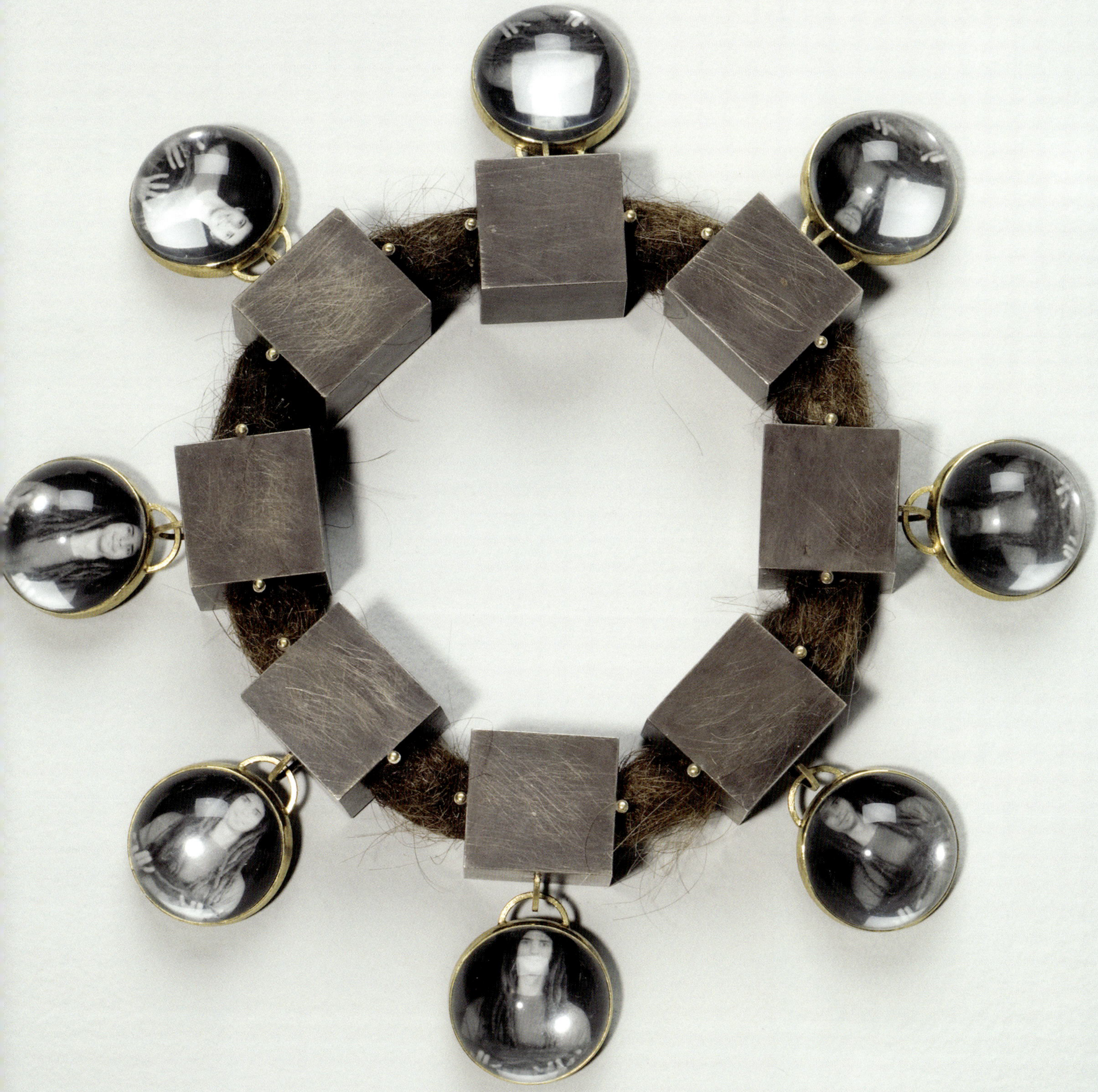

MARTIN PAPCÚN

Ring | *Ring (1)*

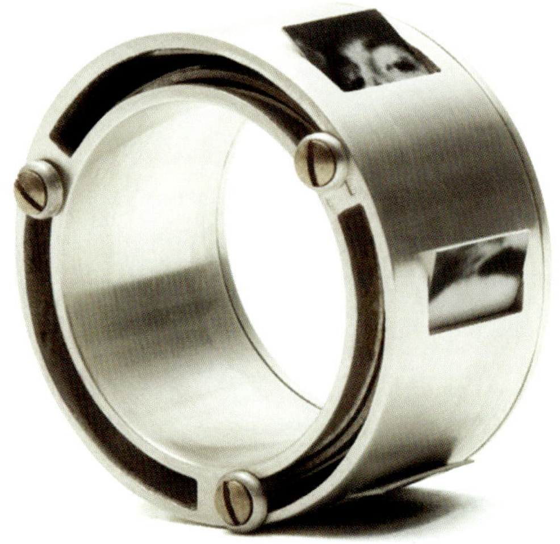

A big part of my life has been spent moving from one city or country to another and from one house or flat to another. This separated me from my close friends and girlfriend, and I missed them a lot. I wanted a way to keep them secretly with me and to remember their faces so I made mechanical rings to hide black-and-white photographs that I had taken of them and of myself. With one turn of the ring around the finger, the pictures emerge, and by reversing the movement, they disappear again.

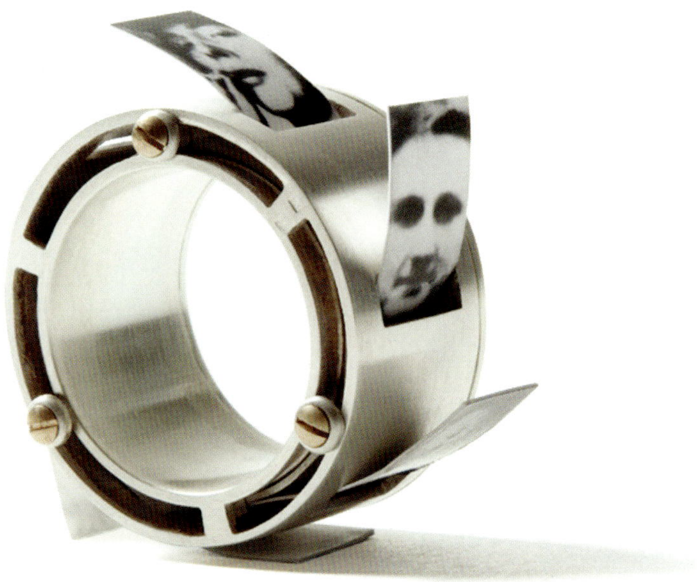

22 LEFT

Martin Papcún

Ring, 1999

Artist's analog photographs, silver, brass

1 1/8 in. (2.8 cm), diameter, closed;

5/8 in. (1.6 cm), width

SUPŠ A VOŠ TURNOV,

The Secondary School of Applied Arts and

The College of Craft

Turnov, Czech Republic

23 OPPOSITE PAGE

Martin Papcún

Ring (1), 1999

Analog photograph, silver, brass, steel

4 7/8 x 1 1/8 x 1 3/4 in. (12.5 x 2.7 x 4.4 cm)

SUPŠ A VOŠ TURNOV,

The Secondary School of Applied Arts and

The College of Craft

Turnov, Czech Republic

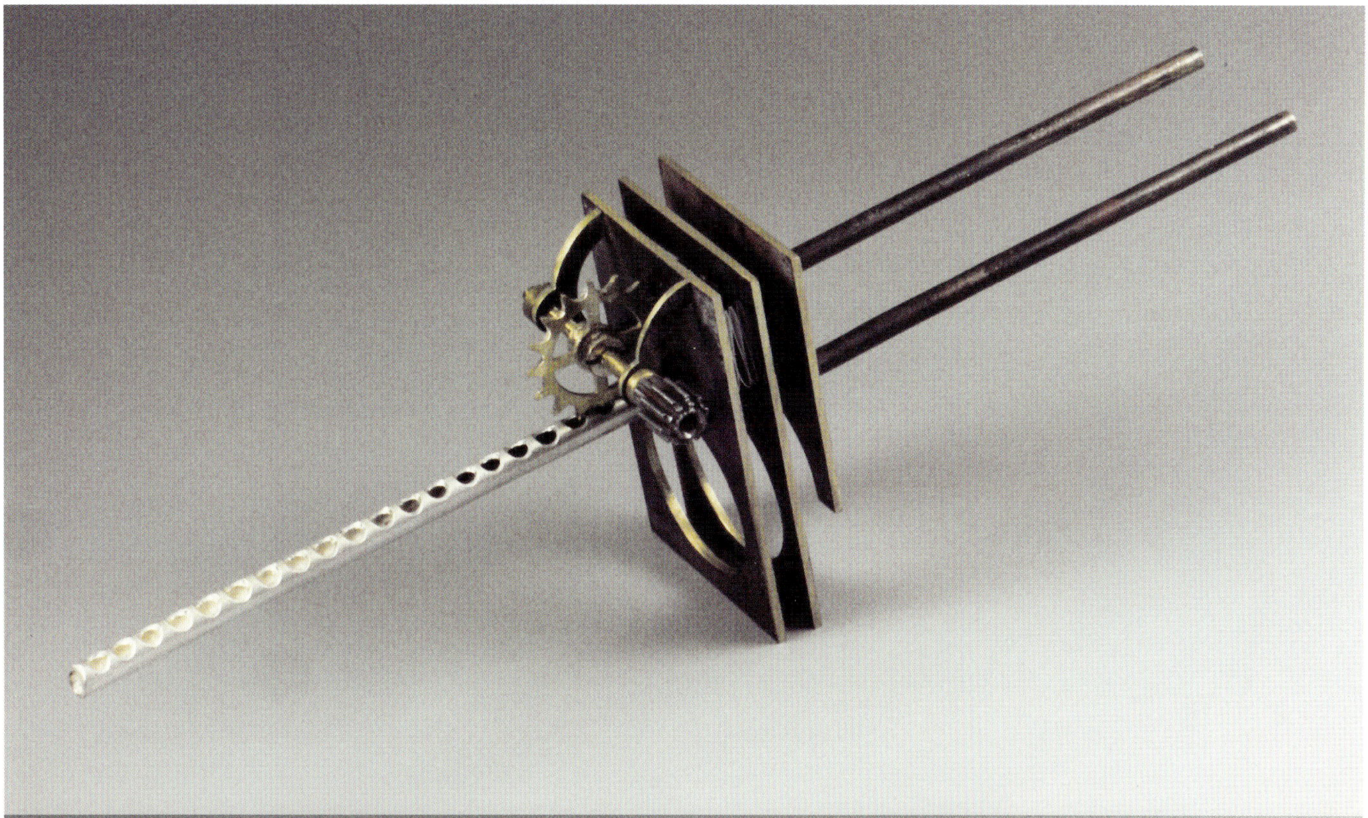

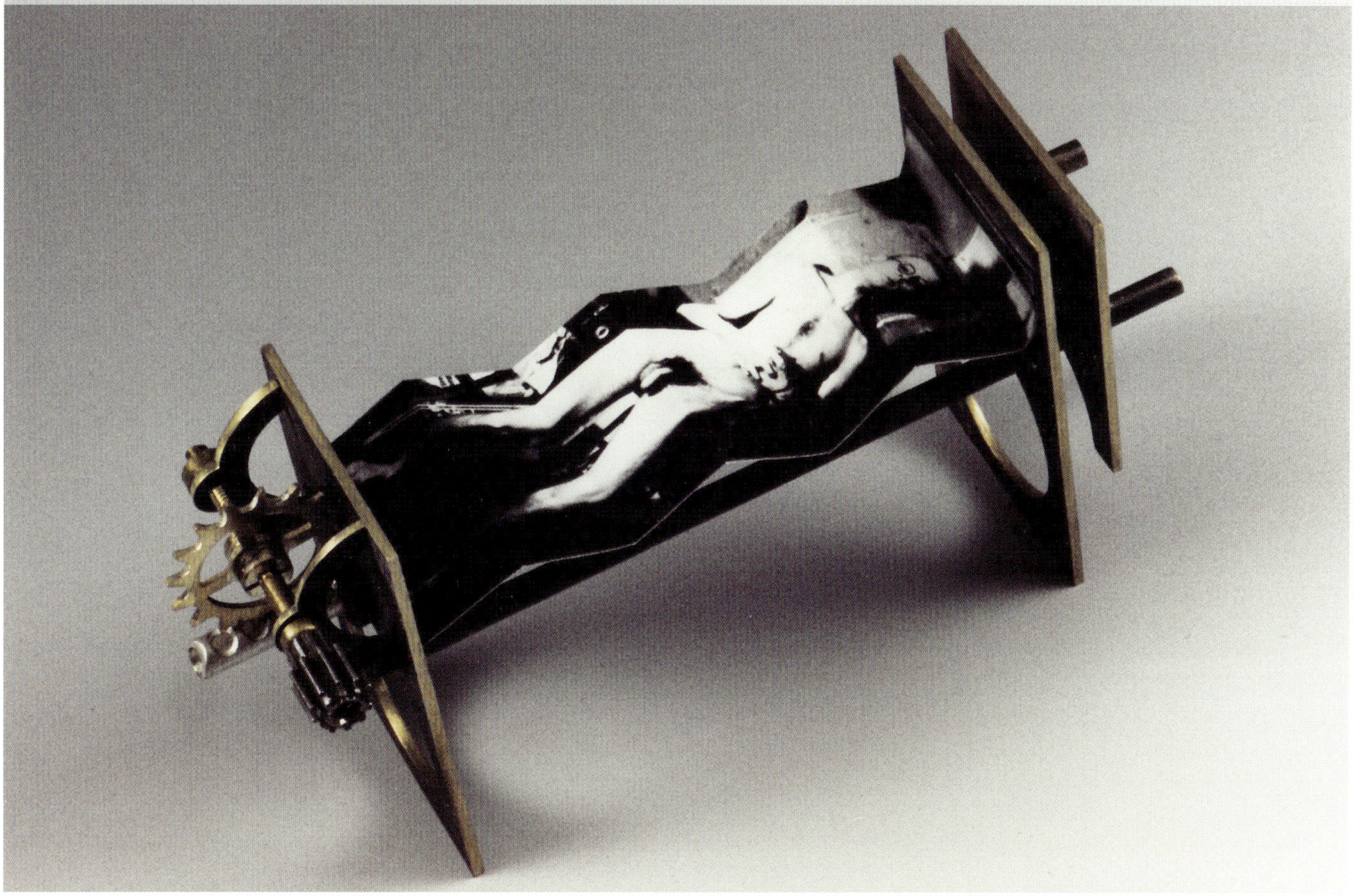

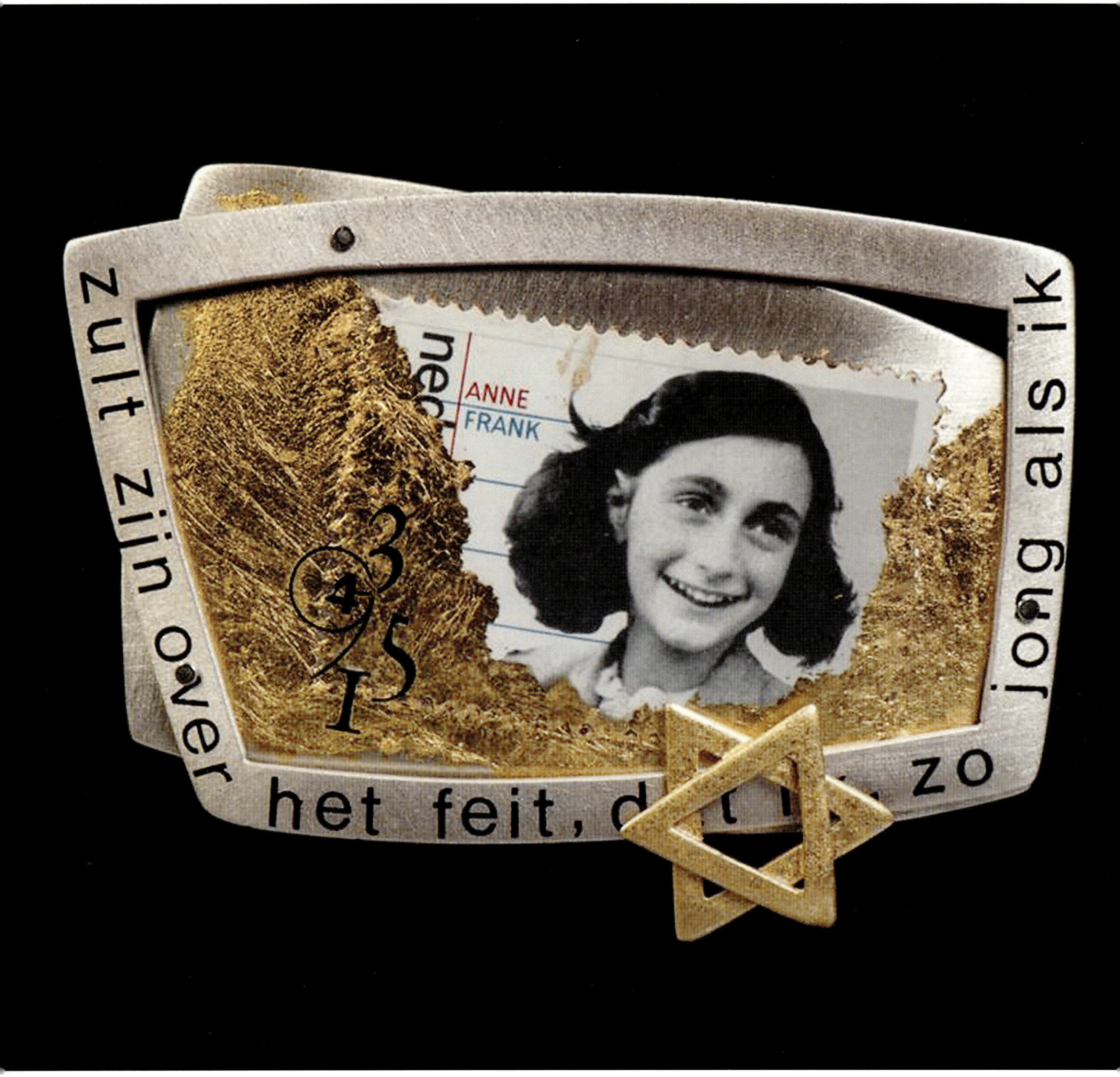
zult zijn over
het feit,
zo
jong als ik
ANNE
FRANK

LOES VAN RIEL and ROBERT PFUELB

Saturday, 20 June 1942

Our series of portrait brooches was inspired by a stamp featuring Anne Frank's likeness that I found in my native city of Amsterdam. I had grown up with my parents' stories about World War II and my father's role in the Dutch Resistance, so the subject was close to my heart, and together, Robert and I decided that I should focus on surface design, while he would design and fabricate the silver backgrounds. Along with a postage stamp, each piece features a partial sentence from Anne's diary, and if the three hundred brooches we made were laid in a long line, one would be able to read more than five full chapters of her thoughts in Dutch.

24 OPPOSITE PAGE

Loes van Riel and **Robert Pfuelb**
Saturday, 20 June 1942 (brooch), 1991–92
Postage stamp issued in the Netherlands in 1980, sterling silver, gold leaf, Letraset type
2 x 2 1/2 x 1/4 in. (5.1 x 6.4 x 0.6 cm)
Collection of Mr. and Mrs. Lou Grotta

BEVERLEY PRICE

Contemporary Interpretation of Nelson Mandela's Neckpiece from the Time of the Rivonia Trials in 1963–64

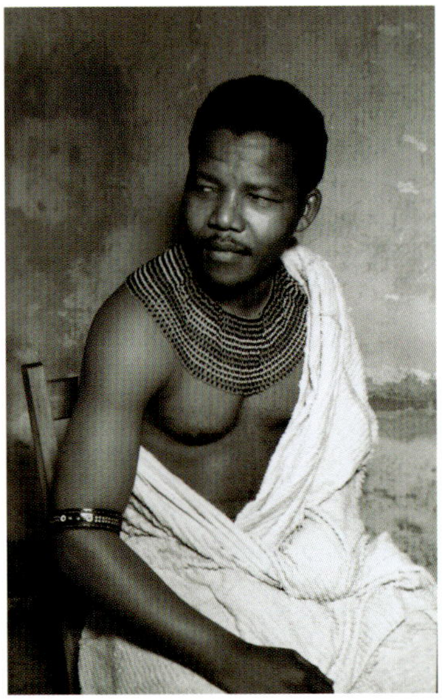

My neckpiece is a tribute to Nelson Mandela (1918–2013), who became our nation's first freely elected president in 1994. It was inspired by the traditional *ithumbu*, a venerated adornment of the indigenous South African Xhosa people from whom Mandela was descended, but it is a cultural hybrid, since Xhosa traditions are not part of my own culture.

In 1964, during the historic Rivonia trial leading to his twenty-seven-year imprisonment on Robben Island, Nelson Mandela sat for a photo portrait wearing an *ithumbu* (see figure on left). The picture was taken by Eli Weinberg and testified to Mandela's cultural sovereignty and political defiance. I was a child at the time, but as I grew up under apartheid, I became increasingly impressed by Mandela's resolve and was eventually inspired to reference his Xhosa neckpiece in a work of my own.

Using miniaturized, hand-foiled photographs taken of Mandela by apartheid photographers such as Jürgen Schadeberg, I created a concentric chronology of his life that can be read from the neck to the outer circumference of the piece. The images are linked in chain mail fashion, and the resulting form is lined with synthetic leather and trimmed with beadwork in dusty pink, blue, and white, colors symbolic of the Xhosa culture. The images for the neckpiece were acquired from the Bailey Archives belonging to the publishers of *Drum*, a magazine produced for the black population during apartheid, as well as from the photo collection of the Mayibuye Centre on Robben Island.

25 RIGHT AND OPPOSITE PAGE
Beverley Price
Contemporary Interpretation of Nelson Mandela's Neckpiece from the Time of the Rivonia Trials in 1963–64, 2006
Miniaturized foil-backed and linked copies of analog photographs by apartheid photographers, aluminum, plastic, wire, synthetic leather, glass beads, buttons
18 7/8 in. (48 cm), diameter
Collection of Natalie Knight, Johannesburg, South Africa

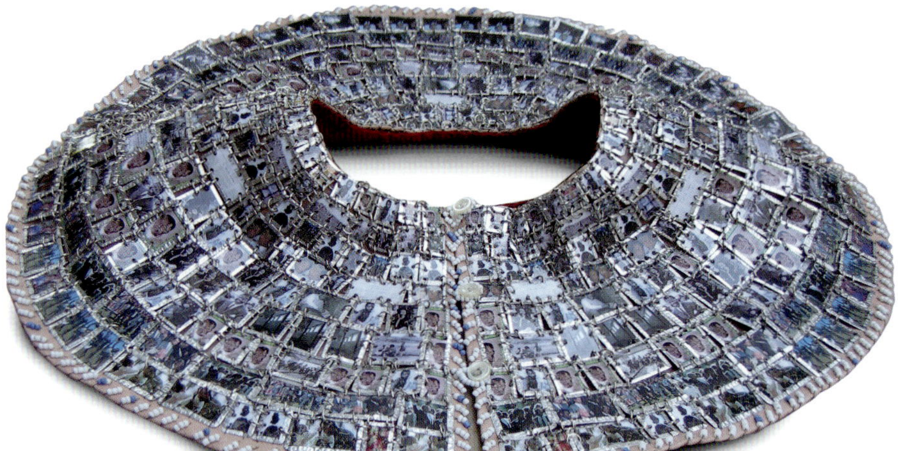

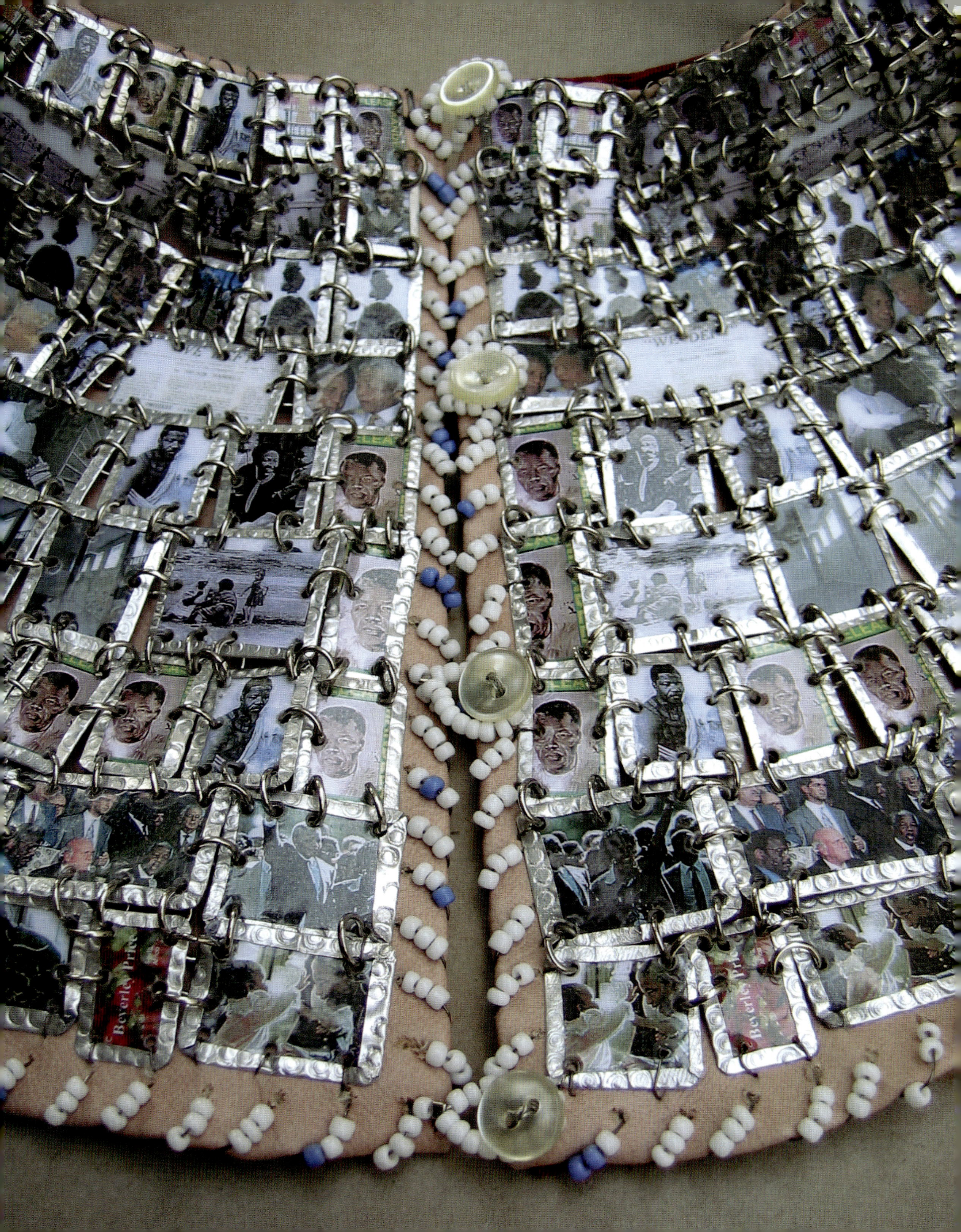

Zerrissene Photographie is about destroyed and recreated histories, the past as an incomplete picture, partial facts in changed positions. I made this necklace intuitively without any conceptual planning. I saw the fragments of the photograph in our rubbish container and immediately got the idea.

BERNHARD SCHOBINGER

Zerrissene Photographie

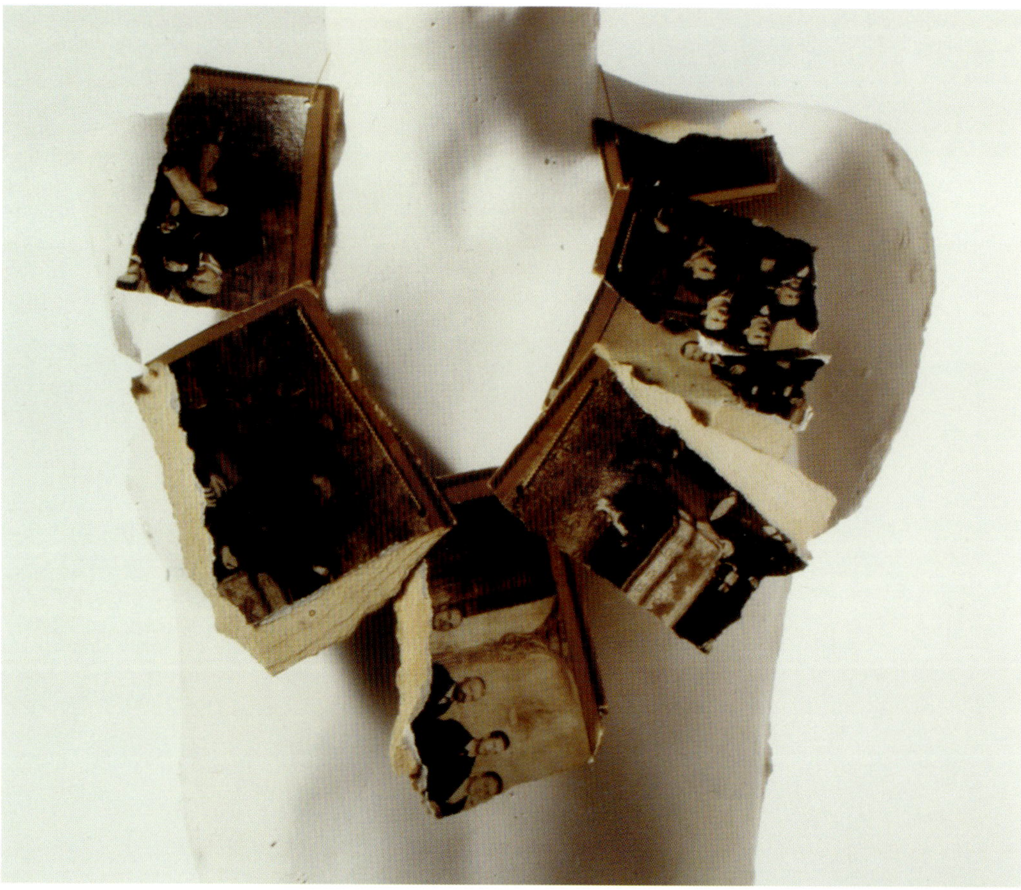

26
Bernhard Schobinger
Zerrissene Photographie
(necklace), 1985
19th-century gelatin silver prints, baryta paper, gold chain
11 7/8 in. (30 cm), diameter
Courtesy of Hiko Mizuno College of Jewelry, Tokyo

SONYA CLARK

Remembrance

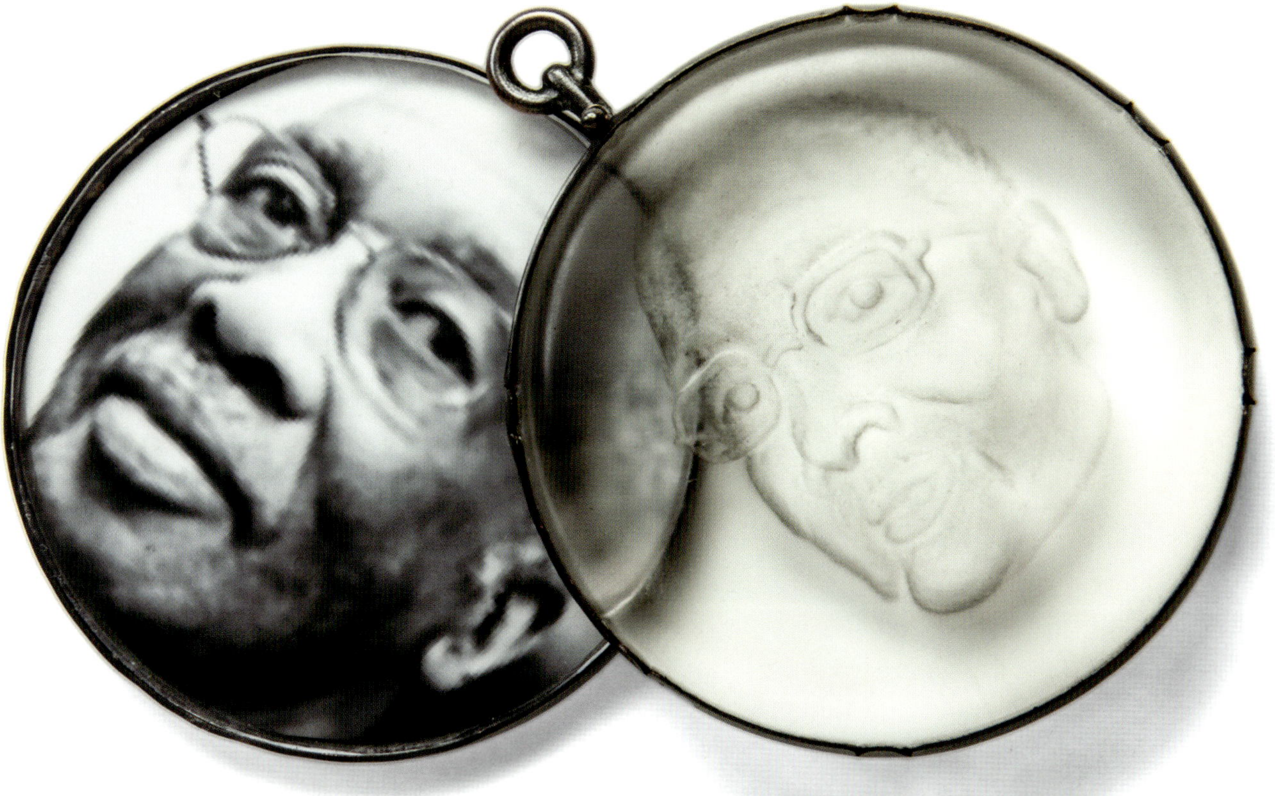

Is it possible to become immortal through objects? This question led me to make *Remembrance* in homage to my late father. It is not my memory of my father's physical presence that endures but rather the qualities of his spirit. He was a man of incredible kindness, grace, and warmth. *Remembrance* is an object that refers to lockets (memory keepsakes) and watches (measurers of time). The piece is a repository for my father's presence (embodied in the last photograph I took of him) and his spirit (etched in glass). It is an attempt at immortality, merging his intangible qualities with a tangible object.

27

Sonya Clark
Remembrance (pendant), 2012
Digital artist's photograph, hand-blown and etched glass, copper
2 1/2 in. (6.4 cm), diameter
Collection of the artist

IRIS NIEUWENBURG

Family

I like to look at classical jewelry and use the ideas I find as blueprints for my own jewelry. Traditional ways of presenting images, precious objects, and collections such as butterflies or dollhouse furnishings also interest me, and I adapt these ideas to provide context in my jewelry.

The inspiration for *Family* came from a visit I made to a frame shop in Paris. In addition to rows and rows of antique frames, many of them beautifully gilded, I came upon a cabinet filled with old photographs of individuals who had once formed part of a living, loving family. It saddened me to look at the images and realize that the people had all died, but as I pondered them, I began to realize that it was irrelevant whose family this was. It was everyone's family. Families and the celebrations and sorrows that bind them together are universal. *Family* became the first in a series entitled Gilded Frames and Reflections from Paris.

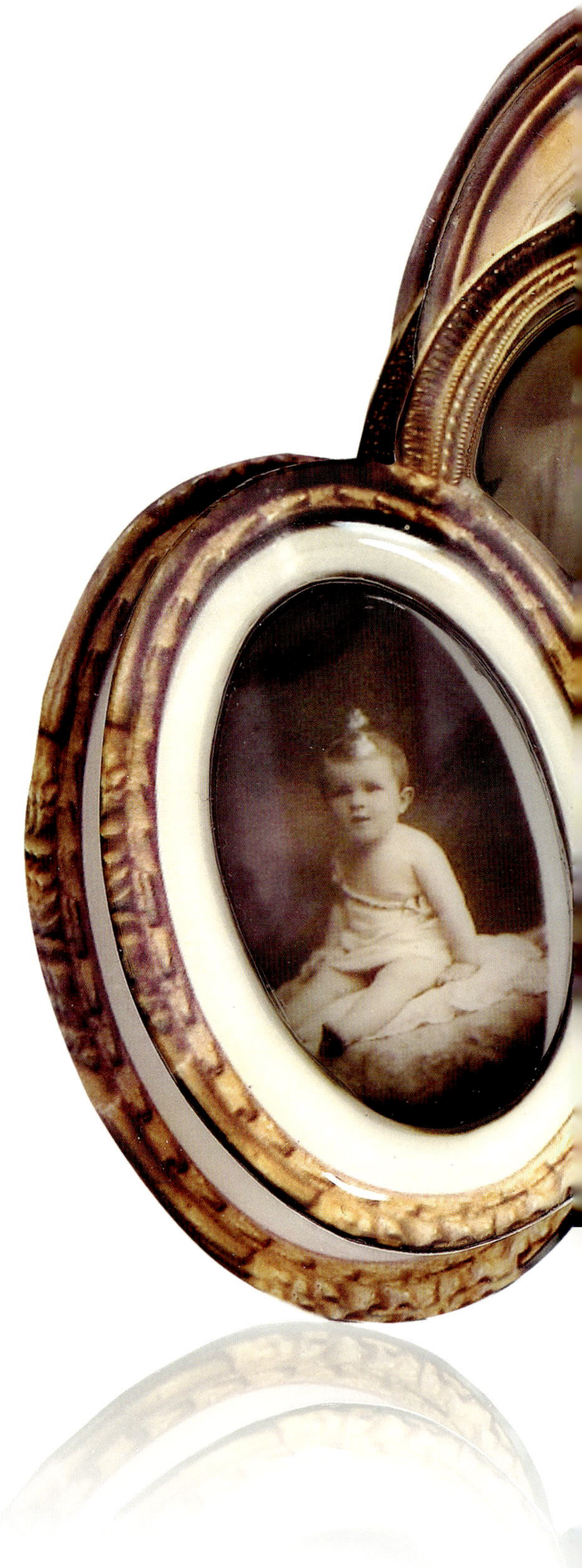

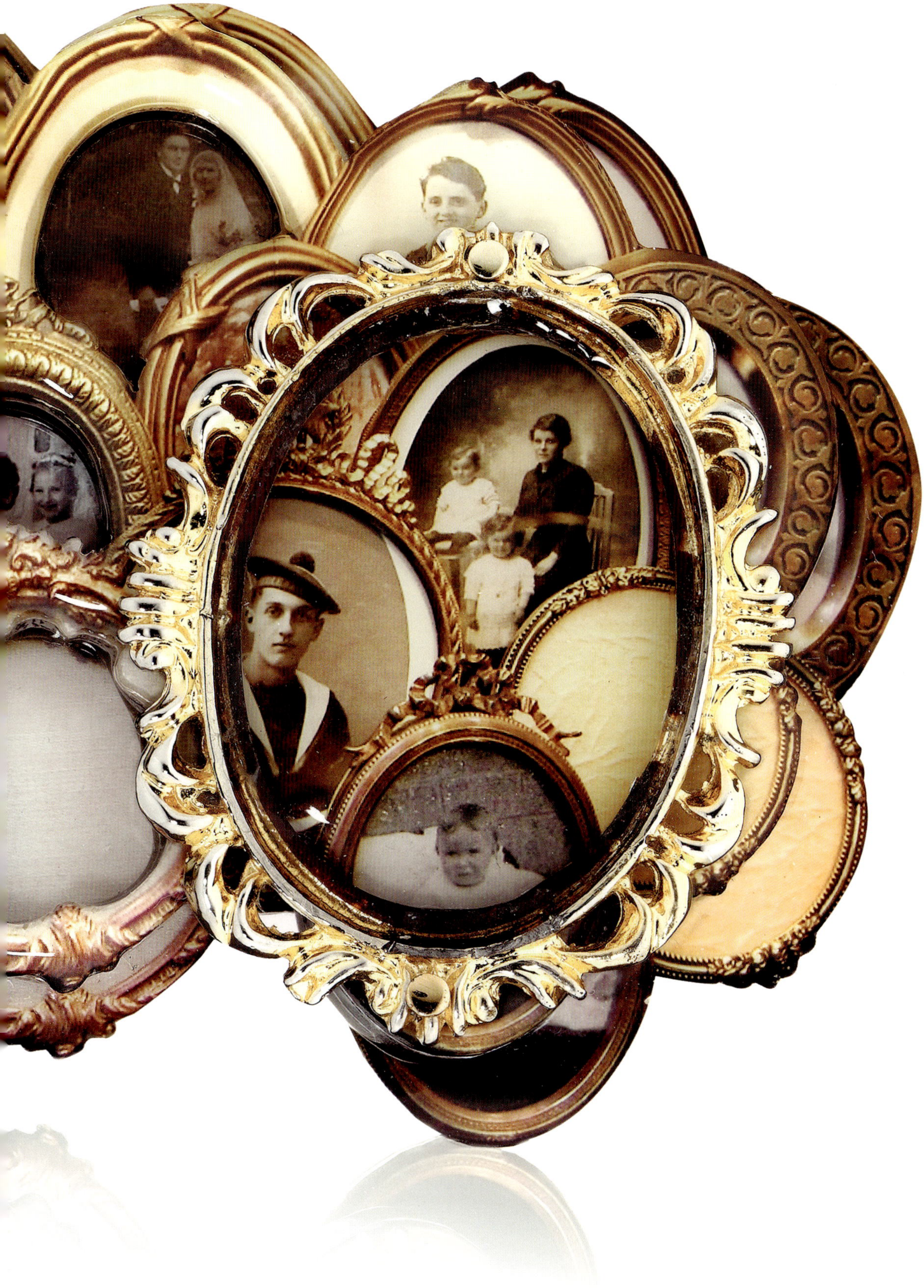

28

Iris Nieuwenburg
Family (brooch), 2010
Digital photographs, silver, wood, veneer, lacquer, gold-plated dollhouse frame, 24k gold
$2^{3}/_{4}$ x $3^{3}/_{4}$ x $^{1}/_{2}$ in. (7 x 9.5 x 1.3 cm)
Museum of Arts and Design, with funds provided by LOOT! 2011 Purchase Committee, 2011

BABETTE BOUCHER

Souvenir #3 | *Souvenir #8* | *Souvenir #9*

My work is a reflection on memories, how to materialize them and how to turn them into jewelry. Memory, so intimate, so fragile and ephemeral, is a personal and universal reality. Time disfigures it; faces and emotions fade away.

For the Dead Class series, a reference to Tadeusz Kantor's theater piece, I used faces from pictures of my mother's classmates in 1949, printing them on silky paper and then setting them in resin. As if I were a taxidermist of memory, I played with transparency and light so that the portraits would emerge—or not—when the brooches are worn.

29 TOP (FRONT AND BACK)
Babette Boucher
Souvenir #3 (brooch)
from the Dead Class series, 2005
Photo transfer on silky paper, iron, 18k gold, resin, magnet
1 1/4 in. (3 cm), diameter
3/8 in. (1 cm), depth
Collection of the artist

30 CENTER (FRONT AND BACK)
Babette Boucher
Souvenir #8 (brooch)
from the Dead Class series, 2005
Photo transfer on silky paper, iron, 18k gold, resin, magnet
1 1/4 in. (3 cm), diameter
3/8 in. (1 cm), depth
Collection of the artist

31 BOTTOM (FRONT AND BACK)
Babette Boucher
Souvenir #9 (brooch)
from the Dead Class series, 2005
Photo transfer on silky paper, iron, resin, magnet
2 3/4 in. (7 cm), diameter
7/8 in. (2.3 cm), depth
Collection of the artist

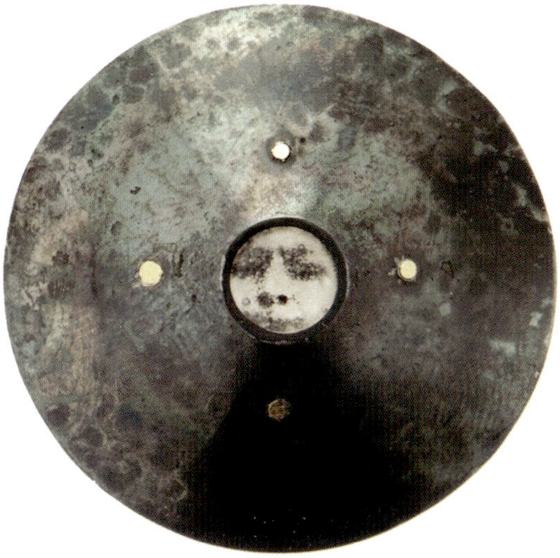
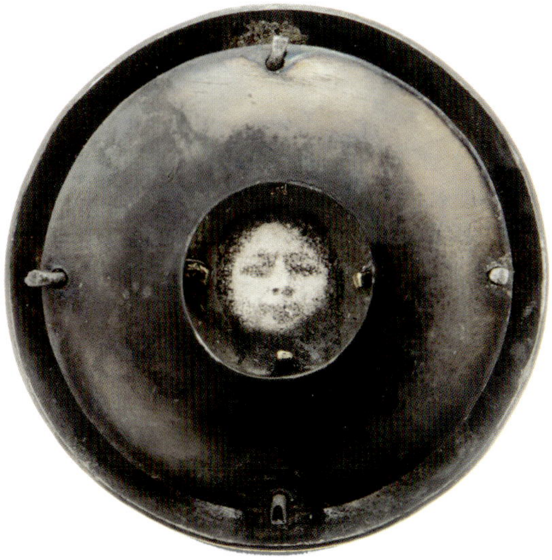
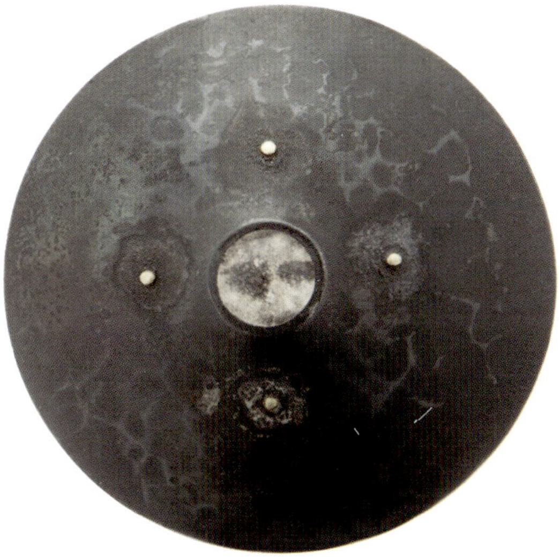
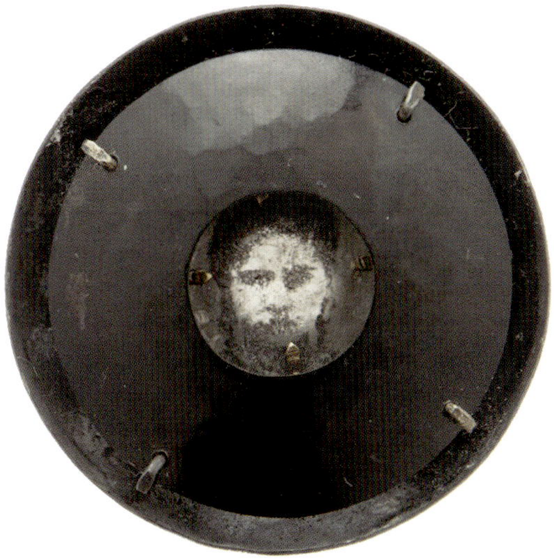
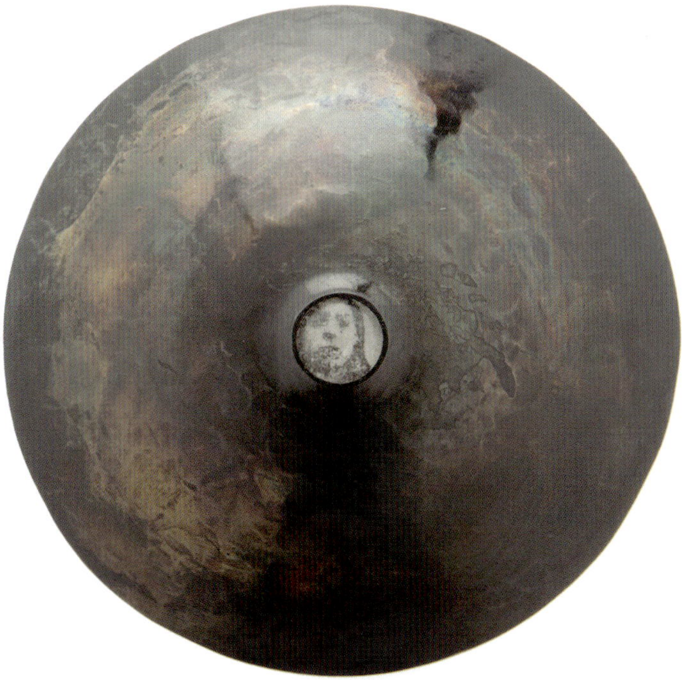
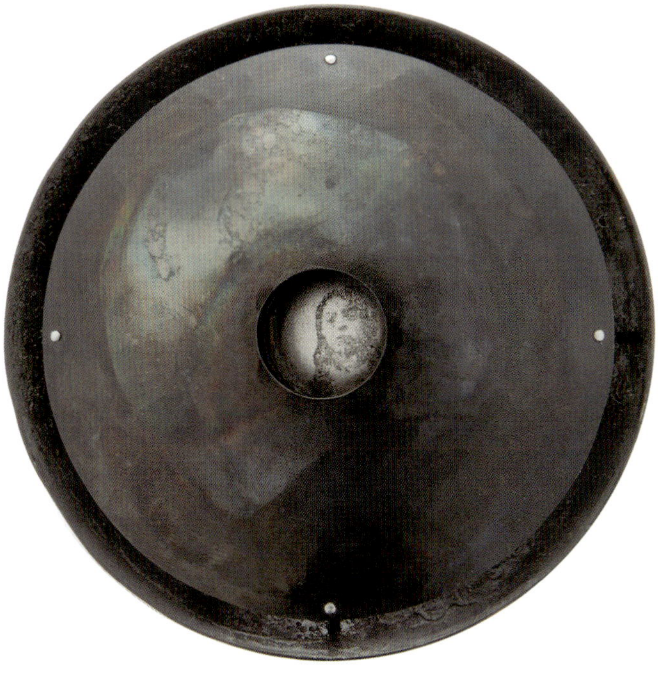

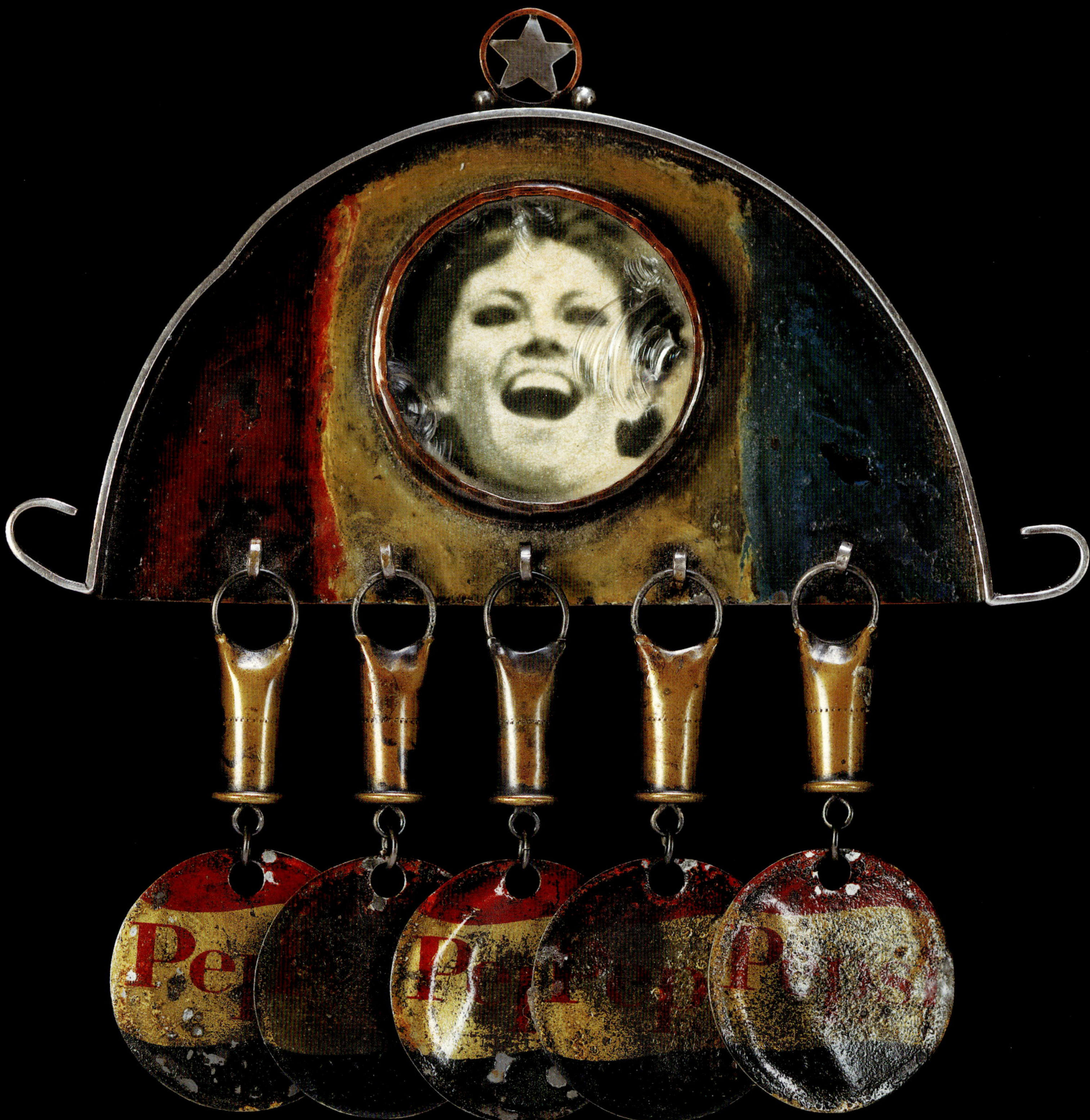

J. FRED WOELL

Come Alive, You're in the Pepsi Generation

I consider myself to be more of a social-political commentator than a maker of jewelry. I make things I hope people can laugh at and yet take seriously. I use my work as a platform to make the nature of things bearable. *Come Alive* was my response to an ad Pepsi-Cola ran continuously in the early 1960s to promote Pepsi. My aim in making this piece was to make it look complete, with an intimate, spontaneous quality that gives it a presence of its own. I tried to keep the freshness of my fingerprint on the work in an effort to give the piece a timeless character.

32 OPPOSITE PAGE AND RIGHT

J. Fred Woell
Come Alive, You're in the Pepsi Generation (brooch), 1966
Analog photograph, sterling silver, copper, brass, steel, glass, found objects
4 x 4 x 1/4 in. (10.2 x 10.2 x 0.6 cm)
Renwick Gallery of the Smithsonian American Art Museum, gift of Kathleen Kriegman, 2006

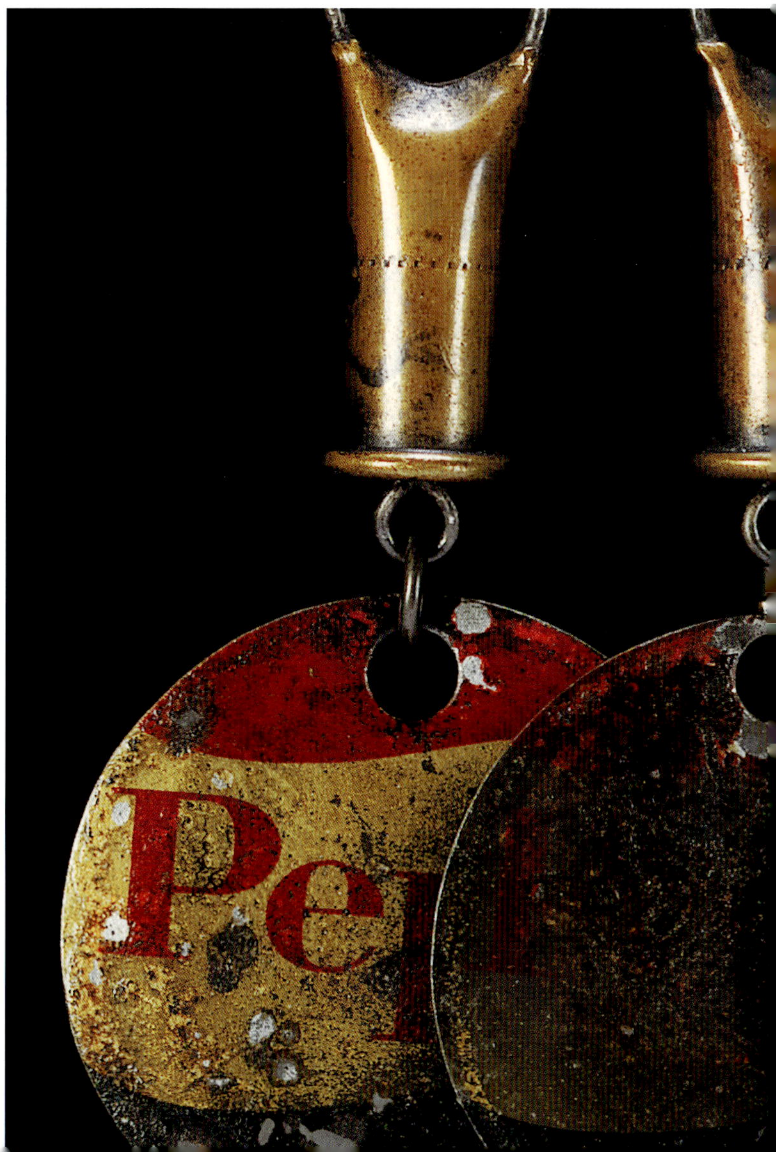

DONALD PAUL TOMPKINS

Janis Joplin Commemorative Medal | Minnesota Fats Commemorative Medal

My brother was a very passionate man, drawn to extremes. He had a great affection and admiration for people who gave themselves fearlessly to their beliefs and talents, and he delighted in a "Damn the torpedoes" philosophy. It didn't matter whether or not he thought a person was nuts; he appreciated bravery of conviction and the depth of dedication and delivery.

A sense of irony figured big into his work, as did compassion and sly humor. The subjects of the pieces in this show are cases in point. The image of Minnesota Fats came directly from a *Time* magazine article. I'm not sure where the Janis Joplin picture came from, but obviously he was a loving fan and was moved by the tragedy of her death.

— Merrily Tompkins

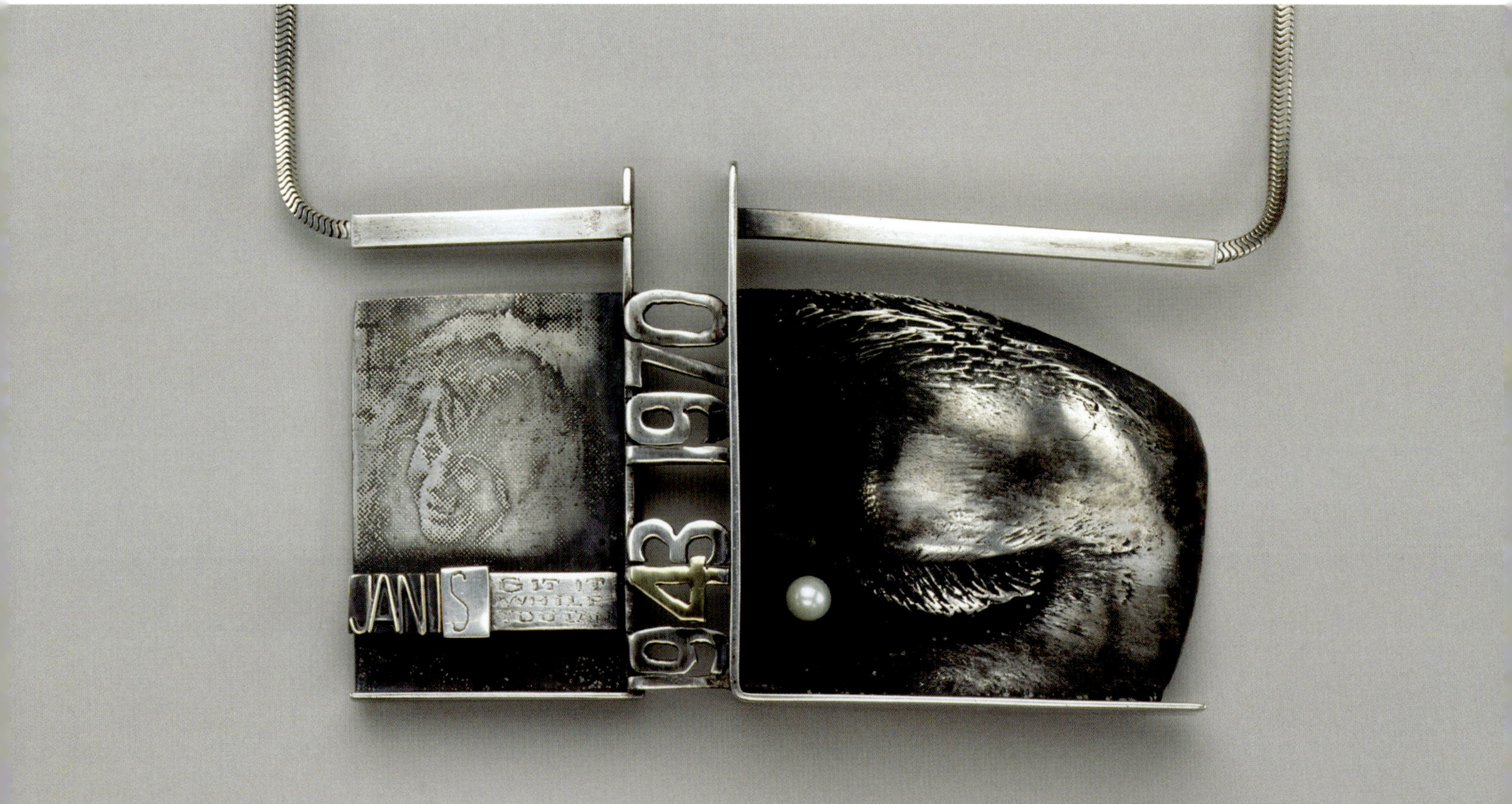

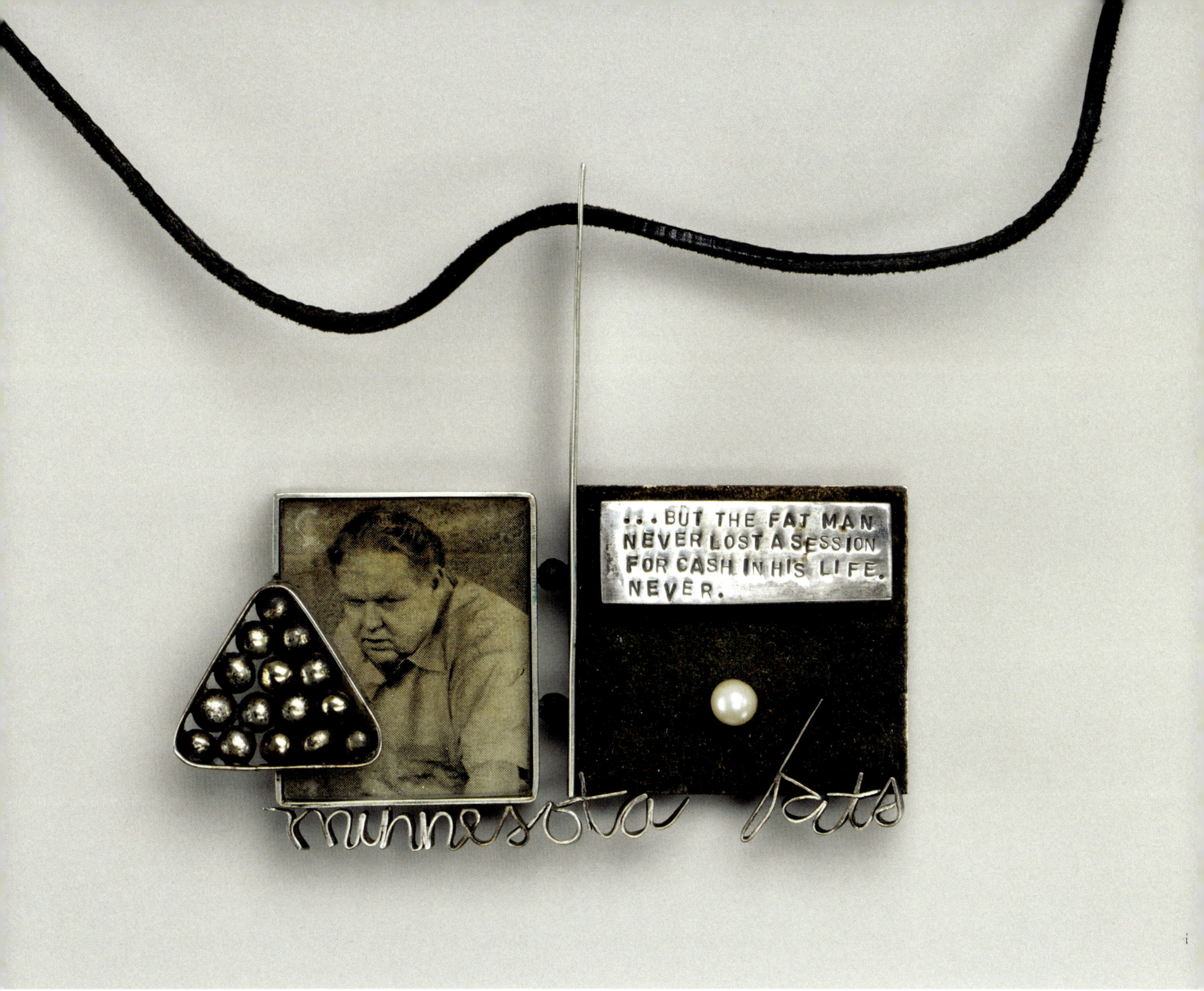

33 LEFT

Donald Paul Tompkins (1933–1982)
Janis Joplin Commemorative Medal
from the Commemorative Medals series, 1970
Photo-etching, sterling silver, brass, pearl
$9\frac{3}{4} \times 4\frac{1}{4} \times \frac{3}{4}$ in. (24.8 x 10.8 x 1.9 cm), overall
$2\frac{1}{4} \times 3\frac{5}{8} \times \frac{3}{4}$ in. (5.7 x 9.2 x 1.9 cm), pendant
The Museum of Fine Arts, Houston, Helen Williams Drutt Collection, gift of Helen Williams Drutt English, 2006.657

34 ABOVE

Donald Paul Tompkins (1933–1982)
Minnesota Fats Commemorative Medal
from the Commemorative Medals series, 1971
Half-tone photomechanical reproduction, sterling silver, pearl, Plexiglas, flocking, leather
$3\frac{5}{8} \times 3\frac{3}{4} \times \frac{5}{8}$ in. (9.2 x 9.7 x 1.6 cm)
The Museum of Fine Arts, Houston, Helen Williams Drutt Collection, museum purchase funded by the Morgan Foundation, 2002.657

ROBERT EBENDORF

Fishman | *Man and His Pet Bee*

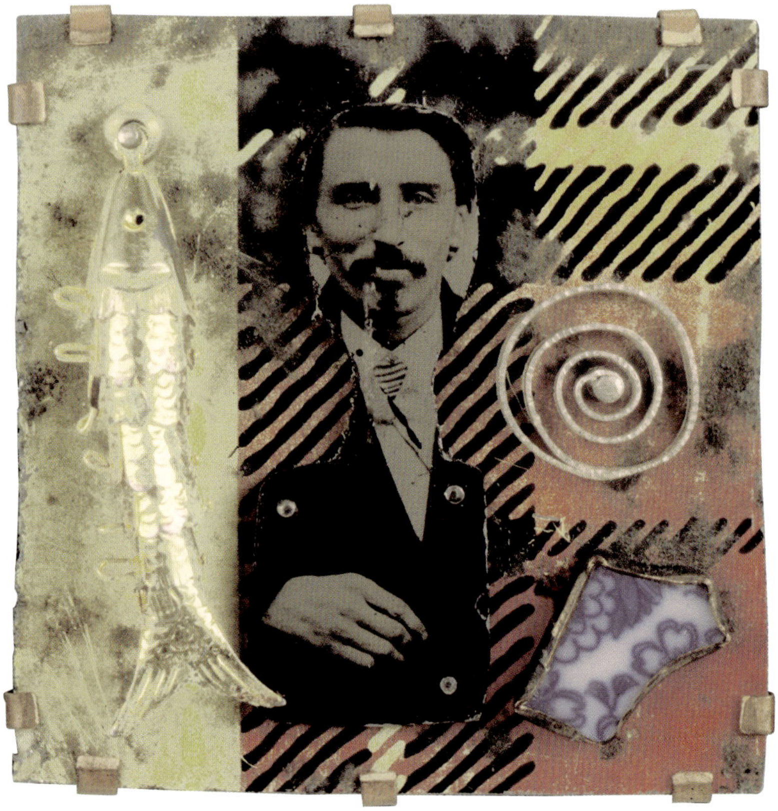

My inspirations for the *Fishman* brooch were a tintype I acquired and a fish market I visited in Norway. The visual character and activities of the local market are suggested through a small brass fish, a broken piece of blue-and-white china reminiscent of that used by the fishmonger to hold loose change, and the brooch's multi-colored tin background.

Oftentimes my ideas and compositions reflect the unusual people and places I encounter in my dreams. The *Man and His Pet Bee* came from a dream I had about a man who was sitting in a room carrying on a conversation with a pet bee that was situated in the crotch of his trousers.

35 ABOVE
Robert Ebendorf
Fishman (brooch), 2010
Tintype, silver, tin, ceramic shard, jointed brass fish
3 x 3 in. (7.6 x 7.6 cm)
Collection of the artist

36 OPPOSITE PAGE
Robert Ebendorf
Man and His Pet Bee (brooch), 1968
Tintype, silver, brass, copper, aluminum, glass bead, turquoise bee, found objects
$6\frac{3}{4}$ x $4\frac{3}{8}$ x $\frac{1}{2}$ in. (17.1 x 11.1 x 1.3 cm)
Museum of Fine Arts, Boston, The Daphne Farrago Collection, 2006.50

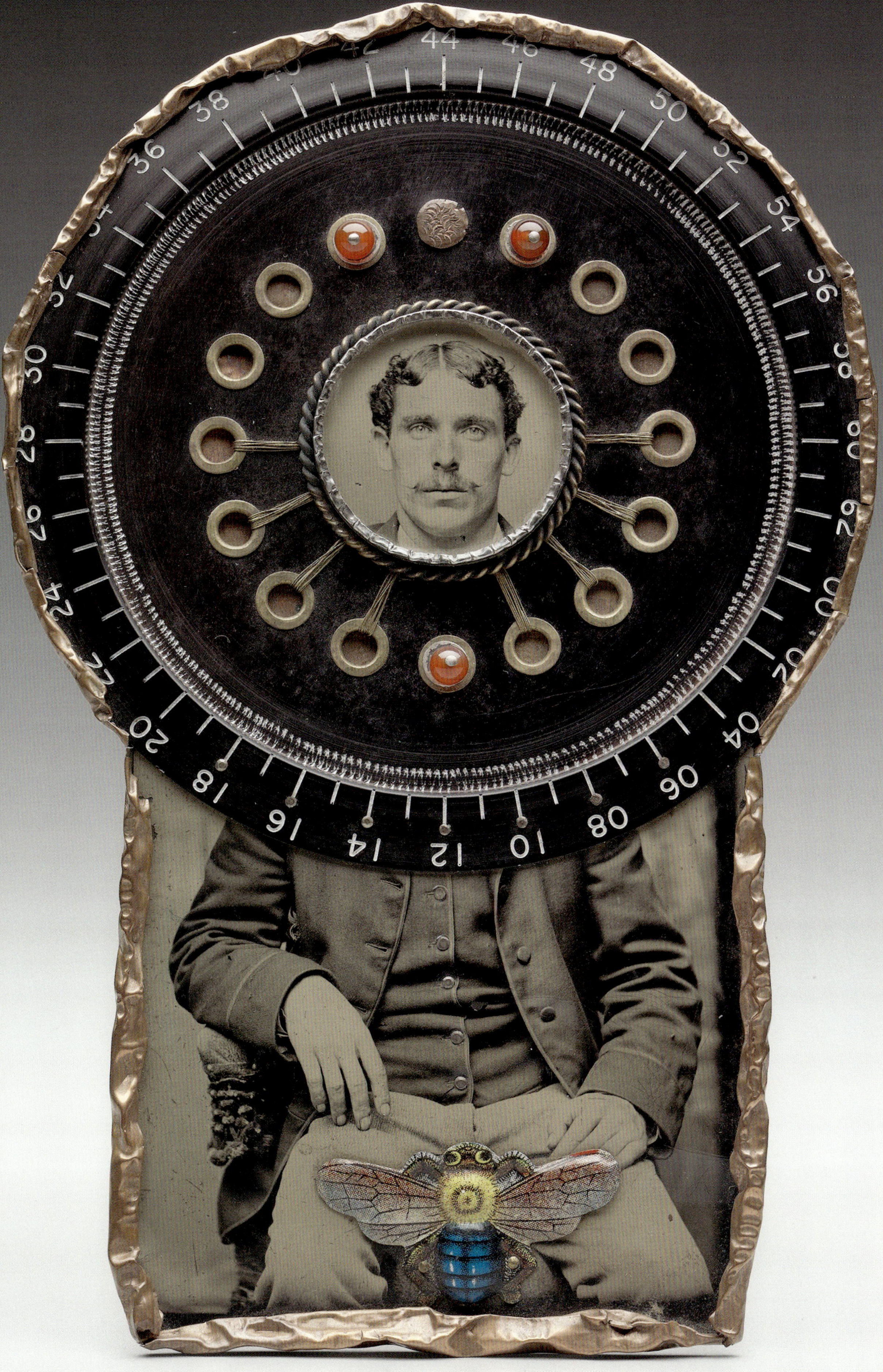

JOYCE J. SCOTT

Ancestry / Progeny

37 OPPOSITE PAGE

Joyce J. Scott
Ancestry/Progeny (necklace), 2013
Tintypes, glass beads, thread
$14\frac{1}{2} \times 8\frac{1}{2} \times 1\frac{1}{8}$ in. (36.8 x 21.6 x 2.9 cm)
Courtesy of the artist

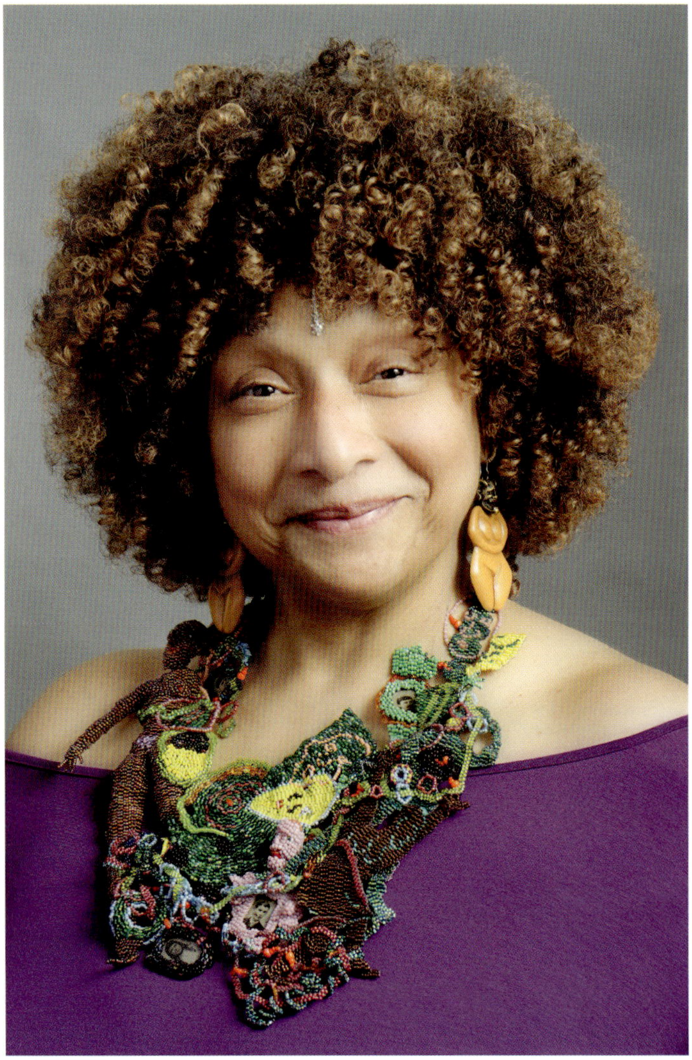

Photograph of the artist, 2013.

Sometimes, making a new necklace is akin to writing a letter—I mean “old style” with paper and pen, with each word I write conjuring the recipient’s special charms. My necklace is a daydream made real. The beaded figures and the photos embody each person’s attributes, igniting the particular aroma, rhythm, and spirit of each. Handling of the beads, thread, and tintypes—my crafting of these simple components—is my pledge to do right by honorable souls.

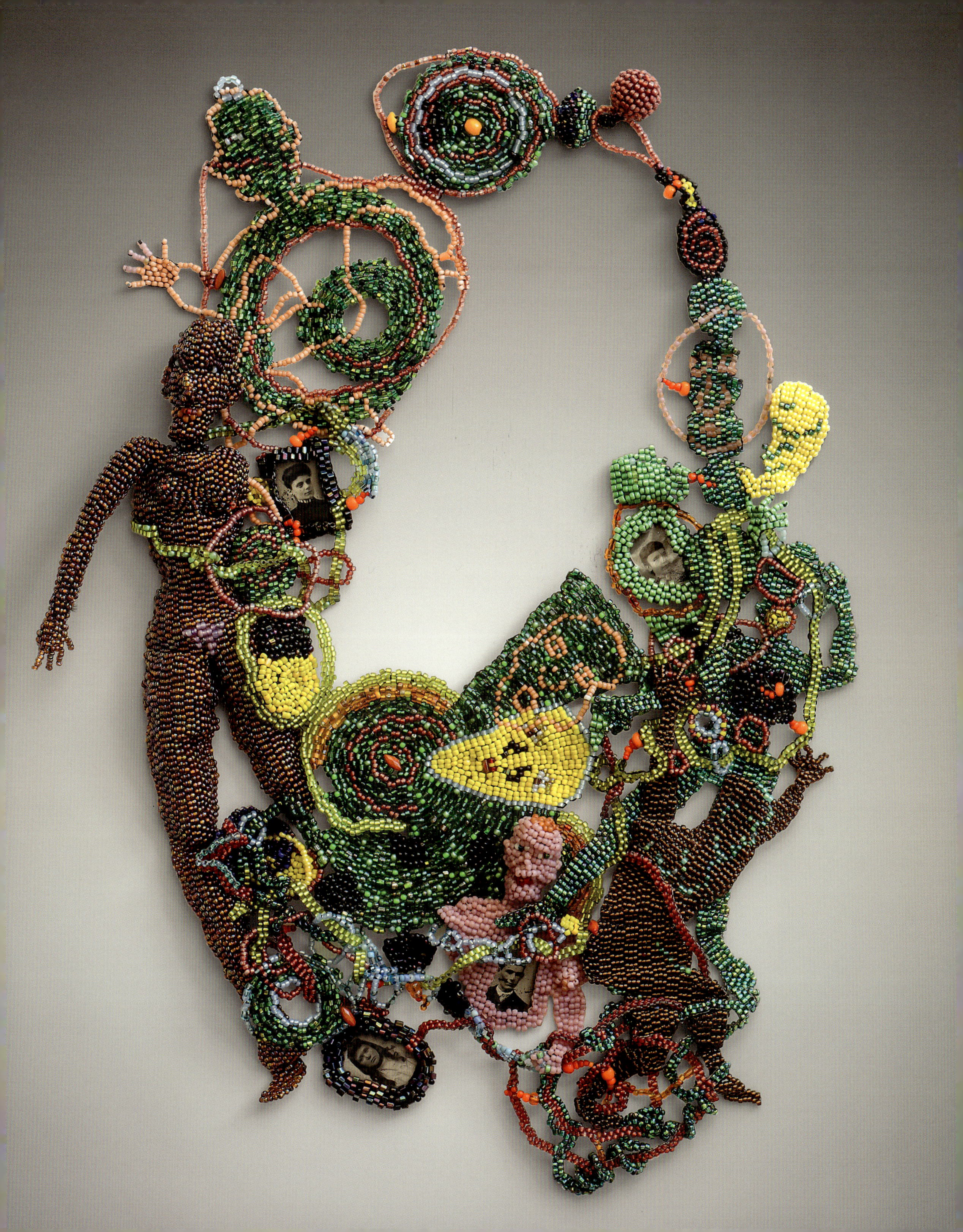

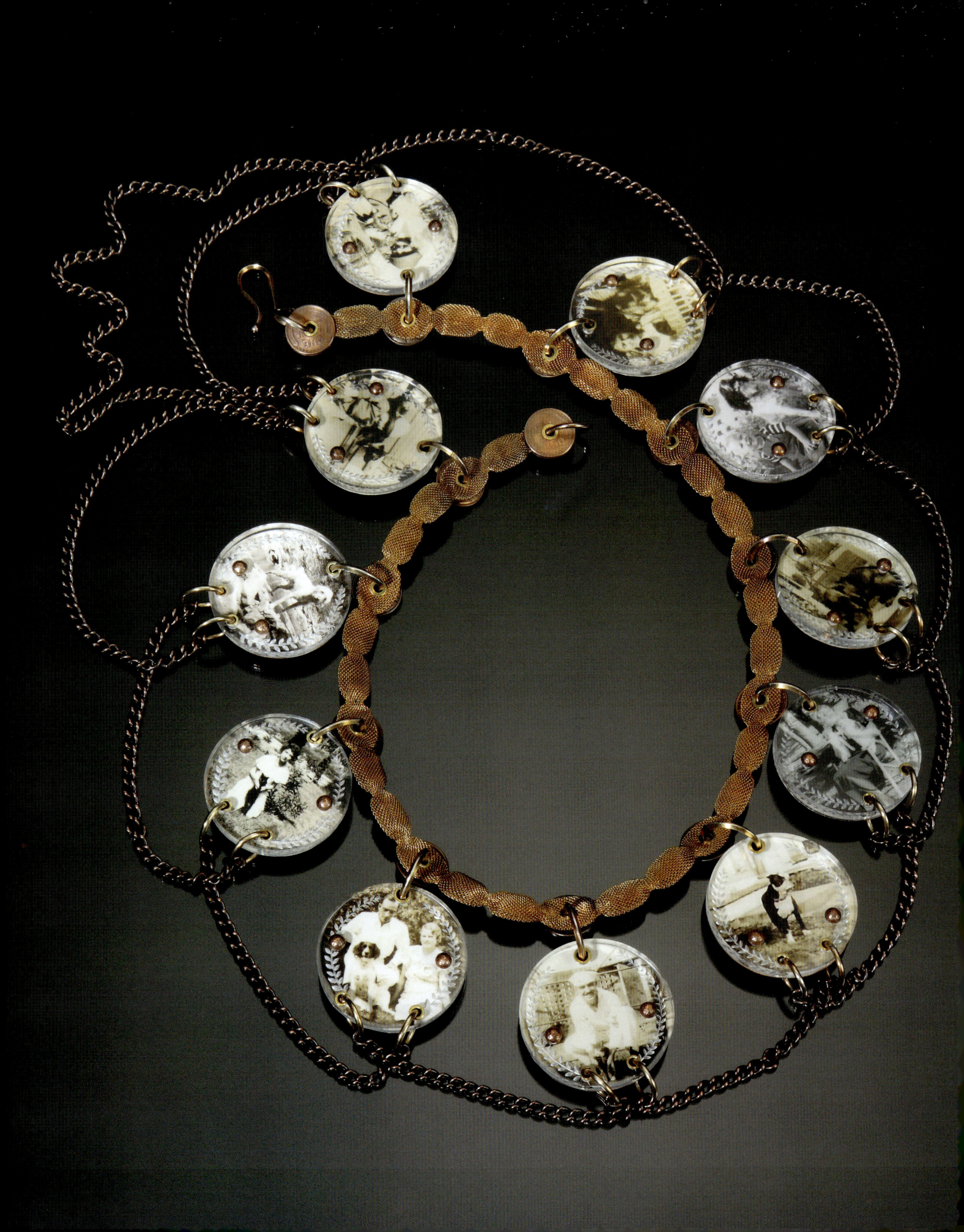

NANCY WORDEN

The Revenants

This necklace was inspired by the Billy Collins poem "The Revenant," which is told in the voice of a dead dog addressing his former owner. Working with old snapshots I found in my grandmother's estate, I created a personal narrative for each pet. All of the pets in the photos are deceased, and each one has a complaint told from the pet's perspective. Their stories are etched on the reverse of each photo medallion.

38 OPPOSITE PAGE AND BELOW
Nancy Worden
The Revenants (necklace), 2011
Scanned vintage photographs, copper, woven gold-plated brass, brass, acrylic
29 1/2 in. (74.9 cm), length
7/8 in. (2.2 cm), medallion depth
Collection of the artist

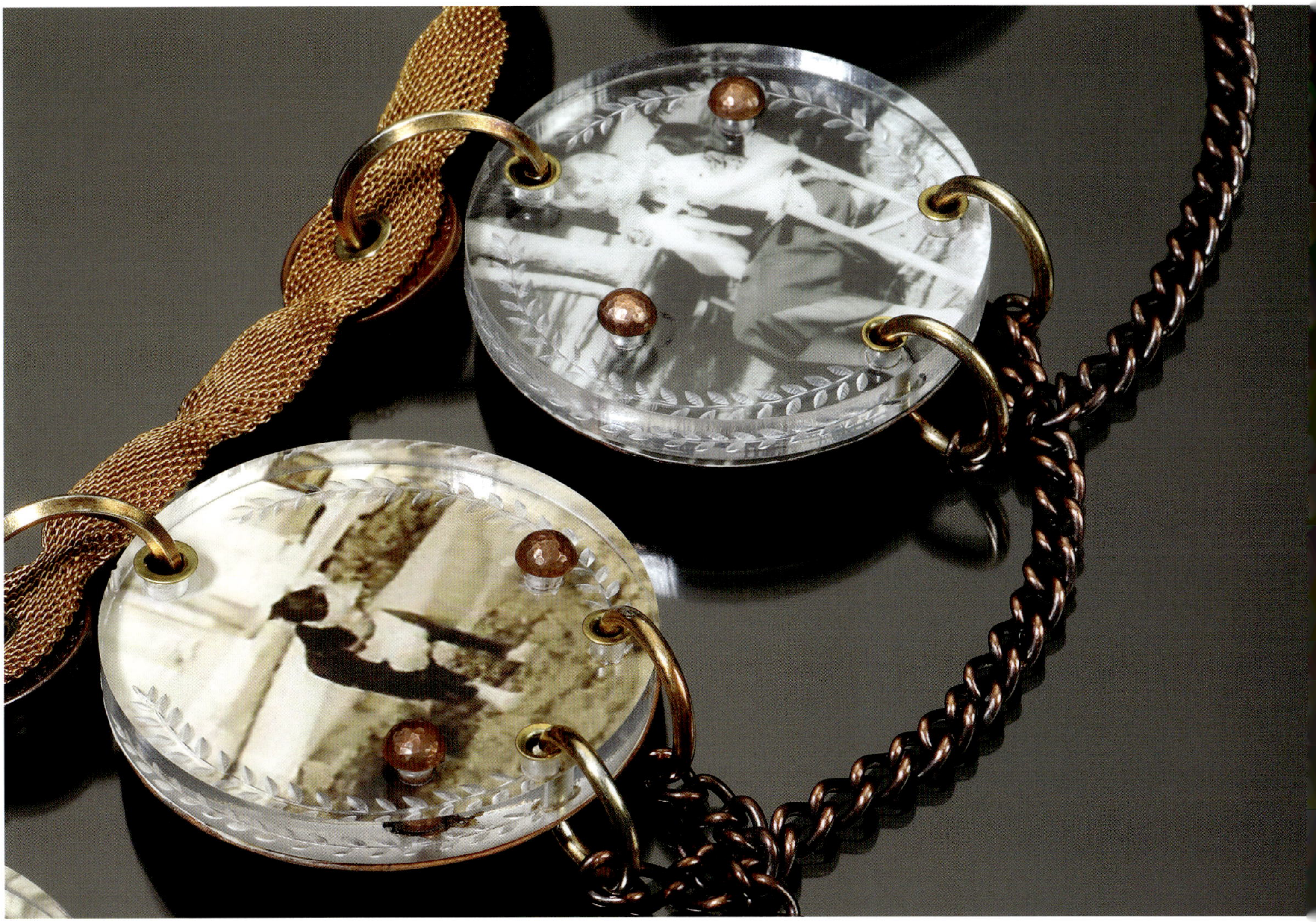

PAMELA MORRIS THOMFORD

My Father, My Children, My Worry... A Mother's Prayer

The complex and personal narrative in *My Father, My Children, My Worry . . . A Mother's Prayer* links three generations. The subject is war and loss, and the rosary format communicates an attitude of prayer and concern. With vivid memories of my father's struggles post–World War II, the social turmoil surrounding America's war with Vietnam during my youth, and worry over the possibility of my children's future calls to battle, I combined a wartime photo of my father in uniform, a casting of his World War II bombardier metal, a coin from his year and country of birth, my mother's Red Cross nurse's badge, and photos and pennies from the birth years of my four children, in order to make a personal declaration regarding the tragedy of war, the devastation of loss, and the absence of godliness during conflict.

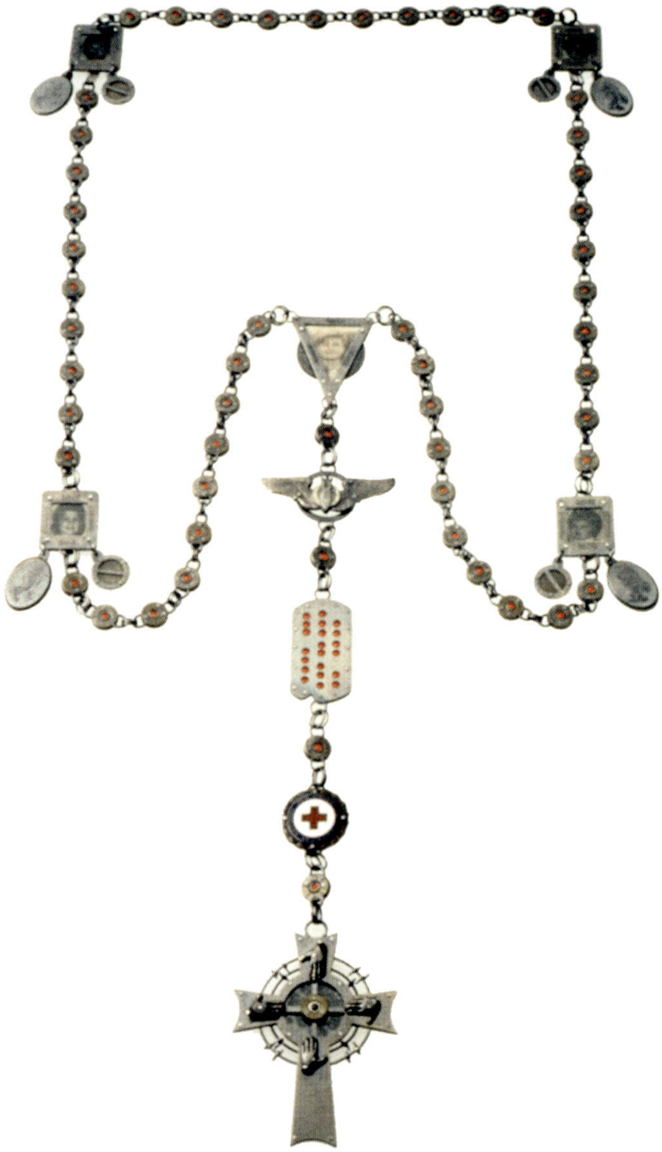

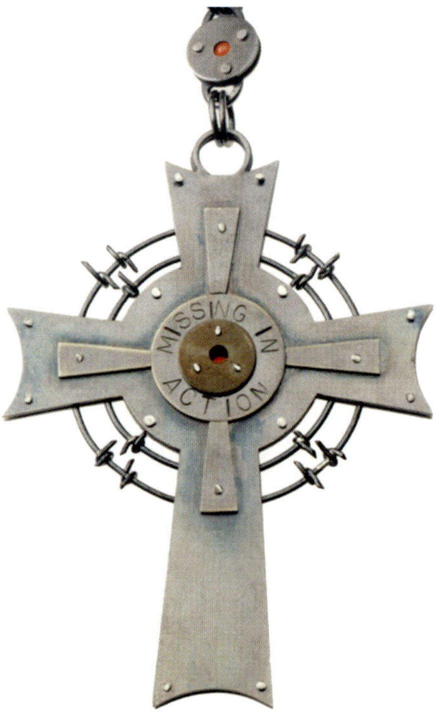

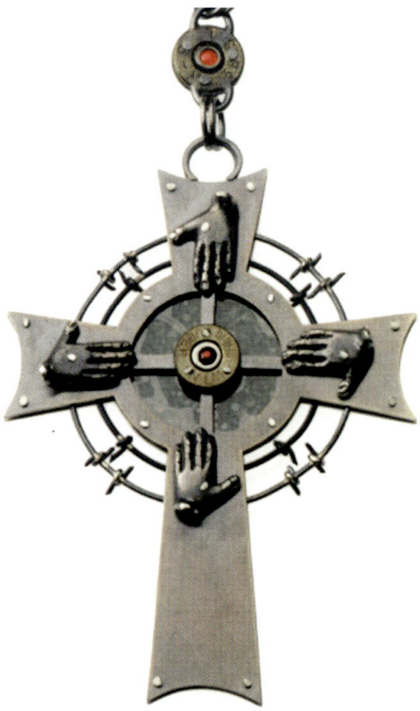

39 ABOVE AND LEFT

Pamela Morris Thomford

My Father, My Children, My Worry . . . A Mother's Prayer (rosary), 1999

Analog photographs, rubies, sterling silver, Precious Metal Clay, mica, rifle castings, American and British coins, copper, Red Cross medal

40 x 2½ x ½ in. (101.6 x 6.4 x 1.3 cm)

Collection of the artist

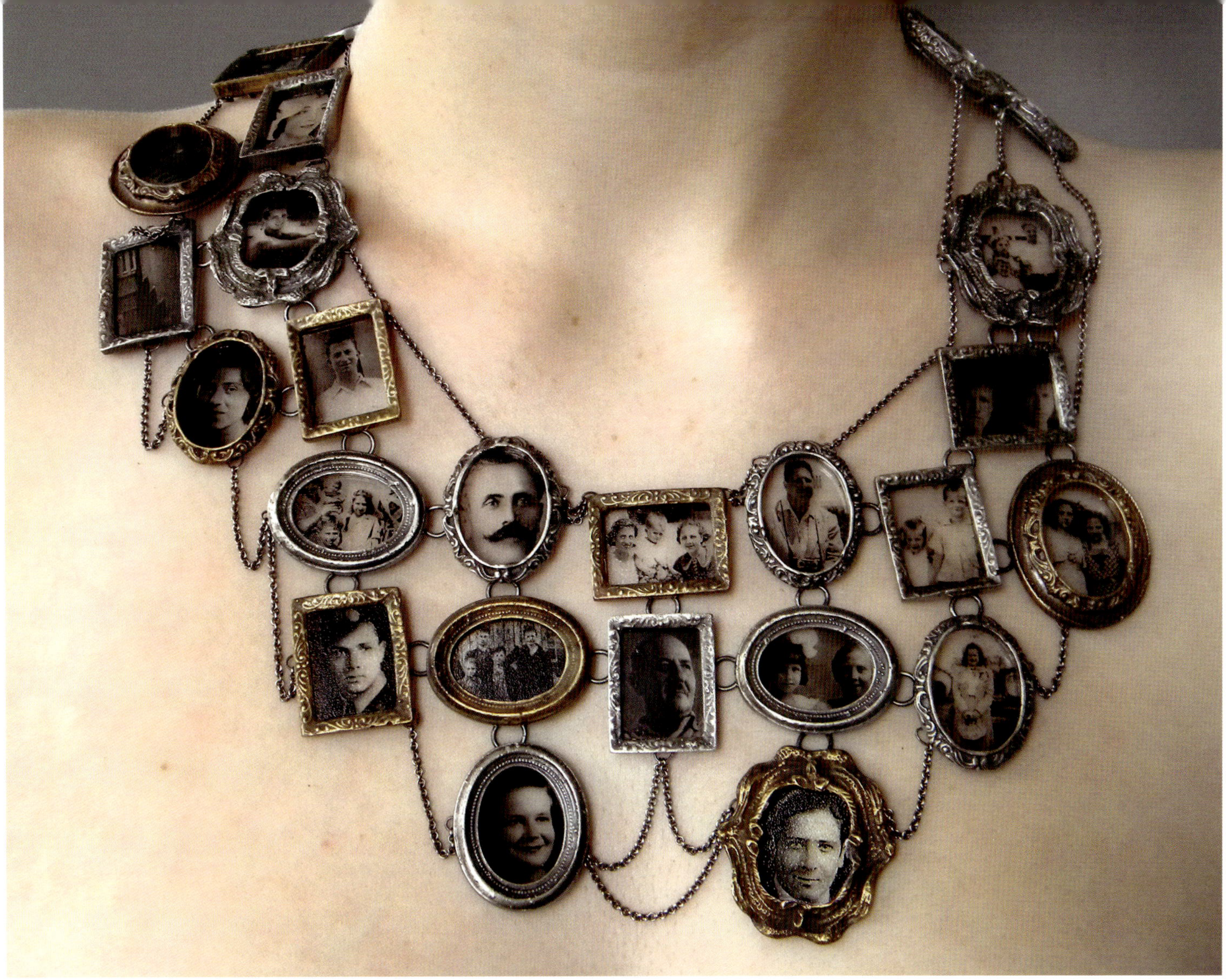

40

Ashley Gilreath

I Am Who They Were (necklace), 2011

Decal photographs, sterling silver, bronze, optical glass

10 x 8 1/2 in. (25.4 x 21.6 cm)

Collection of the artist

ASHLEY GILREATH

I Am Who They Were

Hanging on the walls and hidden in the corners of our homes are the photographs and objects of those who came before us. These seemingly mundane and irrelevant items are the indexical records of family and human history. Accumulating in layers and decaying through time, these remnants of our physical world provide tangible reference points for how we understand one another, and ultimately ourselves. With this necklace of family portraits, I am referencing the tradition of heirloom jewelry while recreating the illusion of ascending and descending through time. My skin shows through the glass as my ancestors' skin so that who I am becomes who they were.

SALLY VON BARGEN

Elegy

Elegy is a monumental neckpiece consisting of more than forty-two hundred digital portraits of American men or women who lost their lives in Iraq during the Bush presidency. It is my hope that this work engenders feelings of respect for those who died, sympathy for their loved ones, and disdain for the politicians who manipulated the truth to wage an unjustifiable war. Each portrait was digitally printed, mounted, and then sandwiched back-to-back with another portrait to form a simple unit. These units were connected by brass eyelets and rings and formed into seventy strands.

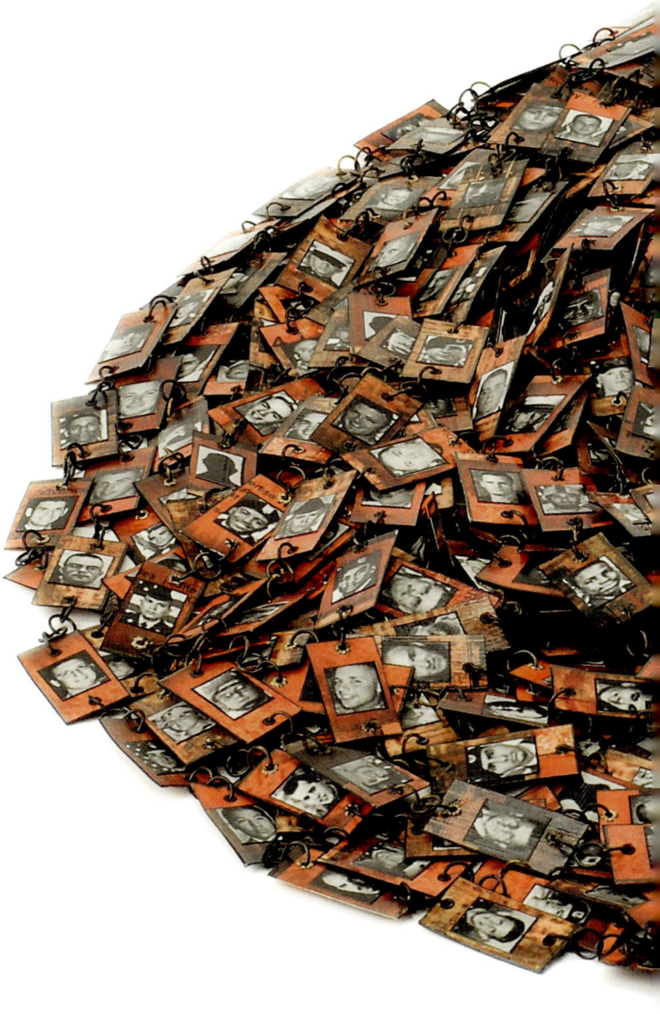

BETTINA SPECKNER

Untitled | *Untitled* | *Frau Holle, Mother of Snow*

It is important to me that the images I use in my jewelry have a timeless quality, whether I use photos I have found or ones I have taken myself. The portraits in these pieces are old ferrotypes in which the image was printed onto a thin "blackened" metal plate, a relatively simple photo-technique that was patented in the United States and England in the 1850s and offered the advantages over the daguerreotype process of being faster and simpler and of producing less fragile images. I collect old ferrotype plates and work on the images to develop them and transform them into jewelry. I don't work with the intention of decorating things or making them look prettier. I try to discover the soul of an object or the essence of a photograph and try to make something new of it beyond its mere optical appearance that will appeal to me and to other people.

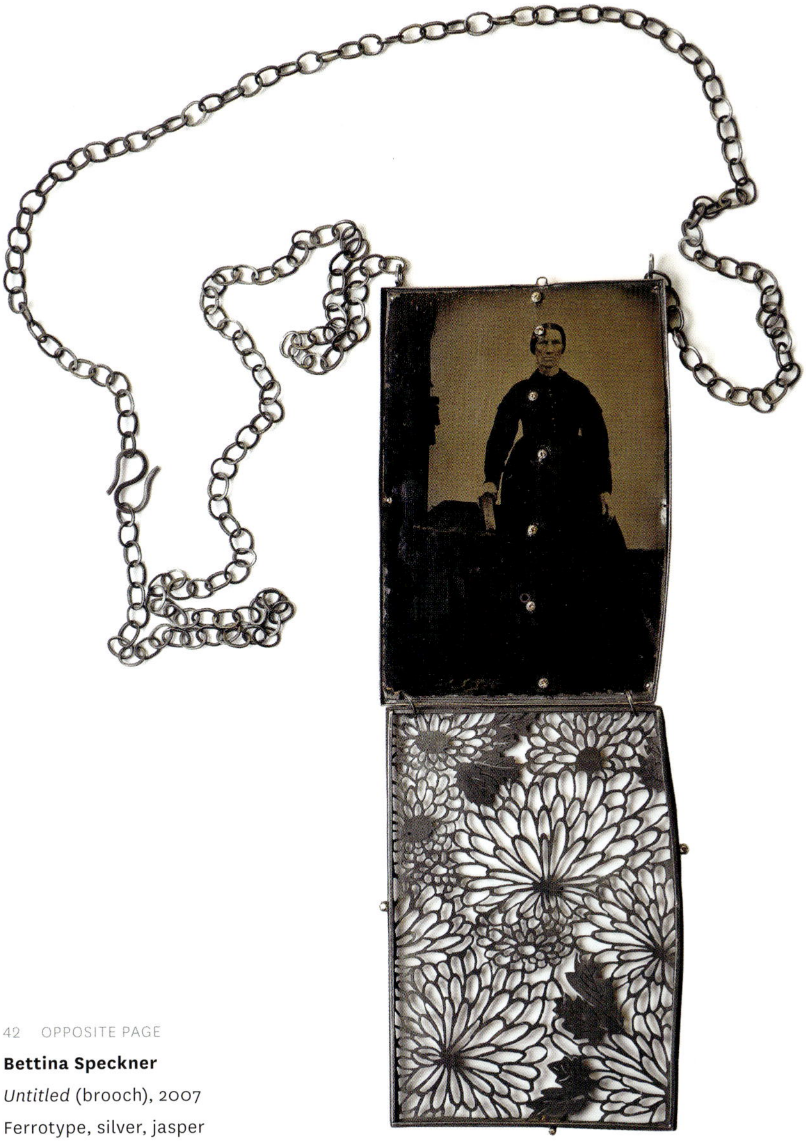

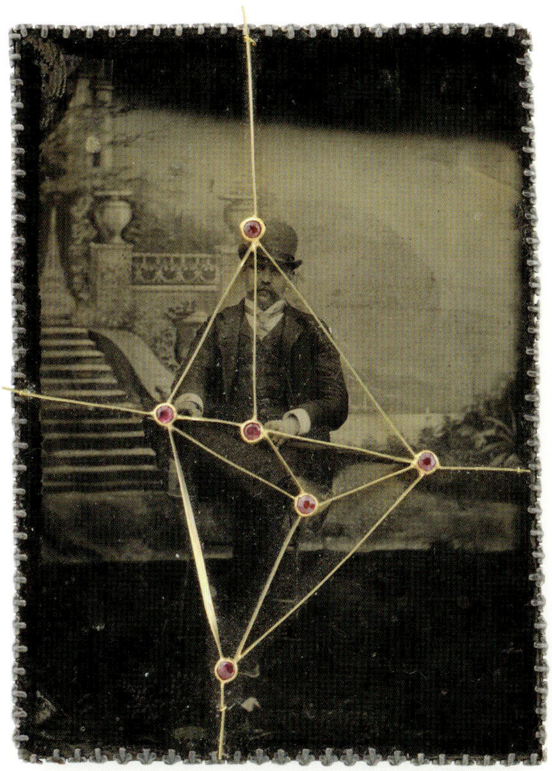

42 OPPOSITE PAGE
Bettina Speckner
Untitled (brooch), 2007
Ferrotype, silver, jasper
$3^{1}/_{4}$ x $2^{1}/_{4}$ x $^{1}/_{2}$ in. (8.4 x 5.7 x 1.2 cm)
Stedelijk Museum 's-Hertogenbosch

43 FAR RIGHT
Bettina Speckner
Untitled (brooch), 2004
Ferrotype, rubies, gold, silver
$3^{3}/_{4}$ x $2^{3}/_{4}$ x $^{1}/_{4}$ in. (9.5 x 7 x 0.6 cm)
Collection of Susan C. Beech

44 ABOVE
Bettina Speckner
Frau Holle, Mother of Snow (pendant), 2010
Ferrotype, champagne diamonds, silver
$3^{3}/_{4}$ x $2^{1}/_{2}$ in. (9.5 x 6.4 cm), without chain
Rotasa Trust Collection

ELEANOR MOTY

Dual Image | *Fan Brooch*

45

Eleanor Moty
Dual Image (brooch), 1974
Artist's Polaroid photograph photo-etched on sterling silver, quartz crystal, obsidian
$2^{3}/_{4} \times 3 \times {}^{1}/_{2}$ in. (7 x 7.6 x 1.3 cm)
Collection of Robert L. Pfannebecker

Having taken a Polaroid photograph of a woman posing with a book open to an August Sanders photograph, I later processed the image as a halftone transparency for use in photo-etching, and the photo-etched silver was incorporated into the fabricated brooch. The juxtaposition of the historical image and the contemporary one was the impetus for the brooch. A natural quartz crystal replaced the woman's face, giving the image a sense of mystery, and an obsidian star emphasized the formality of the Sanders portrait.

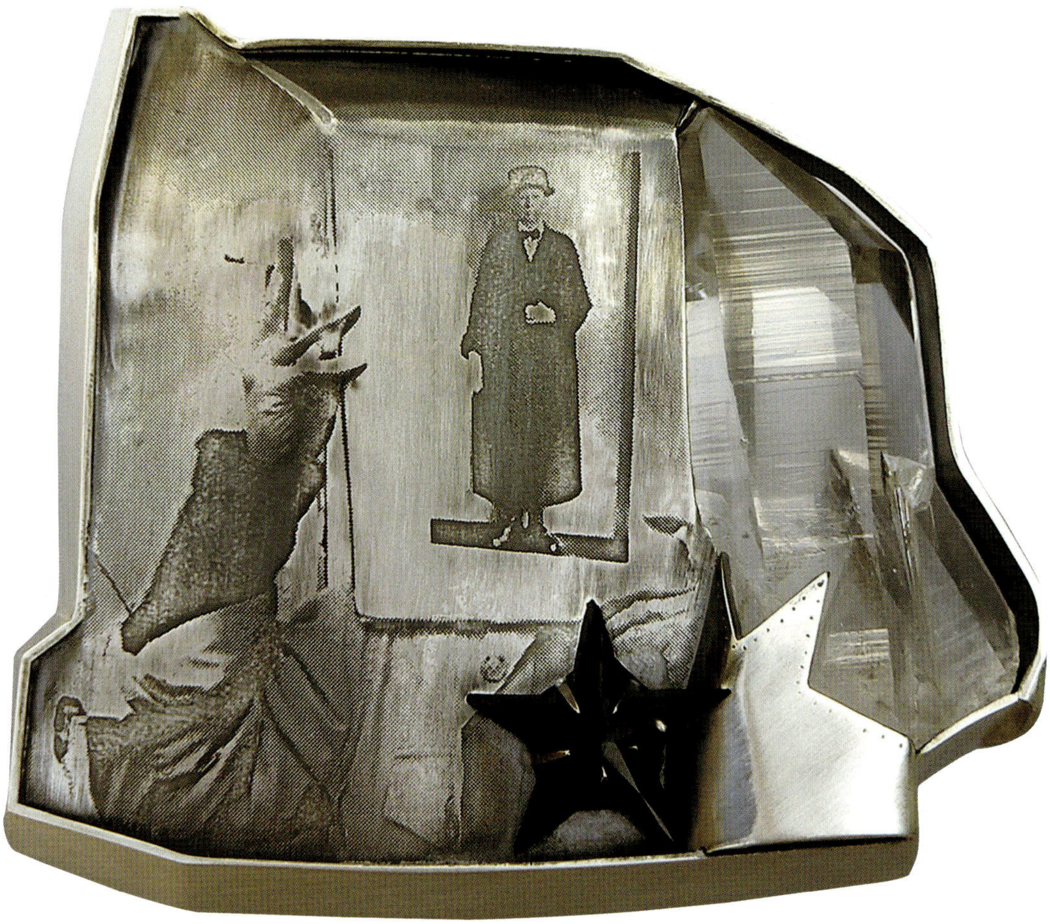

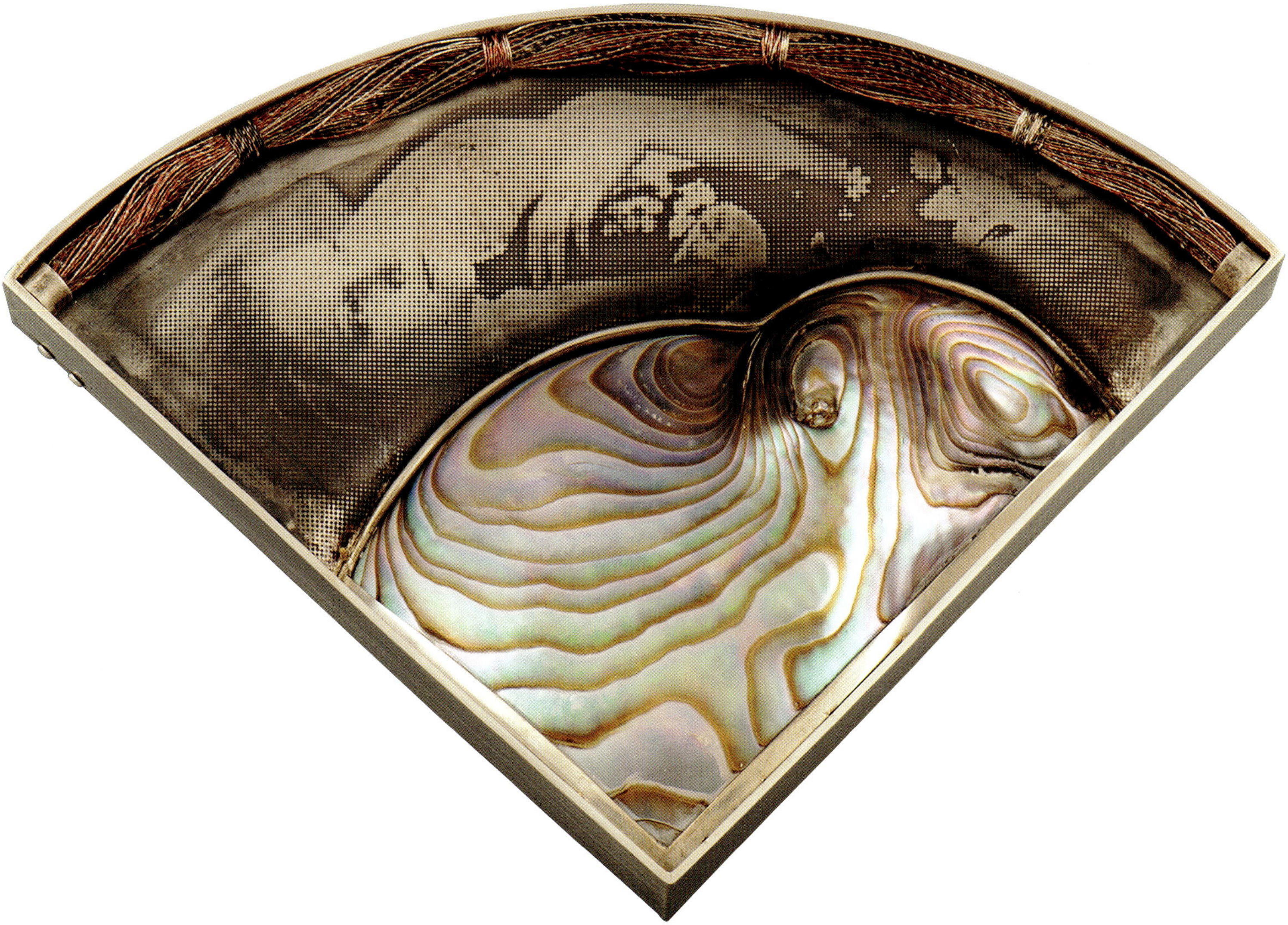

With a student at the Haystack School of Crafts in Deer Isle, Maine, serving as model, I created a series of Polaroid images of her dressed in a kimono. In *Fan Brooch*, she strikes a pensive pose, and the pattern and imagined color of the kimono are referenced by carved abalone shell. The iridescence of the abalone shell is repeated by the bundled metallic silk thread typical of that used in embroidered kimonos, and the fan shape adds emphasis to the Asian influence of the design.

46

Eleanor Moty

Fan Brooch, 1981

Artist's Polaroid photograph photo-etched on sterling silver, abalone shell, silk thread

4 x 3 x 1/2 in. (10.2 x 7.6 x 1.3 cm)

Collection of the artist

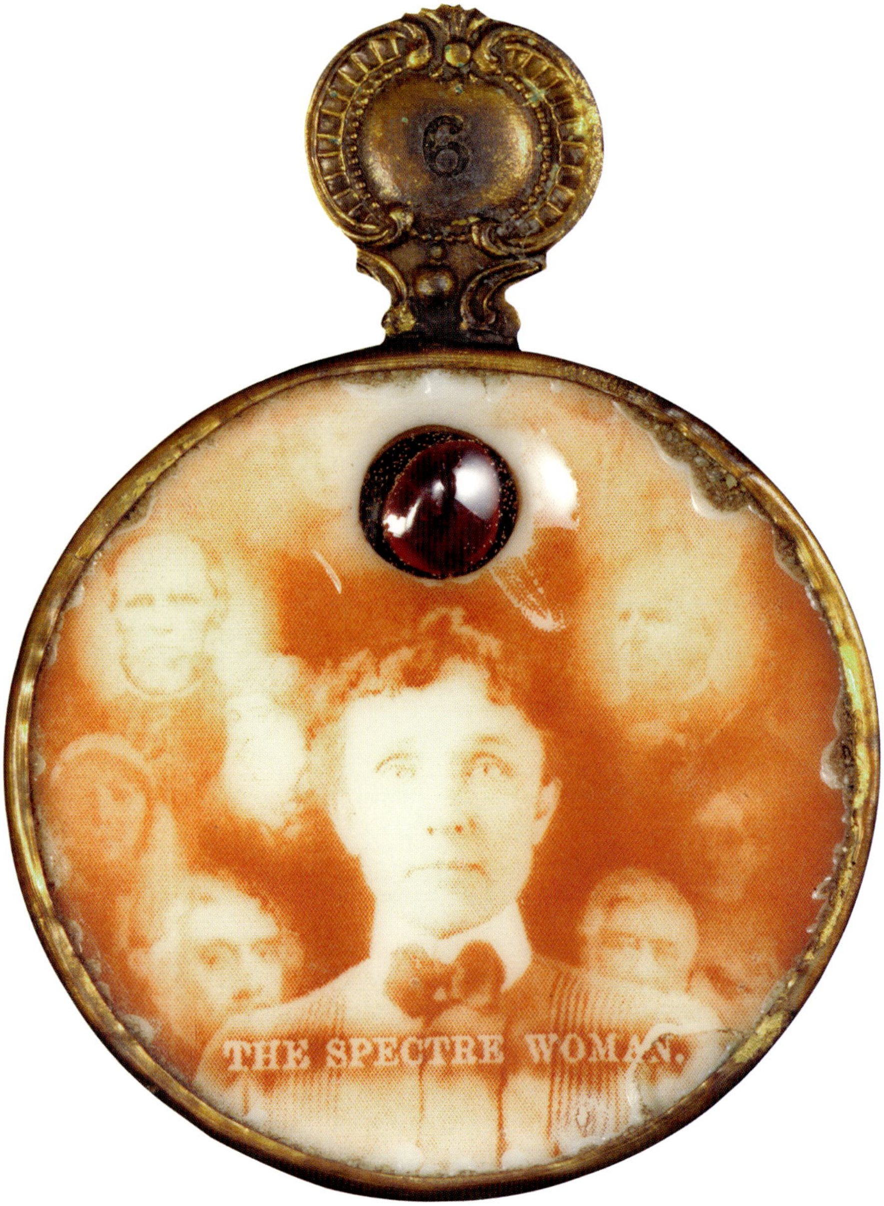

47
Keith Lo Bue
The Spectre Woman (brooch), 2010
Vintage photographs fused onto glass, uncut ruby, resin, optometrist's lens frame
2 x 1½ in. (5 x 4 cm)
Collection of Claire L. Ramsey

KEITH LO BUE

The Spectre Woman

In learning the process of kiln-fusing photographic images onto glass, I was reminded of early "spirit photographs" in which otherworldly entities were claimed to have been captured from the ether onto glass plates. How fitting, then, to use this newly learned process to affix a Victorian multiple-exposure "spirit" to my own glass. The frame, an optometrist's test lens from the same time period, is a punning reinforcement of the act of seeing into this invisible world.

KLAUS BÜRGEL

Ghost Ring

I was not interested in photography per se when I made this ring—I mean, I was and I wasn't. What I was really interested in was faces. I do not know this person. There was no indication of why the picture was taken, and the original photograph was somewhat blurry. Quite possibly this is what turned me on to this image—its lack of importance, the blank stare, the humble gesture, the empty canvas.

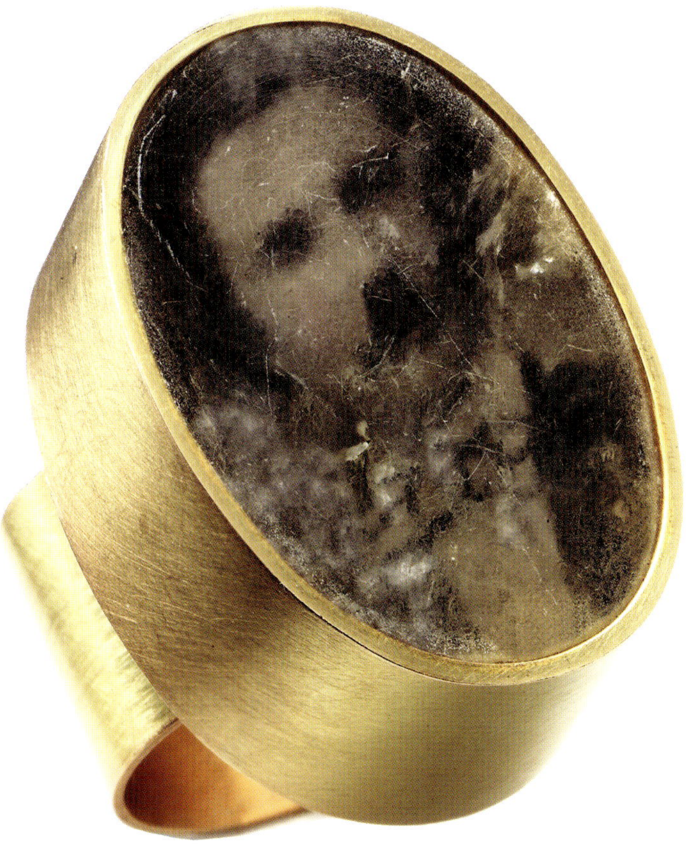

48
Klaus Bürgel
Ghost Ring, 2001
Tintype, gold, ulexite
$1^1/_4$ in. (3.2 cm), height
$1^1/_4 \times {}^3/_4$ in. (3.2 x 1.7 cm), setting
The Susan Grant Lewin Collection

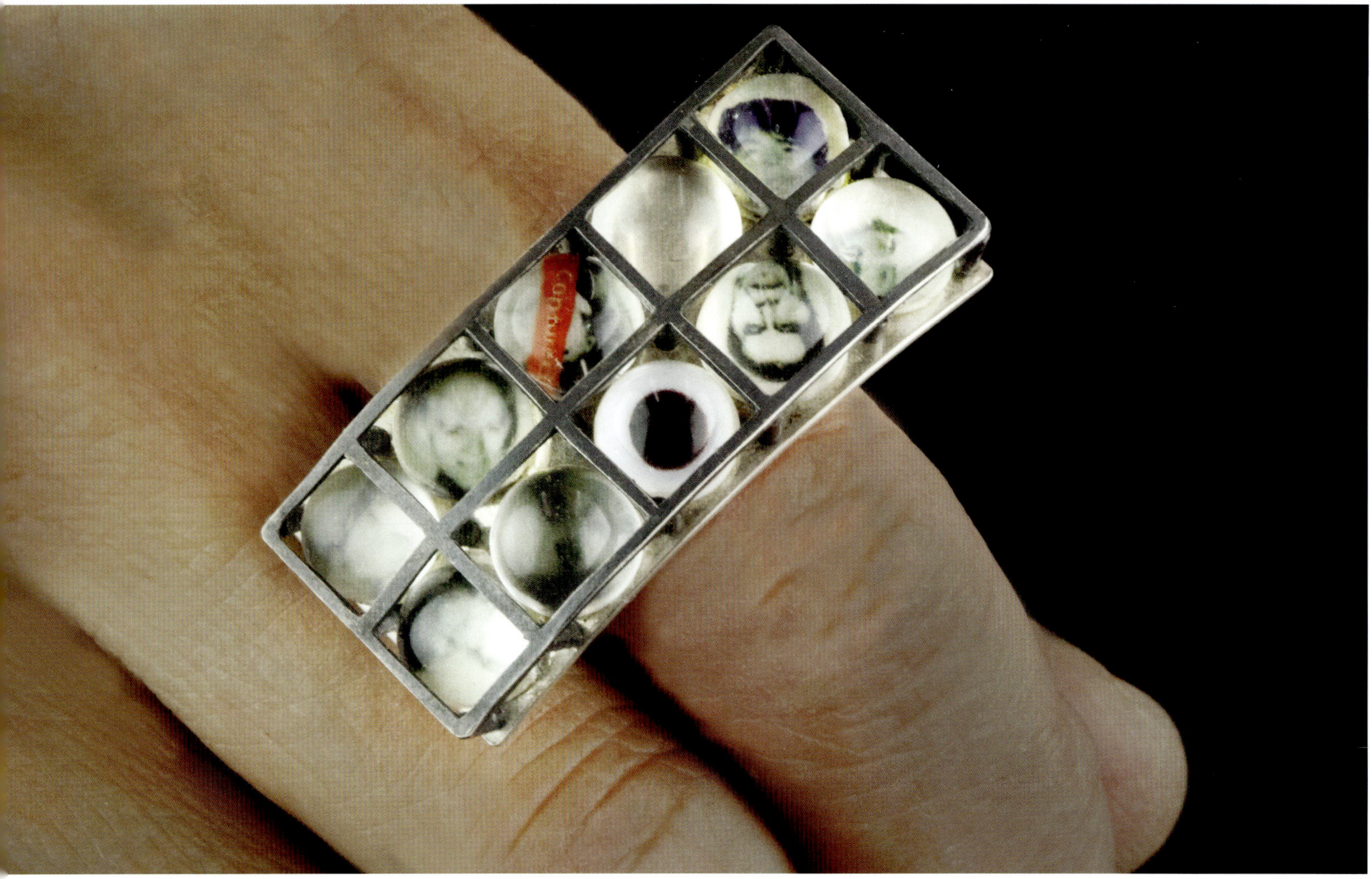

PETER DECKERS

Ten Most Wanted

The *Ten Most Wanted* ring portrays images that provoke fear. It contains nine images from the FBI's 1999 "Most Wanted" list. The tenth image is of a glass eye that a taxidermist used in an attempt to give a lifelike appearance to an endangered bird. Traditionally gemstones are fundamental to the value of jewelry, but these "gemstones" are symbols of what we turn our faces from, trying to ignore what we do not like to see.

49
Peter Deckers
Ten Most Wanted (ring), 2000
Photographic reproductions, sterling silver, glass, taxidermy eye
1 in. (2.6 cm), overall height
3/4 in. (1.8 cm), diameter
Ring top: 1 1/2 x 3/4 x 1/4 in. (3.7 x 1.7 x 0.5 cm)
Collection of Gina Matchitt

SHARI PIERCE

34 Sex Offenders and 2 Sexual Predators from within a 5-Mile Radius

Particularly in the U.S., girls grow up thinking that receiving jewelry is evidence that a man loves them, but jewelry can just as easily remind us of the dark side of being the object of desire. The combination of a decorative form, particularly one that violates one's privacy as jewelry does, with terrifying content has changed how I view my creations. I see this necklace as a kind of "awareness ribbon" that can alter the wearer's and the viewers' perceptions of themselves and the world they inhabit. I found the images for this necklace online, in the U.S. Sex Offenders database.

50 BELOW AND RIGHT
Shari Pierce
34 Sex Offenders and 2 Sexual Predators from within a 5-Mile Radius (neckpiece), 2010
Photos from U.S. Sex Offender database transferred onto silk
66 7/8 in. (170 cm), length
Collection of the artist

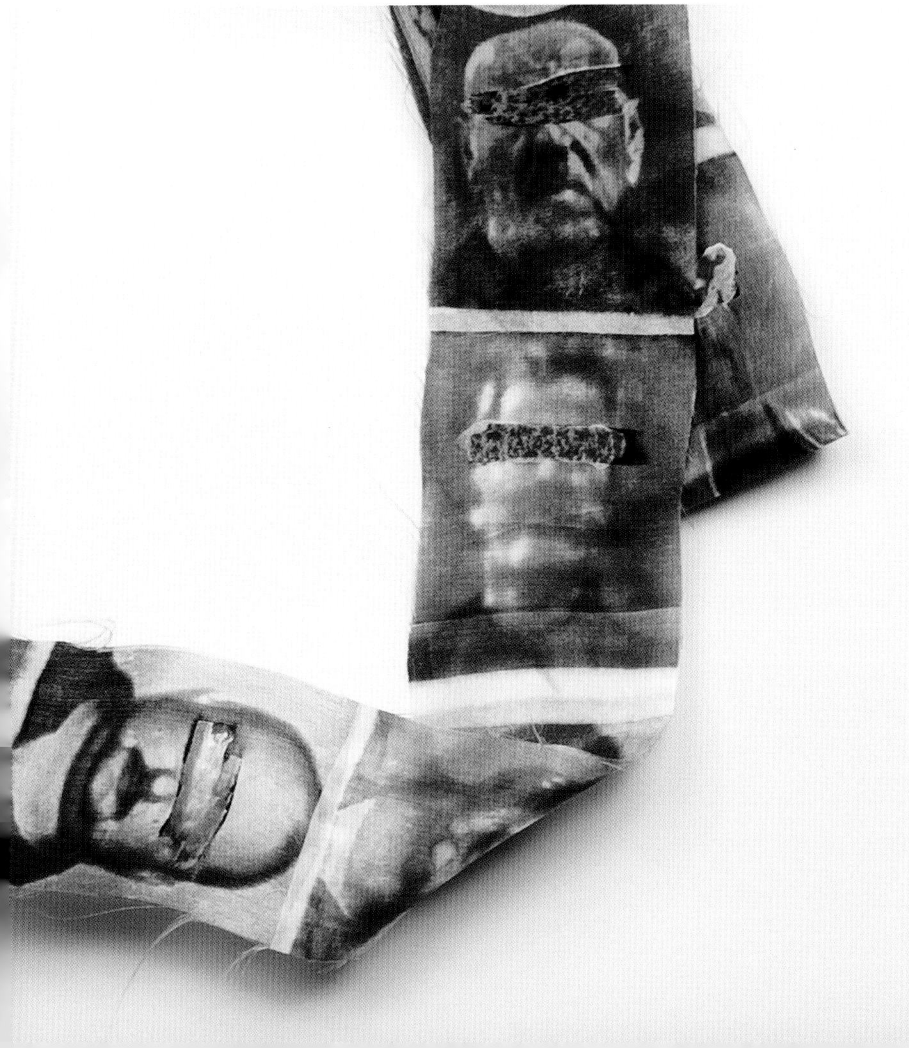

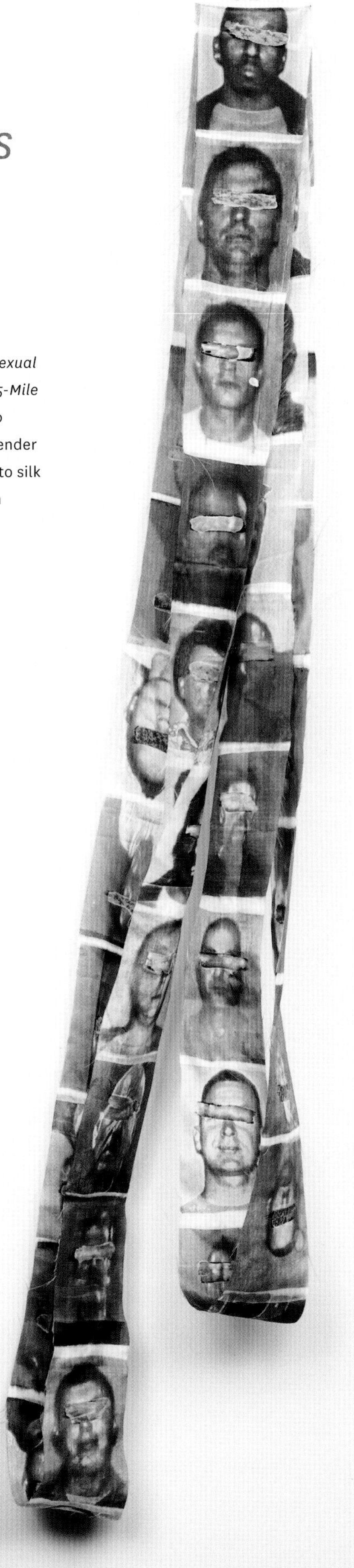

JORDAN DONER

Display Cuff | *Surveillance Pendant*

51 BELOW
Jordan Doner
Display Cuff, 2014
LED screen, rutile quartz, sterling silver, laser-cut calf's leather
5 in. (12.7 cm), diameter
$2^1/_2$ in. (6.4 cm), width
Collection of the artist

Jewelry is ornament and instrument in my *Surveillance Pendant* and *Display Cuff*. Nestled in the necklace's smoky quartz faceted heart is an HD video camera suspended by a ribbon of soft laser-cut calf's leather so that it remains centered and steady between the clavicles in order to archive the field of view and capture portraits and self-portraits as reflected in mirrors or people's responses. With the body as dolly, and with vantage and framing determined by the auteur's footwork and body motion, the necklace is interloper, witness, and intruder.

Display Cuff offers an analog overlay of the digital. Glowing through the intricate imperfections of rutile quartz, and enshrined and distorted by the minerals, the LED screen provides continuous and uneven display of the *Surveillance Necklace's* surreptitious, illicit voyeurism. The screen is encased in animal skin that is tanned and precision-sliced, and it is bound to the wrist with soft laser-cut calf's leather. Necklace and cuff are both elevated and diminished through materials that span from the primordial to the present.

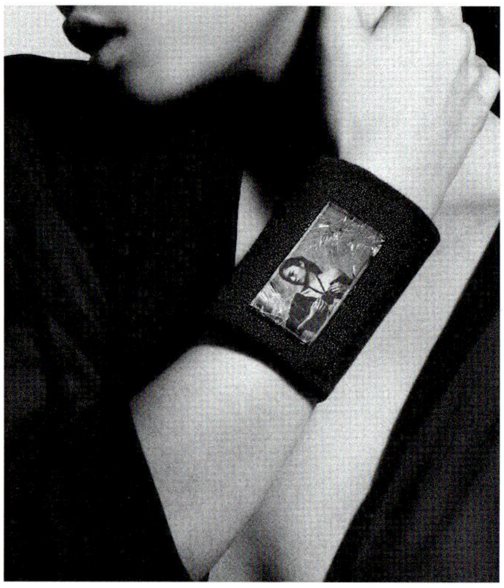

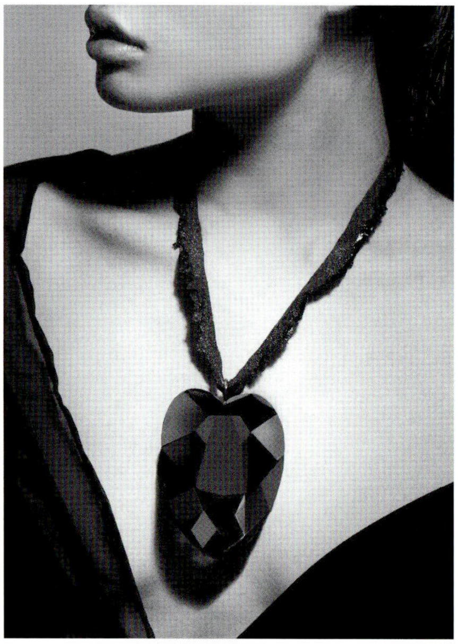

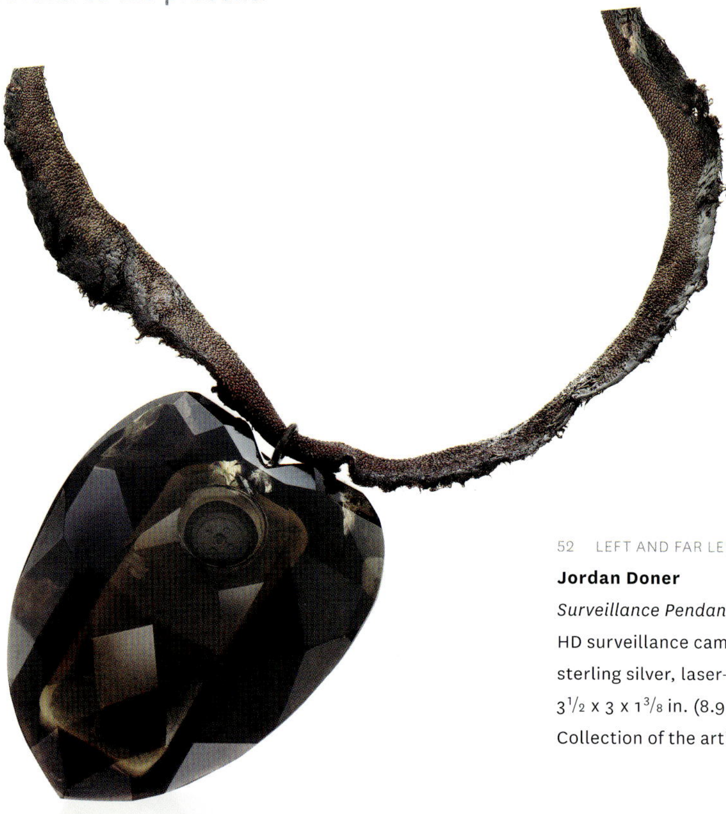

52 LEFT AND FAR LEFT
Jordan Doner
Surveillance Pendant, 2014
HD surveillance camera, smoky quartz, sterling silver, laser-cut calf's leather
$3^1/_2$ x 3 x $1^3/_8$ in. (8.9 x 7.6 x 3.5 cm)
Collection of the artist

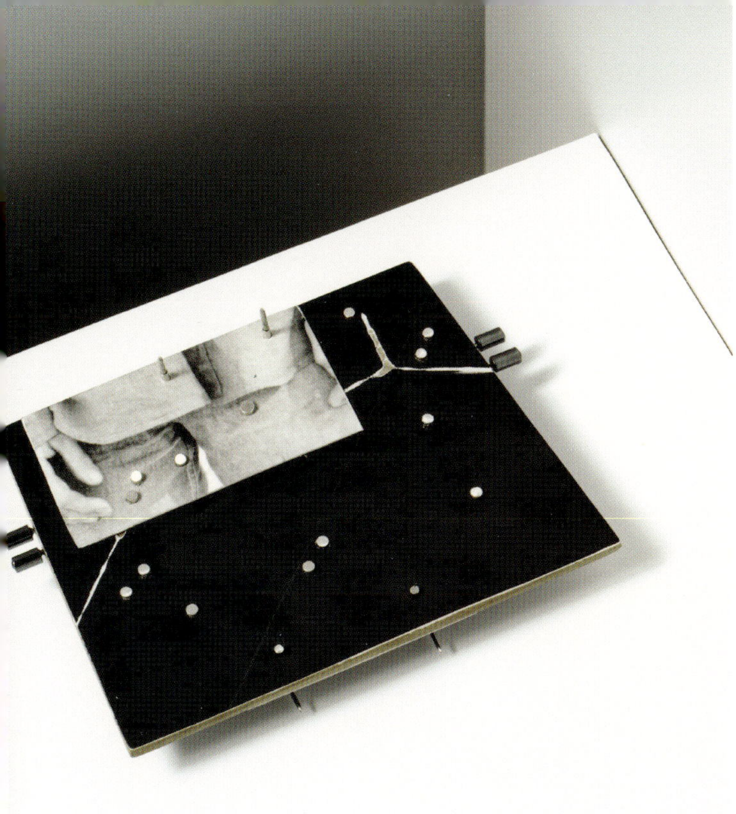

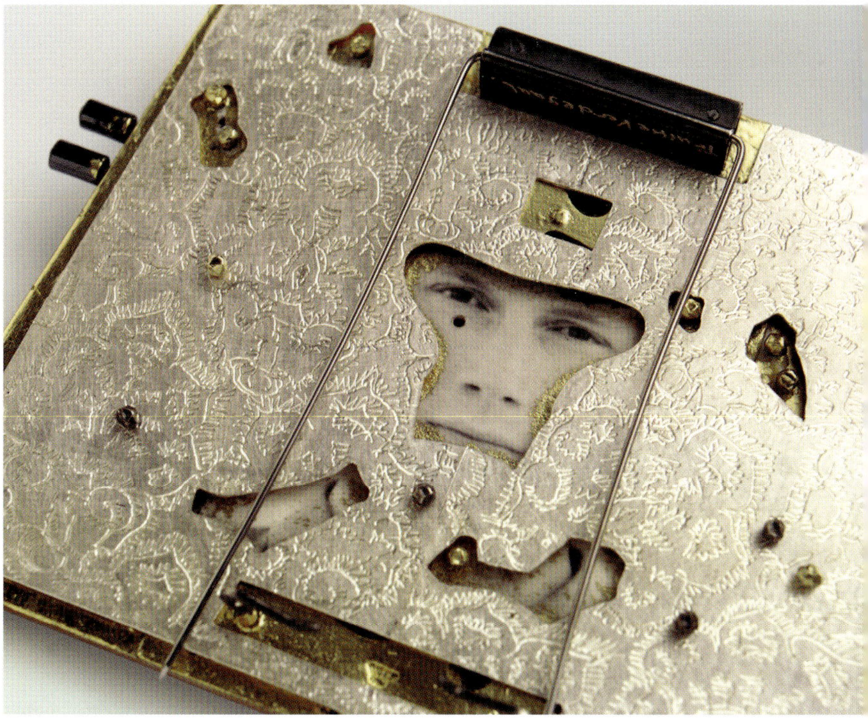

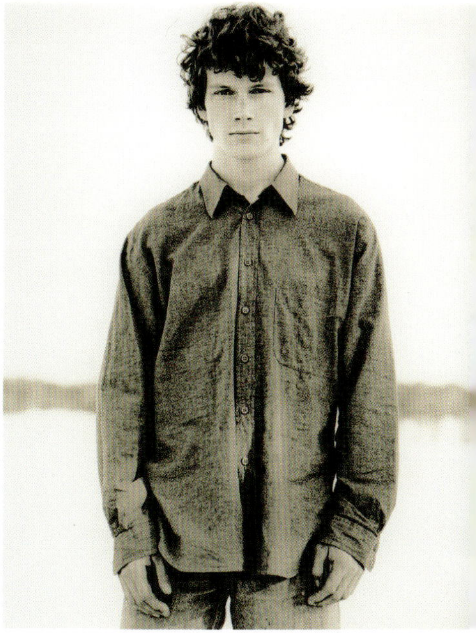

TRUIKE VERDEGAAL

Muhu

Jewelry fascinates *and* communicates. So do faces. I have used portraits by the Dutch photographer Eddo Hartmann to explore the effect of jewelry that looks back at you. Young people look straight into the lens. I have put some of these portraits behind ulexite, a transparent mineral with unusual optical properties, in a way that the portrait is only visible when you are positioned directly in front of the piece. This is the only way to make "eye contact" with this forceful face. In the brooch *Muhu*, a man's portrait is just visible from behind a sheet of engraved silver. On the reverse side he is standing in an empty, dark room, and his vulnerability shows. His loneliness is communicated.

53 TOP LEFT AND RIGHT
Truike Verdegaal
Muhu (brooch), 2003
Analog photograph, gold leaf, silver, oak, hematite, paint
$2^{3}/_{4}$ x $3^{5}/_{8}$ x $^{7}/_{8}$ in. (7 x 9 x 2 cm)
Collection of Susan Kempin

ABOVE
Eddo Hartmann photograph.

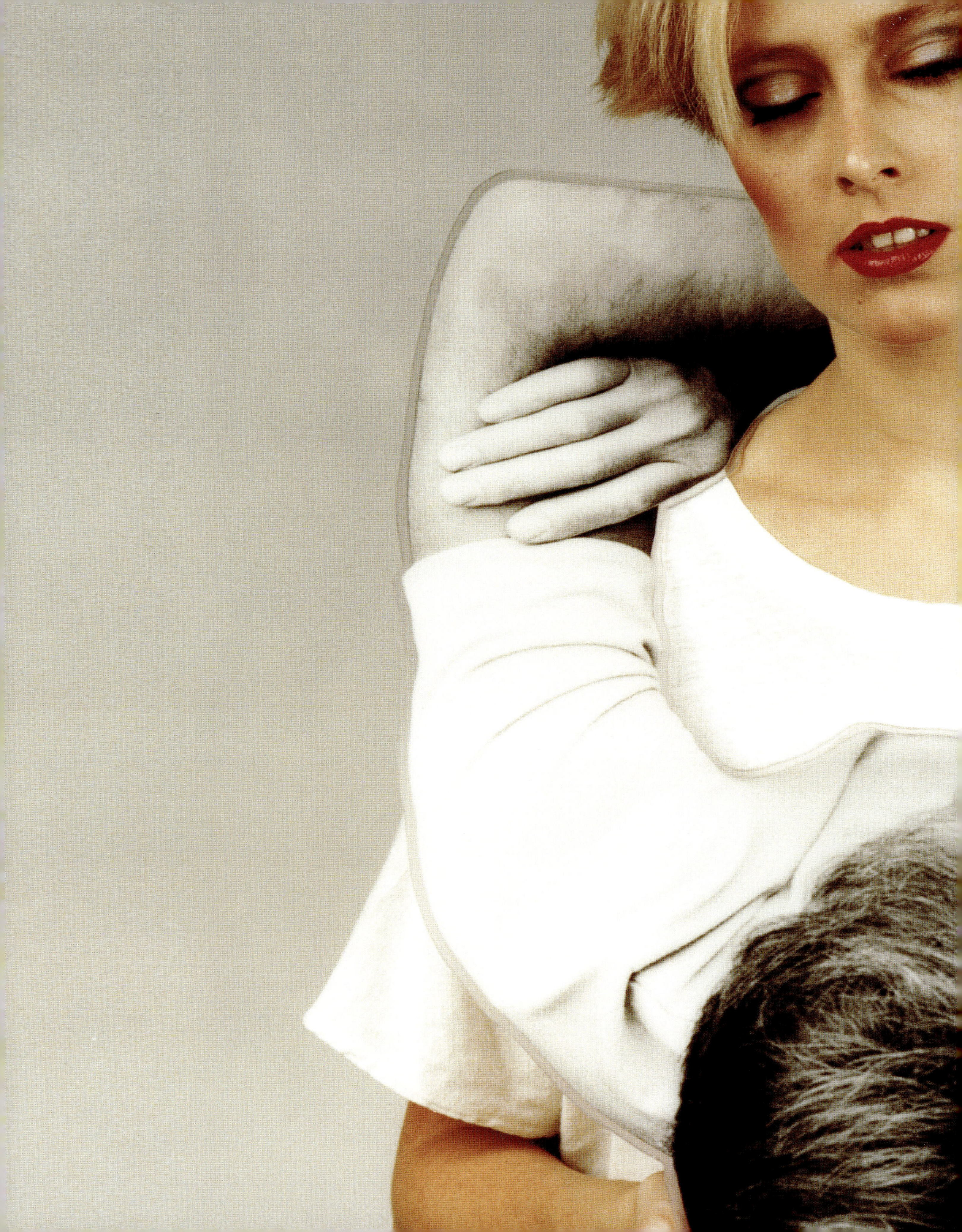

“...BODIES FROM BOTH A PHYSICAL AND PSYCHOLOGICAL PERSPECTIVE...”

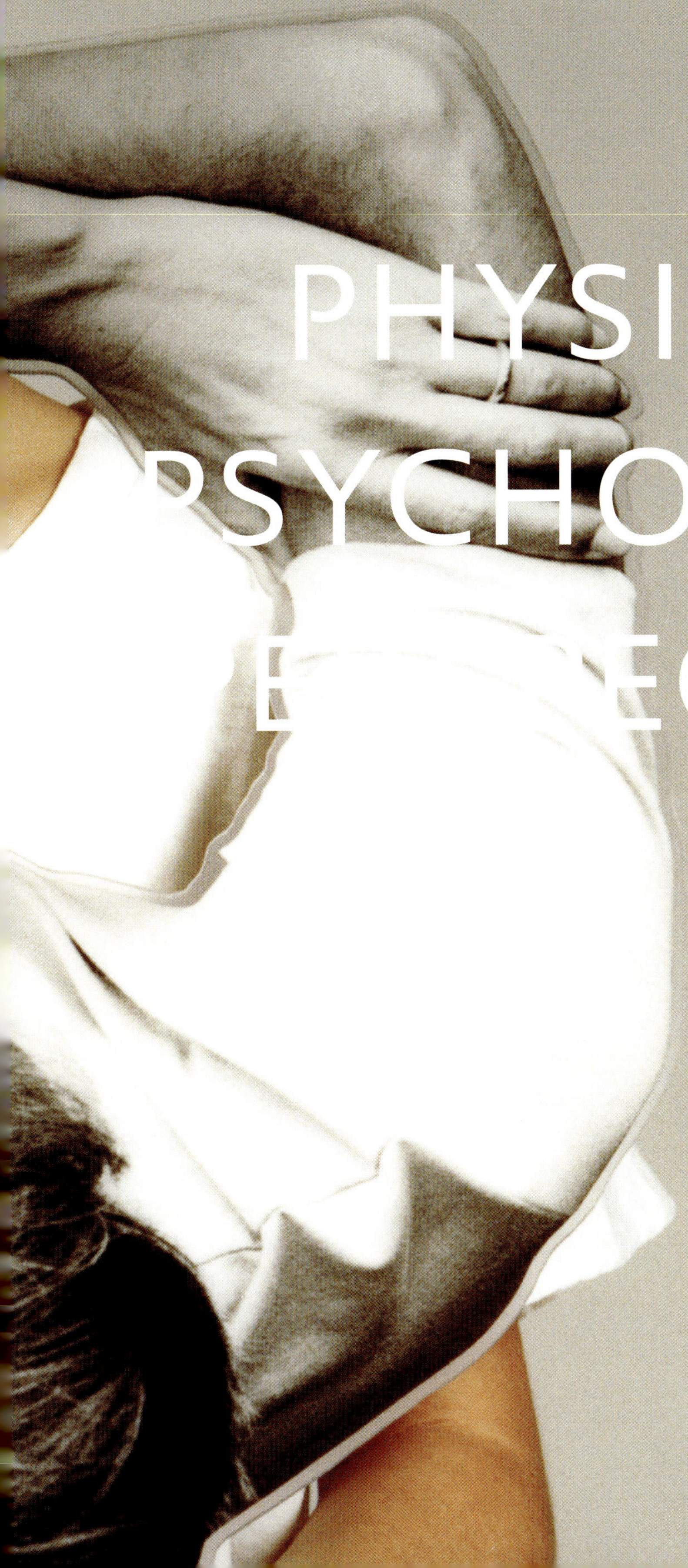

WEARING THE BODY

LOWERY STOKES SIMS

IN THE 1980 SUPERMAN MOVIE SEQUEL (*Superman II*), General Zod and his henchmen, Ursa and Nod, who have threatened the security of the planet Krypton, are sentenced to be banished to the "Phantom Zone."[1] In the film this "zone" appears as a floating, mirrored sheet that descends from an unknown source and literally absorbs their three-dimensional corporal states as flattened entities within the confines of its two-dimensional form.

Indeed, the Zone functions like photography, echoing its predatory character in "capturing" likenesses and "freeze-framing" fleeting motions that might otherwise escape notice. The comparison between photography and the Phantom Zone can be carried even further. In the cinematic device, the images of Zod and his companions are literally contained within a form that holds or frames them, however mobile it may be. The Phantom Zone is not unlike a large pendant floating in space. When it is smashed, the likenesses are freed and return to their corporal state.

From its invention, photography's conflation of the two-dimensional and the three- has complicated our understanding of the relationship between the "*real*-istic" and the "*imagin*-ative" and worked against the medium's self-proclaimed veracity.[2] The stage for this ongoing dialogue between reality and illusion was set during the Victorian era with its penchant for lovelorn expressions and postmortem mementos that sometimes included clothing and hair as well as photographs. When worn as adornment, these mementos can be said to have collapsed the distinction between the "mori" and the "vivant."

Given this historical precedent, today's incorporation of photographic depictions of the body into jewelry can be seen as an update of a long-standing fascination. Through a diversity of concepts, materials, and forms, contemporary jewelry artists speak of our adoration of the body beautiful (as well as the flip side of this adoration—our fear of the ugly and abnormal), our drive to understand the body inside and out, and our preoccupation with its psycho-sexual meaning.

So at one end of the spectrum, we have *Waterman*, Gijs Bakker's appropriation of a photograph of a bodybuilder pouring a bucket of water over his muscular, nude body (NO. 58); at the other end, we have Gabriela Sánchez y Sánchez de la Barquera's (Ab)normal Cameo series featuring photographs that document and publicize people's insecurities about specific parts of their bodies (NOS. 73, 74, 75). As is often the case in contemporary art jewelry, references to luxury are combined with the use of mundane materials. Without a doubt, all this serves to highlight the fetishism that is frequently associated with luxury adornment.

We can also single out examples in photo jewelry of bodies that reflect moods or convey an attraction-repulsion impulse, or simply defy the modes of habitation we have come to expect from instruments of adornment.

In further deconstructing photographic images of the body in contemporary jewelry, several categories emerge: full-blown representations of the body (frequently in narrative scenarios); isolated body parts that speak to a fascination with a dysmorphic or reliquary approach; and X-rays and sonograms that penetrate and probe the inner body.

The Netherlands has taken a strong lead in the contemporary jewelry world, giving rise to artists whose ideas are influencing contemporary jewelry round the globe.[3] Gijs Bakker, one of the country's stellar citizens, created a stir back in 1976 with his *Bib/Slab* necklaces featuring photographic images of actual nude male and female torsos (NOS. 61A, 61B). When worn, the torso depicted on each bib actually covers the "real" torso beneath it. Framing plays a crucial role in these works, informing the witty visual puns in the necklaces' photographic images. As artist/activist Theaster Gates noted in a 2011 interview with critic Lilly Wei, "[P]eople miss things when they're unframed, when no context is given."[4] Bakker's *Bib/Slab* also brings to mind painter Kerry James Marshall's 2002 painting *Heirlooms and Accessories* (fig. 1). Here the artist extracts the heads of three white women spectators from a 1930 photograph by Lawrence Beitler of a lynching of two African American men (Thomas Shipp and Abram Smith) and sets them within elaborate pendants with chains.[5] This framing device effectively forces us not to "miss things," and the fact that the three women who are among the spectators to this horrific event glance back at the photographer implicates us, the viewers, in this historical event. The social, political, and personal ramifications of photography into which we the viewers have always been included are potently present in this instance.

Bakker's visual framing of the female (although it could just as well be male) body in the arms of a man in his *Embrace* necklace is an almost overpowering depiction of carnal passion (NO. 62). That one can wear the object of one's affection in such an obsessive way is also exemplified by Michael Petry's neckpiece *Laying Low* (NO. 63). Here the photograph of the figure is positioned over the heart in a winding and curling length of paper embellished with acrylic medium and gold and silver leaf. Whereas Bakker's creation takes forthright possession of the wearer, Petry's is more sinuous and perhaps a little insidious—in a delicious way.

This prurient quality is also glimpsed in Célio Braga's *Golden Boys Collection/Silver Boys Collection*, in which he has assembled fragments of photographs of male actors from feature films as well as from male porn films, embellished them with gold and silver glitter, and mounted them on double-sided tape (NO. 67). That the source photograph is transformed into what could be called geometric patterns achieves an encoding that speaks to his personal obsession.

And in this context, what are we to make of Bakker's unusual "cut-off" profile of a black man provocatively sticking out his diamond-tipped tongue (NO. 60)? Peter Dormer describes this cheeky expression as having "some style and irony,"

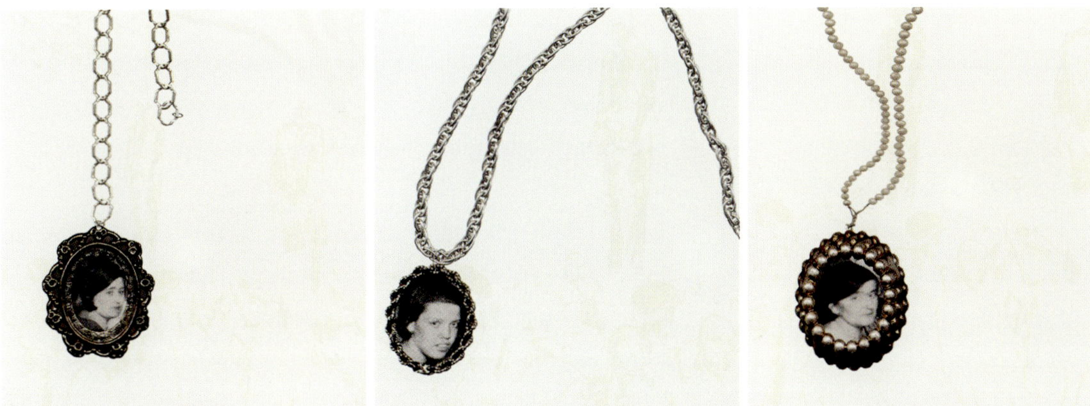

FIG. 1
Kerry James Marshall
Heirlooms and Accessories, 2002
Inkjet prints on paper, wood, rhinestones
57 x 54 1/4 x 3 in.
(144.8 x 137.8 x 7.6 cm), each
Studio Museum in Harlem; museum purchase made possible with funds provided by anonymous donor

noting that while in cultures such as the Maori "the protruding tongue is a gesture of power . . . in Western culture, the tongue is used to poke fun at something—and Bakker is well known for trying to prick what he regards as the pretensions of 'precious' jewelry."[6] Mecky van den Brink evokes an obsession of the maternal kind in her *Wedding Necklace*, made from a magazine advertisement for baby cream that caught her eye after the birth of her daughter (NO. 71).

Thomas Mann turned to a sepia-colored photograph by contemporary photographer Stephen John Phillips for his brooch *Stretch* (NO. 65). Contrasting the sensuality of the photographic image— a female body seen from the back, with outstretched arms that at first glance recall depictions of the crucifixion—Mann adds hand-fabricated metal parts that have an almost machine-like precision, resulting in a theatrical setting the artist refers to as "Techno-Romantic."[7]

While these artists all worked with images from contemporary media, in *Broken Tie*, Kiff Slemmons made use of a late nineteenth- or early twentieth-century photograph of a young girl, dividing the child's body in half, down the middle, with the two sides askew and appearing to be in a different scale. The left and right sides are joined by a bold squiggle of silver that incorporates her head, tightly framing it in the manner of a cameo or locket (NO. 56).

Slemmons further evokes photographic history—specifically Eadweard Muybridge's serial studies of motion from the late 1800s—in her *Manual Locomotion* necklace (NO. 55). Mimicking Muybridge's sequencing of motion, the artist presents gloved hands in different gestures, each an inkjet print of her own hand. In *Hindsight*, Slemmons focuses on eyes (NO. 54), framing them with a lorgnette made from a clock-hand and thereby bringing unity to the cut, collaged, and juxtaposed images that form the face of this brooch.

Suska Mackert presents individual disembodied eyes in her series of *Augen* brooches, an ongoing project since 2005 (NO. 57). One thinks of the early work of video/installation artist Tony Oursler, who in the 1990s often projected disembodied eyes and mouths onto stuffed figures, orbs, and other objects, providing a tragicomic commentary on contemporary existence. Mackert's eye pieces were inspired by eighteenth- and nineteenth-century brooches and rings that display the painted eye of someone the wearer lost or of a secret love. Her versions are created out of newspaper and cardboard and feature the eyes of contemporary individuals who are famous in the media.

In 1967 the famed collagist, painter, and installation artist Robert Rauschenberg literally visualized a type of existential torment in his color lithograph and screen print entitled *Booster* by combining a life-sized X-ray of himself with an astrological chart and magazine images of athletes. Rauschenberg's use of the X-ray sets the context for the work of Julia Barello and Viktoria Münzker. In *Brooch with Window I*, Barello makes use of the X-ray's ability to reveal hidden aspects of the human body (NO. 72). By eliminating exterior details that can allow us to discriminate according to such attributes as skin color, nationality, and gender, she reminds us that we are the same under the skin. Before medical privacy laws were passed in 1996, she would include the patient's name on the X-rays she used in her work because for her medical film became a stand-in for the individual.[8] Münzker's brooches from her Secret series are more personal and autobiographical in nature, featuring sonograms of the fetus of her son Sebastian at sixteen, twenty-four, and twenty-seven weeks (NO. 70). The sonograms are a scientific revealing of what previously was totally hidden or "secret."

While Münzker ponders her own body and emotional state in her work, Claire Lavendhomme turns to engravings by her contemporary, the artist Kiki Smith, to reflect on women's bodies from both a physical and a psychological perspective (NOS. 68, 69).

The uterus appears prominently in Smith's linoleum block relief print entitled *How I Know I'm Here*, which consists of four sheets, each 11 1/2 by 43 inches, that she worked on between 1985 and 2000 (p. 120). In this work various human organs and body parts float in dense environments where the shapes suggest muscles, veins, and nerves, occasionally punctuated by a face or "a pair of hands performing various activities."[9] Lavendhomme's interest in the permeability of states of being in the cycle of life parallels that of Smith, and in an age where the beginning of life is still fiercely debated, these works provide cogent and pertinent statements.

In her video *Constellation*, Lauren Kalman displays an obsession with corporal maladies (fig. 2), dramatizing sores and other syphilis-produced skin lesions using random patterns of tiny, colorful LED lights. Kalman cultivates a high degree of discomfort in the viewer by having these twinkling lights pierce the skin. Her aim is to force viewers to confront their own apprehensions and even shame about the disfigurement caused by disease through her depiction of a grotesquely "bejeweled" body.

Mary Hallam Pearse and Eva Tesarik use photographs to present narrative sequences that play on our fascination and infatuation with pearls. Pearse's *Feeding Desire* shows a woman lying with her right arm extended in an exaggerated gesture of enjoyment and desire as pearls literally fall from her hand to her open mouth (NO. 59). The original image was taken from an advertisement in a magazine and reflects the common practice of using sexualized images to promote and sell a wide range of objects, jewelry not excluded. A rich panoply of sexual references can also be seen in Tesarik's

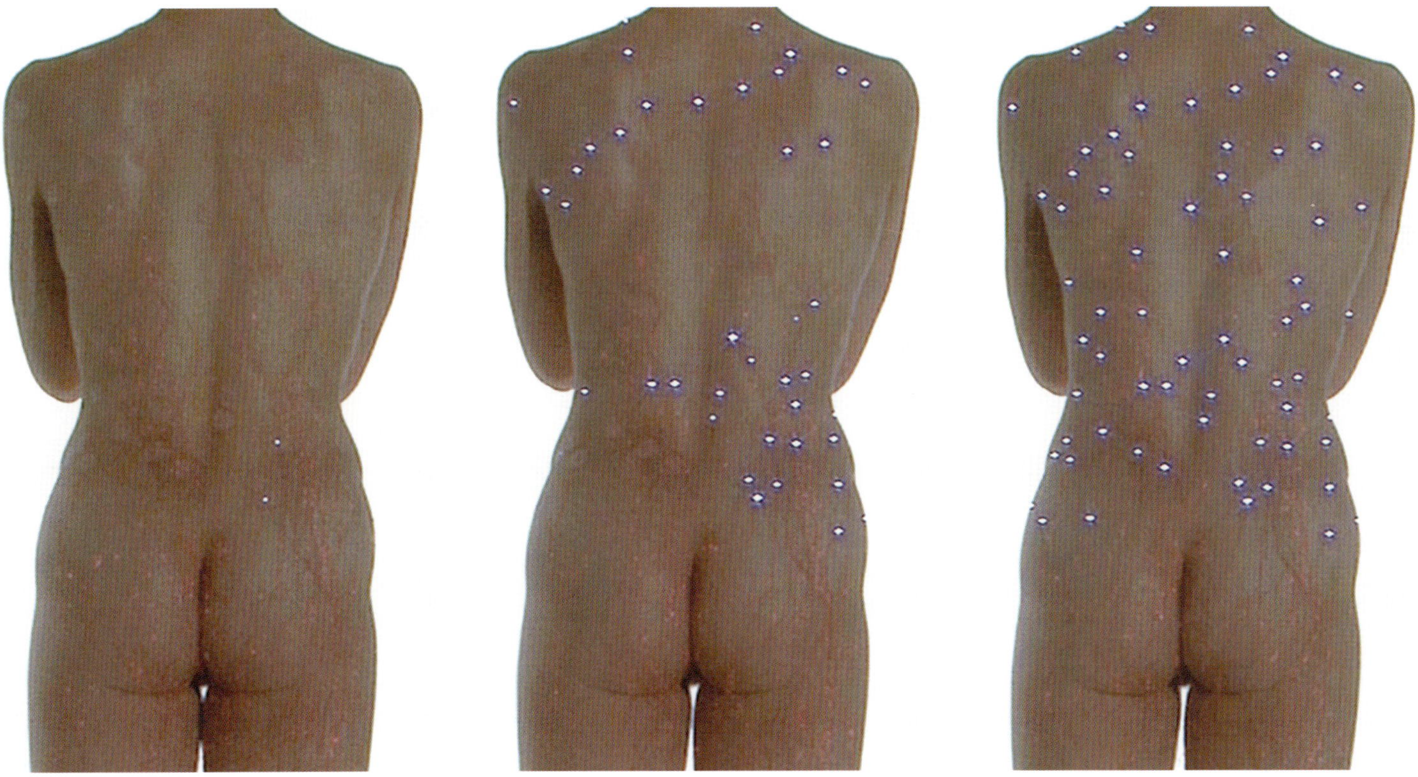

FIG. 2

Lauren Kalman

Constellation (video), 2010

12 minutes, 13 seconds

Courtesy of the artist and Sienna Patti

Time of Pearls (NO. 64). An erudite evocation of the historical *Wunderkammer*, her necklace incorporates rock crystals and pearls with photographs of a reclining nude, various nautilus and conch shells, and what seems to be a photograph of a geological formation whose original image is distorted when seen through the matrix of the crystal.

A final example of wearing the body, Thomas Gentille's brooch *Woman with Stockings*, is a tongue-in-cheek representation of the artist as voyeur (NO. 66). In this case, the photograph of a shapely pair of women's legs in black net hose and high heels was taken by the jeweler himself as the eye-catching woman walked up the stairs, ahead of him. The power of this work derives from the furtive, partial view of the female body, particularly in retreat from the pursuing viewer. Emblematic of the voyeuristic age we live in and the vanishing notion of personal privacy, the photograph staged as jewelry allows us to see the human body not through the eyes of a mere voyeur but through the discerning lens of the artist.

Lowery Stokes Sims *is William and Mildred Lasdon Chief Curator at the Museum of Arts and Design.*

1

The Phantom Zone is a fictional prison dimension featured in the Superman comic books and related media published by DC Comics. It first appeared in *Adventure Comics* #283 (April 1961) and was created by Robert Bernstein and George Papp. See http://en.wikipedia.org/wiki/Phantom_Zone. Accessed January 5, 2012.

2

One cannot help but refer to tales from anthropology that "natives," when shown moving images of themselves projected on a screen, looked behind the screen to see where the figures went off sight of the camera lens.

3

See, for example, Yvonne G. J. M. Joris, ed., *Jewels of Mind and Mentality: Dutch Jewelry Design, 1950–2000* (Rotterdam: Museum het Kruithuis, 2000).

4

Lilly Wei, "Theaster Gates," *Art in America* 11 (December 2011): 120–27; http://www.artinamericamagazine.com/features/theaster-gates. Accessed January 13, 2012.

5

Marshall discusses this work at http://www.artbabble.org/video/smart/kerry-james-marshall-heirlooms-and-accessories.
Accessed August 12, 2013.

6

Peter Dormer, "The Body and Jewellery," in Susan Cohn, ed., *Unexpected Pleasures: The Art and Design of Contemporary Jewellery* (London: The Design Museum and Skira Rizzoli, 2012), 108–13.

7

Patricia Harris and David Lyon, "Thomas Mann: The Business of Reinvention," *Metalsmith* 23, no. 2 (Spring 2003): 19–24.

8

Gussie Fauntleroy, "E Pluribus I-ray," *American Craft* 72 (June/July 2012): 30–31; http://www.craftcountil.org/magazine/article/e-pluribus-x-ray. Accessed August 12, 2013.

9

See http://www.fawbush.com/artists/kiki_smith/artwork.

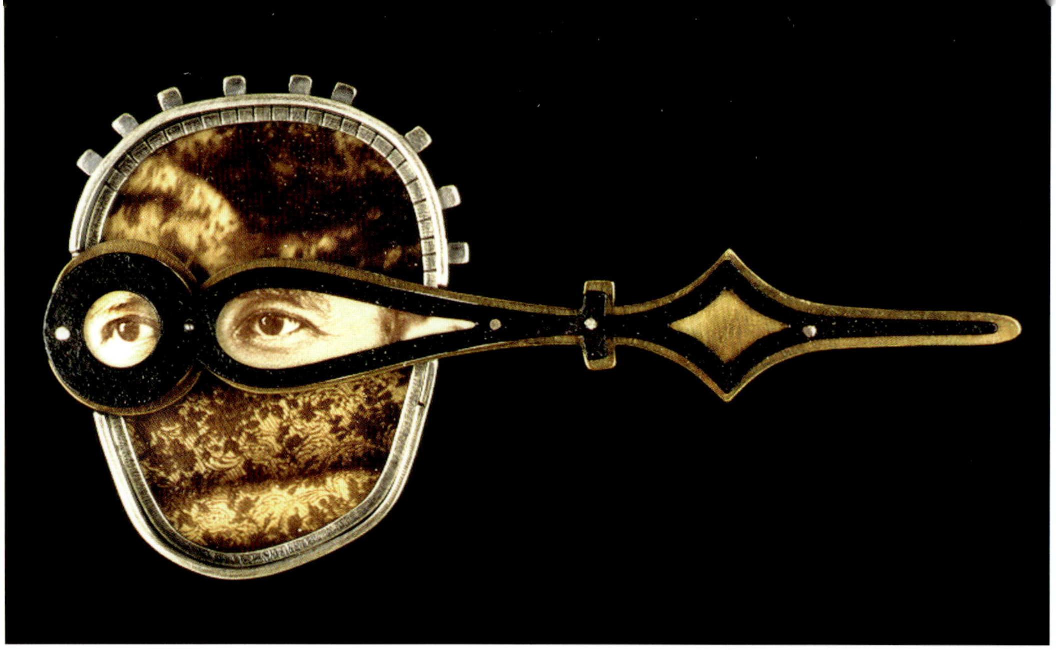

54 LEFT
Kiff Slemmons
Hindsight (pin), 1997
Found photographs, silver, clock hand, mica
2 x 4 x 1/4 in. (5.1 x 10.2 x 0.5 cm)
Collection of Helen Kornblum

The reference in this necklace is to Eadweard Muybridge's late nineteenth-century photographic exploration called *Animal Locomotion.* In my *Manual Locomotion,* each gesturing gloved hand (digital inkjet prints of my hand) is a separate wheeled pull toy that actually rolls. Hooked together and upside down, they become a necklace.

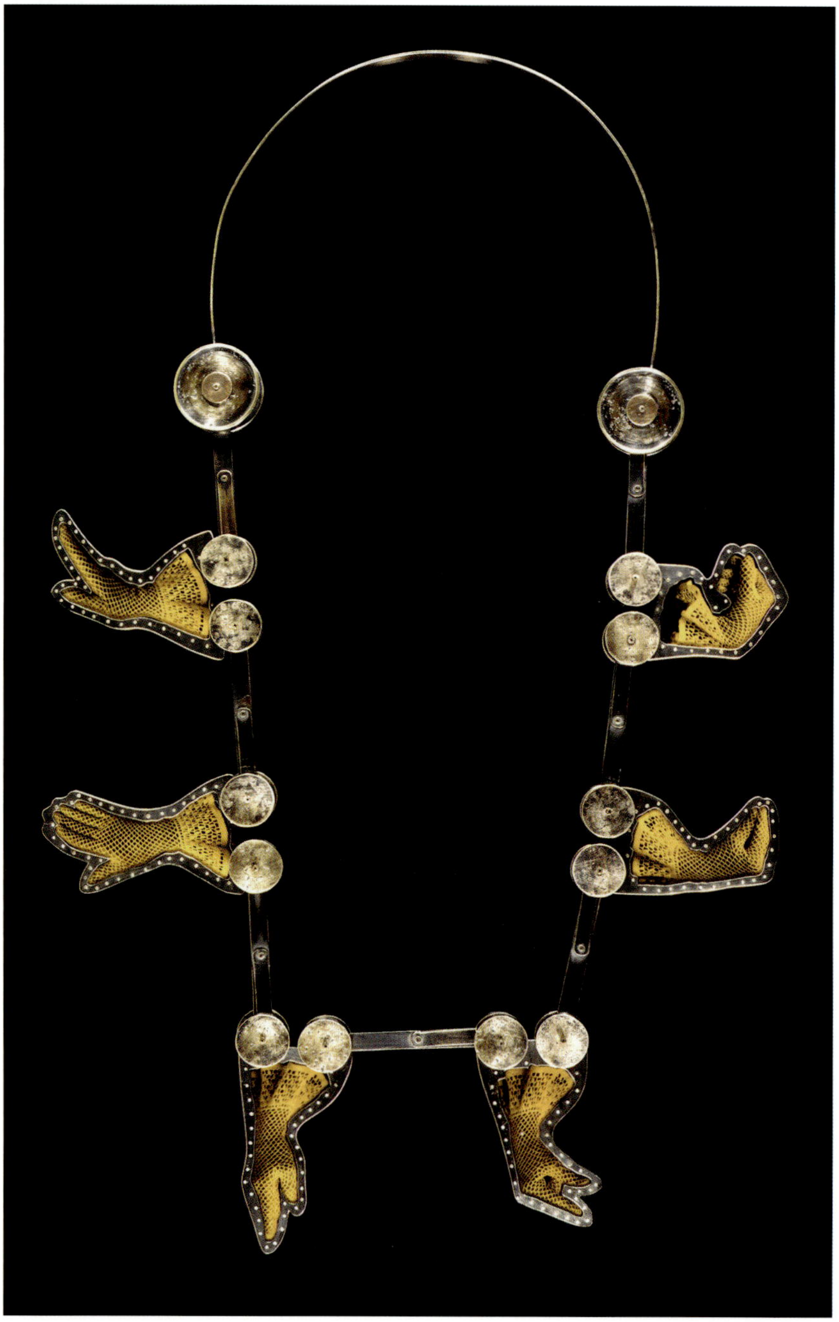

55 RIGHT
Kiff Slemmons
Manual Locomotion (necklace), 1999
Digital inkjet prints, silver, mica
13 x 7 7/8 x 3/8 in. (33 x 20 x 1 cm)
Collection of Susan C. Beech

KIFF SLEMMONS

Hindsight | *Manual Locomotion* | *Broken Tie*

The photo portraits for *Broken Tie* and *Hindsight* were extracted from late nineteenth- and early twentieth-century paper photographs that lost their previous value and potency when they became disconnected from their identities. Reconnecting them to the present with another kind of preciousness is possible through jewelry. Juxtaposing off-kilter cuts from the same image can have an unsettling effect, adding a link to the surreal and a take on dislocation, two prevailing themes in my work.

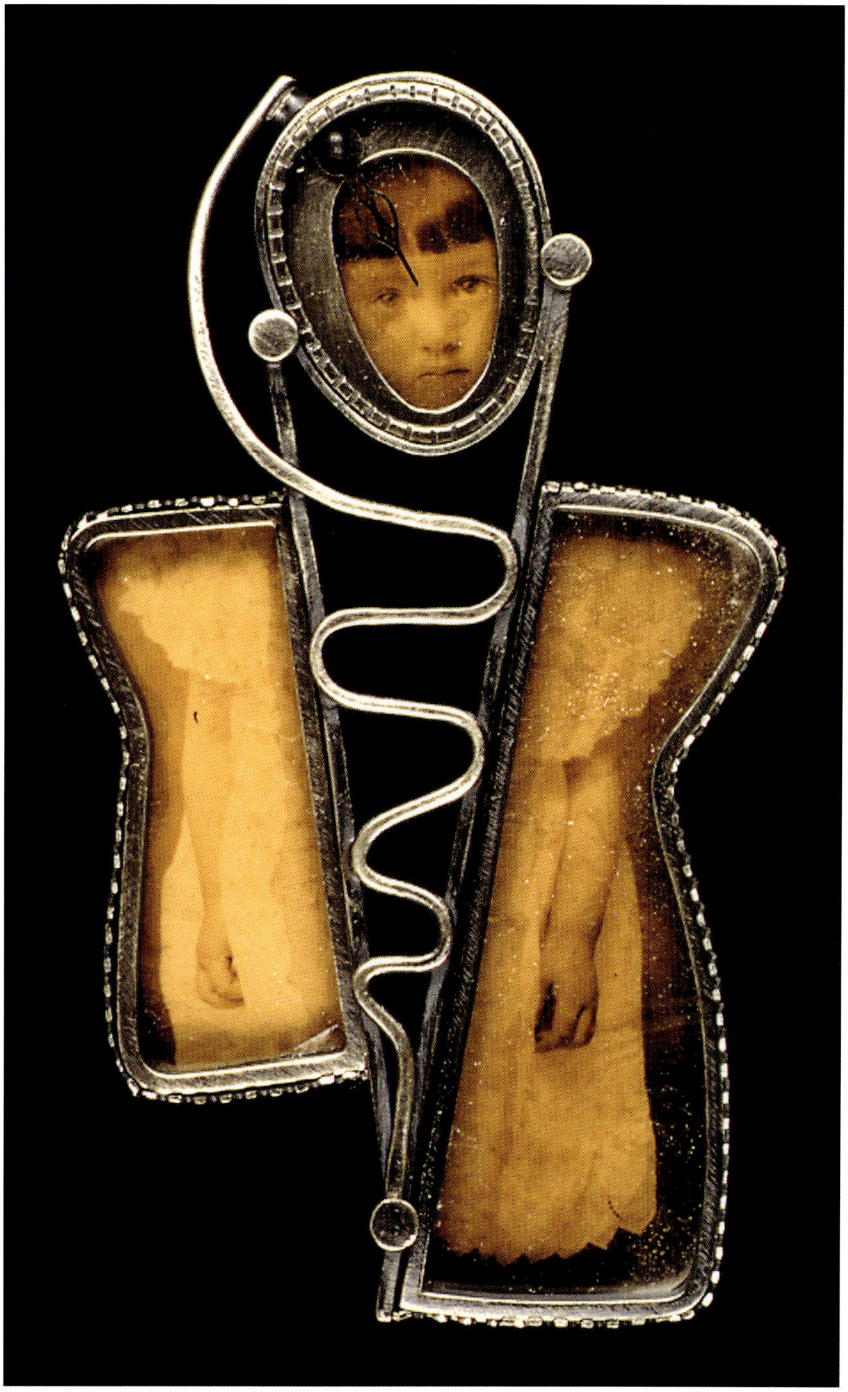

56
Kiff Slemmons
Broken Tie (pin), 1997
Found photograph, silver, mica
$2\frac{3}{4}$ x $1\frac{1}{2}$ x $\frac{1}{4}$ in. (7 x 3.8 x 0.5 cm)
Collection of Sandra Donnell

SUSKA MACKERT

Augen

In the 1800s it was fashionable to wear eye jewelry—brooches or pins decorated with the painted or enameled eye of someone the wearer loved and someone who was truly close—a spouse, a fiancé, a secret lover, or even a friend or family member who had died. With my brooches, people wear the visages of someone known to them only through the media—people they have never met personally and whose lives are very different from their own. My *Augen* project includes newspaper images of the eyes of several hundred such personalities, some whom we admire and love, and others, like Saddam Hussein or Fidel Castro, whom we know to have played a dubious role in the world. What does it mean to wear the eye of such a person? Through the *Augen* project I question the role and meaning of jewelry in our daily lives.

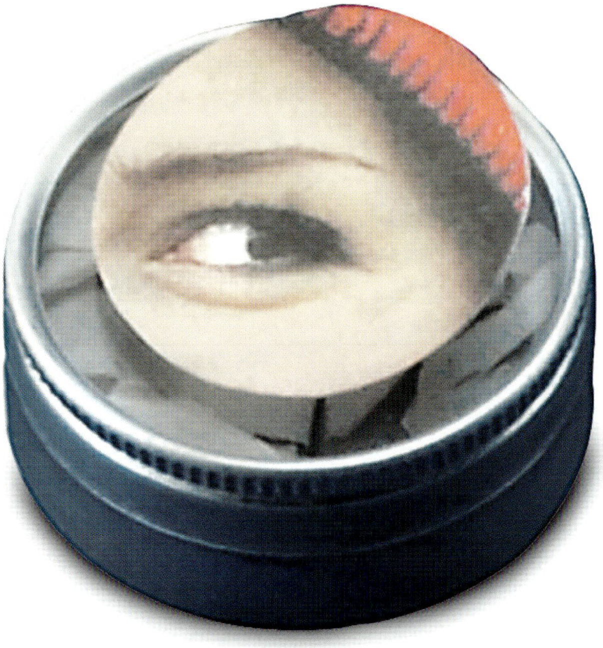

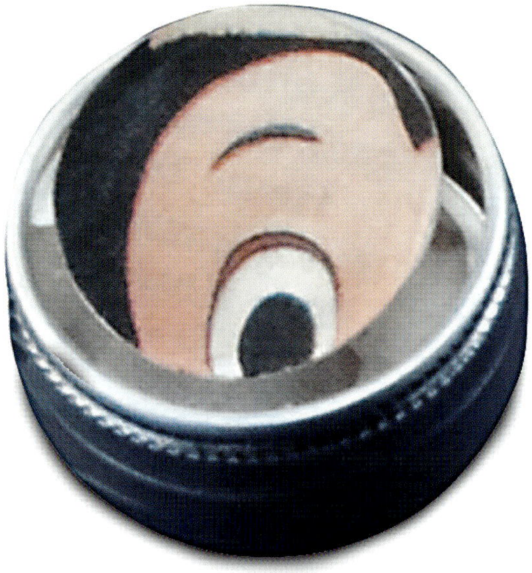

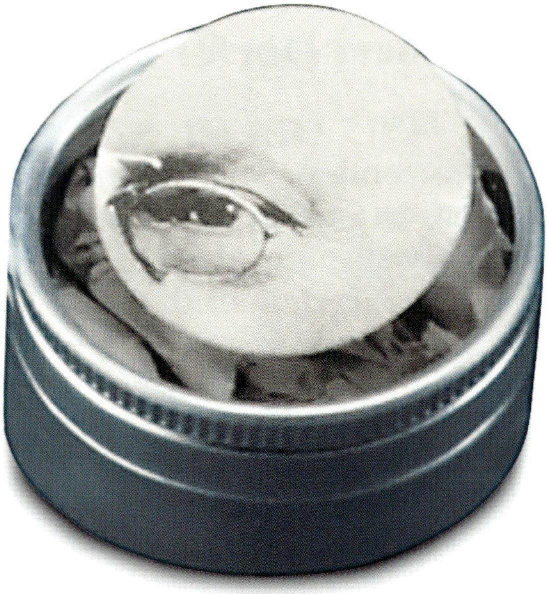

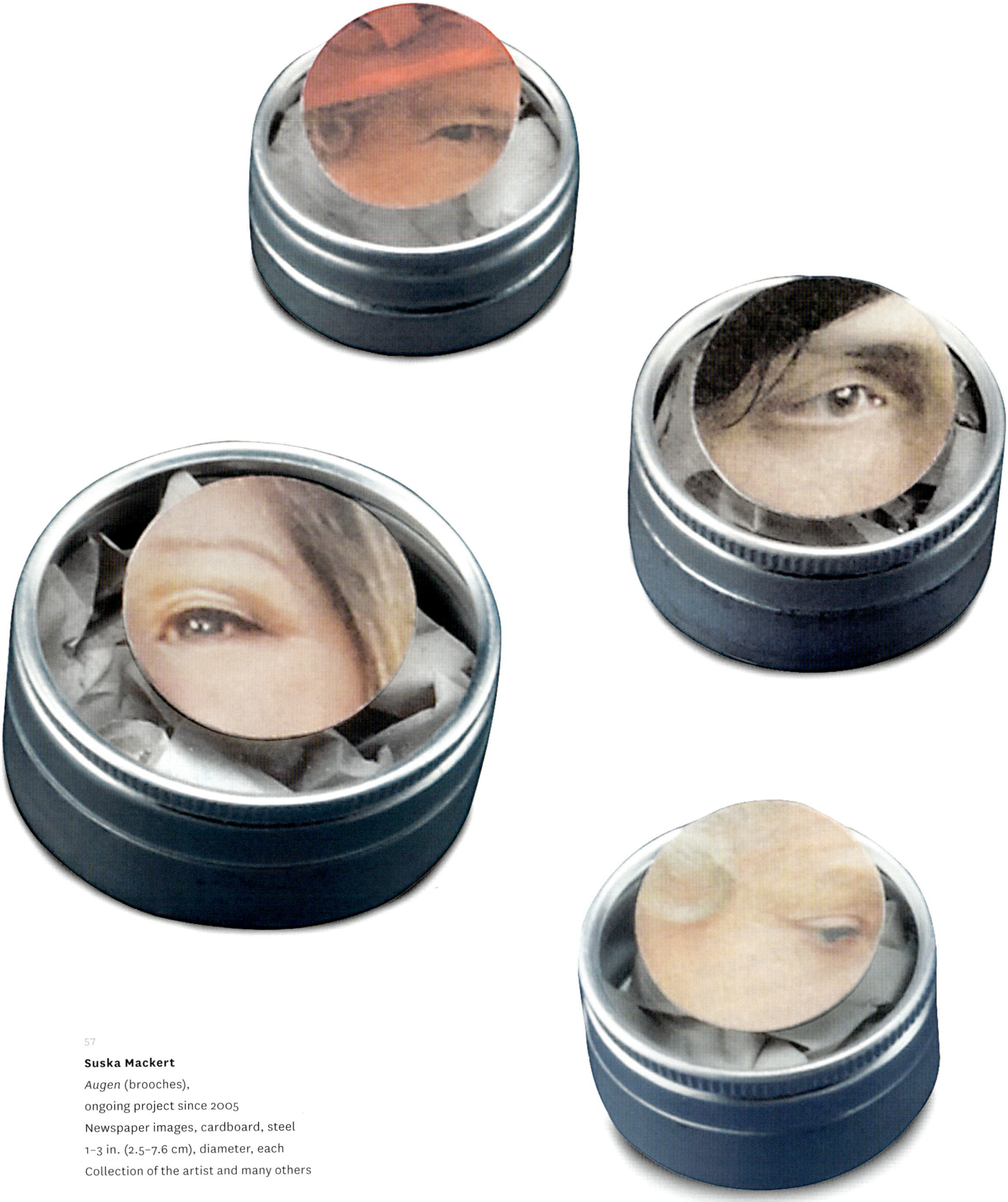

57

Suska Mackert
Augen (brooches),
ongoing project since 2005
Newspaper images, cardboard, steel
1–3 in. (2.5–7.6 cm), diameter, each
Collection of the artist and many others

GIJS BAKKER

Waterman

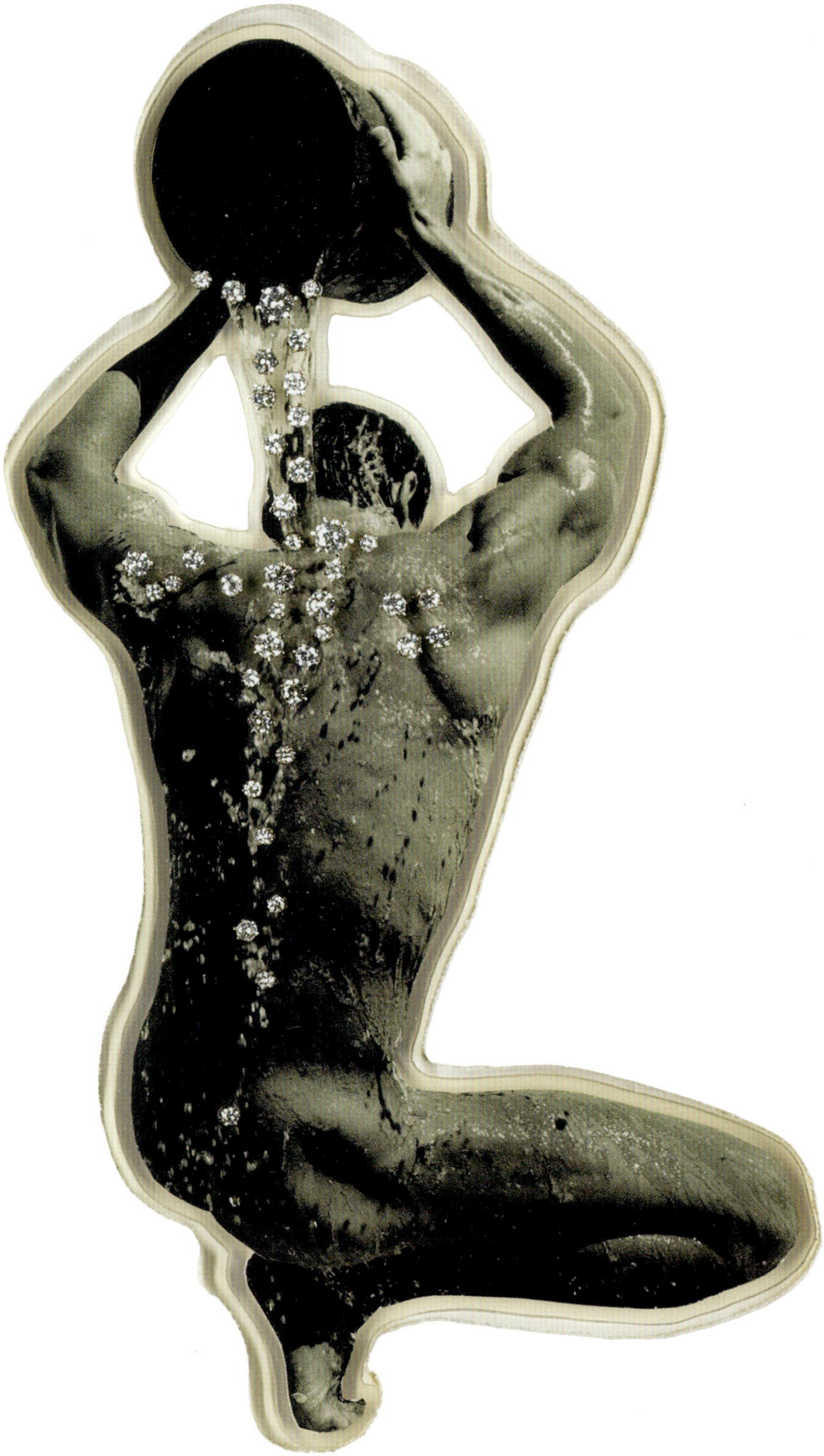

During a workshop in San Diego many years ago, I visited a souvenir shop and was struck by a postcard I found showing a naked man throwing a bucket of water over his back. I had been working on a different series (Sportfiguren) and had discovered that a powerful statement could be made about vulgarity and luxury by combining newspaper clippings laminated in PVC with precious stones and gold settings. Many years after I used the postcard to make the *Waterman* brooch, I discovered that renowned photographer Bruce Weber had taken the picture.

58

Gijs Bakker
Waterman (brooch), 1991
Copy of a postcard, diamonds, white gold 585, PVC
$5^{7}/_{8}$ x $3^{5}/_{8}$ x $^{3}/_{8}$ in. (15 x 9 x 1 cm)
Collection of Angela Schaefer

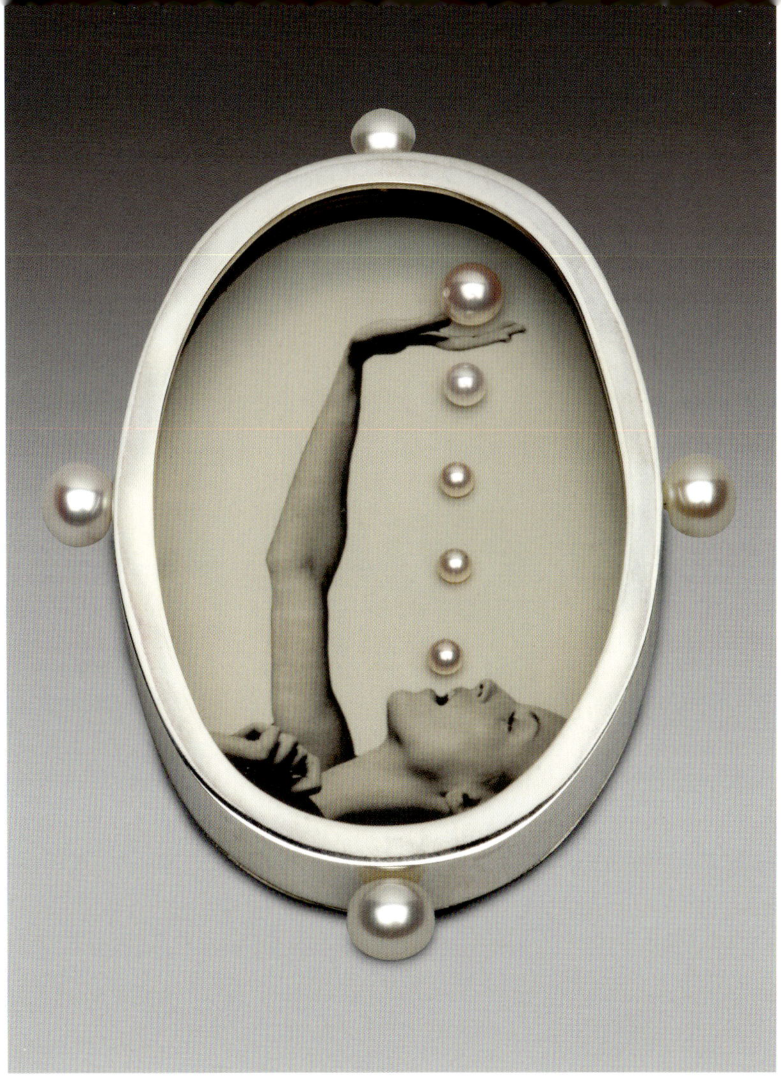

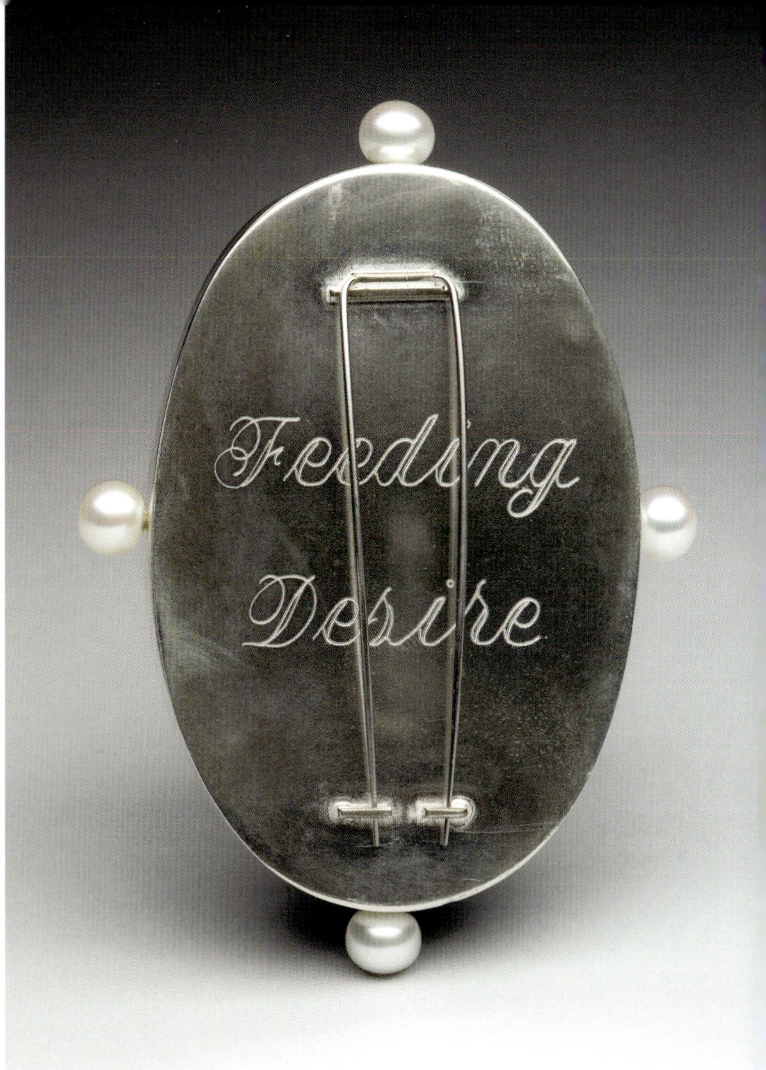

59 ABOVE LEFT AND RIGHT

Mary Hallam Pearse

Feeding Desire (brooch), 2008

Digital photograph, aluminum, silver, pearls, glass

$3^{1}/_{2}$ x $2^{1}/_{2}$ x $^{1}/_{2}$ in.

(8.9 x 6.4 x 1.3 cm)

Collection of Sally von Bargen

MARY HALLAM PEARSE

Feeding Desire

Feeding Desire is based on conventions of nineteenth-century portrait jewelry and classic children's dexterity games. The work's playful and ironic image is only completed when the viewer plays the "game of desire" and manipulates jewels in the brooch into indentations in the image of the woman's body. I am interested in incorporating past traditions such as engraving and images such as this magazine ad into my jewelry as a way of commenting on material culture today. I altered the image for this brooch in Photoshop and then digitally printed it on a thin sheet of aluminum and made a sterling silver frame to complement the image.

GIJS BAKKER

The Tongue Brooch | *Bib/Slab* | *Bib/Slab* | *Embrace*

In many cultures (such as that of the Maori), the protruding tongue is a gesture of power, and in this brooch the balancing of a cut diamond on the tongue gives that gesture some style and irony. . . . In Western culture, the tongue is used to poke fun at something, and Bakker is well known for trying to prick what he regards as the pretensions of "precious" jewelry.

— Peter Dormer

"The Body and Jewellery," in Susan Cohn, ed., *Unexpected Pleasures: The Art and Design of Contemporary Jewellery* (London: The Design Museum and Skira Rizzoli, 2012), 108–13.

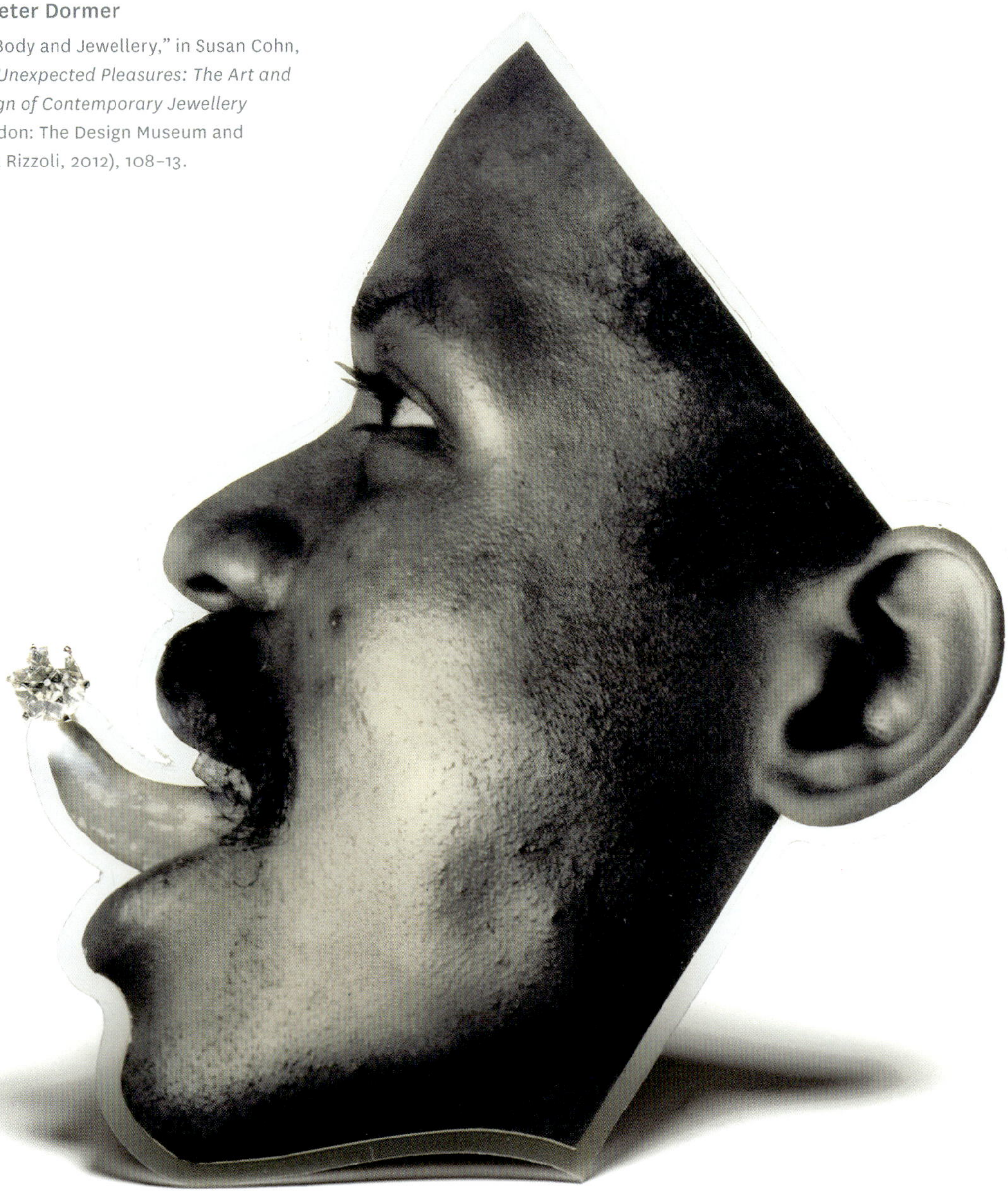

60
Gijs Bakker, executed by **Pauline Barendse** and **Tobias van Roojen**
The Tongue Brooch, 1989
Analog photograph printed on paper, diamond, rhodium-plated white gold 585, silver 925, PVC
$4\frac{1}{2}$ x $3\frac{1}{2}$ x $\frac{3}{8}$ in.
(11.5 x 8.8 x 1 cm)
Helen Williams Drutt, Philadelphia

62 OPPOSITE, LOWER RIGHT
Gijs Bakker
Embrace (necklace as worn), 1982
Analog photograph printed on paper, PVC
23 x $18\frac{3}{4}$ x $\frac{1}{8}$ in. (58.5 x 47.5 x 0.2 cm)
Loan Cultural Heritage Agency of the Netherlands, on loan to CODA Museum Apeldoorn

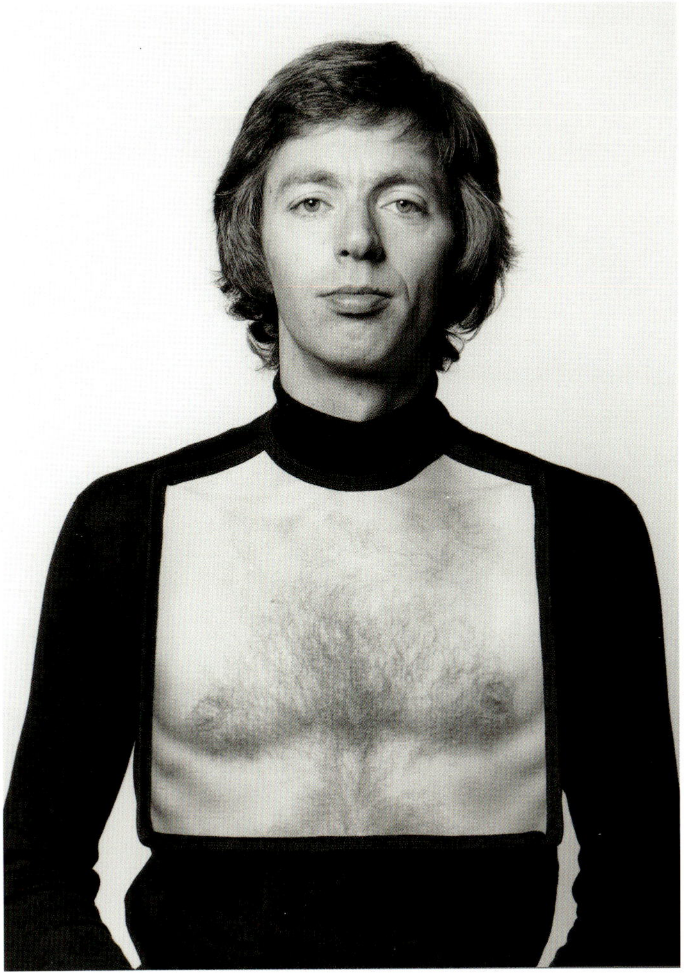

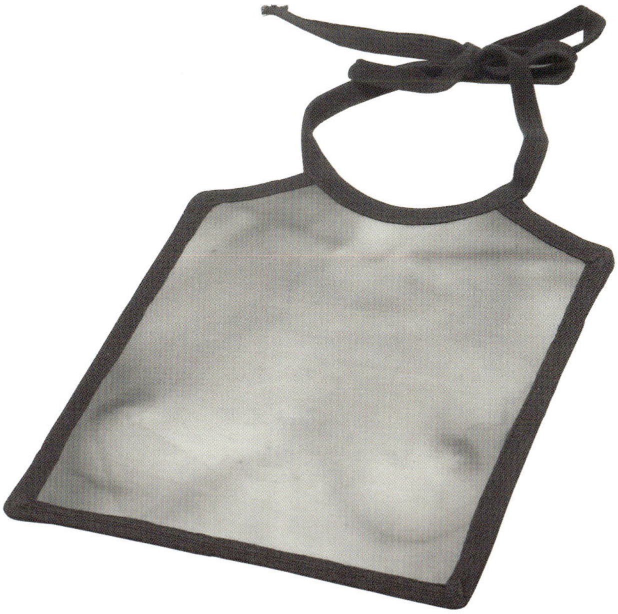

The question I asked myself before I made *Bib/Slab* was, "Why must a piece of jewelry be made from metal? Why not feature skin?" I decided to take photographs of men's and women's chests, print the images on fabric, and produce bibs.

61A ABOVE (AS WORN BY ARTIST)
Gijs Bakker
Bib/Slab, 1976
Analog photograph
printed on fabric, cotton
13 x 12 3/4 x 1/8 in.
(33 x 32 x 0.3 cm)
Stedelijk Museum, 's-Hertogenbosch

61B TOP RIGHT
Gijs Bakker
Bib/Slab, 1976
Analog photograph printed
on fabric, cotton
13 1/4 x 11 1/4 x 1/8 in.
(33.5 x. 28.5 x 0.3 cm)
Collection of the artist

My goal with *Embrace* was to create a more personal form of wedding jewelry than the traditional wedding ring—something that would include the partner showing his or her love. The photo for this necklace was shot from above in black and white, laminated in PVC, and cut out so it could hang around the beloved's neck.

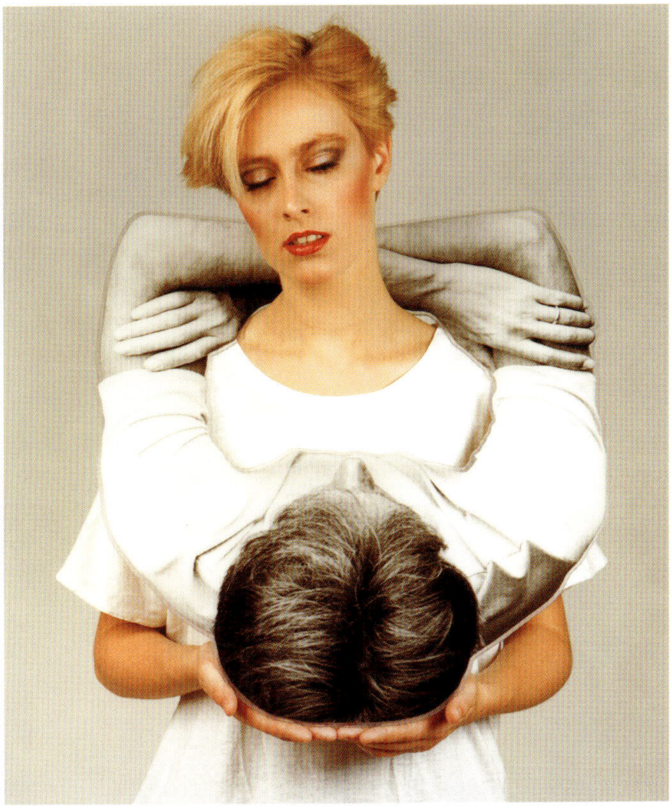

MICHAEL PETRY

Laying Low

The main component of this neckpiece is a photograph I took of a nude man in a bed. As in other pieces from my Almost There series, the image has been built up on the back with many layers of gold and silver leaf and then torn into a spiral shape. An erotic undertone pervades the piece: the actual object is flexible, feels like skin, is warm to the flesh, and tangles about the wearer in much the same way the sheets tangle around the nude man. The piece can also be flattened out into a traditional photographic shape (a rectangle), black and white on one side, silver and gold on the other.

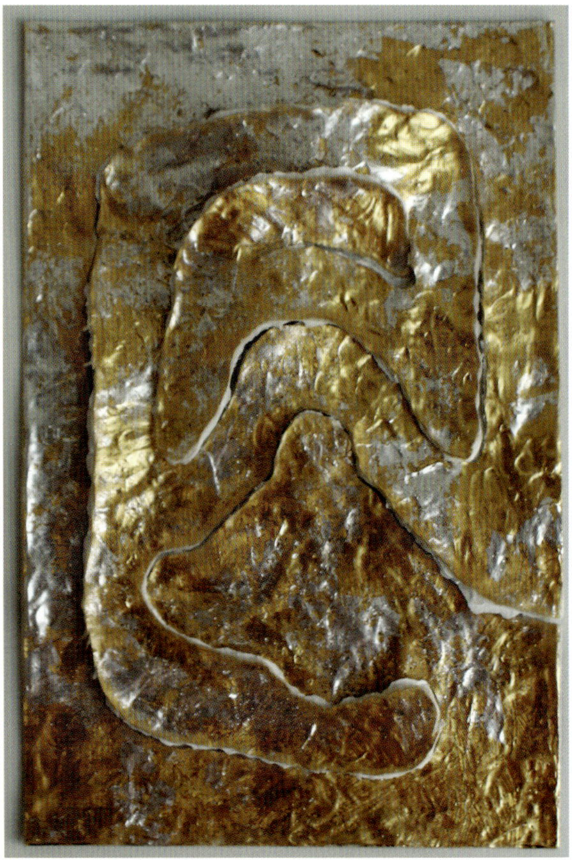

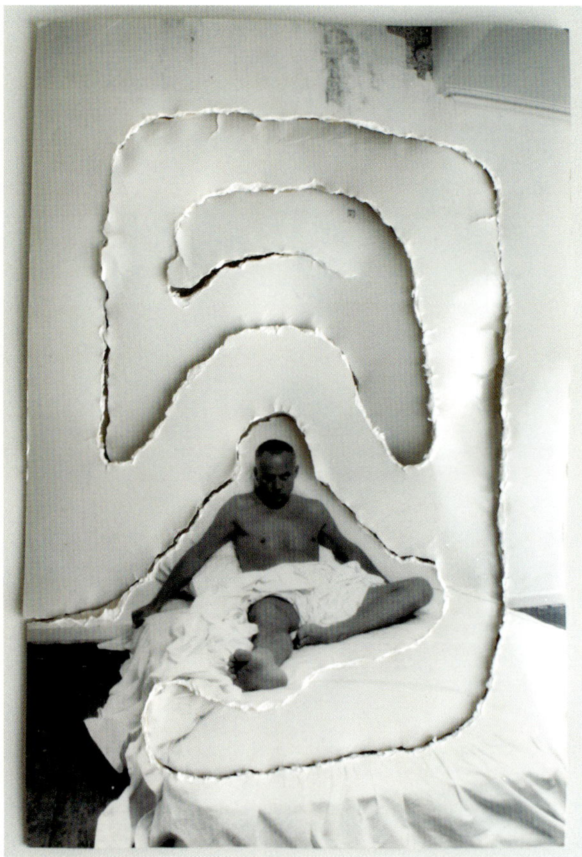

63 OPPOSITE PAGE AND RIGHT

Michael Petry
Laying Low (neckpiece) from the Almost There series, 2012
Gelatin silver print, 23k gold leaf, silver leaf, acrylic
$9^{3}/_{4}$ x $6^{1}/_{4}$ x $^{1}/_{8}$ in.
(24.8 x 15.9 x 0.2 cm)
Collection of the artist

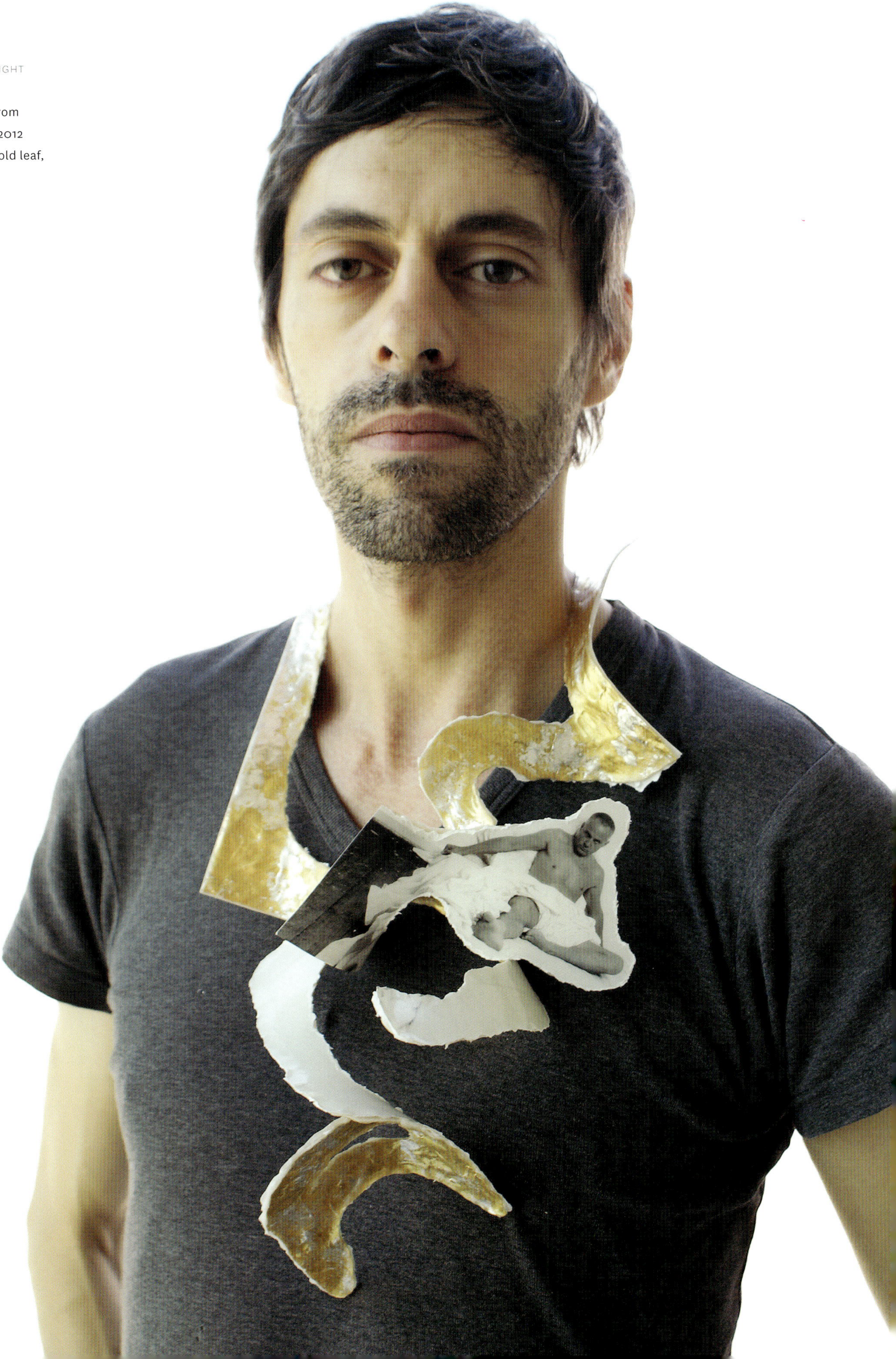

EVA TESARIK

Time of Pearls

Twenty-five years ago, I enjoyed collecting things, putting them together as if they were on display in a *Wunderkammer*, or curiosity cabinet, and then capturing these still lifes in photographs. Rock crystal changes reality, moves it into another dimension. Time shifts, light is refracted, and the viewer is ushered into another world. In *Time of Pearls*, an earlier moment has been transformed into a broken view of the past.

64
Eva Tesarik
Time of Pearls (necklace), 2005
Artist's digital photograph, silver, pearls, rock crystal
12 5/8 in. (32 cm), diameter
Courtesy of a private collection, Austria

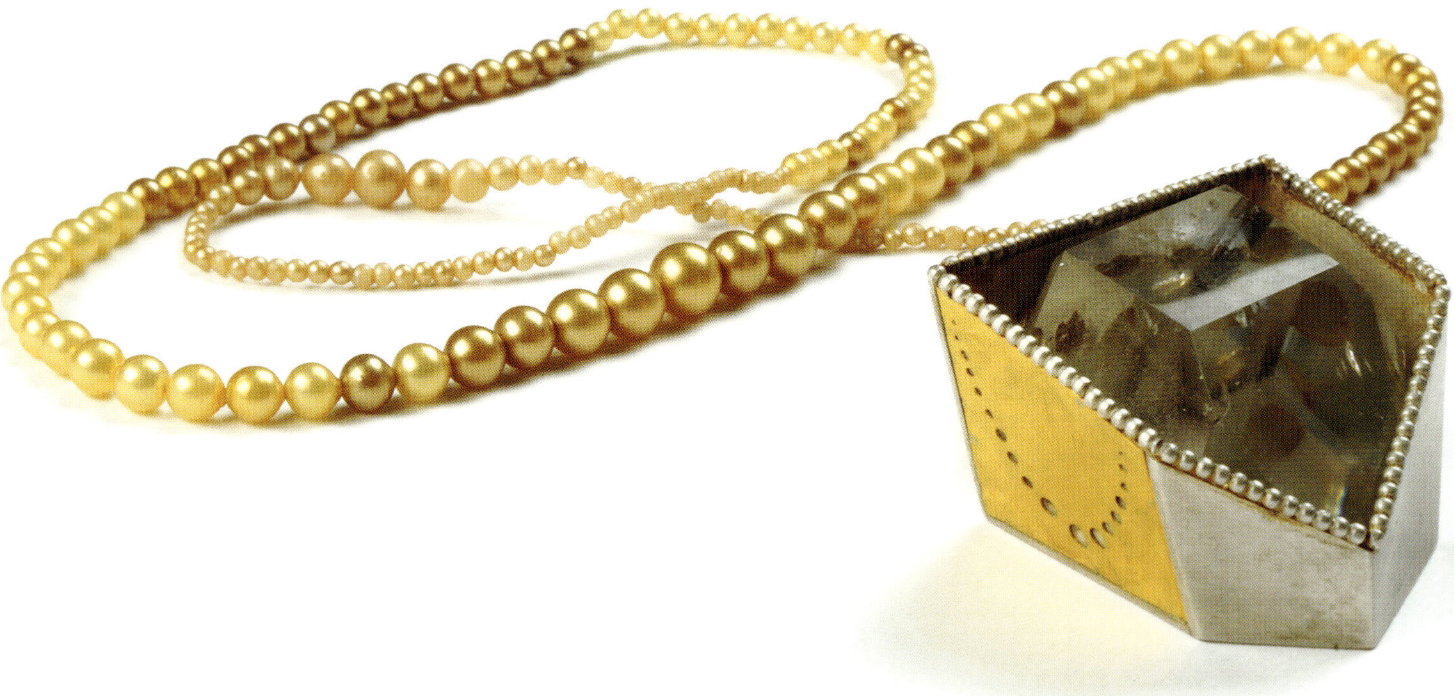

65

Thomas Mann
Stretch (brooch), 1988
Stephen John Phillips analog photograph, sterling silver, nickel, brass, bronze, acrylic, steel, found objects
$3\,{}^{5}/_{8}$ x $2\,{}^{3}/_{8}$ x ${}^{3}/_{8}$ in. (9.2 x 6 x 1 cm)
Museum of Arts and Design, Gift of Mimi S. Livingston, 2008

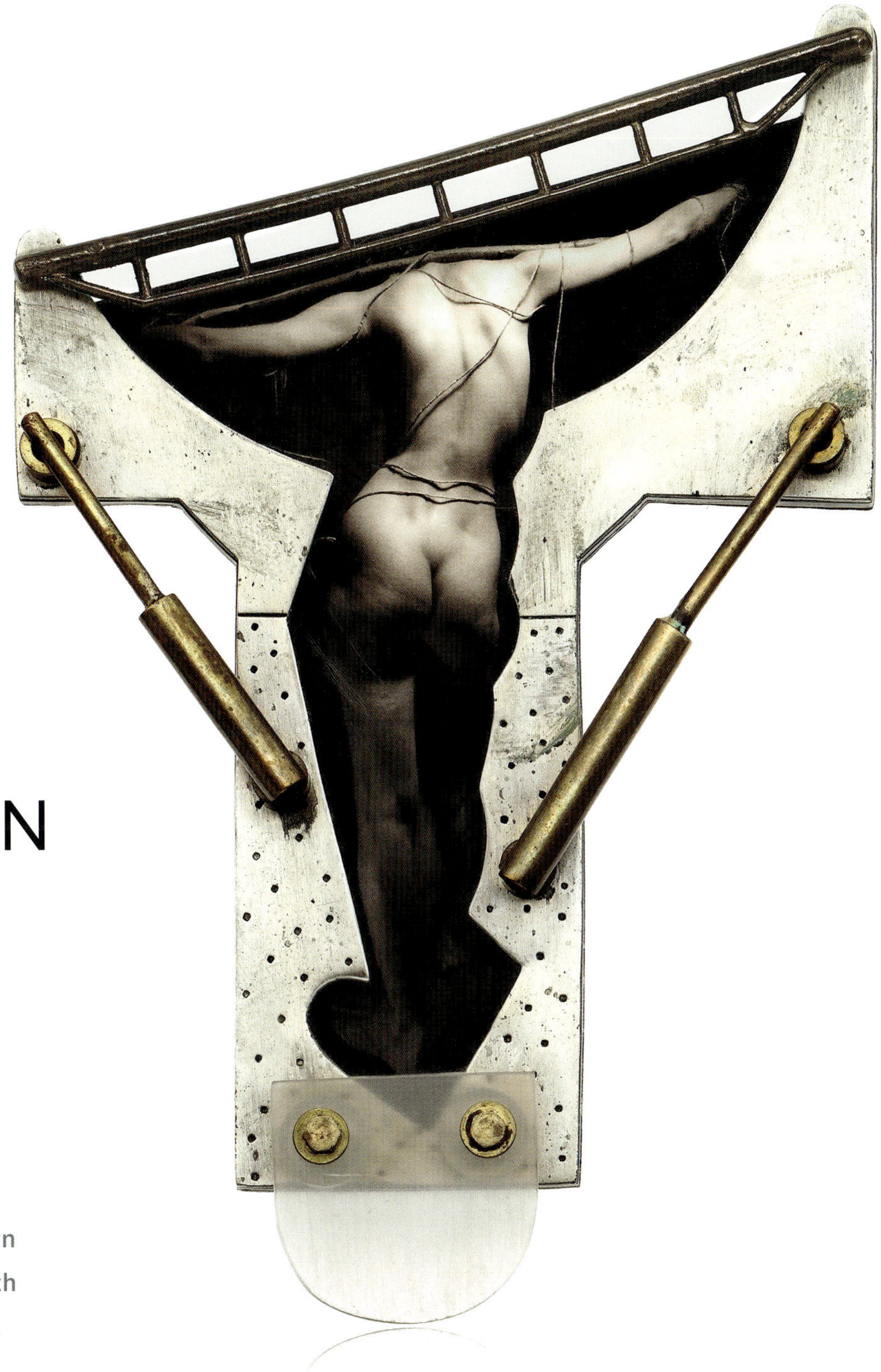

THOMAS MANN

Stretch

I began treating photographs as the thematic focus of my jewelry objects in the mid-seventies. At first, I used tintypes and daguerreotypes, but I swiftly progressed to creating my own images and eventually to working with those of professional photographers.

My goal is always to augment, reflect, or enhance the photograph's composition. In some pieces, the specific message is portrayed; in others, a delightful design exercise results, as was the case with *Stretch*.

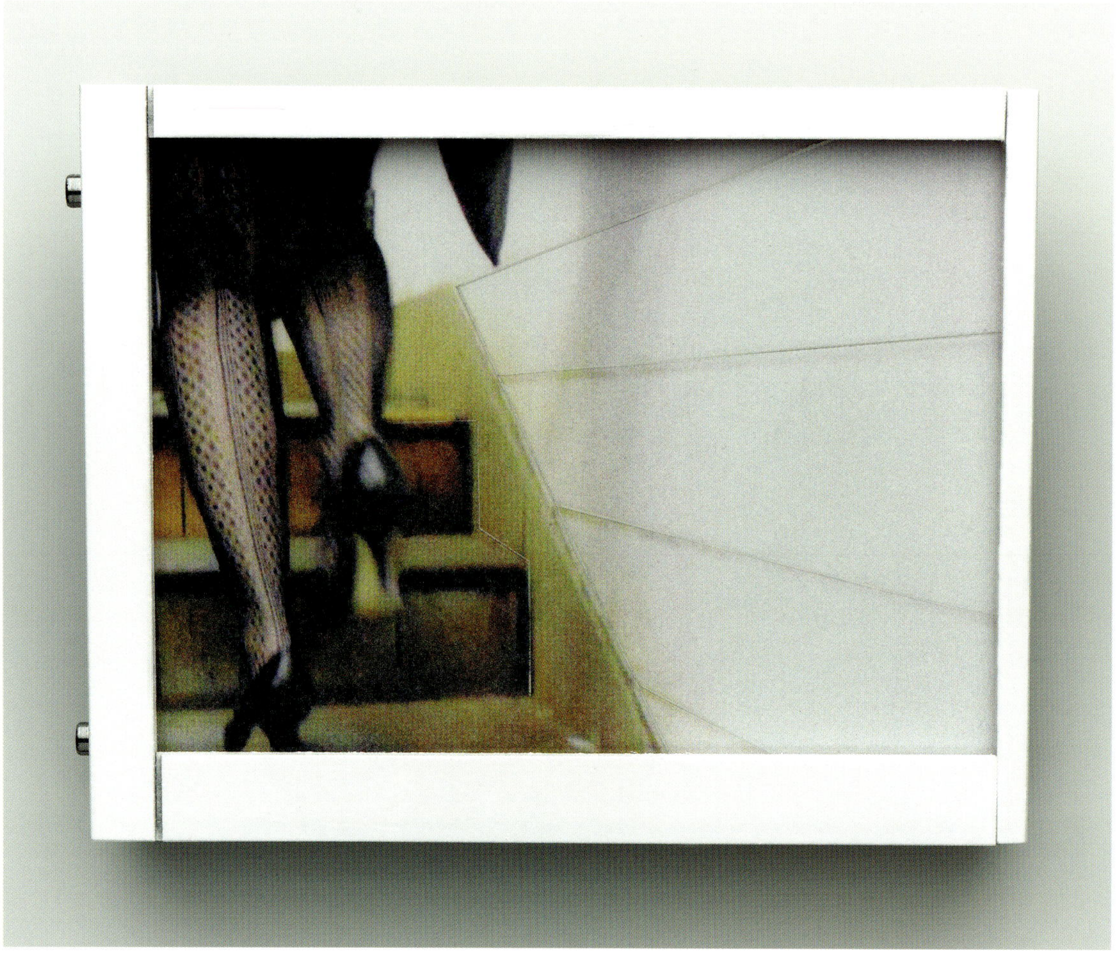

66

Thomas Gentille
Untitled (brooch), 21st century
Artist's digital photograph, acrylic, cherry, stainless steel, paint
3 x 3 3/4 x 3/4 in. (7.7 x 9.6 x 1.7 cm)
Collection of the artist

THOMAS GENTILLE

Untitled

On a crowded subway train, in a forest of passengers' legs, I caught a glimpse of a young woman sitting across from me, her beautiful legs marvelously encased in stockings. By the time I got my camera out, it was too late. I only had a few seconds before the next stop. Hoping I might get a shot of her walking on the platform, I hustled anxiously through the crowd, trying to prevent exiting passengers from getting between us and struggling desperately to achieve the desired settings on the camera without losing sight of her. As she turned to climb the stairs, I thought, "I'll never make it," and at that exact moment everything fell into place. I managed to photograph the woman with stockings.

CÉLIO BRAGA

Golden Boys Collection/ Silver Boys Collection

Photography has always played an important role in my “oeuvre,” either as inspiration or as material to be included in my works. The *Golden Boys/Silver Boys* collections have been inspired by gay-/queer-themed films such as Todd Haynes’s *Poison* (1991), Jean Genet’s *Un Chant d’Amour* (1950), Gus Van Sant’s *Gerry* (2002), and Gregg Araki’s *Mysterious Skin* (2004). In general, my works investigate memory, love, desire, lust, and loss, which are constantly shifting between shimmering hopefulness and existential torment.

67

Célio Braga
Golden Boys Collection/Silver Boys Collection
(strings/colliers), 2010–11
Fragments of digital C-prints, double-sided tape, glitter
185 3/4 in. (472 cm), total length; 5/8 in. (1.4 cm), width
Collection of the artist

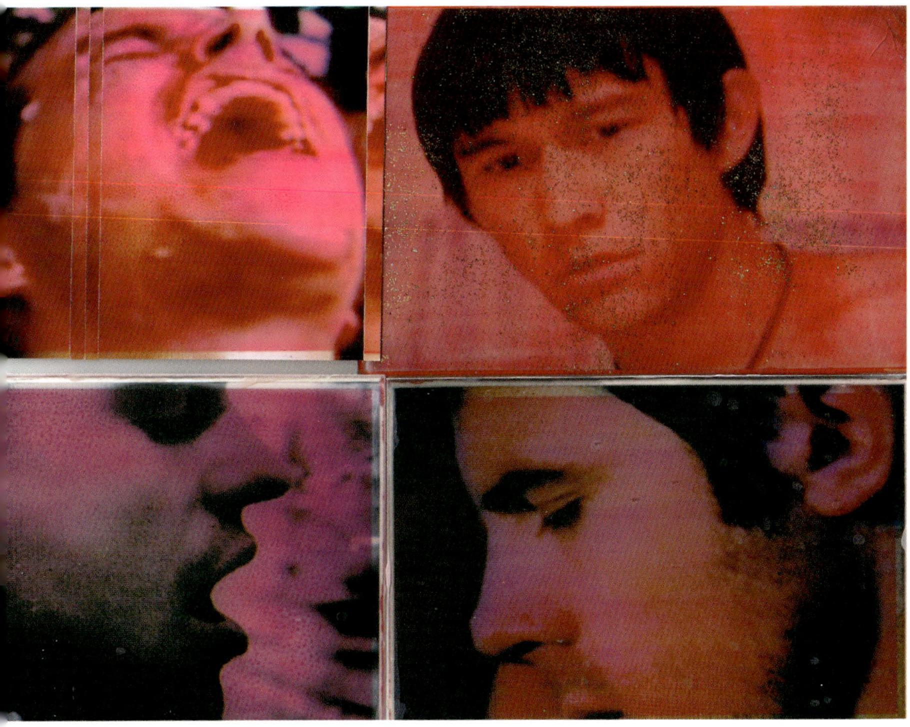

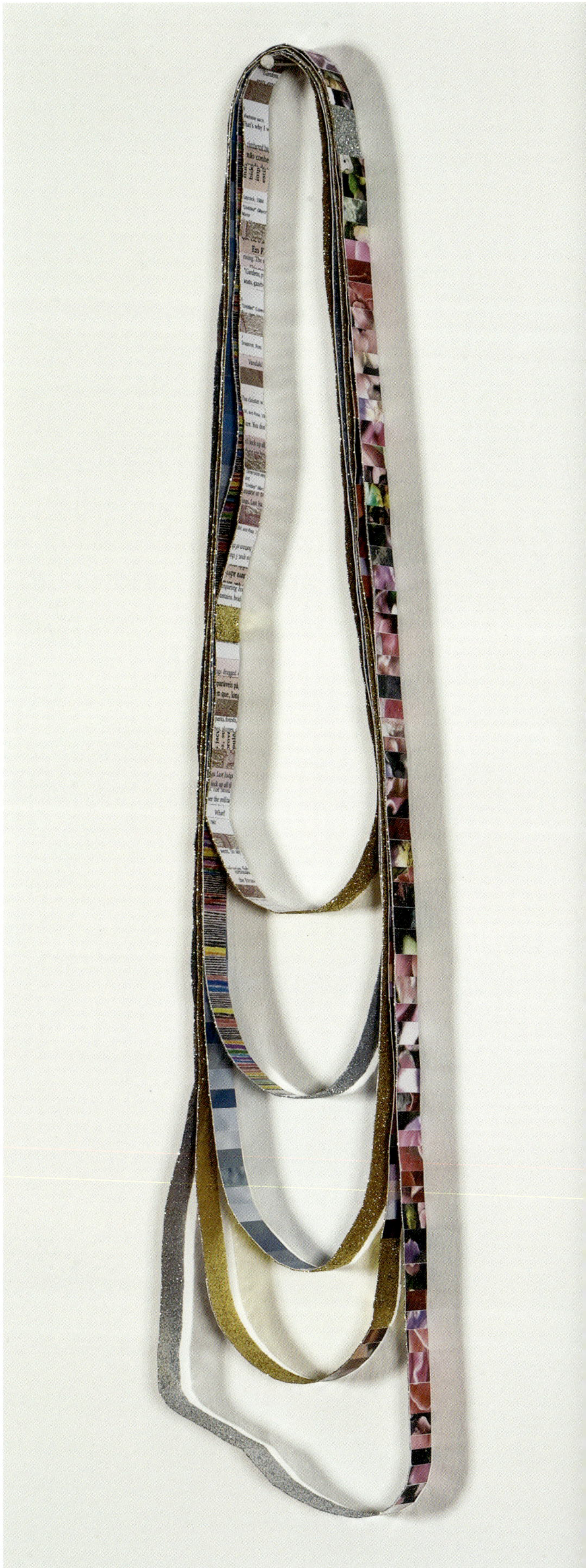

CLAIRE LAVENDHOMME

Brooch | *Brooch*

When we talk about jewelry, we're talking about the body. Jewelry travels with the body. In the How series, I try to maintain a close symbolic, formal, and metaphorical relationship with the body. I play to both a direct sensual relationship and a veiling of the tactile in order to move toward something more visual and more suggestive. The images in these brooches are details from artist Kiki Smith's engravings *How I Know I'm Here* and *Black Flag*, which I photocopied from a book and then photographed and covered with a thin opaque resin to create a kind of visual distance. The beauty of these pictures can be experienced only by sensitively unveiling them.

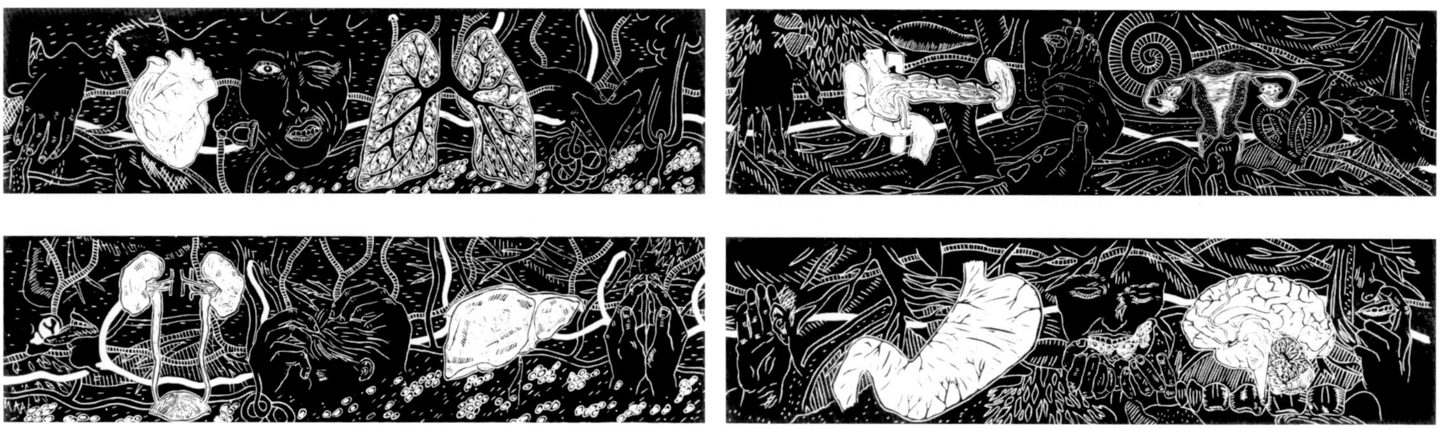

Kiki Smith
How I Know I'm Here, 1985/2000
Linoleum-block relief print in four sheets, printed in indigo on Thai Mulberry paper
11½ x 43 in. (29.2 x 109.2 cm), each
Courtesy of the artist and Editions Fawbush, New York

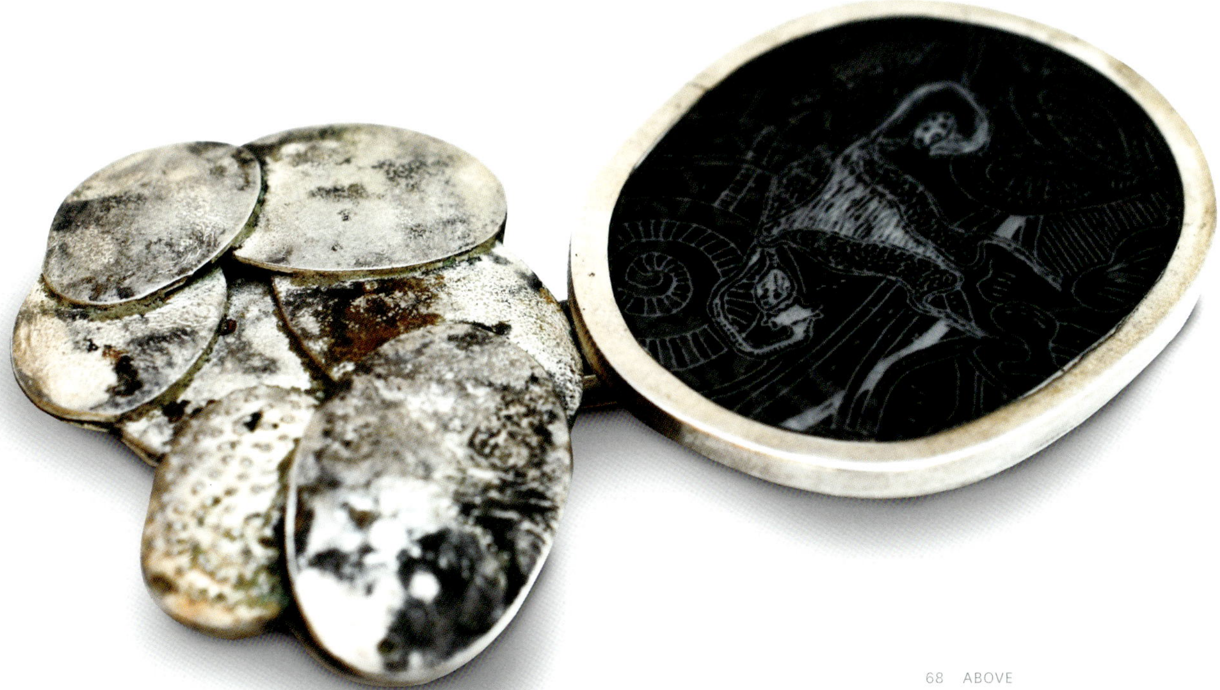

68 ABOVE

Claire Lavendhomme
Brooch from the How series, 2009
Photograph of a photocopy from a Kiki Smith engraving, resin, silver
$2^{3}/_{8}$ x 3 x $^{3}/_{8}$ in. (6.1 x 7.5 x 1 cm)
Collection of the artist

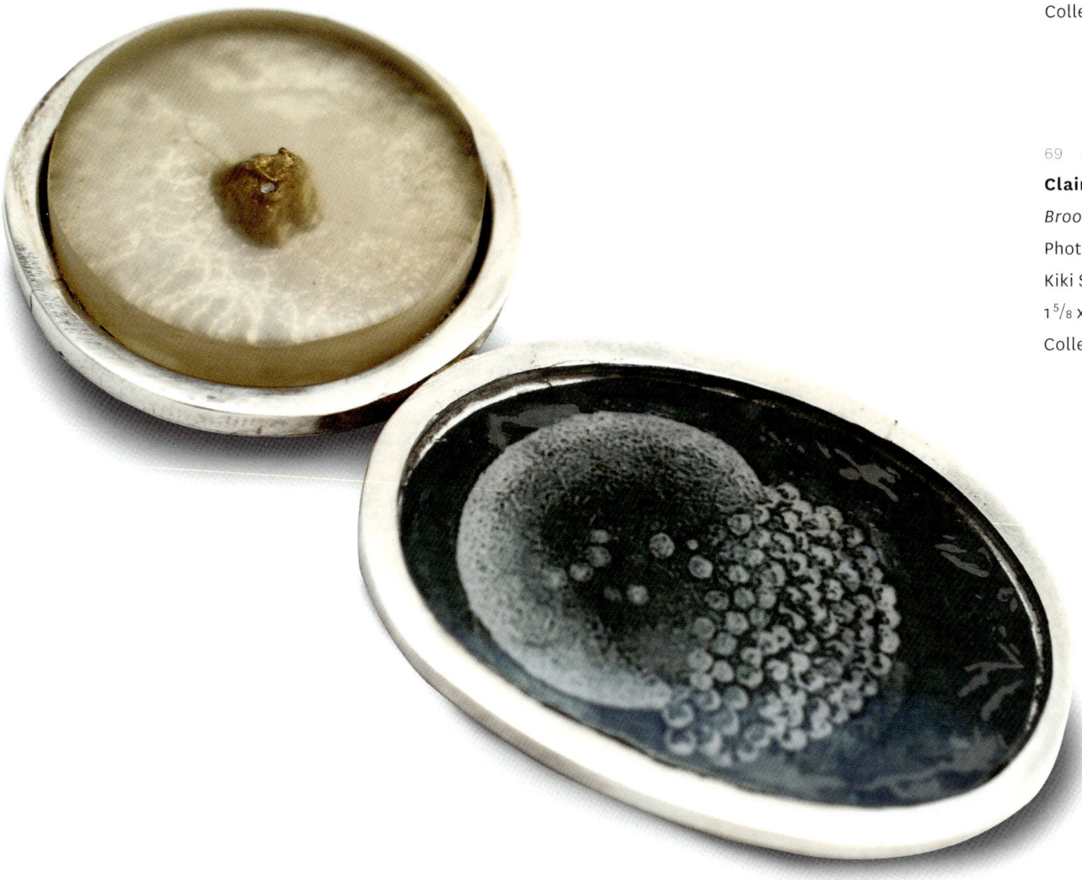

69 LEFT

Claire Lavendhomme
Brooch from the How series, 2009
Photograph of a photocopy from a Kiki Smith engraving, resin, silver
$1^{5}/_{8}$ x $3^{1}/_{4}$ x $^{3}/_{8}$ in. (4 x 8.2 x 1 cm)
Collection of the artist

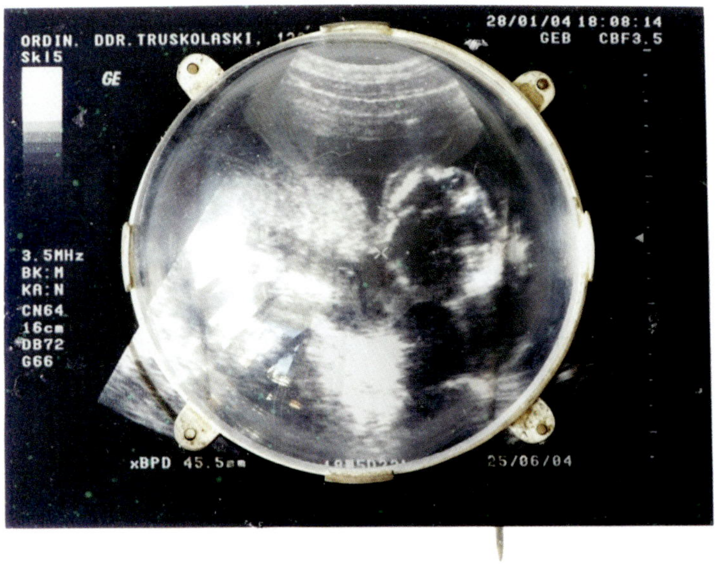
ORDIN. DDR.TRUSKOLASKI.
Sk15
28/01/04 18:08:14
GEB CBF3.5
GE
3.5MHz
BK:M
KA:N
CN64
16cm
DB72
G66
xBPD 45.5mm
25/06/04

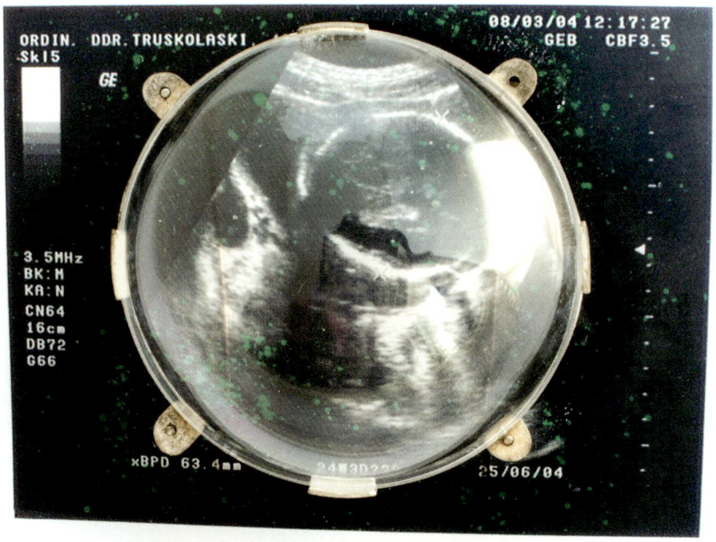
ORDIN. DDR.TRUSKOLASKI
Sk15
08/03/04 12:17:27
GEB CBF3.5
GE
3.5MHz
BK:M
KA:N
CN64
16cm
DB72
G66
xBPD 63.4mm
25/06/04

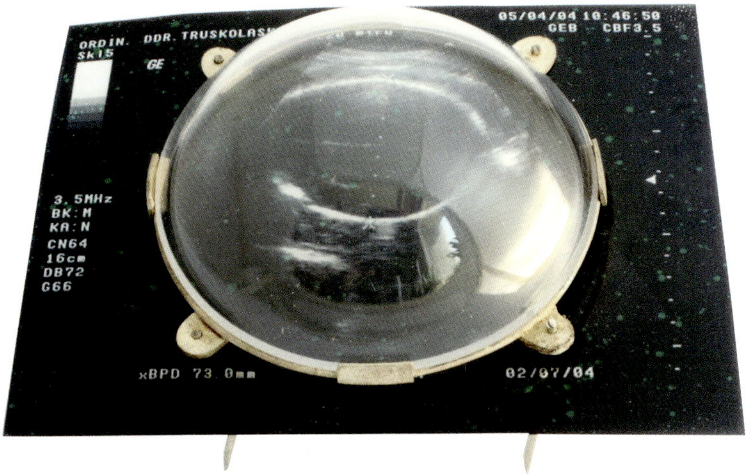
ORDIN. DDR.TRUSKOLAS
Sk15
05/04/04 10:46:50
GEB CBF3.5
GE
3.5MHz
BK:M
KA:N
CN64
16cm
DB72
G66
xBPD 73.0mm
02/07/04

VIKTORIA MÜNZKER

18th Week | 24th Week | 27th Week

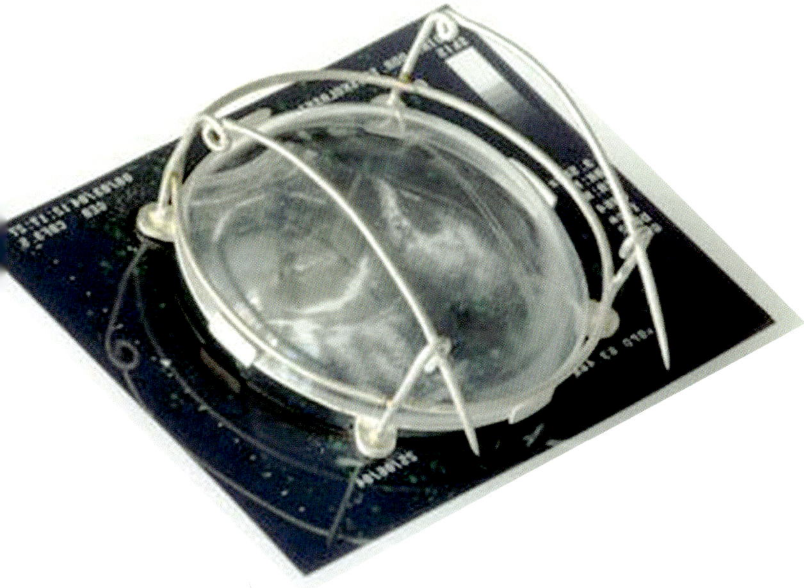

Feelings, emotions, and stories are important in my jewelry. For the first three months of my pregnancy, I didn't know I was carrying a "secret." Then, when I found out, my feelings were mixed. I was doubtful about what lay ahead and at the same time happy and full of expectation. I became so emotional that I had to process the experience in my work. These brooches show three stages of my child's growth in my uterus. Each brooch contains a plastic foil photocopy of an original sonogram print that I got from my gynecologist and a plastic hemisphere ringed by silver to guard and protect the fetus. I used a fragile construction to keep the brooches lightweight. These brooches are my message to my son, Sebastian. They express how much I care.

70 OPPOSITE PAGE AND ABOVE

Viktoria Münzker
18th Week, *24th Week*,
and *27th Week* (brooches) from the
Secret series, 2004
Sonograms printed on transparent
plastic foil, silver, plastic hemispheres
$2\,^{5}/_{8}$ x $3\,^{5}/_{8}$ x $1\,^{3}/_{8}$ in. (6.7 x 9 x 3.5 cm)
Collection of the artist

RIGHT

Artist's sonograms, 2004.

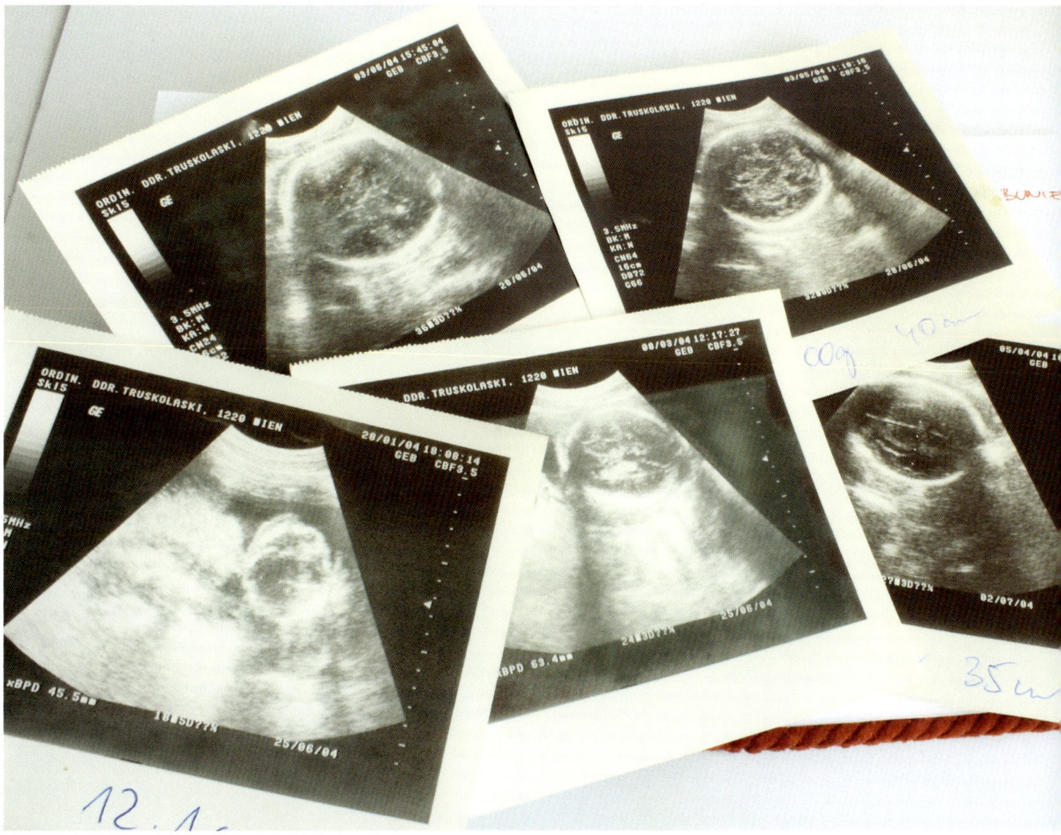

MECKY VAN DEN BRINK

Wedding Necklace

The idea for this necklace came during the hectic period when I was obsessed with mothering my newborn daughter. I photocopied a baby-cream ad from a magazine, wrapped plaster of paris around an inflated inner tube from a wheelbarrow tire, and glued lots of copies of the photocopied images onto the set plaster. Back then, jewelry had to be wearable, so I only made three different necklaces in this series, each to be worn once and then repurposed as a wall decoration or sculptural ornament.

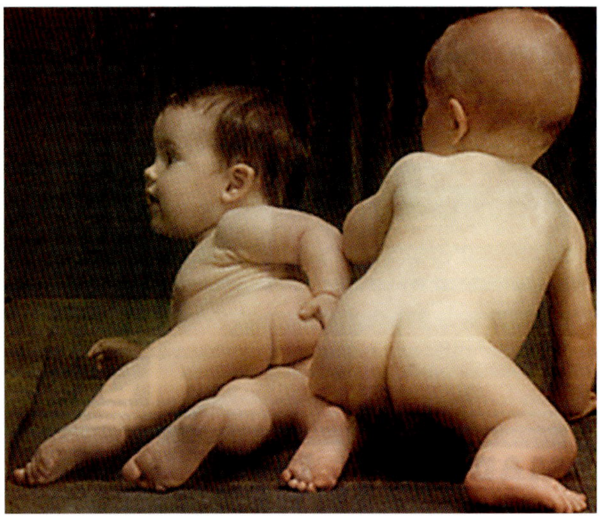

LEFT
Original magazine advertisement.

71 OPPOSITE PAGE
Mecky van den Brink
Wedding Necklace, 1989
Photocopies of a magazine advertisement, plaster of paris, paint
$14\,^{5}/_{8} \times 17\,^{3}/_{8} \times 2\,^{3}/_{4}$ in.
(37 x 44 x 7 cm)
Collection of the artist

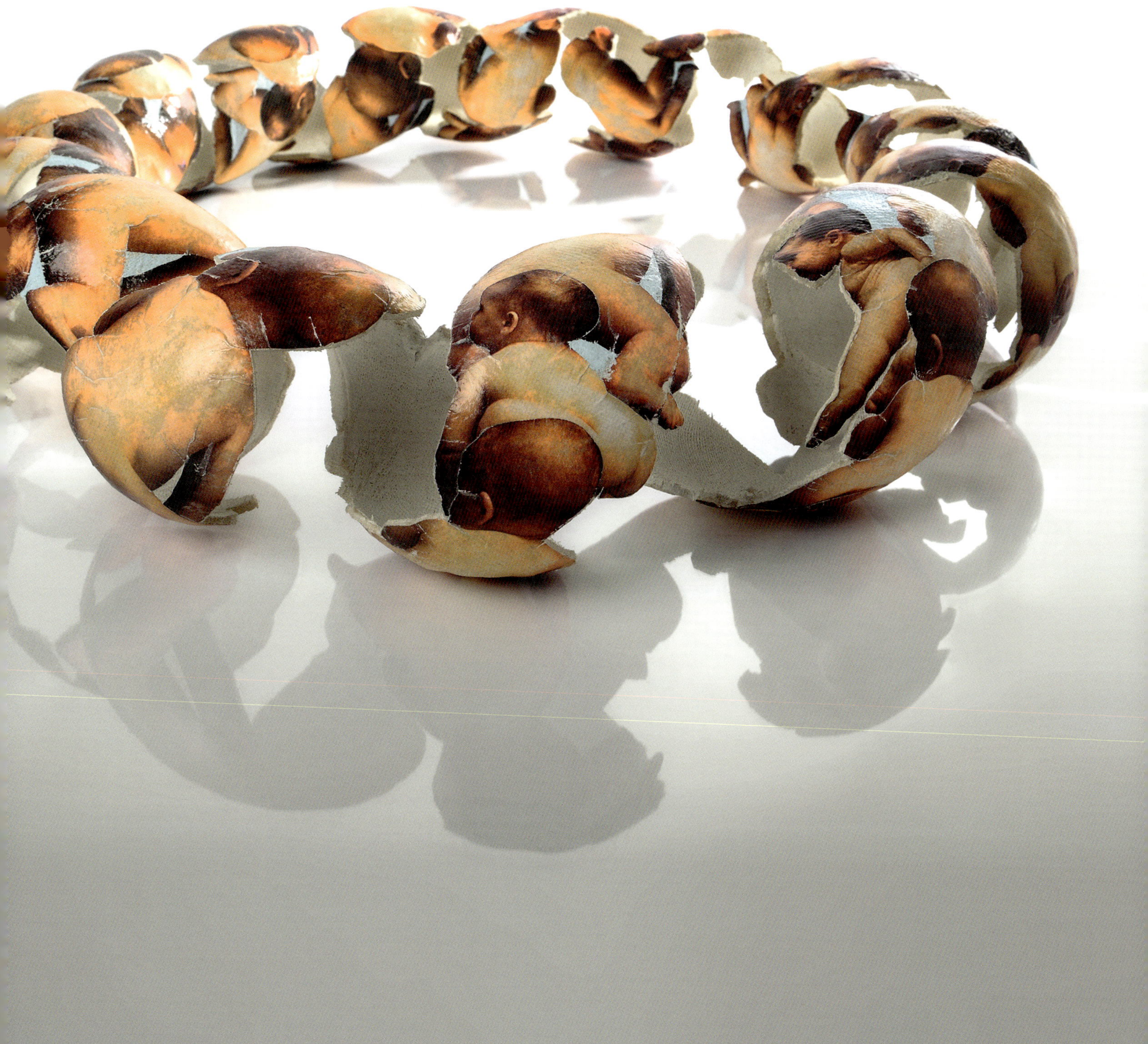

JULIA BARELLO

Brooch with Window I

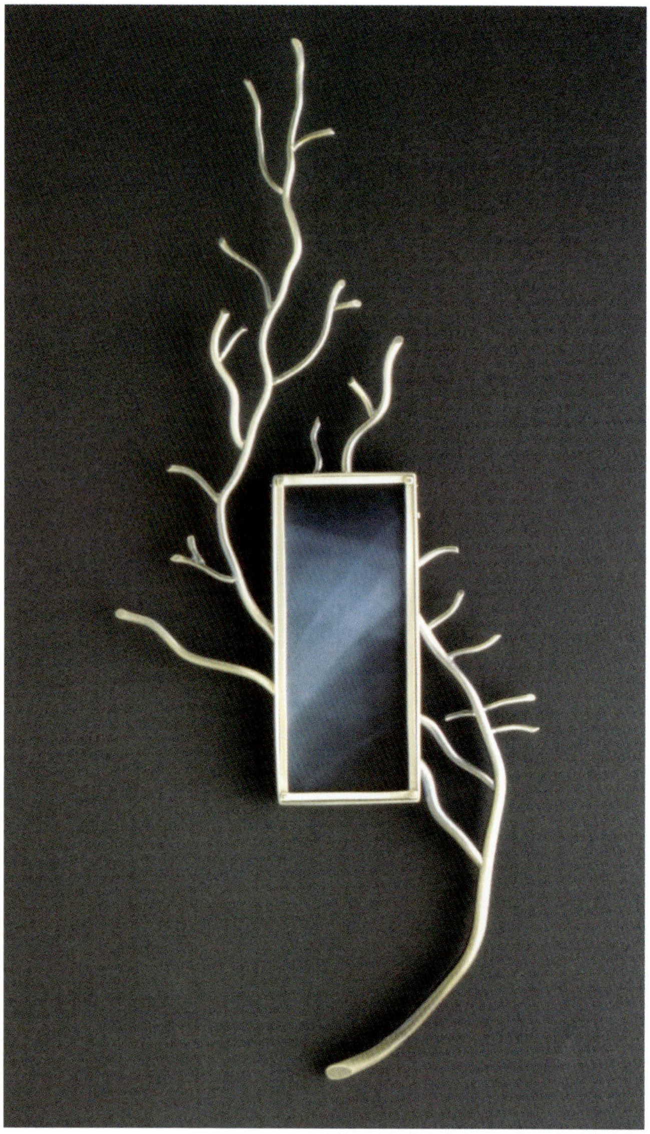

My interest in making jewelry that was gender free and spoke to the physicality of the human body led me to explore X-rays. They are the result of a non-invasive examination of the interior of the body, and they have a clarity and truth to them. They reveal systems that, with some variations, we all share as humans.

72

Julia Barello
Brooch with Window I, 1999
X-ray film, sterling silver
$7\frac{1}{2} \times 3\frac{1}{2} \times \frac{1}{4}$ in. (19.1 x 8.9 x 0.6 cm)
Collection of Ron Porter and Joe Price

GABRIELA SÁNCHEZ Y SÁNCHEZ DE LA BARQUERA

Piece II | *Piece X* | *Piece XI*

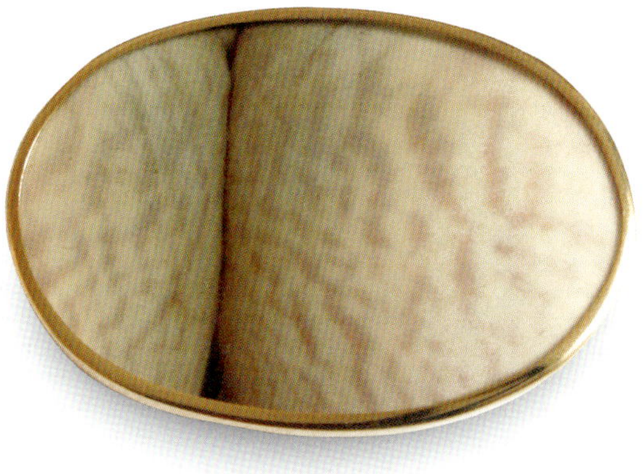

Humans reject ugliness. We aspire to being appreciated and beautiful and tend to hide our physical defects and try to repair our imperfections. We fear being repulsive and are disgusted by deviations from the norms of beauty.

Traditionally, cameos—carved pieces of jewelry framing aesthetically admired images such as elegant feminine profiles, flowers, or picturesque landscapes—have been worn by wealthy women as a means to represent status. My cameos invite people to question the social ideals of beauty. I asked people to photograph what they perceive as ugly spots on their bodies and framed the unmodified digital photos so they could be worn as jewelry. My cameos raise questions: How real is the beauty we see? How abnormal is the ugliness we hide?

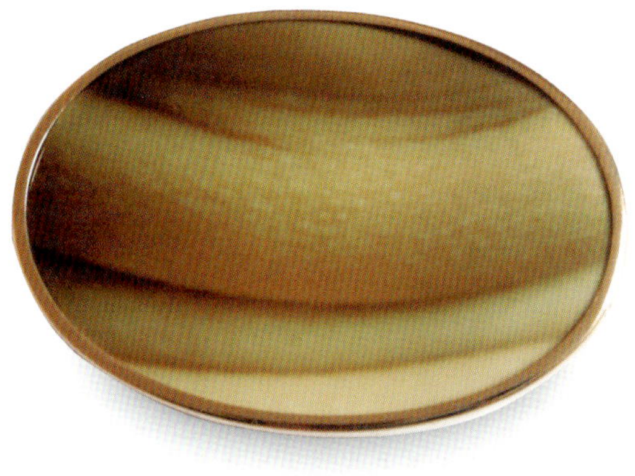

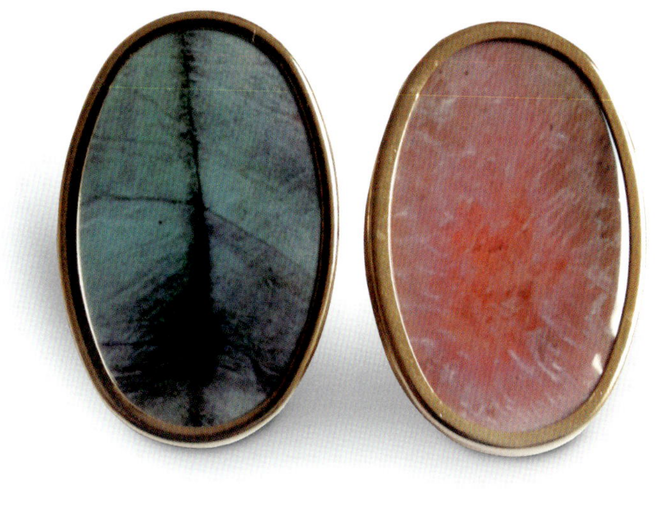

73 LEFT
Gabriela Sánchez y Sánchez de la Barquera
Piece II (earrings) from the (Ab)normal Cameo series, 2011
Digital photograph, gold-plated silver, epoxy
$1^{3}/_{4}$ x $1^{1}/_{8}$ in. (4.5 x 2.8 cm)
Collection of the artist

74 TOP
Gabriela Sánchez y Sánchez de la Barquera
Piece X (brooch) from the (Ab)normal Cameo series, 2011
Digital photograph, gold-plated silver, epoxy
2 x $2^{3}/_{4}$ in. (5.2 x 7.2 cm)
Collection of the artist

75 BOTTOM
Gabriela Sánchez y Sánchez de la Barquera
Piece XI (brooch) from the (Ab)normal Cameo series, 2011
Digital photograph, gold-plated silver, epoxy
2 x $2^{3}/_{4}$ in. (5.2 x 7.2 cm)
Collection of the artist

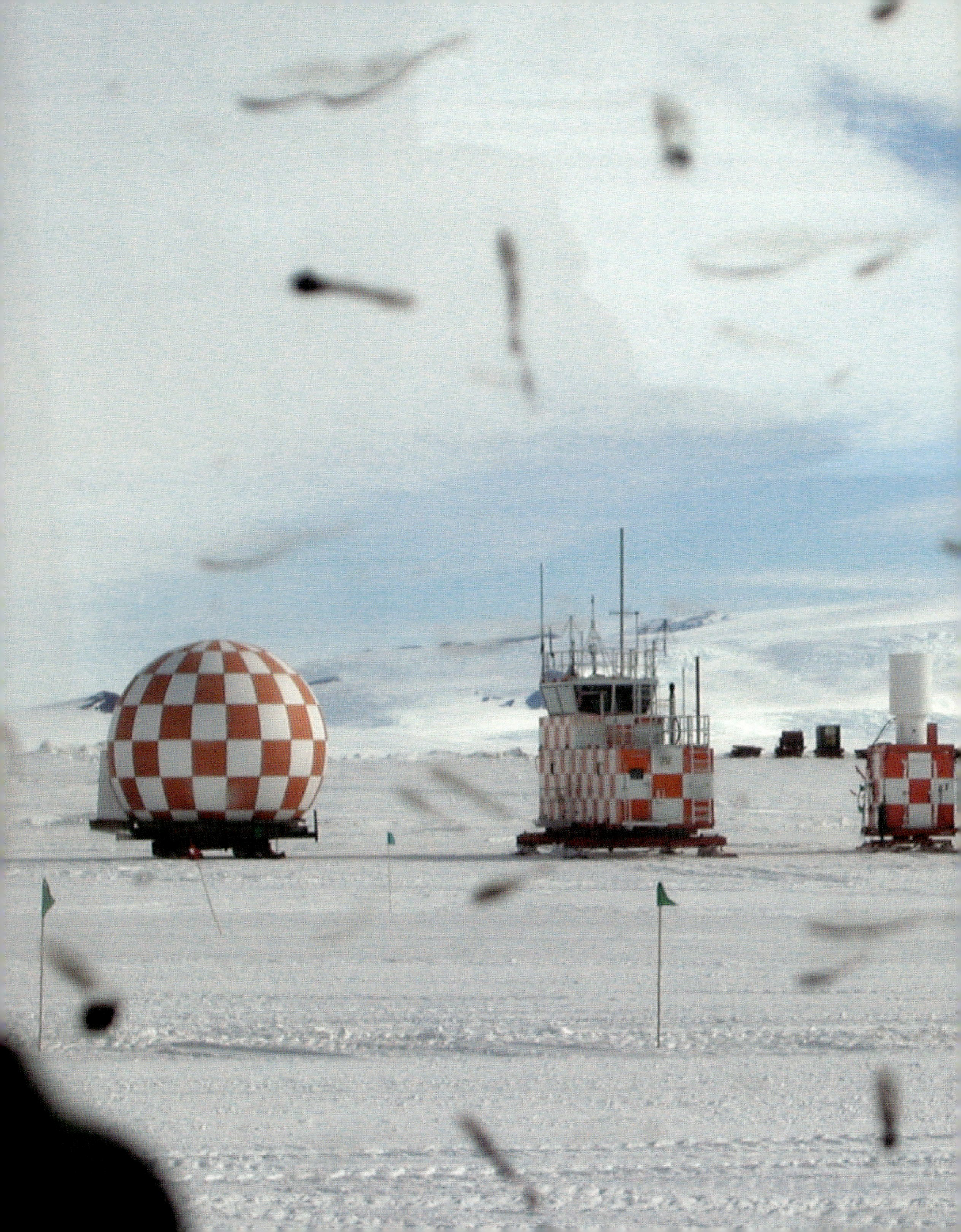

"... LANDSCAPE IMAGERY LOST ITS INNOCENCE ..."

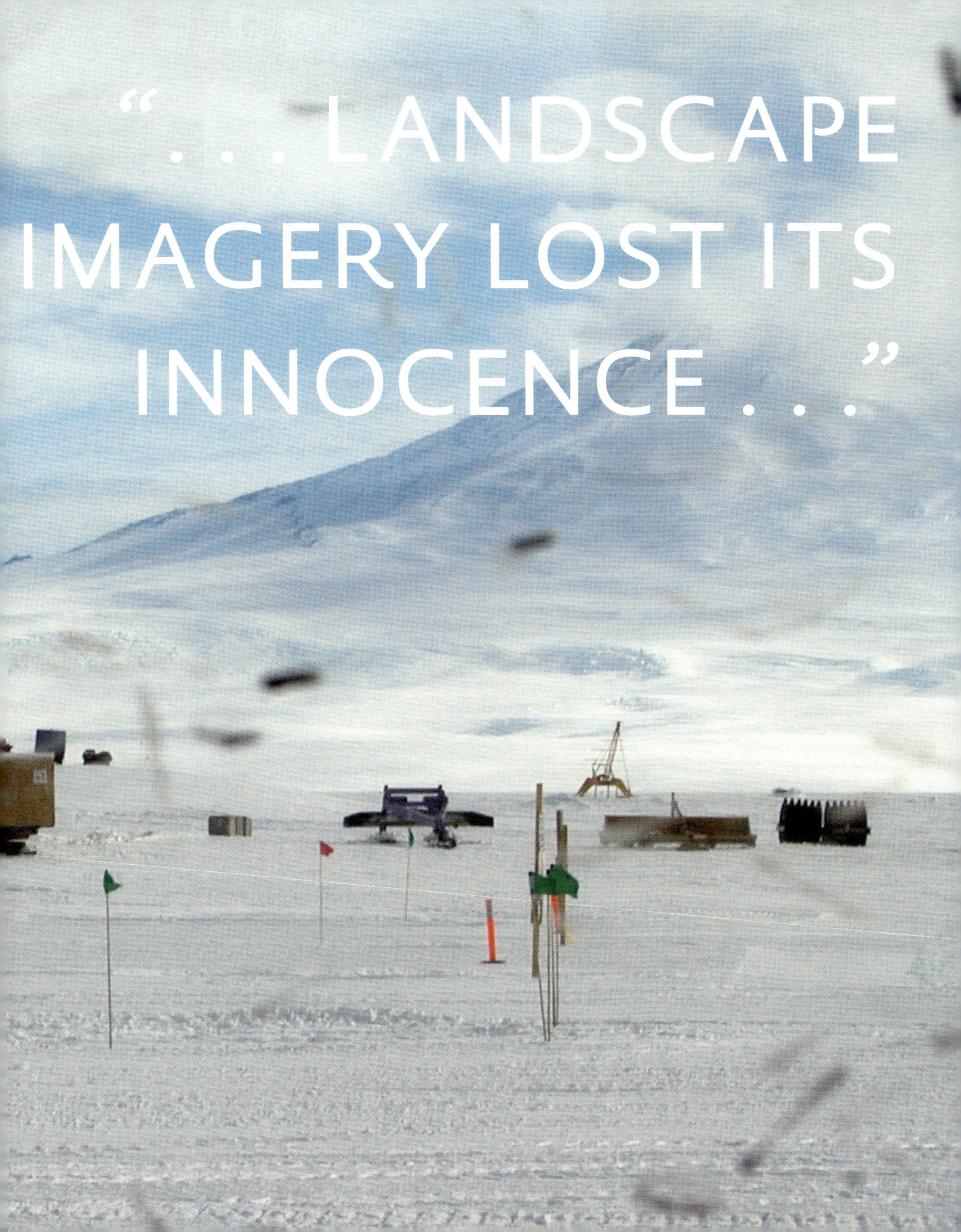

REMEMBERED PLACES—IMAGINED SPACES

Primitive society had its masks,
bourgeois society its mirrors.
We have our images.

—JEAN BAUDRILLARD

ELLEN MAURER-ZILIOLI

CREATORS OF JEWELRY who employ photography as a design element in their work contribute to the ongoing discourse on the representation and transformation of pictorial reality in art. As summarized by Jean Baudrillard, photography has changed, expanded, and even deluded our perceptions. It testifies to the disappearance of things, to the "state of the world in our absence,"[1] while at the same time producing images that simulate reality. Contemporary photo-jewelry is both a witness and an accomplice to this process as it takes on the contradictory role of being a vessel of memory, yet also a corrective instrument thereof. Reality, dream, and imagination may take effect in parallel fashion through dialogue, confrontation, and interpretation. Photography provides a bridge that enables jewelry creators to find their bearings in this artistic milieu without leaving the historical premises of their discipline completely behind.

Whether the photographic imagery in contemporary jewelry originates with the artist's taking the picture or comes from print media is not necessarily relevant. Identifying and gathering each motif, on the other hand, play a significant role in the creative process: essential artistic decisions are made during these activities. Georg Lukács spoke of the constitution of artworks through "aesthetic positing,"[2] with the completed work falling between daily life and art, and with a given piece of jewelry ultimately manifesting itself as a sensory aesthetic experience. The recognition of artistic purpose always takes place, after all, at that specific threshold of our perception where common practice and banality are transcended.[3]

Through and with imagery, memory and creative activity can achieve congruence. In the context of jewelry, this connection is referred to as a souvenir. Miniature pictures on enamel and various tokens of love have long expressed our need to preserve things past or absent in small sanctuaries near our own bodies. This is what inspired Kirsten Haydon in her latest series of works: "In my work, jewellery and object are used to connect with human experience and place through the notion of the souvenir."[4] In 2004, the New Zealand Artists to Antarctica program made Haydon, who has explored the subject of souvenir photos in jewelry since 1993,[5] the first jewelry artist to visit the South Pole. She then offered a summary of her experiences in a remarkable dissertation at RMIT University (Melbourne, Australia).[6] Through drawings, sketches, and photography, Haydon familiarized herself with the expanse and spectacular nature of Antarctica. She based the works that followed on sketches of photographs to capture shadow, horizon, and atmosphere—as is evident in her *Ice Arrival* brooch from 2008 and her *Ice Valleys* neckpiece from 2011

(NOS. 80, 79), where the seemingly immaterial white of the ice formations dominates. Later, Haydon began to incorporate her own personal photos, with overlaid reflector beads lending crystallized ice a textured appearance while simultaneously referencing the historical use of micro-mosaics in souvenirs (NO. 81).

In 1851, France's Commission des Monuments Historiques, an agency of the French government, charged the Missions Héliographiques with taking a comprehensive photographic inventory of the architecture of France's provinces. Around the same time, photographers were beginning to capture the American West, thanks to the propagation of the daguerreotype process in the 1840s and 1850s.[7] These efforts were among the first to demonstrate the links between travel photography, landscape photography, and photography of architecture. The objective was to produce an exhaustive account of the world, explore the fascination of exotic faraway lands, document human civilization's achievements, and make the resulting findings accessible to all. Commenting on the tireless expeditions undertaken to every imaginable corner of the world, Louis de Cornemin stated in 1852: "We need no longer . . . undertake dangerous journeys. In the hands of some intrepid individuals, photography will tour the world for us and bring back the universe in a portfolio. . . ."[8] As Susan Sontag affirmed, one of the greatest effects brought on by the invention of photography "is to give us the sense that we can hold the whole world in our heads—as an anthology of images."[9] Sontag interpreted the act of taking photos as appropriation, as offering certifiable proof of the past "by converting experience into an image, a souvenir."[10] By its nature, photography thus wanders between reality and fiction—in the very arena in which Haydon's works can be found. Landscapes float dreamily over white oval and round backgrounds, recalling the concept of the medallion in the history of jewelry, at once supporting and subverting it with surprising motifs.

Landscape imagery lost its innocence in the twentieth century, with photography and other art forms devoting themselves to climate change, industrialization, and the pollution of the environment and providing a territory where a longing for the idyllic could be projected. Throughout this transition, the souvenir has remained inescapable and proven itself subversive by affirming how potent images are in constructing autonomous systems of language in jewelry. In her works, Haydon follows a conceptual approach that resembles a systematic preservation of evidence. For Bettina

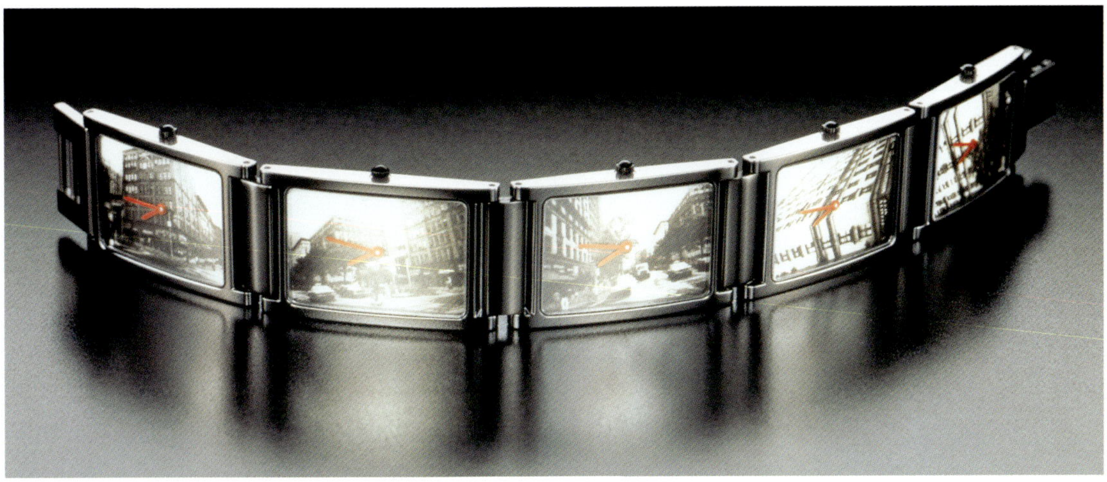

FIG. 1
Movado / Andy Warhol
Times 5 (bracelet watch), 1988
Reproductions of artist's photographs, stainless steel, red baton hands
$8\frac{7}{8}$ in. (22.5 cm), length
$\frac{1}{4}$ in. (0.6 cm), depth
Collection of Vincent Fremont

Speckner, on the other hand, compositional considerations chart out a general direction, with photographs she has taken herself on her extensive travels now representing a key component of her work.

Regardless of the effect Speckner's cloud-covered landscapes, dreamy green spaces, and enchanted nature scenes might have—many of them reproduced in finely balanced tones of gray—the artist herself states that neither melancholy nor nostalgic evocations of the past guide her in selecting her motifs. Rather, she strives for a synthesis of past and present: her additions of seashells, pearls, gemstones, and framing elements are to be interpreted as a jeweler's intervention on photography (NOS. 76, 77). The backgrounds of Speckner's works reveal connections to Germany's photographic history (the Becher school comes to mind, along with Thomas Struth's earliest attempts at portraits and interiors) that merge seamlessly with the purpose of her designs and mirror the souvenir character of Kirsten Haydon's works.

Mari Ishikawa, meanwhile, focuses on details in images of nature. It has been some time since Ishikawa, herself an ardent photographer, began placing delicate black-and-white photos of plants alongside her jewelry (NO. 78). Leaves, blossoms, and trees stand as models of creation and the cosmos; Eastern philosophy interweaves with Western notions of plant symbolism, whereas the destruction of nature and other environmental issues go unaddressed. Ishikawa conjures the "48 browns, 100 grays"—the traditional Japanese embodiment of elegance and style. Between darkness and light, one can find nuances that accentuate the kind of beauty and atmosphere better developed in shadow.[11] Nature serves as an idealized projection surface, an imagined space in which things can exist.

The democratization of photography has gone hand in hand with the popularity of commercially produced picture postcards. The dissemination of images is no longer subject to any limits, although the postcard established itself as a form of mass culture only after World War II (thus corresponding to the explosive growth witnessed in tourist travel at the time). In her 2008 series Dolomiten Sagen [Tales of the Dolomites], Jantje Fleischhut uses postcard images sketched over with miniature structures and phrases and embellished with words, to spin a timeless fairytale (NOS. 84, 85). The Dolomites' imposing mountain-scape undergoes a radical transformation brought on by ironic inquiry: Fleischhut's works involve examples of classic landscape photography whose expressions of distance and grandeur are drawn back into tangible dimensions by her own additions. Kiko Gianocca, on

FIG. 2
Fritz Maierhofer
Crumblestone Farm Brooch, 1976
Artist's analog photograph transferred onto aluminum printing foil, gold, silver, acrylic
3 1/8 x 2 1/4 in. (8 x 5.5 cm)
Collection of the artist

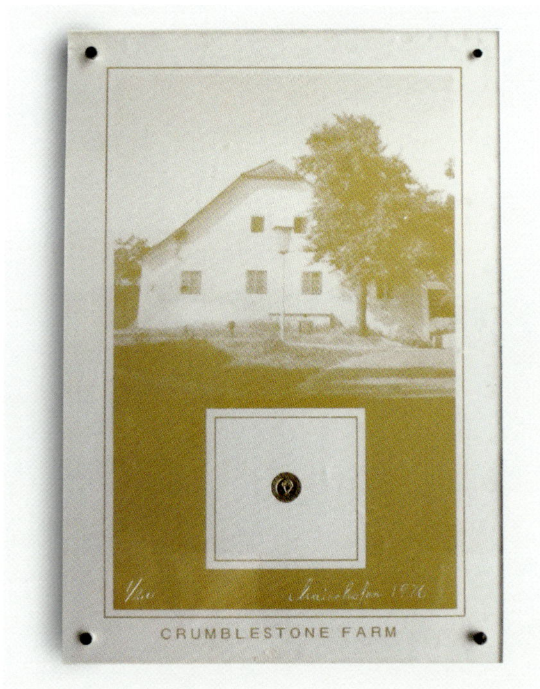

the other hand, goes so far as to banish a mountain image to the reverse side of a postcard-shaped brooch (NO. 83). His placement of the pin stem suggests a window for the image that lends the entire piece a purely practical appearance.

"Photographs are made of time"[12]—indeed, are bound to perceptions of time and space, enabling the two elements to converge. Personal memories are often at the heart of the general interest in photography. In 1970, Eleanor Moty enhanced a nineteenth-century image of a schoolhouse in Dodge City, Kansas, with a mirror silhouette of amethyst, which supports the motif like a pedestal (NO. 87). The Austrian jewelry artist Fritz Maierhofer would later immortalize a recently acquired and renovated farmhouse in his 1976 *Crumblestone Farm Brooch* (fig. 2). The visual concept of the house evinces phenomenological character traits with respect to literature and art. In *The Poetics of Space*, Gaston Bachelard offers an in-depth definition of the subject as an expression of the intimacy of personal existence—as a symbolic dwelling for reverie, disengagement, and memory: "For our house is our corner of the world . . . it is our first universe. . . ."[13] The "aesthetic of the hidden" manifests itself in images of the home.[14]

While Maierhofer's work is an evident portrait of his new abode, in the series Sichten I–VI, Susanna Kuschek covers pictures of building façades in Berlin with ornamental cast-resin patterns that offer further insight into the underlying subjects (NO. 86), vividly illustrating Bachelard's theory that "the house is one of the greatest powers of integration for the thoughts, memories, and dreams of mankind."[15] Given the premise that jewelry is particularly suited for tucking away intimate objects, Maierhofer and Kuschek have achieved a perfect congruence of image and form.

"Buildings embody time."[16] Since the advent of photography, cities and architecture have been among its most privileged motifs.[17] With the growth of the world's major cities, the focus shifted to phenomena of the modern age, and the introduction of Kodak's Brownie (1900) and the Polaroid Land Camera (1947) mark important milestones in the documentation of this development. Adjusting to keep pace with the current times, photographs increasingly featured broken perspectives that reflected aspects of mobility and acceleration. One witness to this evolution, Walter Benjamin, describes in his *Berliner Chronik* (1906–1932) how people began obsessively to integrate the camera into their existence: "We now see the world in terms of the 'snapshot,' and according to the mechanism of the camera itself."[18] The avant-gardists—works by Hans Richter or Alexander Rodchenko come to mind, along with Bauhaus series by Lucia Moholy-Nagy and Laszlo Moholy-Nagy—dissected and reassembled our view of the world. "Photographs can act as a window on the architecture they depict."[19] This photographic window corresponds to perception. Sooyeon Kim's neckpiece *House on Benefit Street* demonstrates this dynamic using a photograph of a home in Providence, Rhode Island (NO. 90).[20] In this piece, she manages to lend the individual elements and illustrations a bold, deconstructivist character.

At the beginning of the twentieth century, New York was considered a new breed of city—and one of the most photogenic—and Alfred Stieglitz, Paul Strand, Berenice Abbott, Lewis Hine, and many others proceeded to create unforgettable photographic icons of its uniqueness.
Since the 1950s, New York City's cultural vitality has been celebrated in a number of photo books, including *Andy Warhol's Index (Book)*. The Movado/Andy Warhol bracelet watch *Times/5*, designed in 1987 as the second piece in the manufacturer's Artists Collection series and realized in 1988, consists of five separate stainless-steel casings. Images of the West Side of Manhattan serve as its multiple faces, with red watch hands hovering above the black-and-white photographs (fig. 1). Their progression and arrangement again recall

filmstrips or contact prints, thus corresponding to the serial nature of Warhol's oeuvre. In a certain sense, we can even make out a connection to his early photo-booth pictures. These as-yet unidentified snapshots were taken from Warhol's immense archive of photographs and clocks. A Minox 35 EL (a "James Bond camera," as Warhol put it[21]) accompanied the avid collector on his tireless wanderings through "his" city. Warhol seems to have chosen his motifs simply by turning in place; only the transition to upright format interrupts the panorama. Warhol's "fragmented attempts at a systematic, non-hierarchical, infinitely expandable photographic inventory"[22] were made in the context of what occupied artists' minds in the twentieth century. Rodchenko had already recognized this in 1928, interpreting casual photography "as a form necessary for contemporary subjects" that "takes account of the change and inherent contradictions that accompany the passage of time and the various forms of pressure generated by modern life."[23] Warhol's approach correlates fully with this observation.

At virtually the same time, Peter Skubic, then a professor of jewelry design at the Cologne University of Applied Sciences in Germany, began exploring reflection, a subject that informs his work to this day; indeed, it has nearly become his trademark. The 1986 portrait of Skubic wearing glasses reflecting the Cologne Dome (fig. 3) illustrates a radical departure from conventional thinking toward a more conceptual process of creating jewelry. The round "lenses" of his glasses are filled with old reproductions of the Cologne cathedral, initiating a paradoxical interplay among projection, duplication, and illusion. From the artist's perspective, reality is replicated, while other observers see a reflection. "In this case, reality is 'plus,' the reflection is 'minus,' and the plane of the mirror itself is 'zero.' If I set 'zero' to NOTHING and 'minus' to LESS, I see LESS THAN NOTHING in the mirror."[24] Reality fades in the supposed reflection, revealing itself as fiction.

Thomas Gentille, meanwhile, takes on the myth of the "architectural cityscape" by blending a photographic foundation with the painterly atmospheric character oftentimes exhibited in his works (NO. 82). With her necklace *Transformations* (NO. 88), Kara Ross references a current event: the development of Hudson Yards on the West Side of Manhattan, ground for which was broken on December 4, 2012. Ross commemorates this spectacular intrusion on the city's previous image with a classical assemblage of photographs and concrete fragments whose contours evoke the silhouettes of skyscrapers. In a way, the piece conceptualizes a miniature version of New York's future skyline—a utopian souvenir of a memory not yet experienced.

Gathering, cataloguing, and exploring the noteworthy characteristics of a subject are part of a jeweler's artistic research. Herman Hermsen illustrates the concept of collection with his necklace *Booklets*, with its fifteen booklets of five pages each, whose tiny images come together over and over to form new constellations (NO. 94). The fifteen booklets become architectural elements that encircle the wearer's head. The structure of a building can be considered a metaphorical counterpart to a worn ornament, and references to architecture generally account for a significant portion of the photographic components woven into pieces of jewelry. Thus Rebecca Hannon's poetic narratives unfold through a series of symbolic images depicting secondary structural elements—cornices, beams, façade arrangements, and pavement patterns (NO. 95). Hannon created her own personal "souvenirs" during a stay in Munich, Germany, where they offered a means of analyzing, comprehending, and overcoming her unfamiliar surroundings, much as if the key to it all were hidden in the details. Suzanne Beautyman's focus in her Opulent Boarders series (NO. 96) is on the transience and fragility of once-proud structures, the deterioration of which is integrated gracefully into her jewelry through the use of sharp angular contours and rough, mottled surfaces.

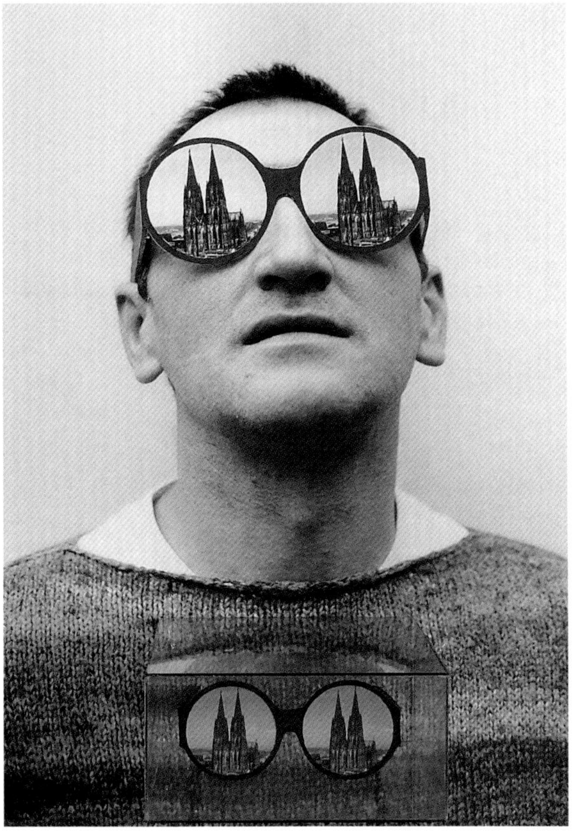

FIG. 3
Portrait of Peter Skubic Wearing Eye Glasses Reflecting Cologne Dome, 1986
Collection of Peter Skubic

One can observe a further permeation of photographic imagery in works by Craig Arnold and Margit Hart. Like Suzanne Beautyman, Arnold seeks to relegate contemporary images to the surface of his *Corrosion* brooches (NO. 91), which then transform during the creation process into an abstract signature, an "*écriture automatique*," as Baudrillard termed the act of photography.

After creating her first pieces in 1995–96, Margit Hart began exploring vegetative structures through macrophotography. The things we fail to see at first glance fascinate Hart, as does the confrontation of unfamiliar materials. Her latest works are dominated by grid and lattice patterns, which develop their own detached visual qualities (NOS. 92, 93). They reveal internal micro-spaces with structures that protrude outward, an adroit technique the artist employs to lend the pieces the impression of plasticity. Spaces real and imagined intertwine to define a new dimension: synthesis.

Observing these works in their entirety, one can see that the intended purpose is to explore (and constantly scrutinize) the reiterative reflection of reality, the construction of identity, and the occupation of space. If, on the one hand, we consider the trend toward extending the body's confines through jewelry, thus granting it additional metaphorical "extremities," so to speak, we can contrast this tendency with the manner in which photographic images appropriate the outside world. If the body can grow, can allow itself an imaginary second layer thanks to jewelry,[25] the use of photography triggers a complementary motion: not an outward projection, but rather an internalization of space. Instead of expanding into emptiness, jewelry then absorbs and incorporates it. All of these artist-protagonists are themselves storytellers; they tread the fine line between fantasy and objectivity, constantly fashioning new supposed circumstances. They create a metaphysical construct that combines elements of memory, the world, and the quotidian on a diminutive stage, fascinated by the as-yet unprecedented in jewelry, by "remixes" of tradition and innovation, by the pursuit of self-reassurance. After all, every place in their imagined topography is close at hand and yet far off in the distance.

Ellen Maurer-Zilioli *is an art critic, freelance curator, and gallery owner in Munich.*

Translated from the German by Miriam Levy.

1

"Jean Baudrillard: Denn die Illusion steht nicht im Widerspruch zur Realität," in *Jean Baudrillard: Photographies 1985–1998* (Graz: Peter Weibel, 1999), 21 (epigraph), 28.

2

Georg Lukács, *Heidelberger Ästhetik, 1916–18* (Darmstadt: Neuwied, 1975), 12; as cited in Konrad Paul Liessmann, *Das Universum der Dinge: Zur Ästhetik des Alltäglichen* (Vienna: Paul Zsolnay Verlag, 2010), 64.

3

Liessmann, *Das Universum der Dingum*, 35–36.

4

Kirsten Haydon, Introduction to *Micromosaic: Antarctic Landscapes* (Melbourne: RMIT University, 2013), 6.

5

As in the preceding groups of works *Poppy's poppies* (2000–2001) and *In the Drawer* (2004–2005) in the context of the grandfather's memories of war, for example; the 2003 work *Projections* as a diary between Australia and New Zealand; and the work *Number 128 N.Z Scenic Cameos*, which references landscape images from old Christmas postcards.

6

http://researchbank.rmit.edu.au/eserv/rmit:6690/Haydon.pdf.

7

See Martha A. Sandweiss, *Print the Legend: Photography and the American West* (New Haven: Yale University Press, 2002).

8

As cited in Graham Smith, *Photography and Travel* (London: Reaktion Books, 2013), 8.

9

Susan Sontag, *On Photography* (New York: Farrar, Straus and Giroux, 1977), 3.

10

Ibid., 9–10.

11

See Tanizaki Jun'Ichiro, *Lob des Schattens* (Zürich: Manesse, 1987).

12

Joel Smith, *The Life and Death of Buildings: On Photography and Time* (New Haven: Yale University Press, 2011), 14.

13

Gaston Bachelard, *Poetik des Raumes* (Frankfurt: Fischer Taschenbuch Verlag, 2003), 31.

14

Ibid., 26–27.

15

Ibid., 33–35.

16

Joel Smith, *The Life and Death of Buildings*, 13.

17

See the exhibition catalogue *Ansicht Aussicht Einsicht:Architekturphotographie*, with contributions from Andreas Gursky, Candida Höfer, Axel Hütte, Thomas Ruff, and Thomas Struth (Bochum: Monika Steinhauser in cooperation with Ludger Derenthal, 2000).

18

As cited in Neil Leach, "Walter Benjamin: Mimesis and the Dream World of Photography," in *Reconstructing Space: Architecture in Recent German Photography* (London: Michael Mack, 1999), 12–17.

19

Ibid., 13.

20

See Otto Künzli, "Bericht aus Providence," *Art Aurea*, no. 3 (1989): 50–61, who says that a girlfriend of Edgar Allan Poe once lived in the house.

21

As cited in Bruno Bischofsberger, "Andy Warhols visuelles Gedächtnis," in *Andy Warhol: Fotografien 1976–1987* (Hannover: Carl Haenlein, 2001–2002), 13–26, 20–21.

22

Mark Francis, "Stilleben: Andy Warhols Photographie als eine Form der Metaphysik," in *Andy Warhol: Photography* (Hamburg / Pittsburgh, 1999), 19–24.

23

Ibid., 24.

24

Helen W. Drutt, *Peter Skubic: Between* (Stuttgart: Arnoldsche, 2001), 125.

25

See Luiza Palancino, "De l'imagocratie: Corps, bijoux et autres anneaux dans la tête," in *Peter Skubic: Between*, 79–89.

BETTINA SPECKNER

Untitled | *Untitled*

My focus is on simplicity. I photograph the "normal," the day-to-day, the everyday, what is the same all over the world, in order to discover the "essential." Photo-enameling was used to produce the image in the piece below. I work with a very small company in Portugal that still knows how to do this process. Mostly I use pictures I have taken, which they enamel for me in the cut I want.

My images do not talk about situations; they give access to stories. But who owns the stories? The beholder of the piece or the piece? The images for the brooch on the right have been etched on zinc plates. This process comes from the old heliogravure printing technique, which works well for jewelry. Unfortunately, no one does this kind of work anymore, so I do it myself, mostly for pictures I have taken.

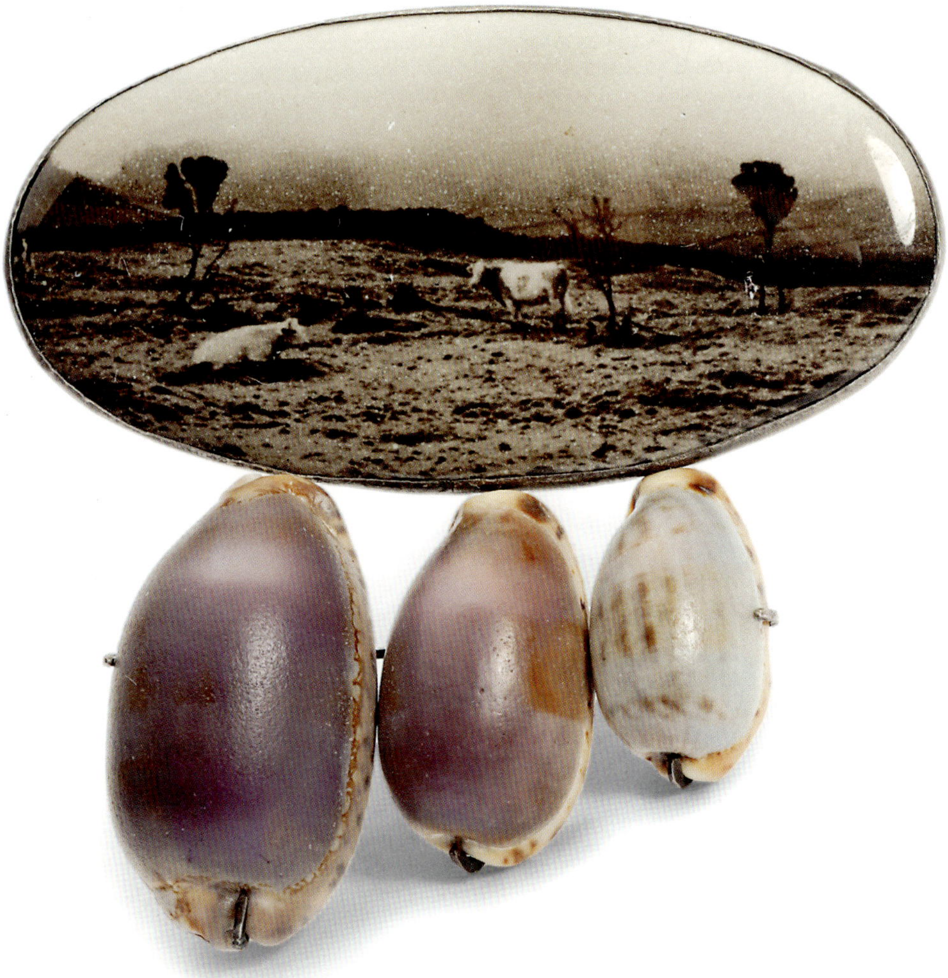

76

Bettina Speckner
Untitled (brooch), 2004
Artist's photograph enameled on silver, cowrie shells, amethysts
$2^{3}/_{4}$ x $2^{3}/_{4}$ in. (7.1 x 7.1 cm)
Courtesy of a private collection, Finland

77

Bettina Speckner

Untitled (brooch), 2004

Artist's photograph etched on zinc, silver, sapphires

$2^{3}/_{4}$ x 2 x $^{1}/_{4}$ in. (5.1 x 7 x 0.5 cm)

The Olnick Spanu Collection, New York

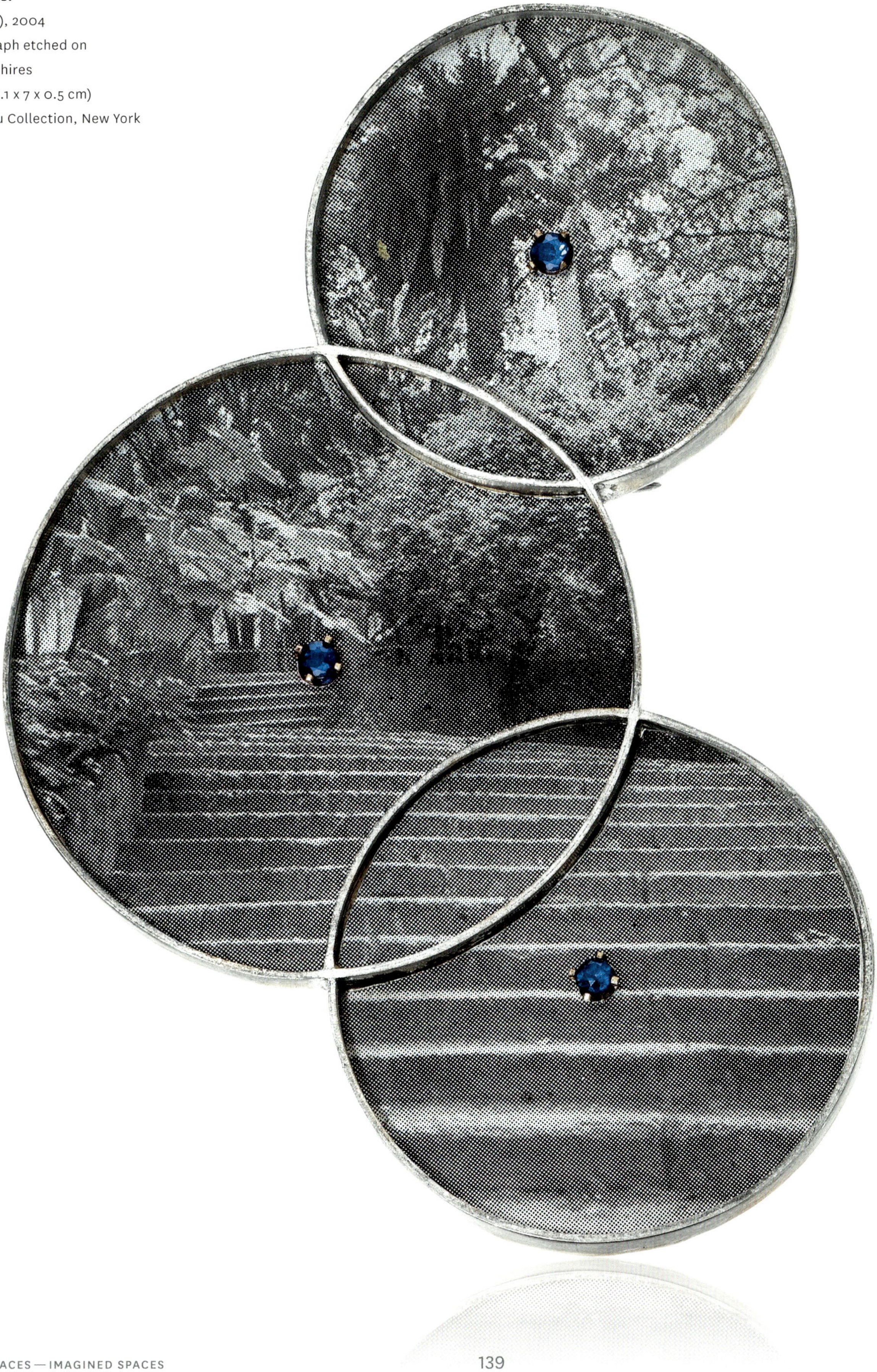

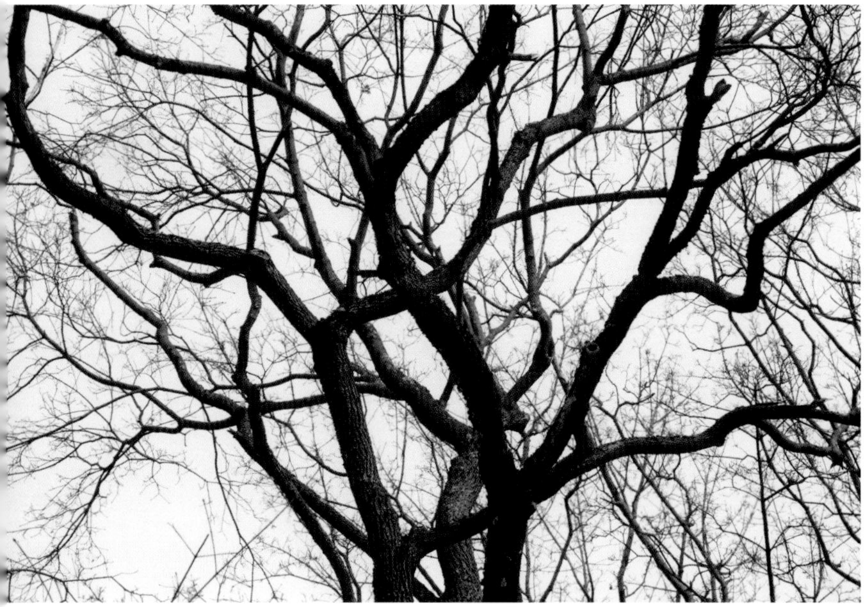

People are fascinated by nature. Plants, especially, have always been part of our lives. Plants are silent and do not openly demonstrate their power; they simply blossom and grow. The color, fragrance, and vitality of plants strengthen our senses. They can affect us more than a thousand words. In the shade of the tree we share our lives with nature.

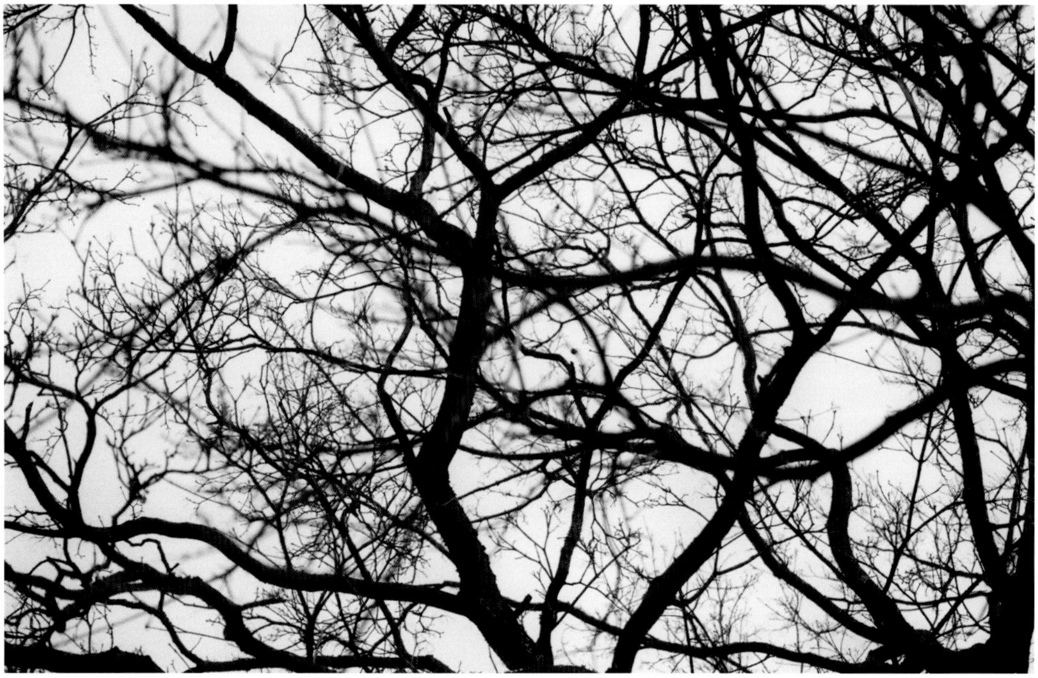

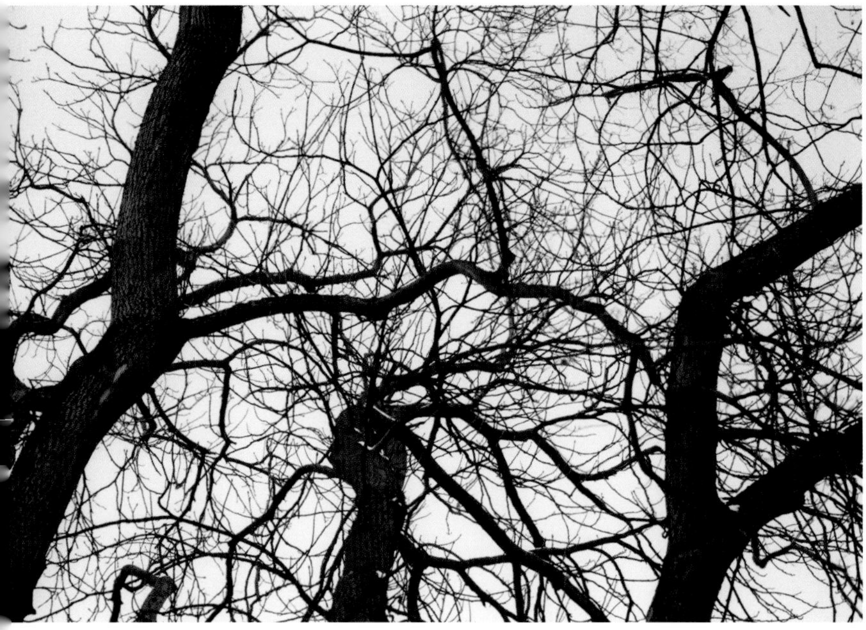

Mari Ishikawa
In the Shade of the Trees, 2006
Analog photographs
$23^{5}/_{8}$ x $15^{3}/_{4}$ in. (60 x 40 cm), each
Collection of the artist

MARI ISHIKAWA

In the Shade of the Trees | *Rings*

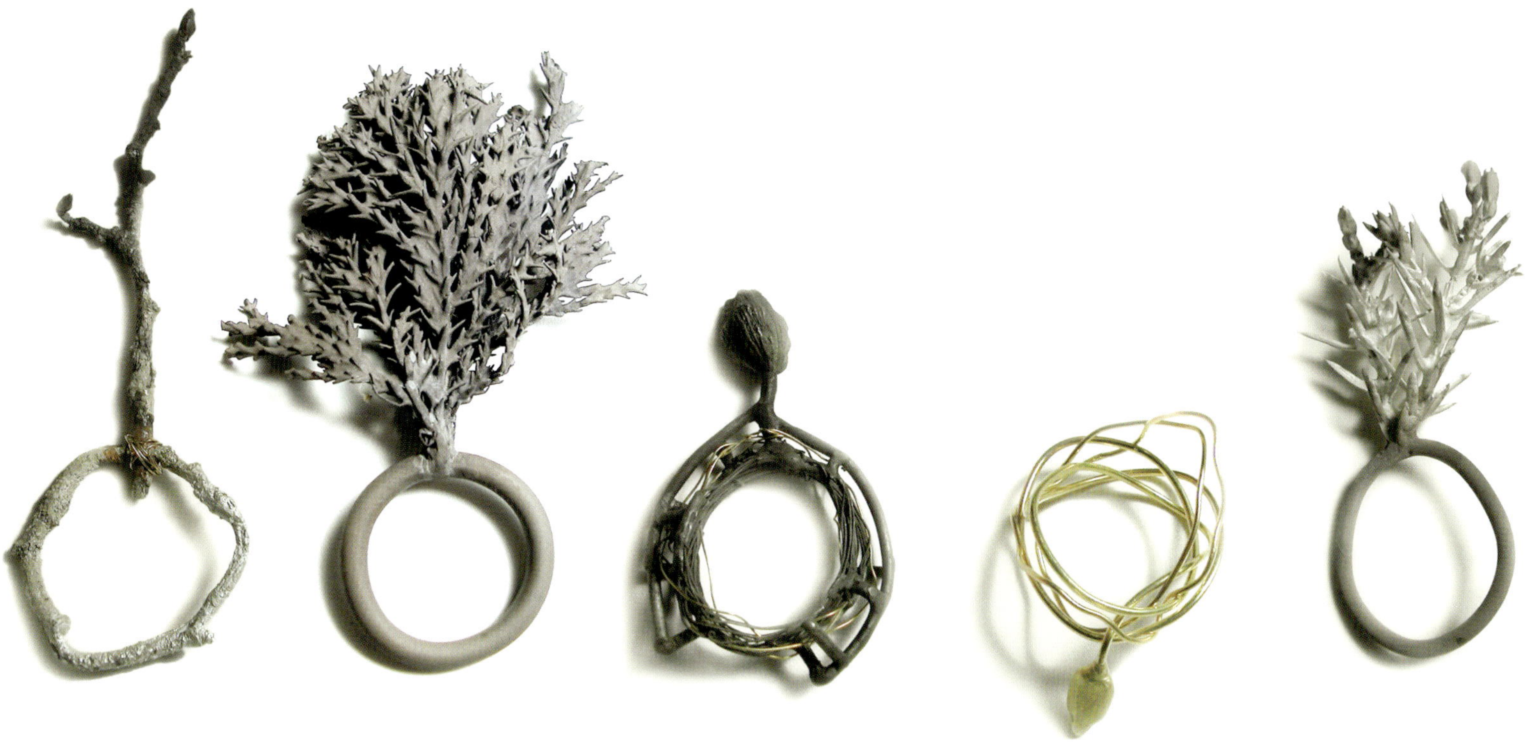

78

Mari Ishikawa

Rings from the In the Shade of the Trees series, 2006

Gold 750, silver 925

from left to right: $2\frac{3}{4} \times 1\frac{3}{8} \times \frac{3}{8}$ in. (7 x 3.5 x 1 cm);
$2\frac{5}{8} \times 1\frac{3}{4} \times \frac{3}{8}$ in. (6.5 x 4.5 x 1 cm); $1\frac{5}{8} \times 1\frac{1}{4} \times \frac{5}{8}$ in. (4 x 3 x 1.5cm);
$1\frac{3}{8} \times 1 \times \frac{5}{8}$ in. (3.5 x 2.5 x 1.5 cm); $2\frac{3}{8} \times 1 \times \frac{5}{8}$ in. (6 x 2.5 x 1.5 cm)

Collection of the artist

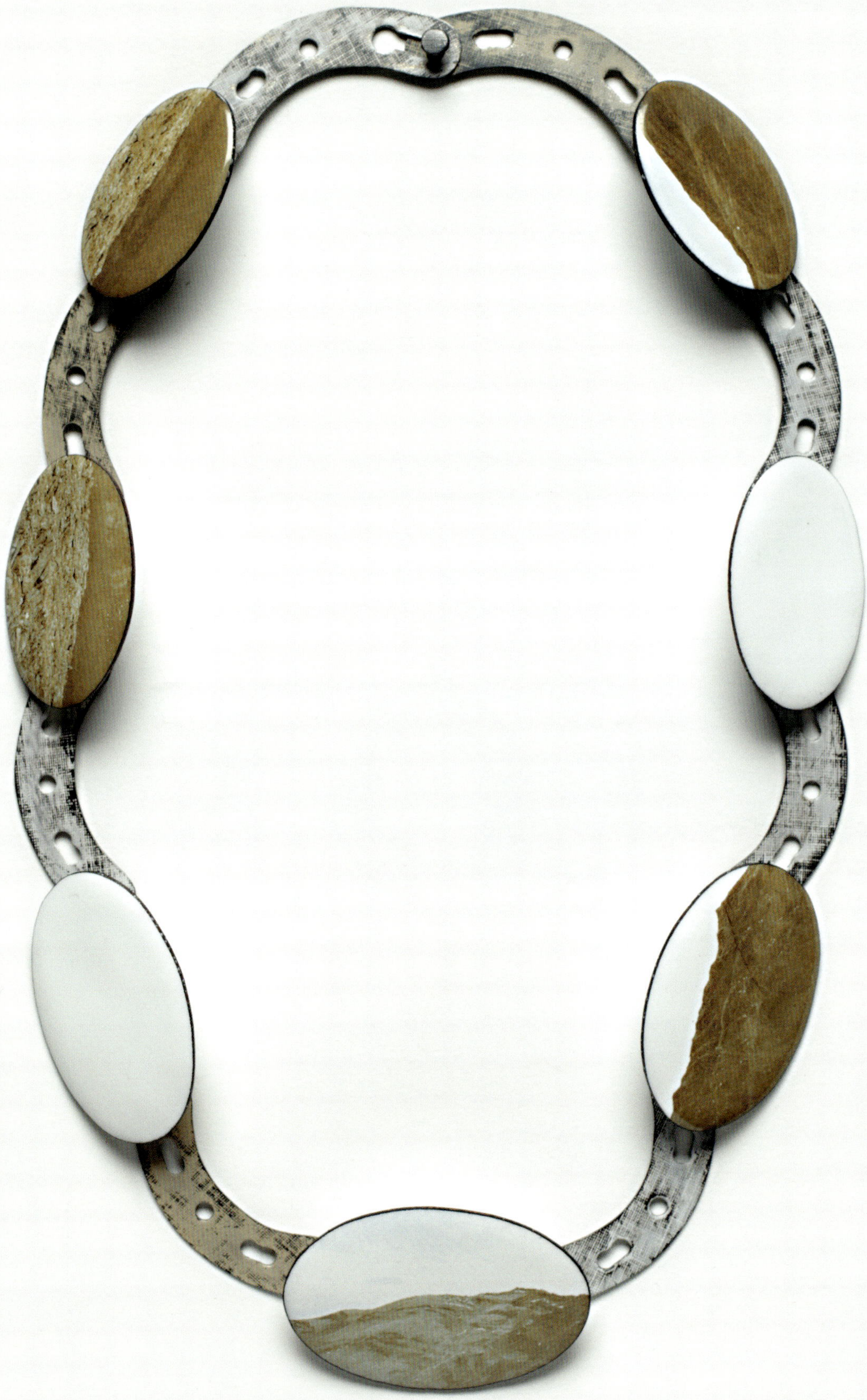

KIRSTEN HAYDON

Ice Valleys

79 OPPOSITE PAGE
Kirsten Haydon
Ice Valleys (neckpiece), 2011
Artist's analog photographs digitally altered and transferred onto enamel, silver, paint, copper
11 x 6 3/8 x 5/8 in. (28 x 16 x 1.5 cm)
Collection of the artist

BELOW
Artist's photograph taken in Antarctica.

The environment of Antarctica, both natural and constructed, provided me with a vantage point from which to consider how personal meaning and memory of place have presence in objects. The images in these pieces were taken in the field in 2004 when I was a New Zealand Antarctic Arts Fellow. These photographs and others have since informed my research into how the souvenir can represent and draw awareness to environments we risk losing. The pieces reference precious souvenir-making techniques and forms such as enameling, micro-mosaics, and painted miniatures in order to highlight Antarctica's significance culturally and environmentally.

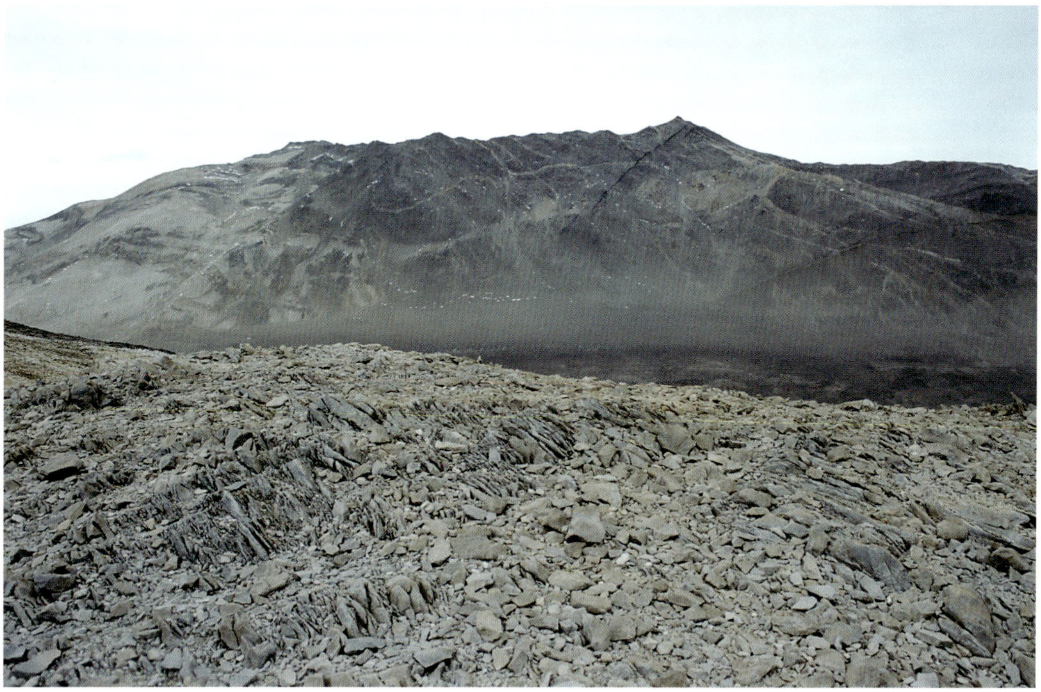

Ice Arrival | *Ice Airfield*

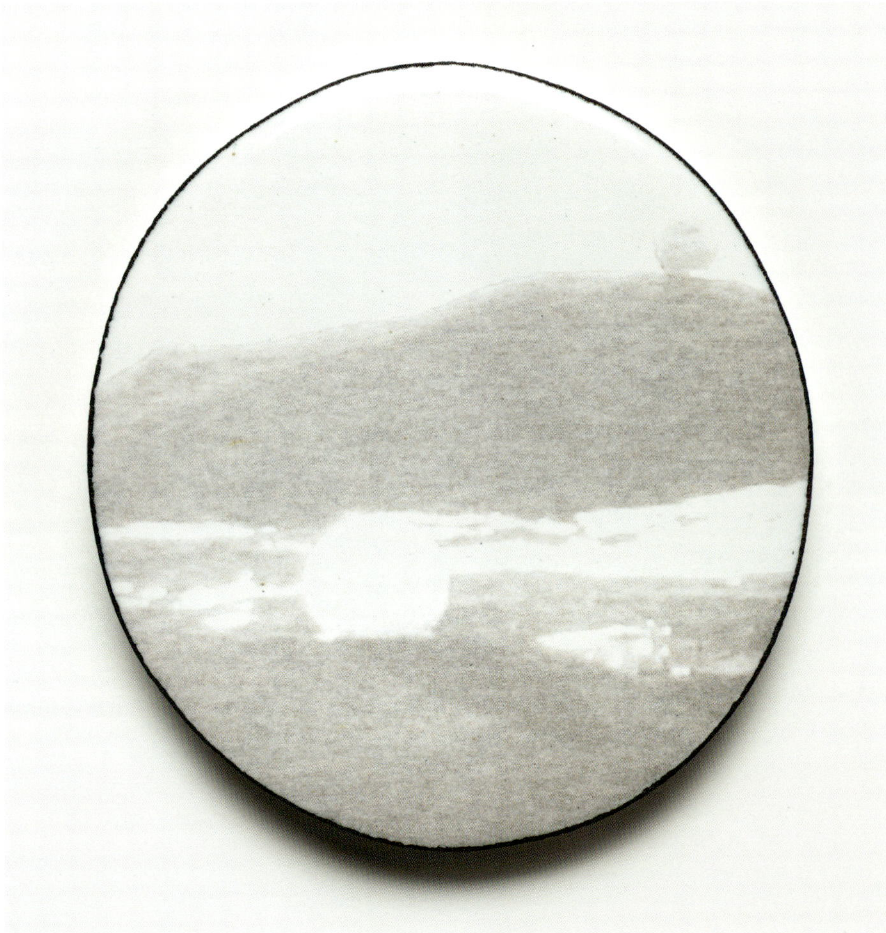

80 RIGHT

Kirsten Haydon
Ice Arrival (brooch), 2008
Artist's analog photograph digitally altered and transferred onto enamel, silver, copper, steel
2 7/8 x 2 5/8 x 5/8 in. (7.2 x 6.5 x 1.5 cm)
Collection of the artist

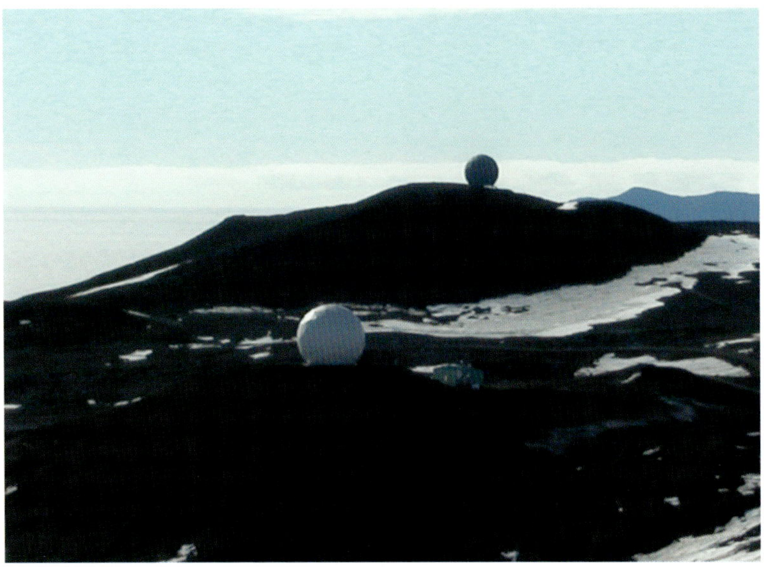

LEFT
Artist's photograph taken in Antarctica.

RIGHT

Artist's photograph taken in Antarctica.

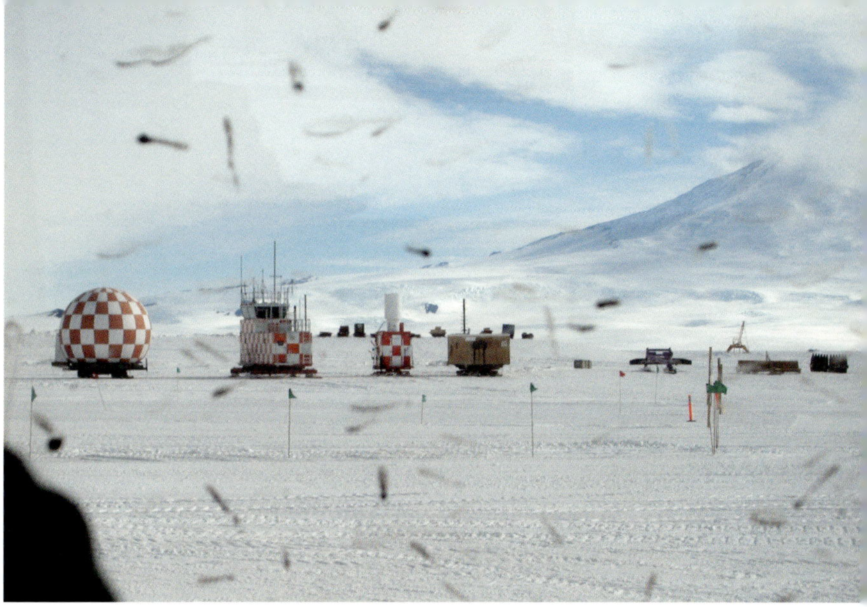

81 BELOW

Kirsten Haydon

Ice Airfield (brooch), 2008

Artist's analog photograph digitally altered and transferred onto enamel, copper, reflector beads, silver, steel

3 x 5 1/8 x 5/8 in. (7.5 x 13 x 1.5 cm)

Collection of the artist

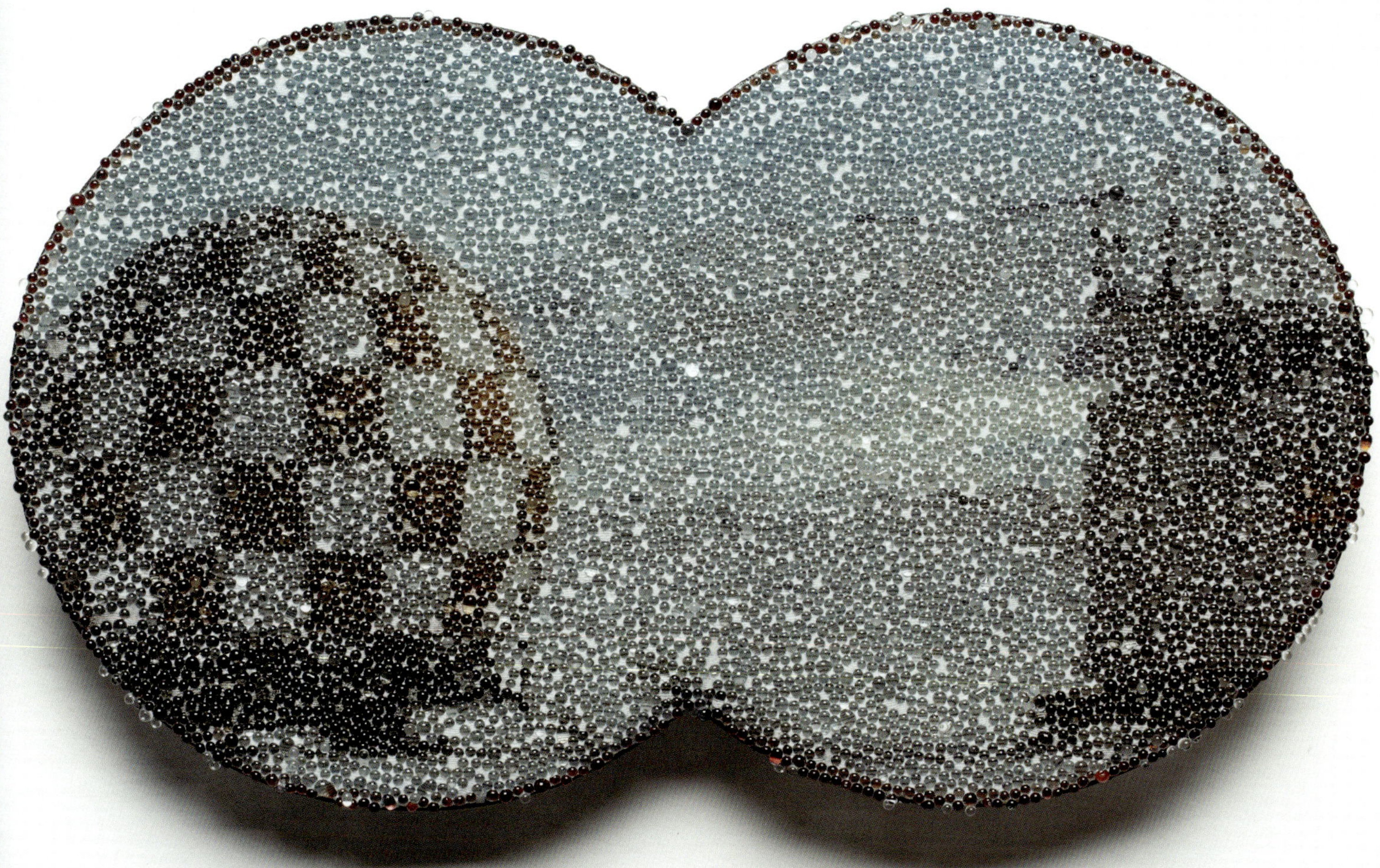

THOMAS GENTILLE

Untitled

I live in Manhattan. It is magical in its weather complexities. New Yorkers are so apt to complain about the weather they forget to see it. To great reward, I sometimes remember. This is a direct digital photograph. Nothing has been altered in any way.

82 LEFT
Thomas Gentille
Untitled (brooch), 21st century
Artist's digital photograph, acrylic, maple, mica, stainless steel, pigment
$5^{1}/_{2}$ x $2^{5}/_{8}$ x $^{3}/_{4}$ in. (14 x 6.5 x 2 cm)
Collection of the artist

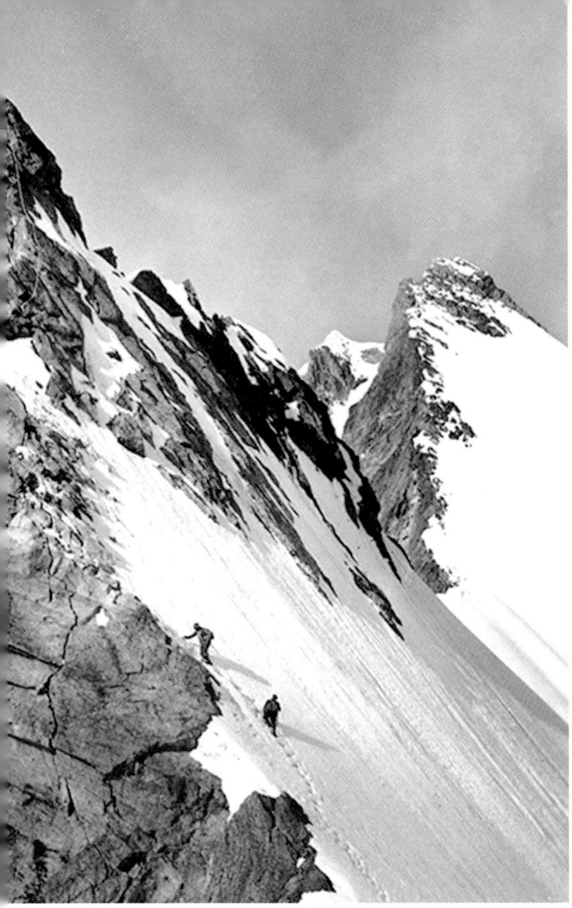

KIKO GIANOCCA

The Way Up

LEFT

Original photograph, 2006.

83 BELOW

Kiko Gianocca

The Way Up (brooch)

from the Never Been There series, 2010

Found analog photograph digitally printed on PVC, silver, polyurethane resin

$5^{1}/_{2}$ x $3^{3}/_{8}$ x $^{3}/_{8}$ in. (14 x 8.4 x 0.8 cm)

Collection of the artist

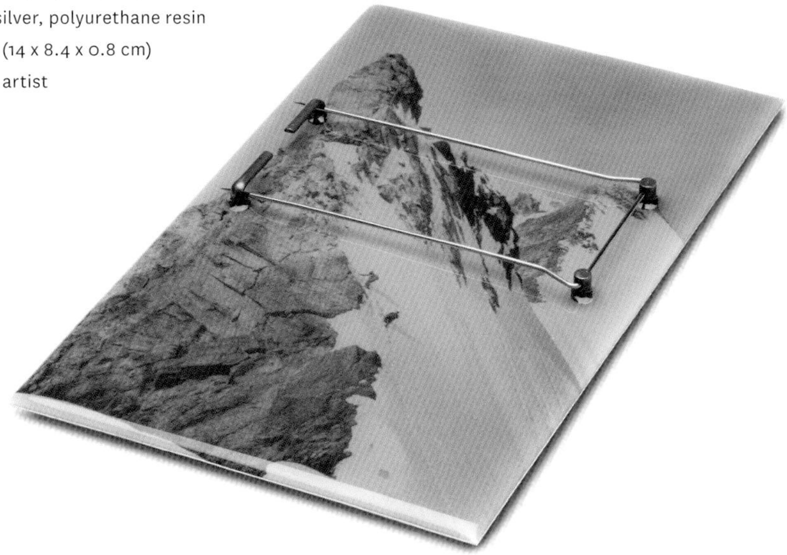

Found images, frequently old photographs that I have noticed at flea markets or that people sell on the Web, are the starting point for my brooches. I search for pictures that, from my perspective, have the power to enter the realm of an archetypal moment in time. I am curious about how memories are shared and the ways in which somebody's personal recollection can become the start of someone else's imagery.

For the pieces in the Never Been There series, I scanned old pictures and digitally printed them at the original size onto rigid PVC. Both sides of these brooches were then covered with resin. The blackened fronts of the brooches intentionally erase any information of what could be represented on the photos. The images, now the backs of the brooches, face the wearer's body, almost secretly attaching themselves to the new owners of these memories.

JANTJE FLEISCHHUT

Morgen | *Surmountable*

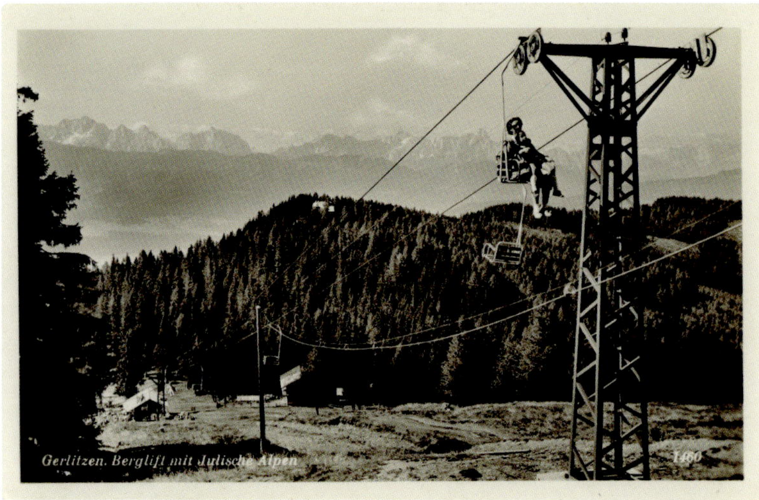

A brooch that tells a story. Drawings and photographs are encased between layers of transparent resin to produce a multilayered image. Light shines through this image because it is mounted on a mirror-finished sheet of gold. The word *Morgen* is cut out of the gold, which amplifies the associations, as do the two gemstones at the bottom. If the brooch is reversed, the viewer looks at his own reflection.

ABOVE
Vintage postcard.

84 RIGHT
Jantje Fleischhut
Morgen (brooch)
from the Dolomiten Sagen series, 2008
Digital silkscreen on foil, gold,
topaz, quartz, resin
$3^1/_2$ x $2^1/_2$ in. (8.9 x 6.4 cm)
Collection of Susan C. Beech

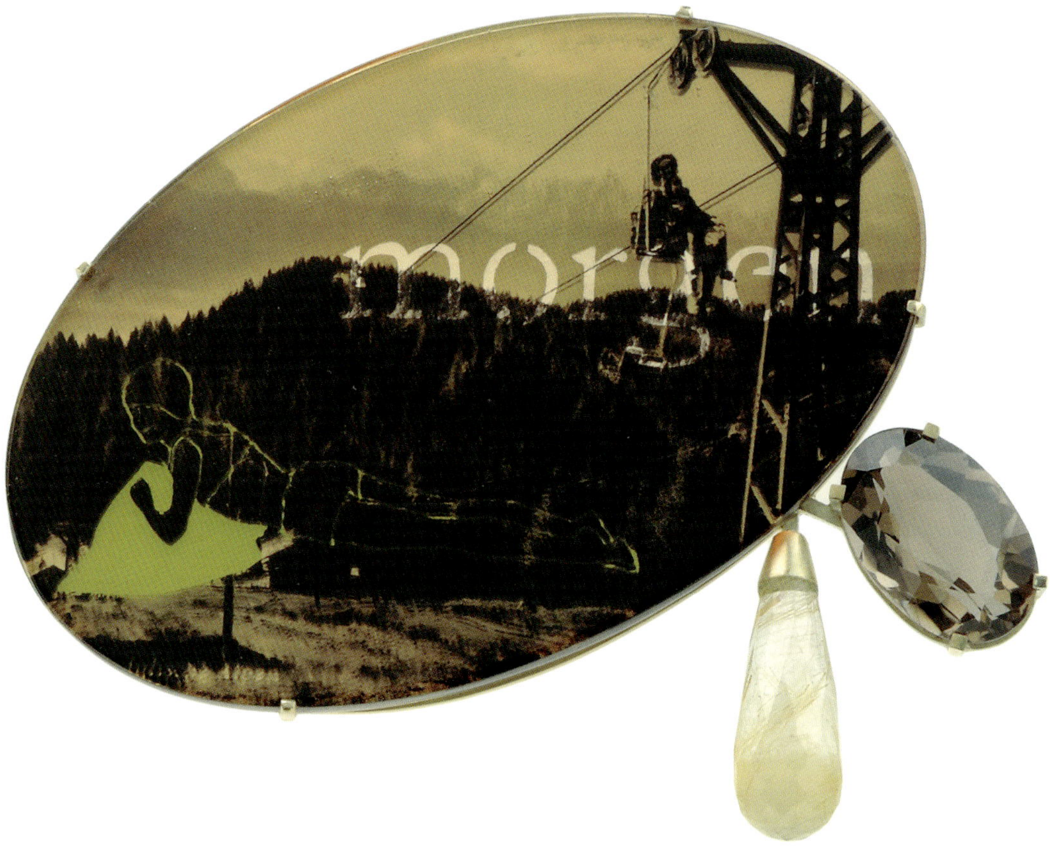

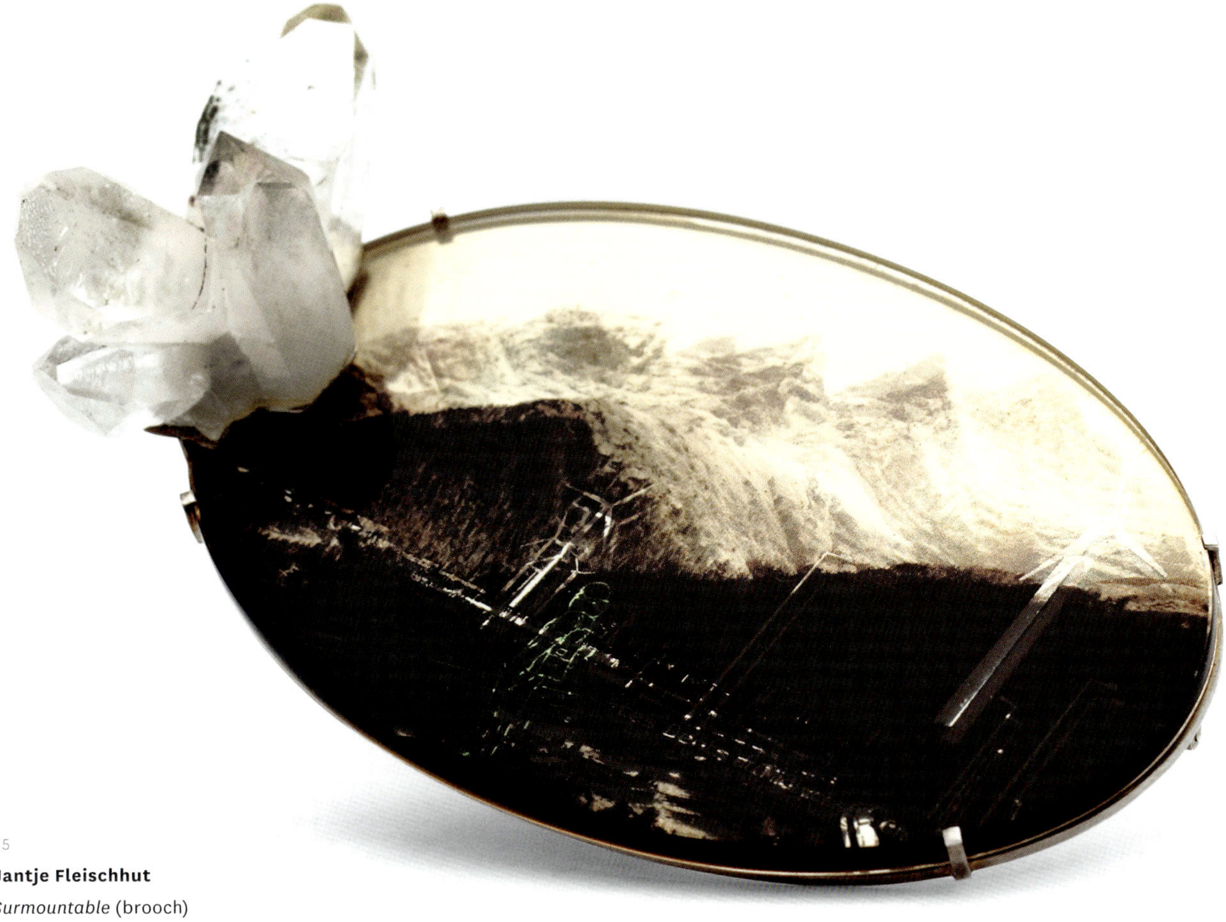

85

Jantje Fleischhut
Surmountable (brooch)
from the Dolomiten Sagen series, 2008
Digital silkscreen on foil, silver,
rock crystal, resin
$2^1/_2$ x $3^1/_2$ in. (6.4 x 8.9 cm)
Courtesy of Galerie Rob Koudijs

Another story about the Dolomites. Digital silkscreen allowed me to capture a legend of the "pale" mountains, as they were once known, in my favorite material: plastic. The original fairy tale spoke about a bright glistening moon shining in the dark night; about an aloof princess and the prince who loved her. Nowadays wind turbines, buildings, and highways dominate their world but behind the mountains the alluring shine of precious metal can still be perceived.

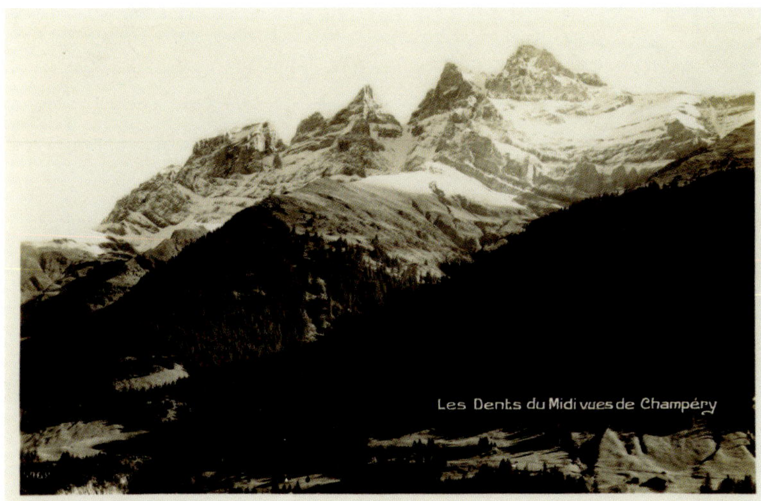

ABOVE
Vintage postcard.

SUSANNA KUSCHEK

Sichten II

The buildings on the brooches in the Sichten series are in Berlin. A good number of them were instrumental in shaping the appearance of the city; others, such as the one on this brooch, are simply ordinary but representative apartment buildings. They have no personal significance in my life but interest me because of their structural characteristics, their ornamental facades, and especially because of the daily life that I imagine took place in them.

I photographed the buildings myself and layered the images with resin. What appears as pure documentation has been altered to create and lay bare different memories and perceptions of the city. The brooches bring out a nice interplay between architecture and ornament and jewelry as ornament. Architecture is embellished by ornament and architectural ornament becomes body ornament.

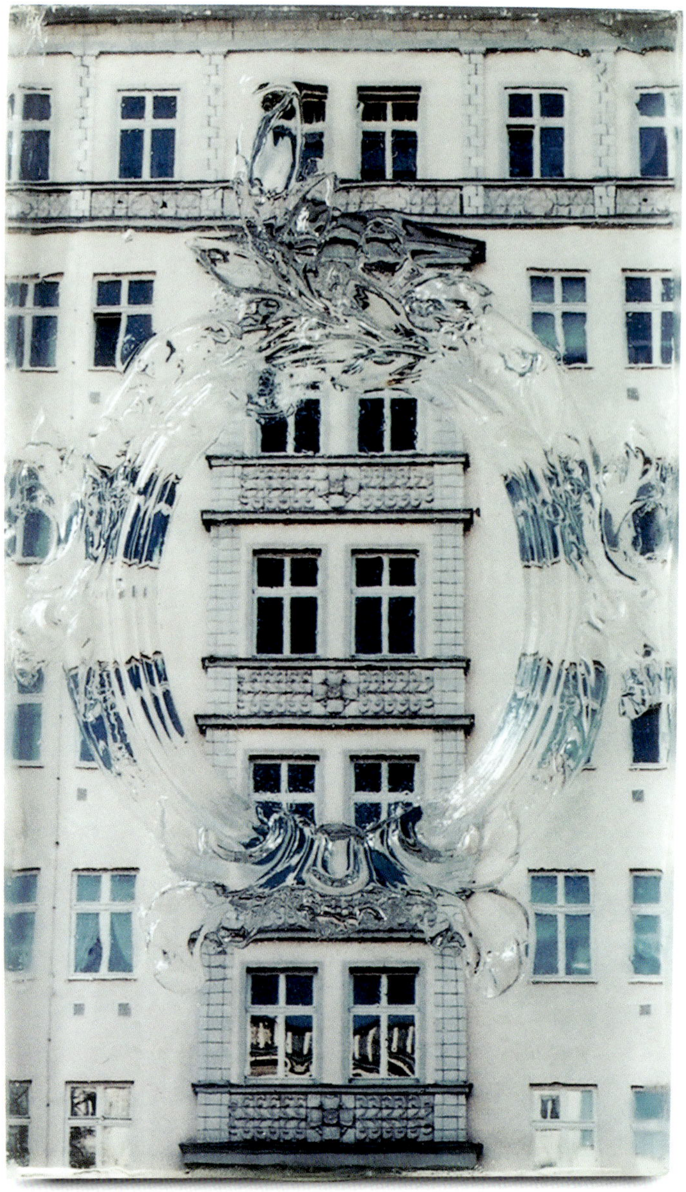

86
Susanna Kuschek
Sichten II (brooch)
from the Sichten series, 2002
Artist's analog photograph, silver, resin, acrylic, glass
$3^{3}/_{8}$ x $1^{7}/_{8}$ x $^{3}/_{8}$ in. (8.6 x 4.8 x 1 cm)
Collection of the artist

ELEANOR MOTY

Reflected Schoolhouse

The image for this brooch was taken from a glass negative of a nineteenth-century prairie schoolhouse in Dodge City, Kansas, with the students and teacher standing in front of the building. Elements and materials were combined to enhance and enrich the photo image. A halftone transparency was used to create the nickel-silver photo-etched image for the brooch, and a piece of phantom amethyst and a tourmaline crystal were selected to "reflect" the roof line of the building.

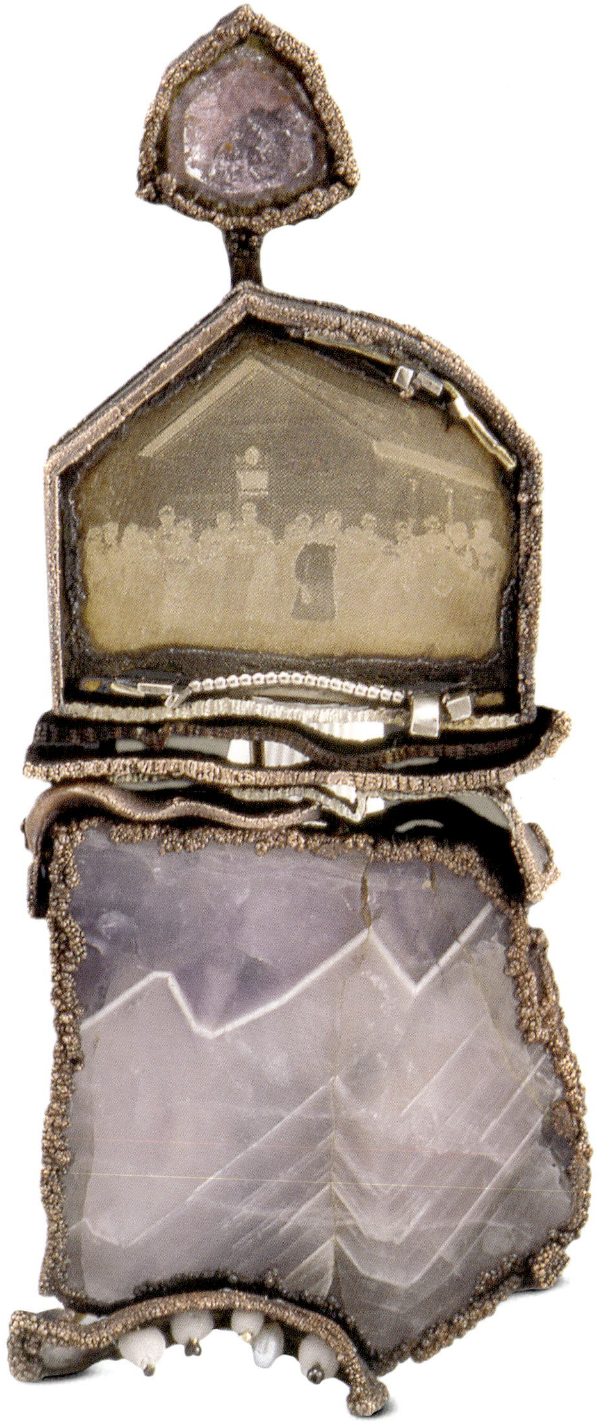

87

Eleanor Moty
Reflected Schoolhouse (brooch), 1970
Vintage glass negative photo-etched on nickel-silver, gold, sterling silver, bronze, electroformed copper, phantom amethyst, tourmaline, pearl, porcelain beads
$5^{1}/_{4}$ x $2^{1}/_{4}$ x 1 in. (13.3 x 5.7 x 2.5 cm)
Courtesy of Tyler School of Art, Temple University, Philadelphia, Pennsylvania

KARA ROSS

Transformations

Hudson Yards is a twenty-six-acre stretch of property on the West Side of Manhattan that has served for years as an exposed train storage and maintenance yard but is now being redeveloped to serve twenty-first-century interests and needs. My necklace seeks to mirror this transformation and growth. It was created from hand-carved and polished geometric pieces of concrete debris from a building formerly located on the site. These concrete pieces are held together in a manner similar to the way in which train cars are linked. Black-and-white images in sterling silver frames show the railroad yards as they existed, the debris from demolition, and renderings of buildings that are soon to come. Black diamonds and white sapphires indicate the anticipated splendor. Transformation and growth are what New York City is all about, and my necklace mirrors this process.

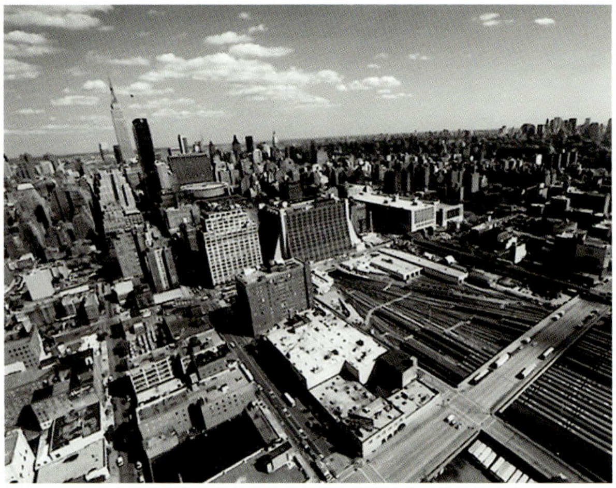

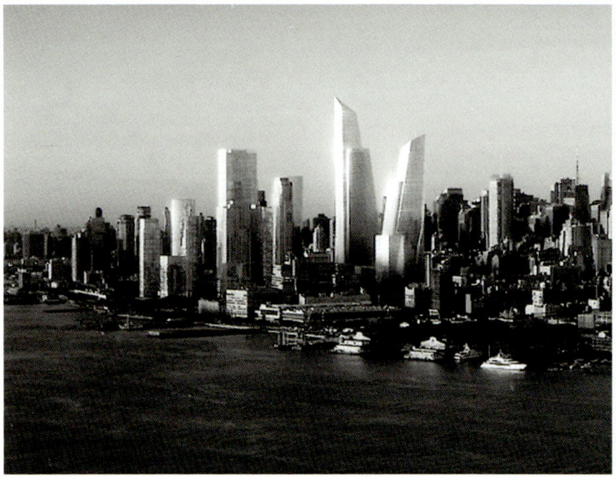

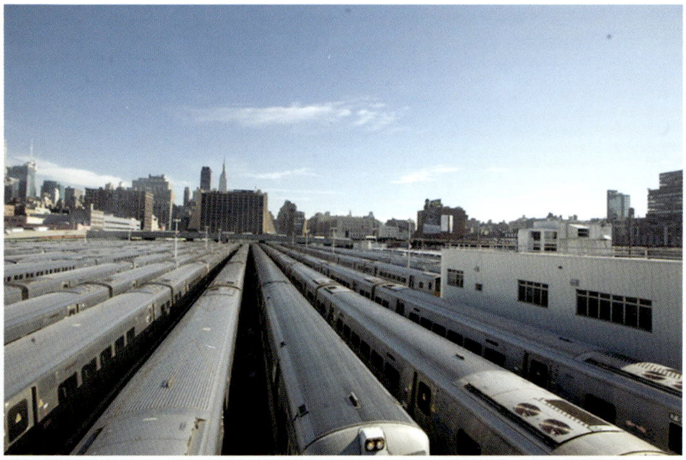

ABOVE AND RIGHT

Artist's source images of the Hudson Yards development project.

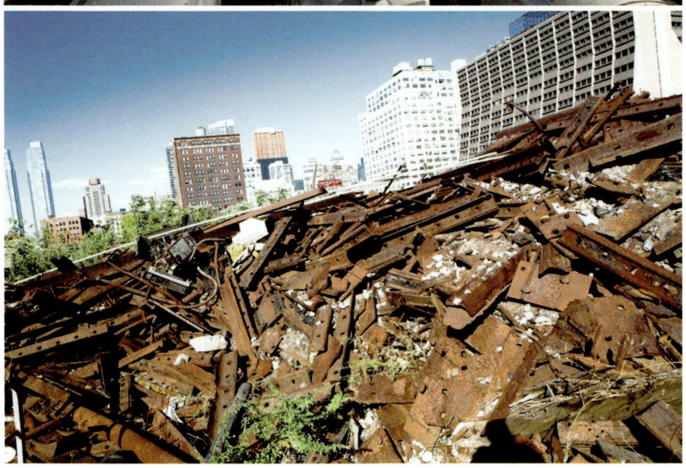

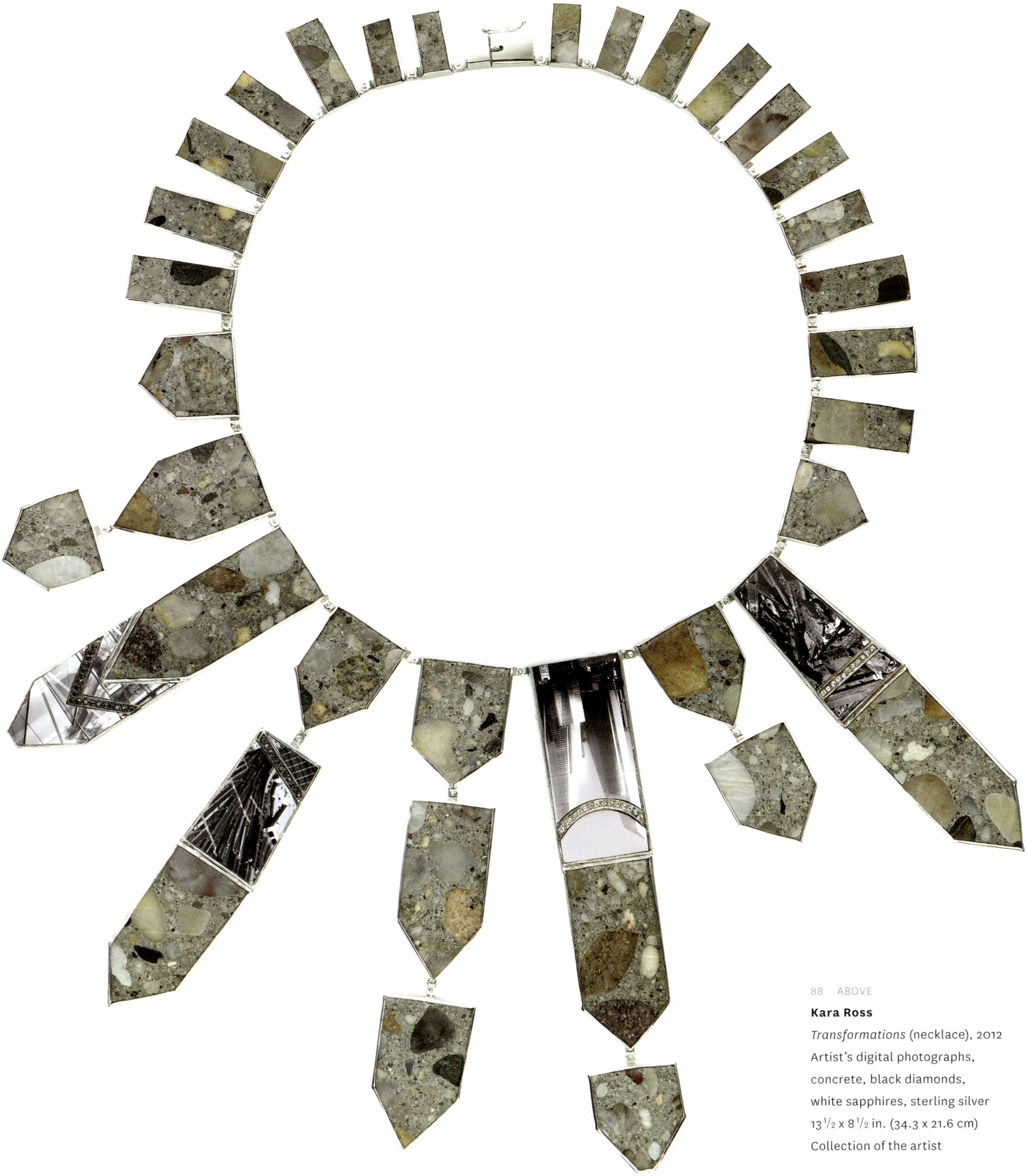

88 ABOVE

Kara Ross
Transformations (necklace), 2012
Artist's digital photographs, concrete, black diamonds, white sapphires, sterling silver
$13\frac{1}{2}$ x $8\frac{1}{2}$ in. (34.3 x 21.6 cm)
Collection of the artist

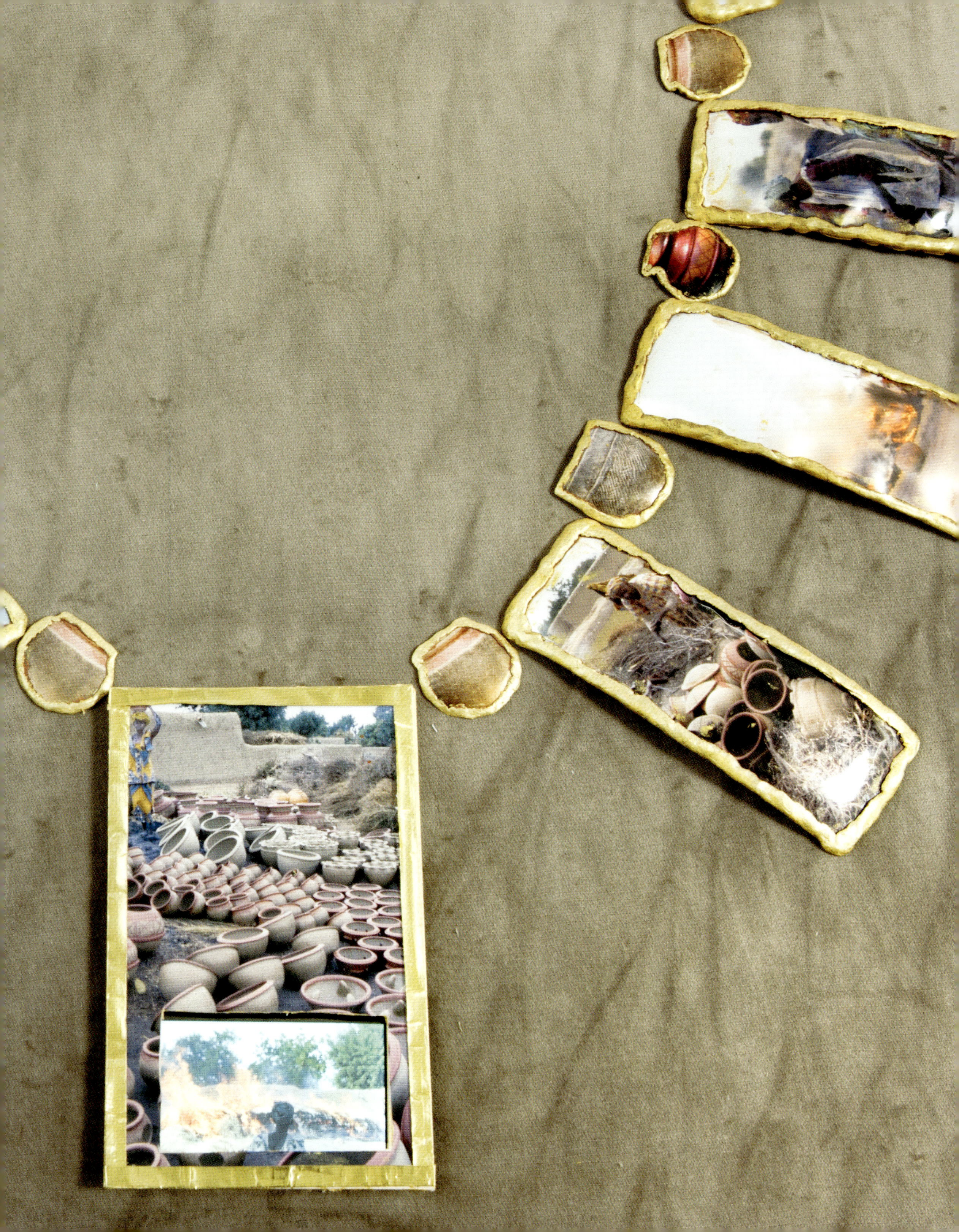

JANET GOLDNER

Wealth in Africa

Wealth in Africa is a mixed-media sculpture in the form of a necklace. In this work, I use photographs, video, and sound I recorded in Kalabougou, a village in Mali where I lived and conducted research for several months. This work pays homage to the renowned women potters, upholders of a long tradition of skill, resilience, and humanity. Inspired by my long connection to the continent, *Wealth in Africa* highlights the richness of Africa—the people and their cultures.

89

Janet Goldner

Wealth in Africa (mixed media sculpture), 2013

3-minute video with sound, artist's photographs, mixed media, velvet

10 x 32 x 40 in. (25 x 81.3 x 101.6 cm)

Collection of the artist

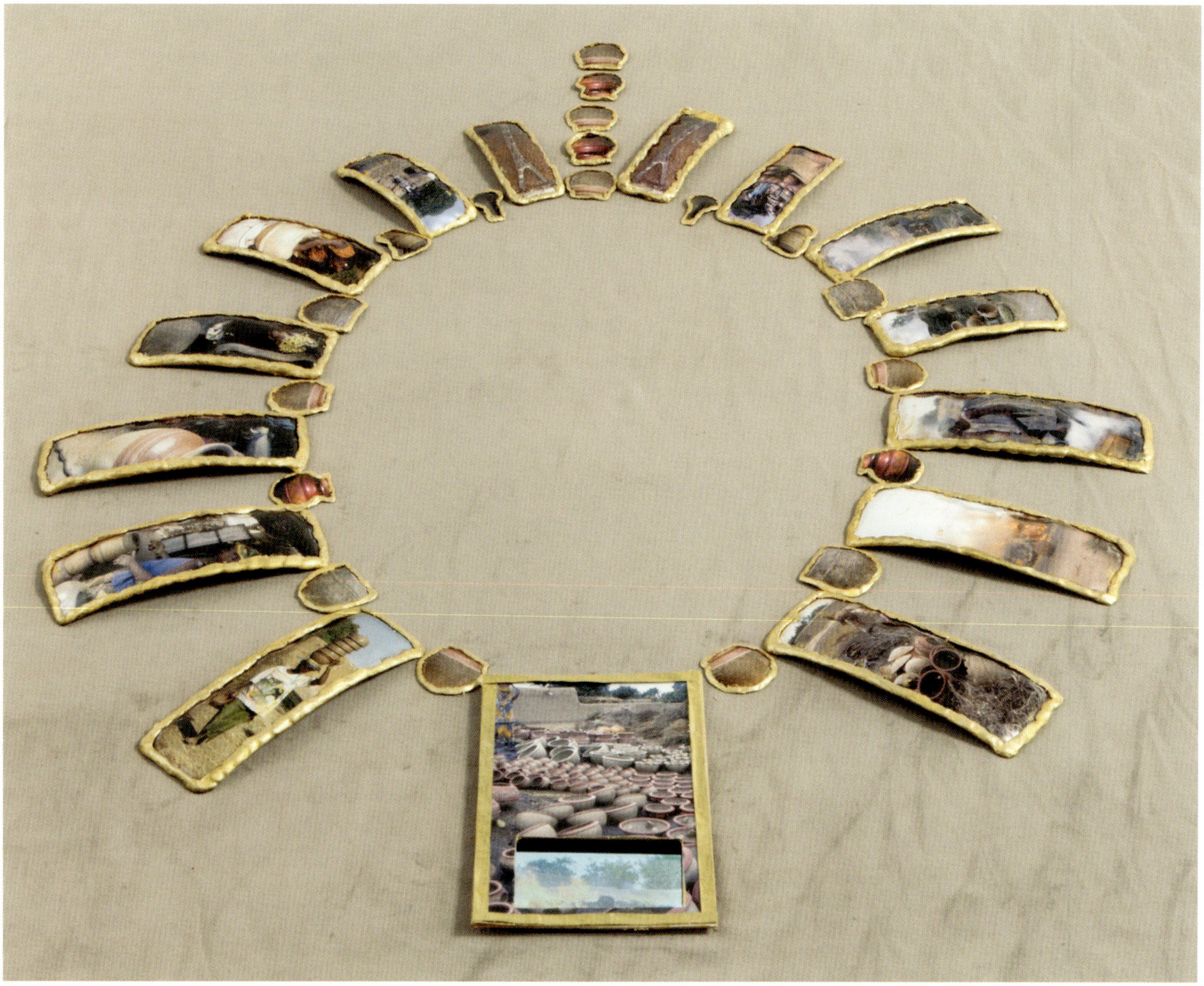

SOOYEON KIM

House on Benefit Street

I explore the experiences that memories are made of through the lenses of my eyes and camera and through my computer, and in the course of my investigation my memories are transformed into spatial forms.

My paper ornaments emerge through the digital and physical manipulation of photographs of places I have visited. The process requires hand cutting, duplicating printed images, and repeatedly tracing the outlines of my memory until the white space on paper acquires its own identity. The experiences become tattoos on my mind, and the spaces where images are absent yield to the imagination's discovery of the hidden and unknown.

The house that is memorialized in this neckpiece is in Providence, Rhode Island, where I once lived. Benefit Street was special to me because of its beautiful Colonial homes. One day when I was passing by, I noticed a tiny loft atop one of the houses. I drew a picture of an intimate moment, which is captured in my neckpiece. Thinking of Benefit Street makes me nostalgic for the moments I spent there with loved ones and for my school days. It evokes pleasant and sad memories.

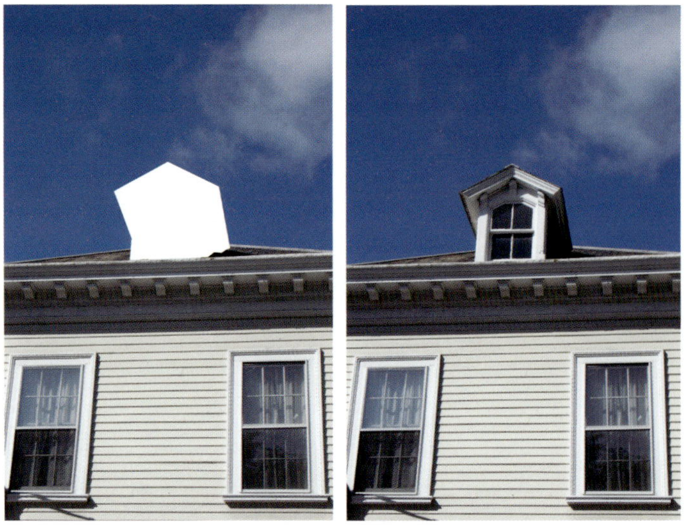

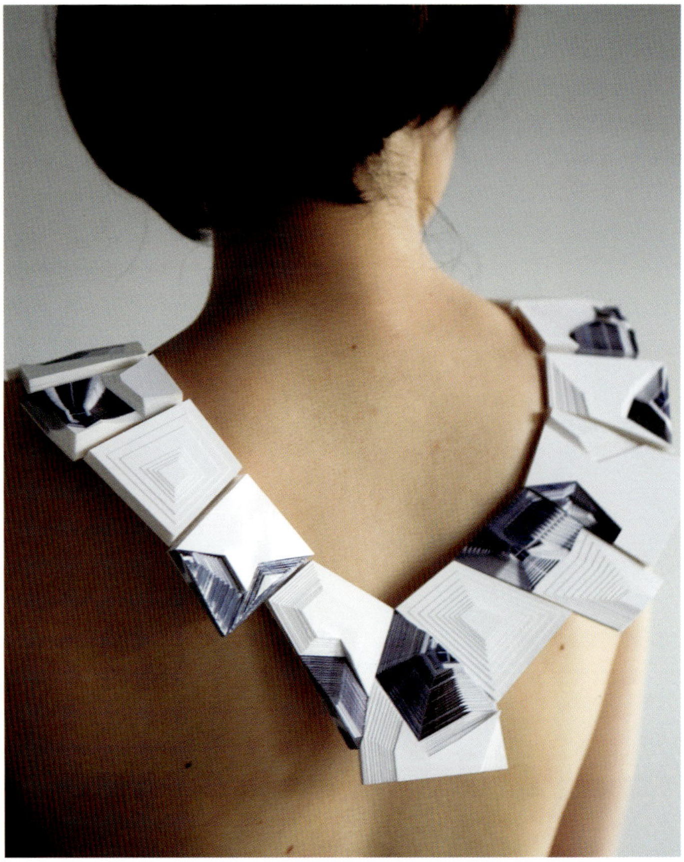

ABOVE
Artist's original photographs.

90

Sooyeon Kim
House on Benefit Street (neckpiece), 2010
Artist's digital photographs on
paper, fabric, magnets
12 x 12 x 1/4 in. (30.5 x 30.5 x 0.6 cm)
Collection of the artist

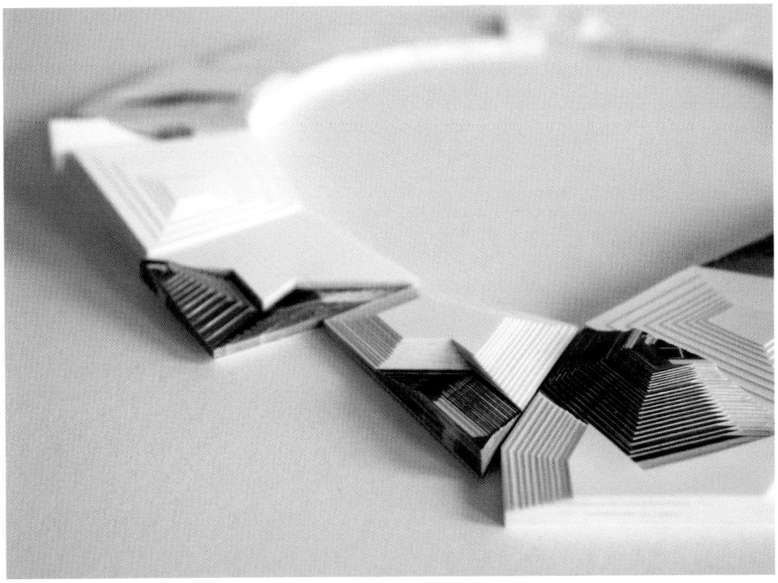

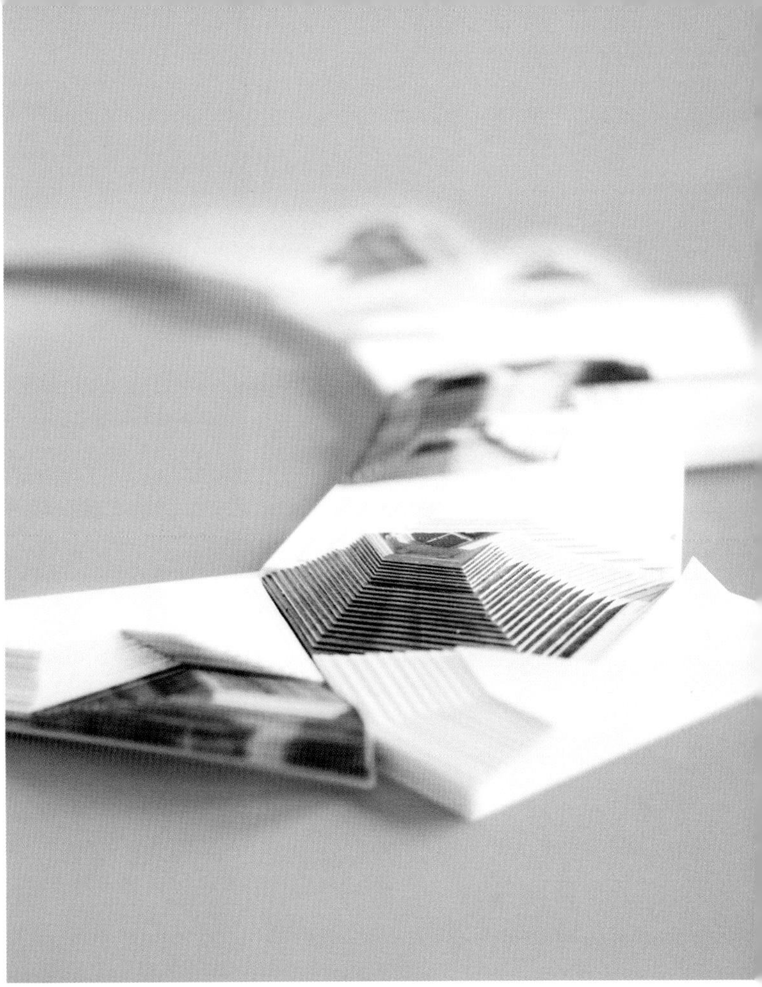

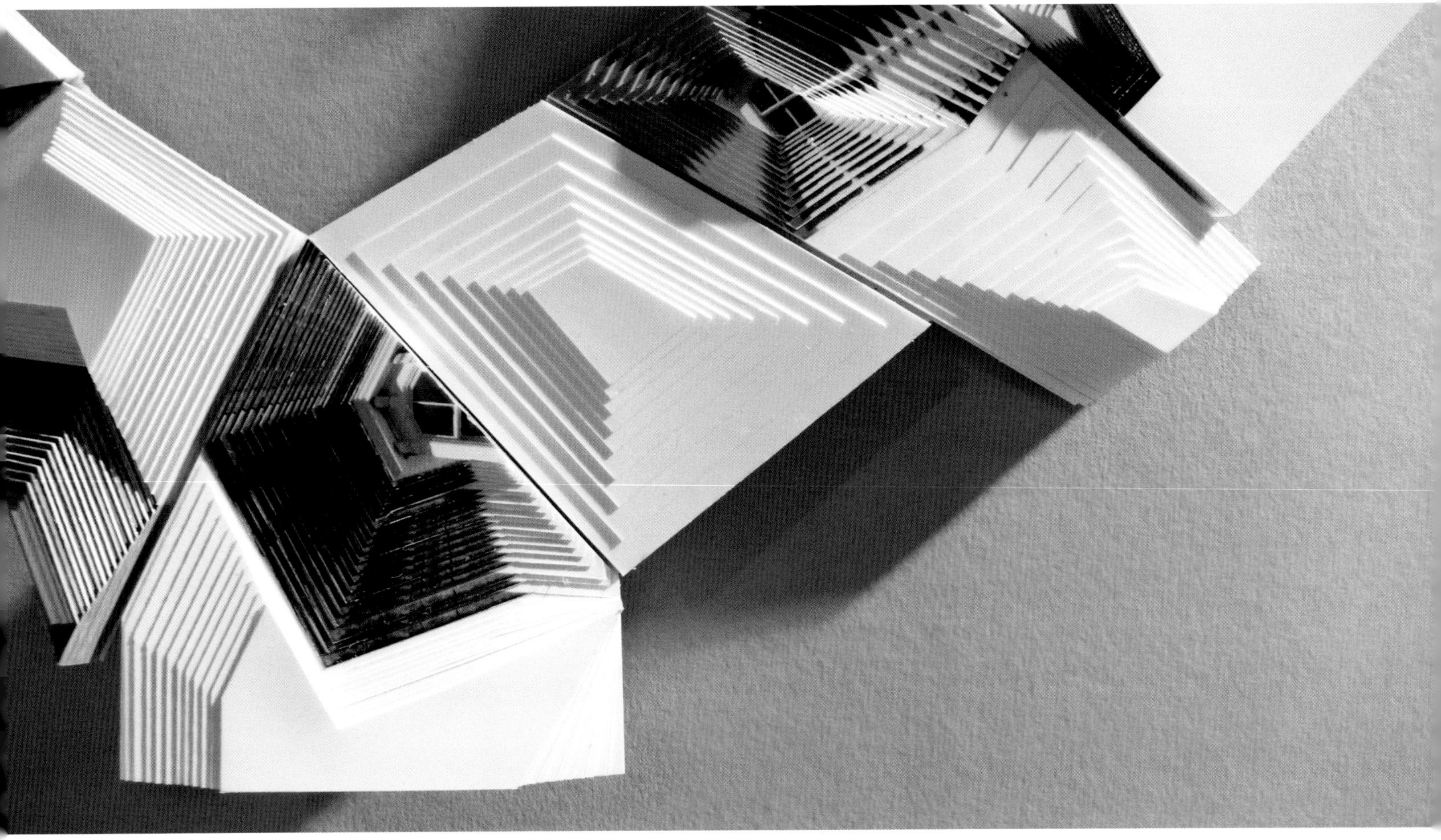

CRAIG ARNOLD

Corrosion Brooches

As a photographer and jeweler, I have long been interested in the concept of what is beautiful, useful, and image-worthy. Many "ugly," unwanted objects have fascinating details when scrutinized closely. Looking at twisted, damaged metal in a junkyard, I couldn't help but be drawn to the fascinating patina that age and corrosion had produced on the once-functional objects discarded there. My photographs of the metal, and the brooches made with these images, are concise statements concerning the finite nature of our constructions and the inevitability of decay. The idea that the detritus of our industrial age can be inspiration for objects of adornment is a central theme in my work.

91
Craig Arnold
Corrosion Brooches, 2010
Color negative film reproduced on sublimated steel backed with camera leather, magnetic clasp
$1\frac{1}{2}$ x $1\frac{1}{2}$ in. (3.8 x 3.8 cm), each
Collection of the artist

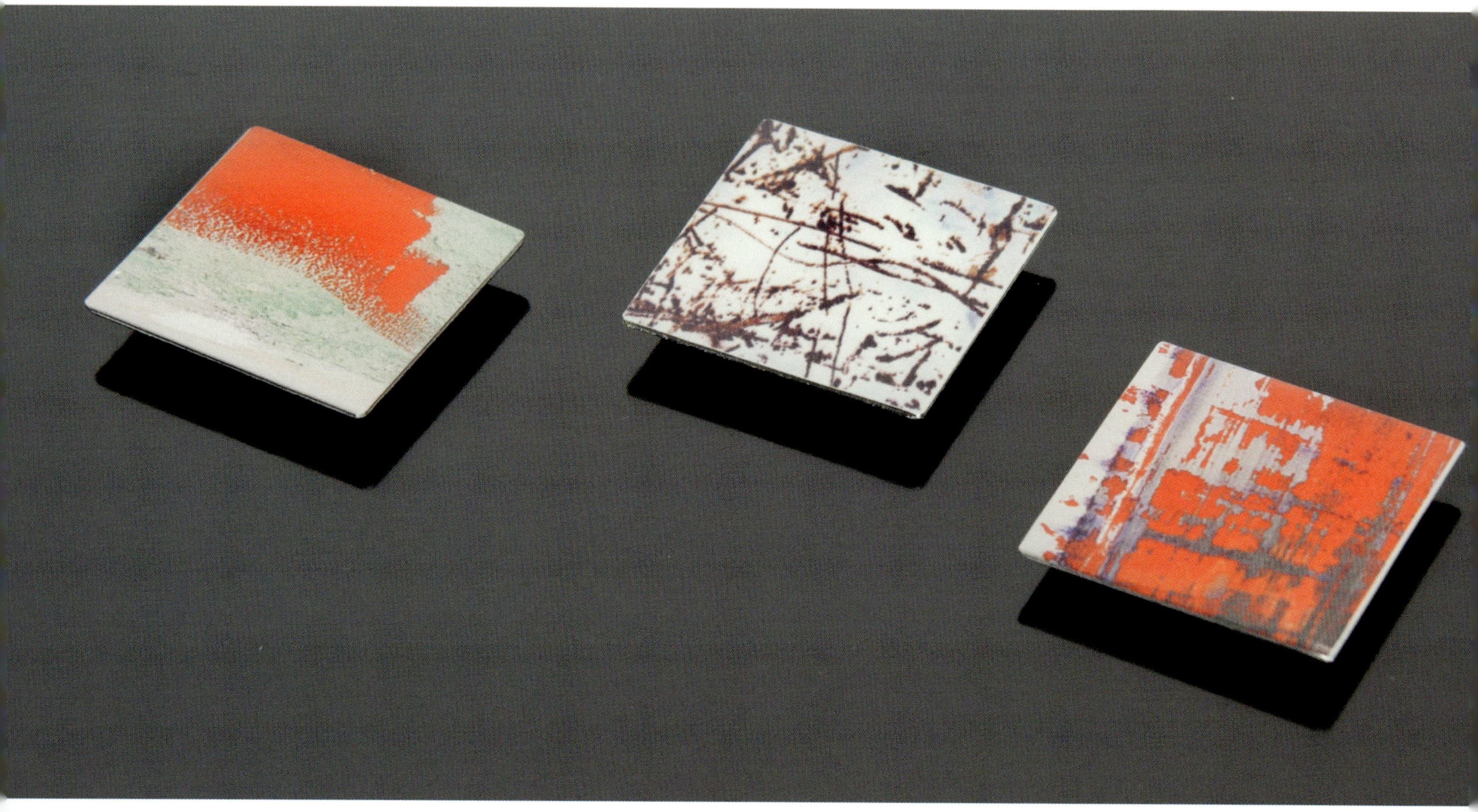

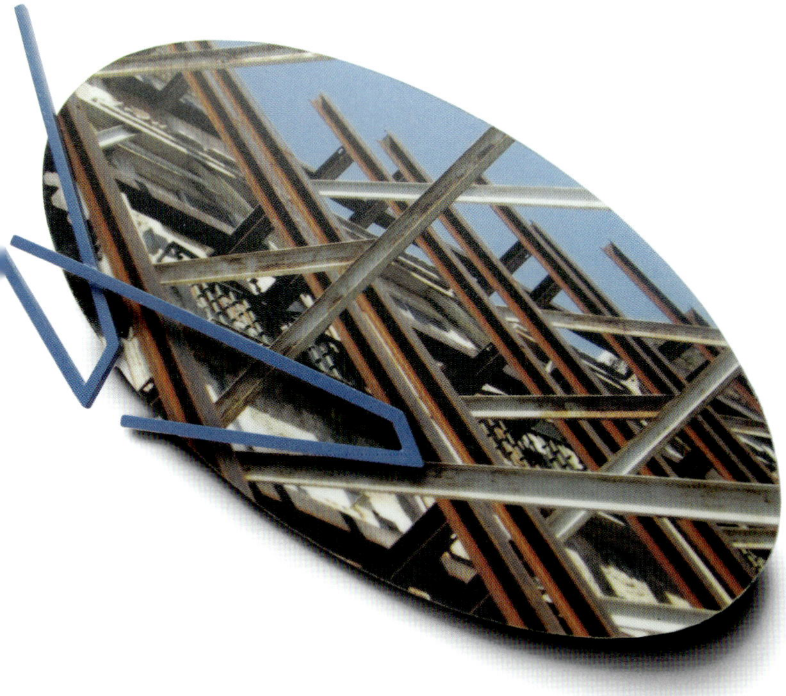

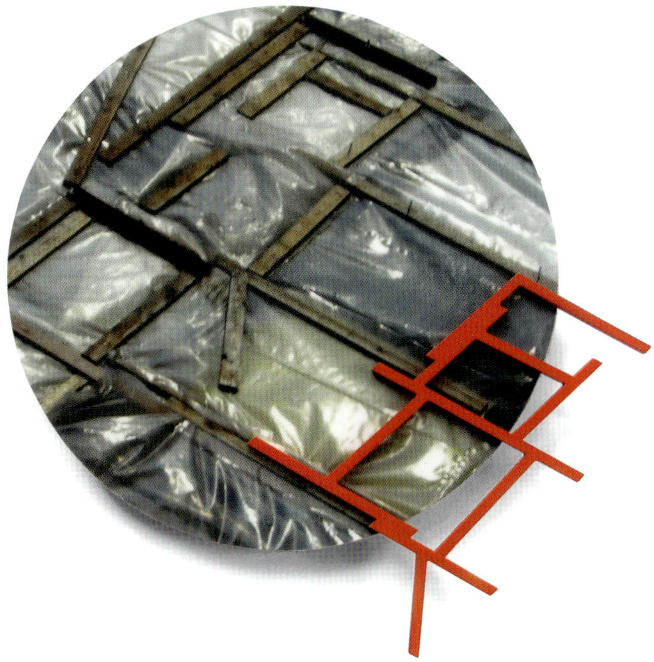

MARGIT HART

Brooch | *Brooch*

The digital photos in these brooches depict buildings in Lisbon and Belfast. My interest goes beyond merely capturing something as a memory. The oval and round crops convert the scaffoldings into semi-abstract designs, a transformation that is emphasized through the addition of silver elements on the surfaces of the pieces. The memory of the real space might still be retained in the brooch, but through changes in size and scale, realities become indistinct, turn into something new, and give space for a variety of novel and unexpected connotations, especially as the brooches are worn in different surroundings.

92 ABOVE LEFT
Margit Hart
Brooch, 2011
Artist's digital photograph on Dibond®, silver, paint
6 1/8 x 3 x 1/2 in. (15.5 x 7.5 x 1.2 cm)
Collection of the artist

93 ABOVE RIGHT
Margit Hart
Brooch, 2011
Artist's digital photograph on Dibond®, silver, paint
4 3/4 x 4 3/8 x 1/2 in. (12 x 11 x 1.2 cm)
Collection of the artist

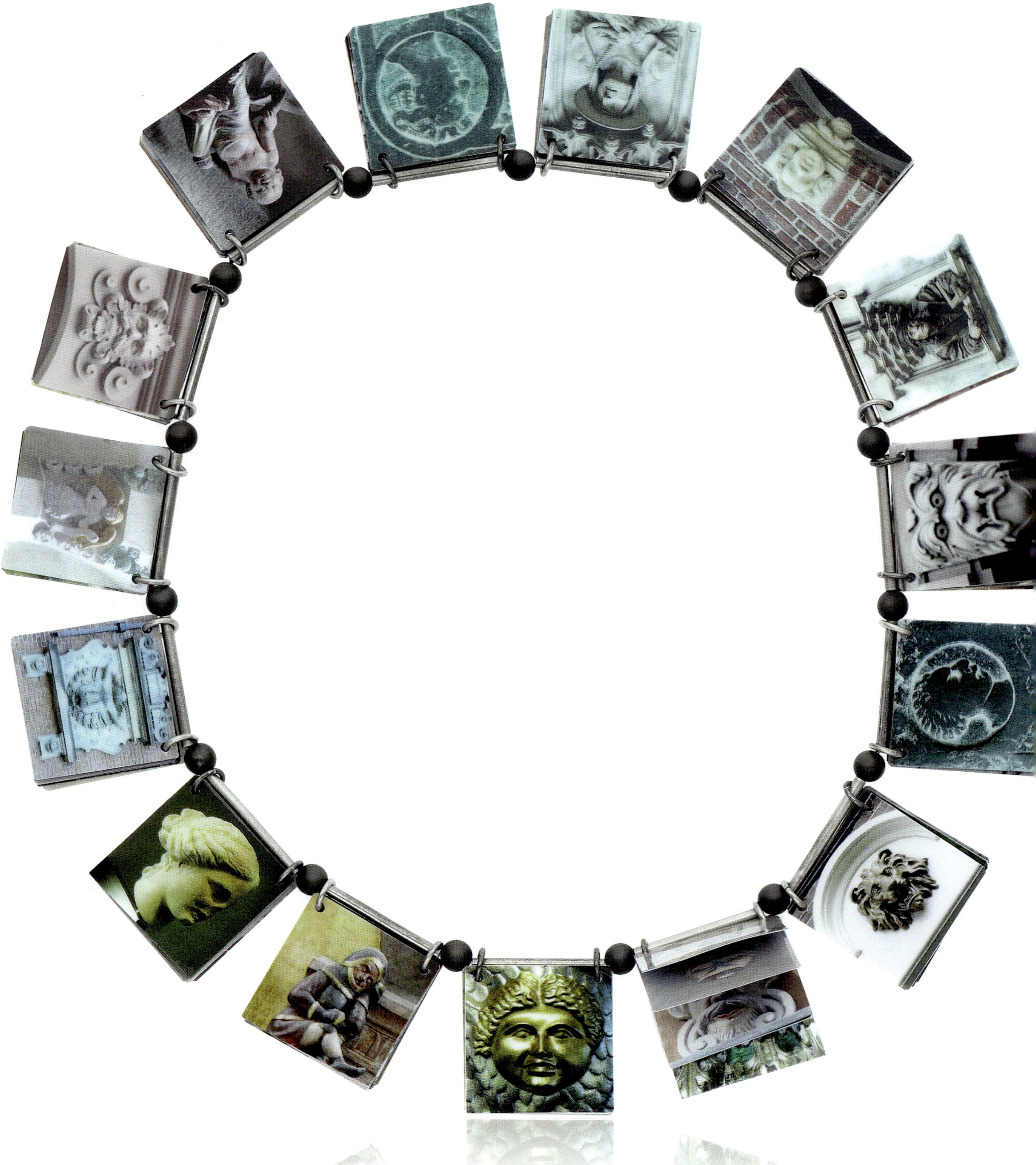

HERMAN HERMSEN

Booklets

The design concept for this necklace goes back to 1997, when I decided to develop a variable piece of jewelry that could be changed and worn with different combinations of images. Out of an immense collection of photos that I took of decorative reliefs on buildings all over Europe, I made a selection of seventy-five images and mixed and ordered them into the fifteen small five-page booklets that form the necklace. Turning the pages of the books results in different expressions of the necklace. I made several necklaces based on this idea, with each necklace having a unique selection of images and expressing its own theme. Among the many views offered in this necklace are a hotel in the center of Erfurt, Germany; the cathedral in Lisbon, Portugal; the town halls in Arnhem and Bolsward, The Netherlands; and a bank building in Helsinki, Finland.

94 OPPOSITE PAGE AND BELOW
Herman Hermsen
Booklets (necklace), 2011
Artist's digital photographs
laser-printed on paper, laminated PVC
8 3/4 in. (22 cm), diameter
1 1/2 x 1 1/2 in. (3.8 x 3.8 cm), each booklet
The Olnick Spanu Collection, New York

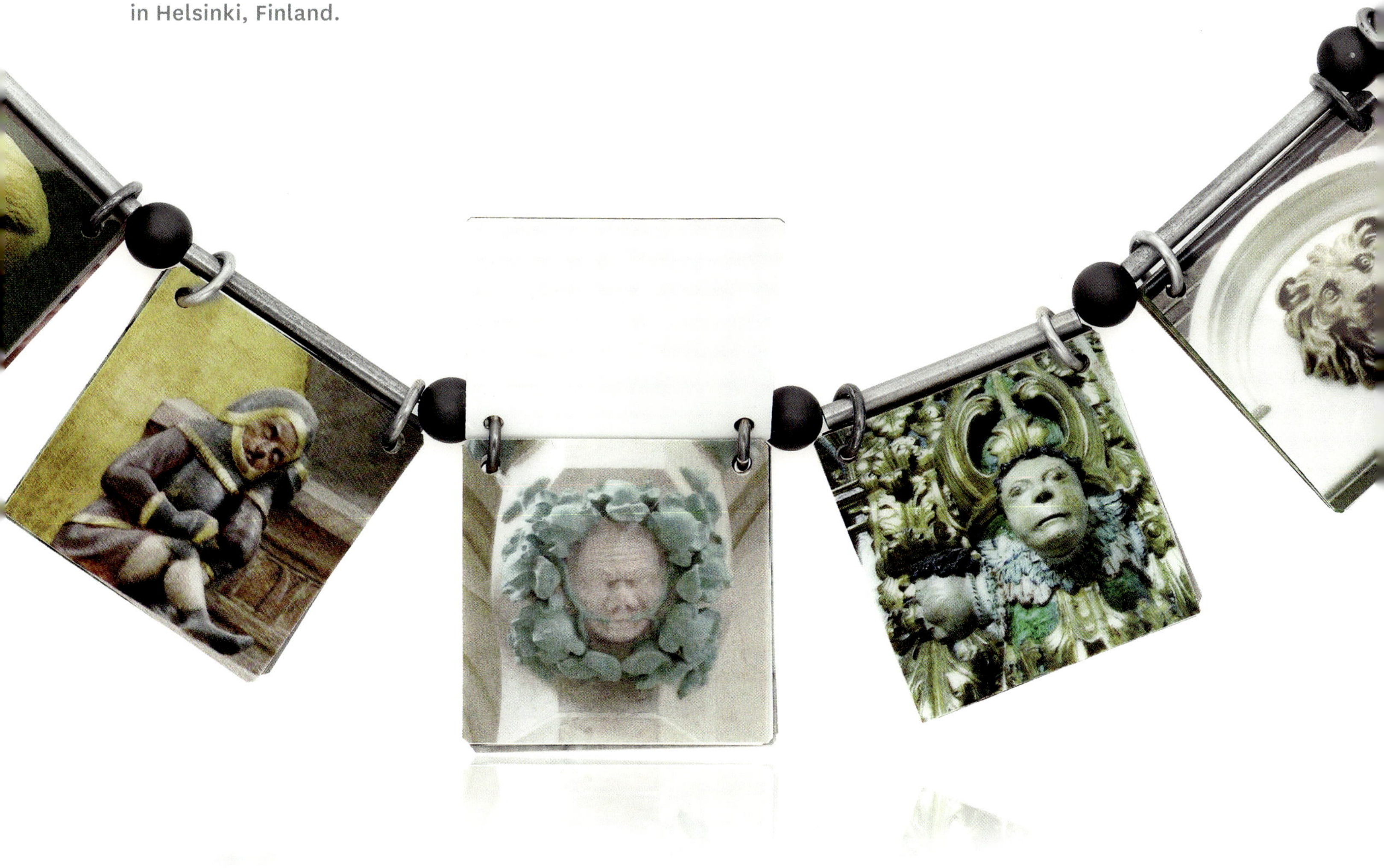

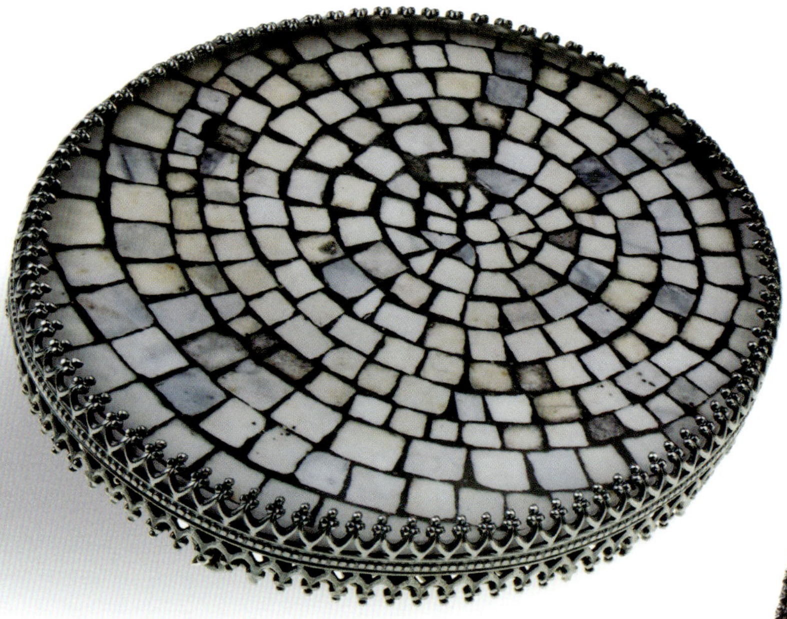

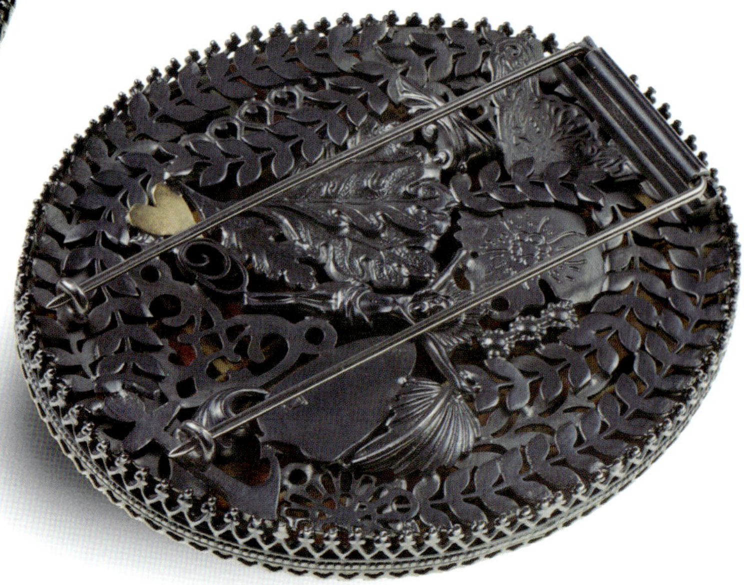

REBECCA HANNON

Cobblestone

When I first arrived in Munich, I biked around like a madwoman, taking pictures of all the new things I was seeing. Inside some of the churches, however, photo exhibitions documenting the destruction and reconstruction of buildings in the city told a different story. Back in my workshop, I sat with double prints of my photos, cutting them and forming collages to see what they might become. Deconstruction and reconstruction of the photos is a good metaphor for the deconstruction/reconstruction that has taken place in Germany itself. The images are encased between pieces of Plexiglas and held in a prong setting just as a traditional gemstone would be. Oftentimes these brooches hide a private message only the wearer knows about, and holds close to her heart.

95
Rebecca Hannon
Cobblestone (brooch), 2005
Artist's digital photograph, gold, silver, Plexiglas
$1\frac{1}{2} \times 2 \times \frac{1}{2}$ in. (3.8 x 5.1 x 1.3 cm)
Collection of the artist

LEFT: Front
RIGHT: Back

SUZANNE BEAUTYMAN

Interior Blinds

The deteriorated architectural forms in my Opulent Boarders brooches belie jewelry's historical function as adornment as well as its traditional association with wealth. Exploring the folded forms of my brooches reveals faded and worn surfaces from a forgotten past.

The images for these pieces were shot digitally while I was exploring abandoned homes and industrial sites in and around Detroit, Michigan. They were distorted or augmented using digital software and applied to enameled steel brooch forms as ceramic decals.

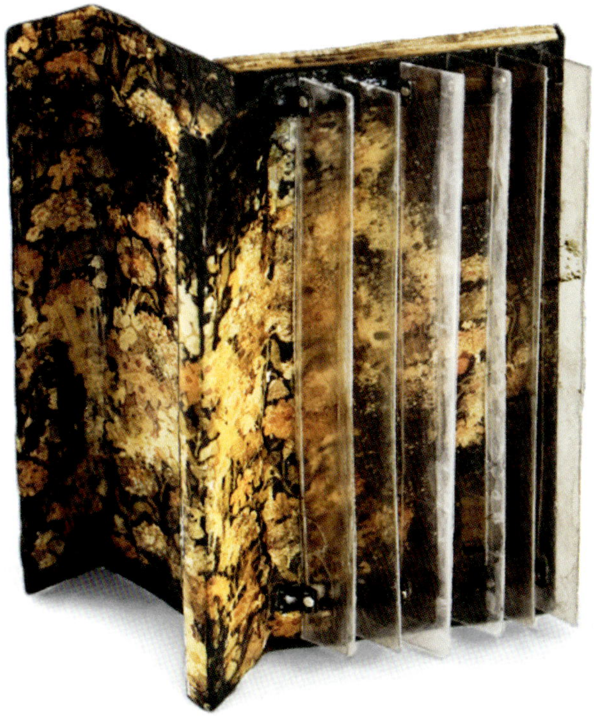

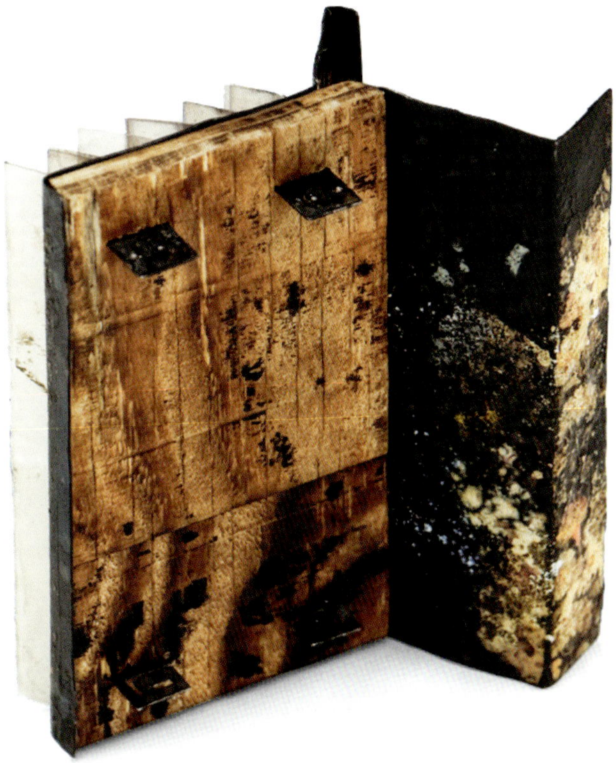

96 TOP (FRONT) AND RIGHT (BACK)
Suzanne Beautyman
Interior Blinds (brooch)
from the Opulent Boarders series, 2010
Artist's digital photographs printed on decals, enamel, silver, iron, mica
4 x 4 x 1½ in. (10.2 x 10.2 x 3.8 cm)
Collection of the artist

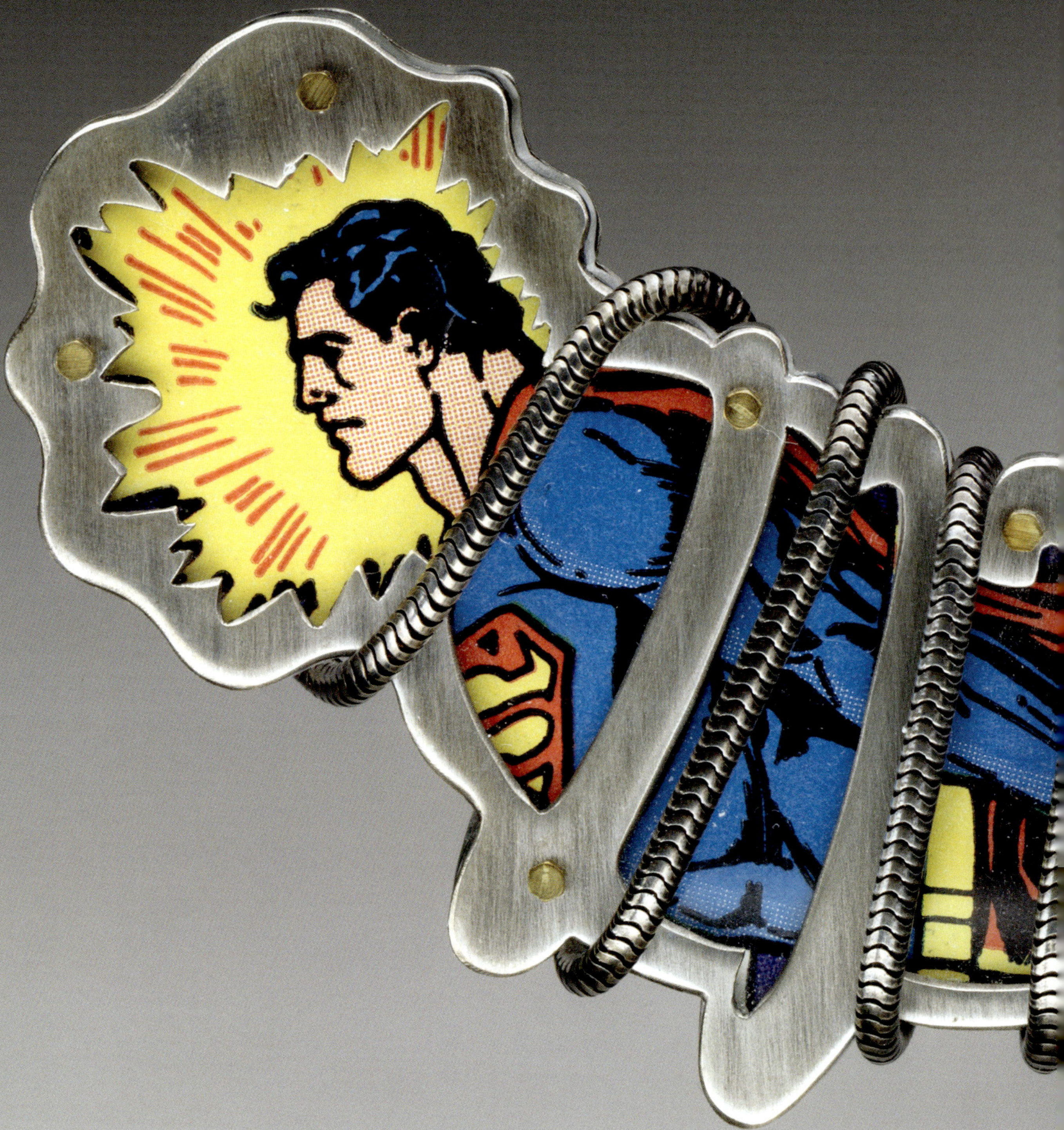

"...THEY IMPROVE UPON, EMBELLISH, RIDICULE, SATIRIZE, AND PAY HOMAGE TO OTHER ARTISTS' IDEAS ..."

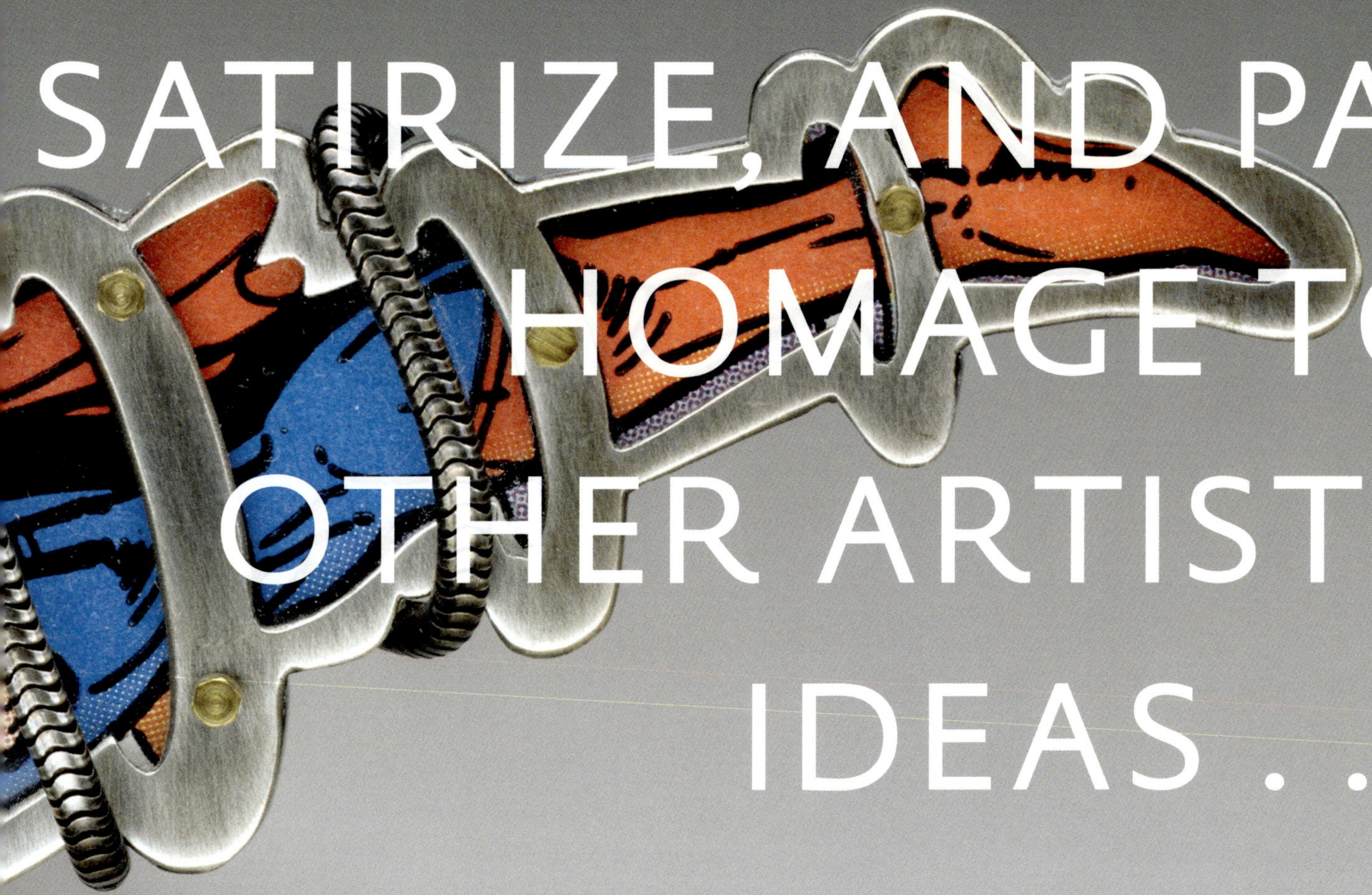

THE APPROPRIATED IMAGE IN CONTEMPORARY JEWELRY

JUTTA-ANNETTE PAGE

APPROPRIATING IMAGES—taking visuals from an existing creation and adapting, altering, and recontextualizing them—has been a long-standing practice in art, architecture, and design. Artists from Italian Renaissance painter Raphael (Raffaello Sanzio da Urbino) to eighteenth-century English potter Josiah Wedgwood to postmodernist architect Michael Graves and American photographer Sherrie Levine have quoted or copied work originated by others in creations of their own.[1]

In the last thirty years, the widespread availability of photographic images in color, along with the means to copy, manipulate, and resize them, has made their use irresistible to contemporary jewelry artists. Referencing art icons, images from popular culture, and personal adornment from earlier times, they improve upon, embellish, ridicule, satirize, and pay homage to other artists' ideas through the jewelry they create.

In 1985, the visionary Dutch jeweler Gijs Bakker created a two-dimensional photographic tongue-in-cheek comment on value in jewelry (NO. 97). Entitled *Pforzheim 1780*, his collar referenced an eighteenth-century French necklace crafted from precious metals, gems, and pearls that is in the Schmuckmuseum Pforzheim. Responding to the original neckpiece's inherent materiality and spatial perspective, Bakker transformed the museum masterpiece's opulence and tactile richness into a flat and stiff biblike ornament by laminating a photographic color print of the necklace between sheets of PVC. The physical reality of his slick plastic collar with its photographic gems strips the traditional jewelry of its light-catching glamour and intrinsic value, wittily exposing it as a symbol of pointless materiality and old-guard aesthetic.

Photography, whether analog or digital, not only readily captures a pre-existing work and facilitates easily printed images of it in a desired size, it also enables an artist to produce jewelry in a limited series. Generating multiple images, Bakker was able to produce a limited number of nearly identical Pforzheim necklaces, further emphasizing his radical viewpoint on traditional notions of value.

Whereas sizing the photographs for the Pforzheim necklace was relatively simple, scaling the images Ruudt Peters adopted for his 1983 tribute to architect Andrea Palladio was of paramount importance. Thinking of the body in architectural terms and architecture in terms of the body, Peters photographed drawings from Palladio's *Quattro Libri dell' Architettura* from 1570 and incorporated these images into a brooch and bracelet (NOS. 111, 112), scaling down from the original rendering in the case of the column brooch and scaling up in the case of the bracelet. The resulting jewelry speaks to the conceptual intelligence of Peters. Off the body, the brooch's long, double pin-stems delineate the vertical mass of Palladio's column as negative space; when the brooch is worn, the metal pin-stems connecting the Corinthian capital and base disappear. Peters's bracelet depends on an unusual appropriation—a cross-section of the top of an Ionic capital from the ancient Roman Temple of Portunus in Rome, with the interior mass of the column perceived as negative space, resulting in a flat and lightweight ornament. In both his brooch and his bracelet, Peters has transferred images of Palladio's drawings onto marbleized Formica, referencing the material for which the engraved designs were originally intended. Novel and unexpected, these photographic representations of Palladio's genius float in elegant testimony to the effortless strength and timeless validity of classical architecture.

The undeniable beauty of historical masterpieces is only one of the reasons contemporary jewelry artists feel compelled to appropriate imagery from the past. Within the canon of Western art, the enduring communicative power of works with traditional religious symbolism has been a lure for a good number of contemporary artists. Whether they incorporate this imagery as affirmation of their own religious beliefs or as critical commentary, the statements they make through their use of photographs in jewelry are intentionally strong and thought-provoking.

In his *Tree* brooch from 2011, Ruudt Peters manipulates and assembles monochromatic photocopies of a crucifixion image that he found on the Internet to create a Christ figure with ten arms resembling the branches of a tree, an original depiction of avowed Christian devotion (NO. 102). Before the advent of the Internet, colorful lithographic prayer cards and prints served to popularize devotional imagery, particularly among the Catholic faithful. A digital photograph of one such *ecce homo* portrait of Christ, the original perhaps a neoclassical rendition after Guido Reni (making the photograph itself at least twice removed from the original) is featured in Finnish artist Maria Nuutinen's 2006 pincushion bracelet entitled *Passion* (NO. 104). The head of Christ has been cut out in a circle and mounted onto a padded wrist ornament. Removable yellow-topped sewing pins project from around his head, conflating his iconic crown of thorns and saintly golden halo into a somewhat fetishistic, commodified religious symbol.

Works that combine Christian with profane iconography are an appropriation paradigm in postmodern painting that intentionally strikes a controversial chord. In 1975, when American painter Alfred Leslie created *The Killing of Frank O'Hara, 1966*, some viewed his work as sacrilegious because he visually equated the figure of the dead poet with Caravaggio's *Deposition of Christ* by using a similarly striking figural composition and stark chiaroscuro. In his *Münster da Vinci* brooch from 1998 (NO. 110), Bakker comments on contemporary society's reverence for soccer stars: through computer montage, he replaces the head and arms of the crucified Christ from an early Renaissance painting with those of the soccer player Krzysztof Bociek (born 1974), whose gesture of triumph was to pull his shirt over his head and run with his arms outstretched whenever he scored a goal. Bakker positions his hooded athlete in the iconic stance of Leonardo da Vinci's *Vitruvian Man*, against a gold ground recalling early Italian Renaissance altarpieces. The frozen movement of the athlete, a subject repeatedly explored by Bakker, also recalls Robert Longo's appropriation of movie actors cut from freeze frames, their movements suspended in mid-air.

Ramon Puig Cuyàs excels at layering erudite historical, scientific, and cultural references. In his brooches, *N° 1279, Ita est* and *N° 1320, Ad longa manu*, both from his UTOPOS series, he incorporates magazine and Internet images with materials such as enamel, resin, silver, nickel silver, onyx, shell, pearl, coral, and plastic in order to create complex compositions of stunning beauty and intelligence (NOS. 100, 101).

In the nascency of the digital age, jewelers took their historical imagery almost exclusively from printed materials such as books, magazines, photographs (found and self-generated), prints, postcards, and photocopies. Bakker, for example, obtained the figure for his 1988 *Adam Necklace* from a glossy book on Michelangelo Buonarotti's Sistine Chapel, trimming the figure to its contours and floating it on a circular, gold-plated brass wire (NO. 109). Dramatic changes in technology since the 1990s notwithstanding, the practice of "cutting-out" appropriated imagery continues. For her *Pompeian Frieze* necklace of 2009 (NO. 105), Marianne Schliwinski turned to a book on Pompeii and carefully cut out images of a well-known but little understood Roman frieze in Pompeii's Villa of the Mysteries that depicts life-size figures of women of various ages whose diaphanous flowing garments and deliberate gestures hint at ancient rituals that have not passed easily across social borders or through time. Schliwinski set the small printed reproductions of the scenes in oxidized silver frames that are mounted with cast profile busts in shallow relief that recall ancient Roman cameos. These citations of the artistic past invoke what Jan Verwoert describes as "ghosts of unclosed histories," which "allows them to appear . . . and reveal the nature of [their] ambiguous presence."[2] The fresco's still elusive meaning demands that both wearer and viewer of Schliwinski's necklace draw their own conclusions.

Interiors and the interaction of people therein are also the focus of Dutch artist Iris Nieuwenburg. She, by contrast, creates vignettes of imagined lives in miniature settings that are often inspired by books on eighteenth-century French interiors and presented in distorted perspectives. Computer enhancements and found objects, frequently from dollhouses, are combined in collages that suggest narratives about people with opaque pasts or futures that are lived out in delicate historical decor (NO. 113), here referencing the famous rococo interior of the Salon Ovale at the Hôtel de Soubise in Paris.

Women, especially famous women (real or mythical) and their sexuality, remain a popular topic for jewelers of both genders. In Diane Falkenhagen's 1998 brooch *Folly* (NO. 107), a photographic image from Agnolo Bronzino's Italian mannerist painting *Venus, Cupid, Folly, and Time* was clipped from a magazine and through heat-transfer directly imprinted onto a lozenge-shaped base of polymer clay and then enhanced with colored pencil and sealed. The isolated image of Venus and Cupid hones in on the nude figures and their tender embrace, while the faux-jeweled frame creates a peep-hole effect and suggests clandestine voyeurism.

Appropriations of highly recognizable images—favorites of European art history such as Leonardo da Vinci's *Mona Lisa* and Raphael's *Sistine Madonna* (and its associated adoring and adored putti) can be generically identified as "Famous Art." *Mona Lisa*, in particular, is low-hanging fruit in appropriation jewelry, and works citing this icon of Western beauty risk seeming formulaic and trite. Still as Rinaldo Alvarez demonstrates in his 2009 puzzle brooch, *Peep-Show* (NO. 108), in the right hands, a new "take" is always possible, and humor and playfulness are useful agents in countering predictability. Emphasizing the veiled sexuality that some perceive in Mona Lisa's smile, Alvarez combines an image of her head with a black-and-white image of bare breasts from an old erotic postcard. Then, taking a cue from a dime-store game, he tempts the viewer to play with her by coaxing two small pearls—symbols of virginity—into two circular hollows in the place of her nipples.

Not surprisingly, society's current fascination with pop culture and celebrities is also reflected in contemporary jewelry. The blonde bombshell in Petra Zimmermann's *Diva III* brooch (NO. 115) stands for a generic type of beauty, and although the image itself is derived from a magazine clipping, it has been carefully painted and built up by hand. Betsy King's *Bound to Be Back* brooch from 1992 (NO. 114) features an image of Superman that she photocopied from a vintage comic book. Following a decline in popularity, the iconic superhero had undergone several visual updates and rewrites in the 1980s in an effort to engage new generations with changing attitudes towards characters with superhuman powers. In King's brooch, the bound hero is about to break free from the restraining coils of the past and return "full force" to the top of comic book sales charts.

Another comment on popular culture comes from Norman Weber, who harnesses the popularity yet empty perfection of Barbie and Ken dolls in his portraits from 2005 and 2006 (NOS. 116, 117). While King selected a printed image from a comic book, Weber photographed "real" dolls, icons of popular culture and consumerism as well as his favorite childhood toys, and then created a realm of suspended belief by partially concealing the well-known duo behind enigmatic structures.

Flawed or troubled "stars" are also aspects of "star mythology" and are often just as popular and fascinating to the public. Kathleen Browne honed in on images of women taken from a 1950s pulp magazine, *Secrets*, that visually moralized their predicaments and social demise in stark black-and-white portraits with exaggerated expressions and gestures. Browne's *Mood Swing* pendant (NO. 106) is a sharp-eyed exposé of a suppressed and often desperate gender, formally underscored for emotive emphasis by mirror images of the woman's face.

The interest that Bakker and other artists showed early on in creating jewelry that refers to other types of jewelry continues today, but now on a global scale. Beverley Price's large textural necklace is made of photographs of Zulu love-letter necklaces that have been backed by tinfoil product labels and chain-mailed together with galvanized wire (NO. 98). Out of deference to the makers of the traditional beaded necklaces, Price, a second-generation white immigrant to South Africa, deliberately uses photographs of their work rather than appropriating actual beaded "love-letters." Her hybrid construct comments on both indigenous and colonial jewelry traditions.

Dutch artist Mecky van den Brink chooses a more minimalist approach involving clever mimicry for her comment on ethnic ornament. Her Moroccan necklace, seemingly made of colorful broken shards of Moroccan tiles, reveals on closer inspection to rely on several different shards for its structure and design, with the rest of the necklace composed of repeated photographic images of these shards (NO. 99). Through photographic reproduction, the work turns the absurdity of a necklace with identical shards into a poignant statement about the relationship of the fake to the real.

The lively dialogues that ensue when contemporary jewelry artists incorporate photographic imagery taken from the visual arts of earlier times or from today's popular culture, adapting these artistic expressions to their own interests and restaging them within the context of their work, all but guarantee the continued use of this popular practice. Jewelry citing, copying, or modifying original works of art is jewelry by and for thinkers.

Jutta-Annette Page *is Curator of Glass and Decorative Arts at the Toledo Museum of Art in Toledo, Ohio.*

1
Raphael's *Deposition* of 1507 depends on Perugino's *Lamentation* of 1495; Michael Graves draws on earlier architectural styles such as classicism, Art Deco, and Beaux Arts; Sherrie Levine has appropriated photographs by Edward Weston and Walker Evans.

2
Jan Verwoert, "Apropos Appropriation: Why Stealing Images Today Feels Different," http://www.artandresearch.org.uk/v1n2/verwoert.html .

GIJS BAKKER

Pforzheim 1780

People's expectations are always related to the known. The unknown makes them nervous, or, in the best case, curious. My goal is to reach people and communicate my thoughts and feelings through my jewelry, so curiosity is what I hope for. When I made the *Pforzheim* necklace, the Schmuck Museum in Pforzheim collected only jewelry that was made of precious materials. To tease them I copied one of the star pieces in their catalogue and laminated it in PVC. Years later I discovered that they acquired my piece, and it is now in their permanent collection.

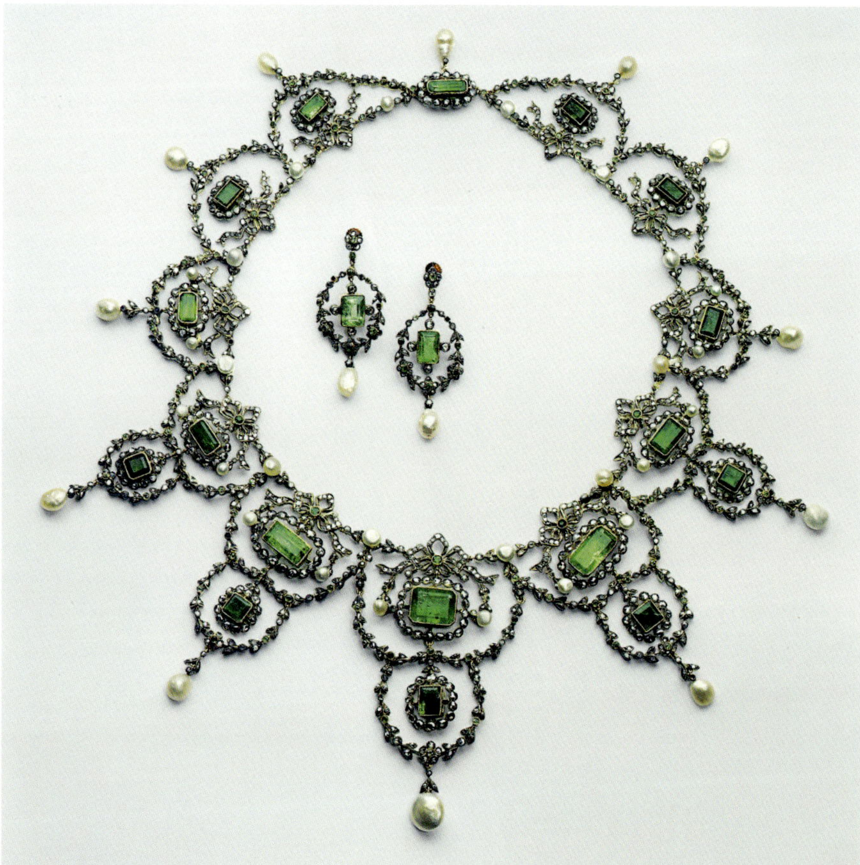

Maker unknown, France
Parure (necklace and earrings), ca. 1780
Silver, gold, emeralds, diamonds, pearls
7 7/8 in. (20 cm), diameter, necklace
1 7/8 x 3/4 in. (4.8 x 2 cm), earrings
Schmuckmuseum Pforzheim

97

Gijs Bakker

Pforzheim 1780 (necklace), 1985

Analog photograph, PVC

$14\frac{1}{2} \times 14\frac{1}{2} \times \frac{1}{8}$ in. (36.8 x 36.8 x 0.3 cm)

Courtesy of Friedman Benda

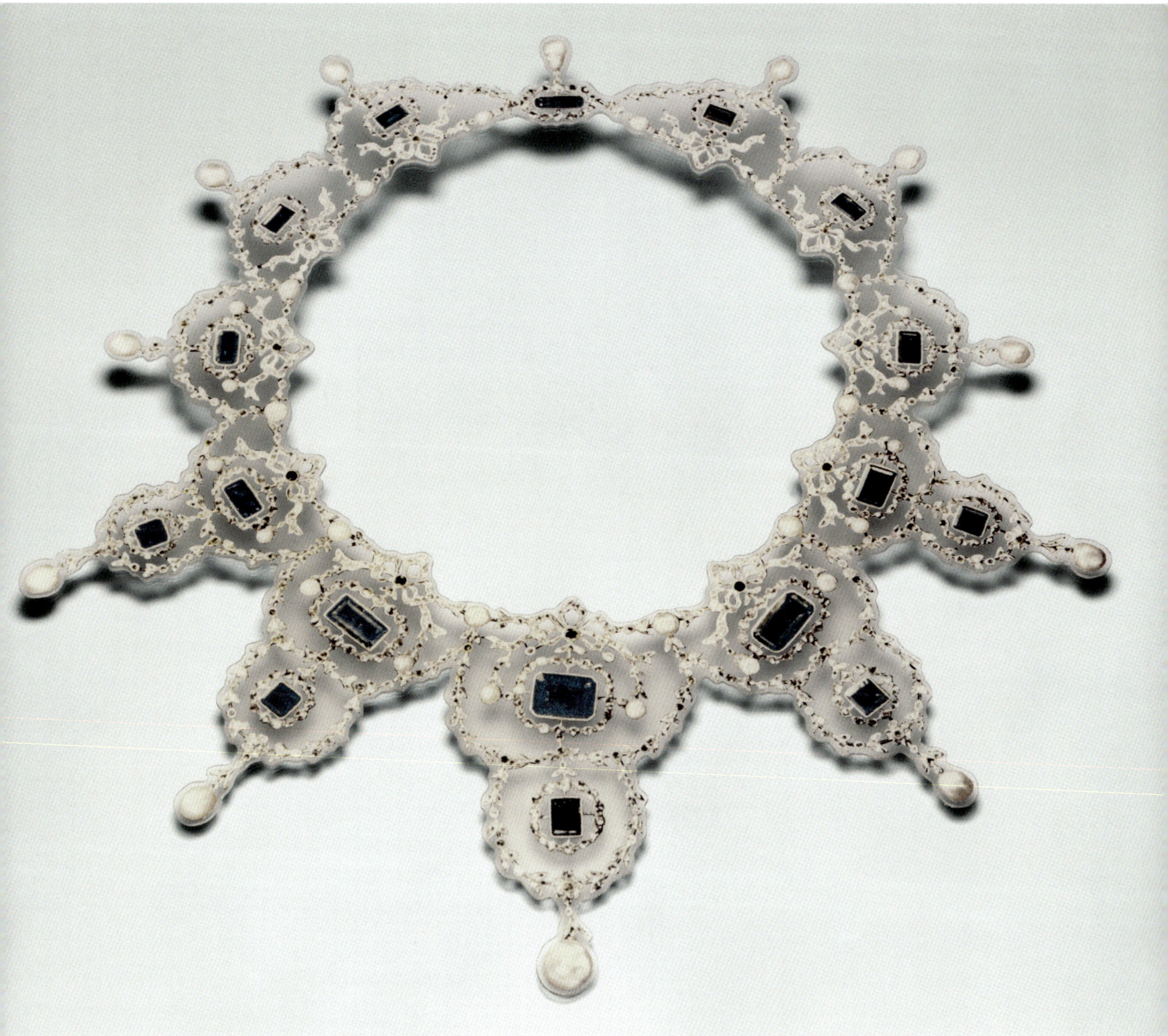

BEVERLEY PRICE

Untitled

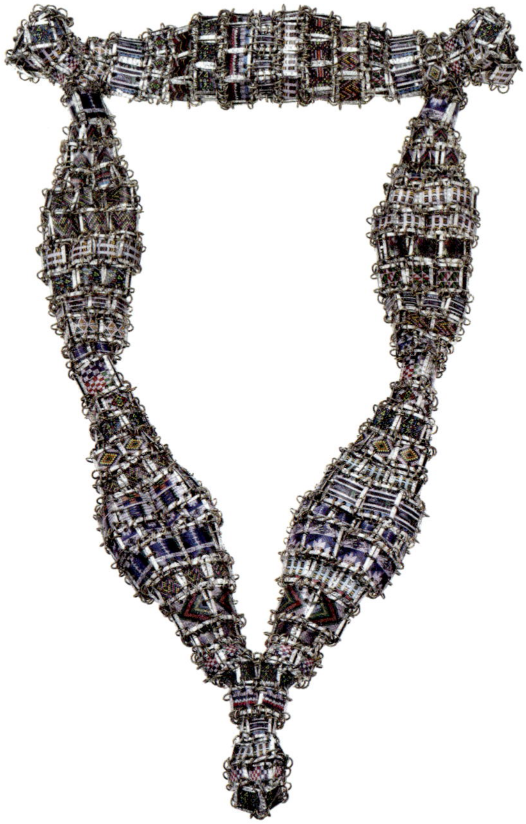

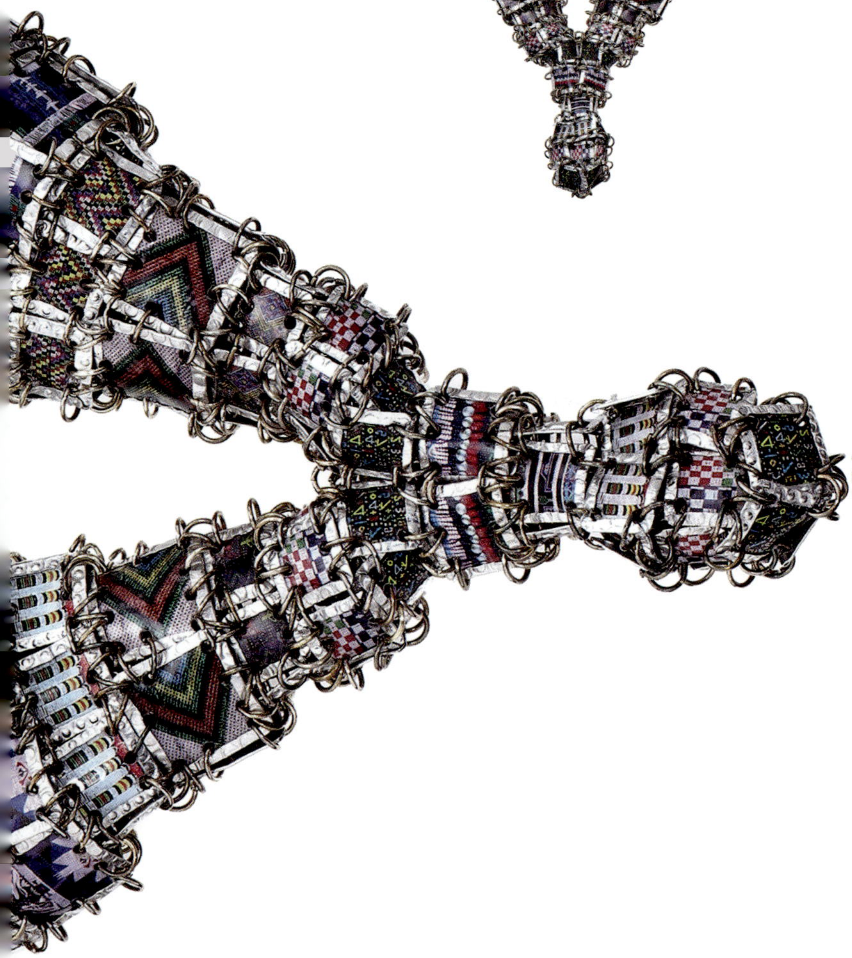

Living in South Africa in the post-apartheid era, I am part of a cultural flux that is exploring our national identity, and I am using this new freedom to make cross-cultural hybrid jewelry.

I have tremendous admiration and respect for the cultural commitment—ancestral and contemporary—of the indigenous South African peoples to adorn the body. To create their ornaments, even during periods when favored materials such as glass beads and leather have been unavailable, they have innovatively used alternative materials in ways that are beautiful and astonishing.

Love-letter beadworks are characteristic of the Kwa Zulu Natal (East coast) province of South Africa, where single Zulu men and women wear them to indicate to one another their availability for marriage. For my necklace, I have used beads in a secondary manner, referencing them through photographs of traditional beaded love letters and then foiling and joining the images to each other to create a hollow, light adornment that can be worn easily in spite of its considerable size. The individual platelets of the necklace rustle with movement, reminding us that like many traditional South African ornaments, this creation is fully realized only when worn.

98

Beverley Price
Untitled (necklace), 2009
Digital photographs of Zulu love letters beadwork, aluminum, plastic, galvanized wire
$19^{1}/_{2}$ x $11^{1}/_{2}$ x $1^{3}/_{4}$ in. (49.5 x 29.2 x 4.4 cm)
Museum of Arts and Design, gift of Rosamund Fokschaner, London.
Facilitated by Jessica Deutsch, Arts to Life, Ltd., London, in honor of the late Leona Price, sister-in-law of the artist, 2010

MECKY VAN DEN BRINK

Marokko

For this necklace, I was inspired by the beauty of old ceramic shards I found while traveling in Morocco, so I picked them up and took them home. I discovered that through photocopying and lamination I could make shards that were identical to the ones I had found. Some shards in this necklace are ceramic; some aren't. Because of this composition of "fake and real," the necklace is light in weight and easy to wear.

99 RIGHT
Mecky van den Brink
Marokko (necklace)
from the Fake or Reality series, 1991
Photocopies on PVC,
ceramic shards, metal
$15^{3}/_{8}$ x $^{1}/_{4}$ in. (39 x 0.8 cm)
Museum Arnhem

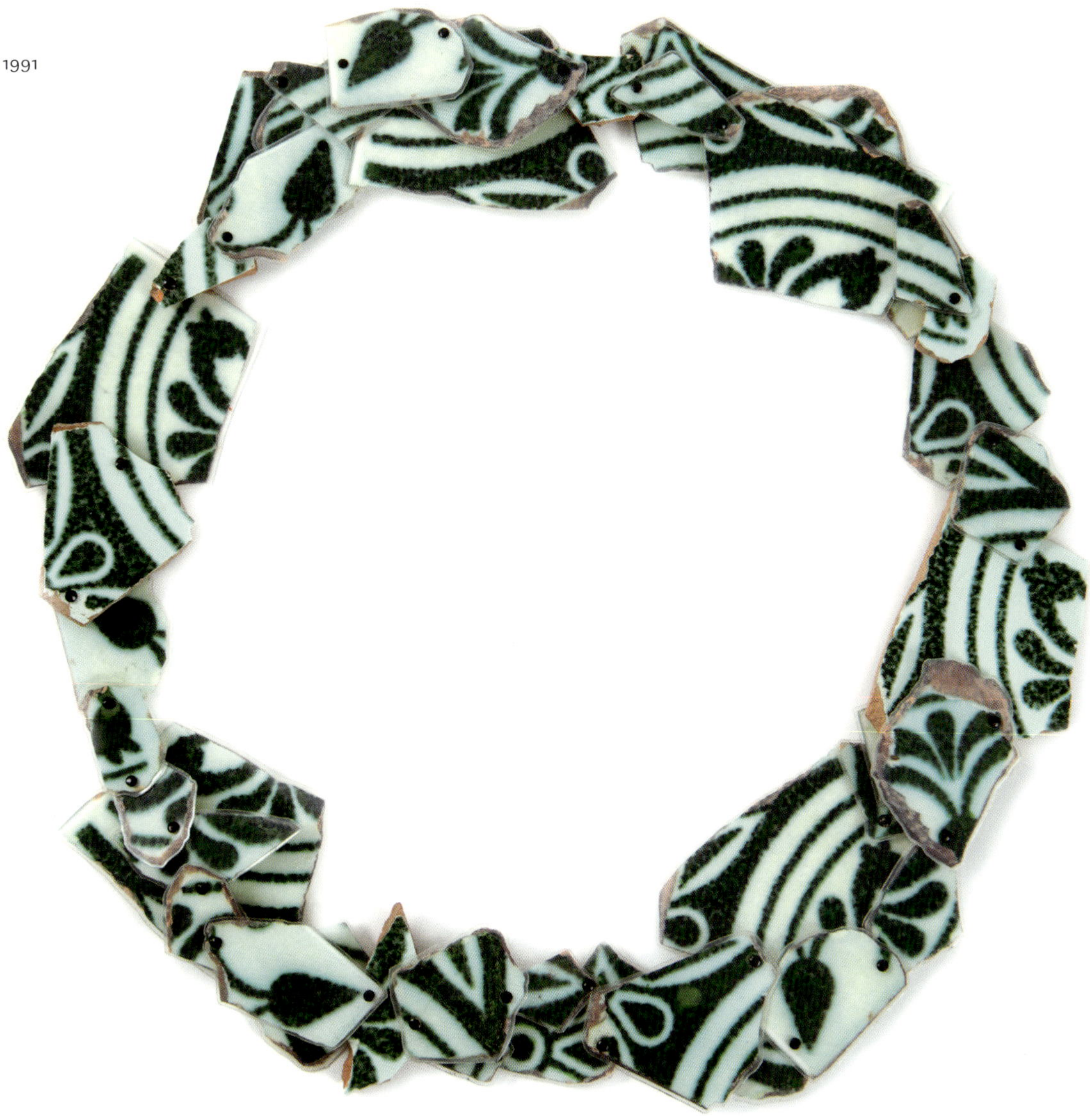

RAMON PUIG CUYÀS

N° 1279, Ita est | *N° 1320, Ad longa manu*

It is the eye of the White Goddess. It is the outlook of scientific man, of the artist who wants to see, to discover, to make visible what we cannot see, to penetrate the darkness. This is the look that asks and wants to understand the existence of the universe. It is the eye that wants to see everything, that looks beyond the black hole. It's like an artist's eye that seeks to recognize and order amid chaos.

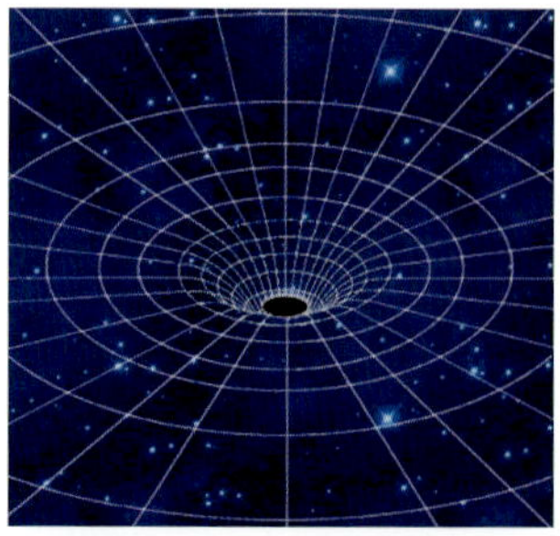

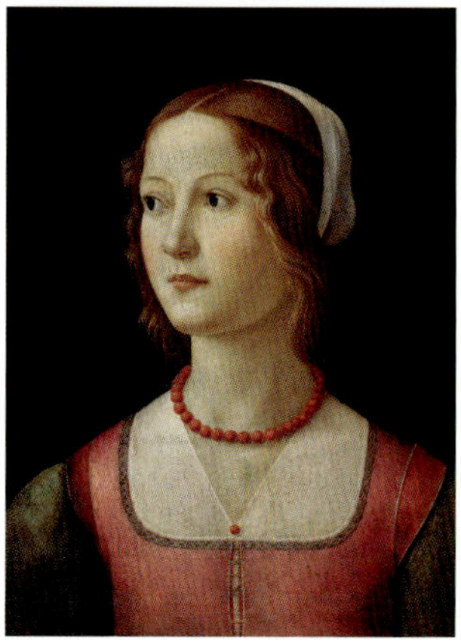

100 BELOW
Ramon Puig Cuyàs
N° 1279, Ita est (brooch)
from the UTOPOS series, 2009
Internet images, enamel, acrylic resin, silver, nickel silver, onyx, shell, pearl, coral, plastic
$2\frac{5}{8}$ x $1\frac{5}{8}$ x $\frac{1}{2}$ in. (6.5 x 4 x 1.2 cm)
Courtesy of a private collection, New York

TOP
Image found by the artist on the Internet.

RIGHT
Domenico Ghirlandaio (1448–1494)
Portrait of a Young Woman, ca. 1485
Tempera on wood
$17\frac{1}{4}$ x $12\frac{5}{8}$ in. (44 x 32 cm)
Lisbon Gulbenkian Museum: The Calouste Gulbenkian Foundation, Inv. No. 282

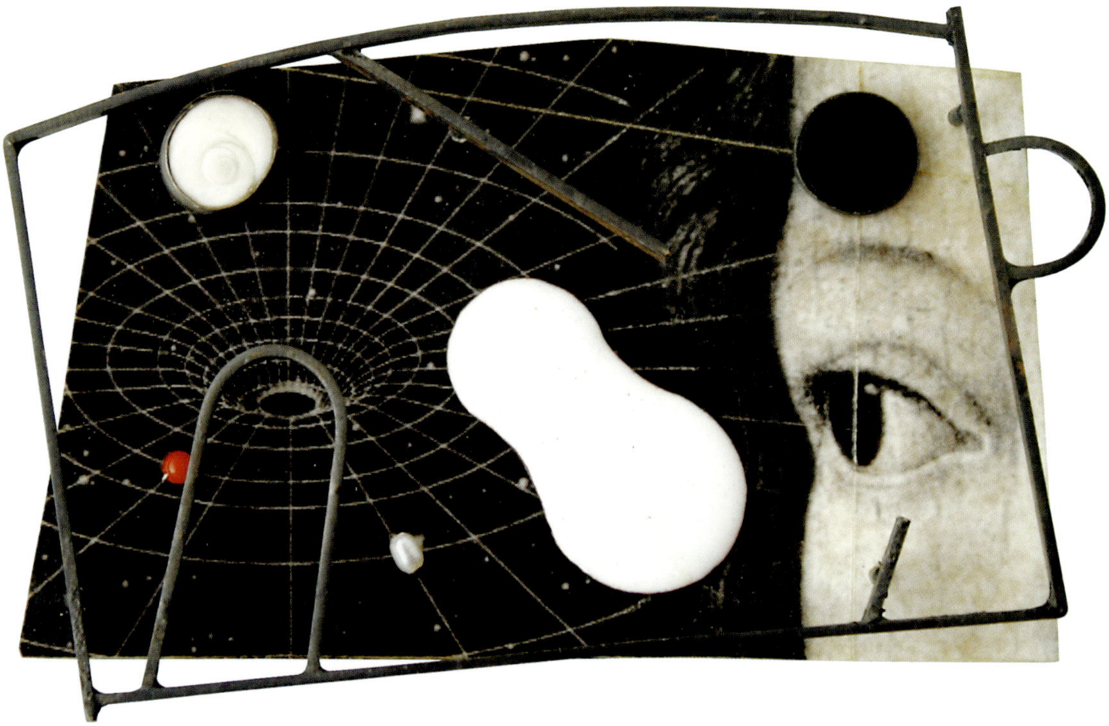

101 RIGHT

Ramon Puig Cuyàs
N° 1320, Ad longa manu (brooch)
from the UTOPOS series, 2009
Internet images, enamel,
acrylic resin, silver, nickel silver,
quartz, pearl, plastic
$2^{3}/_{4}$ x $2^{3}/_{8}$ x $^{1}/_{2}$ in.
(7 x 6 x 1.2 cm)
Collection of the artist

BELOW

Hermann van der Mijn (1684–1741?)
Venus and Jupiter with Cupido (?), ca. 1712
Oil on canvas, bonded on oak panel
72 x $46^{1}/_{4}$ in. (183 x 117.5 cm)
Courtesy of Düsseldorf,
Stiftung Museum Kunstpalast

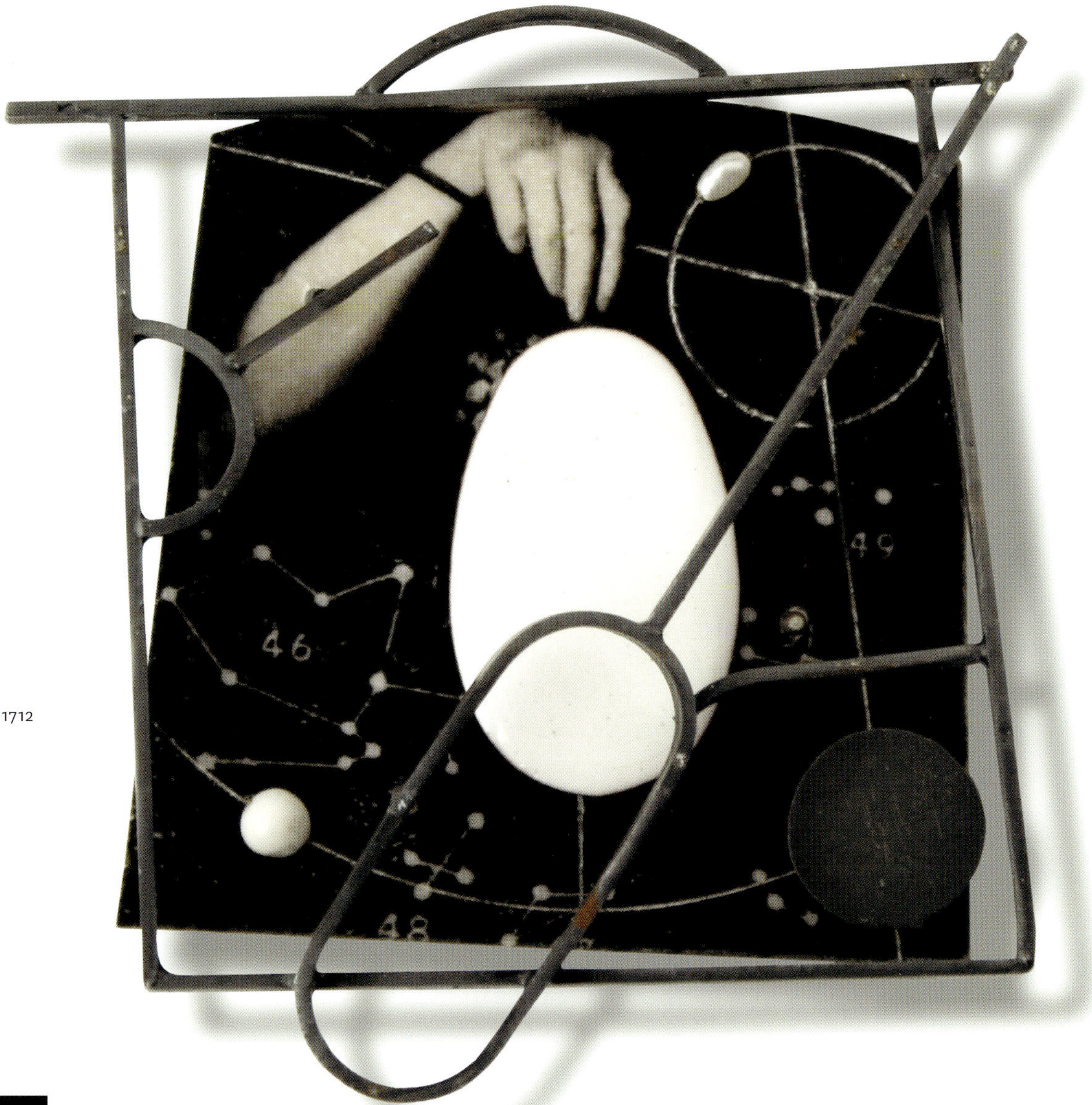

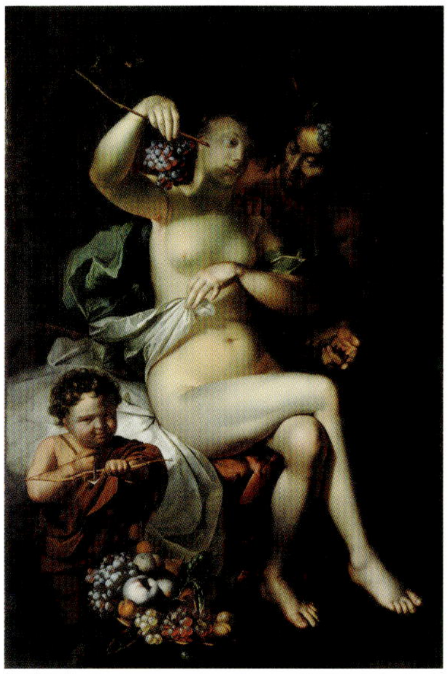

Knowledge comes through the hand of the expert craftsman, who like a magician can bring light. The hand makes contact with the indefinable. A hand holds the world as it comes to birth. It searches for order and balance. Everything depends on everything. For both brooches, I manipulated the online images by computer, converted them to grayscale, printed them, affixed them to a plastic plate, and covered them with epoxy resin.

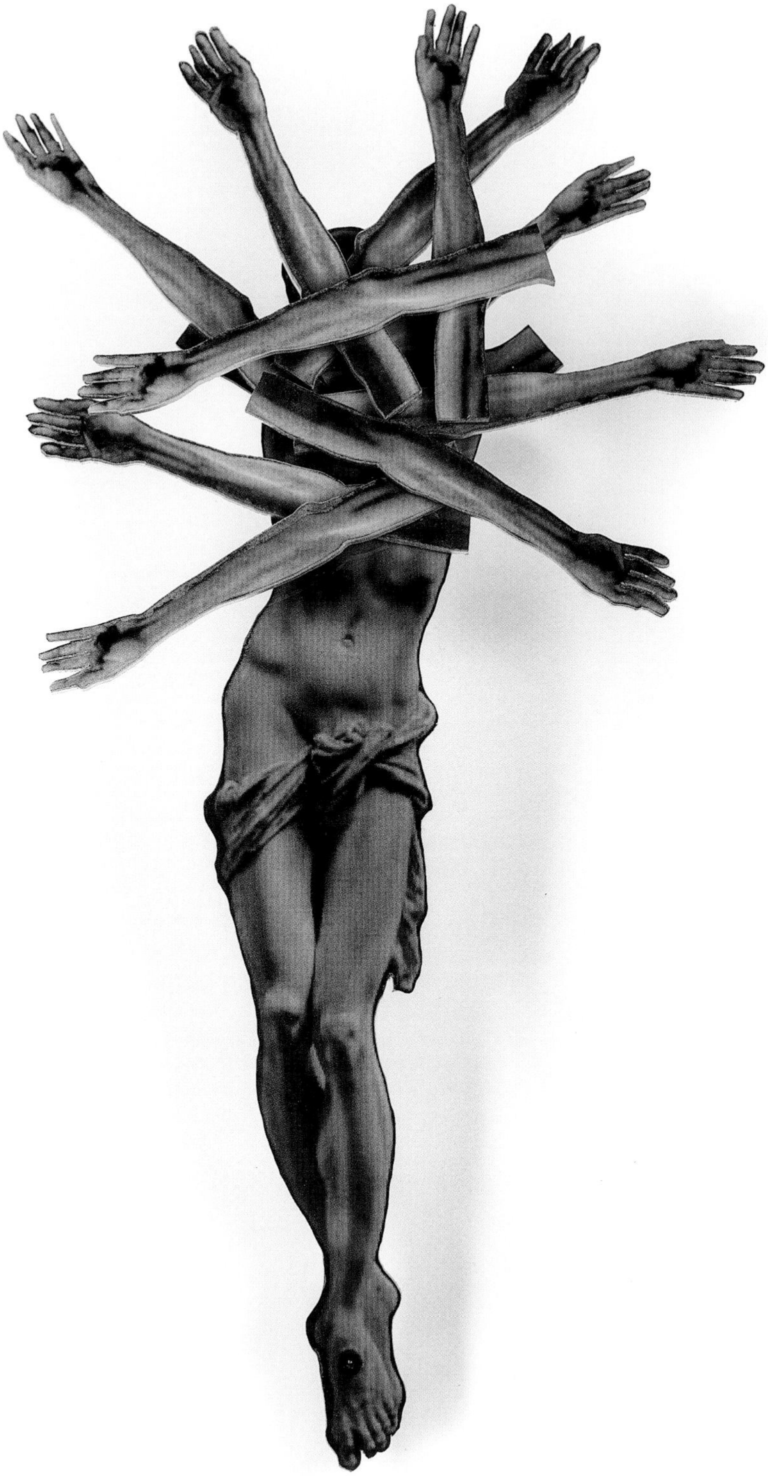

As a young boy, I was impressed by the naked body of Jesus Christ in our churches, many of them beautifully painted and sculpted by great artists, and I would never have dared to alter such an important Christian symbol. Now, I see Christ as an alchemist—a tree with his branches in the air. I made this brooch using a photocopy of a beautiful image of Christ I found on the Internet.

102
Ruudt Peters
Tree (brooch), 2011
Internet image,
aluminum, polyester
10 3/4 x 5 1/2 x 5/8 in. (27.3 x 14 x 1.6 cm)
Collection of Susan C. Beech

RUUDT PETERS

Tree

MARIA NUUTINEN

Madonna | *Passion*

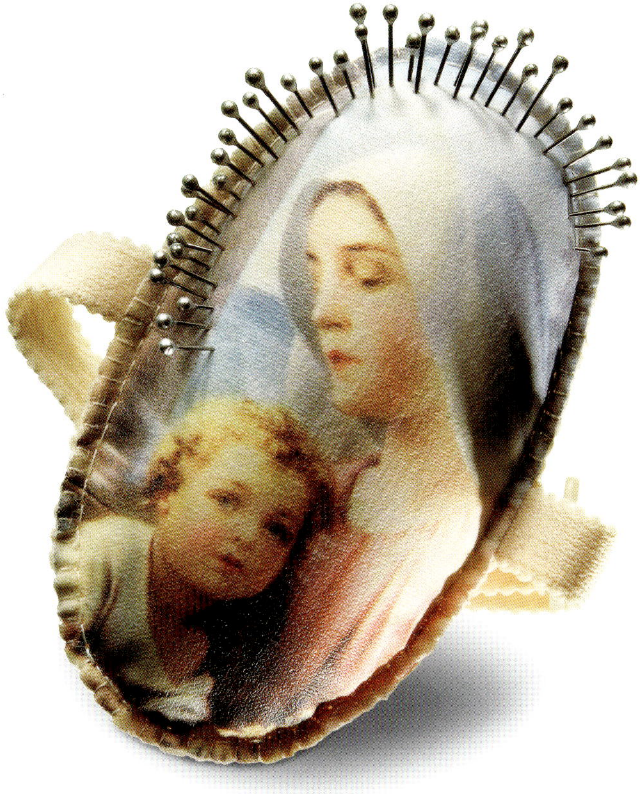

The pretentiousness of “art” that was inexpensively mass-produced for people to hang in their homes during the first half of the twentieth century, and especially the exaggerated way these pictures express emotions like misery and love, fascinates me. The images for *Madonna* and *Passion* came from printed reproductions of paintings that I digitally photographed hanging on the wall of a secondhand shop. Converting these sentimental images into pincushions offered me the opportunity to test limits, although I worked respectfully with the images, carefully considering the color of the pins and their layout in order to enhance the compositions. Even so, the use of religious images and pins arouses conflicting feelings in viewers.

103 TOP
Maria Nuutinen
Madonna (pincushion bracelet), 2006
Digital photograph, fabric,
plastic, pins, filling
$6^{3}/_{4}$ x $3^{5}/_{8}$ x $1^{1}/_{4}$ in. (17 x 9 x 3 cm)
Collection of the artist

104 RIGHT
Maria Nuutinen
Passion (pincushion bracelet), 2006
Digital photograph, fabric,
plastic, pins, filling
$6^{3}/_{4}$ x $3^{5}/_{8}$ x $1^{1}/_{4}$ in. (17 x 9 x 3 cm)
Collection of the artist

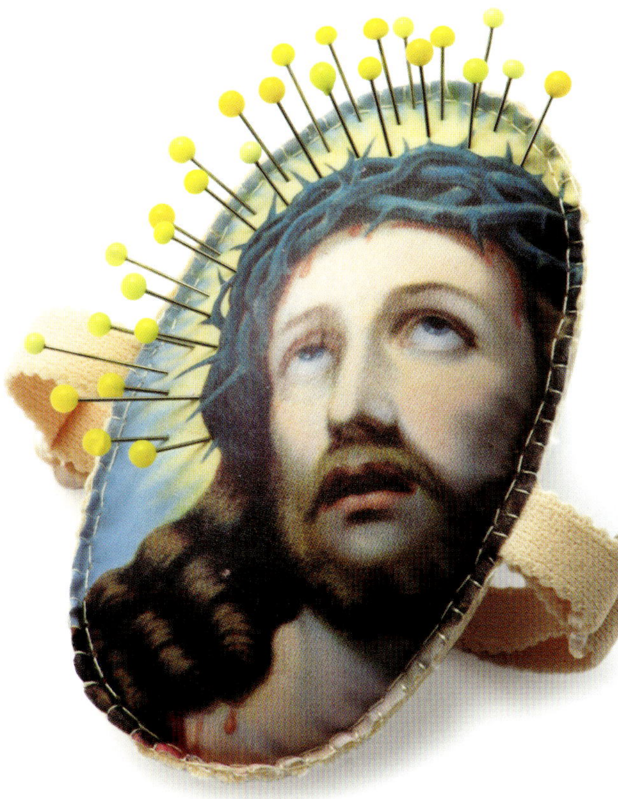

MARIANNE SCHLIWINSKI

Pompeian Frieze

Although there has never been a clear explanation for the controversial scenes depicted in the "mystery frieze" that was discovered in 1909 on the walls of a newly excavated Pompeian villa, there can be no doubt that the central theme of the cycle revolves around women. It is what these frescoes suggest about the role of women in this ancient Roman city that attracted my attention and made me want to incorporate the images into jewelry. I leave it to the wearer and viewers of this necklace to come to their own conclusions about the "true" meaning of the scenes portrayed.

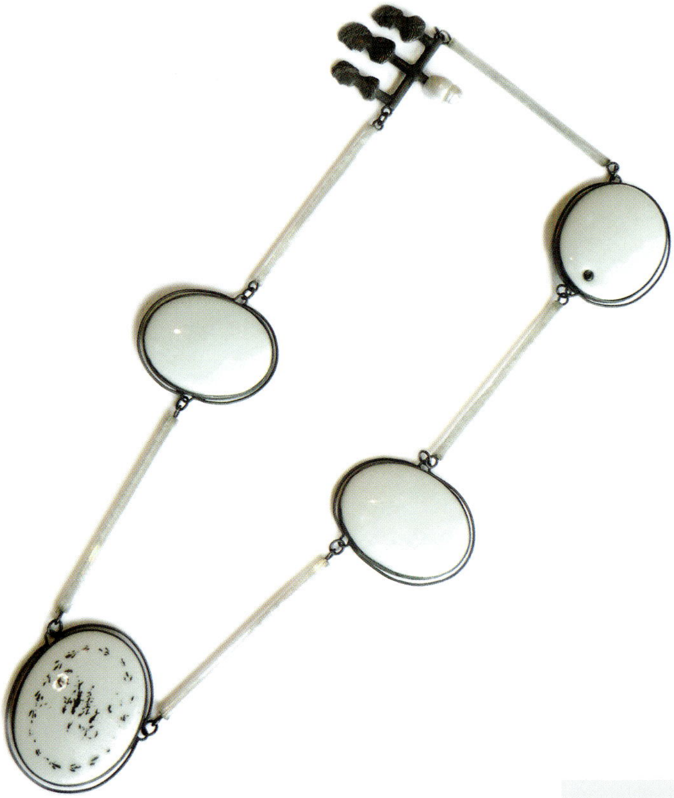

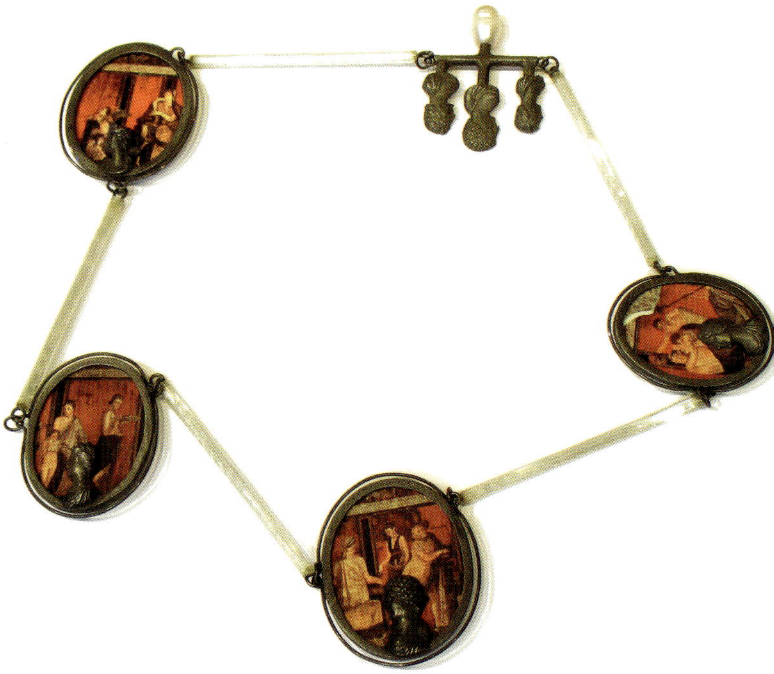

105 ABOVE LEFT (FRONT) ABOVE RIGHT (BACK) RIGHT (DETAILS OF BACK)

Marianne Schliwinski
Pompeian Frieze (necklace), 2009
Artist's digital photograph, black sapphire, porcelain discs, oxidized silver, antique Venetian glass tubes, baroque pearl, lamination
$11\frac{7}{8}$ x $7\frac{1}{8}$ in. (30 x 18 cm)
Collection of the artist

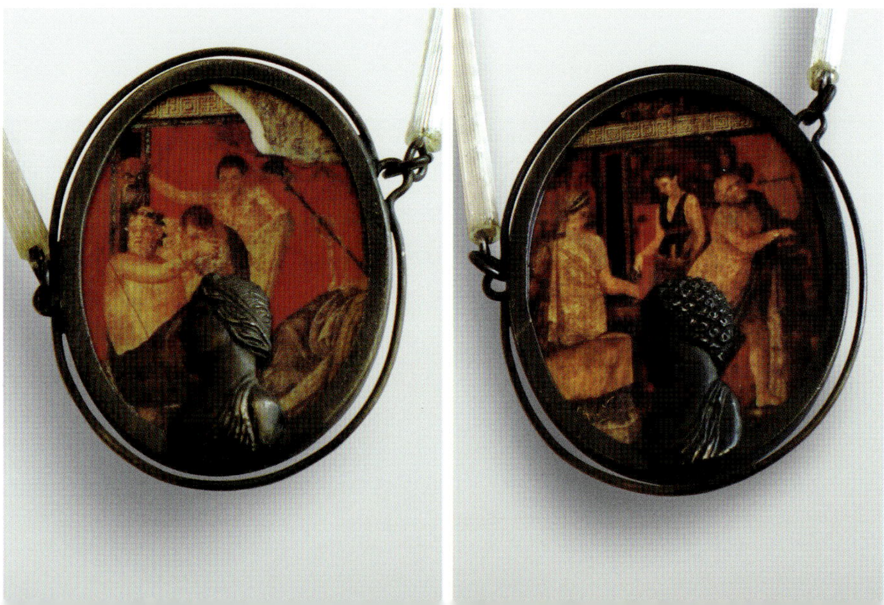

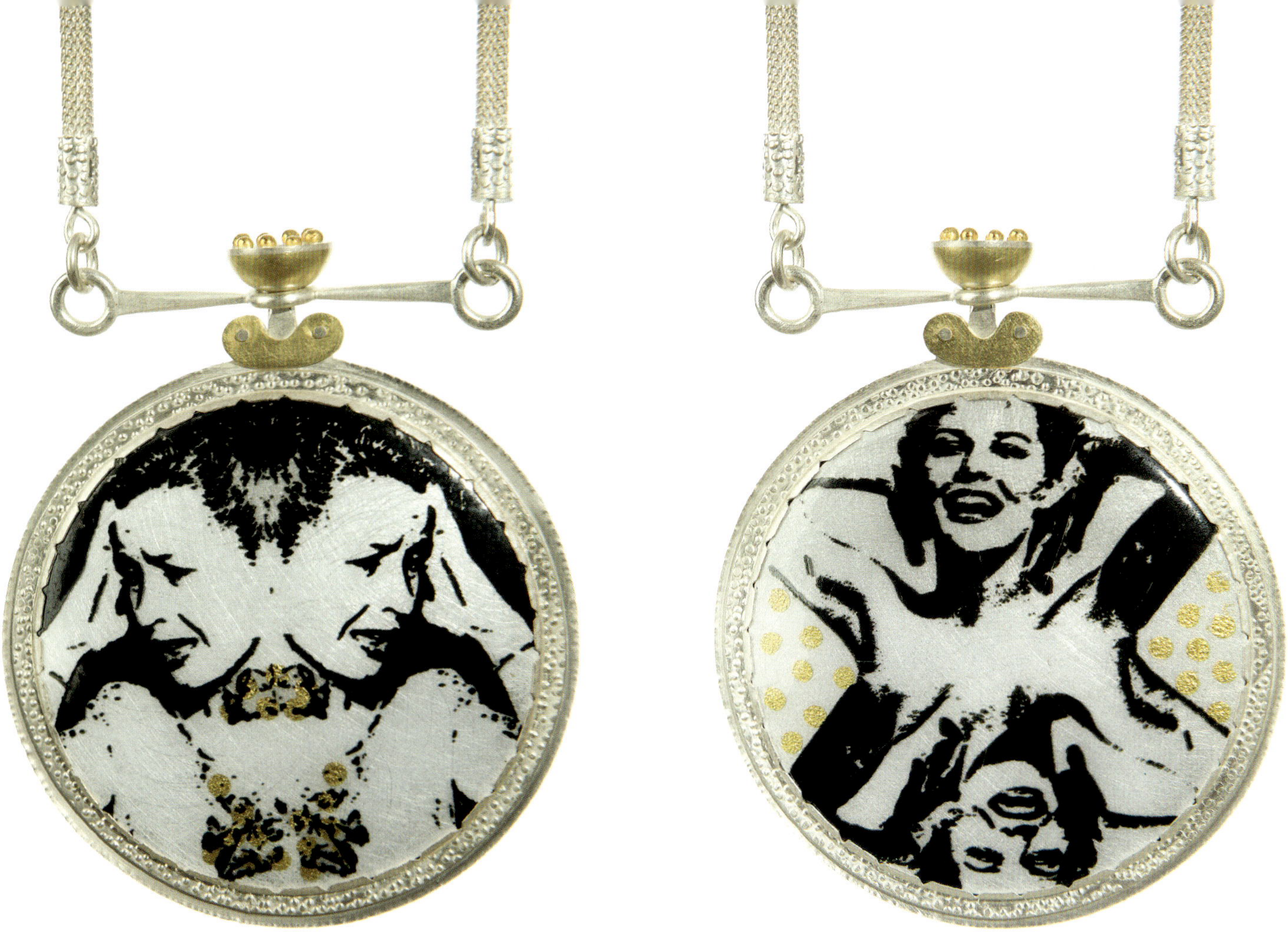

KATHLEEN BROWNE

Mood Swing

106

Kathleen Browne
Mood Swing (pendant)
from the Daily Confidential series, 2002
Magazine images, enameled decals, 24k gold, 18k gold, fine silver, sterling silver, Plexiglas
20 x 3 x 1/2 in. (50.8 x 7.6 x 1.3 cm)
Collection of the artist

The images for the *Daily Confidential* series were appropriated from a 1950s pulp magazine titled *Secrets*. The magazine photos were overly dramatic and stagy, both tragically so and unintentionally comic, but somehow they captured the spirit of the time regarding female transgression. I manipulated the magazine images both by hand and through xerography and ultimately processed them into enamel decals. These reconfigured images freeze a moment in the daily drama of our lives, and, set as jewels, they memorialize the most quotidian of events.

DIANE FALKENHAGEN

Folly

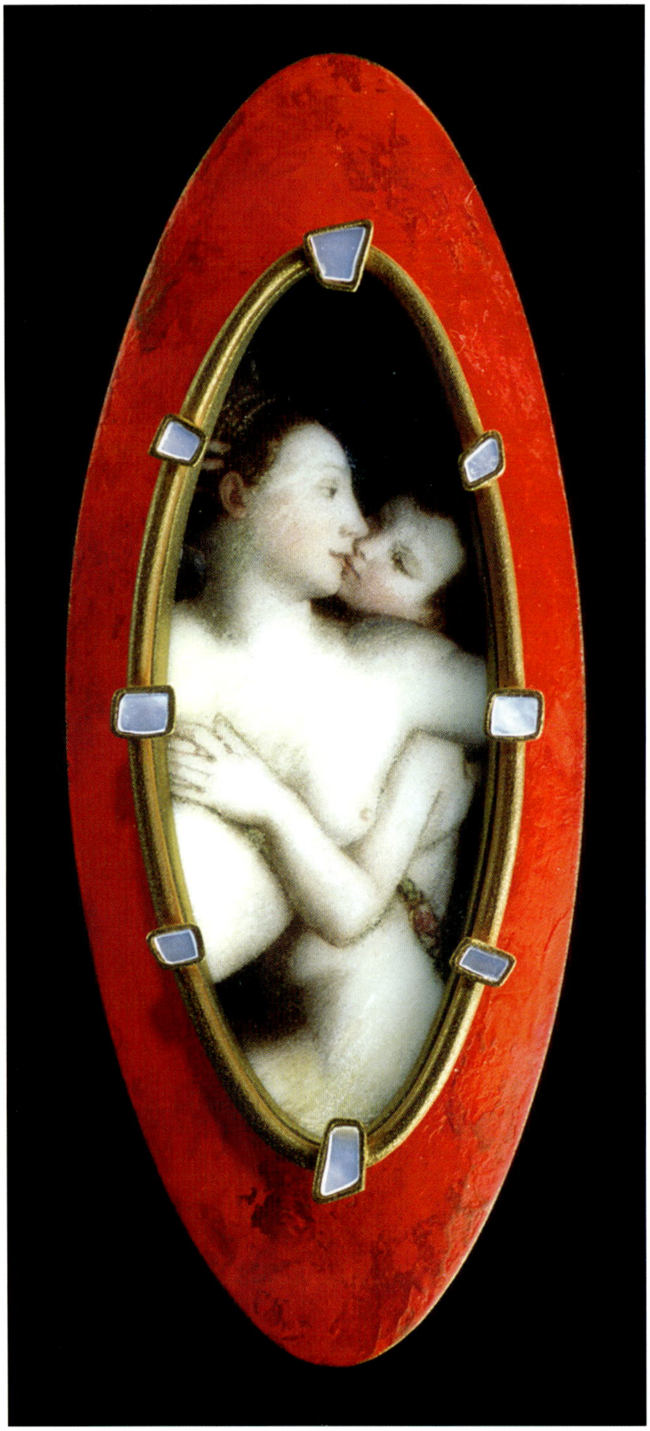

In my mixed-media jewelry, I often combine two-dimensional or low-relief pictorial space with three-dimensional jewelry forms. My starting point for *Folly* was a magazine image of the painting *Venus, Cupid, Folly, and Time* by sixteenth-century Italian mannerist Agnolo Bronzino. Using the simple direct heat-transfer technique, I conveyed the inks from the printed magazine image onto polymer clay and then soaked off the paper backing. The result was a reverse/mirror image of the original, which I slightly modified and enhanced with layer upon layer of colored pencil and sealer.

107

Diane Falkenhagen
Folly (brooch/pendant), 1998
Mixed-media image on polymer clay, 24k gold-plated copper, wax patina, mother-of-pearl, stainless steel
4 x 1 1/2 x 1/2 in. (10.2 x 3.8 x 1.3 cm)
Collection of Ron Porter and Joe Price

RINALDO ALVAREZ

Peep-Show

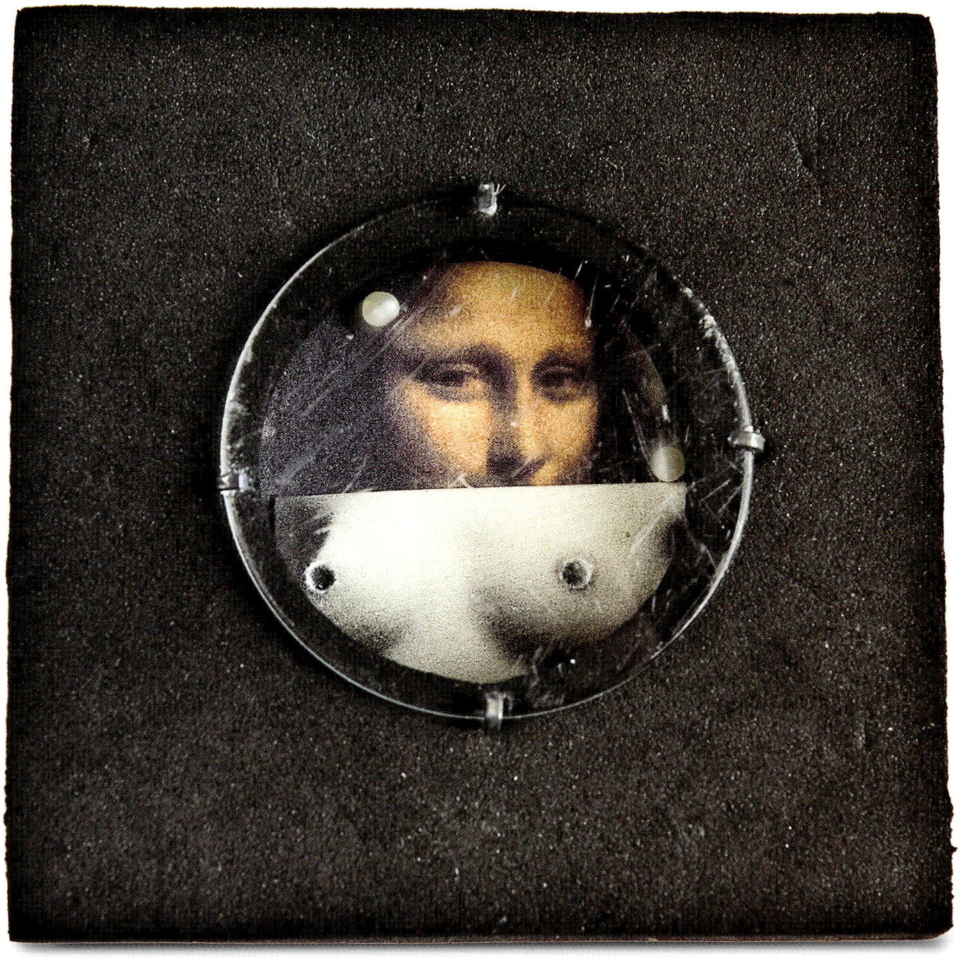

108

Rinaldo Alvarez
Peep-Show (brooch), 2009
Photographic reproductions, silver, glass, pearls, foam
$2^{3}/_{8}$ x $2^{3}/_{8}$ x $^{5}/_{8}$ in. (6 x 6 x 1.5 cm)
Collection of Ulrike Knab

Like children's games in which you have to roll a ball around until you can put it in a hole drilled in an illustrated paper or guide a ball through a small labyrinth, this brooch has two pearls that must be moved into position on the woman's nipples. But in this game, someone is looking at you while you play—while you peep—and her expression is ambiguous. Is she allowing you to play? Is the brooch a mirror? The feelings that arise can be traced back to childhood. Games, nipples, secret labyrinths, and the visage of an inscrutable woman are a subtly constant presence when we are growing up. They form a second amniotic fluid that we move in throughout life.

The images for *Peep Show* are photographic reproductions of *La Gioconda* by Leonardo da Vinci and a part of an old erotic postcard, both of which I cut from books. Most of the elements for the frame were salvaged and reused.

GIJS BAKKER

Adam Necklace | *Münster da Vinci*

I am interested in playing with the context of an image to find out if the image still has impact when used in a completely different environment. The *Adam Necklace* came about as I was leafing through a book on the Sistine Chapel in the library of the Royal College of Art in London and was inspired by the brilliance of the painter, sculptor, and architect Michelangelo Buonarotti, and especially by the sensuality of his figures. The neck and the shoulder determine the position of the figure in this necklace every bit as firmly as does the roundness of the vault on which Michelangelo's fresco was painted.

109
Gijs Bakker
Adam Necklace, 1988
Photographic reproduction, gold-plated brass 750, PVC
10 3/4 x 10 3/4 x 1/8 in.
(27.3 x 27.3 x 0.3 cm)
Collection of Mr. and Mrs. Lou Grotta

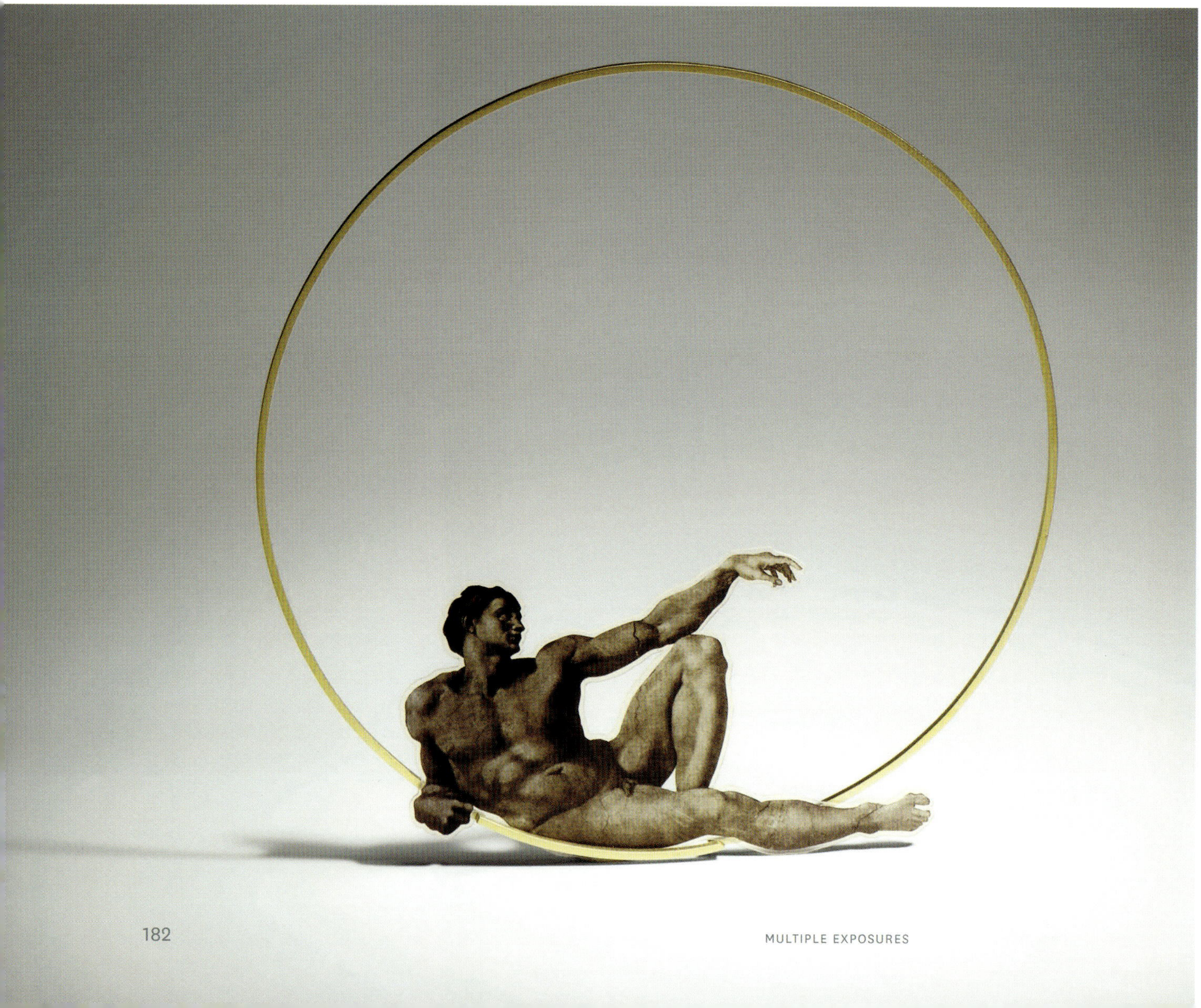

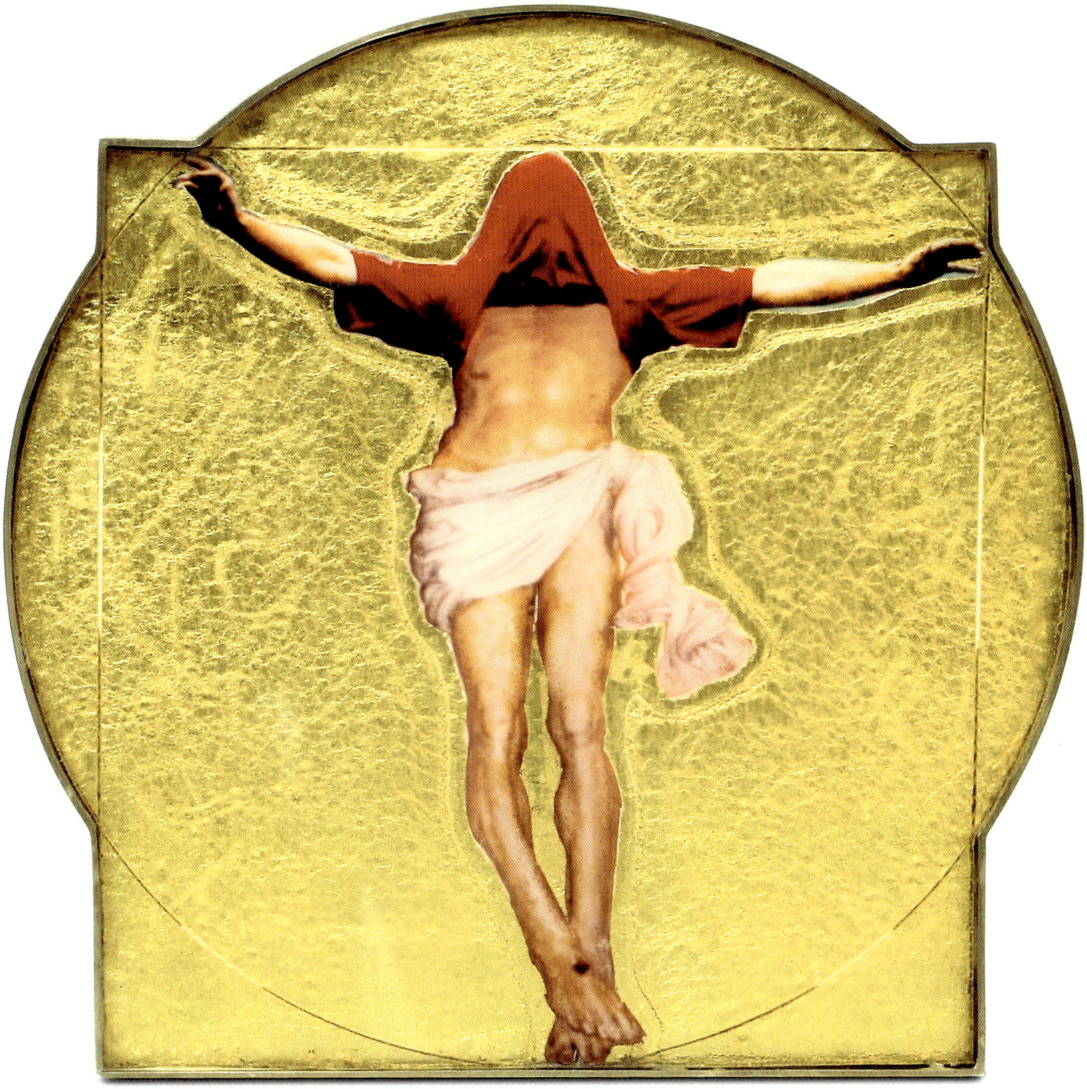

In my morning newspaper, I saw a soccer player running in victory, his red shirt pulled back over his head after making a goal, and I spontaneously said, "Jesus Christ!" I had to wonder, "Is soccer playing more important than religious services?" With this thought in mind, I began photographing church crucifixes and then putting the pictures into my computer so I could combine them with images of sports figures.

110

Gijs Bakker, executed by **Pauline Barendse**
Münster da Vinci (brooch) from
the Holy Sport series, 1998
Digitally manipulated photographs,
gold leaf 916, silver 925, glass, Plexiglas
$4^{1}/_{8}$ x $4^{1}/_{8}$ x $^{1}/_{4}$ in. (10.4 x 10.4 x 0.8 cm)
Collection of Susan C. Beech

RUUDT PETERS

Bracelet | *Brooch*

In the 1980s, I was intrigued by architecture and dedicated this bracelet and brooch to Palladio in appreciation of his important influence on the field. I see the arm as a column, with the bracelet as the capital, on top of it. The dimensions of the brooch are harmonious with the human body, and the piece is a statement that architecture is an expression of and related to humans. I created the base and capital of the column by printing a photo from a book on Palladio onto marble-patterned Formica. The column itself is almost invisible between these two architectural elements.

111 BELOW LEFT
Ruudt Peters
Bracelet, 1983
Photographic reproduction of architectural drawing, marble-patterned Formica
4 1/4 x 4 1/4 x 1/8 in. (10.8 x 10.8 x 0.2 cm)
The Museum of Fine Arts, Houston, Helen Williams Drutt Collection, museum purchase funded by the Caroline Wiess Law Foundation, 2002.4011

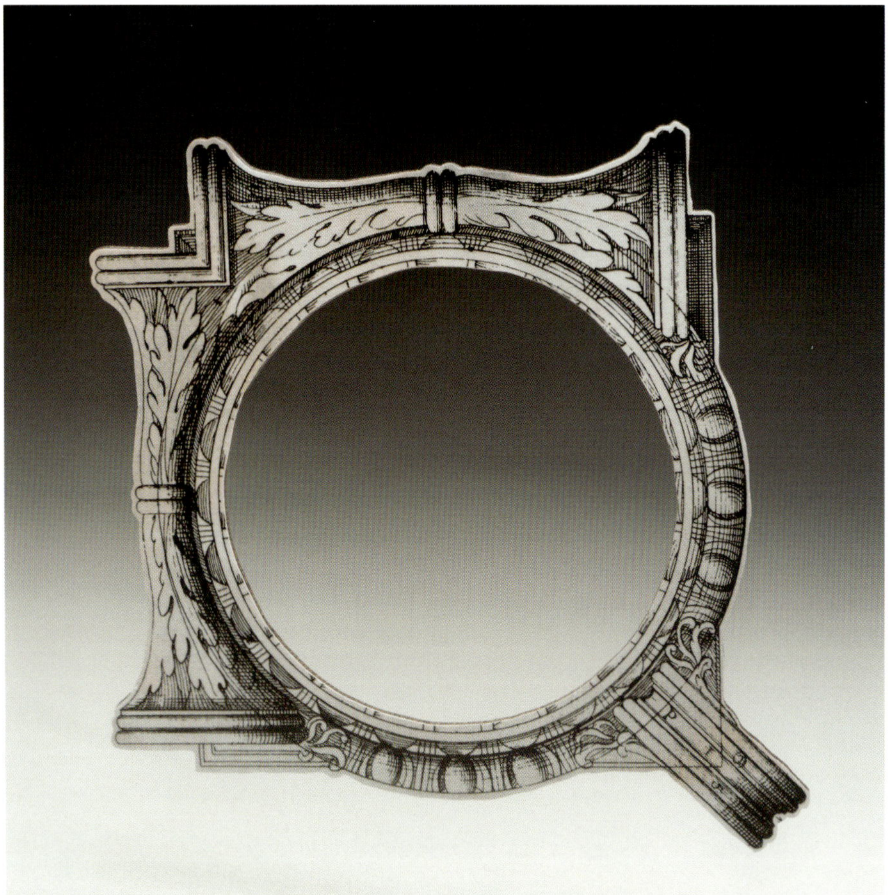

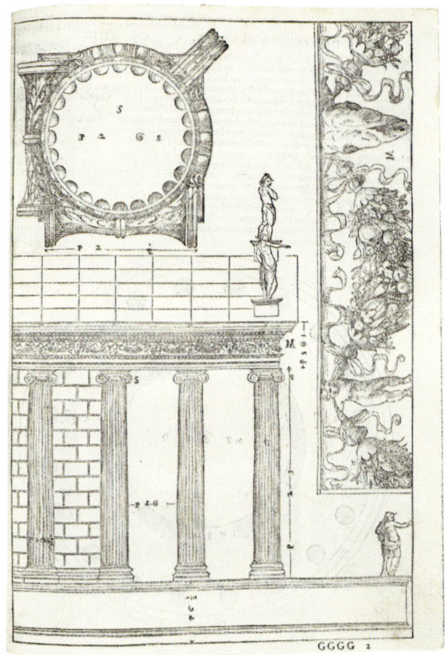

ABOVE
Andrea Palladio (1508–1580)
I Quattro Libri dell' Architettura, 1570
Wood engravings with letterpress text
11 1/2 x 8 1/2 in. (29.2 x 21.6 cm)
Toledo Museum of Art, gift of the Apollo Society, 2009.25

112

Ruudt Peters

Brooch, 1983

Photographic reproduction of architectural drawing, marble-patterned Formica, metal wire

9 3/4 x 2 1/8 x 1/8 in. (24.7 x 5.3 x 0.2 cm)

The Museum of Fine Arts, Houston, Helen Williams Drutt Collection, museum purchase funded by the Caroline Wiess Law Foundation, 2002.4014

IRIS NIEUWENBURG

Love Story

My jewelry is an assemblage of pictures from books on eighteenth-century decorative arts, dollhouse furnishings, antique glass elements, my grandmother's jewelry, and vintage "finds" that catch my eye. I work with pre-existing or found images that I cut up and reorder or rearrange, and I put the entire assemblage together using traditional goldsmith's techniques. At first glance this craftsmanship is not visible; still, such factors as the riveting and the small screws that hold the piece together play an important part in the setting and in the realization of the piece.

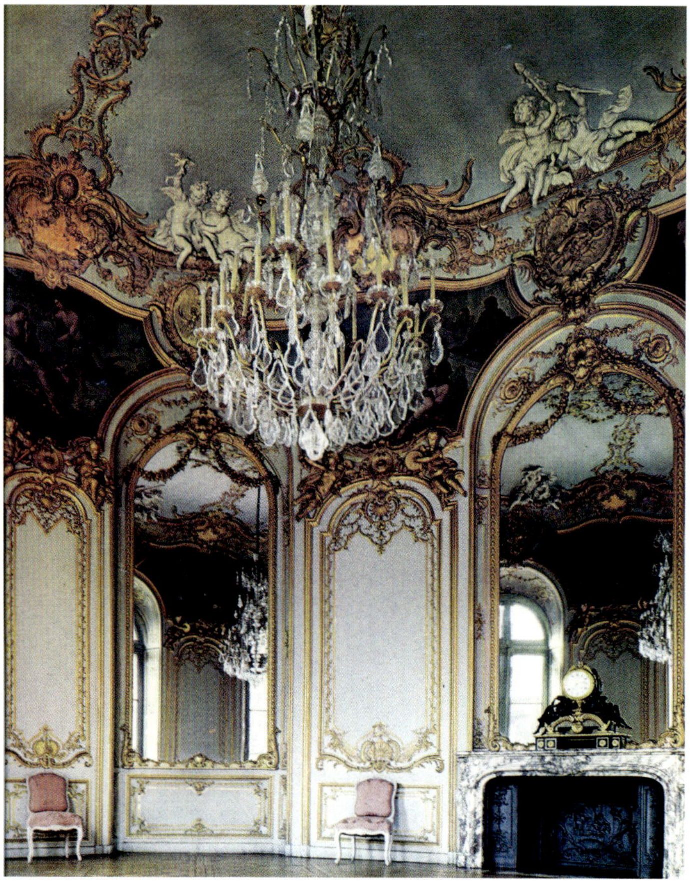

LEFT
The Salon Ovale at the Hôtel de Soubise in Paris.

113 OPPOSITE PAGE
Iris Nieuwenburg
Love Story (brooch), 2009
Photographic reproductions, silver, gold-plating, dollhouse elements, veneer, lacquer, miniature candles
$4^{1/2}$ x 4 x 1 in. (11.4 x 10.2 x 2.5 cm)
Museum of Arts and Design, with funds provided by proceeds from works donated by the American Craft Council, Norman Anderson, Knoll North America, Suzi Pleyte, Daniel Rhodes and Osborn Webb by exchange, 2010

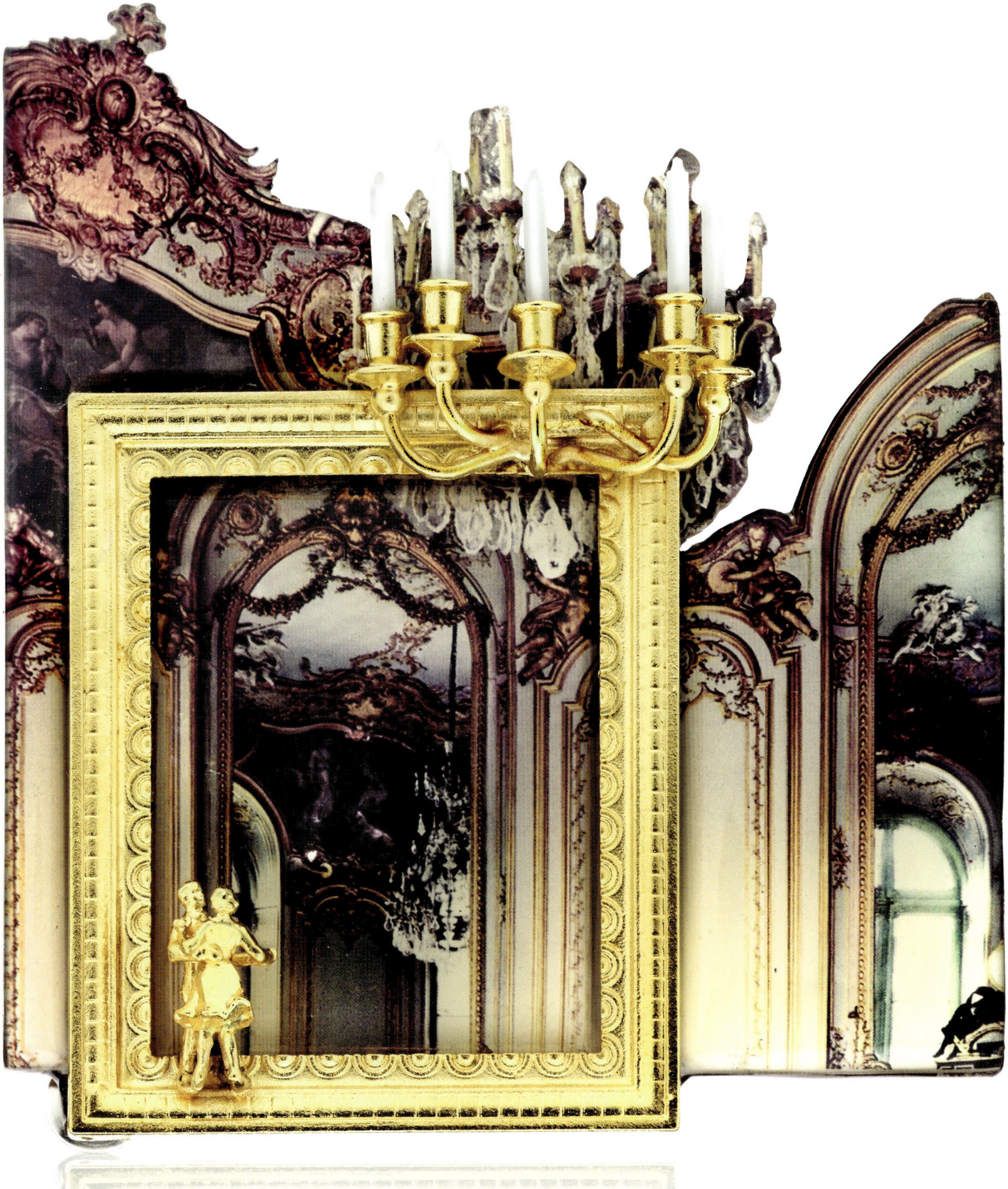

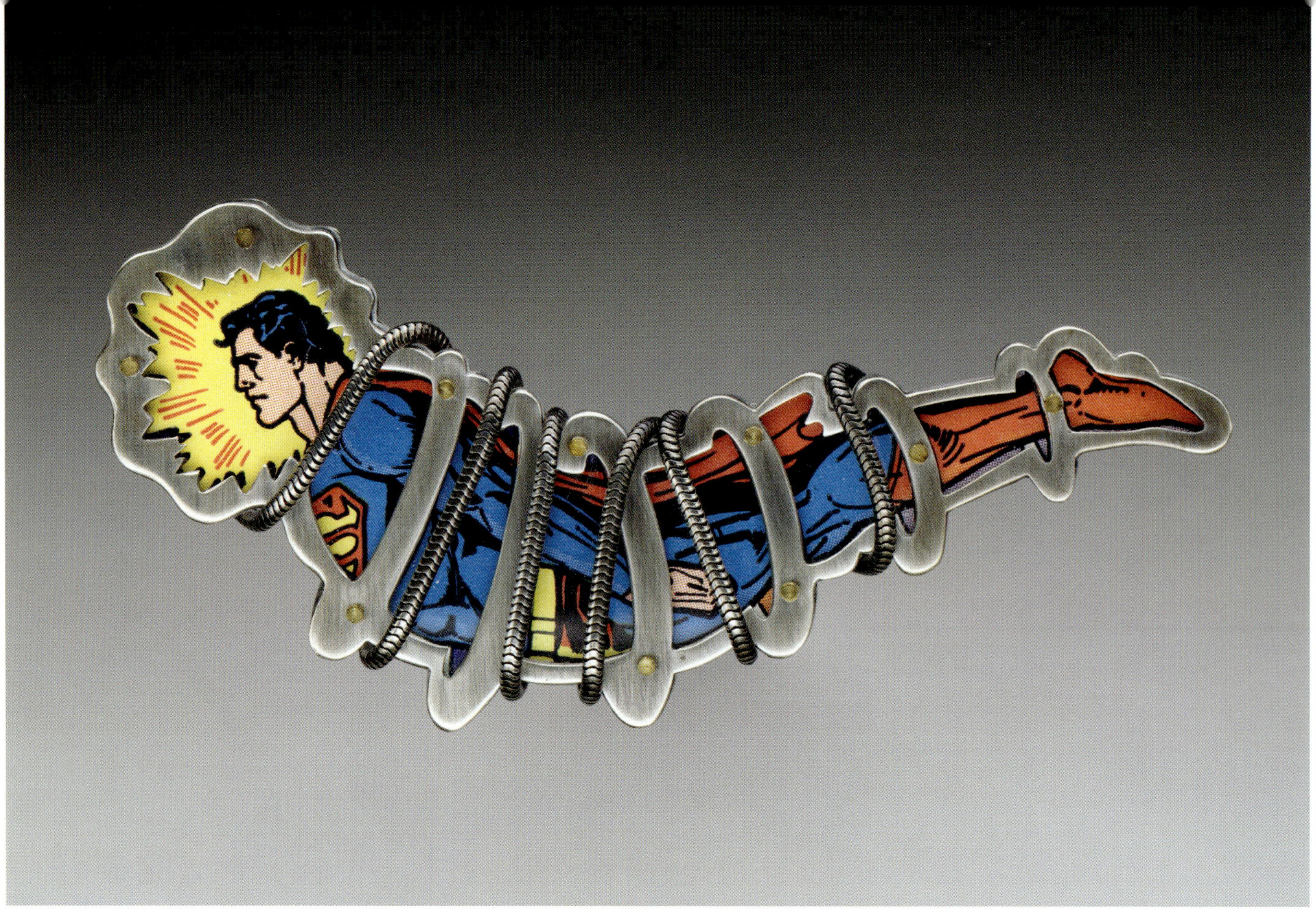

BETSY KING

Bound to Be Back

In late 1992, DC Comics announced the death of Superman, the American superhero icon, provoking a huge outcry from Superman's many fans. This brooch is my reaction to the announcement. I felt Superman was "bound to be back," no matter what they said. And he was. This brooch features a photocopy of an original clipping from a vintage DC Comic Book. The frame is pierced sterling silver sheet and sterling silver rope chain "bound," wrapped, and riveted over Plexiglas.

114
Betsy King
Bound to Be Back (brooch), 1992
Photocopy of comic book character, sterling silver, brass
3 x 5 1/8 x 3/4 in. (7.6 x 13 x 1.9 cm)
The Museum of Fine Arts, Houston, Helen Williams Drutt Collection, museum purchase funded by the Caroline Wiess Law Foundation, 2002.3853

PETRA ZIMMERMANN

Diva III

My selection of motifs for my jewelry has changed over time from scenes showing very intense situations and moments of decision to images we are confronted with all the time through mass media—pictures we almost don't pay attention to anymore because they merely present stereotypical images. *Diva III* was such a picture, but cut from the magazine, painted in several layers of plastic, and worn as jewelry, the image is noticed, and its message is clear.

115
Petra Zimmermann
Diva III (brooch), 2013
Magazine cut-outs, acrylic paint, polymethyl methacrylate, rhinestones, iolite beads, gold leaf, blackened silver
5 3/8 x 4 x 3/8 in. (13.8 x 10.2 x 1 cm)
Collection of the artist

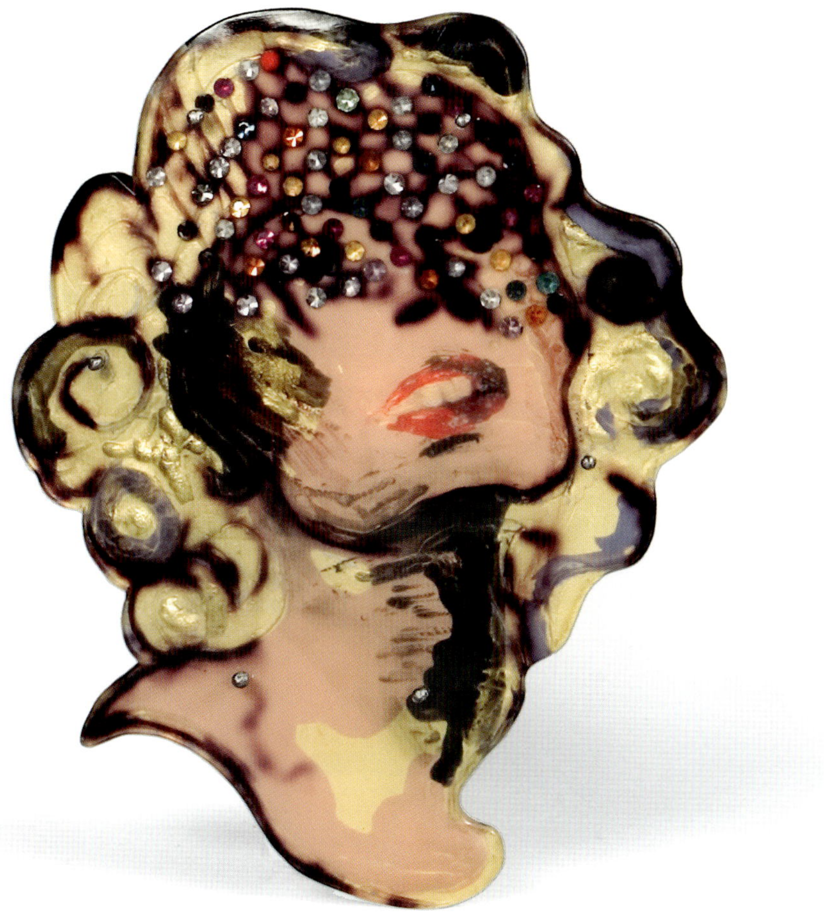

NORMAN WEBER

Porträt #1 | *Porträt #3*

In these brooches, Barbie and Ken descend from the virtual cosmos of Mattel, Inc., from the 1970s. In my childhood, these avatars developed real personalities, but now they are former pop icons that have faded into a distant past. The combination of figurative and constructive elements is what interests me here—the flatness of the picture vis-à-vis the construction of depth. Similar historical examples can be found in mannerist and baroque jewelry. I took the original photographs of these dolls and then worked over them on the computer and prepared them to be digitally-printed on steel.

116 BELOW LEFT AND OPPOSITE PAGE [DETAIL]
Norman Weber
Porträt #1 (brooch), 2006
Digital photograph, steel,
blackened silver, glass, lacquer
$5^{1}/_{4} \times 4^{1}/_{2} \times 1^{7}/_{8}$ in. (13.5 x 11.5 x 4.7 cm)
Courtesy of the artist and
Maurer Zilioli—Contemporary Arts, Munich

117 BELOW RIGHT
Norman Weber
Porträt #3 (brooch), 2006
Digital photograph, steel,
blackened silver, lacquer
$4^{7}/_{8} \times 3^{7}/_{8} \times 1^{3}/_{4}$ in. (12.5 x 9.8 x 4.5 cm)
Courtesy of the artist and
Maurer Zilioli—Contemporary Arts, Munich

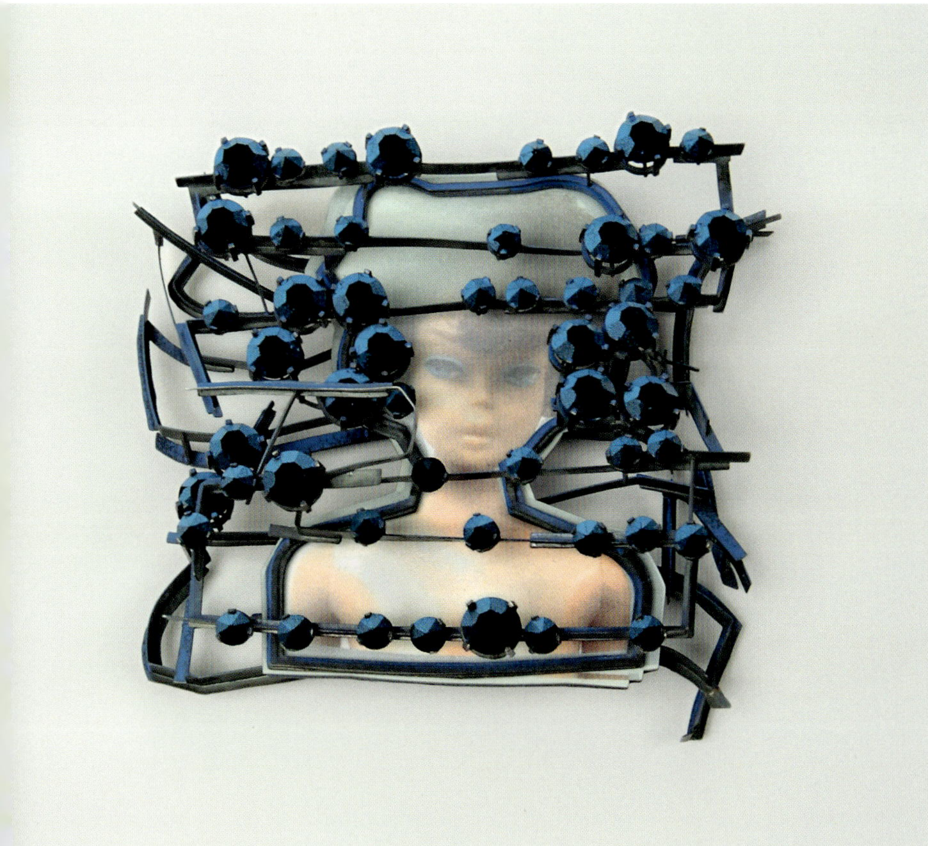

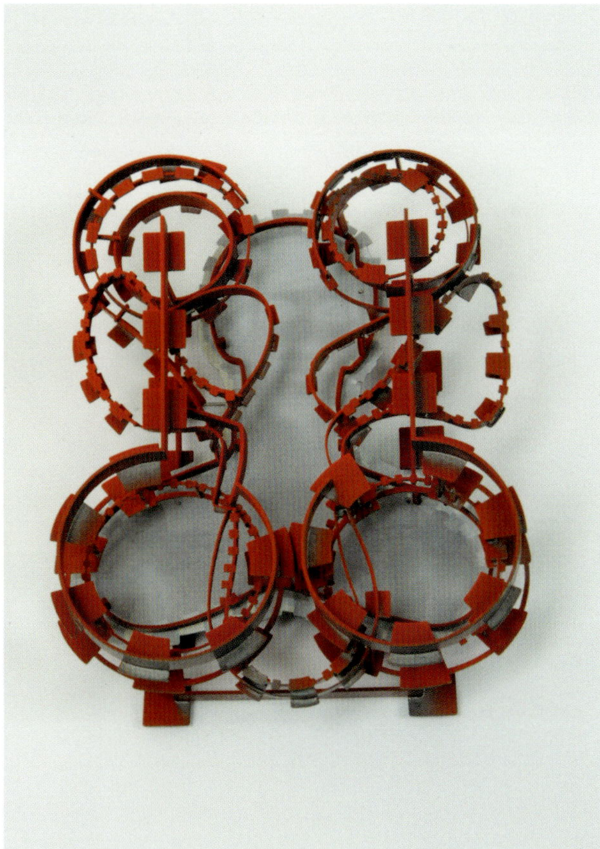

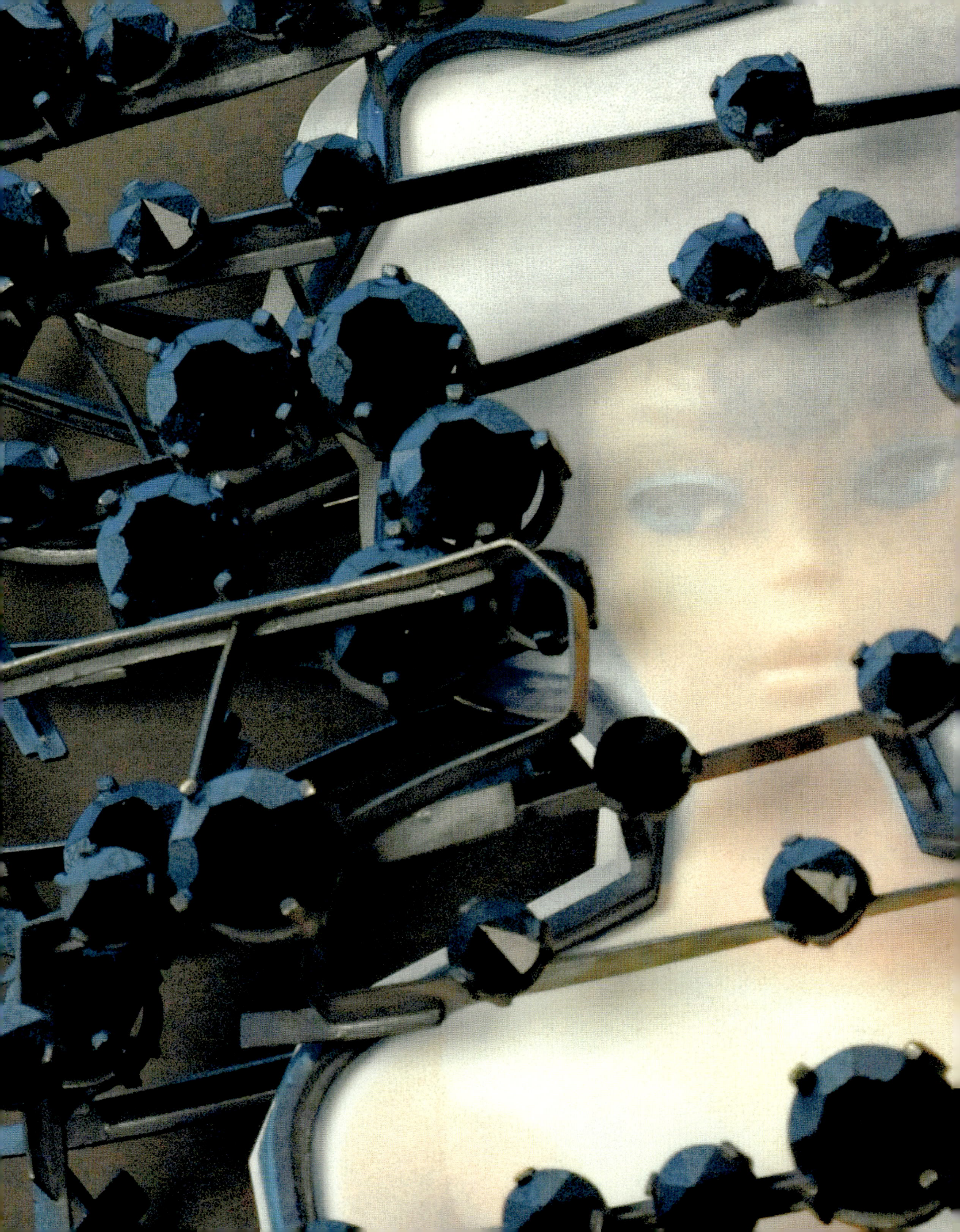

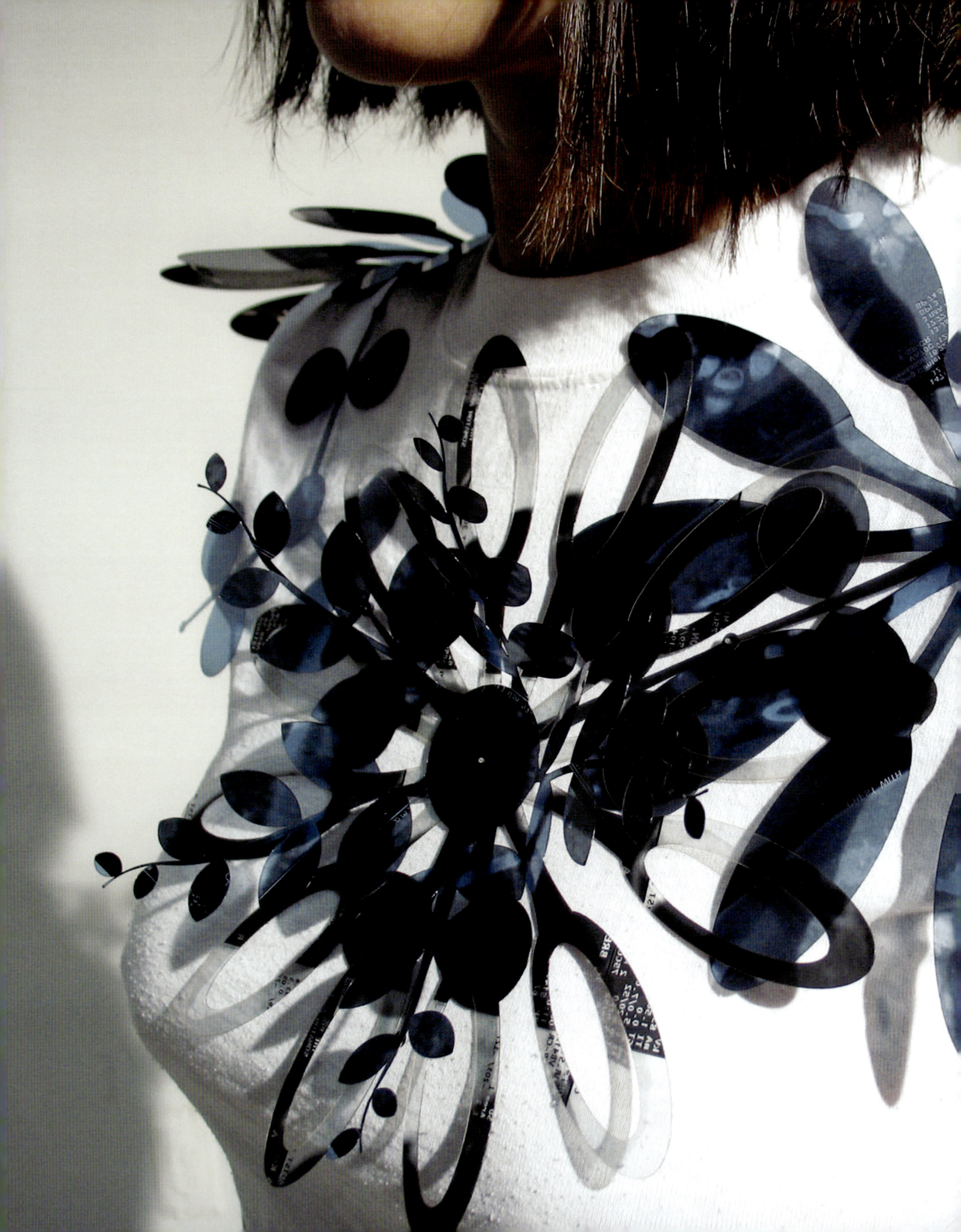

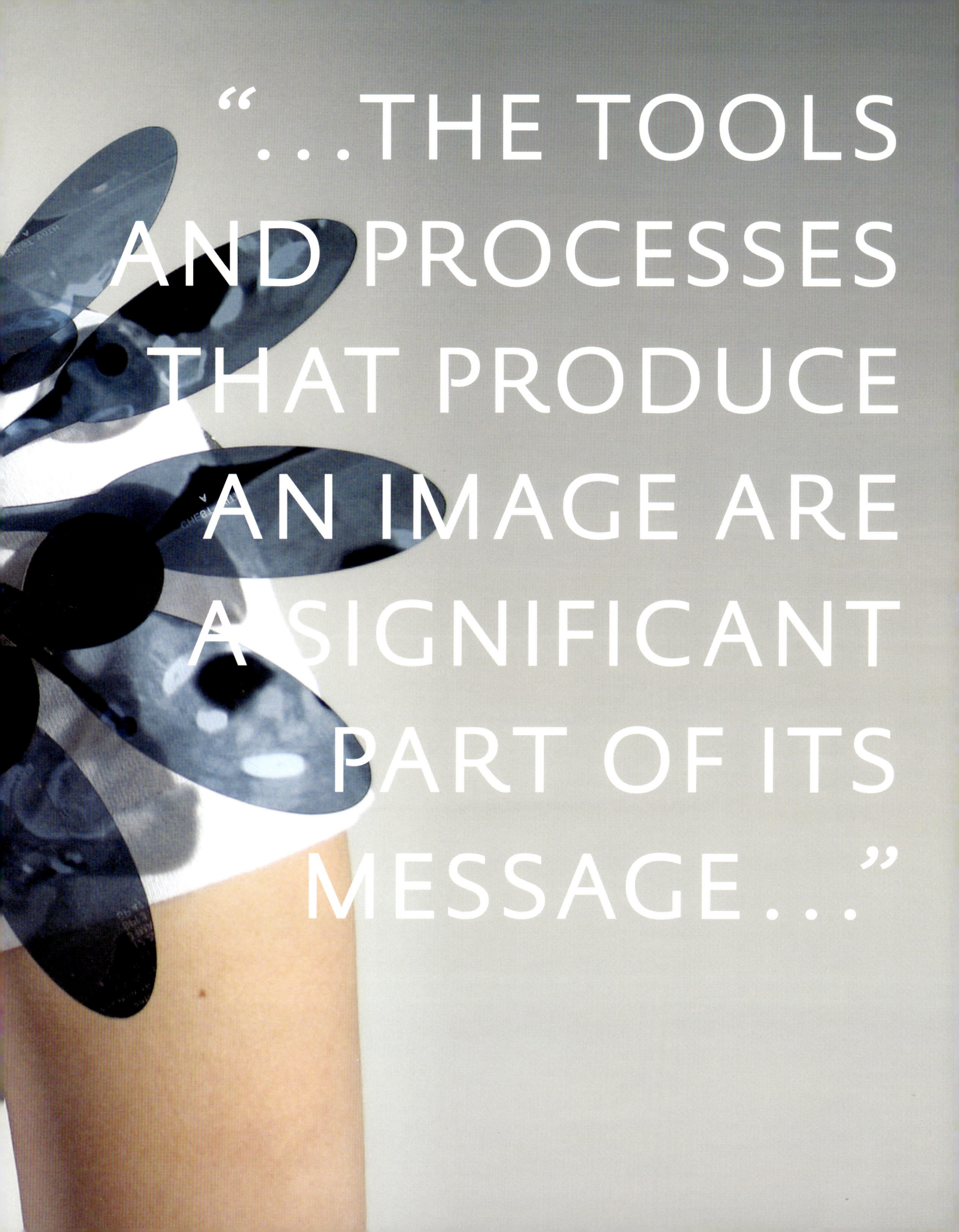

"...THE TOOLS AND PROCESSES THAT PRODUCE AN IMAGE ARE A SIGNIFICANT PART OF ITS MESSAGE..."

LOST LENSES AND ORPHANED APERTURES
APPARATUS TRANS-FORMED

MARK ALICE DURANT

PHOTOGRAPHY'S STORY BEGAN when someone noticed that light passing through a small aperture into a darkened chamber recreated the world in ghostly projection. The fascination with this phenomenon was centuries old by the time a process was patented in 1839 for fixing that elusive glow. Since its inception, the practice of photography has required the marriage of craft, aesthetics, technology, optics, chemistry, and industrial design in an unprecedented formula that has permanently changed the visual landscape of human culture.

Every artistic tradition has its tools and technologies. The materials and processes of a particular tradition give evidence to the time and culture in which they were born and developed. Animal-hair brushes, pigments ground from earth, foundries and heavy metals, sharp tools for scratching into stone all speak to an artisanal relationship to art making. The practices of oil painting, lithography, and bronze casting require an almost alchemical knowledge of elemental materials and a physical commitment that engenders a sensual intimacy.

Since its inception, photography has been at the forefront of technological innovation. In the first fifty years of photography's history, tintypes replaced daguerreotypes, wet plate emulsions were, in turn, succeeded by dry plates, large-format cameras requiring clunky tripods were surpassed by the handheld Kodak Brownie, and glass negatives were made archaic by the rolls of film that filled the Brownie camera. Although the tools and processes of photography continued to be refined over the course of the twentieth century through the development of sharper lenses, faster emulsions, and lighter cameras, until recently the basic characteristics of the mechanisms of photography remained rooted in its nineteenth-century birth.

Photography deals in time-specific imagery. Not only is every photograph a direct record of the instant of its making, turning the present moment into a time capsule, but the very materiality of the image and the manner in which it was made locate it in the chronology of technological process. The tools and processes that produce an image are a significant aspect of its message. To compare the formality of a nineteenth-century daguerreotype portrait with a candid Polaroid from the 1970s, for example, reveals layers of sociological information about fashion and the repertoire of human gesture, but also illustrates a century's worth of technical innovation.

With the rapid rise of digital imaging technologies, analog photography, dominant for over one hundred fifty years, has quietly slipped out the back door to join the exclusive club of highly refined yet somewhat anachronistic mediums that have fallen into disuse. One result of this change is that photographic traditions and esoteric vocabulary consisting of light sensitive emulsions, mechanical apertures, and toxic chemistry have been boxed up and placed among the attic rafters. Thrift stores and eBay are clogged with old cameras, the leather cases they came in, lenses, filters, film canisters, enlargers, developing trays, tongs, and assorted darkroom ephemera. Nevertheless, these artifacts are not simply archaic curiosities or nostalgic objects; they are talismans of memory, catalyzing agents of photography's power and magic. Light passed through apertures, was focused by lenses and absorbed in emulsions to freeze the incessant motion of time and bear witness to histories both large and small. Contemporary jewelry artists, like spelunkers rummaging through the remains of an ancient cave-dwelling culture, have been mining the cast-off treasures of this technological shift.

The very first photographic experiments of Nicéphore Niépce, William Henry Fox Talbot, and Louis Daguerre in the 1820s and 1830s were still lifes or unpopulated city views. Early emulsions required so much light and such long exposures that any attempt to capture an animated being would inevitably produce a blurry ghost. As soon as the technology was up to the task, however, the most fundamental of photographic relationships was established: one person pointing a camera at another to represent his or her body and countenance, proclaiming, irrefutably as it were, "I was here." Since its earliest days then, photography has been capturing bodies—bodies at work, bodies at play, bodies on display—sometimes furtively, sometimes with the conscious intent of arousing desire for commodities and, of course, for sex. The artists under consideration in this essay turn that equation on its head; instead of using the camera to capture the human body, they utilize discarded photographic fragments, ephemera, and detritus in their necklaces, bracelets, pendants, and other ornaments so that the body captures, displays, and refers to the history of photographic apparatus.

Many people are drawn to photography because of all the gadgets and gear that marry polished glass and industrial metal. Cameras, especially film cameras, are precise machines with multiple moving parts. The three basic functions of a camera that shape and control light are focus, aperture, and shutter speed. In most cameras the lenses and aperture share space inside a series of interlocking metal cylinders. Craig Arnold, a photographer by training and a jeweler by happenstance, was fiddling with a broken lens when he realized that the aperture and focus rings might be turned into bracelets or "cuffs" (NO. 130). Depending on whether the lens is wide angle, telephoto or zoom, the width and markings on the focus rings will vary. Arnold's cuffs are materially straightforward, elegant, tough, even manly. The aperture ratios and focus alignments inscribed on the cuffs remain as enigmatic coding, echoes of the obscure language of photographic culture, suggesting membership in a secret society.

Sandy Johanson is both an accomplished photographer and a confident jeweler. Her intimate working knowledge of the mechanics of photography is revealed in her necklaces assembled from camera remnants. Suturing elements such as apertures, ring shutters, winding mechanisms, and filament flash bulbs into industrial elegance (NO. 125), Johanson shares some of the spirit of Steam Punk aesthetics, which resuscitates real and fantasy histories of Victorian-era technologies. Even the title of one such piece—*Selenium Cell Pendant*—suggests that the facts and fictions of industrial culture can be hybridized in unusual ways (NO. 124).

Photography and jewelry have equally contradictory relations to wealth and exclusivity on the one hand and accessibility and popularity on the other. Photography began as a kind of expensive hobby for the leisure classes but was soon transformed into the most democratic of mediums. Photography trades in celebrity, stocking an ever-growing archive of beauty and privilege while simultaneously offering the humblest among us a way of creating a visual record of our sorry existences. Jewelry making, historically associated with guild craftsmen working precious metals and rare gems into filigreed baubles for a decadent aristocracy, is in fact a far more diverse practice that stretches across cultures and social classes.

Francisco Toledo, for example, is a Mexican painter, sculptor, ceramist, and graphic artist who has spent a lifetime developing and refining images that resonate with Pre-Columbian iconography. Toledo's imaginary world is inhabited with fantastical creatures, strange insects, and hybrid beasts representing ancient myths. By cutting X-ray films of the body's interior into the shape of crabs, Toledo's necklace embodies two distinct image forms—the medical and the imaginary (NO. 118). The X-rays literally show us what is below the surface, while the marine life symbols refer to the mysteries of the allegorical deep.

The cyanotype process is one of photography's earliest incarnations. This anachronistic medium produces images of ghostly shapes surrounded by radiant blues that are so otherworldly compared to the hard-edged contrasts of black and white that the process has never really gone out of fashion. Whether manifesting in necklace, brooch, or wall-piece forms, Thea Clark's work combines shaped pink plastic and cyanotype imagery in a unique hybrid of structure and image (NO. 128), the contemporary and archaic, the organic and the architectural. Her *Root Pendant*, for example, suggests a kind of living Eiffel Tower that thrusts upward toward the neck and head of the wearer while finger-like roots stretch down to the lower regions of the body (NO. 127). Interlocking cyanotype imagery encircles the pendant, interrupted by a pink stitching that has attached itself to the pattern like a virus. Ideas of identity, health, secrets, and sources of power resonate from this association of forms and materials. Like much of Clark's work, *Root Pendant* is a deceptively simple miniature ecosystem of organic and cultural references.

Inspired by the way in which photography fragments and represents time and space, Karen Misher's body adornments proffer glass prisms, mirrors, and lenses in place of rubies, sapphires, or other gemstones. Her bracelet *Momentary* (NO. 129) reflects, refracts, and refocuses the persons, places, and moments of the immediate environment. Misher considers her jewelry to be wearable sculpture, and like sculpture, her jewelry activates the social space around it. As the body moves, the mirrors, lenses, and prisms that ornament her bracelets, necklaces, rings, and earrings continually shift and change their color in syncopation with the environment.

Jiro Kamata has similar concerns in relation to time and even coined the term *Momentopia* for one of his series of works to underline his philosophical dedication to the present moment. Using old camera lenses clustered together and set in darkened silver, Kamata's necklace is a study in elegant understatement (NO. 123). While decoratively subdued, the piece is deeply suggestive of darkened pools or, conversely, brightening celestial orbs in the night sky. Kamata insists that despite their apparent transparency, old lenses contain the history of all that has passed through them, and if one begins to contemplate such a fanciful phenomenon, rich associations among time, light, history, spirit, and mortality are evoked. In a more playful, albeit still philosophical vein, Kamata achieves astonishing effects in his Spiegel series by combining lenses with mirrors that draw the viewer into his fantasy realm (NO. 122).

If artists like Johanson and Kamata depend upon the orphaned materials of analog photography, the Korean metalsmith Hyun-Seok Sim revitalizes the camera as object by reinventing it from scratch. Using brass and silver, Sim constructs working miniature cameras—even the screws are handmade—that can be worn as pendants (NO. 126B). The look of these precious, functional cameras is classic industrial design meets Art Deco, as if they were purchased in the gift shop atop the Chrysler Building circa 1930. One might even imagine the characters in Fritz Lang's 1927 dystopian masterpiece *Metropolis* wearing them around their necks. Through his precious miniature cameras, Sim reacquaints us with the functional beauty of these devices. Because every camera is handmade, each one is capable of producing unique images. Some feature the softness, vignetting, and slight distortion of pinhole camera images, while others produce remarkably sharp photographs, as if the light passed through the most refined of lenses, and still others feature dual lenses of stereoscopic imagery.

Among the many progressive ideas of the 1960s and 1970s was a growing sensitivity to the ecological fragility of the Earth. Many photographers fretted over the odious chemicals required to process film and photographs, not to mention all of the metals, paper, and plastics that were used to package photographic materials only to be thrown indiscriminately into the trash. Jaimie MacDonald is a Scottish artist dedicated to reusing discarded materials in her work in order to call attention to both the waste and the potential beauty in our everyday refuse. MacDonald recycles and transforms one of the more mundane artifacts of the analog photography era—the film canister. These formerly ubiquitous plastic containers held rolls of film, and, although occasionally repurposed as pillboxes and the like, they generally were thrown out by the millions with the trash. MacDonald explodes these canisters to reveal wavelike forms before mounting them upon a simple ring (NO. 120).

Swiss-born Verena Sieber-Fuchs has a background in textiles, which gives her an extraordinary sensitivity to patterning no matter how unconventional the materials may be. Her collars made from hundreds of frames of movie stills are burned at the edges to create visceral and unique textures that are then woven into delicate waves (NO. 121). The film material contains an internal contradiction; it is transparent and inhabited by images, in other words, empty and full simultaneously. On first glance the collars appear to be made from clusters of reflective mica or even shell, but on closer inspection hundreds of slivers of images emerge to encircle the wearer like a halo of ghosts.

From silver brooches to dynamic wall installations, Julia Barello's works demonstrate a wide range of materials and presentation strategies. Many of her pieces utilize the somewhat ominous and furtive medical imagery of MRI films and X-rays that map the shadowy images of our internal landscapes, searching for anomalies and fractures. These ghosts of our interiority are fundamental material and fertile metaphor for Barello. She titles her pieces with obscure rhetorical concepts such as *Abcisio*, which means to break off in the middle of a discourse, or *Anacolouthon*, a fragmented sentence without completion, or *Ethopoeia*, which means to put oneself in the place of another. By dyeing, patterning, and externalizing this imagery into flowery clusters that envelop the torso like an exuberant vine or hang from earlobes like exotic fruit, Barello not only recycles these medical artifacts but also transforms them into lovely meditations on the language of the body (NO. 119).

Slipping on a ring or necklace in the morning may seem the simplest of gestures, but that directness belies a ritualistic complexity. As talismans, or symbols of sexual availability, or signs of tribal identity, or declarations of individualism or allegiance, body adornments are essentially performative. The body is a site for activating personal intent, and certain wearable objects can demonstrate a rhetorical power that goes beyond the decorative. The performance becomes real, so to speak, upon stepping outside the intimate boundaries of one's domicile. In the public sphere, the ring, the pendant, and the bracelet activate social space by becoming a sign of the wearer's intent. The body and the ornament agree to a kind of reciprocal activation; the ornament protects and extends the body's presence, while the body provides the ornament with physical and social mobility.

The photographic act has echoes of this performance as well: the camera and its attendant gear can be viewed as wearable sculpture that not only assists vision but also swathes the entire body. There is an almost predatory aspect to the photographer who slings long-lensed cameras over his shoulder and straps on film belts before strutting into the fray. As Marshall McLuhan observed, all technologies extend the human body to amplify or supplement human experience. Photography has expanded humanity's visual consciousness, has intervened in our notion of memory to shape our images of personal and collective history. Throughout its history, especially since the development of portable cameras in the late nineteenth century, the camera has served as a functional instrument and a symbol of intentionality, declaring the presence of an observer, an outsider who is nonetheless there to witness the major and minor events of humanity's narrative.

The dance between the artist's intentions and his chosen medium can be initially awkward, a struggle between personal vision and physical resistance. If the artist is experienced, wise, lucky, or all three, a middle ground will be discovered in which the material gives in a little to move in new directions, while the artist learns a lesson in humility and the fine art of subtle coaxing. All of these jewelers, metalsmiths, designers, and decorative artists have navigated oblique angles, conjured unexpected transformations, and utilized photography's detritus of lenses, apertures, and emulsions in order to conjoin two very distinct mediums. Here, photography's apparatus does not need to spend eternity heaped in the junk pile of antiquated technology but is given a second life, vividly adorning and absorbing the warmth of living bodies.

Mark Alice Durant *is an artist and writer. His website,* saint-lucy *[www.saint-lucy.com], is devoted to writing about photography and contemporary art.*

In my new Spiegel series, I work with translucent camera lenses with mirrors behind them in order to create magical effects. If you look deeply into the *Spiegel Pendant*, you will find your own image inside—but as part of a strange fantasy world. The mirror reflects reality, but the concave lens alters it.

122
Jiro Kamata
Spiegel Pendant, 2010
Camera lens, mirror, blackened silver, stainless steel, nylon string
2 in. (5 cm), diameter
Collection of Susan Grant Lewin

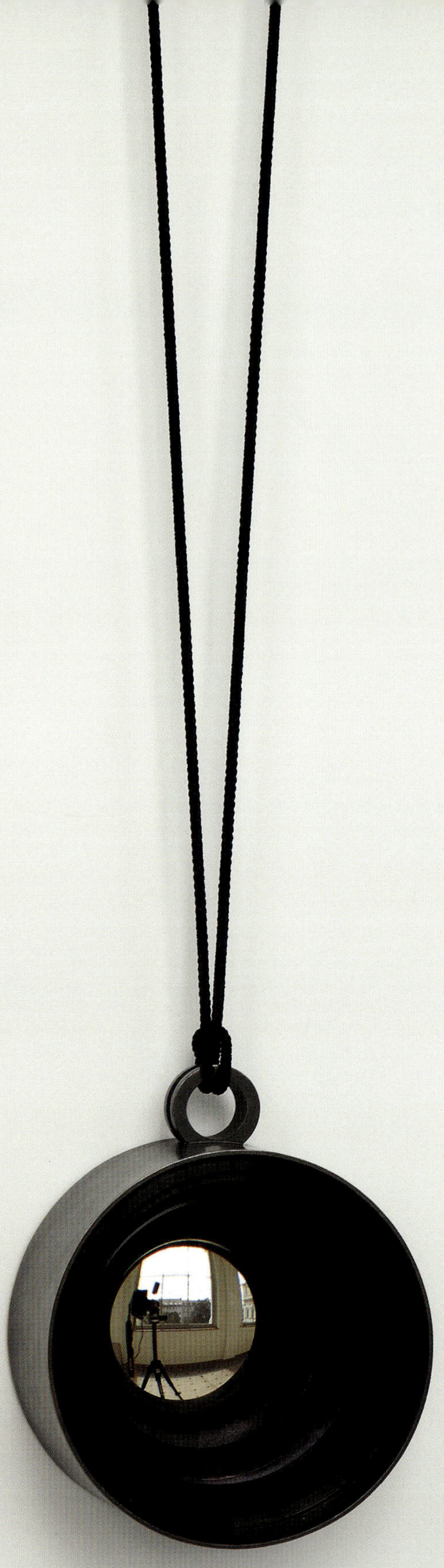

JIRO KAMATA

Spiegel Pendant | *Momentopia Necklace*

Jewelry implies value, but what does this mean? I make jewelry from old camera lenses that have retired from active duty and can be found covered in a light layer of dust, in an obscure corner of some camera shop. Yet those cast-off lenses witnessed the memorable and precious moments of people's lives. I confirm their value by using them as jewels.

123
Jiro Kamata
Momentopia Necklace, 2007
Camera lenses, blackened silver, lacquer
$6^3/_8$ in. (16 cm), diameter
Collection Deutsches Goldschmiedehaus Hanau, Inv-no DG/412

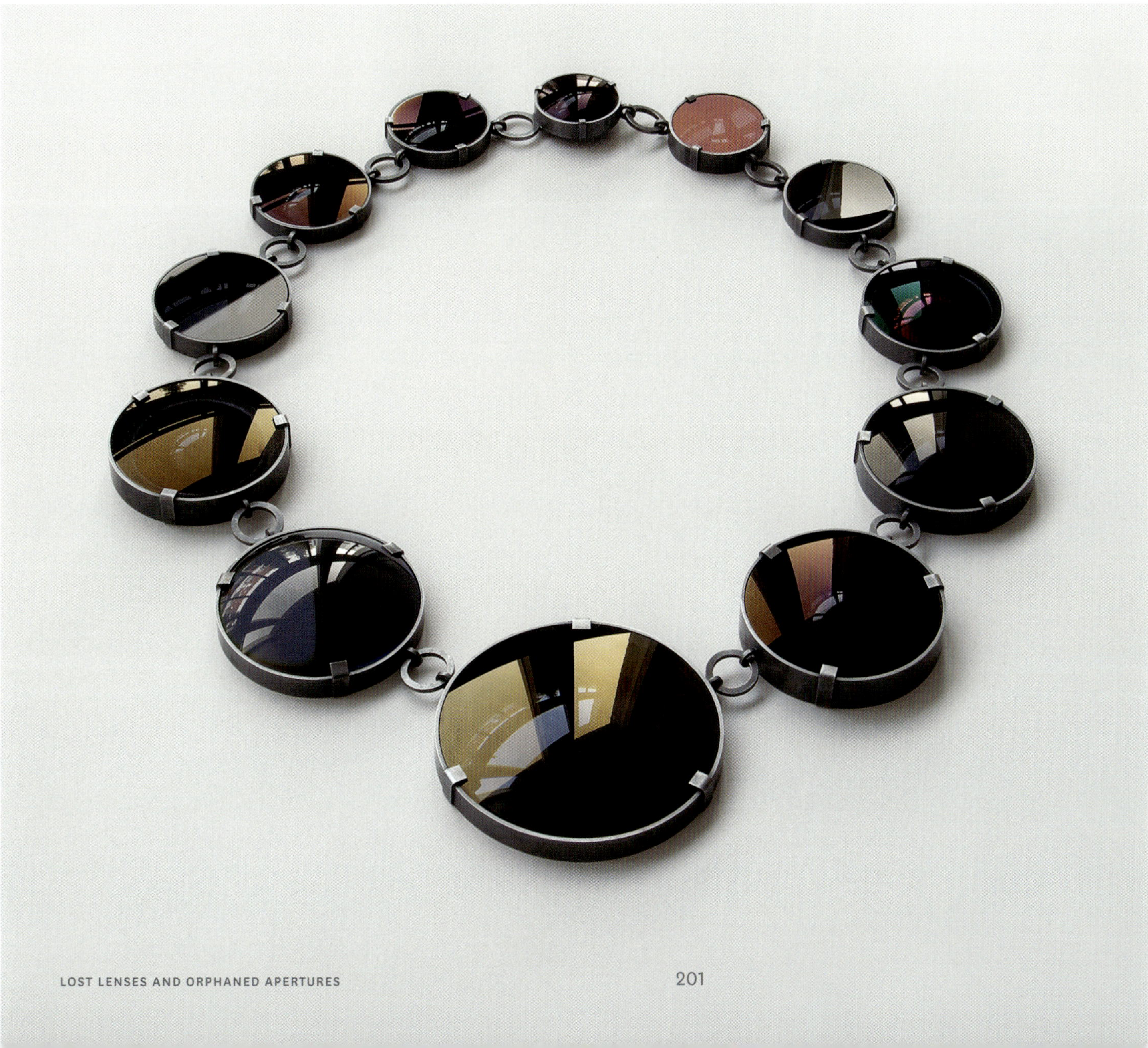

VERENA SIEBER-FUCHS

Neck Ornament

I have been working by hand with various discarded materials for many years. My work is a serious game, a game with the material, the technique, the shape, and overall with the thoughts and events of our everyday lives. I was trained as a textile worker. For *Neck Ornament*, I crocheted snippets of Super 8mm film from the cutting room floor, joining together myriad small pieces to conjure this feathery collar.

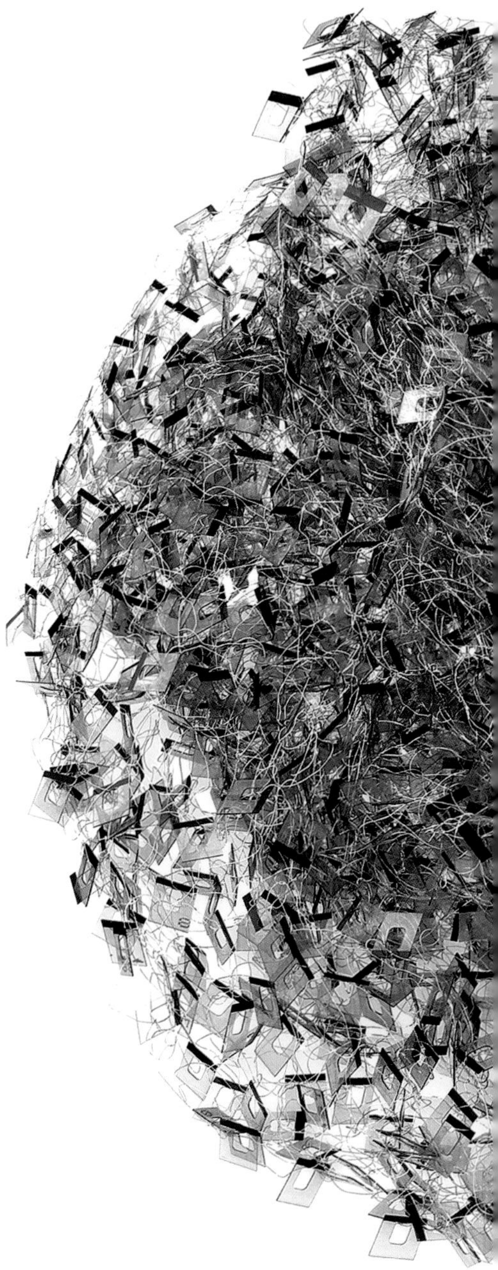

121
Verena Sieber-Fuchs
Neck Ornament, ca. 1998
Photographic film, monofilament
$14^{1}/_{2}$ x 26 in. (36.8 x 66 cm)
Museum of Arts and Design,
gift from the collection of
Barbara Tober, 2013

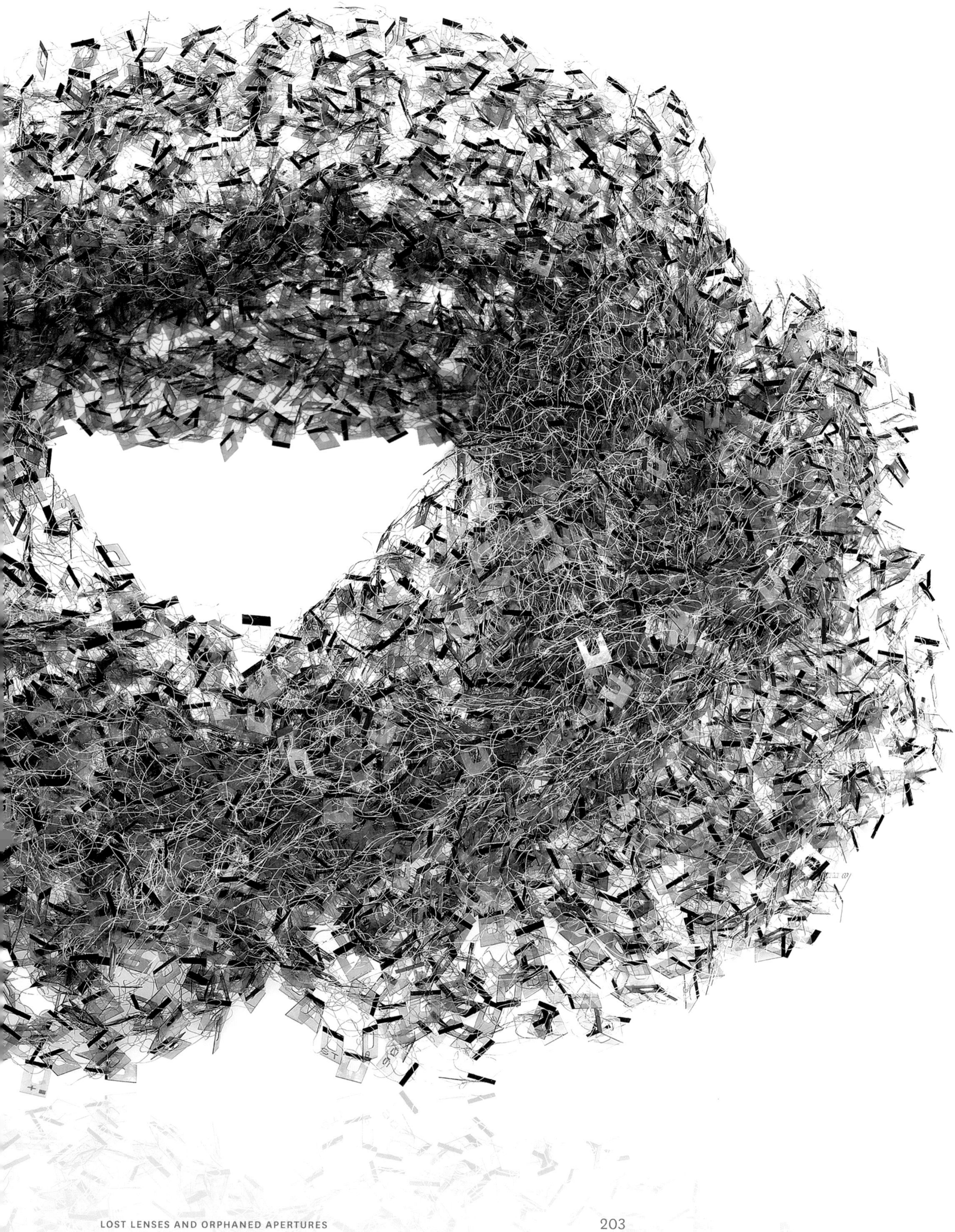

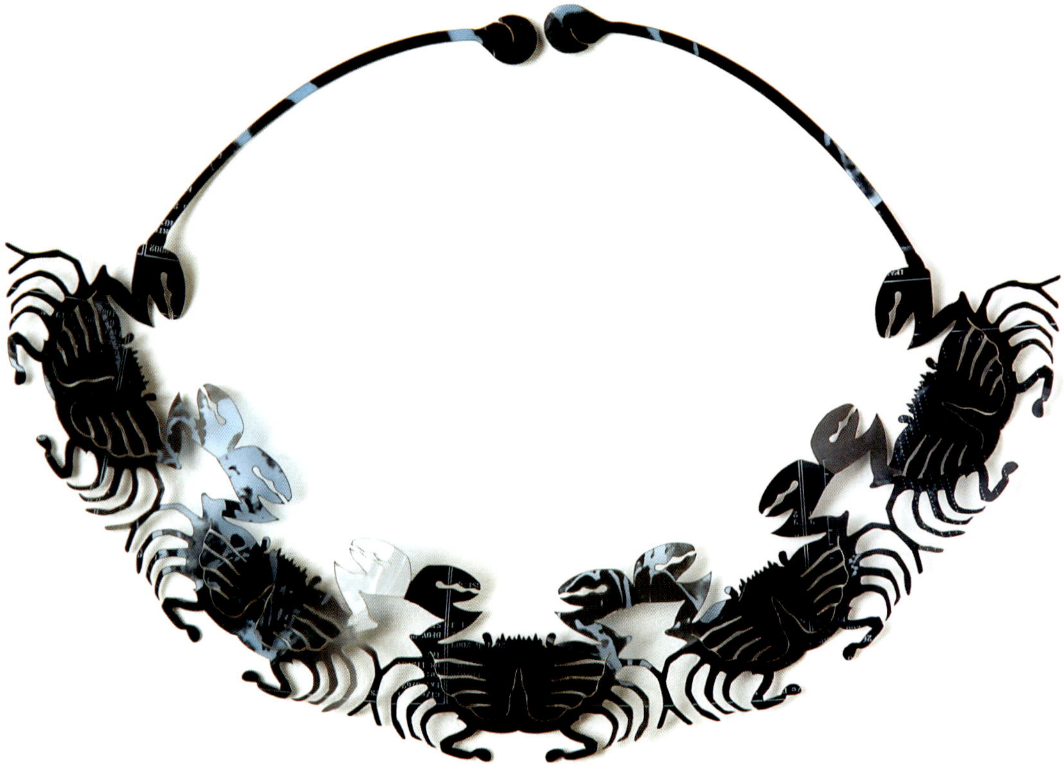

FRANCISCO TOLEDO

Sarta de Cangrejos #2

118
Francisco Toledo in collaboration with
Centro de las Artes de San Agustín
Sarta de Cangrejos #2 (necklace), 2012
X-ray film
6 1/2 x 8 1/2 in. (16.5 x 21.6 cm)
Collection of Kiff Slemmons

Francisco Toledo's necklace functions like his drawings but on film, and in this case laser-cut X-ray film. The crab image derives from the rich vocabulary of nearly all of his art, often sourcing tales and legends of Oaxaca's mythic history. The intricacy of the drawing, its crisp clarity, and its subject as jewelry to be worn around the neck give it an edge. The necklace sets up an additional edge through X-ray film often associated with malady and brokenness, but here it serves to provide the possibility for intricate detail.

Kiff Slemmons on behalf of Francisco Toledo.

JULIA BARELLO

Abcisio

Decorating the body with flowers and floral forms is an ancient practice, yet the flowers in this necklace speak not to our oneness with nature but to our complicated place in it. Our biology is of the world we inhabit, yet the artifacts and structures we create distance us from the basic truths of nature concerning birth, growth, and death. Trace elements of human forms remain in *Abcisio*—sliced, residual imagery from someone who went one day to have a photograph taken of the interior of his body with the hope of gaining insight into his current and continued existence. This necklace is about boldly and willfully dressing up to face the uncertainty of life.

119
Julia Barello
Abcisio (necklace) from the Flowers of Rhetoric series, 2007
X-ray film, monofilament
21 x 21 x 2 in. (53.3 x 53.3 x 5.1 cm)
Collection of the artist

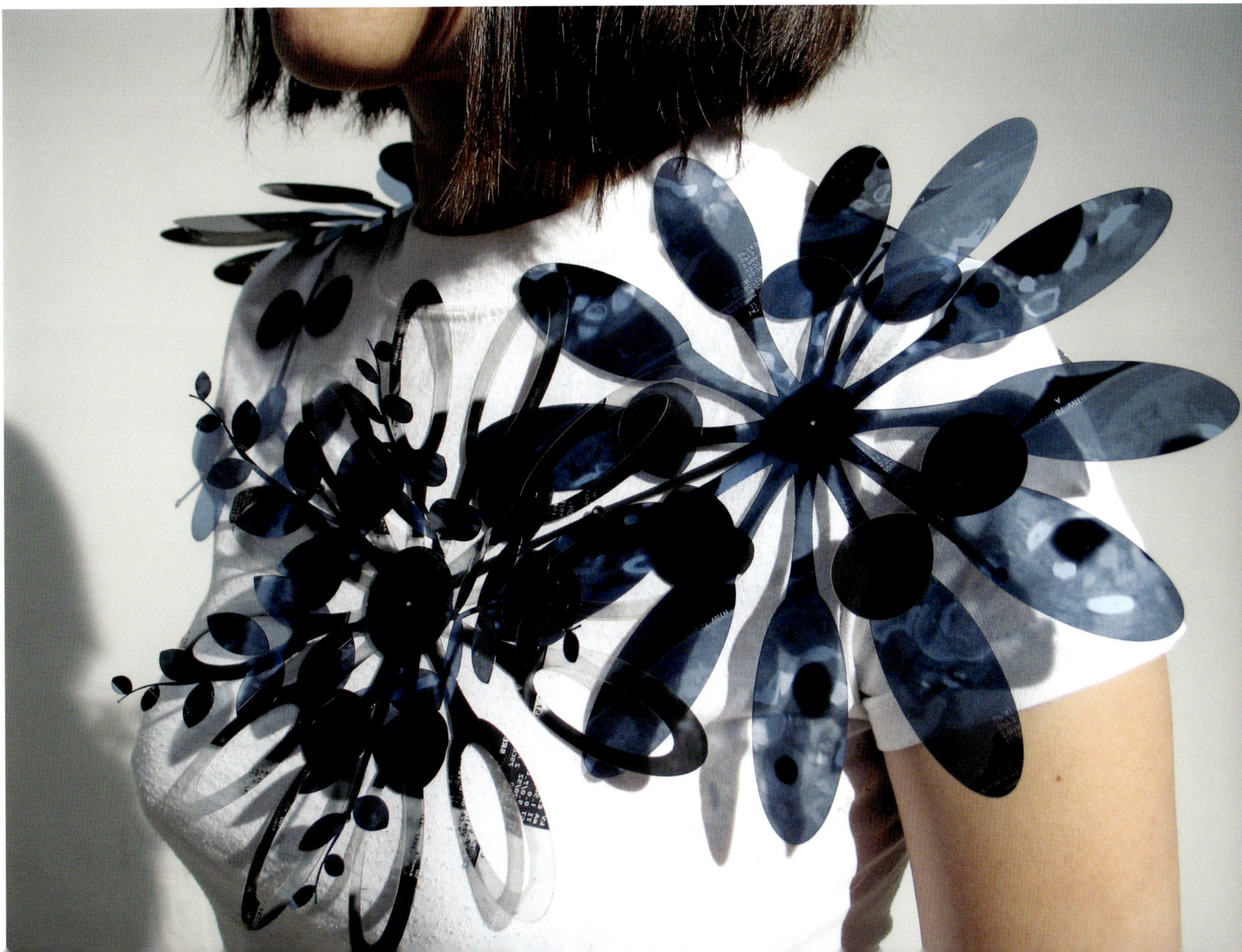

JAIMIE MACDONALD

Wave Goodbye Ring

The *Wave Goodbye Ring* was created at what was the beginning of my journey in transforming reusable materials into beautiful and meaningful objects. After weeks of collecting in local photography shops, I embarked on intensive experimentation in the qualities I could elicit from film canisters. These crisp man-made objects became meaningful to me as the textures and forms that emerged began to reflect features of the landscape I had drawn and photographed on frequent trips to visit my family and my childhood home in the Highlands of Scotland.

120 OPPOSITE PAGE
Jaimie MacDonald
Wave Goodbye Ring, 2005
Plastic film canisters, metal
3 5/8 x 2 3/4 x 2 3/8 in. (9 x 7 x 6 cm)
Collection of the artist

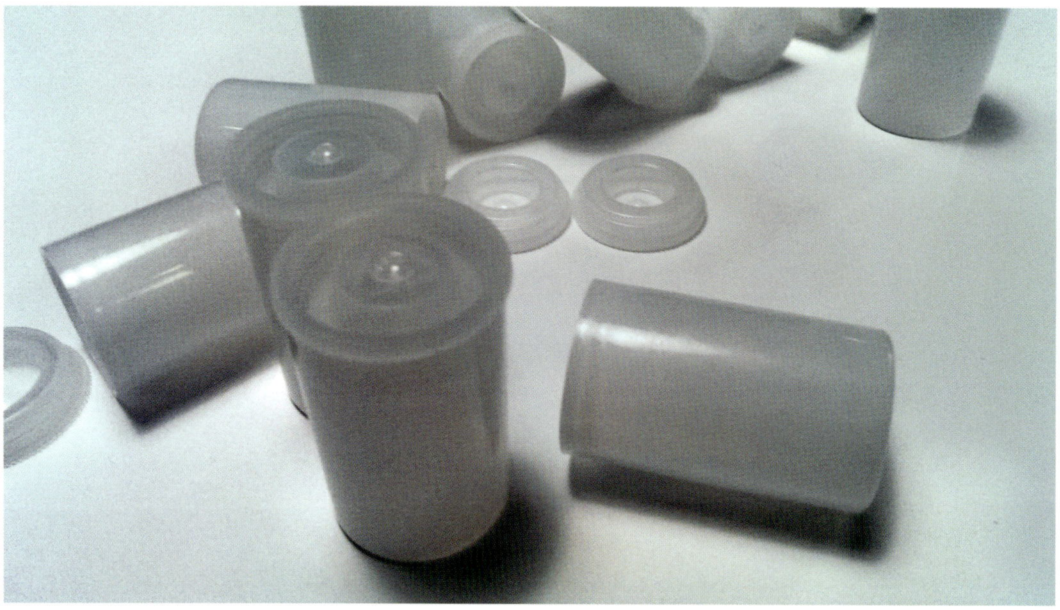

LEFT
Analog film canisters.

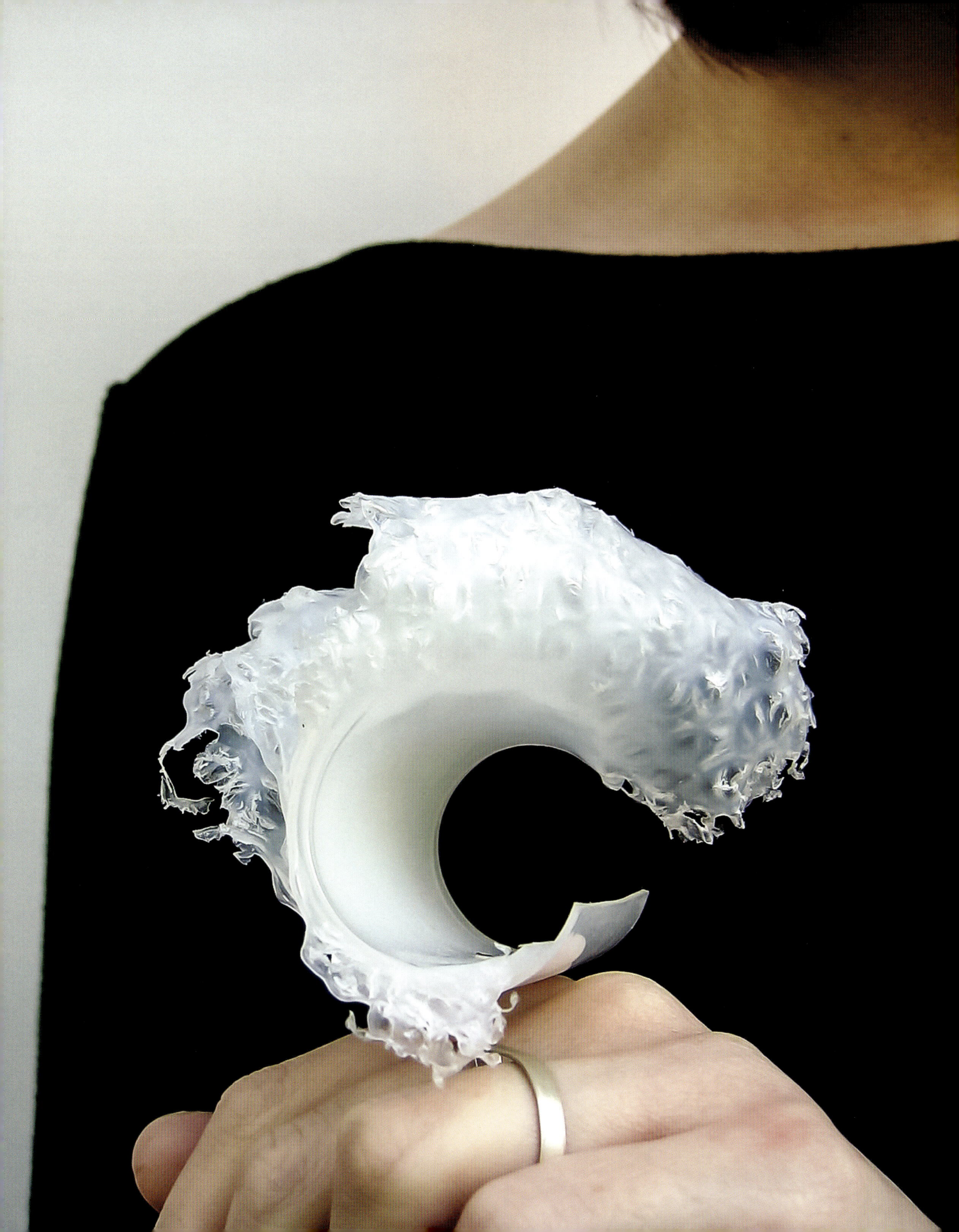

SANDY JOHANSON

Selenium Cell Pendant | *Flash Bulb Neckpiece*

Selenium Cell Pendant **pays tribute to the selenium device that converts light from the visible spectrum into measurable information.**

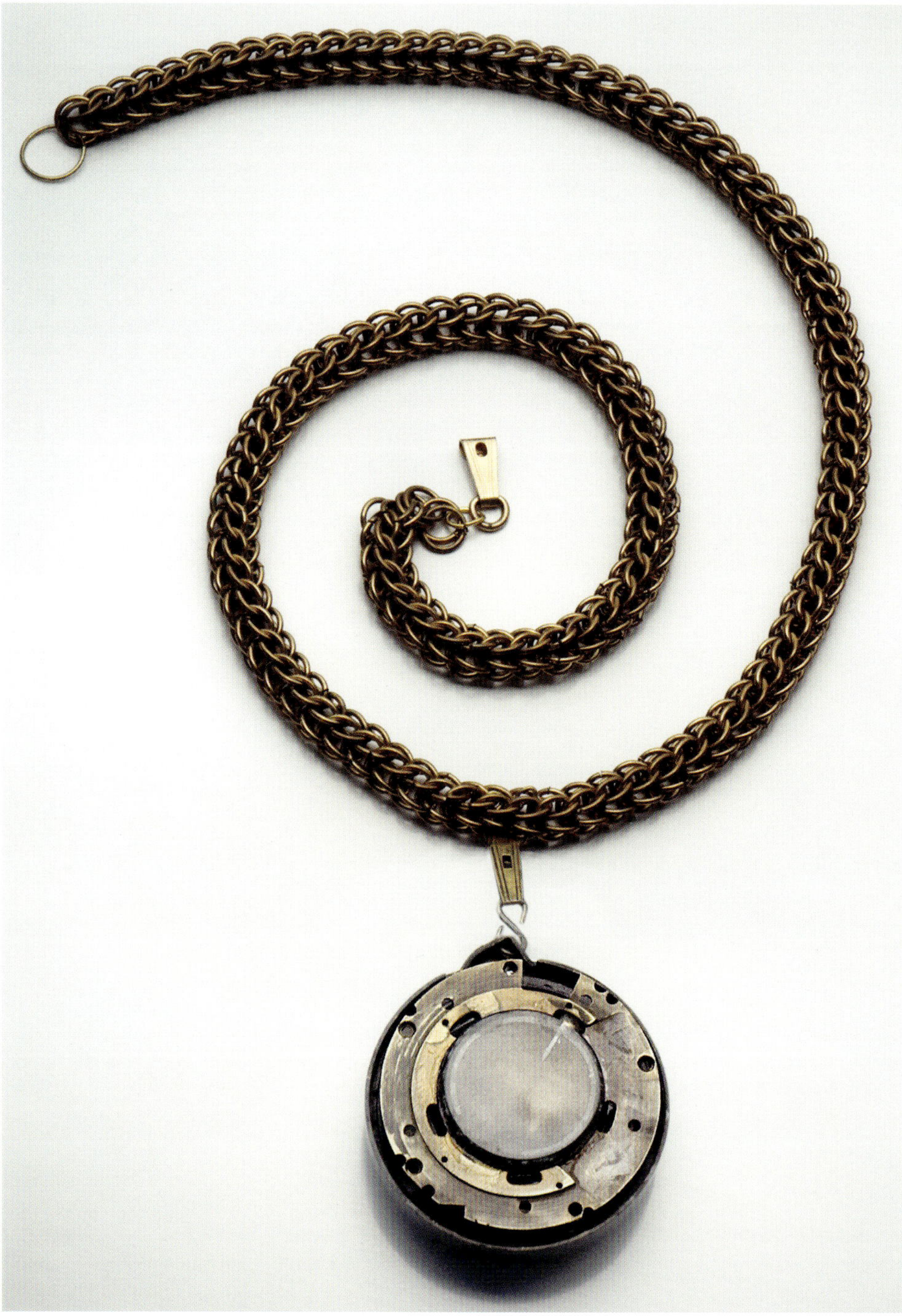

124
Sandy Johanson
Selenium Cell Pendant, 2011
Selenium photovoltaic cell from DeJur light meter, lens housing from Kodak Autographic 1a, brass chain
16 1/2 x 2 in. (41.9 x 5.1 cm)
Collection of the artist

Flash Bulb Neckpiece is made from Sylvania Blue Dot flashbulbs from the 1960s and sterling silver wire. Flashbulbs were coated with blue plastic to match the spectral quality of daylight-balanced color film. This coating also provided a protective shield if the bulb shattered during the flash. By incorporating the fragile, blue flashbulbs into an openwork silver wire structure, I created an updated interpretation of the cartwheel ruff seen in sixteenth-century Dutch portrait paintings and in so doing, united the piece with the constantly evolving history of personal adornment.

125

Sandy Johanson
Flash Bulb Neckpiece, 2011
Unfired Sylvania FP 26 Blue Dot flashbulbs, ca. 1960, patinated sterling silver wire
3 x 8 x 2 1/2 in. (7.6 x 20.3 x 6.4 cm)
Collection of the artist

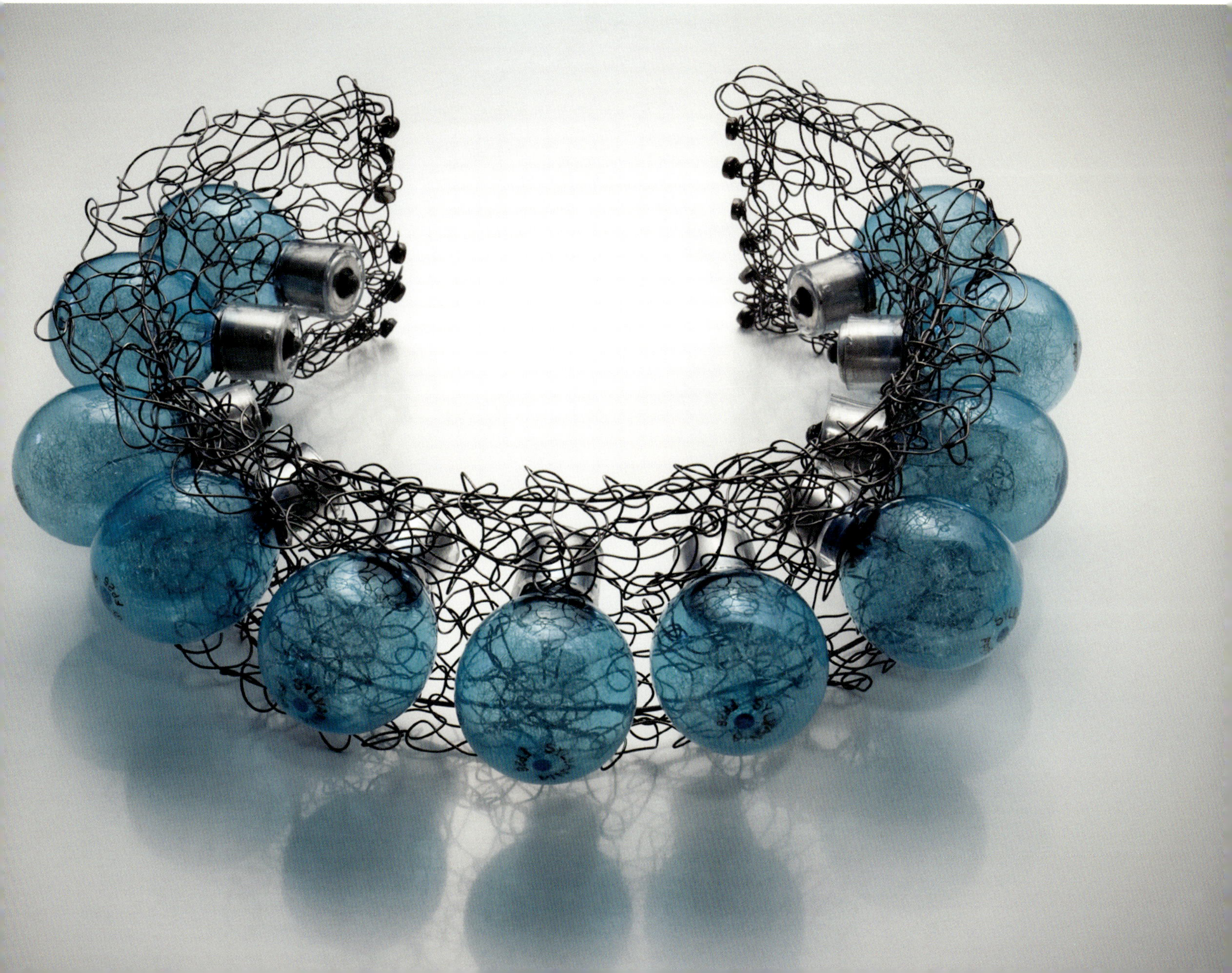

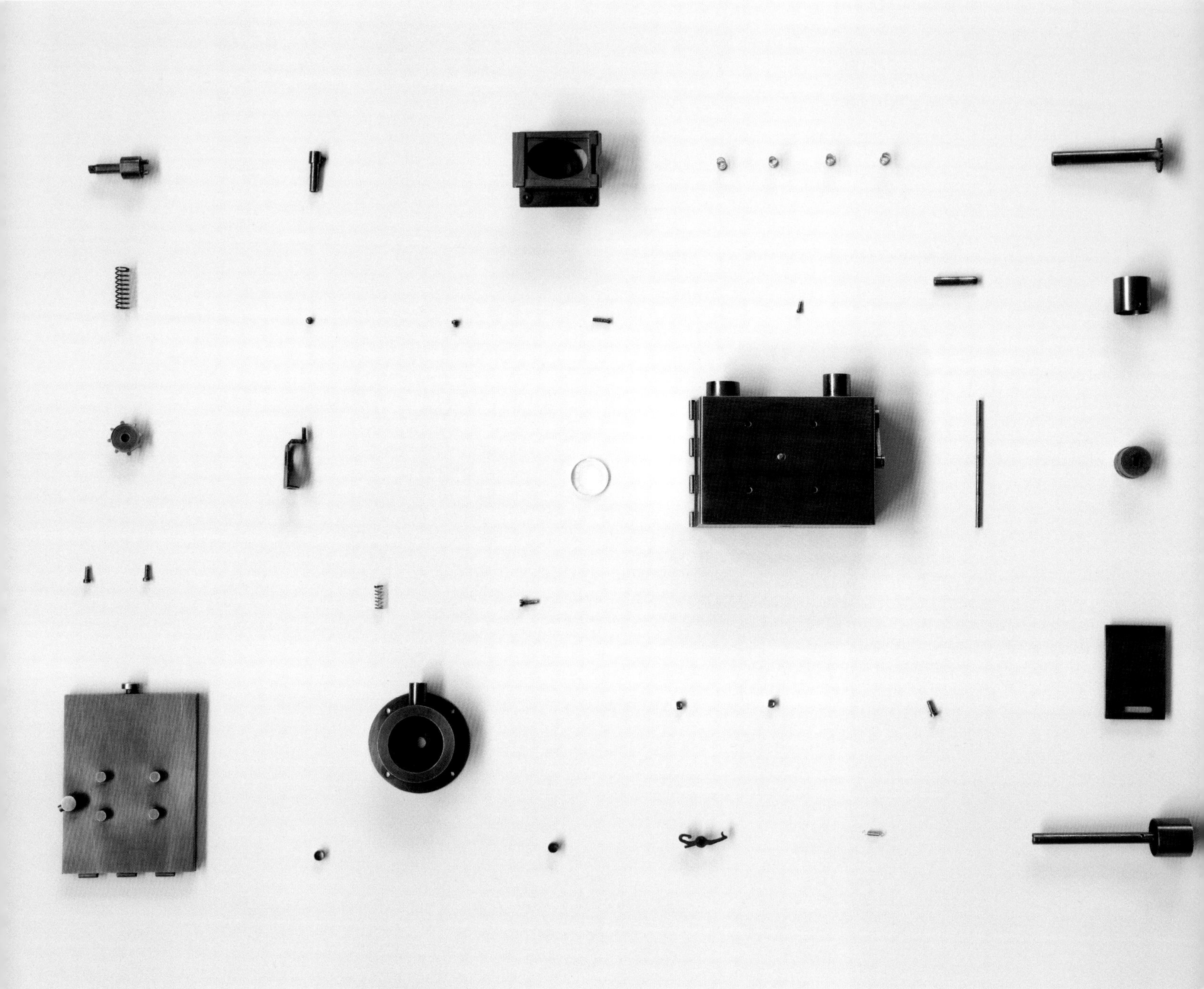

126A OPPOSITE PAGE

Hyun-Seok Sim
Parts of *135 Camera* (pendant), 2007
20k gold, sterling silver, steel, glass
Collection of the artist

126B RIGHT

Hyun-Seok Sim
Panoramic Camera (pendant), 2000
20k gold, sterling silver, steel, plastic
$2^{1}/_{2}$ x $1^{3}/_{4}$ x $1^{5}/_{8}$ in. (6.3 x 4.3 x 4.2 cm)
Collection of the artist

BELOW

Photographs taken by the artist with the *Panoramic Camera* pendant.

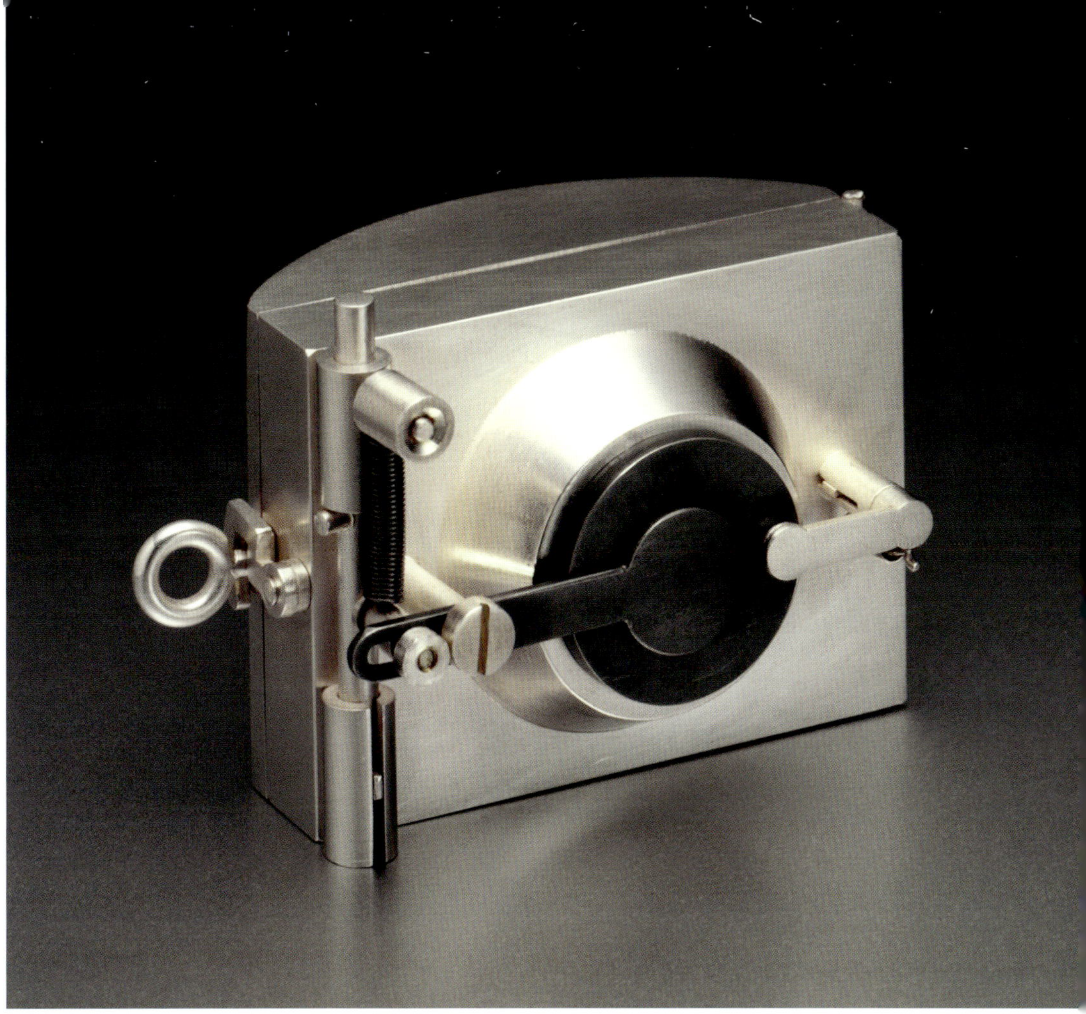

HYUN-SEOK SIM

135 Camera | *Panoramic Camera*

People, especially men, love cameras the way they love cars. In cameras, they see toys, tools, and wealth. I don't wear jewelry, but I like to wear a camera around my neck, and I enjoy using and looking at these precious tools. It makes sense that cameras should be worn as jewelry.

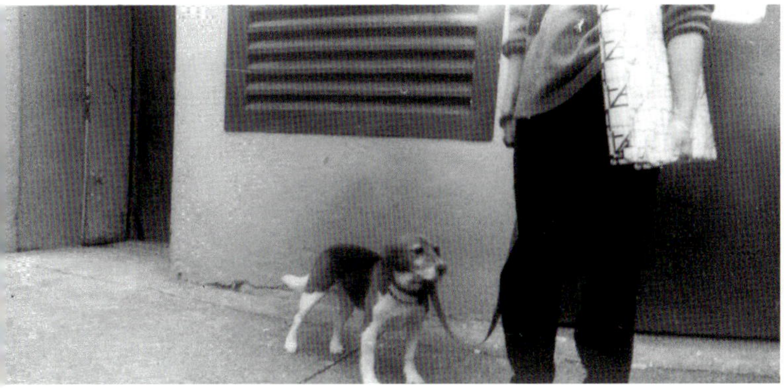

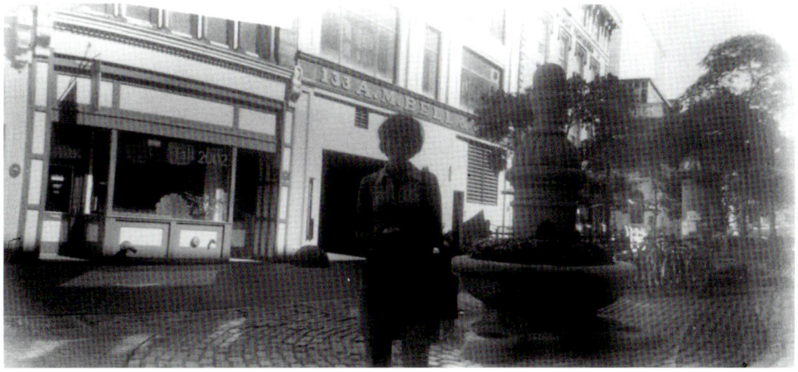

127

Thea Clark
Root Pendant from the
Fluidity and Form series, 2011
Cyanotype on silk, tinted plastic, wood,
nickel, oxidized silver, PVC
6 x 2 x 1 1/2 in. (15.2 x 5.1 x 3.8 cm)
Collection of the artist

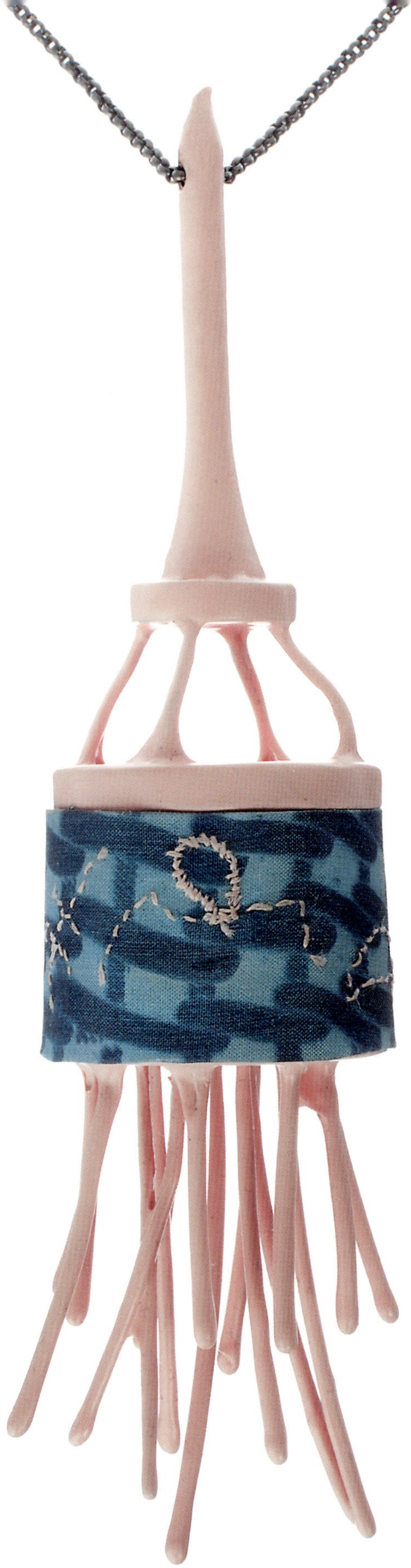

THEA CLARK

Root Pendant | *Six Degrees*

An investigation into the nature of identity provided inspiration for the pink and blue pieces from my Fluidity and Form series. These works evoke dualities: male and female, anima and animus, yin and yang, stasis and change. The cyanotype images can be seen as fragments of memory, abstracted elements of a changing narrative that add up to a notion of self. They were captured on silk using UV light and water and are rendered in the classic blue color of this early photographic process. Like dermis over muscle, the tinted pink plastic both obscures and unifies the structure underlying it. Alternatively, these pink plastic forms can be read in relation to time. Are they becoming? Solidifying the ephemeral? Or reversing the process, dissolving, and disintegrating?

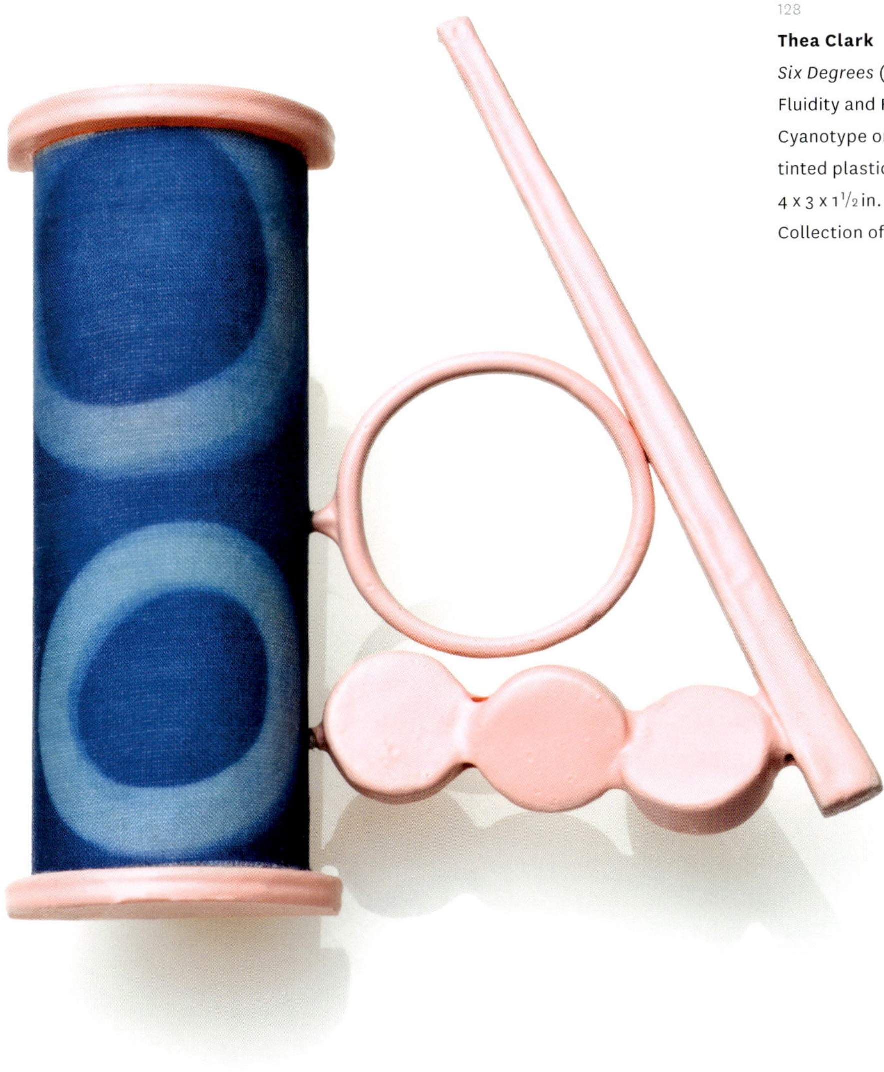

128
Thea Clark
Six Degrees (brooch) from the Fluidity and Form series, 2010
Cyanotype on silk, wood, copper, tinted plastic, acrylic, PVC
4 x 3 x 1½ in. (10.2 x 7.6 x 3.8 cm)
Collection of the artist

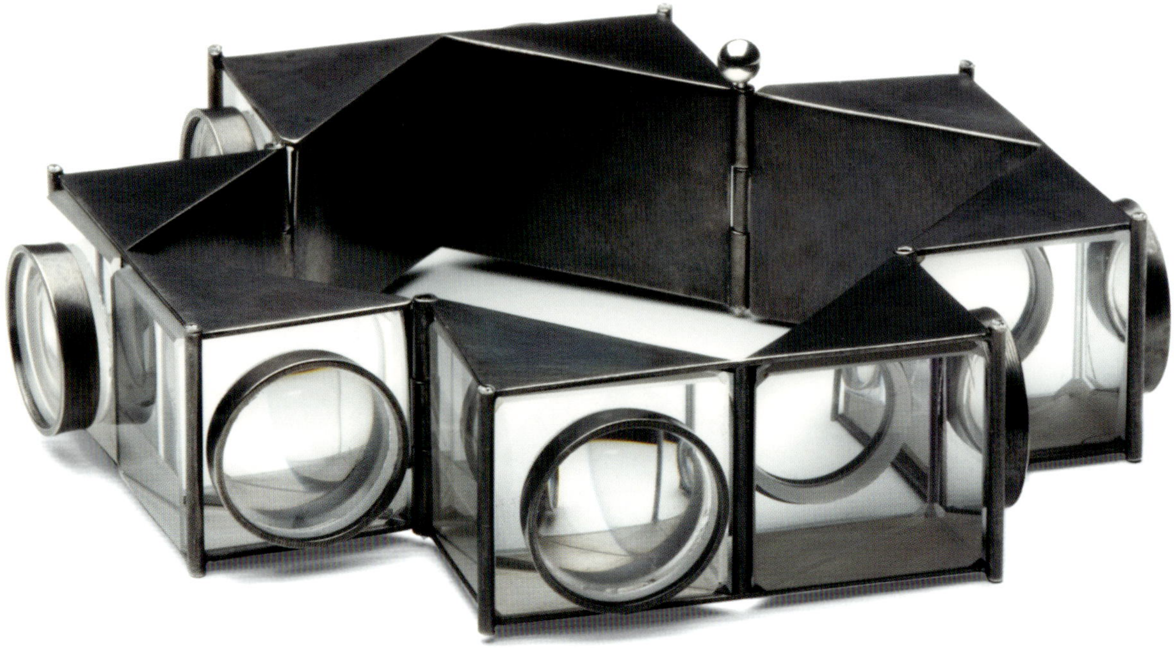

KAREN MISHER

Momentary

As a wearable art form, jewelry enjoys a dual audience: the wearer, who is intimate with the work itself and exchanges energy with it, and viewers who voyeuristically glimpse the work as it passes by. *Momentary* explores the interaction of these two groups. The use of prisms, mirrors, optic lenses, and viewfinders changes one's perspective of the space immediately around the piece, drawing the audience and the wearer closer together. People and surroundings are imaged in the lenses, creating an ever-changing landscape within the work as it moves with the body through the world.

129
Karen Misher
Momentary (bracelet), 2012
Right-angle prisms (view finder), optic lenses, silver, diamonds
$4^1/_2$ x $4^1/_2$ x $1^1/_4$ in.
(11.4 x 11.4 x 3.2 cm)
Collection of the artist

CRAIG ARNOLD

Re:vision

130

Craig Arnold
Re:vision (bracelets), 2009
Left to right: internal zoom cam guide, depth-of-field scale, camera aperture ring
2 x 2 1/2 in. (5 x 6.5 cm); 2 x 2 3/4 in. (5.5 x 7 cm); 2 1/4 x 3 in. (6 x 7.5 cm)
Collection of the artist

In an ideal world, design, function, and technique intersect to create an object of intrinsic aesthetic value and purpose. Why should something that was artfully designed and made be discarded simply because it can no longer fulfill its original purpose?

Rather than simply relegating these film-era camera components to a landfill, I wondered if they could be something other than just a tool for focusing light. Repurposing these camera parts into jewelry has enabled them to have a second life and allows the wearer to reconsider the value of these fragments from another era.

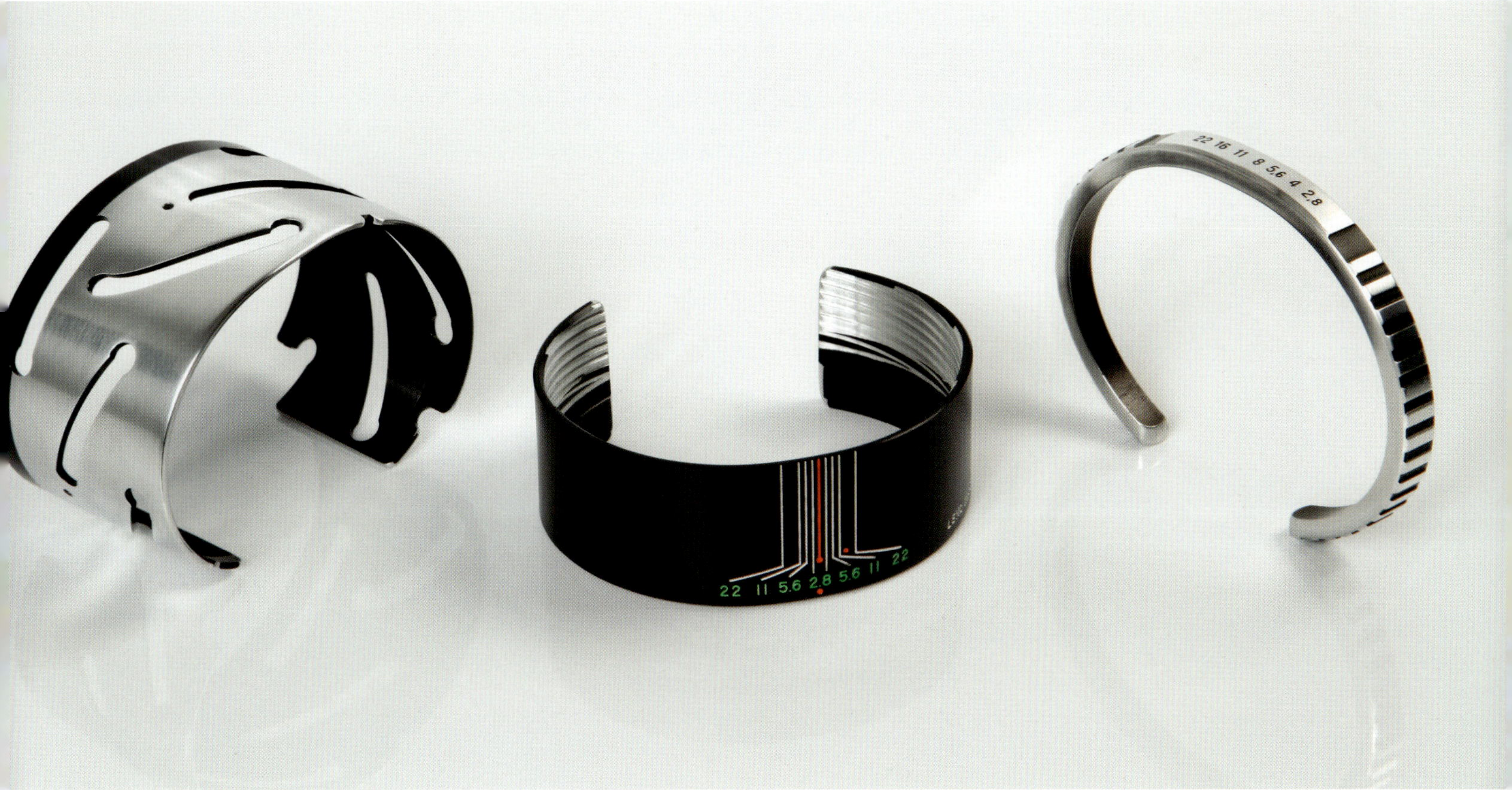

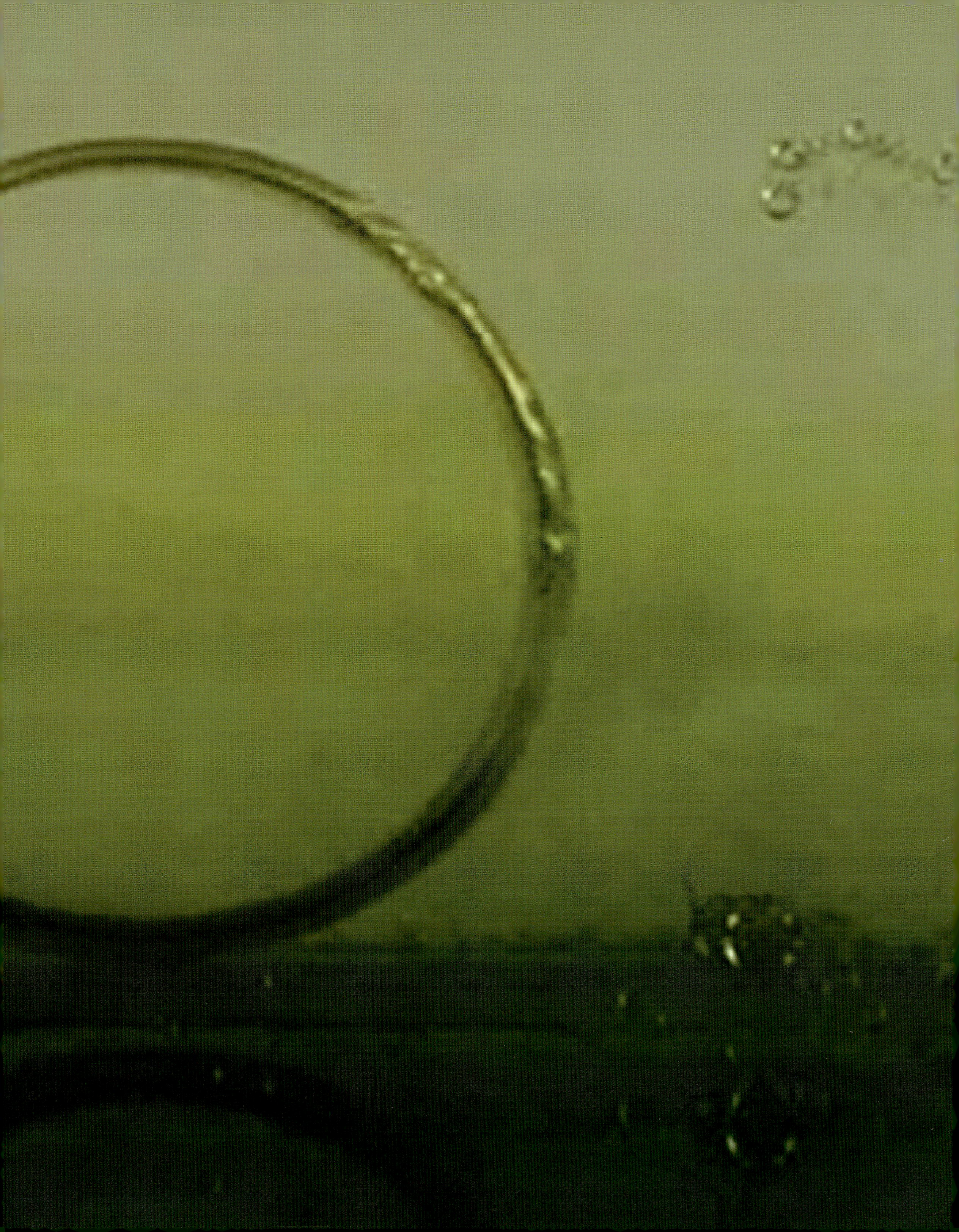

"... FROM MAKING BEAUTIFUL OBJECTS TO REVEALING LESS TANGIBLE ASPECTS OF THE MEDIUM ..."

JEWELRY THROUGH THE LENS

LIESBETH DEN BESTEN

IN 1992, Dutch jewelry artist Dinie Besems made the video *Ice Necklace*, showing a frozen necklace as it slowly melted, with the water being absorbed by the wearer's clothing (fig. 1). Possibly the first jewelry video ever made, Besems's filming of this unusual event transformed viewers' understanding of jewelry as something that was solid and enduring into something that could be dissolvable and temporary. The concept of jewelry was expanded through video.

The use of the lens to explore jewelry as a human and social phenomenon took off in the 1970s, with the moving image becoming more prevalent from the 1990s onward. For many artists, the allure of the photographic medium has been its potential for transmitting conceptual ideas about jewelry and its wearing, and their focus has changed from making beautiful objects to revealing less tangible aspects of the medium. In their photographic explorations, the question "But is it jewelry?" is obsolete; they make it clear that jewelry is an evolving subject.

Sarah Turner is a prime example of an artist who is pushing jewelry's boundaries through her exploration of fleeting images as body decoration. In her imaginative 2004 neckpieces titled *If One Could Wear a Marching Band* (NO. 139), Turner uses a model's body as an uneven, living canvas—a catalyst for the imagination—onto which she projects a series of elusive digital images as if the projections were jewelry. To extend the idea of non-physicality, these images are not printed but can only be realized by being projected onto a wall. What the onlooker sees is in fact a projection of a projection of digitally altered images of a marching band—some altered to the extent that it is impossible to tell that they were of a marching band in the first place. Through this disorienting array of images Turner stretches our ideas about jewelry, while she also questions the hierarchy of imagery that is closely connected with photography.

While Turner plays with our perception of the non-capturable object, Fabrice Schaefer traps a body decoration that is real, although lasting for only a short moment of time. In his 1999 photographs for *Traces* (NO. 135), the artist preserves the fleeting moments when a ring or necklace changes the malleable material of the human body. Unlike Gijs Bakker's *Shadow Jewelry* from 1973, which implied a radical judgment about jewelry itself (see p. 24), Schaefer's images are about the molding effect of a single piece of jewelry on the flesh; they are about the body becoming a temporal living jewel.

Perspectives on beauty and body manipulation are the subject of Lauren Kalman's photo and video work. While her use of jewelry-related materials could almost be seen as playful, *Tongue Gilding*, her video of the tongue's inability to bear its metal coating makes us shiver (NO. 134). The tongue trembles and slobbers saliva, turning the "jewelry" into a slimy mess. In Kalman's hands, gold and gemstones normally used to beautify the wearer have become revolting instruments of torture, effectively documented through photography and video.

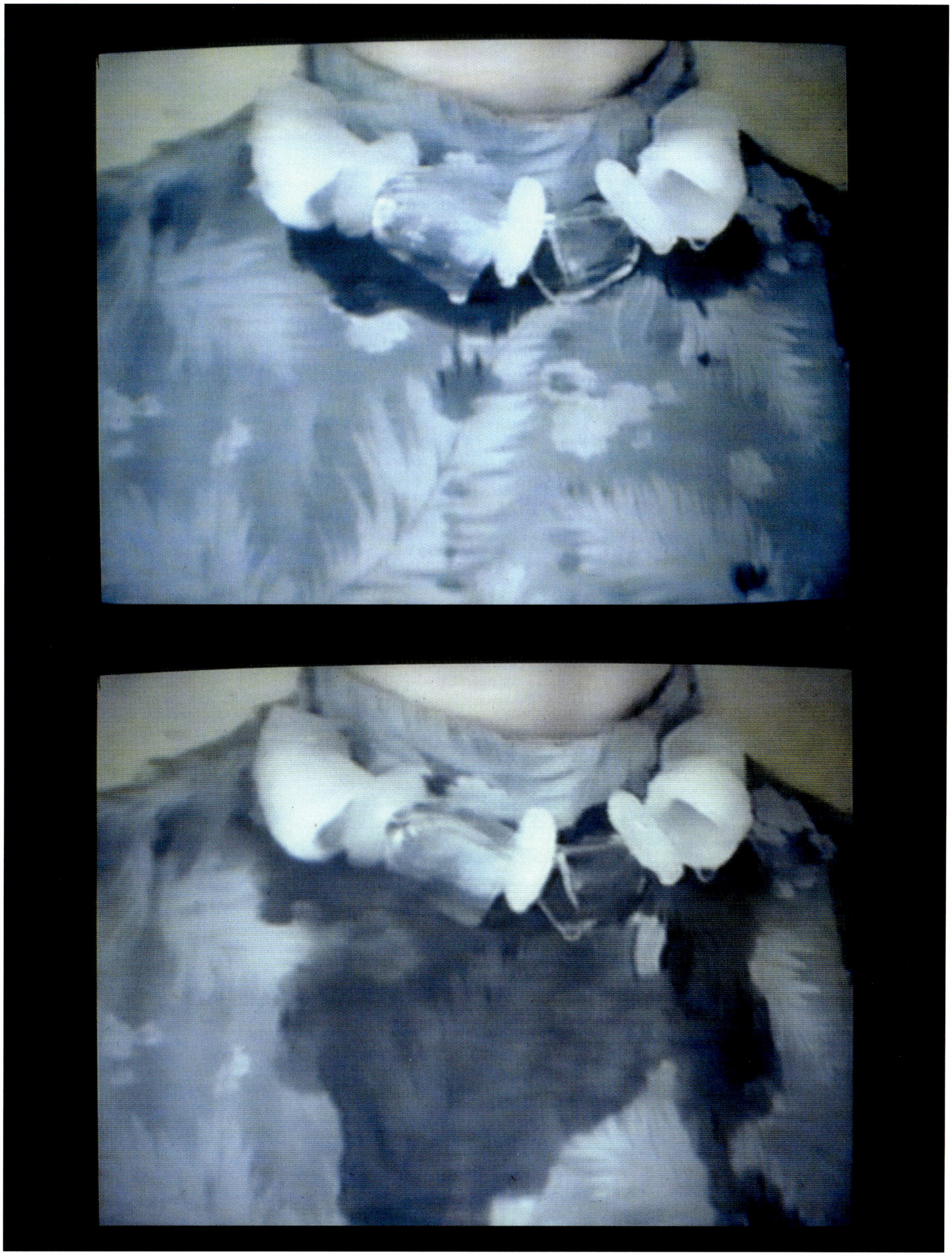

FIG. 1

Dinie Besems

Ice Necklace (video), 1992

13 minutes

Courtesy of the artist

In a different take on jewelry's potential to transform the body, Israeli Noa Zilberman creates a unique wrinkles map of her future face by filling in her wrinkles with gilded metal wire. Documenting the process through her 2012 *Wrinkles* video, Zilberman carefully attaches small golden lines to "problematic" areas of her face, neck, and décolletage (NO. 137). As she adds these precious ornaments to the wrinkles around her eyes and mouth and those that transect her brow, a new face—both impaired and repaired—comes into being, blurring the line between the ugly and the beautiful. The young woman wears her golden wrinkles with pride, and the careful application of precious lines to her face and body can be interpreted as a coming of age ritual. Like Kalman, Zilberman makes use of jewelry semantics by choosing materials, typologies, and rituals that refer to conventional jewelry, and like Kalman, she also undermines the traditional understanding of jewelry as wearable adornment.

Esther Brinkmann focuses on jewelry's social significance. Her video from 2000, *The Present Is the Only Thing without an End*, shows a continuous stream of disembodied hands, though obviously female, male, young, and old, taking rings off their own fingers or someone else's and passing the jewelry around in a consoling affirmation of life and the importance of transmitting heritage (NO. 131).

For Gisbert Stach, the destruction of a piece of symbolic jewelry is as fascinating as the creation of one. In his 2011 video *Maybe Forever* from his Transformations series, the idea of the uncompromising bond between two people, symbolized by two golden wedding rings, is subverted by putting the rings in a tank of acid (NO. 132). Within a couple of minutes, the rings are dissolved forever, forcing the viewer to ponder the symbolism of the rings and the vulnerability of marriage. In a more humorous vein, Stach's 2008 video *Fitting* reflects on the function of jewelry in society, drawing our attention to societal standards of beauty and greed (NO. 133). Luxury turns into abundance and decadence as a woman collapses under the steadily growing number of necklaces and chains around her neck.

Suska Mackert also fosters a conceptual approach, being especially interested in the psychological, social, and cultural meaning of jewelry. Using printed matter and books as a medium, she makes photographic works and videos about jewelry. Her 2002 video *To Be on Display* shows the artist meticulously copying the names of famous jewelry brands such as Cartier and Tiffany in golden letters on a white wall (NO. 149). The activity looks obsessive and appears to be an empty ritual, but it calls to our attention the commercialism of jewelry brands whose names have become mere codes for luxury.

Many jewelers and fine artists who use photography in their jewelry straddle the territory between the applied and the visual arts. In *Wealth in Africa*, her more than life-size neckpiece from 2012, the mixed-media sculptor Janet Goldner focused on the symbolic and representative qualities of jewelry through photography, video, and sound (NO. 89). Goldner's work deals with the continent of Africa, and, more specifically, with a village in Mali where she resided in conjunction with a Fulbright Senior Research Fellowship almost twenty years ago. *Wealth in Africa* contains photographs and a video that pay homage to the women potters who keep the ancient traditions of their small village alive. By presenting the images in a way that turns them into metaphorical gemstones, the artist underlines the value of the women's contributions to their local culture.

In artist and photographer Wafaa Bilal's career, the camera functioned for almost a year as a radiant piece of jewelry that performed a function his own body couldn't accomplish. In 1991, at the age of twenty-five, Bilal left Iraq and moved to the United States. Being aware that the people and places that had been a part of his everyday existence in Iraq were lost to him after his move, he found a way in New York to document his daily life as it slipped away from him so that he would never again be without his past. In 2010, working with jeweler Kristal Romano, he had a small silver camera designed that could be mounted on piercing posts centered on the back of his head (NO. 138). Resembling an extra eye, the *3rdi* transmitted images minute by minute to a website where people could watch Bilal's life as it unfolded through his daily round of activities. Although the camera eventually had to be removed because of a risk of infection, the images of what he left behind live on.

Visual artist Irene Mamiye is interested in using digital imaging techniques to capture light, color, and movement in photography, installations, and video. In *Shattered Gems*, she applies her colorful optical illusions in a piece of wearable jewelry. The necklace is composed of three large components that consist of sixth-generation light-weight iPod Nanos with screens showing various gemstones fracturing: the entire focus is on the pure and intense color of the gems and the dramatic fragmenting and cracking of these precious materials. Mamiye worked closely with jewelry designer Stephen Dweck, who constructed the piece in sterling silver, fabric, and other materials. The iPod Nanos are mounted on slices of black agate, alluding to the traditional setting of gems, while the integration of technology (the charger cords and electronic connections) is celebrated visually. *Shattered Gems* is a rare example of the successful merging of jewelry and technology into a piece of wearable art, thanks to the partnership of a visual artist and a jewelry designer (NO. 148).

Collaboration is an important characteristic of contemporary art, and jewelry artist Karl Fritsch and photographer Gavin Hipkins literally merge two different artistic disciplines to create enigmatic art objects that neither could create without the other. For Der Tiefenglanz, a project that has been ongoing since 2012, their collaboration begins with Hipkins printing black-and-white negatives from his archives and handing the prints over to Fritsch, who is free to modify them in whatever way he chooses. Using jewelry materials (sheets of silver or lead, aluminum, sapphires, cubic zirconia's, native greenstone, synthetic rubies, and semi-precious stones), Fritsch embellishes Hipkins's photos, but in the process he also mutilates them. Fritsch's interventions in the two-dimensional surfaces of these photos constitute a trespassing; they cut through the surface and destroy it, but in so doing, they also create another space, a new dimension, and ultimately, a new work of art. The classical wooden framing of the most recent group of works adds extra meaning to the seemingly unrelated iconography of Der Tiefenglanz (NOS. 140–147).

David Roux-Fouillet also relies on collaboration to make his jewelry and jewelry-related pieces. Working at the cross-roads of jewelry, sculpture, installation, and film, Roux-Fouillet involves animal and man in the creation of his hybrid objects—with a special preference for collaborating with living silkworms and caterpillars. This unusual partnership requires experimentation and study of the behavior of these soft-bodied creatures. In order to let silkworms work for him Roux-Fouillet created refined geometrical open structures in silver that could be used by the worms as a skeleton for weaving their silk cocoons. A man and a woman wore the silver shapes for some time as pieces of jewelry and extensions of their bodies. The woman's piece was mounted on her pierced nipple, and the man's was located in the stretched lobe of his ear. The worms and the people lived together for some time: the silkworms lodging on the body. The *Orna-*

mental Fauna video documents the close and uneasy cohabitation, the cautious movements of the volunteer-participants, and the restless crawling of the insects. With this work Roux-Fouillet proves himself to be a true conceptual artist who directs people and insects in order to create extraordinary pieces of jewelry (NO. 136).

Clearly, in the twenty-some years since Dinie Besems's ice necklace melted on film, jewelry has grown into a medium that can move swiftly and elegantly in undefined territory, where coalitions are formed and collaborations bloom, where jewelry neither needs nor wants to make claims on a "higher status," where it doesn't want to take roots, where it passes by fluently to turn to wearable jewelry again when needed. Through the lens, jewelry is in a perpetual state of flux.

Liesbeth den Besten *is chairwoman of the Françoise van den Bosch Foundation, coach and teacher of Wearable Senses/Industrial Design at Eindhoven Technical University, board member of Art Jewelry Forum (AJF), and writer, lecturer, and curator.*

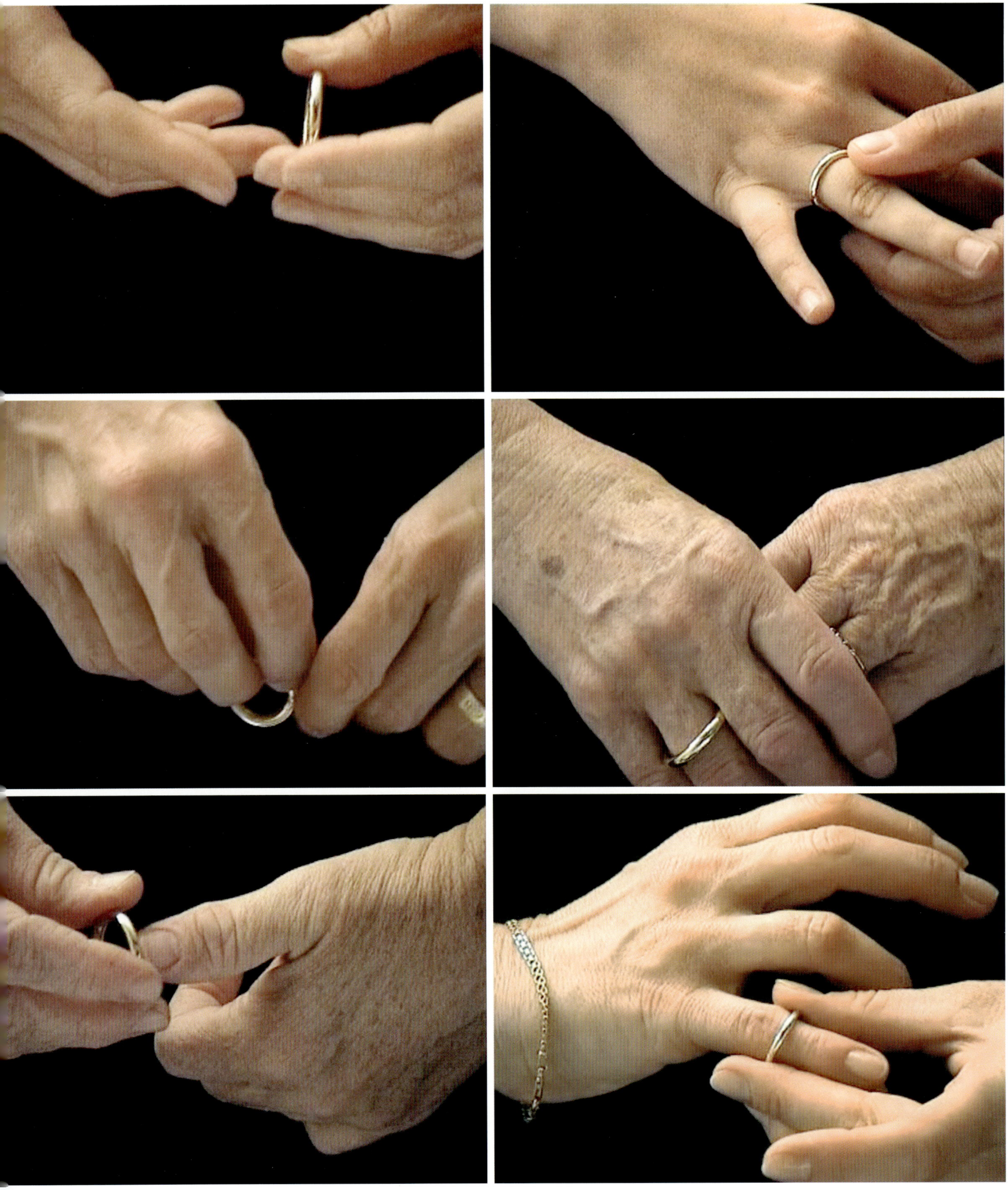

ESTHER BRINKMANN

The Present Is the Only Thing without an End

My video expresses the privileged relationship between jewelry and the body. The viewer enters a silent room where he or she becomes a part of a projection on two walls—a ballet of hands putting on and taking off rings. The hands are big, the movements are slow, and the rings are simple and identical. The viewer senses the unique qualities of the performers' skin, observes their individual movements, and feels the light touch of metal brushing a finger. A piece of jewelry should provoke emotions, should provoke desires!

131 OPPOSITE PAGE AND BELOW
Esther Brinkmann
The Present Is the Only Thing without an End (video), 2000
60 minutes
Filmed by Esther Brinkmann and Philippe Solms
Collection of the artist

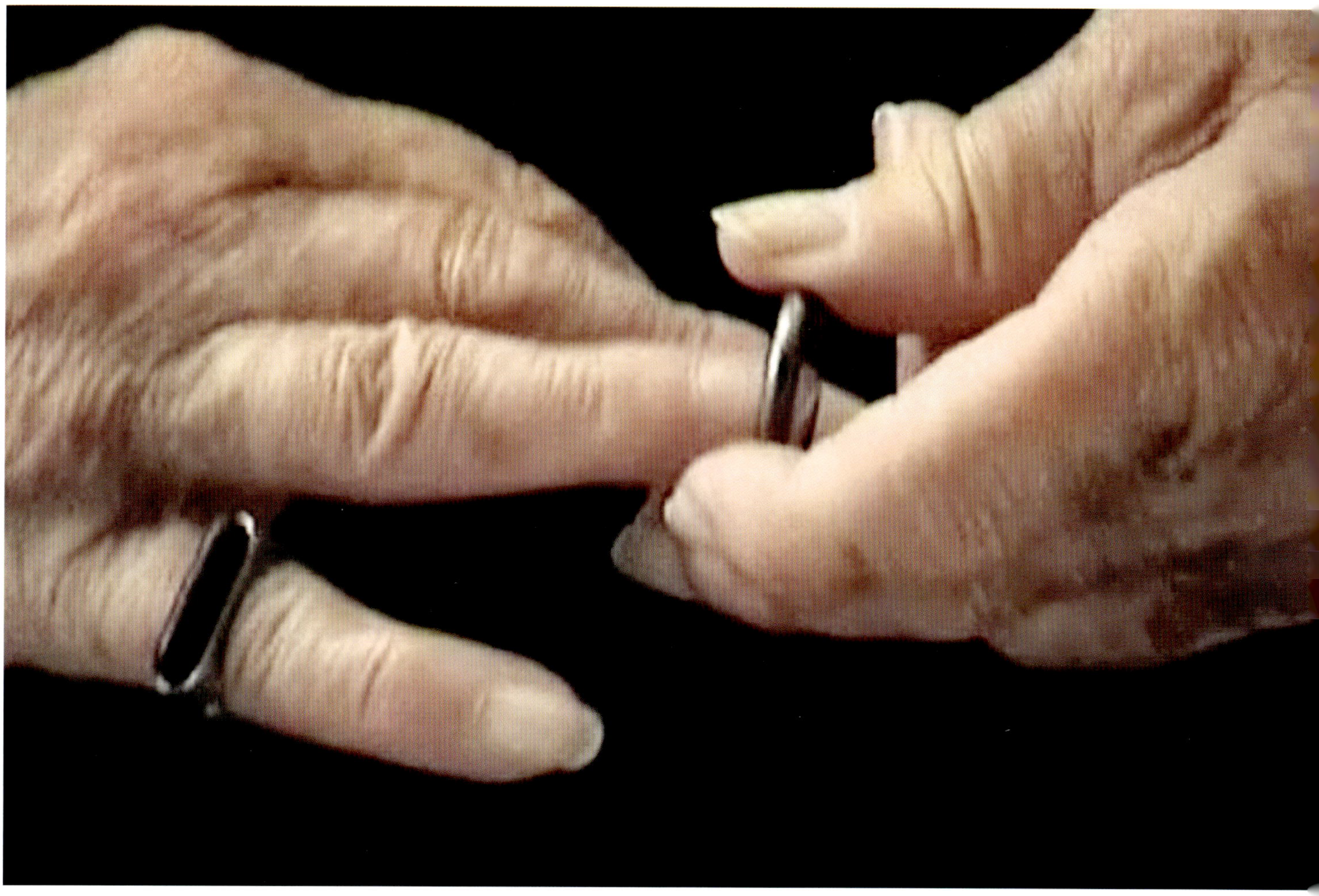

GISBERT STACH

Maybe Forever | *Fitting*

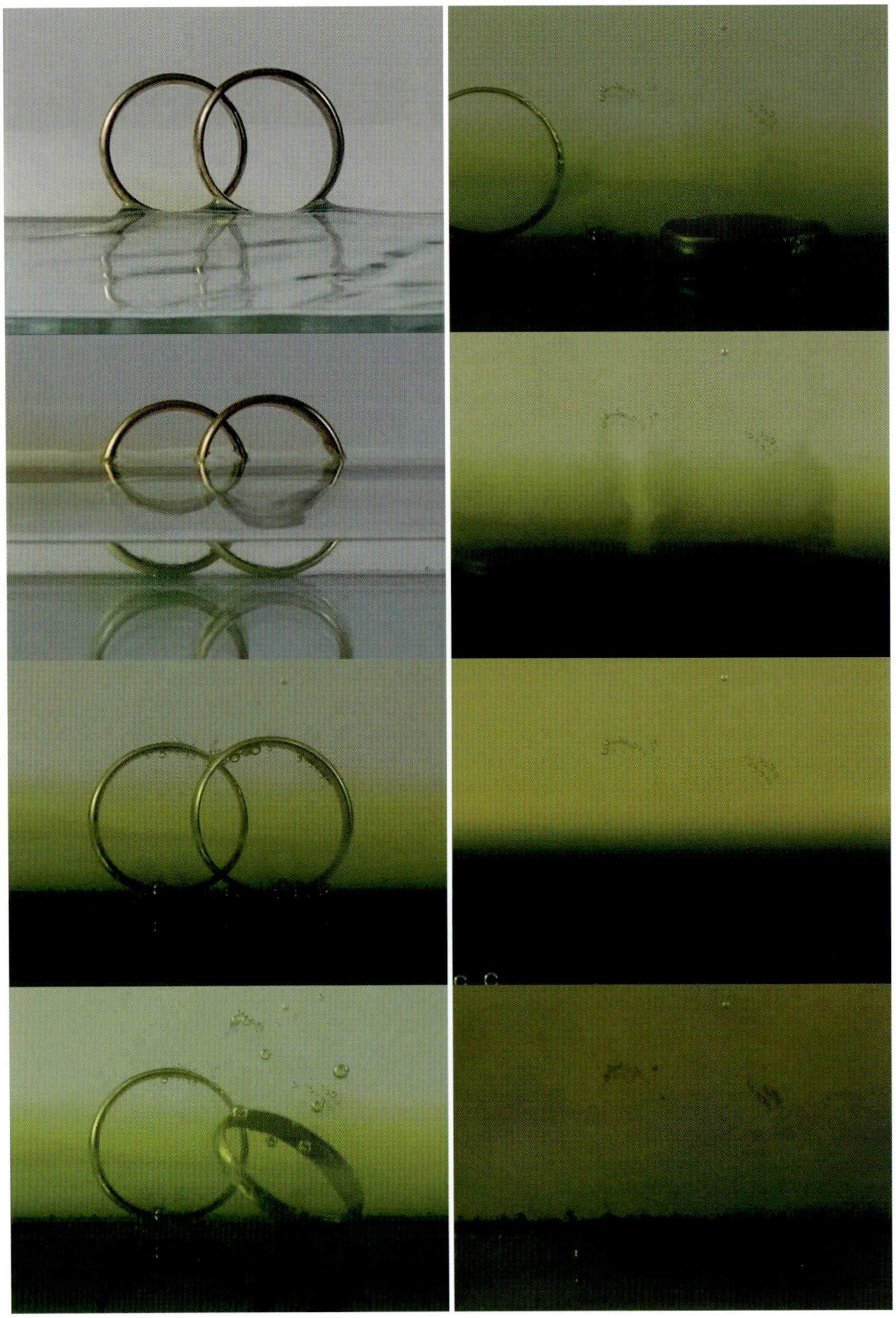

I am almost as fascinated by the destruction of objects as by their creation. The destruction of a symbol produces highly emotional reactions. At the same time, it provides an opportunity to analyze the symbol's importance to individuals as well as to society. In *Maybe Forever*, two upright wedding rings, slightly overlapping as a sign of closeness between two people, are flooded by an acid fluid. Corrosion sets in immediately, and gradually the rings disintegrate and are completely dissolved by the acid. On the positive side, the two rings dissolved in the fluid enter a new material unification. The material and emotional value of the rings has been transformed.

The manner in which societies deal with status symbols and consumer behavior, and in particular the varying cultural attitudes associated with wearing jewelry, intrigues me. In African and Asian cultures, the value of jewelry has traditionally been more existential than in the West, with jewelry even functioning as a form of life insurance for women and a means of fulfilling their obligations toward their families. In contrast, my video *Fitting* reveals the absurdity of adornments. Here, decorating as a means of beautification slowly gives way to burden, anxiety, and existential threat.

132 ABOVE
Gisbert Stach
Maybe Forever (video), 2011
10 minutes, stereo, 4:3
Collection of the artist

133 OPPOSITE PAGE
Gisbert Stach
Fitting (video), 2008
30 minutes, stereo, 4:3
Performance: Sonia Ruiz de Arcaute and Gisbert Stach
Music: Kunst oder Unfall (Kalle Laar, Augusta Laar) 2013, GEMA: Kalle Laar
Collection of the artist

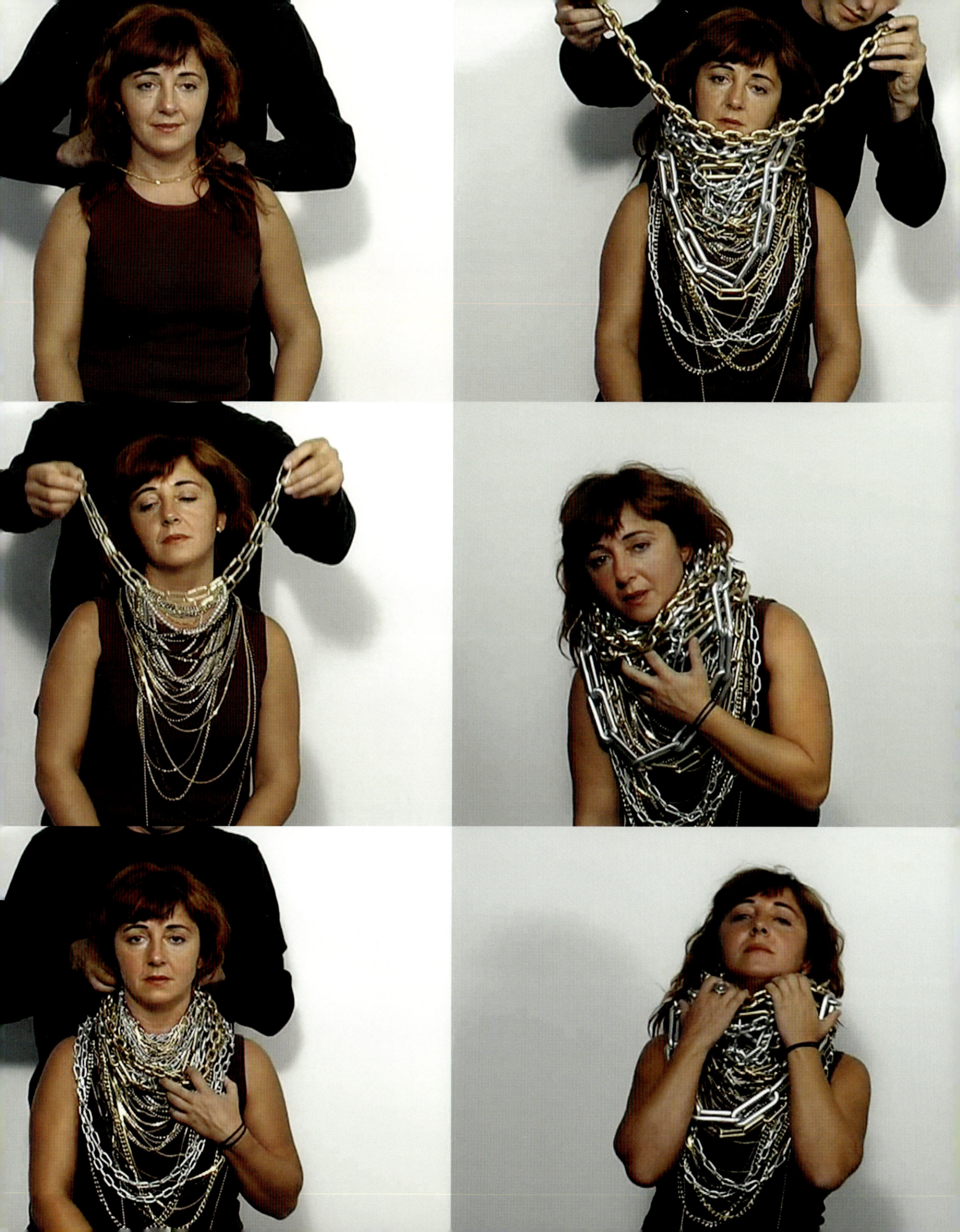

LAUREN KALMAN

Tongue Gilding

I use gold-plating, electro-forming, and semi-precious stones to make hybrid images of grotesque, taboo, or undesirable aspects of the body—in this case the tongue—and objects we associate with beauty, status, health, or wealth. The end results are both beautiful and repulsive.

Photographs are one of the primary formats for my work. Photographs and videos invite the viewer to stare at bodies, playing out a visual power dynamic. Bodies in images become objects that the viewer visually consumes. There is a gendered dynamic created when we stare at a photograph of a body because the vocabulary of the medium was constructed from the vantage point of the powerful majority. Through the act of staring at the relationship between the female body and jewelry, the viewer is implicated in the act of objectifying the body.

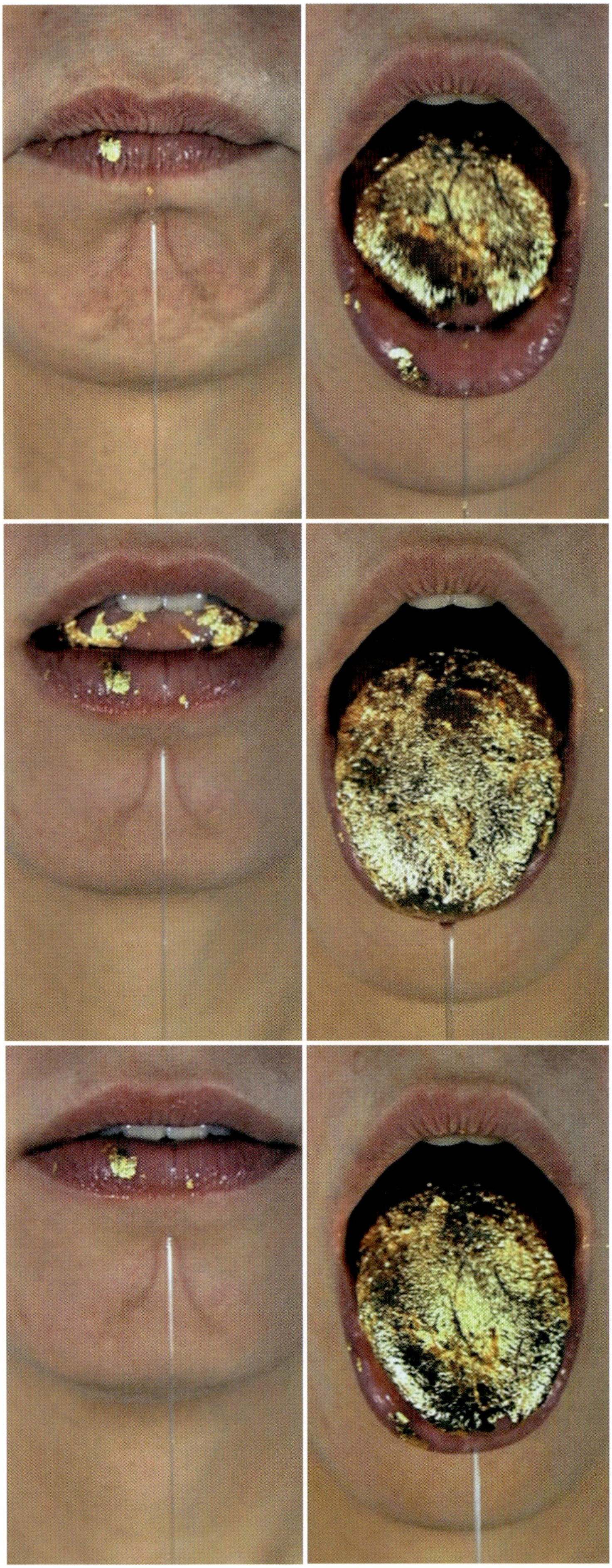

134
Lauren Kalman
Tongue Gilding (video), 2009
12 minutes
Courtesy of the artist and
Sienna Patti

FABRICE SCHAEFER

Traces

When we consider the relationship between the body and jewelry, we usually refer to whichever part of the body catches our eye when a jewel is being worn—how our finger looks with a ring on it, how a necklace frames our face. But this focus excludes another important aspect of wearing jewelry. When we wear a ring or necklace, it presses on our flesh and becomes one with it, and when the jewelry is removed, the skin retains its imprint. Our body, for a brief moment, is a living jewel.

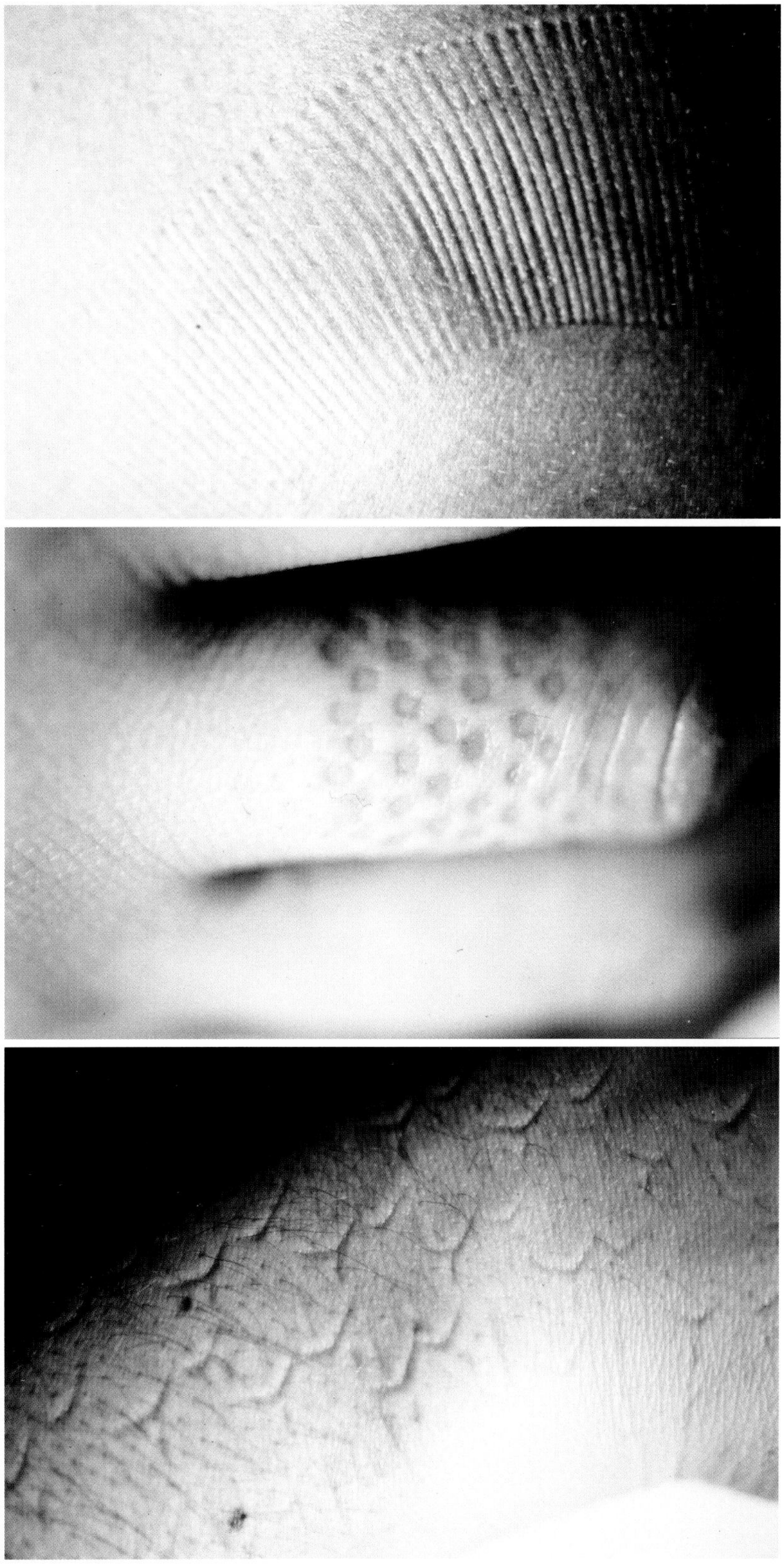

135

Fabrice Schaefer
Traces, 1999
Analog photographs
10 5/8 x 15 3/4 in. (27 x 40 cm), each
Collection of the artist

DAVID ROUX-FOUILLET

Ornamental Fauna

My videos should be viewed as fresh and experimental jewelry projects, part of an exploration of the notion of preciousness in jewelry. *Ornamental Fauna*, in which silkworms can be seen weaving their cocoons on the body, both in the ear and on the nipple, is a reflection on the intimacy that can exist between the wearer and a jewel and also on the broader idea of body modification—connecting the body to an alien element. Some of my pieces were meant to be ephemeral and only had a lifespan of the duration of the process. They constituted "living jewelry," made to be worn while it was alive. Other of my pieces have been made to last, to live on as witnesses to a process.

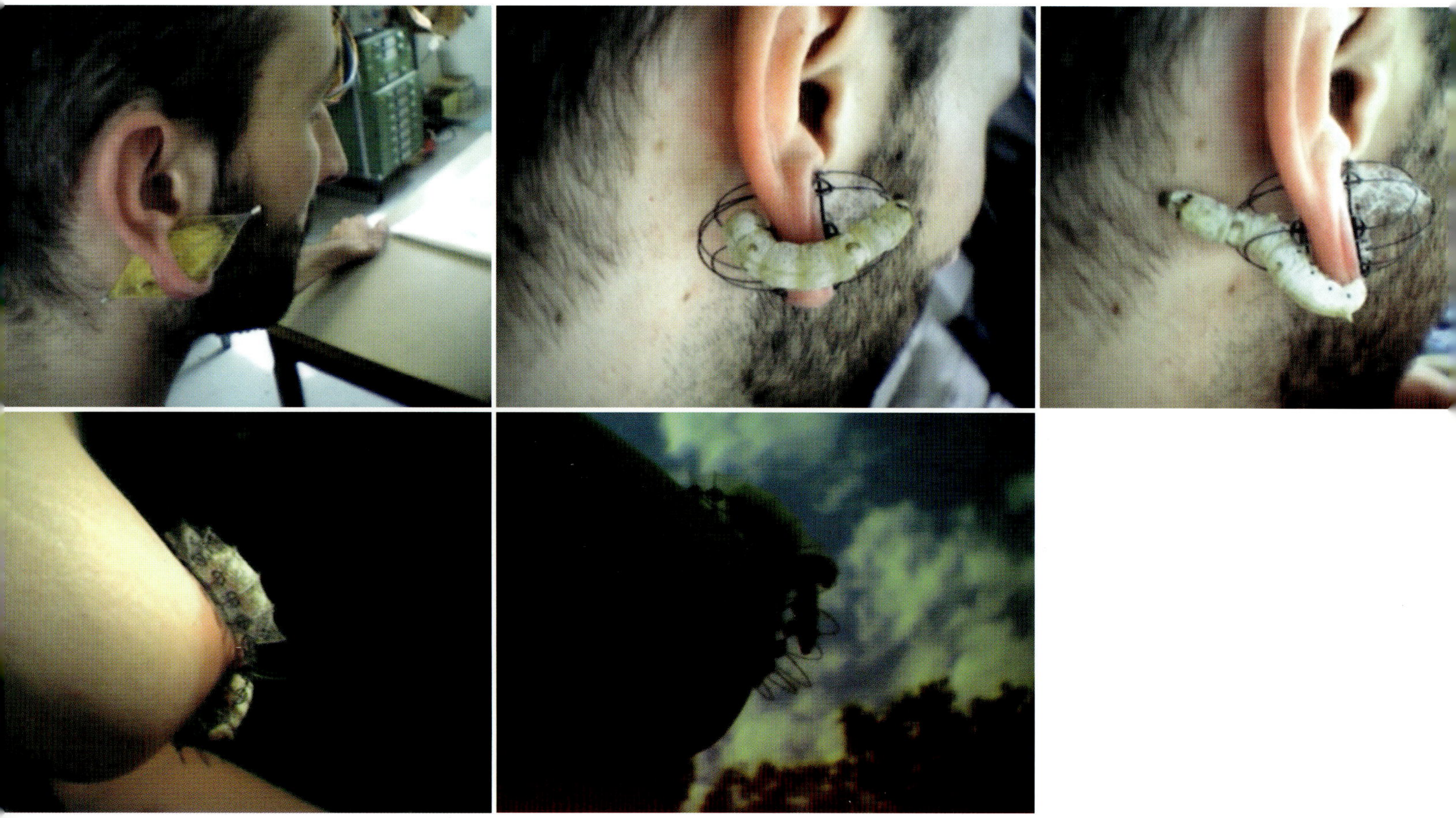

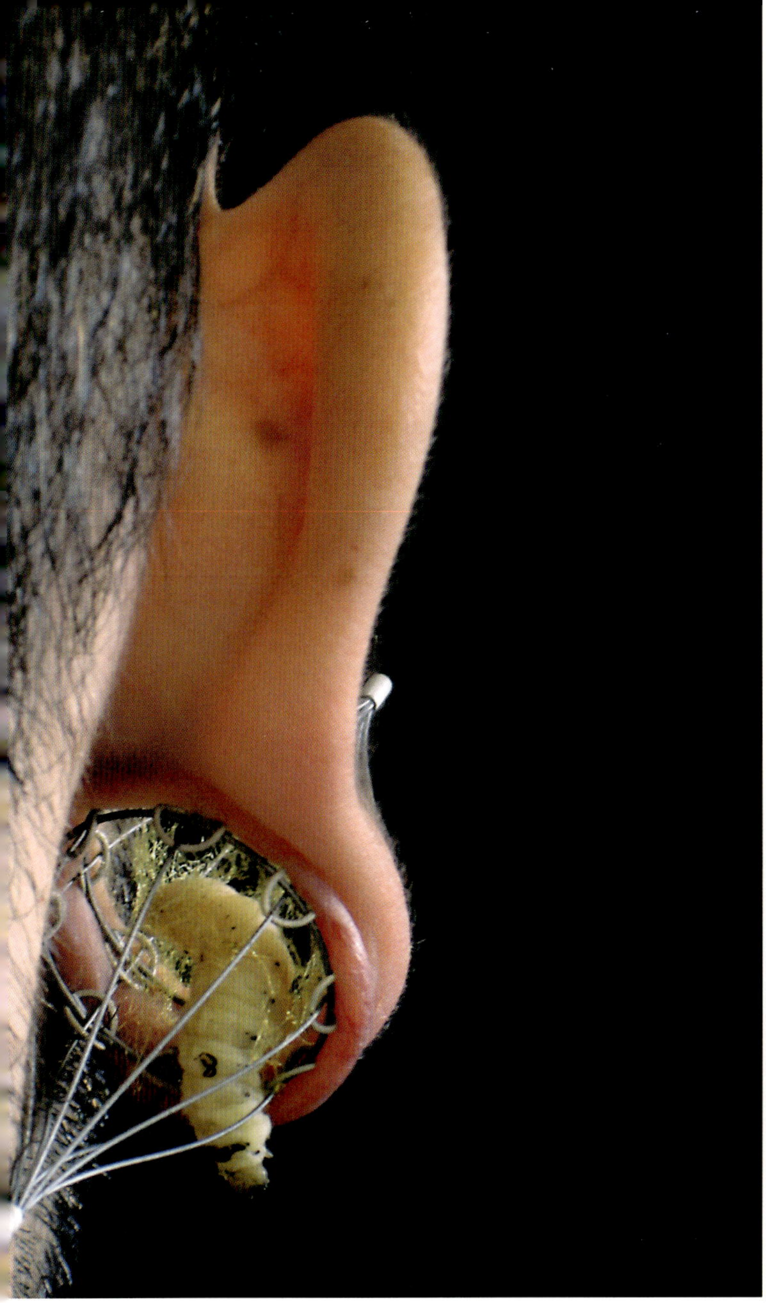

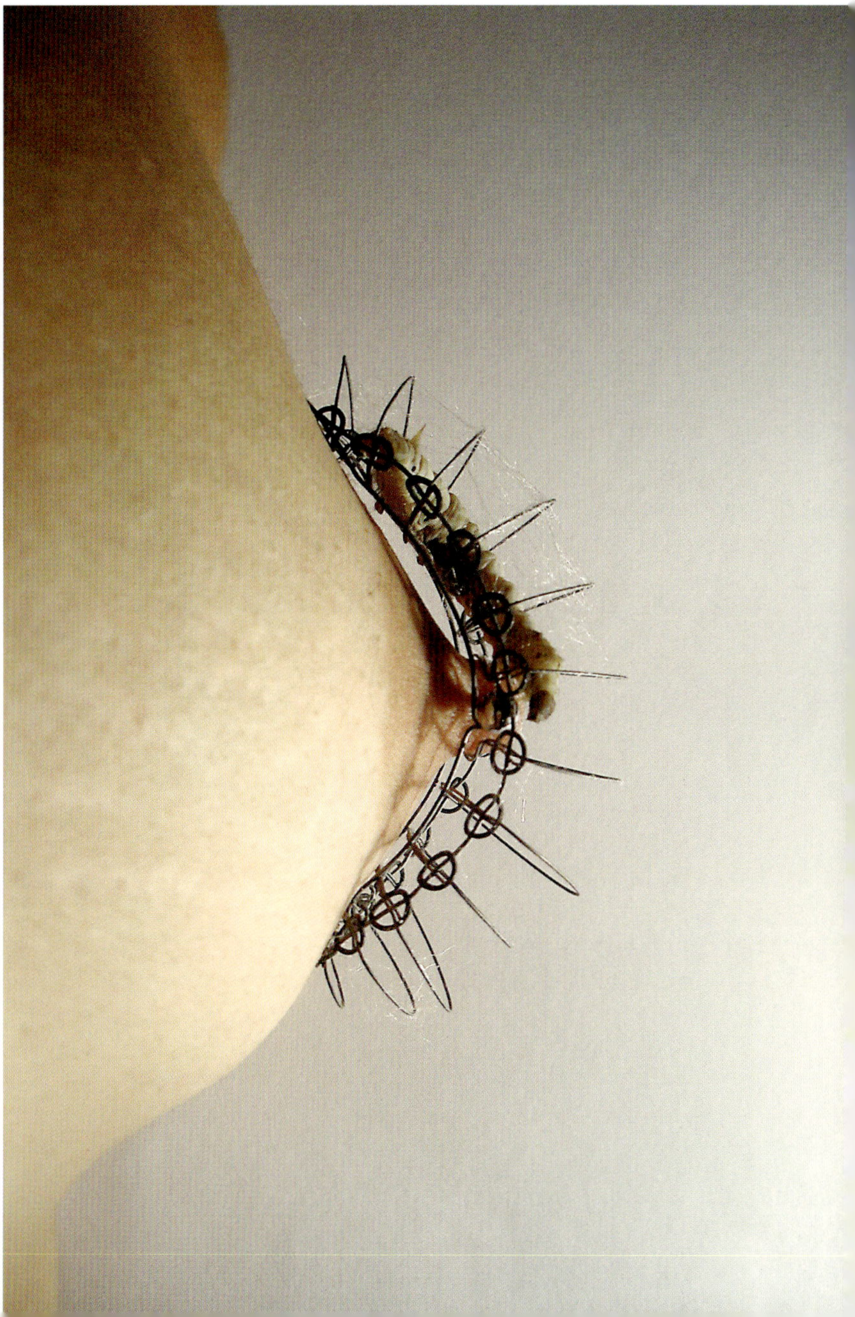

David Roux-Fouillet

Ornamental Fauna (video), 2007

19 minutes

Collection of the artist

NOA ZILBERMAN

Wrinkles

137

Noa Zilberman
Wrinkles (video), 2012
1 minute, 30 seconds
Filmed by Ami Zilberman
Collection of the artist

In my *Wrinkles* video, I examine the aging process of the human face by creating a unique wrinkles map in which my future wrinkles are represented, filled in, and repaired using a gilded metal thread. The resulting "map" led to the design of wrinkle mask jewelry for the face, neck, and décolletage in which the contrast between young facial skin and the unavoidable wrinkles awaiting it provides a platform for morphological transformation and abolishes any timeline associated with the process. It is an intervention that undermines the function of the objects as jewelry and causes us to question the distinction between repairing and impairing and the tenuous basis of our concepts of ugliness and beauty.

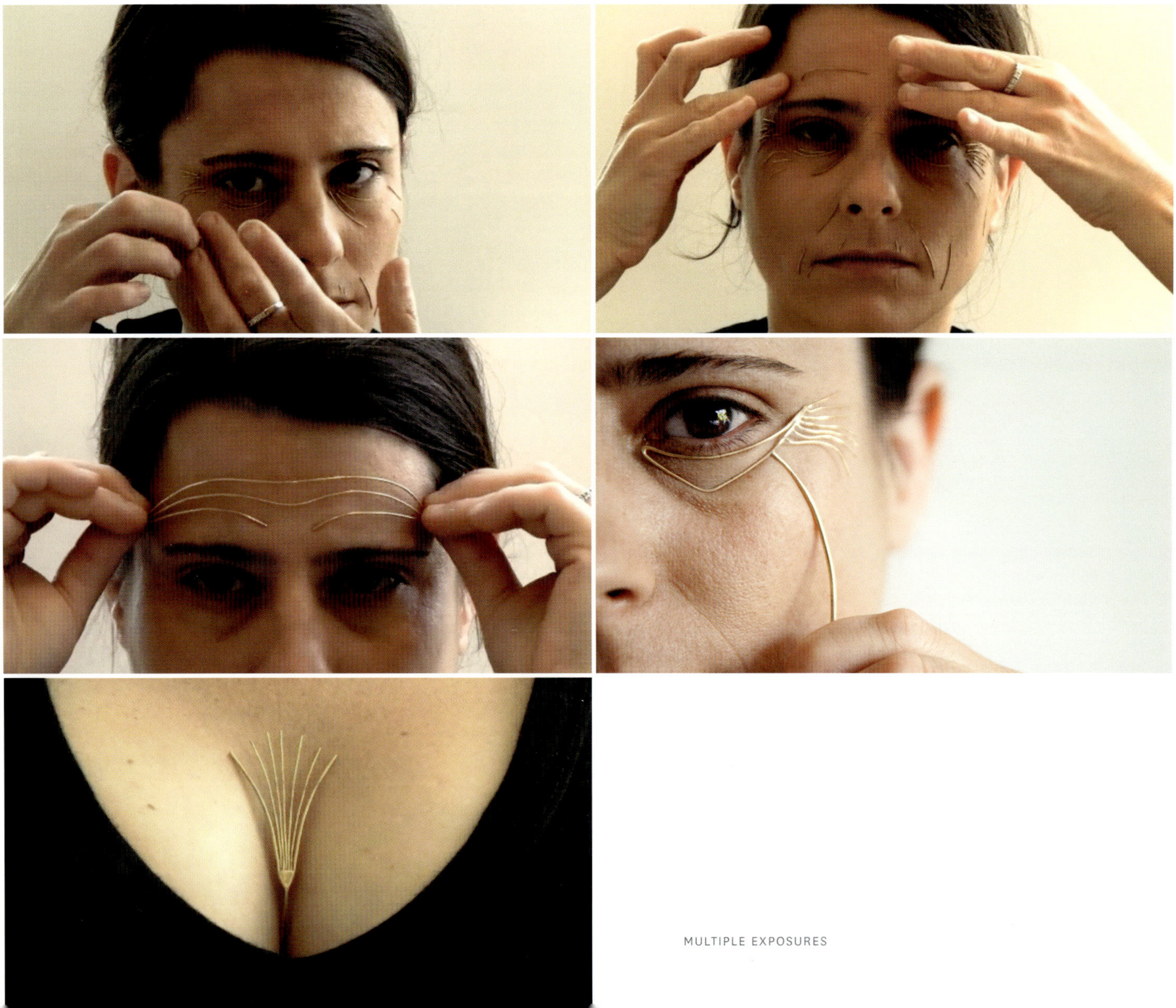

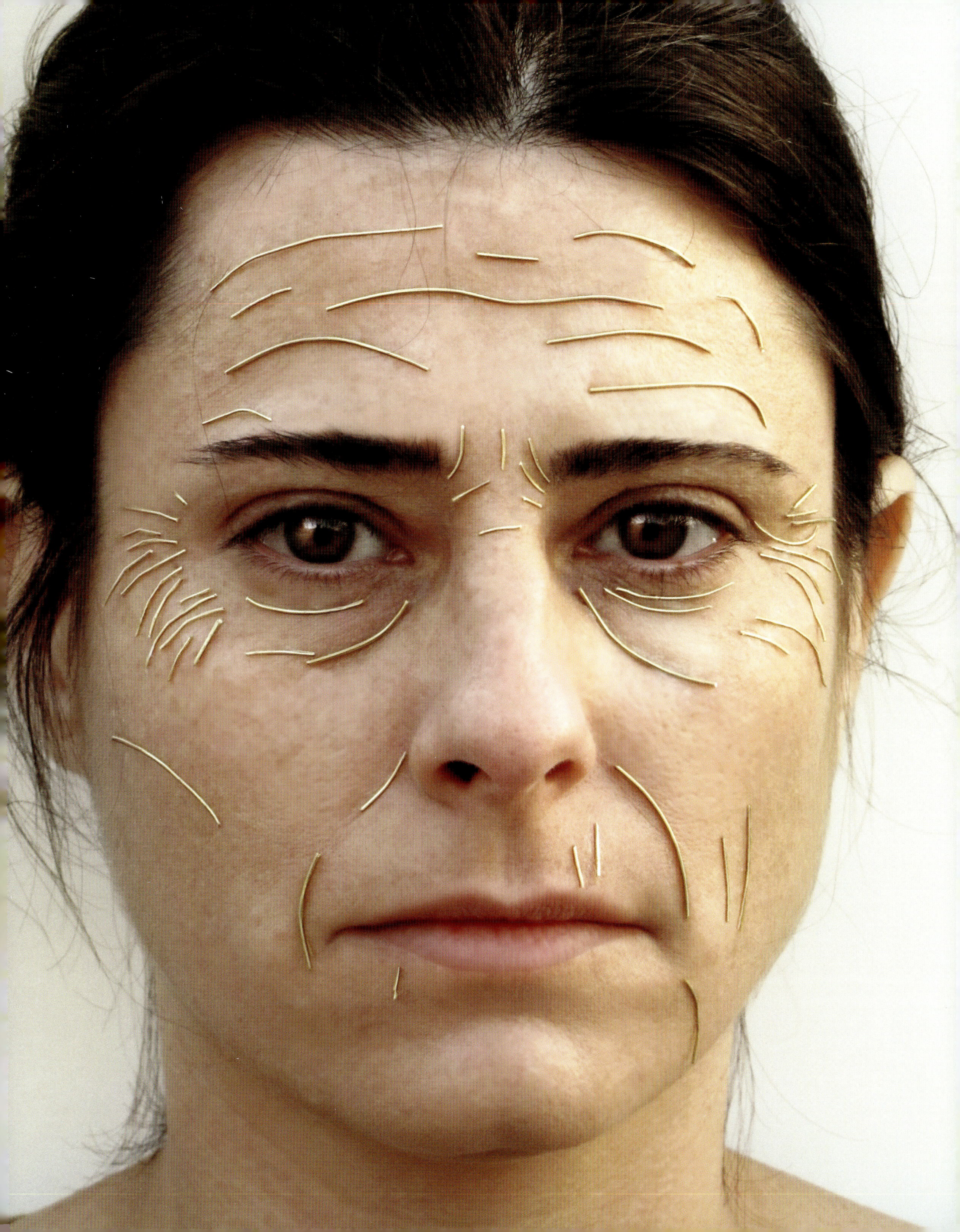

WAFAA BILAL

3rdi

The *3rdi* is an expression of my need to document my past objectively as it slips away from me. When I journeyed from Iraq to the United States, I left many people and places behind, and the images I have of my homeland are ephemeral, held as they are in my own memory. In 2010 I had a camera surgically implanted on the back of my head, and for one year, it spontaneously and objectively captured images of my daily life in New York City and transmitted these images to the Internet. The *3rdi* transformed my body into a mirror reflecting social conditions and created a running commentary on the way in which photographic imagery tells and retells stories.

138 BELOW

Wafaa Bilal
3rdi (implanted camera), 2010
Silver, ABS, high-speed USB cable
2 x 1 1/4 in. (5.1 x 3.2 cm), camera
36 in. (91.4 cm), cord
Collection of the artist

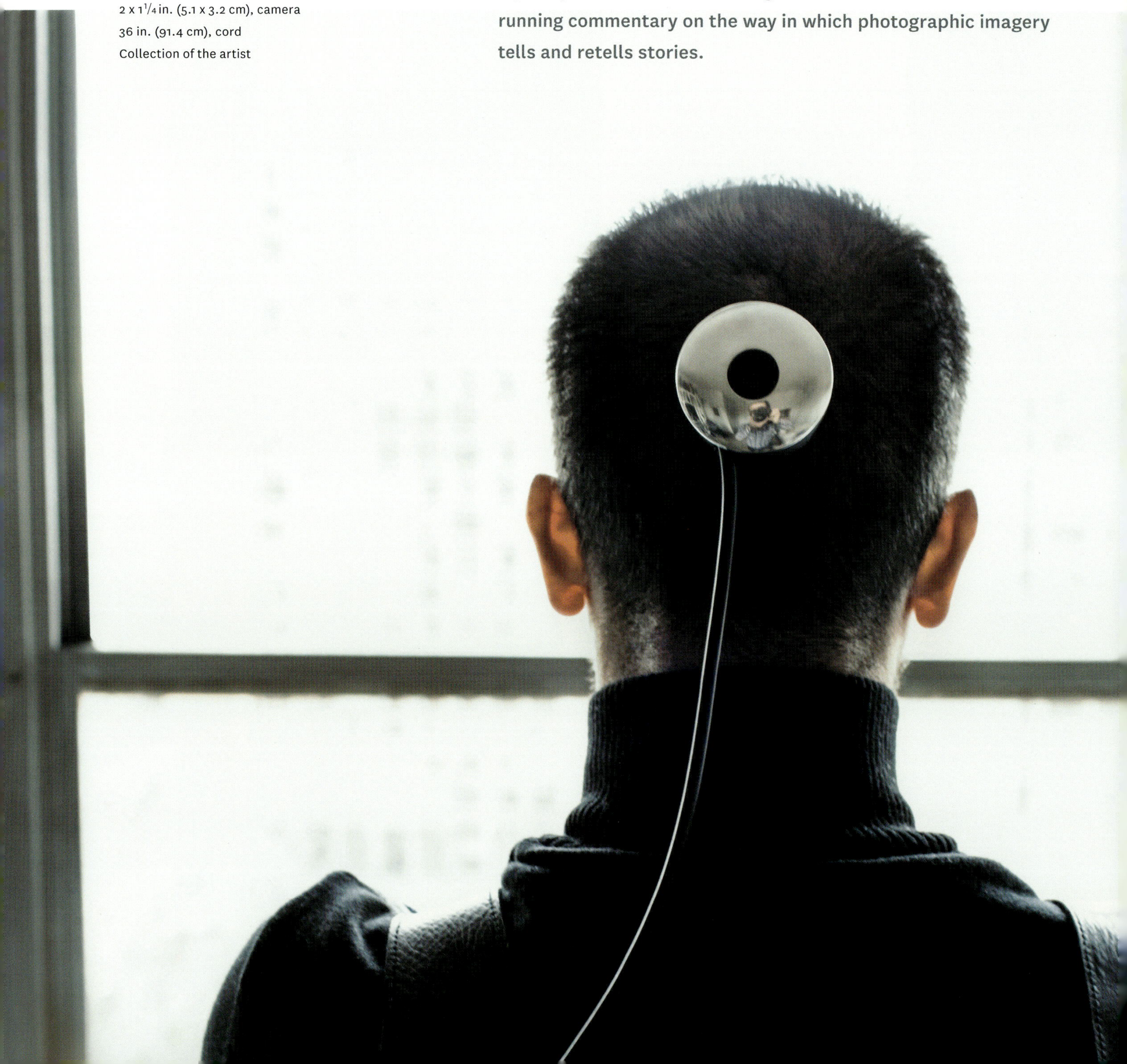

Wafaa Bilal
City Walking, 2011
3rdi camera stills

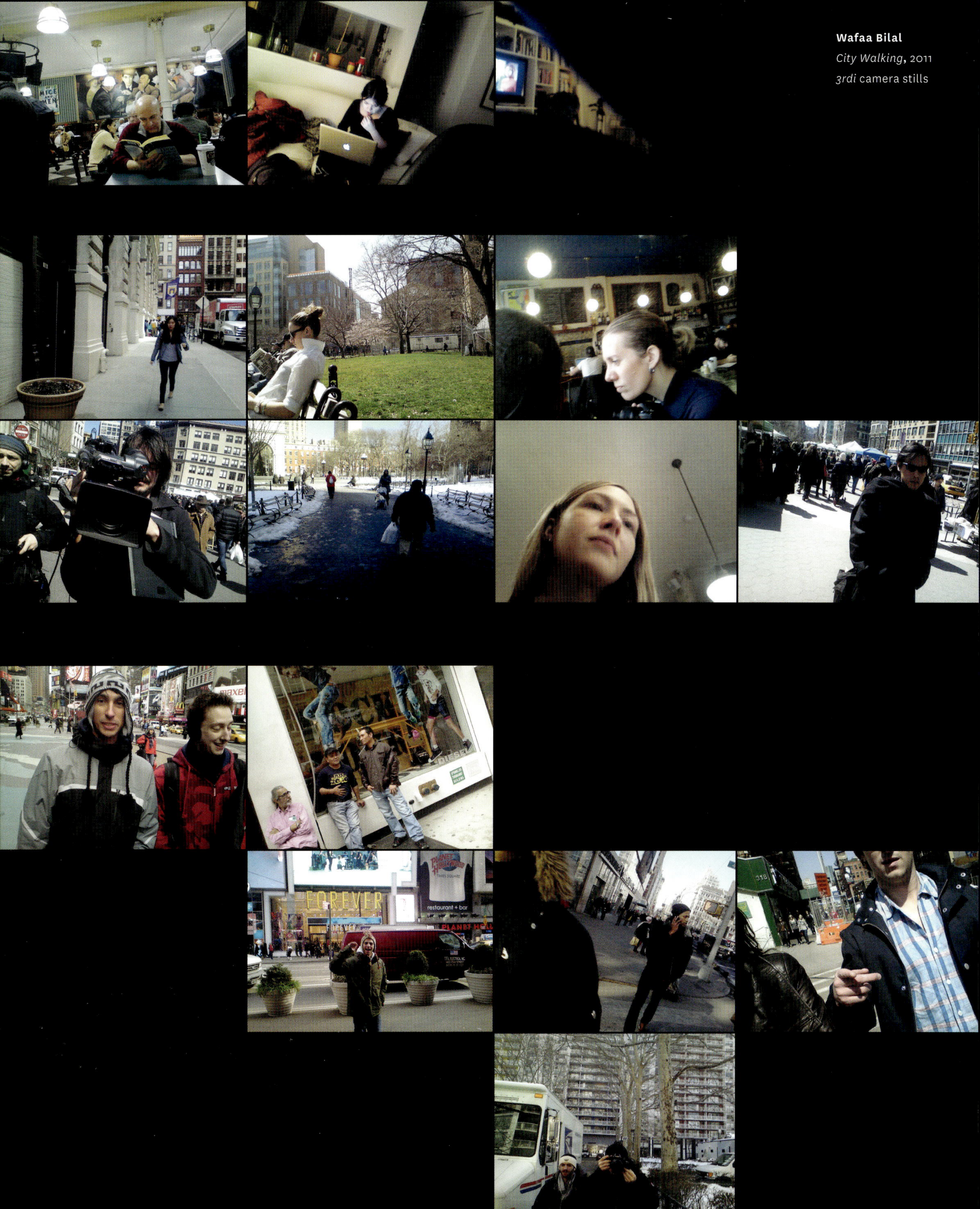

SARAH C. TURNER

If One Could Wear a Marching Band

My series of projected neckpieces is a way to think about the relationship of images and objects. Typically, images serve as representations of, or the context for, original objects—remaining two-dimensional, dependent documents of the things they present. This series is an exercise in sidestepping the hierarchy of source object and representative image. It is also an experiment to push at the conventions, traditions, and expectations of the contemporary jewelry field. It causes one to wonder what could be worn if time, space, and the physical world were not as they are . . . if one could wear a marching band.

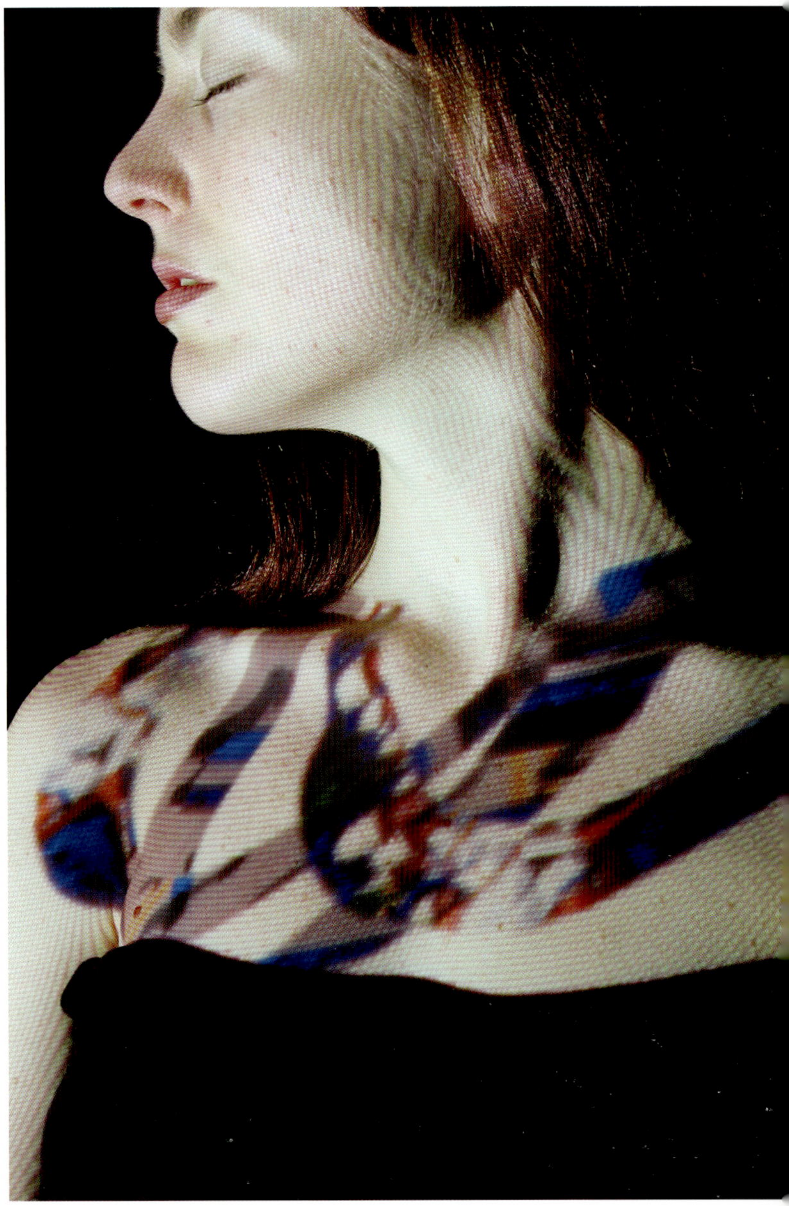

139

Sarah C. Turner

If One Could Wear a Marching Band, 2004

Digital projections

Collection of the artist

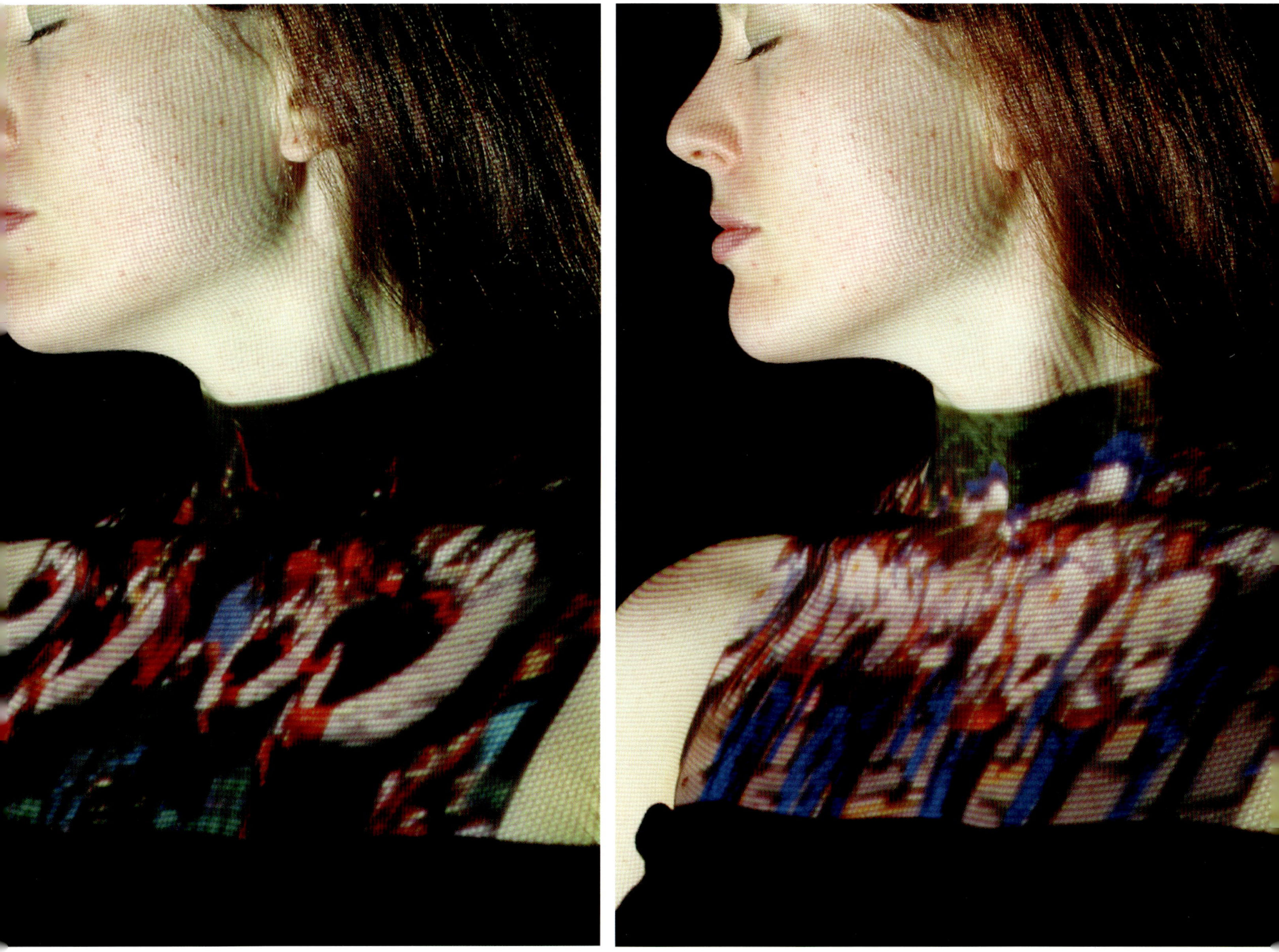

KARL FRITSCH and GAVIN HIPKINS

Der Tiefenglanz

In this most recent cluster of images from our Tiefenglanz series, jewelry is taken from its original context and re-contextualized using motifs from various genres of still life, portraiture, and landscape painting. It is a collaborative undertaking in which seemingly unrelated iconography and objects are brought together to enhance one another in much the same way that contents of a nineteenth-century *Wunderkammer* acquired meaning from being presented together. Nineteenth-century sensibilities are also called on with the erratic scaling of the pictures and the salon-like framing of individual works. Karl's manipulation of my mounted photographs—his carefully considered scarring and embellishing of the pictorial plane with his rings and brooches—ruptures and displaces the photographic imagery and transforms the two-dimensional surface into a montaged relief. The finished works are surrealist in spirit.

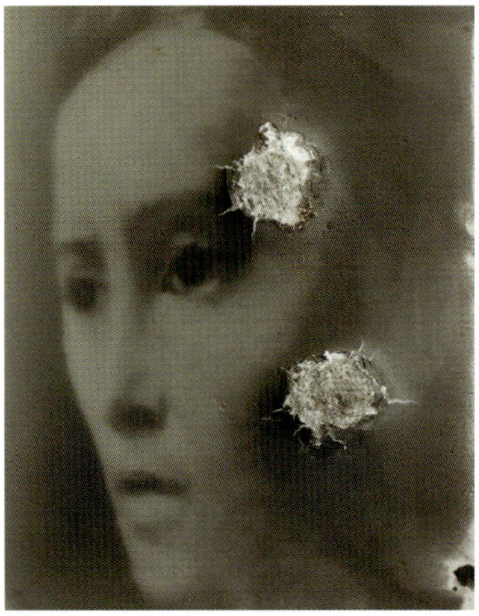

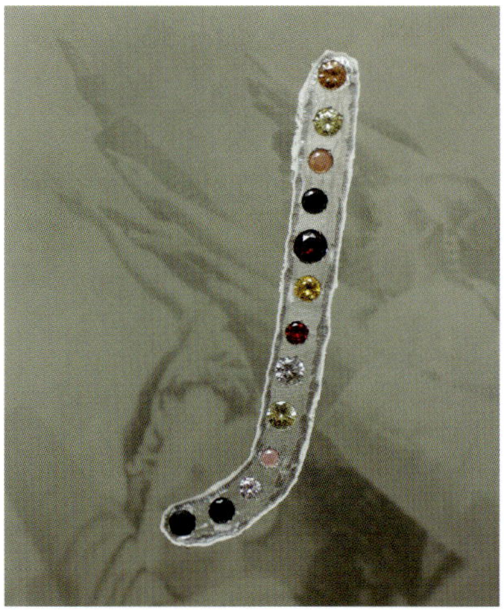

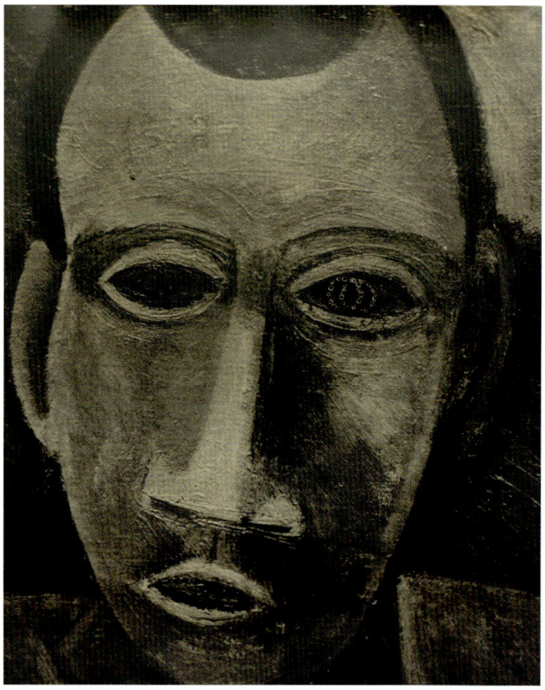

140 ABOVE
Karl Fritsch and **Gavin Hipkins**
Catherine from Der Tiefenglanz series
(jeweled photograph), 2014
Gelatin silver print mounted on aluminum
$14^{3}/_{4}$ x $12^{5}/_{8}$ x $2^{3}/_{4}$ in.
(37.5 x 32 x 6.8 cm), framed
Courtesy of the artists and
Hamish McKay Gallery

141 ABOVE
Karl Fritsch and **Gavin Hipkins**
Kapeu from Der Tiefenglanz series
(jeweled photograph), 2014
Gelatin silver print mounted on
aluminum, cubic zirconia stones
$13^{1}/_{8}$ x $11^{1}/_{4}$ x $1^{3}/_{8}$ in.
(33.4 x 28.7 x 3.5 cm), framed
Courtesy of the artists and
Hamish McKay Gallery

142 ABOVE
Karl Fritsch and **Gavin Hipkins**
Junge from Der Tiefenglanz series
(jeweled photograph), 2014
Gelatin silver print mounted on archival
board, silver, sapphire rings
$21^{1}/_{8}$ x $17^{1}/_{8}$ x $1^{1}/_{2}$ in.
(53.5 x 43.5 x 3.7 cm), framed
Courtesy of the artists and
Hamish McKay Gallery

143 TOP RIGHT

Karl Fritsch and **Gavin Hipkins**
Profil from Der Tiefenglanz series
(jeweled photograph), 2014
Gelatin silver print mounted on archival board,
silver ring, silver fittings
$17^{3}/_{4}$ x $13^{3}/_{4}$ x $2^{1}/_{8}$ in. (45.1 x 34.9 x 5.4 cm), framed
Courtesy of the artists and
Hamish McKay Gallery

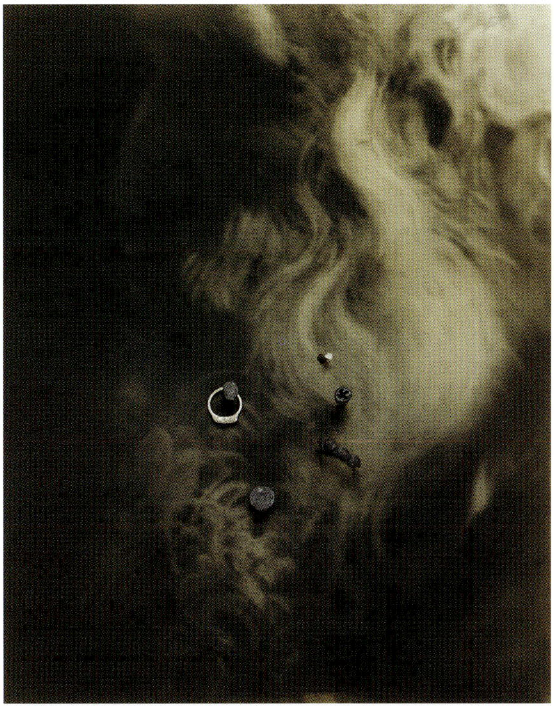

144 TOP FAR RIGHT

Karl Fritsch and **Gavin Hipkins**
Vogel from Der Tiefenglanz series
(jeweled photograph), 2014
Gelatin silver print mounted on archival
board, lead, cubic zirconia stones
$14^{1}/_{4}$ x $11^{3}/_{4}$ x $1^{1}/_{4}$ in. (36.4 x 29.8 x 3.2 cm), framed
Courtesy of the artists and Hamish McKay Gallery

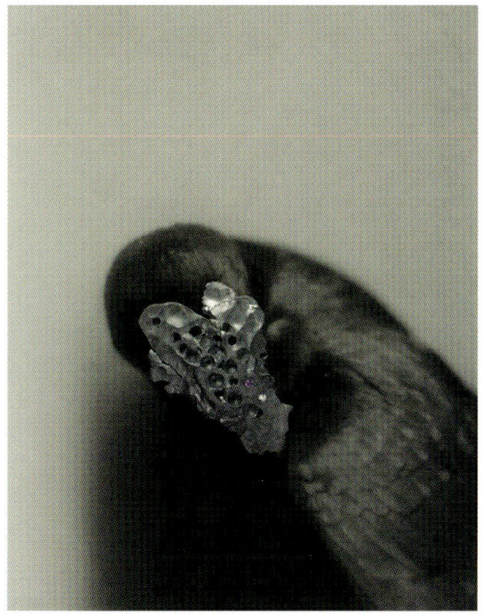

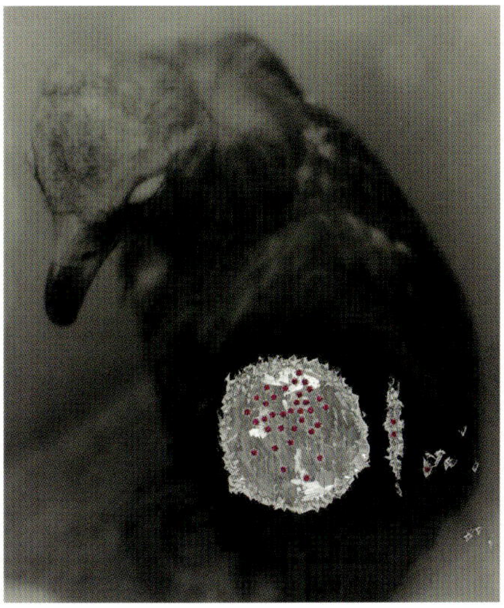

145 ABOVE

Karl Fritsch and **Gavin Hipkins**
Vulture from Der Tiefenglanz series
(jeweled photograph), 2014
Gelatin silver print mounted on
aluminum, synthetic rubies
$18^{3}/_{4}$ x $15^{7}/_{8}$ x $^{3}/_{4}$ in. (47.8 x 40.4 x 2 cm), framed
Courtesy of the artists and
Hamish McKay Gallery

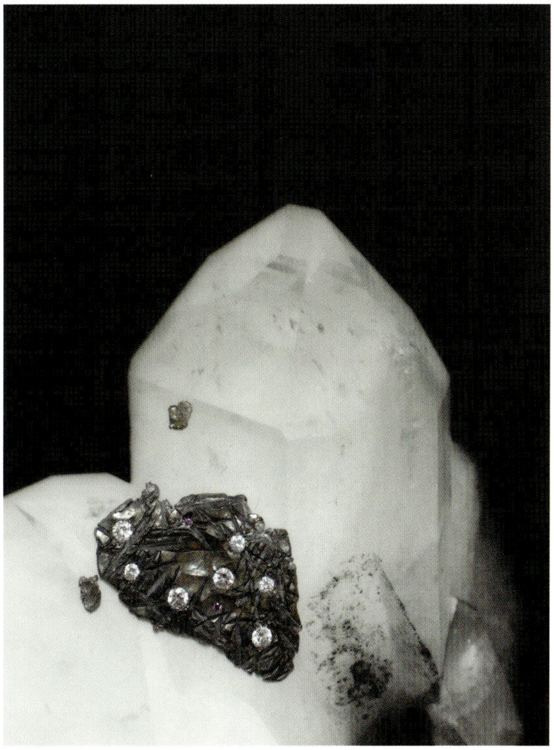

146 ABOVE

Karl Fritsch and **Gavin Hipkins**
Kristall from Der Tiefenglanz series
(jeweled photograph), 2014
Gelatin silver print mounted on archival
board, lead, cubic zirconia stones
$22^{1}/_{2}$ x 18 x $1^{3}/_{4}$ in. (57.2 x 45.8 x 4.4 cm), framed
Courtesy of the artists and
Hamish McKay Gallery

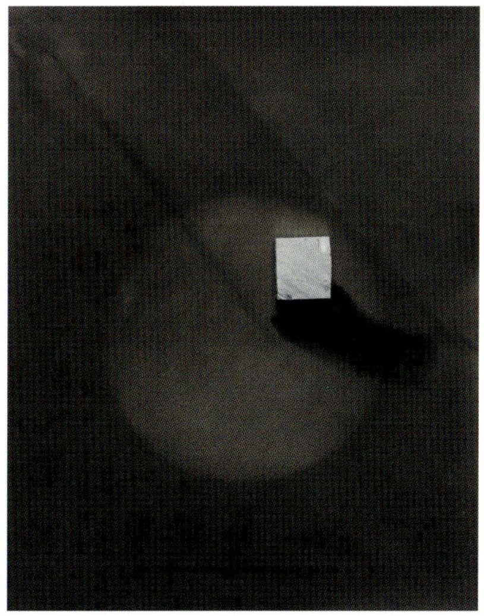

147 ABOVE

Karl Fritsch and **Gavin Hipkins**
Moon from Der Tiefenglanz series
(jeweled photograph), 2014
Gelatin silver print mounted on archival
board, aluminum block
$10^{1}/_{2}$ x $8^{1}/_{4}$ x $2^{1}/_{2}$ in. (26.6 x 21.1 x 6.3 cm), framed
Courtesy of the artists and
Hamish McKay Gallery

IRENE MAMIYE

Shattered Gems

Shattered Gems celebrates its electronic origins through fully visible charger cords and electronic connections. The piece also updates the convention of using still photos in jewelry by incorporating video, and through its images of slowly cracking and exploding gems, it comments on the illusory nature of luxury. The necklace is made up of a group of tiny Nano screens, each displaying the video sequence of the fracturing of a particular gemstone—diamond, ruby, turquoise, citrine, or emerald. I used a digital camera to capture the artificial gems at varied apertures and shutter speeds and then processed those images using software that added the component of movement.

148

Irene Mamiye with
Stephen Dweck and **John Ike**
Shattered Gems (necklace), 2013
iPod nanos (6th generation)
with video loop 16:02, sterling silver,
black agate, black sapphires,
fabric, vinyl cords
17 x 8 in. (43.2 x 20.3 cm)
1 1/2 x 1 5/8 x 3/8 in. (3.8 x 4.1 x 0.9 cm),
each component
Collection of Irene Mamiye

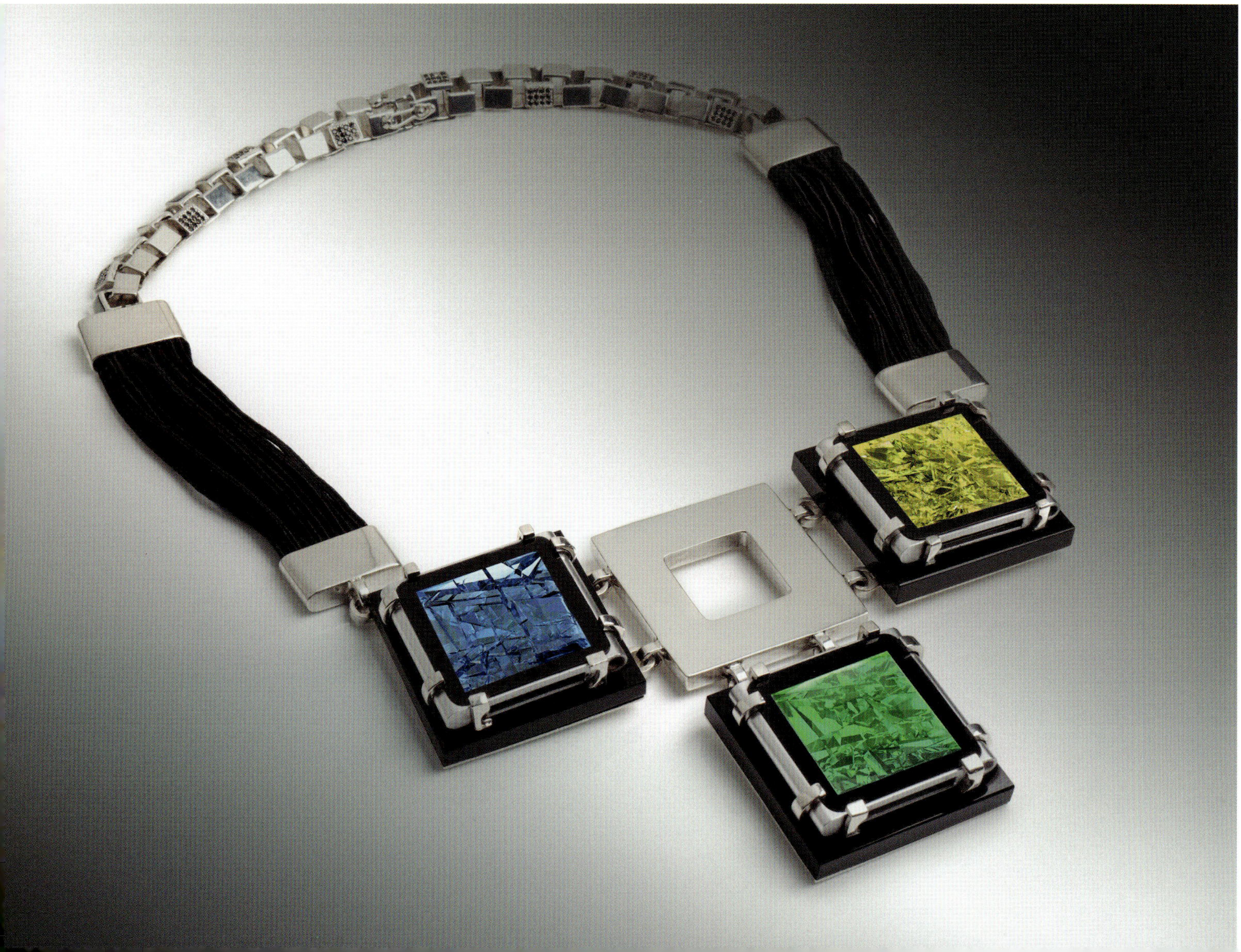

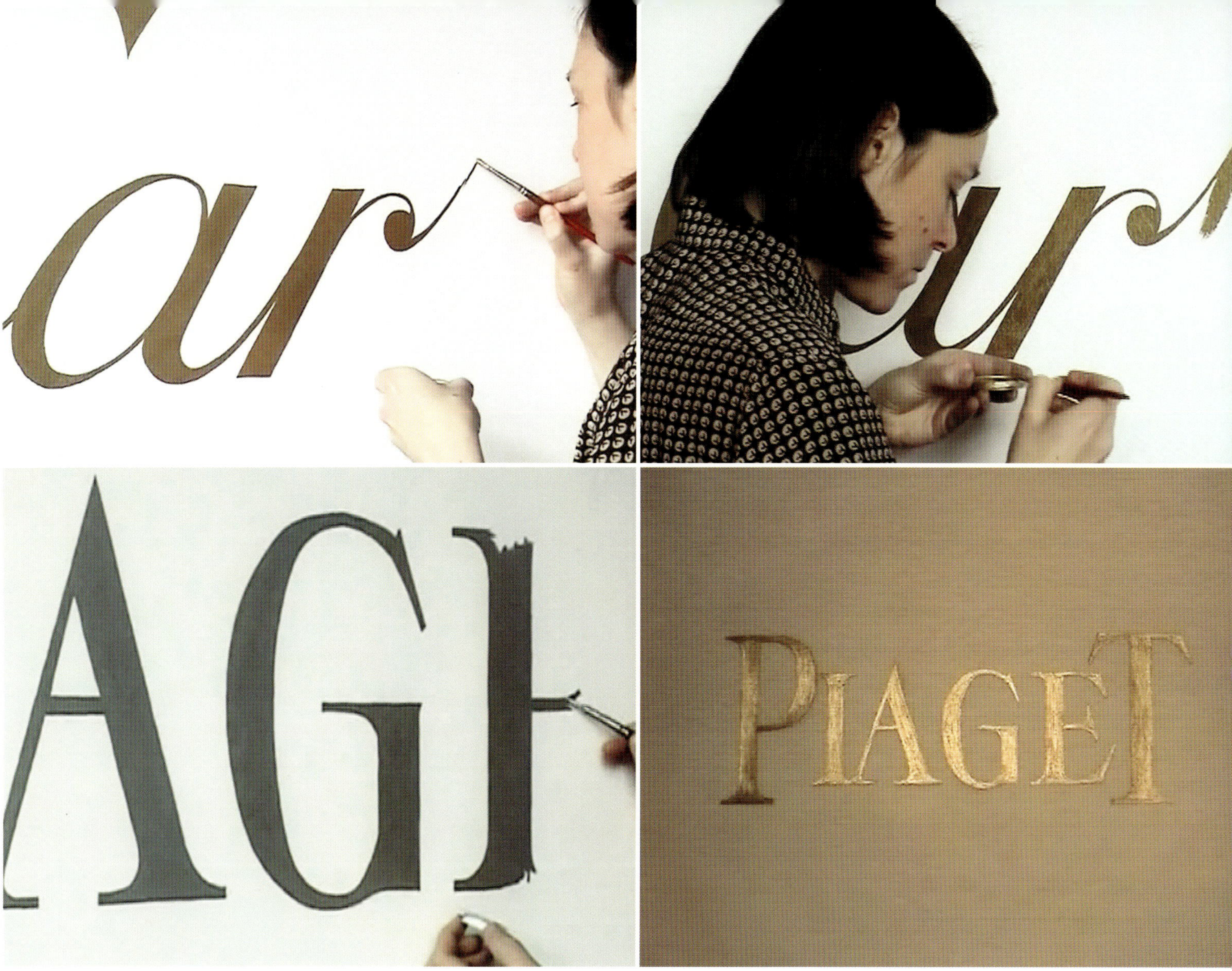

149
Suska Mackert
To Be on Display (video), 2002
4 minutes
Filmed by Suska Mackert and Quirijn Kuchlein
Collection Stedelijk Museum 's-Hertogenbosch

SUSKA MACKERT

To Be on Display

Since 1997 I have rarely made "real," wearable pieces of jewelry. Instead, my work has consisted of artistic transpositions of my thoughts and reflections on jewelry. I regard jewelry as an indicator of fundamental social and psychological mechanisms, and I use photography, video, installation, text, and printed matter to explore the role it plays in our lives. In more than one sense, I am interested in seeking out the breadth of jewelry.

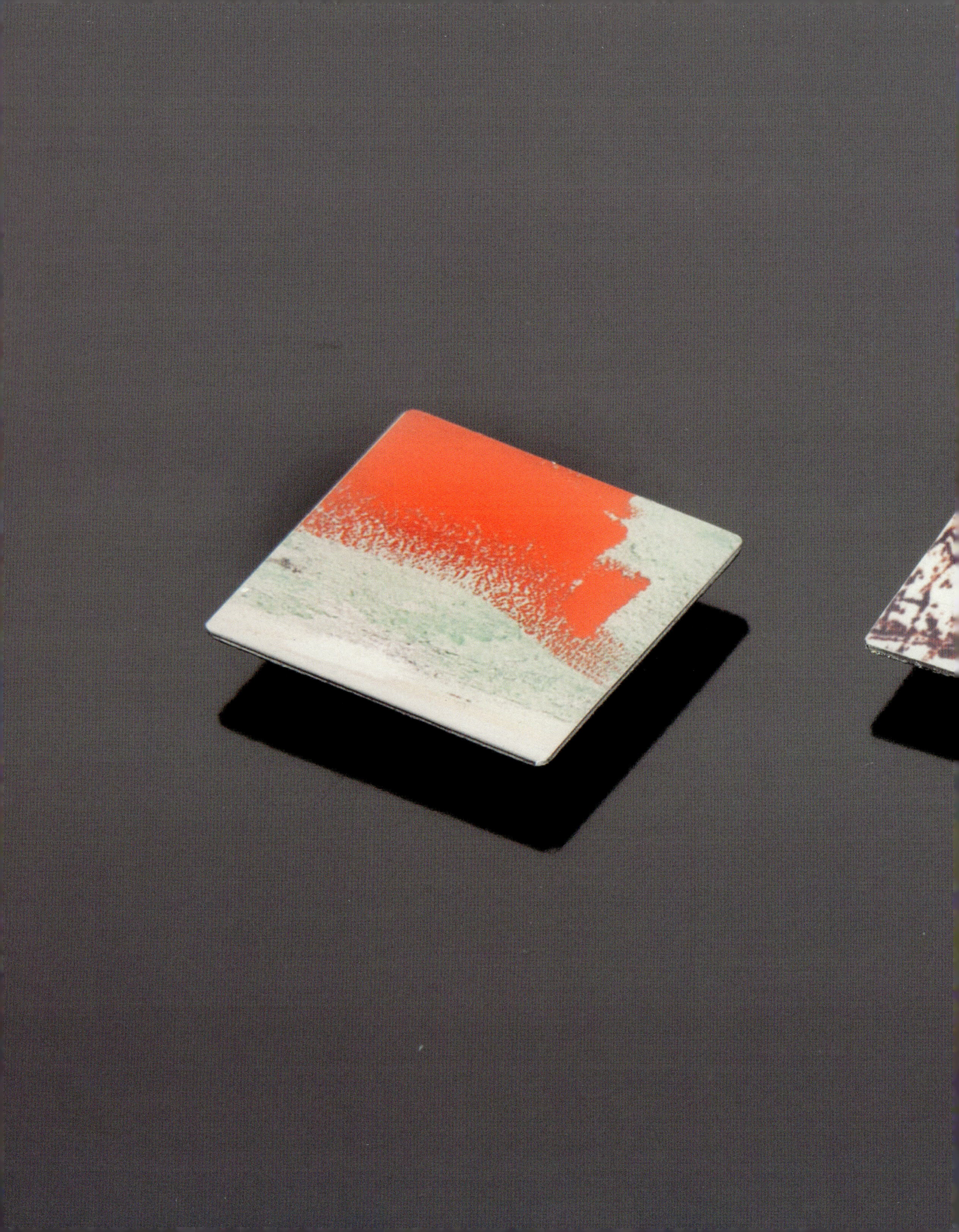

ARTISTS INDEX
SELECT BIBLIOGRAPHY
PHOTO CREDITS

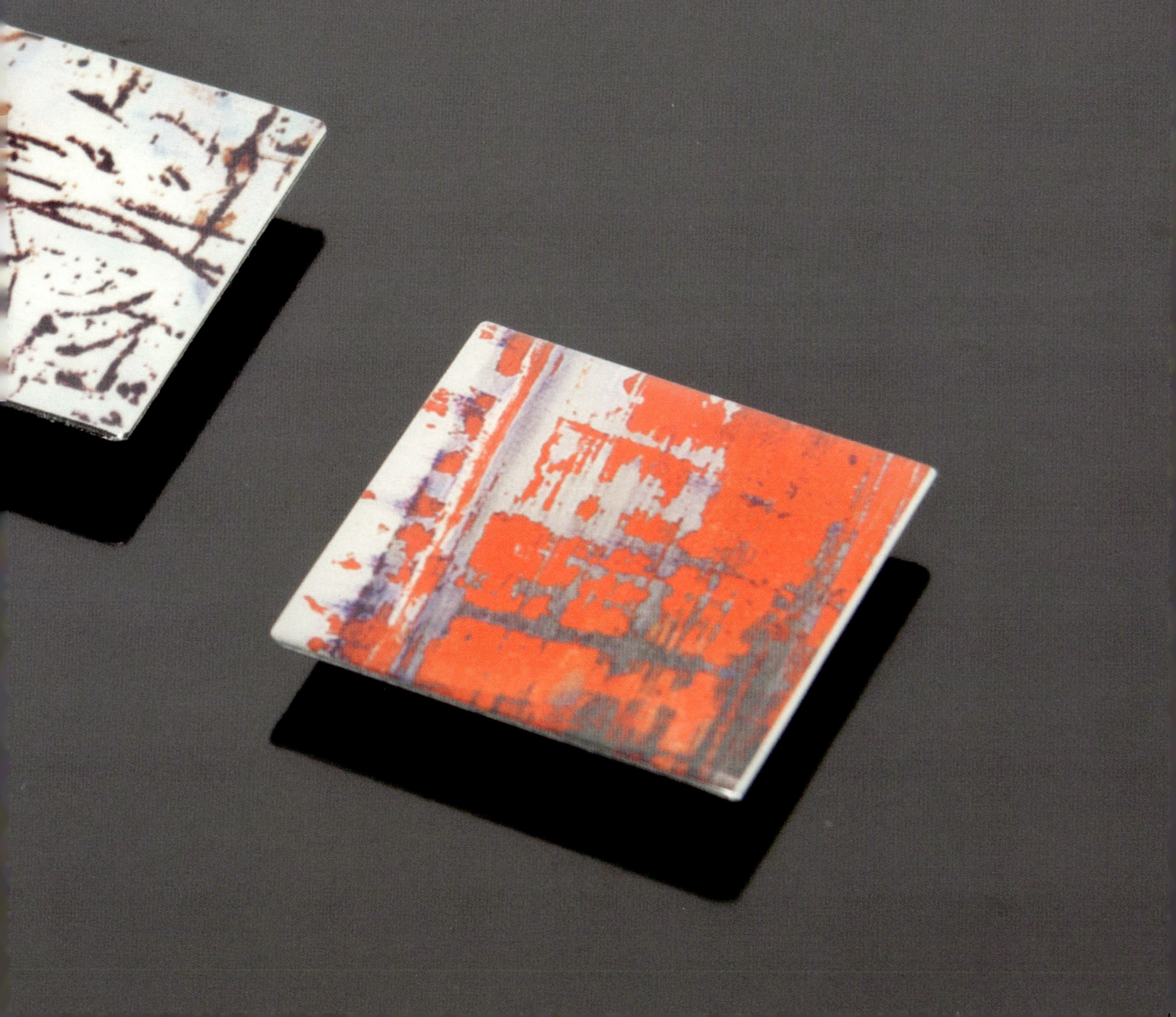

ARTISTS INDEX

Page numbers for images are indicated in **boldface** type

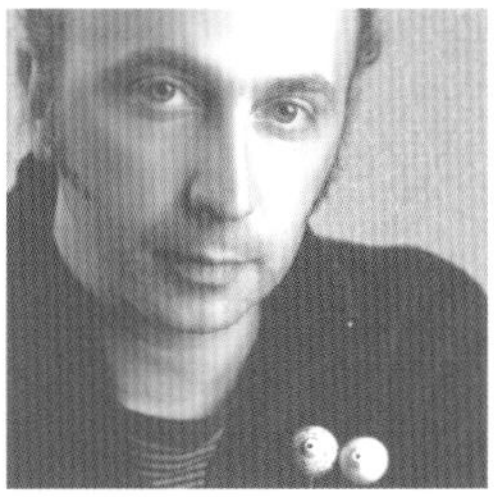

RINALDO ALVAREZ
b. 1971, Spain
Lives and works in Asturias, Spain
168, **181, back cover**

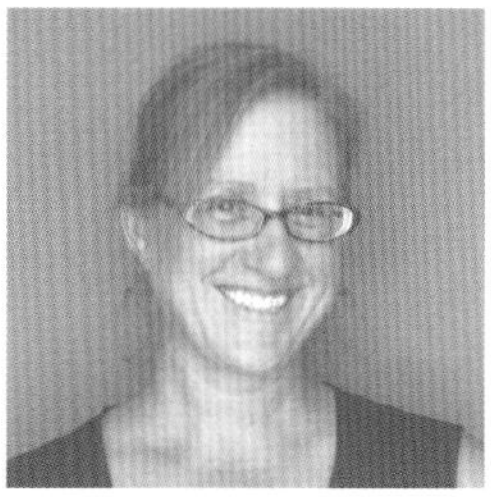

JULIA BARELLO
b. 1957, United States
Lives and works in Las Cruces, New Mexico
102, **126**, 197, **192-93, 205**

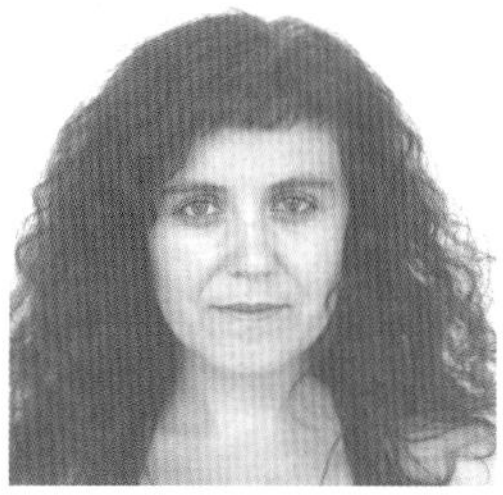

BABETTE BOUCHER
b. 1972, France
Lives and works in Munich, Germany
57, **72–73**

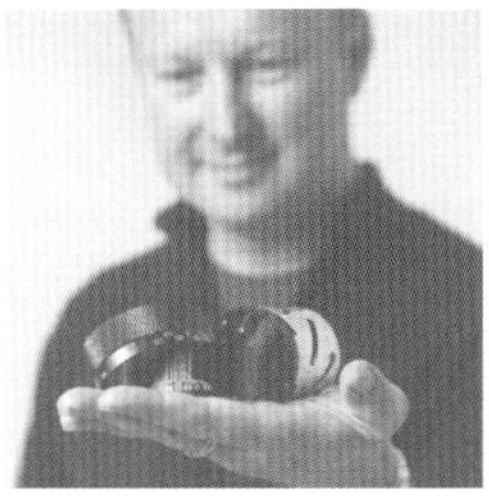

CRAIG ARNOLD
b. 1966, Australia
Lives and works in Adelaide, Australia
135, **158,** 195, **215, 242–43**

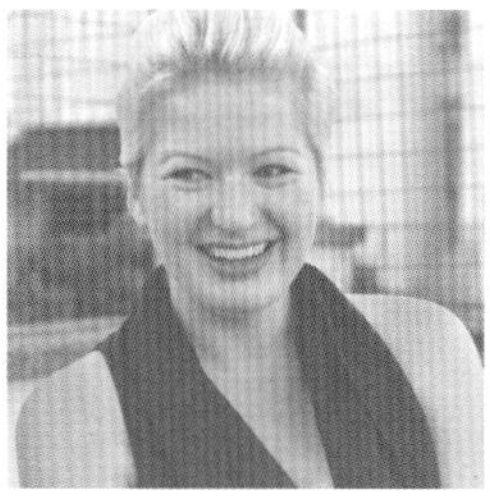

SUZANNE BEAUTYMAN
b. 1979, United States
Lives and works in Birmingham, England
134, 135, **163**

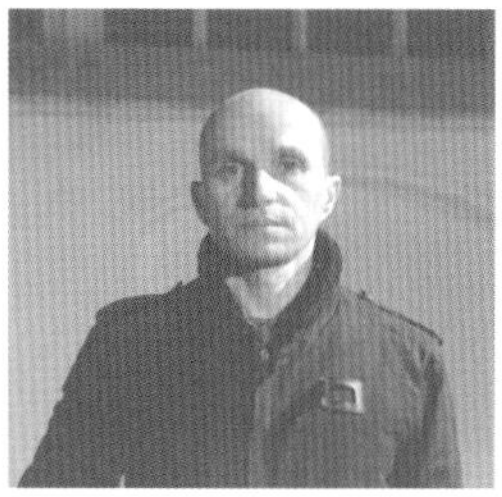

CÉLIO BRAGA
b. 1965, Brazil
Lives and works in Amsterdam,
The Netherlands, and São Paulo, Brazil
101, **119**

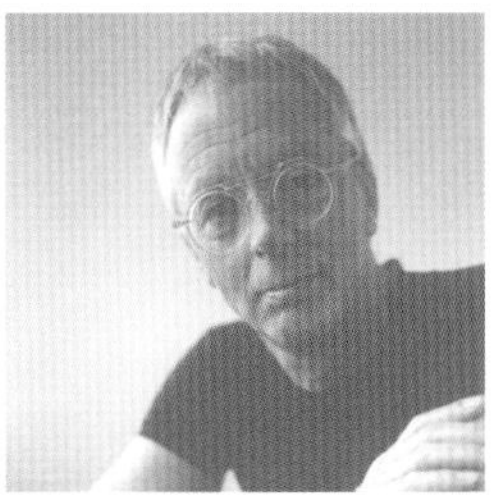

GIJS BAKKER
b. 1942, The Netherlands
Lives and works in Amsterdam,
The Netherlands
15, 17, 19, 20, 21, **24, 98–99,** 100, 101, 102, **110, 112–13,** 166, 167, 168, 169, **170–71, 182–83,** 218, **back cover**

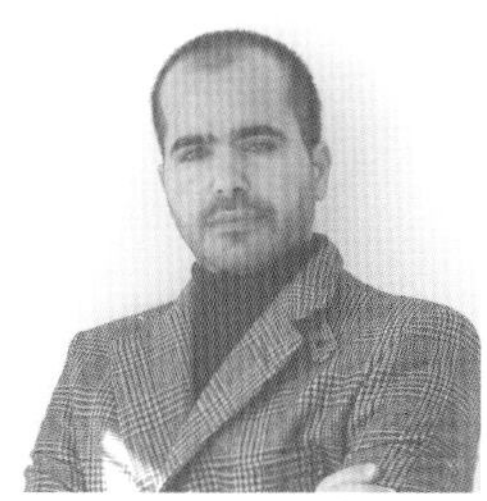

WAFAA BILAL
b. 1966, Iraq
Lives and works in New York, New York
cover, 18, 220–21, **234–35**

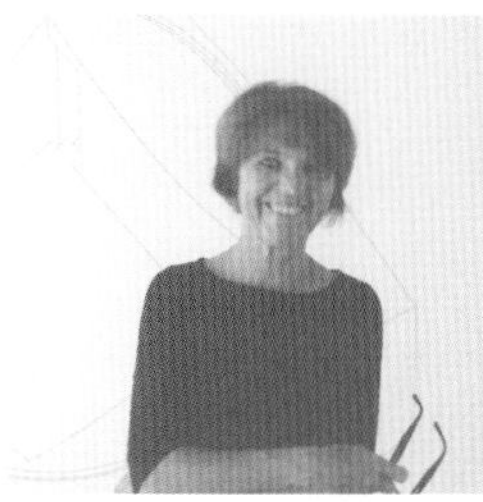

ESTHER BRINKMANN
b. 1953, Switzerland
Lives and works in Mumbai, India
28, 220, **224–25**

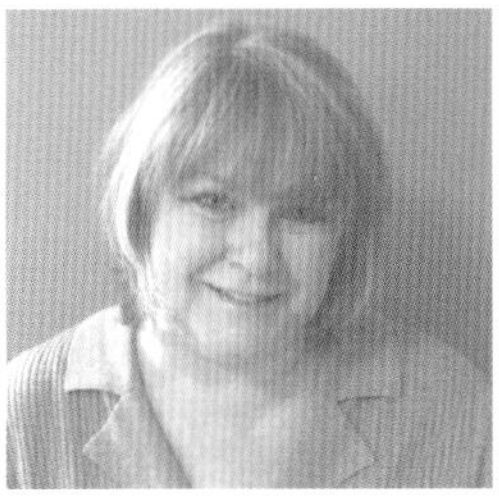

KATHLEEN BROWNE
b. 1950, United States
Lives and works in Ravenna, Ohio
169, **179**

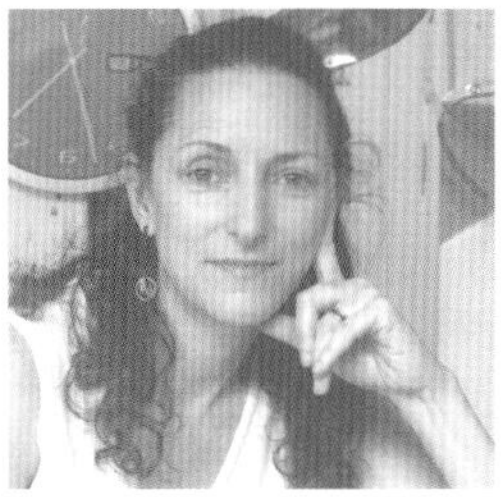

THEA CLARK
b. 1964, Spain
Lives and works in Maplewood, New Jersey
196, **212–13**

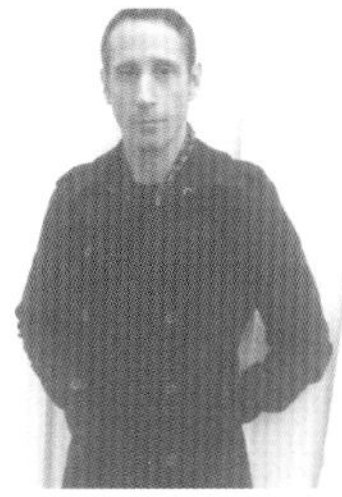

JORDAN DONER
b. 1971, United States
Lives and works in New York, New York
17, 55, **96**

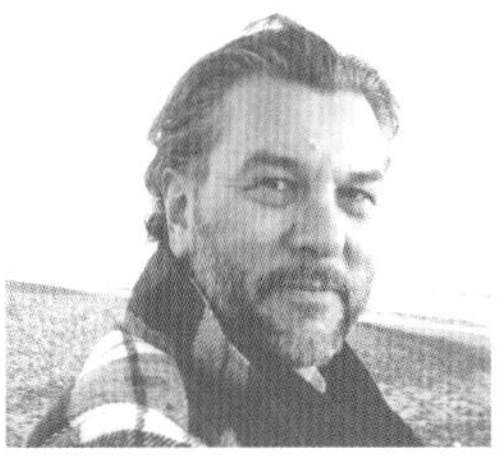

KLAUS BÜRGEL
b. 1958, Germany
Lives and works in New York, New York
57, **93**

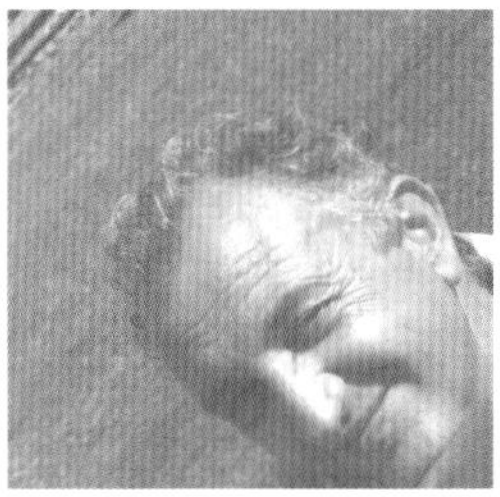

RAMON PUIG CUYÀS
b. 1953, Spain
Lives and works in Barcelona, Spain
19, 167, **174–75**

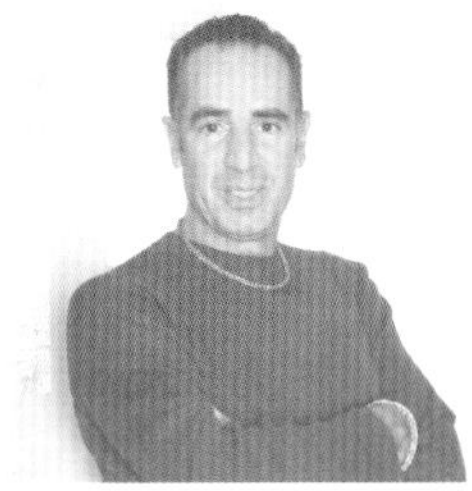

STEPHEN DWECK
b. 1960, United States
Lives and works in New York, New York
221, **240**

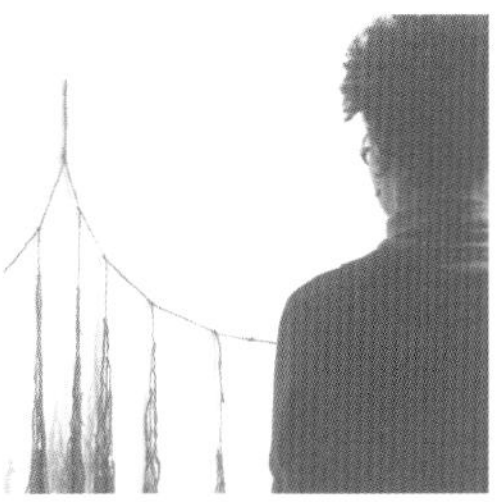

SONYA CLARK
b. 1967, United States
Lives and works in Richmond, Virginia
54, **69**

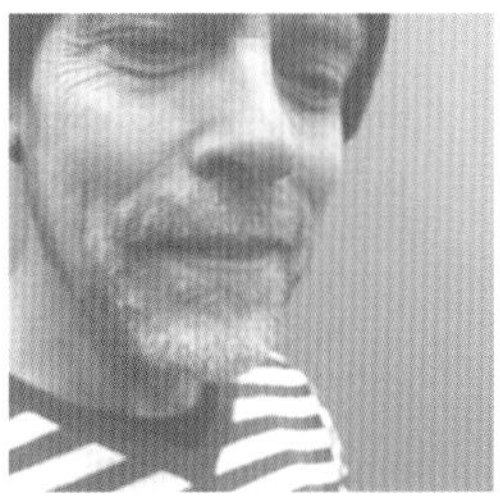

PETER DECKERS
b. 1953, The Netherlands
Lives and works in Wellington, New Zealand
56, **94**

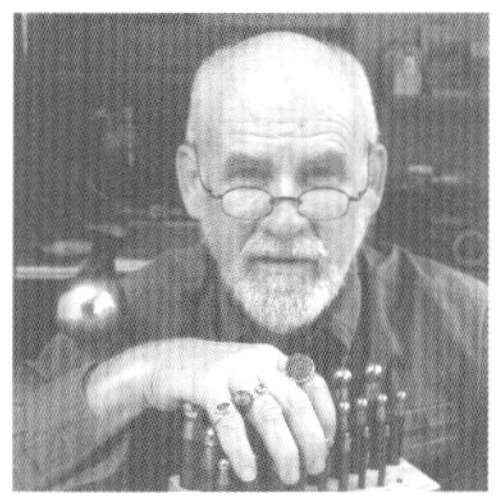

ROBERT EBENDORF
b. 1938, United States
Lives and works in Greenville, North Carolina
15, 56, **78–79**

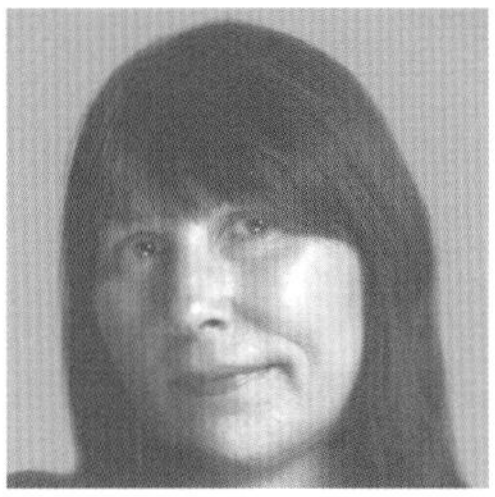

DIANE FALKENHAGEN
b. 1955, United States
Lives and works on West Galveston Island, Texas
168, **180**

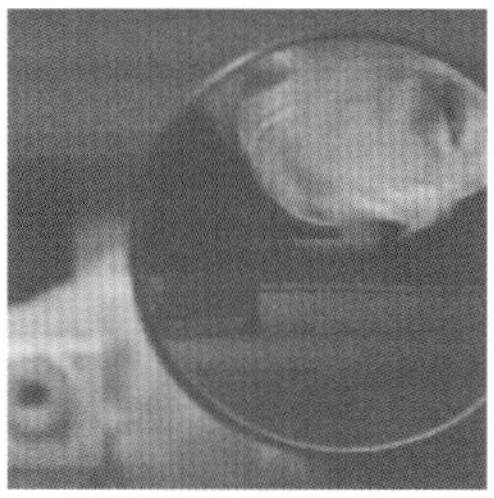

THOMAS GENTILLE
b. 1936, United States
Lives and works in New York, New York
17, 104, **118**, 134, **146**

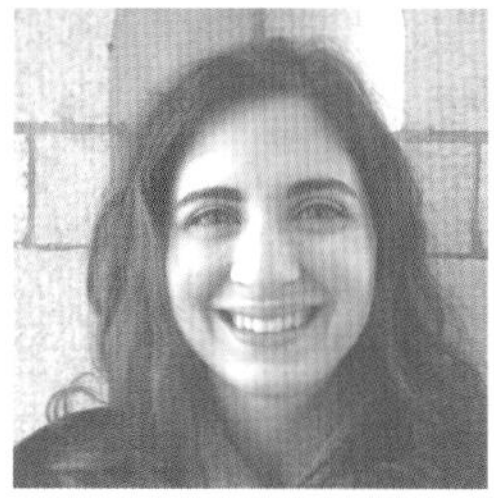

ASHLEY GILREATH
b. 1988, United States
Lives and works in Chicago, Illinois
54, **85**

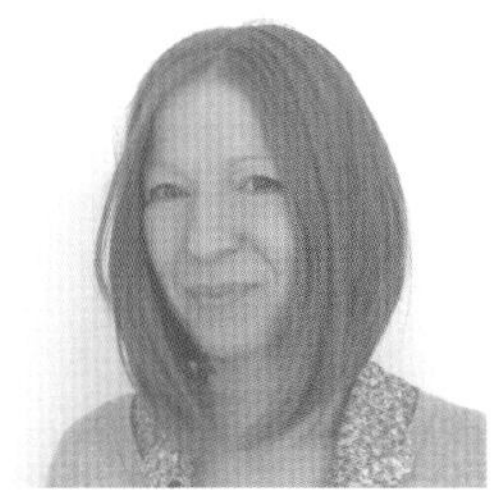

JANTJE FLEISCHHUT
b. 1972, Germany
Lives and works in Amsterdam, The Netherlands
18, 132, **148–49, back cover**

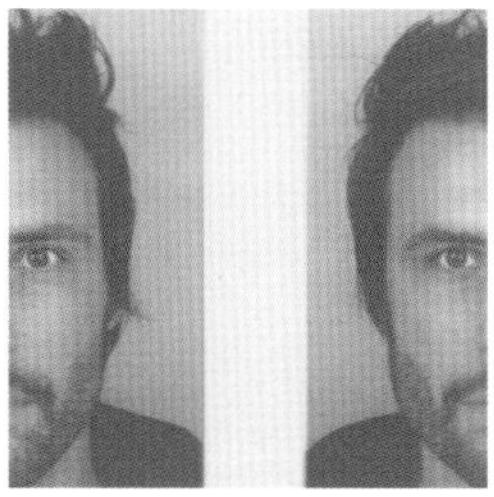

KIKO GIANOCCA
b. 1974, Switzerland
Lives and works in Lugano, Switzerland
132, **147**

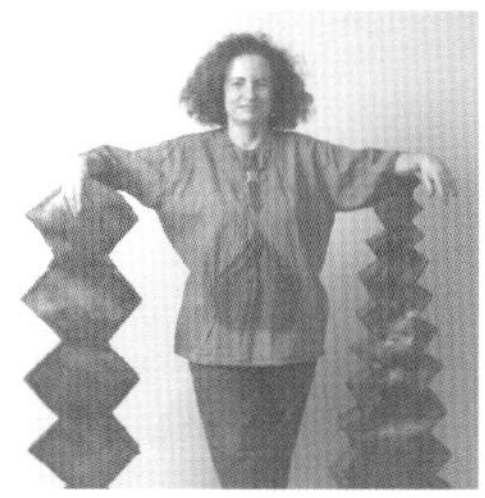

JANET GOLDNER
b. 1952, United States
Lives and works in New York, New York
154–55, 220

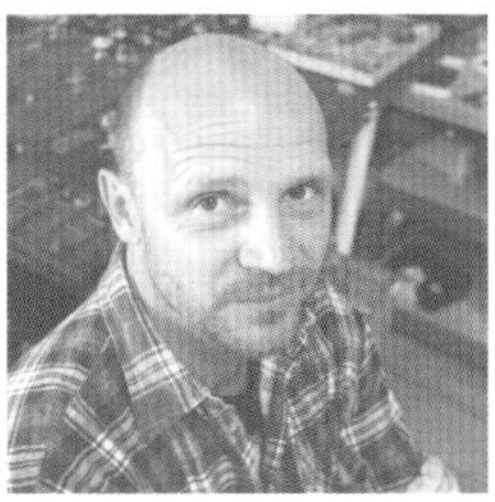

KARL FRITSCH
b. 1963, Germany
Lives and works in Wellington, New Zealand
221, **238–39**

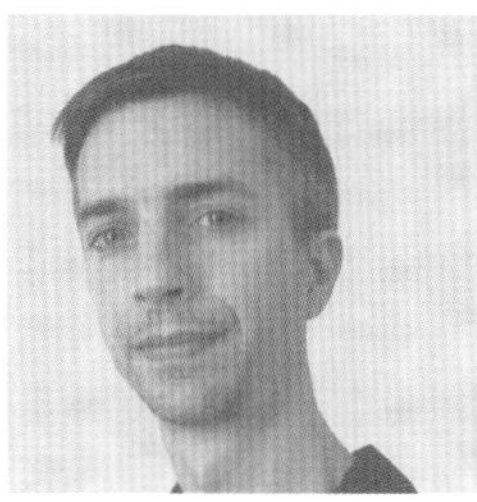

GEOFFREY GILES
b. 1972, United States
Lives and works in Asheville, North Carolina
57, **60–61**

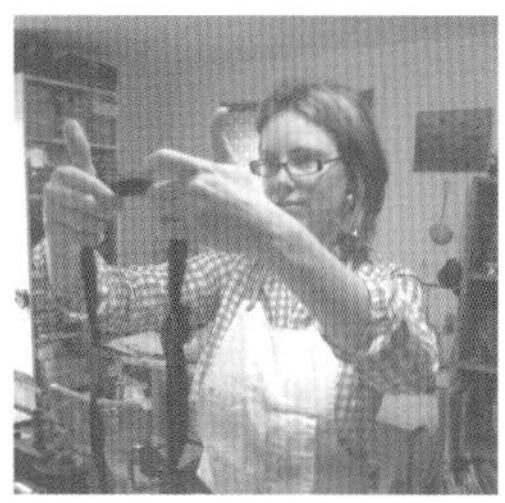

REBECCA HANNON
b. 1973, United States
Lives and works in Halifax, Canada
134, **162**

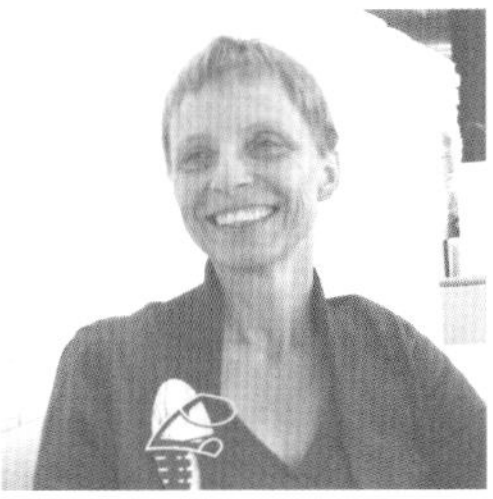

MARGIT HART
b. 1958, Austria
Lives and works in Vienna, Austria
135, **159**

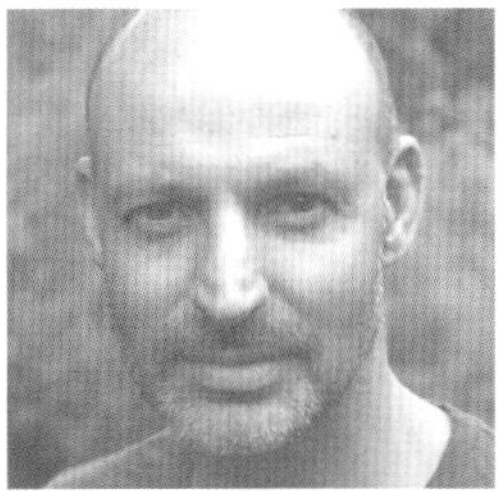

GAVIN HIPKINS
b. 1968, New Zealand
Lives and works in Auckland, New Zealand
221, **238–39**

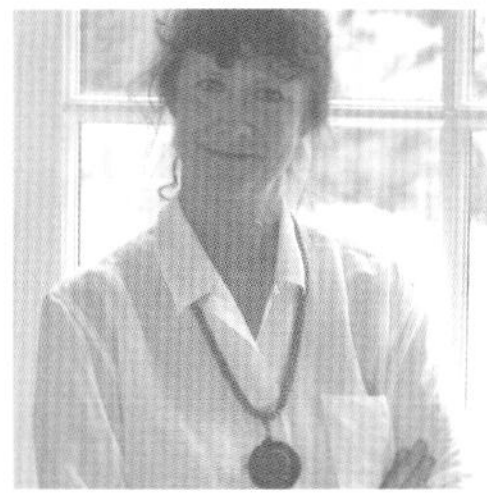

SANDY JOHANSON
b. 1951, United States
Lives and works in Tinton Falls, New Jersey
195, 197, **208–9**

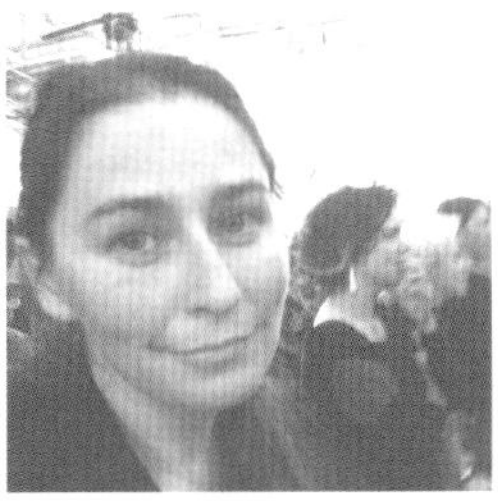

KIRSTEN HAYDON
b. 1973, New Zealand
Lives and works in Melbourne, Australia
128–29, 130, 131, **142–45**

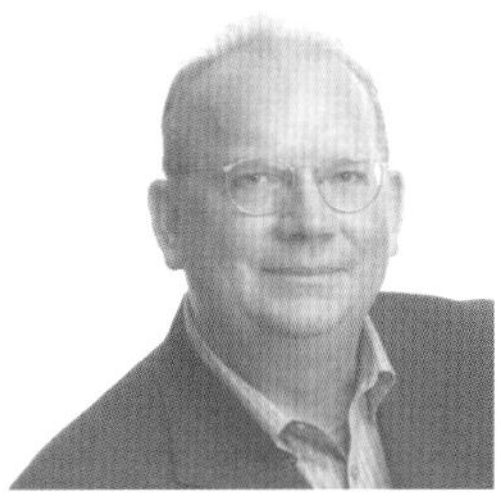

JOHN IKE
b. 1954, United States
Lives and works in New York, New York
221, **240**

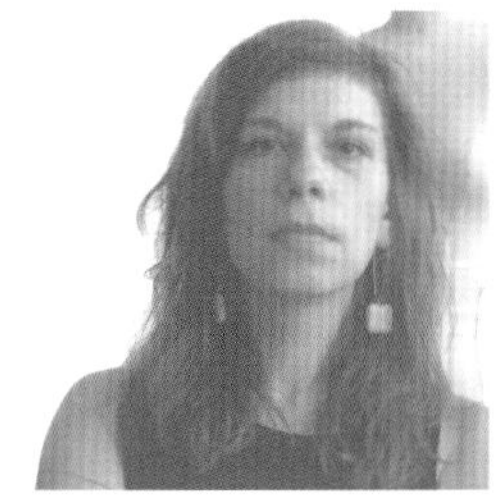

LAUREN KALMAN
b. 1980, United States
Lives and works in Detroit, Michigan
28, 103, 218, 220, **228**

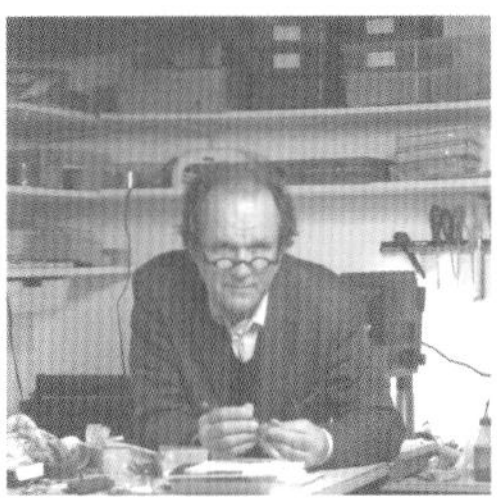

HERMAN HERMSEN
b. 1953, The Netherlands
Lives and works in Düsseldorf, Germany
134, **160–61**

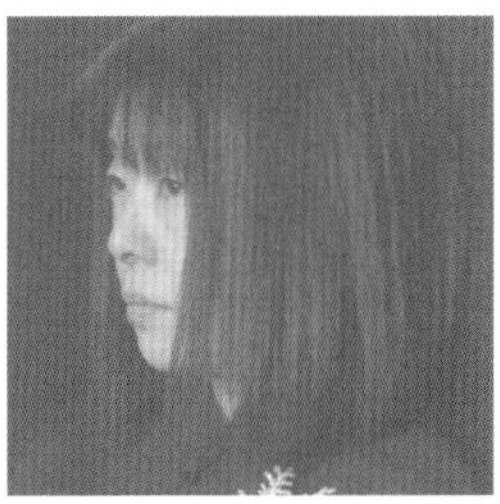

MARI ISHIKAWA
b. 1964, Japan
Lives and works in Munich, Germany
19, 132, **140–41**

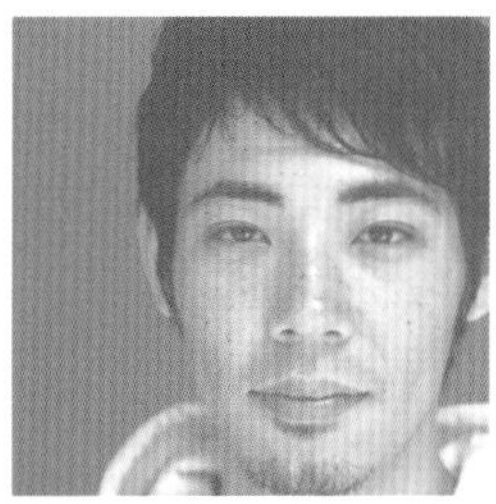

JIRO KAMATA
b. 1978, Japan
Lives and works in Munich, Germany
7, 20, 196, 197, **200–1**

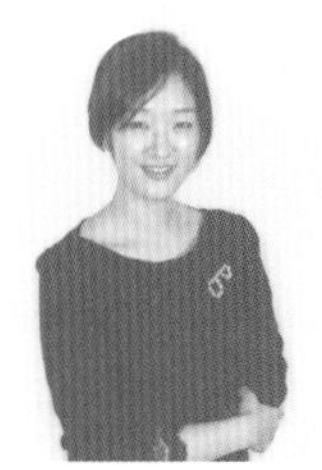

SOOYEON KIM
b. 1983, South Korea
Lives and works in Seoul, South Korea
133, **156–57**

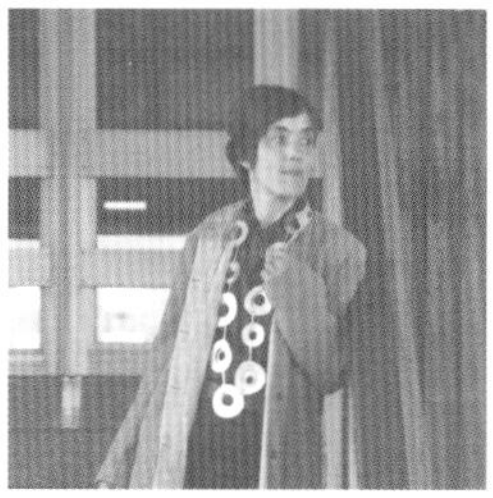

SUSANNA KUSCHEK
b. 1963, Germany
Lives and works in Berlin, Germany
133, **150**

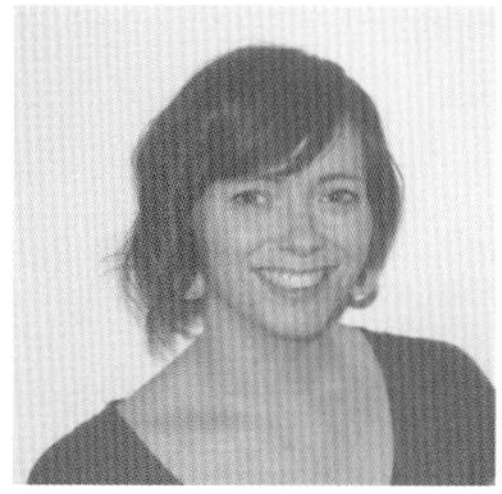

JAIMIE MACDONALD
b. 1981, Scotland
Lives and works in Edinburgh, Scotland
20, 197, **206–7**

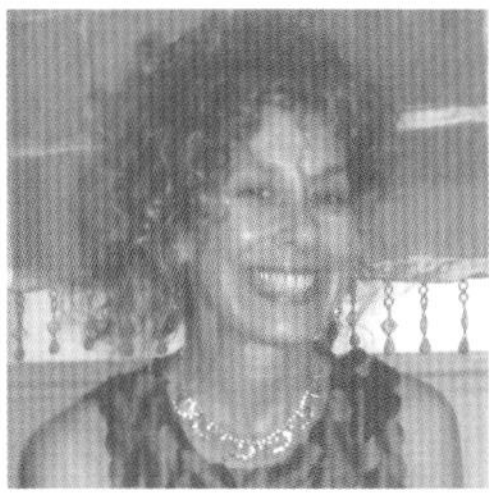

BETSY KING
b. 1953, United States
Lives and works in Ocean City, New Jersey
164–65, 168–69, **188**

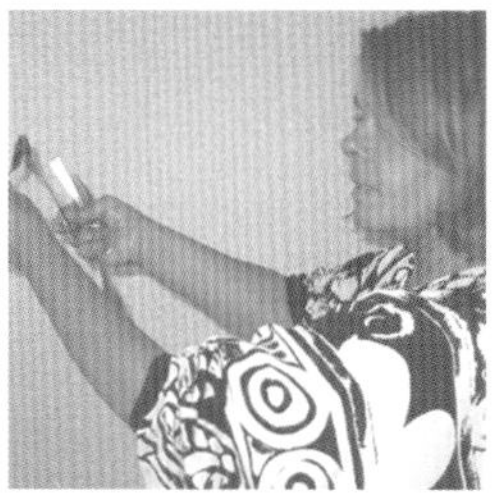

CLAIRE LAVENDHOMME
b. 1959, Belgian Congo
Lives and works in Brussels, Belgium
102, 103, **120–21**

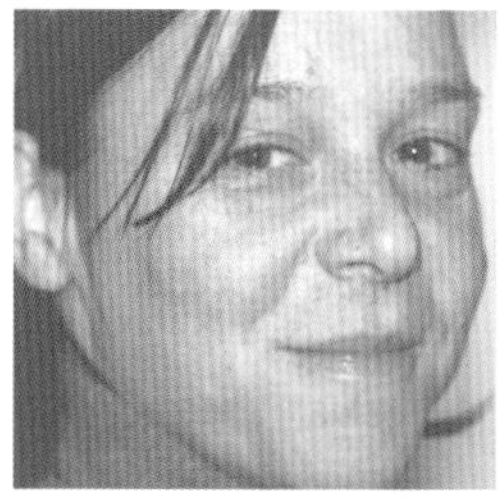

SUSKA MACKERT
b. 1969, Germany
Lives and works in Hamburg, Germany, and Amsterdam, The Netherlands
28, 102, **108–9**, 220, **241**

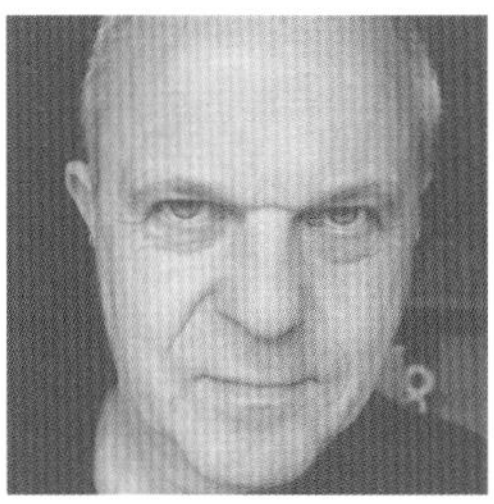

OTTO KÜNZLI
b. 1948, Switzerland
Lives and works in Munich, Germany
21, **22–23**, 28, 59

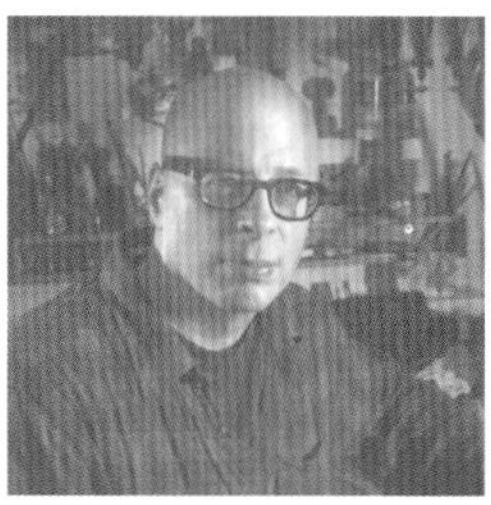

KEITH LO BUE
b. 1964, United States
Lives and works in Sydney, Australia
17, 57, **92**

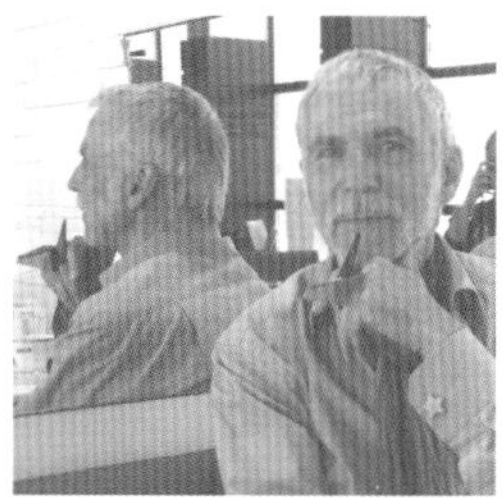

FRITZ MAIERHOFER
b. 1941, Austria
Lives and works in Vienna, Austria
56, **59**, **132**, 133

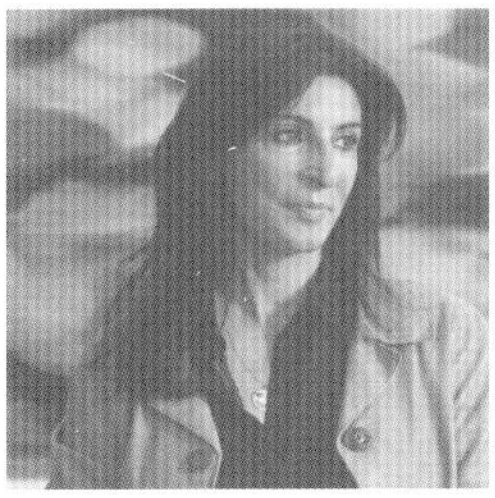

IRENE MAMIYE
b. 1957, France
Lives and works in New York, New York
221, **240**

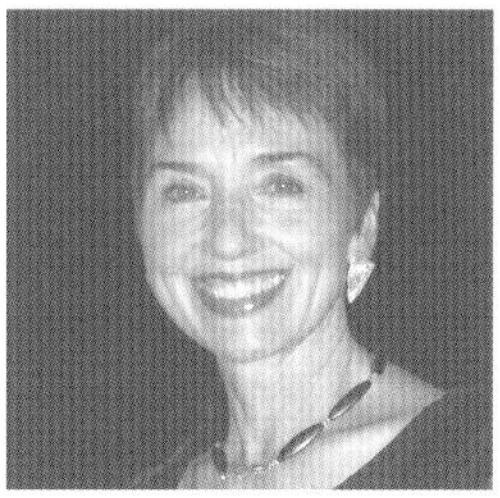

ELEANOR MOTY
b. 1945, United States
Lives and works in Tucson, Arizona
52–53, 57, **90–91**, 133, **151**

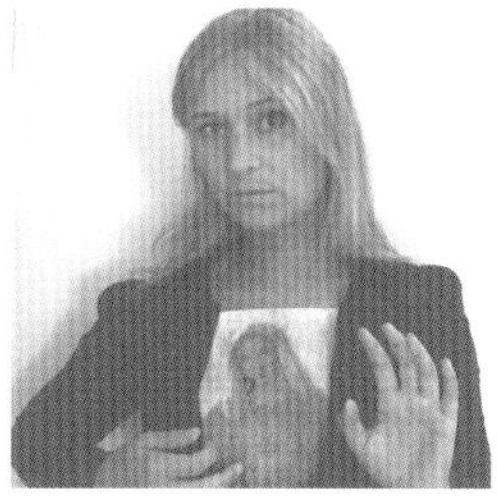

MARIA NUUTINEN
b. 1975, Finland
Lives and works in Lappeenranta, Finland
167, **177**

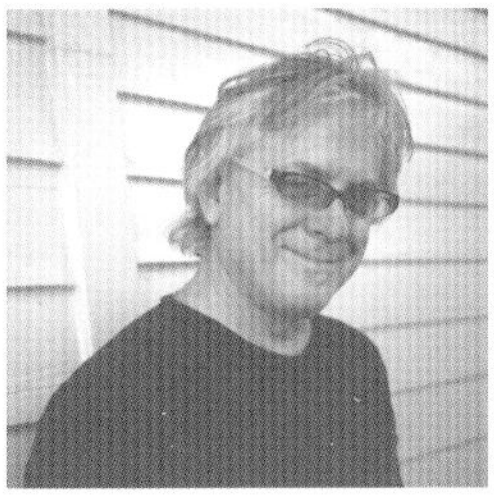

THOMAS MANN
b. 1947, United States
Lives and works in New Orleans, Louisiana
102, **117**

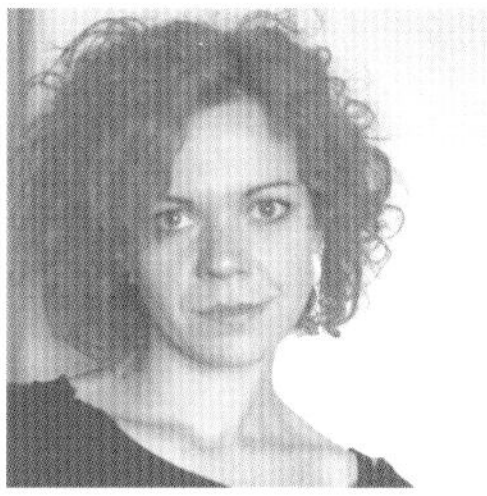

VIKTORIA MÜNZKER
b. 1978, Slovakia
Lives and works in Vienna, Austria
102, **122–23**

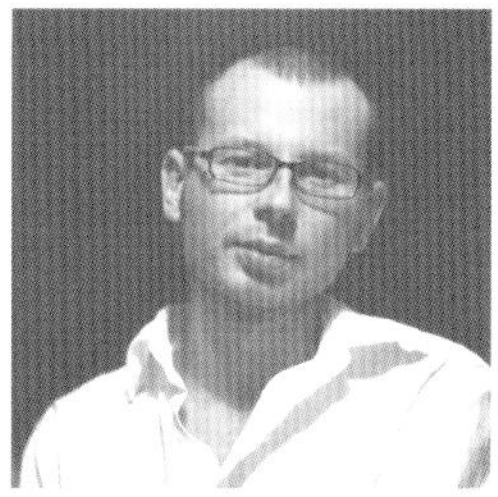

MARTIN PAPCÚN
b. 1979, Slovakia
Lives and works in Munich, Germany
56, **62–63, back cover**

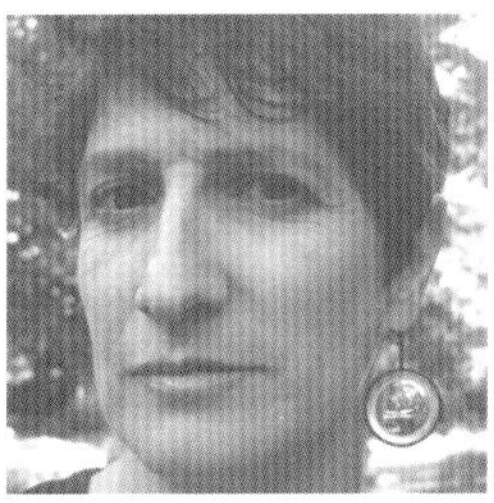

KAREN MISHER
b. 1965, United States
Lives and works in Philadelphia, Pennsylvania
196, **214**

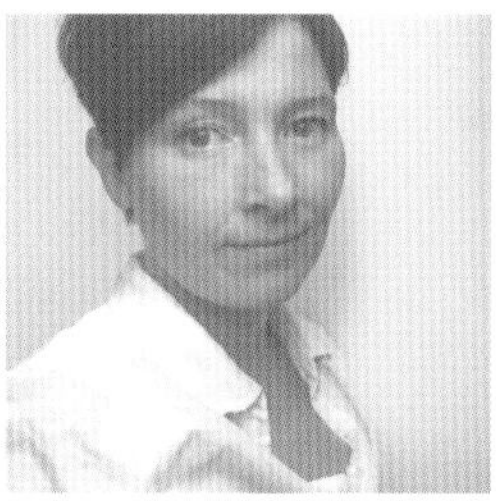

IRIS NIEUWENBURG
b. 1972, The Netherlands
Lives and works in Rotterdam, The Netherlands
54, **70–71**, 168, **186–87**

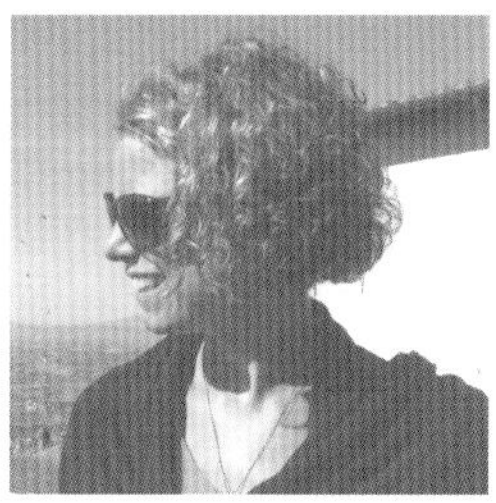

MARY HALLAM PEARSE
b. 1969, United States
Lives and works in Athens, Georgia
103, **111**

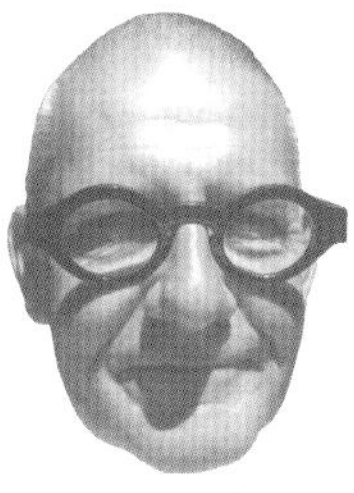

RUUDT PETERS
b. 1950, The Netherlands
Lives and works in Amsterdam, The Netherlands
56, **58**, 166–67, 176, **184–85**

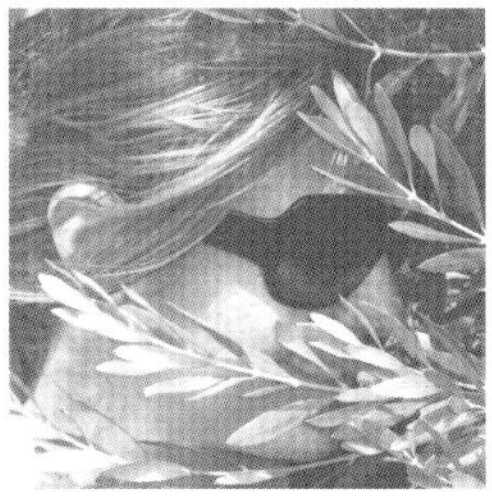

SHARI PIERCE
b. 1973, United States
Lives and works in Munich, Germany
56, **95**

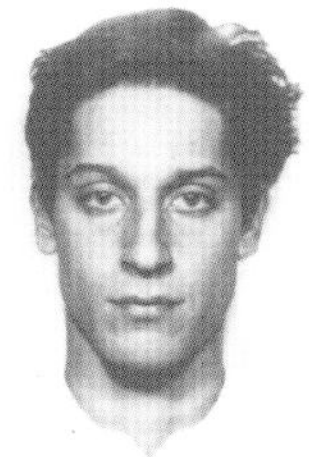

DAVID ROUX-FOUILLET
b. 1978, France
Lives and works in London, England
221–22, **230–31**

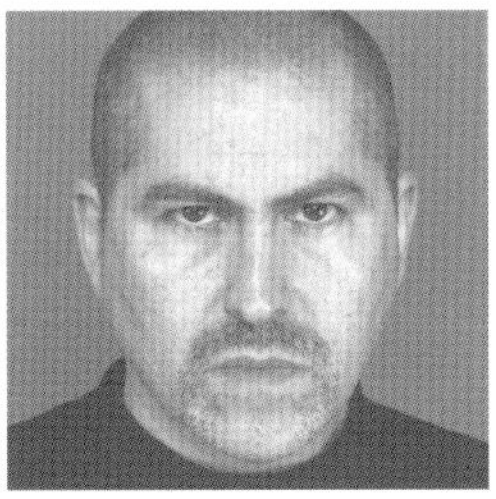

MICHAEL PETRY
b. 1960, United States
Lives and works in London, England
101, **114–15**

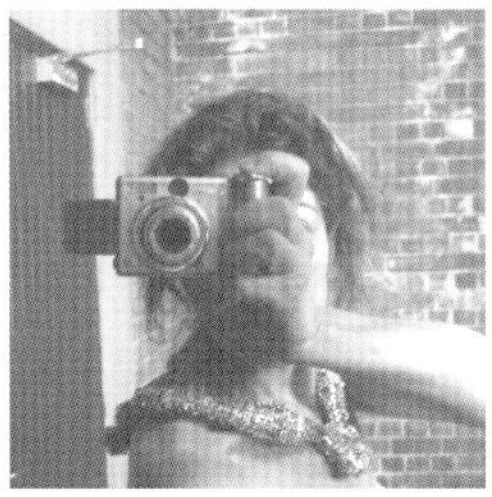

BEVERLEY PRICE
b. 1956, South Africa
Lives and works in Johannesburg, South Africa
55, **66–67**, 169, **172**

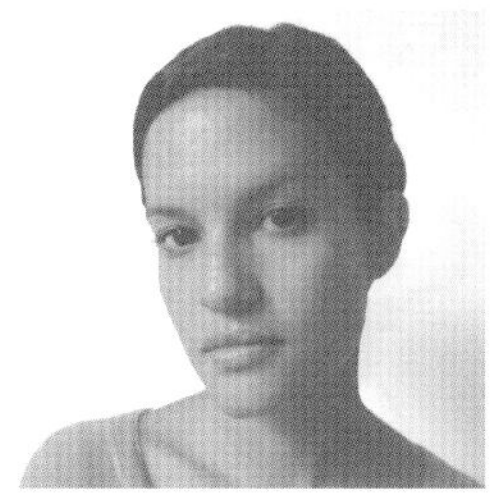

GABRIELA SÁNCHEZ Y SÁNCHEZ DE LA BARQUERA
b. 1982, Mexico
Lives and works in Eindhoven, The Netherlands
100, **127**

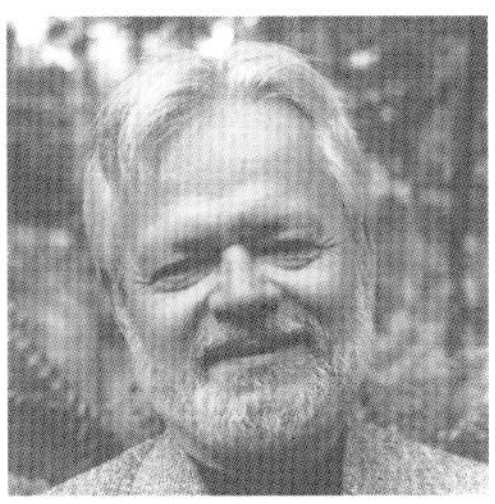

ROBERT PFUELB
b. 1946, United States
Lives and works in Annapolis, Maryland
57, **64–65**

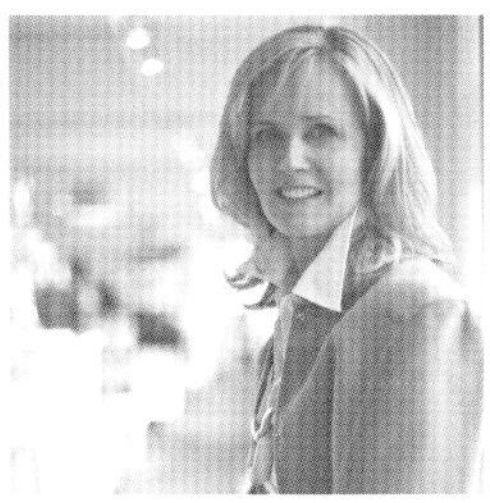

KARA ROSS
b. 1965, United States
Lives and works in New York, New York
18, 134, **152–53**

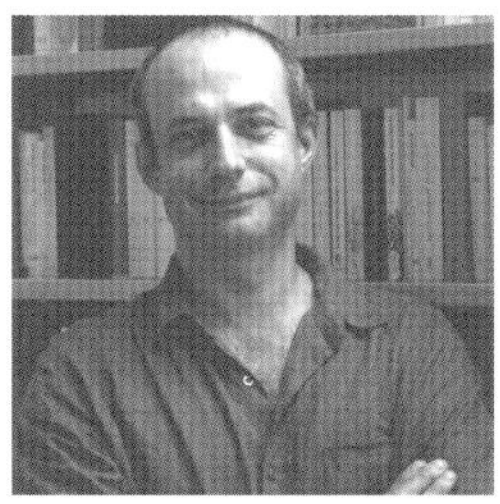

FABRICE SCHAEFER
b. 1969, Switzerland
Lives and works in Geneva, Switzerland
218, **229**

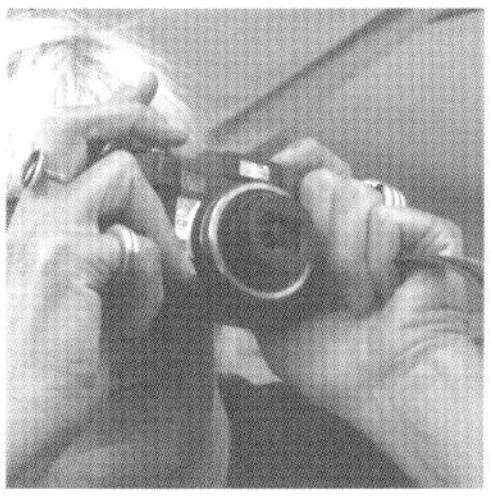

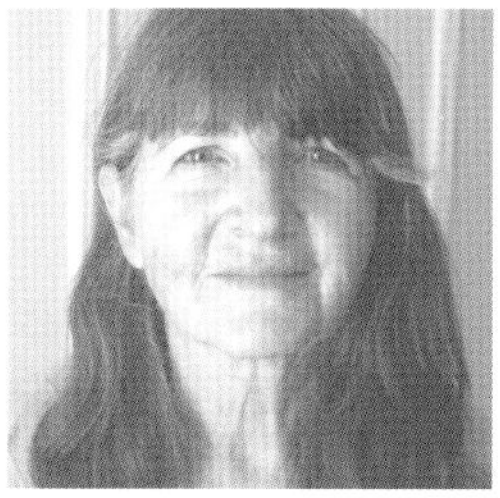

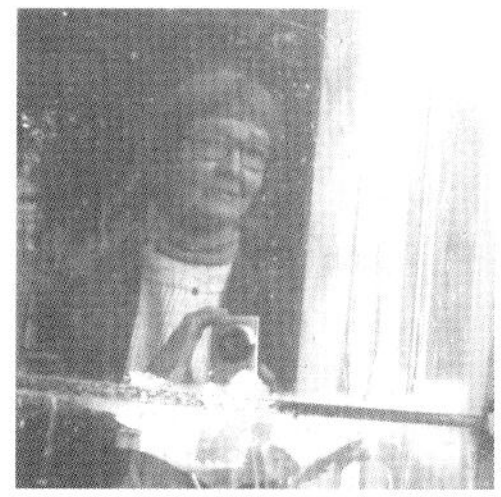

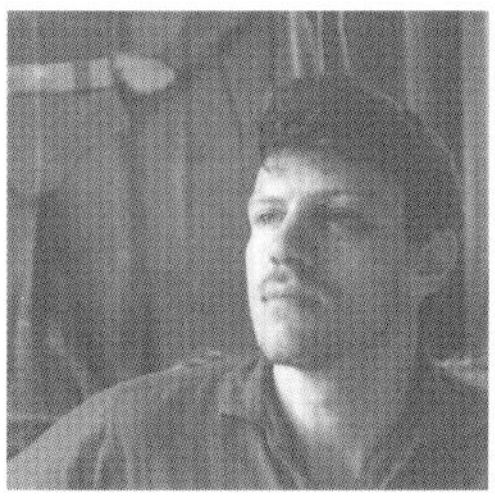

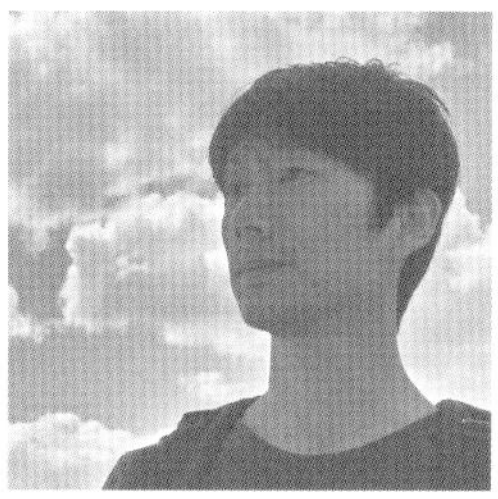

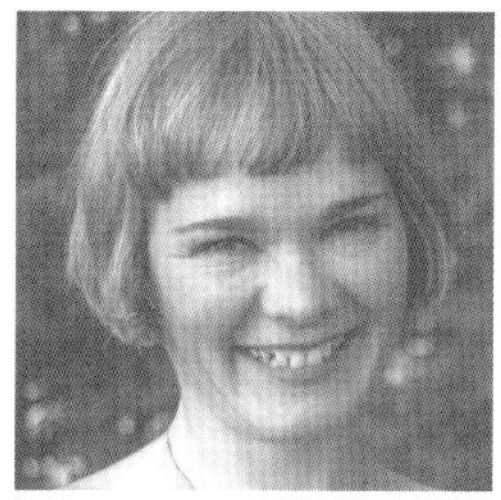

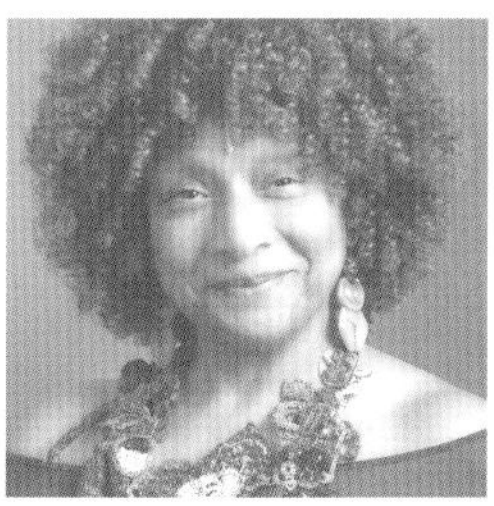

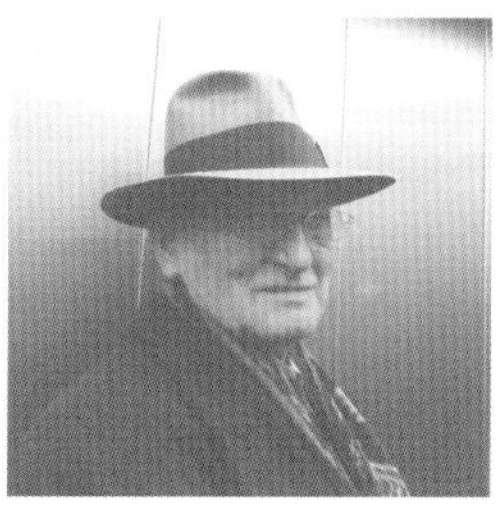

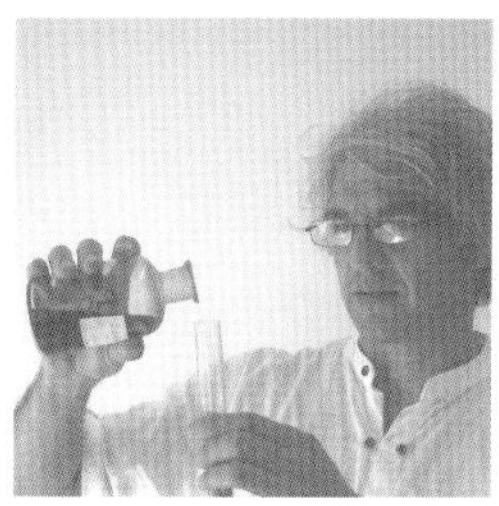

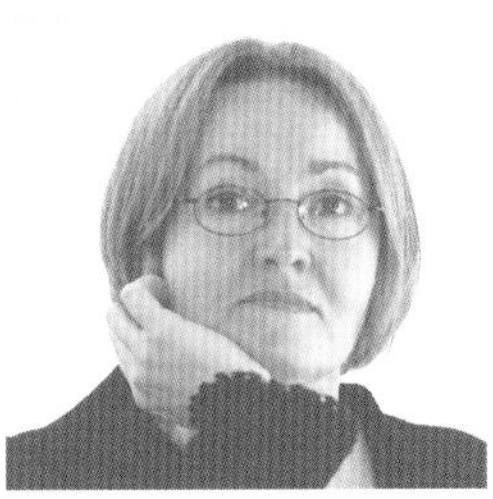

EVA TESARIK
b. 1957, Austria
Lives and works in Vienna, Austria
103, **116**

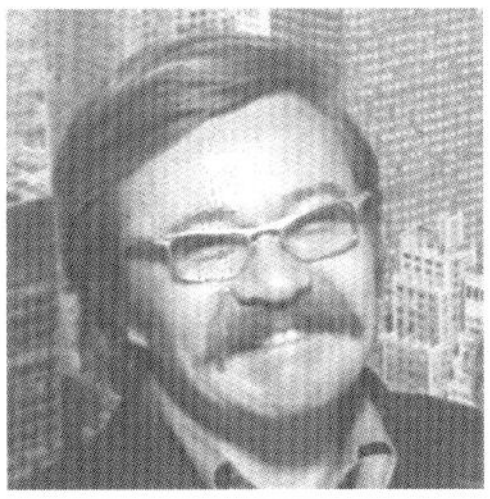

DON TOMPKINS
1933–1982, United States
Lived and worked in Seattle, Washington and New York, New York
12–13, 15, 55, **76–77**

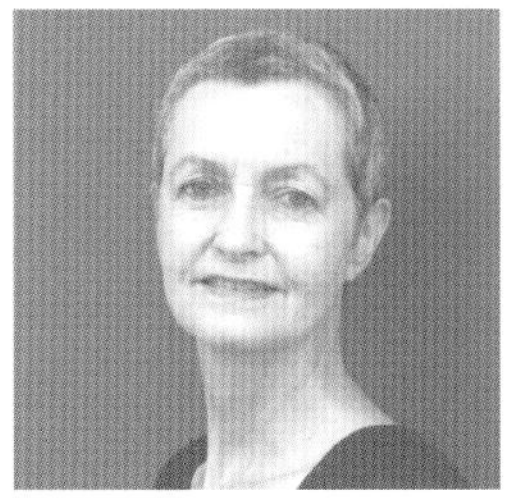

LOES VAN RIEL
b. 1966, The Netherlands
Lives and works in Charlottesville, Virginia
57, **64–65**

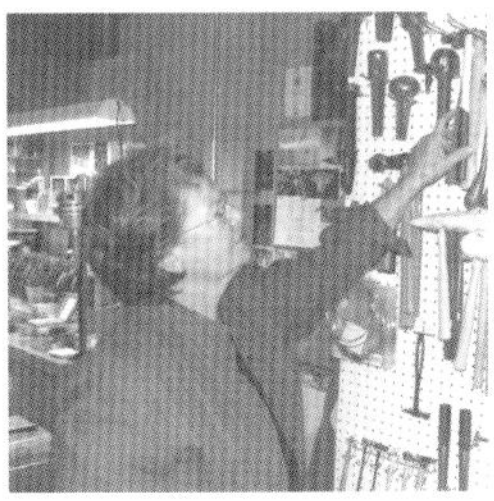

PAMELA MORRIS THOMFORD
b. 1945, United States
Lives and works in Perrysburg, Ohio
54, **84**

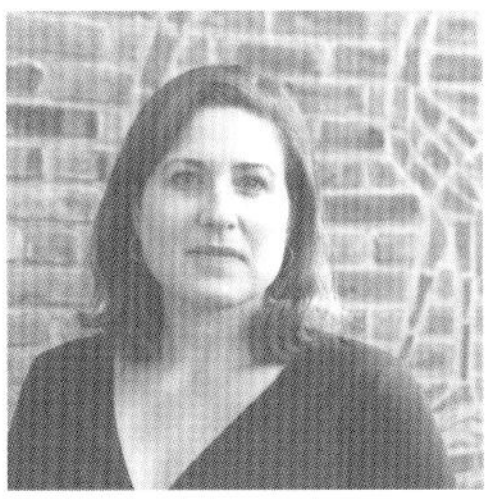

SARAH C. TURNER
b. 1971, United States
Lives and works in Bloomfield Hills, Michigan
28, 218, **236–37**

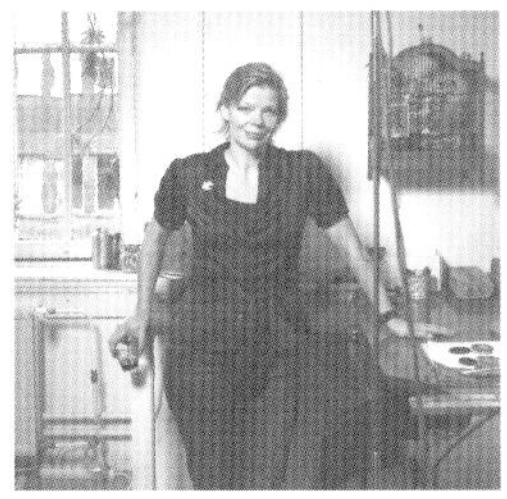

TRUIKE VERDEGAAL
b. 1965, The Netherlands
Lives and works in Amsterdam, The Netherlands
57, **97**

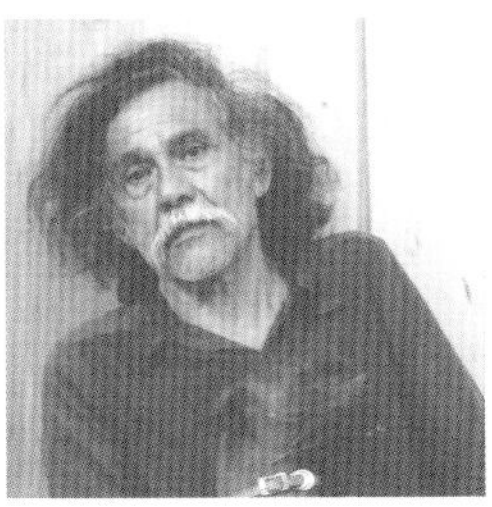

FRANCISCO TOLEDO
b. 1940, Mexico
Lives and works in Oaxaca, Mexico
196, **204**

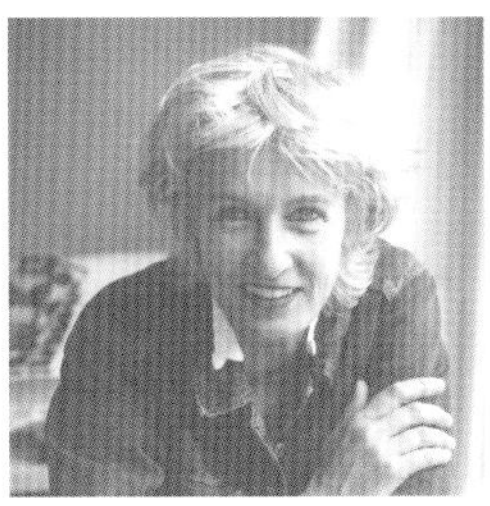

MECKY VAN DEN BRINK
b. 1950, The Netherlands
Lives and works in Amsterdam, The Netherlands
102, **124–25**, 169, **173, back cover**

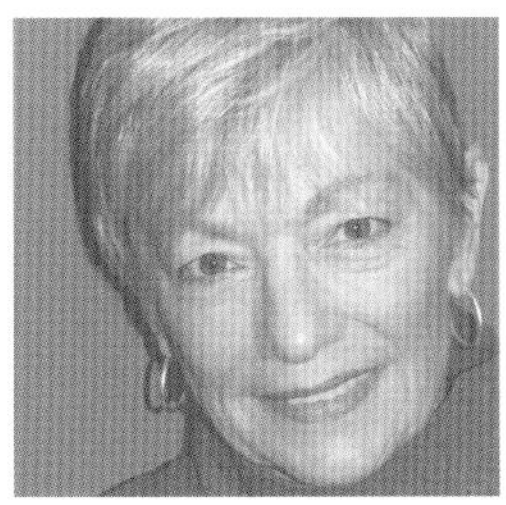

SALLY VON BARGEN
b. 1949, England
Lives and works in Seattle, Washington
57, **86–87**

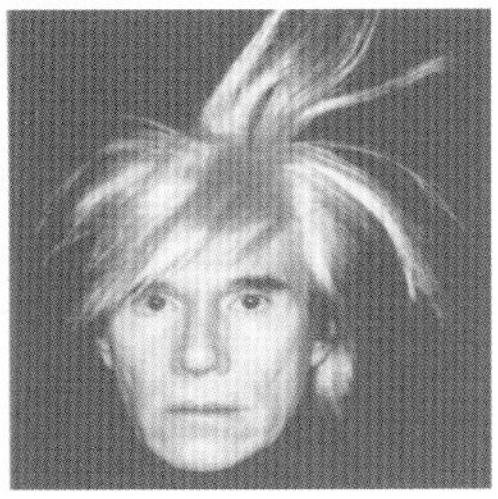

ANDY WARHOL
1928–1987, United States
Lived and worked in New York, New York
131, 133–34

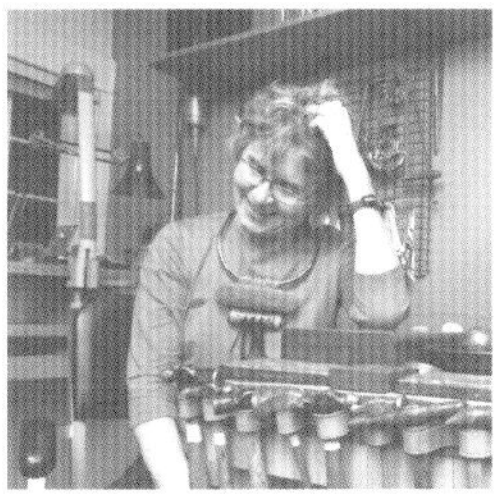

NANCY WORDEN
b. 1954, United States
Lives and works in Seattle, Washington
57, **82–83**

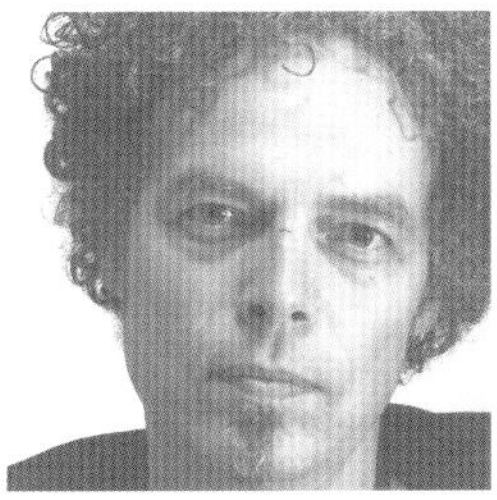

NORMAN WEBER
b. 1964, Germany
Lives and works in Kaufbeuren, Germany
169, **190–91**

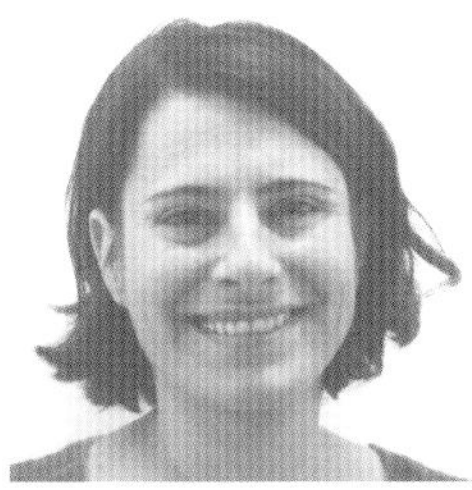

NOA ZILBERMAN
b. 1977, Israel
Lives and works in Jerusalem, Israel
28, 220, **232–33, back cover**

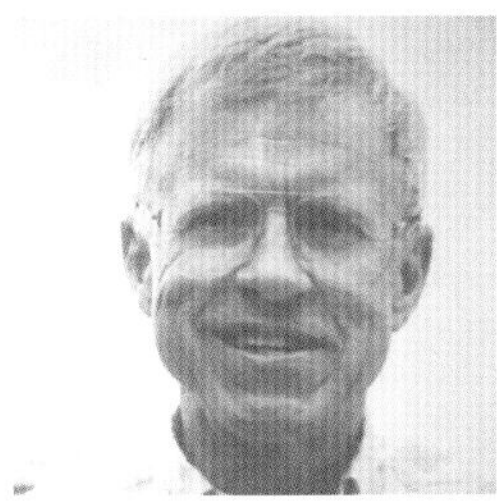

J. FRED WOELL
b. 1934, United States
Lives and works in Deer Isle, Maine
15, 55, **74–75**

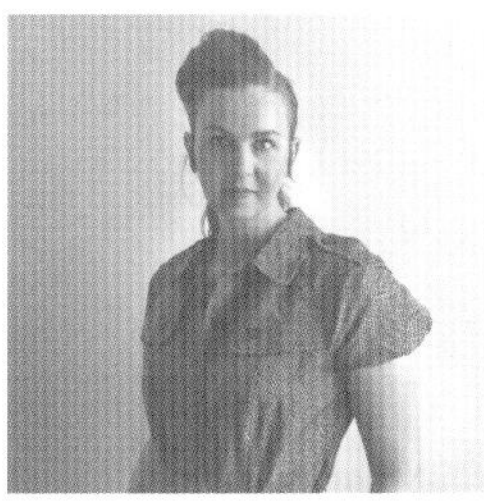

PETRA ZIMMERMANN
b. 1975, Austria
Lives and works in Vienna, Austria
168, **189**

SELECT BIBLIOGRAPHY

Barthes, Roland. *Camera Lucida: Reflections on Photography.* New York: Hill and Wang, 1981.

Batchen, Geoffrey. "From Genre to Generic." *Art on Paper* 3, no. 3 (January–February 1999): 48-49.

Batchen, Geoffrey. *Forget Me Not: Photography and Remembrance.* New York: Princeton Architectural Press, 2004.

Benjamin, Walter. "The Work of Art in the Age of Mechanical Reproduction." In *Illuminations*. New York: Harcourt, 1955.

Bernabei, Roberta. *Contemporary Jewellers: Interviews with European Artists.* New York: Berg, 2011.

Cohn, Susan, ed. *Unexpected Pleasures: The Art and Design of Contemporary Jewellery.* New York: Rizzoli, 2012.

den Besten, Liesbeth. *On Jewellery: A Compendium of International and Contemporary Art Jewellery.* Stuttgart: Arnoldsche, 2011.

Dormer, Peter, and Ralph Turner. *The New Jewelry: Trends and Traditions.* London: Thames and Hudson, 1994.

Frank, Robin Jaffee. *Love and Loss: American Portrait and Mourning Miniatures.* New Haven: Yale University Press, 2000.

Jussim, Estelle, and Elizabeth Lindquist-Cock. *Landscape As Photograph.* New Haven and London: Yale University Press, 1985.

Kappelet, Henriette. "Fotoschmuck: Fotographie in Dekorativer Fassung." *Fotogeschichte: Beiträge zur Geschichte und Aesthetik der Fotografie* 44, no. 12 (1982): 11–22.

Krauss, Rosalind. "Photography's Discursive Spaces: Landscape/View." *Art Journal* 42, no. 4 (Winter 1982): 275–319.

Lindemann, Wilhelm, ed. *Thinking Jewellery: On the Way towards a Theory of Jewellery.* Stuttgart: Arnoldsche Verlagsanstalt, 2011.

Oliver, Valerie Cassel, ed. *Hand + Made: The Performative Impluse of Art and Craft.* Houston: Contemporary Arts Museum Houston, 2010.

Pointon, Marcia. "Valuing the Visual and Visualizing the Valuable: Jewellery and Its Ambiguities." *Cultural Values* 3, no. 1 (1999): 1–27.

Skinner, Damian, ed. *Contemporary Jewelry in Perspective.* New York: Lark Jewelry & Beading, 2013.

Sontag, Susan. *On Photography.* New York: Farrar, Straus and Giroux, 1977.

Strauss, Cindi. *Ornament as Art: Avant-Garde Jewelry from the Helen Williams Drutt Collection.* Stuttgart: Arnoldsche and the Museum of Fine Arts, Houston, 2007.

West, Larry, and Patricia A. Abbott. "Daguerreian Jewelry: Popular in Its Day." *The Daguerreian Annual* (1990): 136–140.

West, Larry, and Patricia A. Abbott. *Tokens of Affection and Regard: Antique Photographic Jewelry.* New York: West Companies, Inc. Larry J. West, 2005.

PHOTO CREDITS

The photographs in Multiple Exposures are by:

Bryan Derballa, front cover; Martin Papcún, back cover (top, right); Ami Zilberman, back cover (first row, left); Gallery S O, back cover (first row, middle); Marc Pluim, back cover (first row, right); Rod Slemmons, back cover (second row, left); Rien Bazen, back cover (second row, middle); Rebecca Sakoun, back cover (second row, right); Fotojuanma-Tapia, back cover (bottom, right); Hyun-Seok Sim, endpapers; J. Gold & Co., frontispiece; Jiro Kamata, 7; Otto Künzli, 21, 22–23; Rien Bazen, 24 (bottom left); Ton Baadenhuysen, 24 (bottom right, top left and right); Harry Ertl, 25 (all); John McKenzie, Edinburgh, 37; Jeremy Rowe, 42 (bottom), 43 (bottom); Matthew Starr, 44 (both), 45, 47 (top); Francesca Moscheni, 48–49 (all); Matthew Starr, 50; Chip Miller, 56; Fritz Maierhofer, 59; Martin Papcún, 62 (both), 63 (both); Carter Grotta, 64; Eli Weinberg, courtesy of Beverley Price, 66 (top); Beverley Price, 66 (bottom), 67; Bernhard Schobinger, 68; Taylor Dabney, 69; J. Gold & Co., 70–71; Babette Boucher, 73 (all); Tara Locklear, 78; Mike Koryta, 80, 81; Nancy Worden, 82, 83; Tim Thayer, 84 (both); Michael Webster, 85; Sally von Bargen, 86–87; John Wilson White, 89 (lower right); Eleanor Moty, 90, 91; Keith Lo Bue, 92; J. Gold & Co., 93; Peter Deckers, 94; Mason Douglas, 95 (both); J. Gold & Co., 96 (pendant); Jordan Doner, 96 (pendant and cuff on model); Eddo Hartmann, 97 (all); Jos Fielmich, 98–99; Marc Bernier, 101; Rod Slemmons, 106 (both), 107; Johannes Kersting, 108–9; ©Thomas von der Heiden, 110; Walker Montgomery, 111 (both); Rien Bazen, 112; Mathilde Jurrissen, 113 (top left); Rien Bazen, 113 (top right); Jos Fielmich, 113 (bottom); Michael Petry, 114–15 (all); Alice Schumacher, 116; J. Gold & Co., 117, 118; Cris Bierrenbach, 119 (right); Claire Lavendhomme,
121 (both); Viktoria Münzker, 122–23 (all); Christina Schumacher, 125; Michael Laurence, 126; Gabriela Sánchez y Sánchez de la Barquera, 127 (all); Kirsten Haydon, 128–29; Fritz Maierhofer, 132; Jürgen Papp, 135; Bettina Speckner, 138; J. Gold & Co., 139; Mari Ishikawa, 140; Frank Vetter, 141; Jeremy Dillon, 142; Kirsten Haydon, 143; Jeremy Dillon, 144 (top); Kirsten Haydon, 144 (bottom), 145 (top); Jeremy Dillon, 145 (below); J. Gold & Co., 146; Jeremy Dillon, 147 (right, top and bottom); Rebecca Sakoun, 148 (bottom); Wouter Stelwagen, 149 (top); Susanna Kuschek, 150; Eleanor Moty, 151; J. Gold & Co., 153; Janet Goldner, 154, 155; Sooyeon Kim, 156 (all), 157 (all); Craig Arnold, 158; Margit Hart, 159 (both); J. Gold & Co., 160, 161; David Kadlec, 162 (both); Suzanne Beautyman, 163 (both); Günther Meyer, 170; Rien Bazen, 171; J. Gold & Co., 172; Marc Pluim, 173; Ramon Puig Cuyàs, 174 (lower left); Catarina Gomes Ferreira, 174 (painting on right); Ramon Puig Cuyàs, 175 (top); Conor Vela, 176; Jaan Seitsara, 177 (bottom); Kimmo Heikkilä, 177 (top); Marianne Schliwinski, 178 (all); Shawn Wood, 179 (both); Bill Pogue, 180; Foto juanma-Tapia, 181; Tom Grotta, Brown Grotta Gallery, 182; Josh Wendler, 183; Eric Zeigler for the Toledo Museum of Art, 184 (right); J. Gold & Co., 187; Petra Zimmermann, 189; Norman Weber, 190 (both), 191; Michael O'Neill, 192–93; Jiro Kamata, 200, 201; J. Gold & Co., 202–3; Rod Slemmons, 204; Michael O'Neill, 205; Henk van Assen, 206; Hugh Mackay, 207; Sandy Johanson, 208, 209; Hyun-Seok Sim, 210; Gwang-chun Park, 211 (right); Hyun-Seok Sim, 211 (bottom, left and right); Steven Brian Samuels, 212; Terry Greene Photography, 213; John Carlano, 214; Craig Arnold, 215; Fabrice Schaefer, 229; Bryan Derballa, 234; Wafaa Bilal, 235 (all); Sarah Turner, 236–37; Karl Fritsch and Gavin Hipkins, 238–39 (all); Morris Gindi, 240; Craig Arnold, 242–43

Images on the following pages have been reproduced courtesy of:

The Museum of Fine Arts, Houston, 12–13; Cult Nation, 16; Jon Rafman and Zach Feuer Gallery, New York, 26–27; George Eastman House, 30–31; Collection of Larry J. West , 33, 34; The Metropolitan Museum of Art, Image copyright © The Metropolitan Museum of Art. Image source: Art Resource, NY, 36; Cathy Gordon, 38 (both); George Eastman House, 42 (top), 43 (top); Thomas Harris, 46; George Eastman House, 47 (bottom); REUTERS/ Jessica Rinaldi, 55; The Stedelijk Museum 's-Hertogenbosch, 58 (top); Gallery S O, 58 (bottom); Mint Museum, 61; Smithsonian American Art Museum, 74; The Museum of Fine Arts, Houston, 76, 77; Museum of Fine Arts, Boston, 79; Sienna Gallery, 88, 89 (left); Michael Petry, 114, 115; Célio Braga, 119 (below); Kiki Smith and Editions Fawbush, New York; Mecky van den Brink, 124; Andy Warhol Foundation for the Visual Arts, Inc., 131; Kiko Gianocca, 147 (left); Jantje Fleischhut, 148 (above), 149 (above); Kara Ross, 152 (all); The Museum of Fine Arts, Houston, 164–65; © Stiftung Museum Kunstpalast - Horst Kolberg – ARTOTHEK, 175 (lower left); The Museum of Fine Arts, Houston, 184 (left), 185; Iris Nieuwenburg, 186; The Museum of Fine Arts, Houston, 188

The video stills in Multiple Exposures have been reproduced courtesy of:

Lauren Kalman and Sienna Patti, 103; Gisbert Stach, 216–17; Dinie Besems, 219; Esther Brinkmann, 224–25; Gisbert Stach, 226, 227; Lauren Kalman and Sienna Patti, 228; David Roux-Fouillet, 230–31; Noa Zilberman, 232–33; Suska Mackert, 241

Imagery on the following pages has been reproduced from the Internet:

16, 27, 174 (top)

Photographs for the Artists Index have been taken by:

Alvarez, Rinaldo: Fotojuanma-Tapia; Arnold, Craig: Rachael Harris; Bakker, Gijs: Yoshiaki Tsutsui; Barello, Julia: Nancy A. Meyers; Beautyman, Suzanne: Federico Cavicchioli; Bilal, Wafaa: Wafaa Bilal; Boucher, Babette: Nanna Melland; Braga, Célio: Renco Veenbrink; Brinkmann, Esther: Werner Nievergelt; Browne, Kathleen: Stephen Litchfield; Bürgel, Klaus: Octavia Bürgel; Clark, Sonya: Abigail Volkman; Clark, Thea: Natalie Dix; Deckers, Peter: Amelia Pascoe; Doner, Jordan: Jordan Doner; Dweck, Stephen: Matt Posey; Ebendorf, Robert: Forrest Croce; Falkenhagen, Diane: Bill Pogue; Fleischhut, Jantje: Rebecca Sakoun; Fritsch, Karl: unknown; Gentille, Thomas: Thomas Gentille; Gianocca, Kiko: Kiko Gianocca; Giles, Geoffrey: Geoffrey Giles; Gilreath, Ashley: Michael Webster; Goldner, Janet: Teri Slotkin; Hannon, Rebecca: Anton Christiansen; Hart, Margit: Fritz Maier-hofer; Haydon, Kirsten: Katie Scott in Munich; Hermsen, Herman: Djim Hermsen; Hipkins, Gavin: Kinstry Smythe; Ike, John: Arthur Cohen; Ishikawa, Mari: Frank Vetter; Johanson, Sandy: Linda Hubbell; Kalman, Lauren: Courtesy Sienna Patti; Kamata, Jiro: Gesa Simons; Kim, Sooyeon: Kang Kun Photography; King, Betsy: Donna Tursi; Künzli, Otto: Otto Künzli; Kuschek, Susanna: Christina Cassim; Lavendhomme, Claire: Dominique Baudon; Lo Bue, Keith: Irena Opacak;

MacDonald, Jaimie: Hugh Mackay; Mackert, Suska: Jens Niehus; Maierhofer, Fritz: Margit Hart; Mamiye, Irene: Martin Diegelman; Mann, Thomas: Angele Seiley; Misher, Karen: Robert Kirsch; Moty, Eleanor: Michael Croft; Münzker, Viktoria: Viktoria Münzker; Nieuwenburg, Iris: Iris Nieuwenburg; Nuutinen, Maria: Maria Nuutinen; Papcún, Martin: Jana Bercelova; Pearse, Mary Hallam: Barbara Tetenbaum; Peters, Ruudt: Ruudt Peters; Petry, Michael: Fin Serck-Hanssen; Pfuelb, Robert: Loes van Riel; Pierce, Shari: Mason Douglas; Price, Beverley: Beverley Price; Puig Cuyàs, Ramon: Ramon Puig Cuyàs; Ross, Kara: Alexander Noe; Roux-Fouillet, David: photo booth in Switzerland; Sánchez y Sánchez de la Barquera, Gabriela: Gabriela Sánchez y Sánchez de la Barquera; Schaefer, Fabrice: Fabrice Schaefer; Schliwinski, Marianne: Marianne Schliwinski; Schobinger, Bernhard: Annelies Štrba; Scott, Joyce: Mike Koryta; Sieber-Fuchs, Verena: Sebastian Sieber-Fuchs; Sim, Hyun-Seok: Serim Kwon; Skubic, Peter: unknown; Slemmons, Kiff: Kiff Slemmons; Speckner, Bettina: Bettina Speckner; Stach, Gisbert: Rose Stach; Tesarik, Eva: Barbara Krobath; Thomford, Pamela Morris: Peg Miller Kern; Toledo, Francisco: Trine Ellitsgaard; Tompkins, Don: Merrily Tompkins; Turner, Sarah: Kelly Kennedy; van den Brink, Mecky: René Gonkel; van Riel, Loes: Alan O'Neal; Verdegaal, Truike: Mark Janssen; von Bargen, Sally: LvB Images; Warhol, Andy: © 2013 The Andy Warhol Foundation for the Visual Arts / Artists Rights Society (ARS), New York; Weber, Norman: Andy Ausschnitt; Woell, J. Fred: unknown; Worden, Nancy: Rex Rystedt; Zilberman, Noa: Ami Zilberman; Zimmermann, Petra: Wolfram Otto

---

BACK COVER

Martin Papcún
Ring, 1999
Artist's analog photographs, silver, brass
1 1/8 in. (2.8 cm), diameter, closed
5/8 in. (1.6 cm), width
SUPŠ A VOŠ TURNOV, The Secondary School of Applied Arts and The College of Craft, Turnov, Czech Republic

Noa Zilberman
Wrinkles (video), 2012
1 minute, 30 seconds
Filmed by Ami Zilberman
Collection of the artist

Bernhard Schobinger
Self-Portrait with Nose (brooch), 2010
Digital photograph on commuter card, hologram, silver, coral
1 1/8 x 1 1/8 in. (2.7 x 2.7 cm)
Courtesy of Gallery S O

Mecky van den Brink
Marokko (necklace) from the Fake or Reality series, 1991
Photocopies on PVC, ceramic shards, metal
15 3/8 x 1/4 in. (39 x 0.8 cm)
Museum Arnhem

Kiff Slemmons
Broken Tie (pin), 1997
Found photograph, silver, mica
2 3/4 x 1 1/2 x 1/4 in. (7 x 3.8 x 0.5 cm)
Collection of Sandra Donnell

Gijs Bakker, executed by **Pauline Barendse** and **Tobias van Roojen**
The Tongue Brooch, 1989
Analog photograph printed on paper, diamond, rhodium-plated white gold 585, silver 925, PVC
4 1/2 x 3 1/2 x 3/8 in. (11.5 x 8.8 x 1 cm)
Helen Williams Drutt, Philadelphia

Jantje Fleischhut
Morgen (brooch)
from the Dolomiten Sagen series, 2008
Digital silkscreen on foil, gold, topaz, quartz, resin
3 1/2 x 2 1/2 in. (8.9 x 6.4 cm)
Collection of Susan C. Beech

Rinaldo Alvarez
Peep-Show (brooch), 2009
Photographic reproductions, silver, glass, pearls, foam
2 3/8 x 2 3/8 x 5/8 in. (6 x 6 x 1.5 cm)
Collection of Ulrike Knab

ENDPAPERS

Hyun-Seok Sim
Parts of *135 Camera* (pendant), 2007
20k gold, sterling silver, steel, glass
Collection of the artist

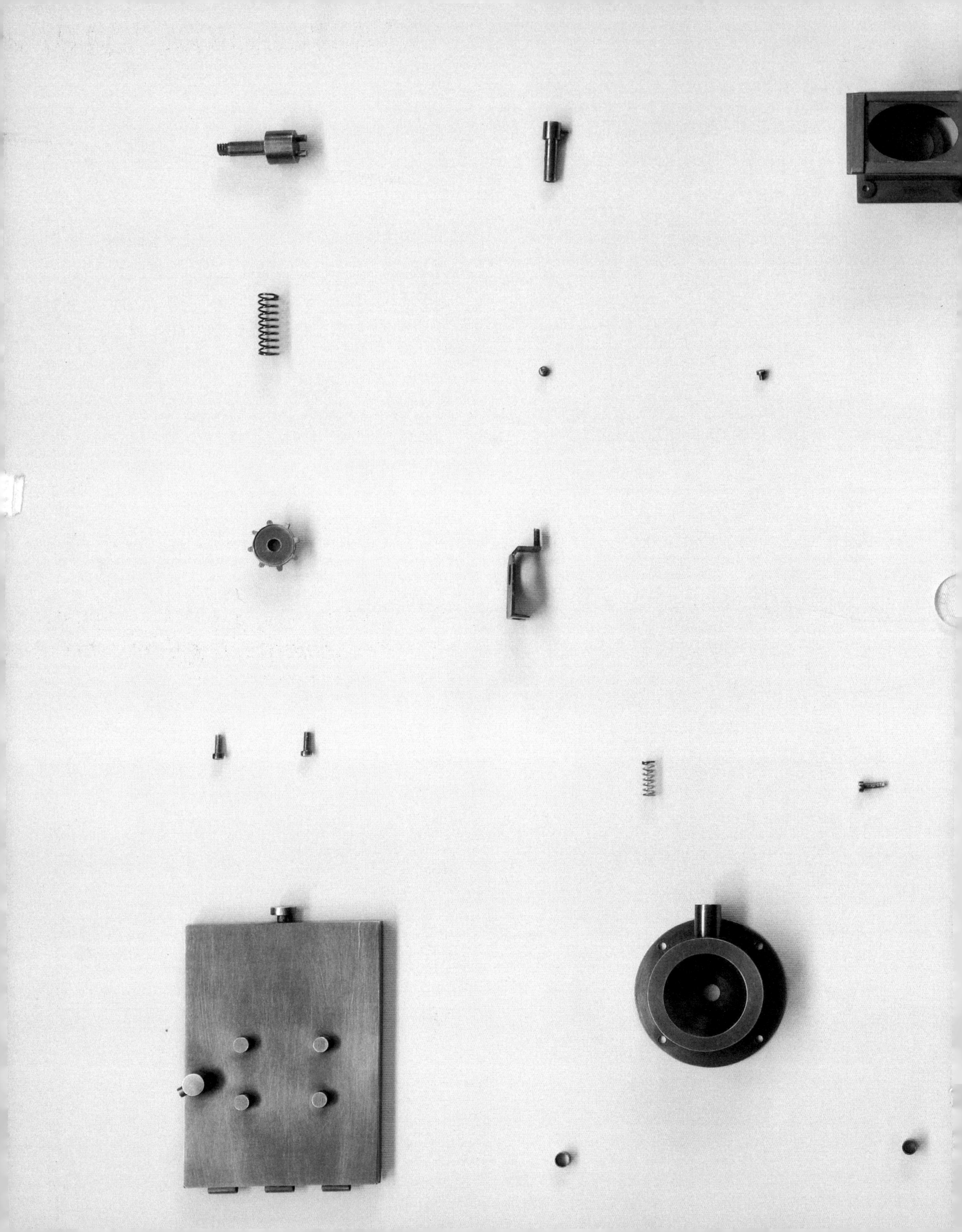